Custom Views and View Switching - Outlook provides built-in views and the ability to create your own custom views. Switching among the different views merely requires selecting the view you want from a combo box.

Notes - Outlook Notes allow you to keep track of miscellaneous thoughts and reminders in memo board fashion, with the ability to change the colors of notes and large numbers of notes.

Word

Letter Wizard - Reduces the time needed to create the structure of a concentrate on the content.

Grammar Checker - As a companion to the spelling checker, the grammar checker proofreads your document either as you type or when you are finished, and informs you of any grammatical errors.

Online Layout View - This new view is the optimal view for reading documents on-screen.

Document Map - This new view makes navigation of large documents simple. With a split-screen view, the left side shows a hyperlink outline of the document while the right side shows the actual document.

Navigational Tools - Combines the ease of a scroll bar with the functionality of the Find and Go To dialog boxes, making it easier to browse through documents.

Multiple Versioning - This new feature allows you to track multiple versions of a document within one file.

Animated Text Formatting - This new formatting feature adds a bit of sparkle to your online text.

Table Drawing Tool - Getting a table just right has always been frustrating. With the Table Drawing Tool, tables can be drawn right in the document to your specifications.

Page Borders - Want a border around your document? The new page borders in Word 97 make it possible—and simple.

Text Borders - Apply borders, shadows, and other effects to text within paragraphs.

In-Place Comments - Allows users to enter comments into a document without altering the content of the document. Comments appear when a user hovers the mouse over the area where the note was created.

MASTERING

MICROSOFT®
OFFICE 97

PROFESSIONAL EDITION
Second Edition

Lonnie E. Moseley

David M. Boodey

SYBEX

San Francisco • Paris • Düsseldorf • Soest

Associate Publisher: Amy Romanoff
Acquisitions Manager: Kristine Plachy
Acquisitions & Developmental Editor: Sherry Schmitt
Editors: Anamary Ehlen and Bonnie Bills
Project Editor: Shelby Zimmerman
Technical Editors: Tanya Strub and Juanita Tischendorf
Book Designers: Patrick Dintino and Catalin Dulfu
Electronic Publishing Specialist: Bill Gibson
Desktop Publisher: Tony Jonick
Production Coordinator: Robin Kibby
Proofreaders: Grey Magauran and Michael Tom
Indexer: Ted Laux
Cover Designer: Design Site
Cover Photographer: David Bishop

Screen reproductions produced with Collage Complete.
Collage Complete is a trademark of Inner Media Inc.

SYBEX is a registered trademark of SYBEX Inc.
Mastering is a trademark of SYBEX Inc.

TRADEMARKS: SYBEX has attempted throughout this book to
distinguish proprietary trademarks from descriptive terms by
following the capitalization style used by the manufacturer.

The author and publisher have made their best efforts to prepare this book, and the content is based upon final release software whenever possible. Portions of the manuscript may be
based upon pre-release versions supplied by software manufac-
turer(s). The author and the publisher make no representation
or warranties of any kind with regard to the completeness or
accuracy of the contents herein and accept no liability of any
kind including but not limited to performance, merchantabil-
ity, fitness for any particular purpose, or any losses or damages
of any kind caused or alleged to be caused directly or indirectly
from this book.

Photographs and illustrations used in this book have been
downloaded from publicly accessible file archives and are used
in this book for news reportage purposes only to demonstrate
the variety of graphics resources available via electronic access.
Text and images available over the Internet may be subject to
copyright and other rights owned by third parties. Online availability of text and images does not imply that they may be
reused without the permission of rights holders, although the
Copyright Act does permit certain unauthorized reuse as fair use
under 17 U.S.C. Section 107.

Library of Congress Card Number: 96-71022
ISBN: 0-7821-1925-5

Manufactured in the United States of America

10 9 8 7 6 5 4 3 2 1

To each other

ACKNOWLEDGMENTS

We would like to thank the many people who contributed their effort and support to the development of this book.

We sincerely thank Sherry Schmitt, our Developmental Editor, who has been a continuous source of good ideas, excellent counsel, and human comfort.

Our editors Shelby Zimmerman, Bonnie Bills, Anamary Ehlen, and Technical Editors Tanya Strub and Juanita Tischendorf honed and sharpened this book in marvelous ways. Their astute questions, clever rewrites, and excellent suggestions helped to make this book outstanding.

A great group of professionals were responsible for the layout, style, and general appearance of the book. Thanks to Production Coordinator Robin Kibby, Proofreaders Grey Magauran and Michael Tom, Electronic Publishing Specialist Bill Gibson, Desktop Publisher Tony Jonick, and others in Sybex's Production and Art departments who were responsible for the look and feel of this book.

Our friend and contributor to the book's Excel chapters, Denise Leo, deserves an award for her patience and tireless efforts to help us create a great product.

We would also like to thank Katherine Murray for her excellent contributions to the PowerPoint chapters and Sheila Dienes for constructing the Master's Reference.

Special thanks go to Kristine Plachy and Amy Romanoff for their added help in the direction of the book.

Our special thanks and gratitude to business partners and friends Cordell H. Sloan and Terese D. Zurzola, without whose continuous support this project would have been impossible to do together.

To our friends and colleagues at CRT for their varying forms of support: Althea, Angela, Audrey, Bob, Bryan, Byron, Carl, Christine, Cordell, Debbie, Denise L., Denise M., Doris, Dwight, Edgar, Eric, Fred, Karon, Ken, Kevin, Matt, Peggy, Rick, Samantha, Sauddah, Scott, Susan, Terry, Tony C., Tony M., and Wynn.

We would also like to thank some very important people who have touched our lives with their support, encouragement, forbearance, and belief.

- William and Winona Moseley, Bill, David, Anthony and Amanda Moseley, Michael Valenoti, Ray Trost, Dave Olson, Deborah K. Batt, Pendeeta, Rona Barufkin-Luber, Barbara Grinnell-Stein, Mary and Thomas Powell, Deborrah Wilkinson, Mildred and Douglas Barton, Francine Araujo, Carole and Charles Stanford, Connie Bell, Maurice Henry, Doris and John Zurzola, Ken Blue, Steve Woodland, Yvonne Flamer, Susan Greco, Catherine McHugh, Mary Sloan, Brenda Kienan, Dan Tauber, Ace Bedford, Dwight Miller, Jim Reinertsen, Norman Spencer, Holly Dawn Hewlett, Bill St. Clair, Peggy Devito, Audrey Reid, Sharon Klein-Leib, Penda Undercoffer, Inez Gibbs, Helene Sloan, Ruth and André Ferber, Linda and Allen Hammond, Aubrey McCutcheon, Steve Dalton, Obra Kernodle, Ed Smith, Harry Watts, Ed Nickerson, Frank and Jan Spezzano, Jerry Fleischman, Rashida Sule, Bernard Watson, Georgia Demopoulos, and Joseph Furlong.

- Robert, Mickey, and Diana Boodey, Grandmom Francis, Blanche Landmesser, Pat and Rob Holdenwang, Bernadette and Dennis Hager, Luke Francis, Bill and Sara Francis, Robert and Kim Francis, Alice Nye, Martha, Leon and Mike Boodey, The Greenwalds, The Petersons, Nadine Medbery, Bryan Becker, Lisa and Larry Grady, and Darren Fromal.

Contents at a Glance

TABLE OF CONTENTS

PART II • COMMUNICATING WITH WORD

PART IV • PRESENTING WITH POWERPOINT

PART V • ORGANIZING WITH OUTLOOK

PART VII • OFFICE 97 INTERNET TOOLS

INTRODUCTION

Business software integration has come into its own with the release of Microsoft Office 97, which combines a new common look and a more polished interface—thanks to Windows 95—with a seamless exchange of information between the Office applications. Thus, we can focus on our documents, rather than on the intricacies of the software that creates them.

The components that make up the integrated Office suite include:

Word
In addition to using Word for anything you'd use a word processor for, you can use it as the foundation for creating letters, memos, reports, and any other document that will include or be included in documents from the other Office applications. For example, you can use a Word document as the basis for an Excel chart or a PowerPoint slide, or you can merge data from Outlook or Access within a Word document.

Excel
Use Excel to formulate and analyze numbers, manage and sort lists, and create graphs, maps, and pivot tables. The lists and numbers can be created and stored in Excel or in an external source, such as an Access database.

PowerPoint
Use PowerPoint to present your thoughts, ideas, and plans to various audiences—for example, your board of directors, sales prospects, or students. Multimedia, animation, and links to your Office data make PowerPoint ideal for timely information and powerful presentations.

Outlook
Outlook is included with Office 97 to manage pertinent information about your contacts, facilitate the scheduling of your time, navigate your hard drive, and provide a Universal Inbox for all of your e-mail sources. A welcome addition to the Office suite, Outlook provides quick access to your contact data for inclusion in a single letter or a mass mailing. Outlook also allows you to coordinate with other users' Outlook schedules—for example, if you need to find the best time that a group of people can get together for a meeting.

Access   Use Access to store, track, and report information. You can also use Access to create databases that track membership lists, client data, student registrations, inventory tracking, and customer invoicing. As a member of the Office, Access can utilize the tools of Excel to analyze and map data. Access also works seamlessly with Word when you need to merge data for mass mailings, and works with PowerPoint when you want to show data that substantiates the points being made in a presentation.

NOTE

Microsoft Office Professional includes Access, but Microsoft Office Standard does not. The Standard version, however, integrates seamlessly with the stand-alone version of Access 97 if you want to purchase it separately (see the Appendix for installation instructions).

Our Approach

Our approach when writing this book was to focus on the skills that you would need when you are on your own in the real world trying to get a job done. The features that we present are the ones that we felt were the most important in order for you to gain a strong understanding of the software.

At the end of each part that covers an application in the Office suite (Parts Two through Six), there is a chapter on integration. Each of these chapters focuses on how to use that program with the other applications in the suite, and provides step-by-step solutions to common business projects. By substituting your documents for the sample documents used in the examples in these chapters, many of your tasks could take advantage of the Office as a whole.

Part One: Welcome to Your New Office

This part is an orientation to your Office environment. This orientation includes an introduction to the individual applications, a primer on the new Windows 95 environment, and the tools made available to facilitate the integration of the Office applications.

Part Two: Communicating with Word

This part covers in detail the features necessary to create polished and professional documents, such as letters, proposals, integrated reports that incorporate information from other Office applications, and reusable form letter, proposal, and report templates that help make your document creation more efficient.

The integration chapter at the end of this part outlines the process for combining multiple Word documents created by multiple users. This chapter also demonstrates how to incorporate Excel charts and PowerPoint slides.

Part Three: Analyzing with Excel

This part delves into the creation of Excel financial workbooks, which allow you to use mathematical expressions and formulas to generate answers from raw data. Also covered is how to analyze, chart, and map your numbers, as well as how to use Excel's powerful list and database features to sort, subtotal, and filter the data.

The integration chapter of this section takes a growing Word table, imports it into Excel for list management, and uses forms and reports while linking the information to Access.

Part Four: Presenting with PowerPoint

This part covers the fundamentals needed for creating colorful and effective slide presentations using PowerPoint. Features explored include everything from the use of Wizards and templates for quickly getting presentations ready to the new animation and multimedia effects that will make your presentations stand out.

The integration chapter of this part follows the process used to create a presentation that incorporates data and charts from Word and Excel.

Part Five: Organizing with Outlook

In this part, the features of the newest member of the Office—Outlook—are introduced. Outlook's features are explored to provide you with the ability to compose and send e-mail; create and manage contacts, appointments, projects, and tasks; and organize your personal and business information.

The integration chapter of this section details the process used to import contact information from other Office applications, and explains how to use the contacts stored in Outlook for mass mailings.

Part Six: Data Management with Access

This part explains how you can create very powerful relational databases, which is easier than it ever has been in the newest release of Access. From basic concepts and helpful Wizards to advanced tips, we cover database design and implementation. Quicker and easier development of forms, reports, and queries are the hallmark of the chapters in this part.

The integration chapter examines how the fictional Northwind Traders company uses Access to do business. The chapter shows how the company merges Access data with Word for a monthly mailing, substantiates PowerPoint presentation points using data stored in Access, and analyzes the data stored in Access using an Excel pivot table on an Access form.

Part Seven: Office 97 Internet Tools

In this part, we explain how to create hypertext documents that can be used on a corporate intranet or the Internet, as well as how to create beautiful Web pages and almost instant Web pages using Word's Web Page Wizard. Step-by-step instruction is provided to create Web pages that incorporate colored backgrounds, hyperlink references, scrolling text, sound, and video. Finally, we demonstrate the ability of each of the Office 97 programs to save their data as Web-ready pages (HTML format) ready for uploading to computers connected to the Internet.

Conventions Used in This Book

We've used some standard conventions and typographer's tricks to make this book easier to read. While most of them will be obvious, you should scan the next few paragraphs just in case.

Keyboard Notations

To simplify instructions and make them easier to follow, we've used a special kind of shorthand notation:

- When you need to hold down one key and then press another, you'll see the key names connected with a plus sign. For instance, Ctrl+S means hold down the Ctrl key while pressing the S key.
- **Boldface** text indicates text you are expected to type.
- Some keys (the arrow keys and the Enter key, to be precise) are indicated by symbols. The symbol for the up, down, left, and right arrow keys are ↑, ↓, ←, and →, respectively. The symbol for the Enter key is a crooked arrow, ↵, as found on many keyboards.

The ➤ Symbol for Menu Commands

As a shortcut and an eye-catcher, we've used a special convention to indicate menu commands. When we want you to choose a command from the menu bar, it will follow this pattern: *menu name ➤ command*. For instance, "Choose File ➤ Save" is a shorter, neater way of saying "Choose the File command from the menu bar, then choose the Save command from the File menu." Sometimes you'll even see a sequence of menu selections that goes three or four levels deep.

PART I

Welcome to Your New Office

LEARN TO:

- *Use the Office 97 Programs*

- *Manage the Windows 95/NT Environment*

- *Link and Embed Data among Programs*

- *Understand the Shared Tools*

Chapter

1

Introducing You around the Office

FEATURING

Introducing You around the Office

Before you jump into working at your desk with your hand glued to the mouse, your head arched at an awkward angle toward the monitor, and your eyes riveted on a font that is much too small, take a minute and read this overview of what's in store when working with Microsoft Office 97. You will begin to relax once you realize just how much you can accomplish by using the tools available in the Microsoft Office suite of products.

What You Can Look Forward To

The new Office is a cohesive group of programs written by the Microsoft programming teams—teams known for their innovative and user-tested software interface designs. The group of Office programs includes:

- Word
- Excel
- PowerPoint
- Outlook
- Access (Professional Edition only)

All of the products have been written to run optimally under Microsoft's newest operating systems, Windows 95 and Windows NT 4.0. The Office programs take full advantage of the powers of these operating systems, from their 32-bit multitasking core to their newly polished interface that makes computing more intuitive than ever before.

Who Is in the Office?

The Professional Edition of Office's product suite includes word processing (Word), spreadsheet (Excel), business presentation (PowerPoint), personal-information management (Outlook), business data management and tracking (Access) programs. Each program can function independently or interact seamlessly, depending on your needs.

Columns of numbers created in Excel can be placed within a Word report and then placed within a PowerPoint Presentation or become the basis for a database in Access. Tables of information created in Word can be copied directly into Excel as the data for a new spreadsheet. Letters typed in Word can be used as the basis of a mail merge of names and addresses contained in Excel or Access.

Architectures of the Future

The Office also includes the Office Binder, which allows you to combine documents from multiple Office applications into one "virtual document." Documents form sections within the Office Binder, providing you with a way to more easily handle large projects.

The Comfort of Team Work

The possibilities are boundless—never has it been easier to revolutionize the way we perform our work. The Office programs share a look and feel—a commonality between menus, toolbars, and other design elements—so as you work in one product, you become familiar with all of the others.

The Office programs share common spelling dictionaries and shortcut word libraries, called AutoCorrect libraries, so productivity tools you create in one application are automatically used in the other applications.

Also available is a new Office Assistant that helps you use the Office programs by providing real-time tips as you work and allowing you to query the help system by typing in questions in the same words that you would use to ask another person. The assistant attempts to parse your question and figure out what it is that you are asking it, and then returns a list of possible topics from which to choose. The Answer Wizard in the last version of Office first introduced the technology to parse real-world questions.

You'll Be Glad You Joined This Office

With the new interface of Windows 95 and Windows NT, you can easily start multiple programs by clicking on the Start button on the Taskbar. Regardless of which program you are working in at the moment, all the names of the open programs appear on the Taskbar. You can easily switch between open programs by clicking on their names on the Taskbar, or you can tile the applications to see all four programs and their data at one time.

The bottom line is this: you will be extremely pleased with your choice of the Microsoft Office suite of products as the tools for redesigning the way you work. Figure 1.1 shows Word, Excel, PowerPoint, Outlook, and Access open in memory and tiled so a part of each is displayed.

FIGURE 1.1

*The Office pro-
grams work
together better
than ever
before.*

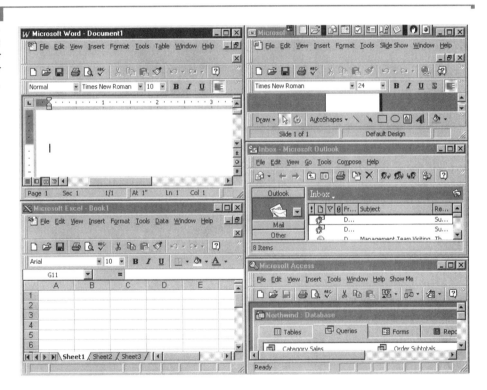

How Much Space Does the Office Need?

The Typical Install of the Standard Edition of Office requires 95MB of disk space and a recommended 12MB of RAM. The Professional Edition of Office, which includes Access, requires an additional 40MB of hard disk space and a total of 16MB of RAM if you want to run Access. If you spend a great deal of your day with more than one program open at a time, it is strongly suggested that you get as much RAM as you can, (at least 16MB) to run multiple Office programs at a time without noticing much of a slowdown in speed.

Introducing the Office Staff

Even though in the subsequent pages of this book you will be sitting down individually with each application in the Office suite to find out exactly how each one can help you with your work, a general introduction is in order so you can decide which application you want to meet with first.

MOSB—The Office Manager

It is a good idea to meet the Office Manager—officially titled the Microsoft Office Shortcut Bar (MOSB)—first, because it allows you to quickly locate the other members of the office and even organizes their functions for you.

By default, the MOSB lies at the top right-hand side of the screen. You can, however, move the MOSB anywhere you want by dragging it to a new position. Figure 1.2 displays a floating Office Shortcut Bar.

FIGURE 1.2

The Microsoft Office Shortcut Bar can be floated and customized.

Word—The Staff Writer

Word for Windows 95 is a seasoned word processing program that you can customize so it virtually writes your letters, memos, and proposals, composes tables, generates monthly reports, and outlines your articles and book chapters. Capable of producing newsletters, brochures, mail-merge letters, and envelopes, you will find virtually every writing feature you might need to produce a wide variety of document types.

Word saves you time and helps you work more efficiently with its AutoText or Auto-Correct features, which allow you to reuse information you have typed in. Word also can walk you through the steps of creating specific kinds of documents with its *Wizards*—predesigned fax forms, letters, envelopes, mailing labels, and Web pages. A Wizard shows you exactly where to type specific information, an especially helpful feature for anyone who doesn't have a background in business typing standards. You will think that it's magic when you see how quickly you can get up and running with this powerful member of the Office team. See Chapter 5 for a full introduction to Word.

You will be quite happy with the way Word works with the finance staff member (Excel) to produce documents that combine technical information with corresponding charts, graphs, and numbers. Figure 1.3 shows a multiple-page print preview of a proposal report that includes Excel budgetary numbers.

FIGURE 1.3

Word works seamlessly with Excel to produce reports that include numbers and graphs created in Excel.

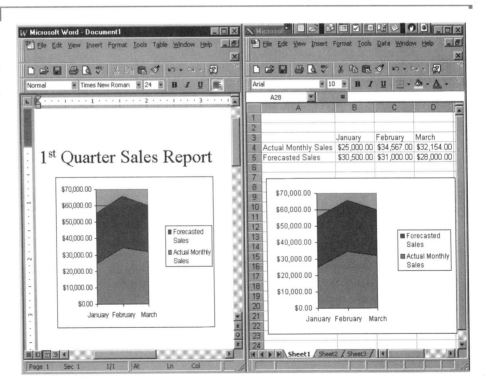

Excel—The Analyst

An equally powerful member of the Office team is Excel, your analyst. Capable of building spreadsheets in a single bound; automatically summing columns of numbers; presenting a graphical representation of your data in the form of pie, bar, line charts, and more; and allowing quick sorts and subtotal tallying, you will be immensely grateful for this member of the team as you begin to work through your budgets, proposals, and other financial documents. Figure 1.4 shows an Excel financial document with the AutoFormat feature applied to the table of numbers.

FIGURE 1.4

You can pick from among sixteen different AutoFormat styles to enhance the attractiveness of your tables.

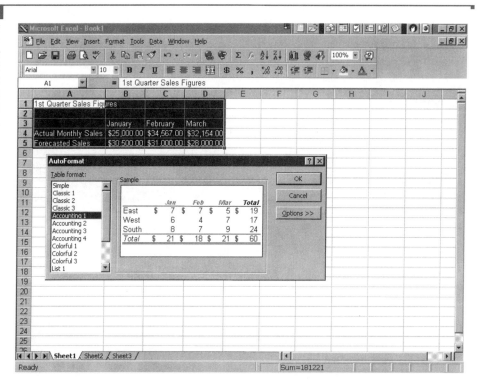

Completely compatible with the other members of the suite, Excel can create numerical analyses that you can then take into a Word report, a PowerPoint presentation, or an Access database. Some of your most pleasurable times at the office will be spent with Excel as you explore the "what-if" possibilities generated by the formulas you create.

Excel incorporates a powerful feature called the Pivot Table, an innovative approach that *flips* and *sums* data in seconds, allowing you to see your financial numbers from various perspectives. You can also design your own screen forms and completely program Excel to automatically perform repetitive monthly tasks. But long before you get to the programming stage with Excel, you will be creating custom toolbars that include the operation buttons you want to use on a daily basis. See Chapter 15 for the hands-on meeting with Excel.

PowerPoint—The Graphic and Presentation Designer

If you failed Straight Line Drawing 101 in school, you will be immensely impressed with and thankful for the next member of your team, PowerPoint, your presentation designer. Because you may not have the time or the background to figure out design elements and the proper color scheme for presentations, PowerPoint has a built-in designer that will give you suggestions on how to lay out and organize your on-screen slide presentations, audience handouts, and 35 mm slides.

PowerPoint works with your financial analyst, Excel, to use numbers and charts in a slide presentation. Also very friendly with Word, the writer, PowerPoint allows you to automatically generate a complete slide show from the outlines generated by Word in Outline mode. PowerPoint then suggests color, flourish, and maybe some clip art pictures to emphasize your presentation.

PowerPoint also helps you decide how dramatic your slide show will be—for example, you can have words and bullet points zoom in from the top or bottom of the screen, or have sounds and music generate from a point highlighted on the screen. You can even write directly on your slide show screen as you are presenting to emphasize a particular point.

When your show is over, PowerPoint will store the presentation for future use—such as inserting it into Word as part of the monthly report information you provide management. See Chapter 26 for a run-through of your designer's capabilities.

Outlook—The Personal Information Manager

More and more responsibilities are being heaped on our personal and business shoulders. Keeping appointments, to-do tasks, and contacts straight has become a full-time job, one for which we need some sort of software tool. In walks Outlook. Outlook is a true personal information manager that can assist you with your daily, weekly, and monthly scheduling of appointments and tasks. Also a business contact manager, Outlook lets you track address and other information about business and personal contacts (date of birth, last meeting date, whether follow-up is needed, and so on). In addition to managing your contacts and appointments, Outlook provides you with an interface to your computer's hard drives and is a universal inbox for all of your e-mail services.

With Outlook, you can designate certain tasks as recurring and only list them once; Outlook will make sure these tasks and appointments appear on your calendar for as long as you specify. A task can be completed in stages and monitored by its percentage of completeness. Outlook also lets you type into and print monthly, weekly, and daily calendar grid layouts; you can use print preview to see exactly how your calendars will look when printed.

As any true manager knows how to do, Outlook works with the other members of the team. For instance, you can directly insert Outlook addresses into a letter you are writing in Word. See Chapter 33 to make an appointment with your personal information manager, Outlook.

Access—The Data Master

Access rounds out the Office suite by providing powerful and easy-to-use data-management tools. With Access, you can enter client information, track legal cases, design a mailing list, register participants for events and training—Access handles any tasks that involve asking questions and getting answers. Aligned with its other Office partners, Access can display a form for data entry in Excel, merge data into Word documents to create form letters or print catalogs and directories, embed a PowerPoint slide in a field, and take information from Outlook. Designed so anyone can create categories, forms, questions, and reports for their data, Access sits in the corner office of the suite (see Chapter 39).

Windows 95 and Windows NT 4.0

Before you sit down with each of the Office suite members, you should understand their underlying environment: Windows 95 and Windows NT 4.0. These operating systems have an interface that lets the Office members work seamlessly with each other.

You also need to understand this innovative, productivity-enhancing technology, so you can better direct the members of the Office team to use the "toys" of the Windows 95/NT interface to their advantage—to link data together, grab back deleted information, receive information from the Internet, route mail around the office, and much more.

The next chapter gives you a tour of the interface before you actually meet the individual Office team members. Become familiar with the Windows 95/NT environment if you aren't already; you can then make the most of the Office team.

Chapter

2

Your Office Environment: The Windows 95/NT Interface

FEATURING

Your Office Environment:
The Windows 95/NT Interface

While Windows 95 and the new Windows user interface have been available for well over a year, many Windows 3.*x* users are just now moving to Windows 95; Windows NT only gained the new interface in its latest release. There are still many users unfamiliar with the basics of the interface, so this chapter reviews those Windows 95/NT features that will help you become more productive when using the Office suite.

New Users - If you are new to computers, take a deep breath and…relax. Microsoft has designed an interface that is much easier to learn than its predecessors. Once pointed in the right direction and made aware of a few of the core navigating tools (which allow you to move from program to program and to manage your files), you will be able to perform a multitude of business tasks more easily than you ever could before.

Users Familiar with the Old Windows Interface - Users already familiar with Windows 3.*x* will have a slightly different experience when switching to the new interface. When taking the interface out for a spin for the first time, you will probably experience a fair amount of frustration, as it's only natural to approach the new interface as if it were what you used before, and of course there are differences. For most people, though, the initial frustration will turn into familiarity and, after a few hours of use, an enthusiastic recognition of the benefits that the changes bring. In fact, after reaching a level of comfort with the interface, you will probably find you want to burrow deeper into the offerings of the interface to discover what other enhancements have been made.

Starting from the Beginning

When your system boots up for the first time with Windows 95/NT, you find yourself facing the *Desktop*, where you will be spending quite a bit of time. Depending on which options you chose during installation, you will see some or all of the objects in Figure 2.1; these objects are described in Table 2.1.

> **NOTE**
>
> This chapter is only an introduction to the Windows 95/NT interface as it applies to Microsoft Office; we assume that you already have Windows 95 or Windows NT installed on your computer. For a broader introduction to Windows 95, please see *The ABCs of Windows 95* (Sybex, 1996).

FIGURE 2.1

The Windows Desktop

PART

I

Welcome to Your
New Office

TABLE 2.1: WINDOWS DESKTOP ICONS	
Icon	**Purpose**
My Computer	Provides direct access to all of your local drives, printers, Control Panel, and the Dial-Up Networking utility.
Network Neighborhood	Access to shared resources on your machine and computers on your local and wide area networks.
Recycle Bin	Provides you with drag-and-drop deletion of files from folders or your Desktop, and provides a second chance to recover files deleted from your hard drive.
Inbox or Microsoft Outlook	Universal in-box for all of your mail sources including faxes, Microsoft Mail, Exchange, and others. If you install Outlook with the Office, the Inbox icon (Exchange) is replaced with an Outlook shortcut.
Start button	Provides single-click access to all of the options you need to manipulate Windows applications and tools.
Taskbar	Displays all open applications and windows.

Start Button and Taskbar

By default, the Taskbar is on the bottom of the screen, with the Start button on the left-hand side. The Taskbar can, if you desire, be placed on the top or either side of the screen by clicking and dragging it to the new location. The Start button and the Taskbar work together to make managing your applications and open windows easier. Figure 2.2 shows the main menu items available when you click on the Start button.

Programs Submenu

Move your mouse pointer over the Programs item on the Start menu, and another menu will pop up. The function of this submenu is to organize your programs. If you're familiar with earlier versions of Windows, this will look like a listing of *program groups*. In fact, if you installed Windows 95 or Windows NT over a previous version of Windows, most of your old program groups will now appear in this list. Once you have Microsoft Office installed, you will be able to access all of the suite's programs from the Programs submenu (see Figure 2.3).

Because you can very easily open programs and files on top of other programs and files on the Desktop, thus obscuring your view of what you have running, Windows 95/NT

First level of the Start menu

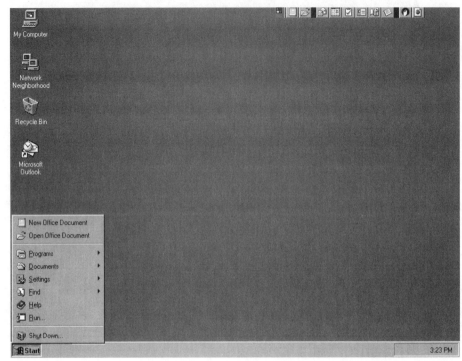

keeps track of all your open windows and lists them on the Taskbar. The benefit of the Taskbar is that when you have multiple applications open at the same time, you can see all of them listed in the foreground, whether or not they are hidden by another window. Even if an application window is minimized on the Desktop, it can still be accessed from the Taskbar. By clicking on an application's window on the Taskbar, you can bring that application to the front of the other windows, and restore it if it was minimized.

The more windows you open, the more items that will be listed on the Taskbar. If you find that you are having more than five windows open at a time, you can increase the size of the Taskbar to allow for multiple lines of open items.

To increase the height of the Taskbar, place the mouse pointer over its top border, the pointer will turn into a double-headed sizing arrow. Then, click and hold your primary mouse button (usually the left one) and drag up as illustrated in Figure 2.4.

FIGURE 2.3

*You have quick
access to
Microsoft Office
programs from
the Start button.*

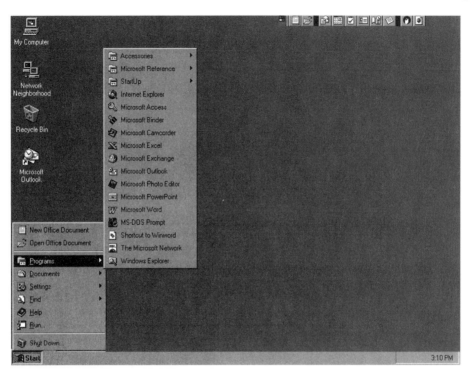

If you click your secondary (right, usually) mouse button on the Taskbar and select Properties from the menu that pops up, you can access the Taskbar's properties. From here, you can check off Auto Hide on the Taskbar Options tab so that the Taskbar disappears when your mouse pointer is not within its area. By selecting this option, you will provide yourself more screen real estate while working within your applications. To view the Taskbar, drag the mouse pointer to the bottom of the screen so that it pops up.

Documents Submenu

The Documents option of the Start menu makes available the last 15 documents you had open in any application (Figure 2.5). The documents are listed alphabetically, not by use, and will be listed whether you open them from within an application or from

FIGURE 2.4

Increasing the size of your Taskbar with the mouse to allow for multiple lines

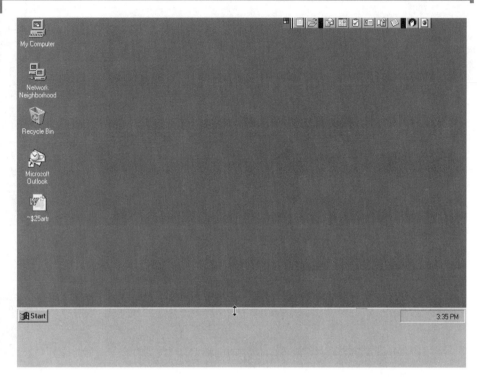

the folder where they are stored. If the list fills with irrelevant documents that you know that you will not want to access, you can clear the list: Right-click on the Taskbar to bring up the Taskbar Properties window; if the Start Menu Programs tab page isn't open in the properties window, click on its tab to display it. Then, click on the Clear button in the Documents Menu area.

Settings Submenu

The Settings option of the Start menu gives you access to the Control Panel, your printers, and the Properties window for the Taskbar. The Control Panel, seen in Figure 2.6, is where you can do most of your customizing of your Windows environment. It contains a great many more options than were available in the Control Panel in earlier versions of Windows. The Printers option shows you your installed printers and the Add Printer Wizard, which assists you in installing new printers. Double-clicking on any of the installed printers will open a window similar to Figure 2.7, showing the current print jobs sent to the printer and a number of menu options available to manipulate the printer and its jobs.

PART

I

Welcome to Your
New Office

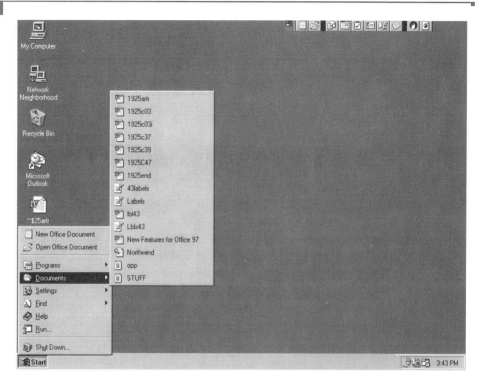

FIGURE 2.5

*Most recently
used document
list, accessed
from the Start
button*

The printer windows are equivalent to the Print Manager in earlier versions of Windows. (Windows 95 and Windows NT differ slightly in what their Control Panel folder and Printer folders hold. The examples in the figures are from Windows 95.)

Find Submenu

A Find submenu provides a universal find option for all of your applications. When you select Find on the Start menu, you can use it to find a file or folder located on your computer, a computer on your network, Outlook items, or areas of interest on the *Microsoft Network*. (The Microsoft Network is an online service that Microsoft provides access to through an interface bundled with Windows 95.)

The file system is broken down into *folders* and files. For those already familiar with older versions of Windows or DOS, folders translate into what you previously knew as *directories*. Those new to computers should consider folders as places to store files, as well as other folders. Folders are used to group files and folders that are used together.

FIGURE 2.6

Start ➤ Settings brings up the Control Panel.

FIGURE 2.7

A printer window opened by double-clicking on an installed printer in the printer window.

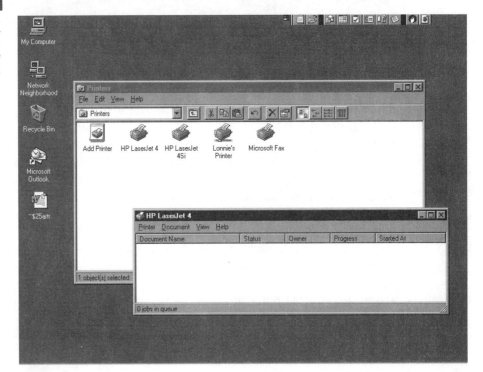

Quick Viewing a File

It is frequently the case when you are looking for files that you do not necessarily know which file contains the information you need. For this reason, looking for and finding the right file can be a long and arduous task if you need to continually open and close files to track down your information. In an effort to provide a more efficient search pattern, a multipurpose *file viewer* called Quick View can display the data content of any application file a find operation turns up.

You can use Quick View to take a peek at a file without having to start the application that created it. (Depending on your machine and its current resources, starting an application can take a few seconds; Quick View is instantaneous.) To use Quick View, locate the file you want to view and click on it with your secondary (right, usually) button. On the menu that pops up, select Quick View. Quick View will open, showing the contents of the document.

NOTE

Depending on how Windows 95/NT was installed, you might or might not see Quick View when you right-click on a filename. Go to Start ➢ Settings and check out the Add/Remove Programs item in the Control Panel to install Quick View.

Help Option

You can find answers to your questions about Windows by selecting Help on the Start menu to open the Help window. To search for help about Windows, type in the desired topic in the text box at the top of the Index tab page. As you type your topic, the help index will try to zero in on your help topic. If it does not come up with what you are searching for, try typing another combination of words under which your topic could be listed.

If your questions concern a specific application that you are using with Windows (for example, Microsoft Word), you should use the Help item found on the menu bar for the application in question, or press F1 from within that application for context-sensitive help.

Run

The Run option on the Start menu is generally an option for the more experienced user. Selecting Run brings up the Run window where you can type the name of a file or folder that you wish to open. If you don't know the entire *path* of folders within which a specific file or folder can be found, you can click on the Browse button within this window to find what you're looking for. Although this is generally not the quickest way to open a document or run a program, sometimes it simply seems more direct than opening a sequence of folders to get to the one you need.

Shut Down

You should "shut down" Windows before you turn your machine off or before you change certain aspects of your "presence" on the system—for example, before you log on to your network with a different user name. Believe it or not, to shut down, you go to the Start button.

Taking a Look Around

There are three primary tools that are available to assist you in finding the files, folders, and other resources on your local machine and network. These are:

- My Computer
- Network Neighborhood
- Windows Explorer

My Computer, which is located on your desktop, gives you easy access to your *local resources* (the ones available on your machine).

Network Neighborhood, which is installed only if your machine is used in a networking environment, is similar in function to My Computer, except it is able to view the printers and directories shared by the owners of computers available to you through your *local area network* (LAN), regardless of network provider (for example, Windows NT Server or Novell Netware).

The Windows Explorer, which is available from the Programs submenu of the Start menu, combines the features of My Computer and Network Neighborhood, giving you an outline view of all of your resources, local and network. Explorer can be considered an enhancement to and replacement of the File Manager found in earlier versions of Windows.

My Computer

My Computer allows you to look at the resources available to you on your local machine. If you have network drives mapped as local drives, they will also show up here. Figure 2.8 shows what a common top-level window of My Computer may look like.

The top level contains all of your lettered drives, local or networked, a folder for access to the Control Panel, a folder for access to your printers, and a Dial-Up Networking folder containing dial-up (modem) connections (if you installed this option at the time of setup).

Double-clicking on a drive in the top level of My Computer will open another window containing the main folders on the selected drive. Double-clicking on any of the folders in the drive window will open another window showing the contents of the folder. You can continue opening folders and subfolders until there are no more folders left in the current folder or you find the file you need.

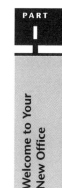

FIGURE 2.8

*My Computer
opening window*

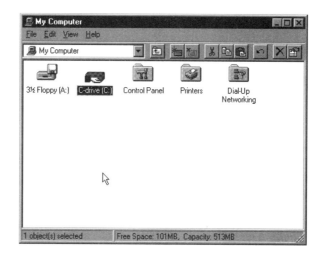

Make Keeping Track of Open Windows Easy!

The process of drilling down into folders of a drive tends to yield a lot of open windows that can become increasingly difficult to keep track of. Here are a couple of techniques to minimize the confusion:

• Remember you don't have to go looking for windows all over the Desktop. Every window that is open will be listed on the Taskbar; you can simply click on the window you want on the Taskbar to bring it to the front of all of the other windows.

• If you select View ➢ Options from the My Computer menu bar, you can choose to drill down into folders and other resources through a *single window*—thereby eliminating the overcrowding of the Desktop with windows you are only opening so you can get to another window. If you select this option, you can easily get back to the windows you opened on your way to the current one by using the Backspace key or the Up One Level button on the drive window's toolbar to backtrack through the windows one at a time.

Double-clicking on either the Control Panel folder or the Printers folder in the My Computer window will let you manipulate the settings for your computer or printer the same way that you would if you were accessing them from the Start menu.

My Computer may very well become your preferred method of accessing everything from folders and files to the Control Panel simply because of its convenient location on the Desktop and its ability to provide direct access to many of the resources you will use on a regular basis.

Network Neighborhood

Network Neighborhood takes the abilities of My Computer and extends them one step further, giving you with the ability to view all of the computers in your workgroup or network, and see what drives or printers may be available for your use.

When you first open Network Neighborhood, a list of the computers within your workgroup are listed along with an Entire Network icon. If you double-click on one of the computers, any resources that computer shares with others in the workgroup—like drives, directories, or printers—will be listed. If you double-click on the Entire Network icon instead, all of the domains or workgroups on the entire network will be listed. Double-clicking on one of these items reveals the computers that can be accessed through that workgroup or domain; from there you can check any resources made available by those computers.

Windows Explorer

Windows Explorer may very well end up being a primary tool for you if you are an advanced user and want to manipulate your resources at a deeper level than is provided by My Computer or Network Neighborhood alone. In addition to drive, folder, and file listings, Windows Explorer can display information such as:

- The current print jobs for available printers
- Identifying comments about other computers in the Network Neighborhood
- Descriptions of Control Panel tools
- The amount of space available on local and network drives

Explorer takes a two-pane viewing approach that permits you to investigate the contents of a folder or drive in the right pane while at the same time manipulating the outline view of the available resources in the left pane. This approach, which in previous versions of Windows required multiple windows in File Manager, is ideal for drag-and-drop copying from one location to another. Figure 2.9 shows this two-pane approach.

Recycle Bin

The Recycle Bin is where your files go when you delete them from your hard drive. You can access the bin to restore or "undelete" any files you inadvertently deleted. You can also drag and drop files onto the Recycle Bin for quick deleting.

The very name *Recycle Bin* suggests that when you delete files, they really do not get deleted. It's a safety feature, built in to protect you against the possibility of deleting something you shouldn't have. Files will be there until you *empty* the Recycle Bin, at which time the files are truly gone and cannot be recovered.

FIGURE 2.9

Windows Explorer allows you to view files from one folder in the right pane while looking at the outline of available folders in the left pane

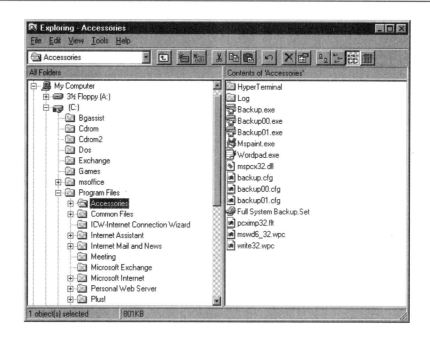

Deleted files in the Recycle Bin still take up disk space. You need to remember, then, to occasionally empty it. To empty your Recycle Bin, right-click on the bin icon and, from the shortcut menu that appears, select Empty Recycle Bin.

TIP

If you want to absolutely, positively delete something from your system and bypass the Recycle Bin altogether, select the file, then press Shift+Delete (that is, hold down the Shift key and press Delete while you still have the Shift key depressed) or hold down the Shift key as you drag a file onto the Recycling Bin. Be careful that you have the correct file before you use either of these options; the file will not be recoverable once it is deleted using the Shift key.

Shortcuts

The icons that you will eventually arrange on your Desktop in Windows 95/NT are fundamentally different from the icons that appeared in the Program Manager in earlier versions of Windows—and not just in appearance. The new Windows interface presents a "true" desktop. What this means is that when you click on an icon and delete it, the file(s) or programs that the icon represents *are* in fact deleted; they're not merely "de-iconized" (removed from the desktop) as was the case in Program Manager.

NOTE In earlier versions of Windows, you couldn't delete files and programs from Program Manager. You had to go to File Manager (or use the long and complicated Find File option in Word), and select by name and directory the files to be deleted.

Because Windows 95/NT makes it so easy to delete files and programs merely by clicking on their icons, you may be reluctant to move them onto the Desktop in the first place. Anticipating this concern, Windows allows you to create "shortcut" icons that work rather like the icons found in Program Manager, only better. Unlike the icons in Program Manager, shortcut icons *keep track* of the files they refer to. If you move a file that you have a shortcut pointing to, Windows will attempt to find it in your system, so the next time you use the shortcut, it will still open the file or folder that you intended. Previous versions of Windows could not keep track of such changes.

There are a number of ways to create a shortcut to a file. The most direct route is to right-click on a file in a window or on the Desktop and drag it to the new location (whether it be another folder or the Desktop); then, from the menu that appears, select Create Shortcut(s) Here.

Once you create a shortcut icon, you can double-click on it to open the file or folder that it is attached to. Most of the time you will be able to pick a shortcut icon out of a group of regular icons, because it will be the one with a little arrow in the bottom left-hand corner.

Special Key Combinations

Table 2.2 lists some keyboard combinations that you may find useful. No matter how devoted you become to your mouse, using key combinations for some of your most frequent tasks will help improve your efficiency while working in Windows.

TABLE 2.2: SPECIAL KEY COMBINATIONS		
Key(s)	**Purpose**	**Where Used**
F1	Call up help for the specific situation you are in	Anywhere in Windows
Alt+F4	Close an application	Anywhere in Windows
Ctrl+Esc	Pop up Start menu	Anywhere in Windows
Alt+Tab	Switch to the last window you were in	Anywhere in Windows

Continued ▶

TABLE 2.2: SPECIAL KEY COMBINATIONS (CONTINUED)

Key(s)	Purpose	Where Used
Shift+F10	View the Shortcut menu for the selected object	Anywhere in Windows
F2	Rename an object	Desktop or Windows Explorer
F3	Find a file or folder	Desktop or Windows Explorer
Alt+Enter	View object properties	Desktop or Windows Explorer
F5	Refresh (update) the view in a window	My Computer or Windows Explorer
Ctrl+Z	Undo file-management actions	My Computer or Windows Explorer
Backspace	View folder one level back	My Computer or Windows Explorer
Ctrl+Tab or Ctrl+Shift+ Tab	Move to the next tab in a dialog box	Dialog boxes

You should now have a basic understanding of the workings of the new Windows interface. Although you may have misgivings at first, as you continue to work within the new Windows environment you will become more and more comfortable. And as you become more comfortable, you will begin to customize the Desktop, the way you perform basic functions, and the overall way you interact with your computer. The best feature of Windows is that it is so customizable that no two people have to use it in exactly the same way.

Chapter

3

Microsoft Office's Integrated Tools

FEATURING

Microsoft Office's Integrated Tools

What makes Microsoft Office stand out the most from its peers is the level of integration between the individual applications. The integration is made possible through common interfaces, shared tools, the ability to link and embed data from one application into another, and the newest, perhaps the biggest, stride towards document integration—the Office Binder, which allows you to keep all of your Office documents for one project in a single file.

Taking a broad look at Microsoft Office is the goal of this chapter. We will start with an investigation of the unique contributions of each product and then move the focus toward the features of Office that will allow you to marry these products and accomplish your document chores.

The Power of One

The integration of applications is understandably the primary area of interest among application users these days. Before you can talk about integration, however, you must know what there is to integrate. Word, Excel, PowerPoint, Outlook, and Access are all valuable resources in their own right, providing the quality ingredients of integrated Office solutions.

Word

The most familiar application among the members of the Office suite is Word. With Word, you can accomplish all of your basic word processing duties and fulfill most of your desktop publishing needs. You will be using Word to generate all of your memos, letters, reports, and other text-intensive documents. Word's most valuable contribution to Office is its flexibility with text and its ability to incorporate data from the other Office applications in their original format to produce comprehensive documents.

Within a Word document, some specific tools you can take advantage of are:

- Built-in and custom templates that allow fast document creation based on boilerplate text and styles, Auto Text, macros, and toolbars stored with individual templates.
- Master Document view that allows you to manage very large documents by incorporating subdocuments into one primary master document.
- The ability to insert fields that make your documents more dynamic by facilitating user input, system input for data (like the current date), and other special features that need to be updated regularly.
- Large-document management features, like the ability to easily create tables of contents, indexes, tables of authorities, tables of figures, and cross references.
- Mail-Merge Helper, which allows you to quickly create merge documents like mass mailings or mailing labels.
- Easy table creation and formatting features such as table AutoFormat, which allows you to focus on your data and let Word handle the formatting.
- Automation through the means of macro creation with the addition of Visual Basic for Applications as Word's programming language.
- AutoCorrect and AutoFormat features that catch typographical errors automatically and allow you to use predefined shortcuts and typing patterns to quickly format your documents.

Excel

Excel is the Office application that you will want to focus on when number crunching and analyzing raw data is a concern. While Excel can be classified as a spreadsheet program, it is misleading to limit Excel by such a definition. Excel can perform all of the general spreadsheet operations with extended functionality in the areas of data entry, data analyzing, and sheer capacity.

Excel is a perfect companion for Word and PowerPoint, letting them provide the presentation while Excel provides the numbers to back it all up. Excel features include:

- Templates that you can use to standardize data entry files that may contain complex formulas.
- Charting and mapping tools that allow you to graphically represent your data.

- The ability to record or edit macros for repetitive tasks with the Visual Basic for Applications language.
- The ability to quickly sort and filter lists of information.
- Subtotaling and grouping features that allow you to see your data in a concise form.
- Importing and exporting tools that help you upscale your data into Excel, or out of Excel and into Access or another database application.
- Scenario tools like Goal Seek and Solver that assist in "What if..." calculations.
- The Pivot Table Wizard, which creates interactive tables that summarize your data every way possible.

PowerPoint

When it comes time to make a presentation, whether it is to prospective clients or your own board of directors, PowerPoint is the application that you will want to have on your side. With PowerPoint, you will be able to get your point across whether it is through a slide show of your presentation on the computer or by using printed overhead slides. PowerPoint will take a combination of the results of your efforts in Word and Excel and add some of its splashy effects to really get your point across. Power-Point features include:

- AutoContent Wizards to walk you through the development of common presentations.
- Templates with over 36 fully designed text and graphical slide formats.
- AutoLayouts, which provide standardized slide formats, reducing the time to build most standard slides.
- An extensive Clip Art library with an Auto Launch button that helps you pull down more clip art from the Microsoft Web Site.
- The ability to add multimedia sound and video to your presentations.
- Animation effects for true incremental display of feature graphics.
- Meeting Minder feature that allows users to annotate presentations during group meetings with action items or minutes of the meeting.
- The ability to create and insert organizational charts into your presentations with Microsoft Organization Chart.

Outlook

A welcome new member to the Office suite is Outlook. A single replacement for Schedule+ and your Exchange client, Outlook provides contact management, an e-mail client, and drive and folder management functionality. Outlook not only allows you to schedule your time, it also facilitates the management of both your personal and business contacts, manages e-mail from various sources, and allows you to gain quick access to folders on your drives. With the inclusion of Outlook in Office, Microsoft is recognizing that to be truly productive, access to the information that we utilize regularly needs to be centralized. This newest innovation in Office will make itself most evident in Word, where you will be able to insert names stored in Outlook into your documents. Outlook features include:

- The ability to record tasks, appointments, projects, and events.
- On-screen daily, weekly, monthly, yearly, and planner views of your schedule.
- The ability to print your schedule in many formats, including popular planner formats.
- The ability to store your contact information, including name, address, multiple phone numbers, birthdays, anniversaries, e-mail address, hyperlinks to home pages, and much more.
- The ability to allow others on the network to have various levels of access rights of your schedule and mail folders.
- The ability to schedule meetings with others using the Meeting Planner, which finds available time for all participants using Outlook over a network.

Access

With Access, everyone from beginners to experts can create and manage databases both small and large. Out of all the other programs in the Office suite, you should look to Access as the sole depository of your data—you need only record your data once, then retrieve it from the other Office applications.

Some of the Access features that you can take advantage of are:

- Database Wizards that create an entire database from tables to reports per your specifications.
- Forms that provide simple data entry and filtering capabilities, allowing you to easily manage your data.
- Sophisticated Report Wizards you can use to create professional looking reports.
- The Report Design Screen, which allows you to create reports from scratch.
- Macros that automate repetitive tasks like importing data.
- Visual Basic for Applications, which you can use to create full-fledged applications.
- The built-in HTML wizards that help you publish your data to the World Wide Web.

The Common Threads That Bind

One of the barriers that many users face when working with multiple software packages is having to remember how each separate system functions. Which key combinations work in *this* application? Where are the font commands on *this* menu bar? With Microsoft Office, this barrier to productive computing is reduced by centering each of the applications around a common user interface. Office also includes tools that are common across all of the applications, providing a familiarity that is conducive to faster learning.

Menu Bars and Toolbars

Probably the most noticeable similarity between the Office applications is the common menu bars and toolbars, which together are called *command bars*. In Office 97, you can place menus on a toolbar and toolbar buttons on a menu bar because their functionality is now the same.

The menu bars, as seen in Figure 3.1, are identical in Word, Excel, PowerPoint, and Access, with the exception of only one application-specific menu item. That application-specific item appears in the same place on all of the menu bars (to the right of the Tools menu), except in Access, where it is to the left of the Tools menu.

FIGURE 3.1

Common menu bars available in the Office applications

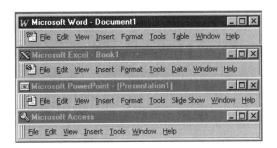

All of the Office applications except Access use common toolbars (including the Standard toolbar, the Formatting toolbar, and the Drawing toolbar) for standard functions, allowing you to move between applications more easily.

To begin working with your menu bars and toolbars, follow these steps:

1. Open Word.
2. From the menu bar, select Tools ➤ Customize. (The customize dialog that opens has three tabs. The Toolbars tab shows all built-in and custom toolbars; the Commands tab lists the commands you can add to your menu bars and toolbars organized by category; and the Options tab that allows you to control the basic functionality of the menus and toolbars.)
3. Click on the Commands tab, select the Edit category, and scroll through the commands until you find Select All.

4. Click and drag the Select All command next to one of your toolbar buttons; the bar that appears at the insertion point when you are on a toolbar indicates where the new button will be placed.

5. Close the Customize dialog box.

6. Try to use your new Select All toolbar button. Notice it functions in the same way as any other toolbar button.

You can also modify your toolbars and menu bars by opening the Customize dialog box and holding down the Alt key while dragging items to a new location:

1. Open the Customize dialog box.

2. While the Customize dialog box is still open, drag the Edit menu to a point on the Standard toolbar, and then release the mouse. The Edit menu will now appear on the Standard toolbar (and not the menu bar).

3. You can then use this same technique to move the Edit menu back to its original location on the menu bar (to the right of the File menu).

NOTE

With the Customize dialog box open, you can also move toolbar buttons *onto* a menu: Drag a toolbar button to a menu; the menu will drop down. Drag the button to the spot on the menu where you want it to appear and release the mouse. The name of the command, as well as the button icon and shortcut key (if any) for the command, will appear at that point on the menu.

Shared Tools

If the words that you are typing are not common words, or are words that are particular to your field of study, chances are that they will not be stored in the dictionaries that come with your applications. You can add such words during a spelling check to a dictionary in an individual application. And since the Office applications all share the same spell-check engine and dictionaries, if you add a word in one application, that word will be recognized in all of your Office applications. Without Office, however, if you add a word to one application, you will still need to add it to the other applications separately.

In addition, the AutoCorrect feature is available in Word, Excel, Access, and Power-Point. AutoCorrect automatically corrects common spelling errors, both built-in and those that you specify. AutoCorrect also allows you to use shorthand entries to insert common symbols (like the copyright or registered trademark symbols); you can also define your own AutoCorrect entries to quickly insert common sections of text or special characters that you use day to day.

To get an idea of the shared spelling checker and AutoCorrect, follow these steps:

1. Launch Excel from the Start button.
2. In cell A1, type **Wunderbar**.
3. Run the Spelling Checker by pressing F7. If you are prompted to decide if the spell-check should start at the beginning of the document, click on Yes.
4. The Spelling Checker will not recognize *Wunderbar* as a word. Choose Cancel in the Spelling dialog box (shown in Figure 3.2).

FIGURE 3.2

Excel spell-checking the word "Wunderbar"

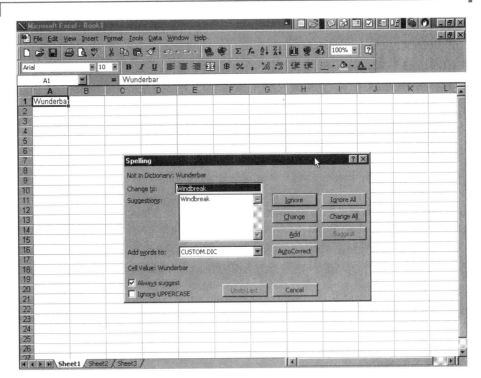

5. Close Excel and launch Word from the Start button.
6. In the blank document opened with Word, type **Wunderbar**.
7. Press F7 to spell-check the document.
8. When Word prompts you to make a decision about *Wunderbar*, click on the Add button.
9. After the spell-check is finished, on a new line type **(c)**. AutoCorrect will replace the characters with a copyright symbol.
10. Your Word screen should look like Figure 3.3

FIGURE 3.3

Adding an Auto-Correct entry in Excel

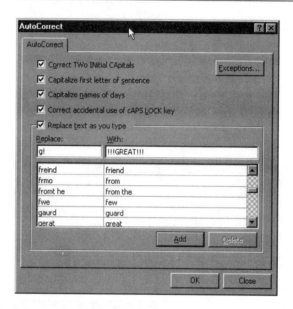

11. Close Word, and don't save the changes.

12. Launch Excel.

13. In cell A1 type **Wunderbar** again. Spell-check the workbook by pressing F7, and notice that because you added the word in the spelling dictionary in Word (step 8), Excel now also recognizes the word.

14. In cell A2 try the AutoCorrect shortcut of step 9; that is, type **(c)**. Notice that Excel also has AutoCorrect: the (c) is automatically changed to a copyright symbol. The copyright symbol is one of the many built-in AutoCorrect entries.

15. In Excel, select Tools ➤ AutoCorrect from the menu bar.

16. In the AutoCorrect dialog box, type **g!** in the Replace text box, and type **!!!GREAT!!!** in the With text box, as in Figure 3.3.

17. Click on the Add button, click on OK, and then close Excel; don't worry about saving any of the changes.

18. Open PowerPoint and go to a section of a slide where you can enter text.

19. Type **g!**.

20. Figure 3.4 shows the result. The custom AutoCorrect item assigned in Excel (step 15) is available in PowerPoint.

The above exercise is a good simple sampling of how the shared tools of Office work together. It is the cooperation of features like these that help make your efforts much more productive and efficient.

FIGURE 3.4

*"!!!GREAT!!!"
inserted into
PowerPoint with
AutoCorrect*

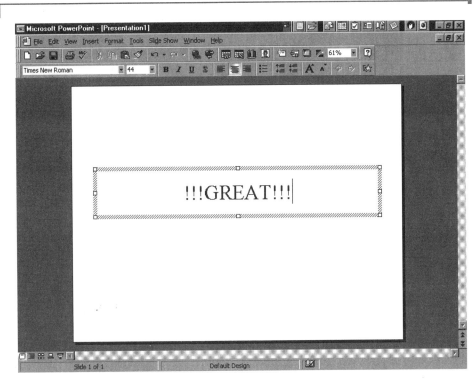

MASTERING TROUBLESHOOTING

When working with multiple Office programs open at the same time, the cross-application availability of the AutoCorrect and Spelling features may not appear to work correctly.

The reason for this is that when you add something to AutoCorrect or the custom spelling dictionaries in one application, the AutoCorrect and custom spelling dictionaries for the suite are not updated until that application is closed.

Therefore, to insure your additions to AutoCorrect or a custom spelling dictionary take effect in another application, close the original application in which you made changes and then open the other application in which you want to use the added items.

Office Assistants and Online Help

You are no longer alone when working with your Office applications—the Office Assistant is always at hand. The online help system takes animated form with the Office Assistant, which provides real-time tips as you work. You can also ask the Office Assistant plain-English questions; it will parse the questions and attempt to provide possible answer topics to help you.

By default, the Office Assistant opens when you open an Office application. You can either leave it on top all of the time, or you can close it until you require its help. To call up the assistant after it has been closed, click on the Office Assistant button on the Standard toolbar. One of the forms the Office Assistant takes is shown in Figure 3.5.

FIGURE 3.5

Office Assistant as an animated paper clip waiting for you to ask it a question.

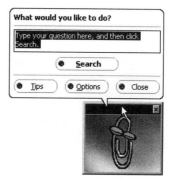

The Office Assistant is a big advance in the features available for online information and help systems. Whether you are a new user or simply a seasoned Office user trying to migrate to this new version, the assistant should prove to be a valuable guide.

Working Together To Get the Job Done

Once you have become familiar with the individual components of Office and the contributions they can make to your projects, you can focus on the building blocks that make Office integration possible. *OLE* is the term that many use to broadly categorize the integration of applications. OLE, which originally stood for Object Linking and Embedding, is now an umbrella term used when people are talking not just about the linking and embedding of objects from one application into another, but also about the ability to programmatically automate and manipulate those objects.

Because an explanation of OLE terminology can quickly become an overwhelming onslaught of information, we'll use the rest of this chapter to take apart OLE, spending time with each piece to make it easier to understand the whole.

Objects

At the center of OLE are *objects*. What are objects? Well, you can say that objects are things that are created by one program and have certain characteristics, like size and color, that can be manipulated by other applications. Objects that you may be familiar with are Excel workbooks, Excel charts, Word documents, PowerPoint slides, and Paintbrush pictures. There is a quick way that you can get a more comprehensive, though far from complete, list of objects you can use within your Office applications.

1. Launch Word.
2. Select Insert ➤ Object from the menu bar.
3. On the Create New tab page, scroll through the list of objects, which you can see in Figure 3.6. (When you've gotten a feel for the number and variety of objects available, click on Cancel.)

FIGURE 3.6

The Create New tab page, available from the Insert ➤ Object menu option

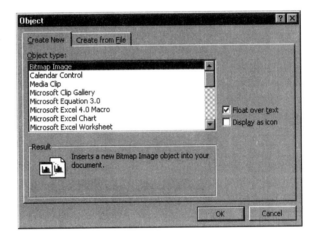

The list of objects on the Create New tab page is an ever-growing list that expands as you add applications to your computer. Using the Insert ➤ Object command is not the only way to move application objects from their native application into another application (say, for example, an Excel chart into a Word document). You can simply make use of the Windows *Clipboard*. By using variations of the Edit ➤ Paste Special command, you can achieve the next part of OLE, linking and embedding.

Linking

Linking is one method of placing an object from one application into another. What sets linking apart from embedding is that with linking, *live data from the original application is used.* For example, you may have numbers in Excel that you want to use in a Word document. You can copy those numbers in Excel and Paste Link them into a Word document. Because the numbers you added to the Word document are linked to the Excel workbook, when the numbers change in the original Excel workbook, they will be updated in the Word document. This quick exercise will show you the power of linking.

1. Launch Excel.
2. Type **100** in cell A1, then type **100** in cell A2. Type the formula **=A1+A2** in cell A3.
3. Save the workbook as Excel Link Test; the worksheet should look like Figure 3.7.
4. Select the range A1 through A3, and select Edit ➤ Copy from the Excel menu bar.

FIGURE 3.7

Excel workbook with three cells containing information

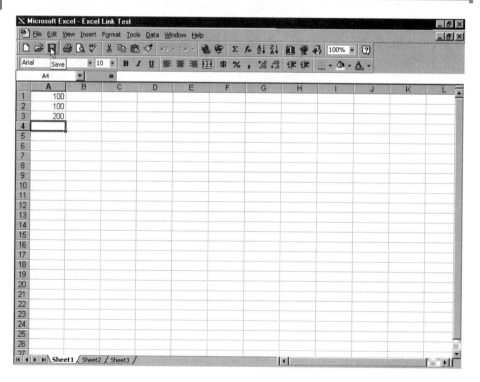

5. Launch Word.
6. Select Edit ➤ Paste Special from the Word menu bar.
7. In the Paste Special dialog box, select Paste Link and Microsoft Excel Worksheet Object; the dialog box will look like Figure 3.8.

FIGURE 3.8

*Paste Special
dialog box set to
link an Excel
worksheet object*

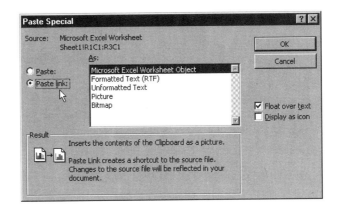

8. Click on OK to paste link the object, then switch to Excel by clicking on its button on the Taskbar.
9. Change the contents of cell A1 to **200**.
10. Switch back to Word. The changes are updated in the Word document, as shown in Figure 3.9.
11. Save the document as **Word Link Test** and close Word.
12. In Excel, change the value of cell A2 to **400**.
13. Save the workbook and close Excel.
14. Launch Word and open the Word Link Test file.
15. Notice that even though Word was closed when the changes were made and Excel is now closed, the information is still updated.

Linked information can be updated either manually or automatically. The default is for links to be updated automatically. If you have a number of linked objects in your document, you may want to update them manually, so that you will not be interrupted whenever information changes and links are updated. To do this, select Edit ➤ Links from the menu bar, highlight the links you want to update manually, and click on the Manual Updating button. Then, if you want to manually update the links, click on the Update Now button in the Links dialog box or press F9 with the links selected.

FIGURE 3.9

Excel data linked into Word

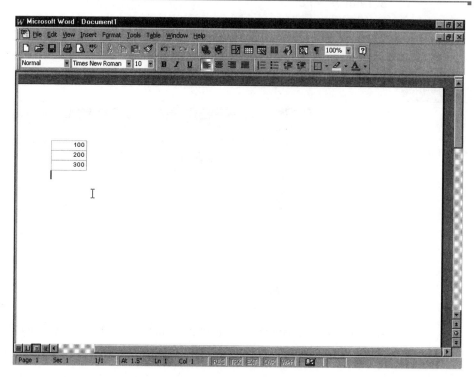

The Print and General tab pages of the Options dialog box also have options for updating linked data. An option on the Print tab page allows you to Update Links just before printing (this updates both manual and automatic links). On the General tab page, you can specify whether or not to Update Automatic Links at Open (to update automatic links when files are opened).

When working with linked data, you can edit a linked object by double-clicking on the object. When you double-click on a linked object, the file that contains the data will be opened in the application it was created in. In the above example, if you were to double-click on the linked Excel data in Word, Excel would launch and the Excel Link Test file would open so that you could edit it.

Embedding

Embedding an object into a document is similar in process to linking an object. Yet while the initial appearance of embedded and linked data is the same, the underlying data is quite different. The biggest distinction between linking and embedding is that in embedding there is *no connection to the original file*. When you embed an object, you

WARNING

When working with linked data, be sure not to move the file in which the linked data originated. When you link information, you are specifying a path to the file. If you move the file, the path is no longer valid. Unlike shortcuts that find the files they are pointing to even if they are moved, OLE does not automatically update file paths. If a linked document does get moved, all is not lost. If you need to modify the path of a linked file, select Edit ➤ Links from the menu bar and click on the Change Source button to update the link.

are taking a copy of the original data from one application and placing it into another application. When you double-click on an embedded object, the menu and toolbars from the original application are brought into the application in which the object is embedded. But if you make changes to the original file or to the embedded object, the other will not be affected. Use the Excel Link Test file you created above with the steps below to see embedding in action.

1. Open the Excel Link Test file.
2. Select the range A1 through A3.
3. Select Edit ➤ Copy from the menu bar.
4. Launch Word.
5. Select Edit ➤ Paste Special from the menu bar.
6. In the Paste Special dialog box, modify the options so that Word is set to Paste (not Paste Link) a Microsoft Excel Worksheet Object, as in Figure 3.10, and then click on OK.
7. Save the Document as **Word Embed Test**.

FIGURE 3.10

Paste Special dialog box set to embed a Microsoft Excel Worksheet Object

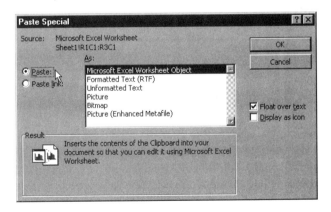

8. Switch to Excel and change the value of cell A1 to **50**.
9. Save the workbook and switch to Word. Notice that the information in the Word document did not change, because there is no link to the original file.
10. Double-click on the embedded object in Word. Note the changes in the toolbar and menu bar that are illustrated in Figure 3.11: the Excel toolbars and menu bar have replaced those of Word.

FIGURE 3.11

Embedded Excel object being edited in Word. The Excel object has been activated, and the Excel toolbars and menu bar are on-screen, making it possible to perform Excel operations on the object

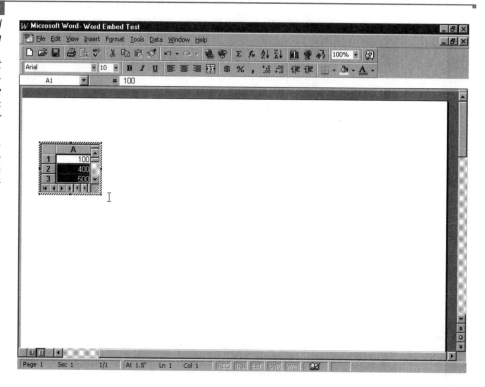

11. Make changes to one of the cells in the object.
12. Click in the document outside of the object. Note that your interface returns to normal (that is, to the Word interface).

The biggest advantage embedding has over linking is that you don't need to worry about the location of the original file an embedded object came from. You will want to be careful about embedding objects, however, if file *size* is an issue. When you embed an Excel Worksheet Object into Word, for example, the entire workbook is embedded, not just the selected portion that you see in Word! A once-small Word document can quickly grow very large with only a couple of embedded objects.

Automation

OLE automation is the ability to control an object programmatically. For example, not only can you run a macro that performs an end-of-month function on a workbook, you can add to that macro to have it then create a Word document, format the document, insert some relevant end-of-month text, place the monthly numbers into the document, print the document, and then close.

OLE automation requires rather deep coding with Visual Basic for Applications, so it is beyond the scope of this book. You can get a better sense of what OLE automation is all about by asking the Office Assistant "What is OLE automation?"

The Office Binder

Microsoft Office Binder is probably the best example of the power of OLE. This application allows you to combine all of the individual documents for a project you are working on into a single entity—a binder. The Office Binder interface, seen in Figure 3.12, consists of two panes, a very narrow "contents" column on the left and a regular document pane on the right. The left pane functions like tabs in a notebook, showing you the constituent elements—the *sections*—of the Office Binder file. The right pane is where you can work on the element selected in the left pane.

Office Binder allows you to edit your section files either directly in a binder itself, or as separate documents outside of the binder. The binders are easy to create, maintain, and distribute. For a quick introduction to Office Binder, walk through these steps:

1. From the Start button, launch Microsoft Office Binder. A new binder will open up.
2. From the Section menu on the menu bar, select Add.
3. Select Word Document from the Add Section dialog box and click on OK.
4. Your binder will now have a Word Document section, which shows up as a Section 1 icon in the left pane. Your binder should look similar to Figure 3.13.
5. Select File ➢ Save Binder from the Office Binder menu bar.
6. Save the binder as **Test Binder.**
7. Type **Main Heading** in the right pane of the binder—the binder's document screen.
8. Center the "Main Heading" text by clicking on the center-alignment button on the Formatting toolbar.
9. Say to yourself, "Neat, I'm working in this section of my binder as if it were a regular Word document!"

FIGURE 3.12

A binder in Microsoft Office Binder containing multiple "sections" (Office files)

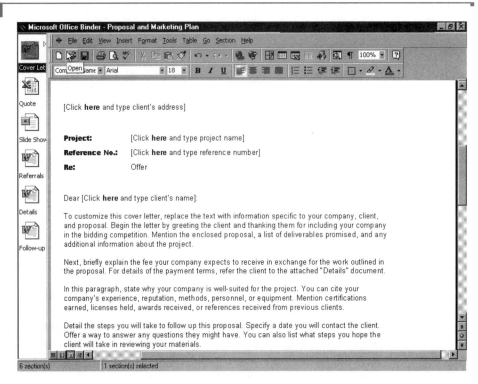

FIGURE 3.13

Office Binder with a Word Document section

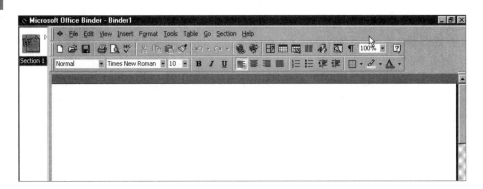

Although working in a binder section is almost exactly like working on a document in its original application, there are a few functions not available when you are inside the Office Binder. To Print Preview a section, for example, you must release the section from the binder. To do this, select Section ➤ View Outside from the Office Binder menu bar. Once the section is outside of the binder you can work with it just like a normal Word document. When you are finished, select File ➤ Close & Return to Binder from the Word menu bar to return the Word section to your binder.

Existing files can be inserted into a binder. From the Section menu on the Office Binder menu bar, select Add from File to insert existing files into your binder. If you have your windows tiled in a way that you can see your files and the binder, you can click and drag files into your binder:

1. Without closing the binder, create a file in Excel and a file in PowerPoint, save them, and then close both Excel and PowerPoint.
2. Select Section ➤ Add from File from the Office Binder menu bar, find your Excel document, and add it to your binder.
3. Using My Computer, find the PowerPoint file you created, and click and drag the file from the My Computer window into the left pane of the binder.
4. Your binder should look similar to the one in Figure 3.14.

FIGURE 3.14

*Office Binder
with Word,
PowerPoint,
and Excel
documents in it*

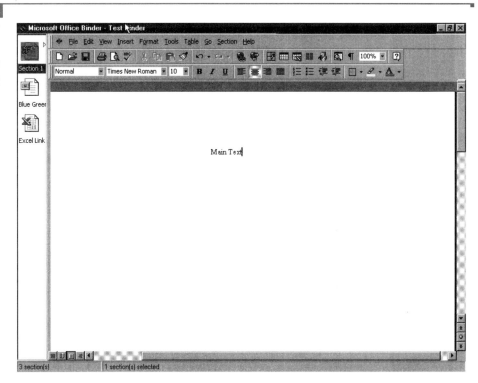

When you are ready to print out the contents of the binder, you can choose to have the entire binder paginated sequentially from beginning to end, or you can have each section paginated separately.

Office Binder will play a key role in your organization of Office documents into projects. In fact, Office Binder may prove to be the best new feature in Office 97.

Chapter

4

Microsoft Office and the Internet

FEATURING

Microsoft Office and the Internet

Bill Gates's 20-year vision of "information at your fingertips" has fully taken form in Microsoft Office 97. This idea began in the late 1970s with the microprocessor's promise of "a computer on every desktop," and continued throughout the 1980s with the development of powerful languages, operating systems, and application software.

Over the last decade, we've seen an increasing integration between applications and operating environments and the emergence of both local area networks (LANs) and the global Internet. Integration has long been a major strength of Microsoft Office, and with the Internet tools added in Office 97, the computer on your desktop now gives you unparalleled access to information. The next twenty years will be very interesting as we see how Microsoft continues to enhance the way we use the Internet, the World Wide Web, and our corporate intranets (internal networks based on the Web and other Internet tools).

This chapter is an overview of Office 97's online and Internet features. The suite's Internet capabilities will be discussed in greater detail in Part Seven.

Information Immediacy

The Office applications have been coming together for the last couple of years, and have finally achieved a truly unified appearance and seamless integration. Office 97 is the product of Microsoft's commitment to use the Internet and intranets to place a powerful information tool in the hands of users. As you work with Office 97 on your desktop, on your corporate intranet, and on the Internet, the product will begin to feel more like one "big" application than a suite of multiple applications.

For now, try to think of Office 97 as a tool for *immediacy*:

- Immediate power provided to your work output via the new Office 97 features.
- Immediate information provided to your corporate colleagues via shared, routed, and hyperlinked documents.
- Immediate facts and feedback provided to the public about your company via information-rich Web pages and sophisticated e-mail routing rules.
- Immediate information about your schedule, tasks, and research needs via a personal information manager and the Internet's plethora of search tools.

What Is the Internet?

Before you can take full advantage of the features available in Office 97 for connection to the Internet, you should be familiar with Internet parts, concepts, and terminology. The next few sections provide you with some Internet basics so that you can understand the purpose of different Office 97 Internet features.

The Internet seems suddenly to be a fact of everyday life—you cannot escape a discussion about the Internet either through your business, the media, or your friends. An exact definition of the Internet, however, seems difficult to come by. This difficulty is in part because of the amorphous nature of the Internet and the Internet's ability to be different things to different people.

We searched the World Wide Web part of the Internet for a definition of the Internet itself. The definition we found is a short, unromantic description of what the Internet is *physically*. (The Internet's *purpose* is still an evolving definition; we'll cover its many uses as we go along.) A firm in Germany—Solutions, E.T.C.—graphically depicted the Internet in the U.S. as a series of interconnected, streaming lines (their Web address is `http://www.solutionsetc.de/home/Internet.html`). The Internet is a global computer network of interconnected networks. The graphic on the next page hints toward the enormity and interconnectedness of the Internet.

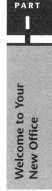

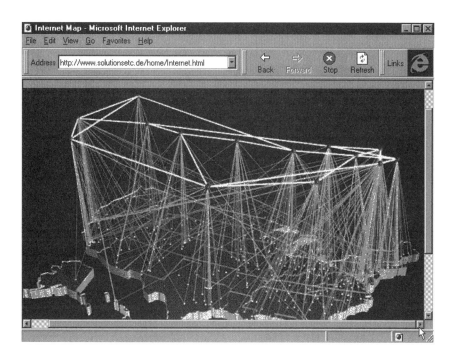

All of the computers connected on the Internet must communicate with each other using a specific set of rules (protocols) called TCP/IP (Transmission Control Protocol/ Internet Protocol). TCP/IP software developed with public funds is considered an open nonproprietary protocol, which means no one owns it and anyone can use it freely. It is the "great leveler"—computers that could never communicate with each other because of their different operating systems can now share information using TCP/IP.

Who Runs the Internet?

No one actually runs the Internet, although there is an Internet Organization (http://rs.krnic.net/1996/map.html) whose committees are concerned with setting up, maintaining, monitoring, and enhancing Internet rules, protocols, and standards; they also monitor the number of new computers being linked onto the Internet at a rate of thousands per day.

The InterNIC (Internet Network Information Center), for example, is a well-known Internet Organization committee responsible for authorizing and registering your Internet name address (domain name).

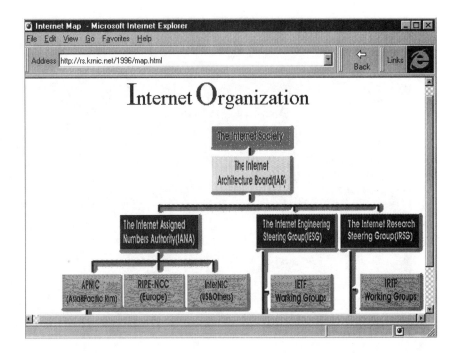

The Internet was originally conceived in 1969 in the United States as part of the American Defense Department's method for exchanging scientific information and intelligence. When the National Science Foundation and other research agencies and universities joined the link, enthusiasm began to grow for the Internet's e-mail, file transfer, and remote login services that enhanced research and collaborative study.

As commercial organizations began providing access to the Internet to people who were not researchers or part of the university community, the Internet's growth exploded. In 1981, 213 computers were registered on the Internet. It is projected that by 1998 there will be over 3 million computers connected through the Internet, with more than 100 million people connecting through these computers. The rough estimates are that about 150,000 people connect each month to the Internet.

Sometimes called the *information superhighway*, the Internet has become an inexpensive, global communication tool capable of sending text, sound, graphics, and videos to computers around the world using telephone lines. The faster your telephone line connection, the more you will enjoy using the Internet.

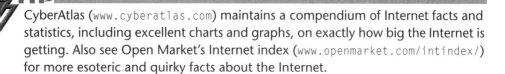

CyberAtlas (`www.cyberatlas.com`) maintains a compendium of Internet facts and statistics, including excellent charts and graphs, on exactly how big the Internet is getting. Also see Open Market's Internet index (`www.openmarket.com/intindex/`) for more esoteric and quirky facts about the Internet.

Internet Backbone

The core or "backbone" of the Internet is a group of host computers linked together by a dedicated (always open) high-speed, telecommunications connection. Some of the companies that maintain the core of the Internet are AT&T, Sprint, MCI, and Cables & Wireless. Service providers and other networks (regional, education, government) get their high-speed connection by connecting into the backbone group; other computers then connect into service providers and the regional or educational networks. This pattern of connecting goes on until you have an intricate network of interconnecting networks.

Online services such as Microsoft Network, America Online, and CompuServe were not Internet networks prior to 1996, but they connected onto the Internet via gateways (intermediary computers that connect networks that have different protocols). These online services then were able to offer Internet access as well as their own information services to the general public.

During 1996, however, we saw these online companies moving a lot of their information to the open Internet for easier access by the millions of people connecting every day. Parts of Microsoft Network, for example, can now be accessed from the Internet instead of having to dial up the network up specifically. America Online will also be bringing parts of its proprietary services to the open Internet.

Internet Activities

Once you are linked onto the Internet and using the TCP/IP protocols, you are able to "visit" and talk with every other computer on the Internet, regardless of where they may be in the world; you can also participate in the different Internet activities. The primary Internet activities allow you to:

- Send and receive electronic messages (e-mail).
- Transfer data files to and from computers around the world (File Transfer Protocol [FTP]).
- View corporate or personal documents containing graphical hypertext content (World Wide Web).
- Share points-of-view on specific subjects with other online groups, (Usenet newsgroups—Network News Transfer Protocol). See Figure 4.1.

PART

I

Welcome to Your
New Office

- Log into other computers to conduct research or view huge databases of information like library databases (remote login or Telnet).
- Chat with other users on the Internet using Internet Relay Chat (IRC).

FIGURE 4.1

DejaNews helps you find a newsgroup of people who share your interests

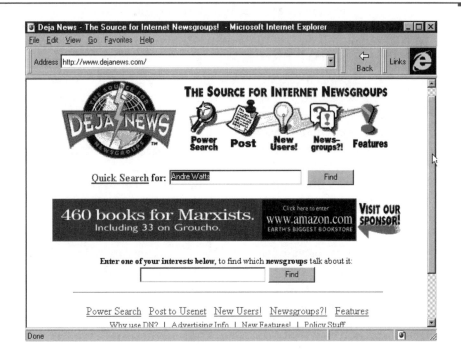

Internet Addressing

Each computer directly linked onto the Internet must obtain a unique address so that it can be located. A computer's *Internet Protocol (IP)* address is a four-part series of numbers separated by periods—for example, 198.137.241.30. Because it is difficult to remember a long series of numbers, a name addressing system was developed called the *domain name system (DNS)*—an example of a domain name is whitehouse.gov. The DNS is a worldwide system of databases that maps domain names with their correlated IP addresses. You can look up an IP address (numbers) and get the name of a host computer or look up a domain name (text) and get the corresponding IP address number. Both the IP address and the domain name are important for an Internet address to be functional.

To obtain an Internet domain name, it is necessary to register with (and pay) a special Internet committee, the Internet Network Information Center (InterNIC). The InterNIC registration services can be accessed on the World Wide Web at http://rs.internic.net as shown in Figure 4.2.

FIGURE 4.2

The InterNIC is the registration organization for domain names.

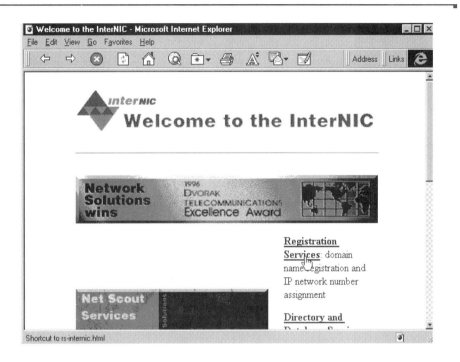

Domain Names

When an organization or company establishes a connection to the Internet either as a high-speed, dedicated provider itself or as an account through a dedicated provider, a domain name must be chosen. The name is unique and comprised of these parts:

```
hostname.subdomain(s).organization.domain
```

For example:

```
amenhotep.training.crtinc.com.
```

The parts of the domain name address are hierarchical as you read the address from right to left. The right-most part of the address name is called the *top-level* specification and is considered the most general description within the name. The top-level domain name categories are:

- com—commercial organizations
- edu—education (universities and education based organizations)
- gov—government (nonmilitary)
- int—international organizations

- `mil`—military organizations
- `org`—nonprofit and research organizations
- `net`—network and service operations
- Two-letter country codes; for example, `us` (United States), `it` (Italy), `uk` (United Kingdom), `de` (Germany), `ca` (Canada), `au` (Australia). Figure 4.3 displays the results from a search done through the AltaVista search engine (`www.Altavista.digital.com`) for country code top-level domain names.

FIGURE 4.3

You can find lists of country code domain names using a search engine such as Altavista.

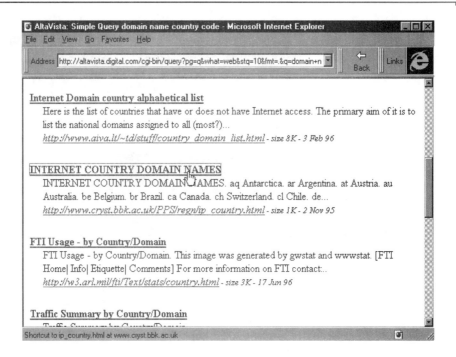

Now we can break down the domain name `amenhotep.training.crtinc.com`, from right to left:

`com`

The top-level part of the name indicates the type of service or organization for the server. In this example, `com` indicates a commercial organization.

`crtinc`

To the left of the domain type is the registered organization or company name. The organization/company name is also called a *second-level* domain name. When you apply to the InterNIC for a domain name, it is the second-level name you are registering. The second-level name can be a maximum of 22 alphanumeric characters and cannot include spaces (although underscores can be used).

```
training
```

To the left of the second-level name is a subdomain name, which in this example represents a department within the organization called crtinc. To the left of this subdomain name, there can be additional subdomain names (although not in this example).

```
amenhotep
```

The first part of the name (left-most) is the host computer itself or *hostname*, which in this example is the name of an actual computer at the organization called crtinc.

This entire domain name is part of a LAN (local area network) connected to the Internet. The network server is connected to the Internet, and each of the computers on the network gain their access to the Internet through the network server. In this example, a class C IP address was obtained so that one registered domain name, `crtinc.com`, could be authorized to *subdivide* its domain name and use subdomain names for each computer on the LAN.

TIP

You can search for the owner of any domain name and also register your own domain name through the WhoIs database at the InterNIC Web site: `http://rs.internic.net/cgi-bin/whois`. Keep in mind that `Microsoft.com` is an already registered name but `Silly-Techs.com` is still available. There is a $100 fee to register each domain name, and you must be able to provide the IP address of the host computer the names will be assigned to.

Domain Name System Portability

A host computer on the Internet has one IP address, but may have several domain names that map to its IP address. A DNS name is portable and can be used for another computer. In other words, an IP address for a computer may change but the domain name stays the same.

For example, Microsoft may exchange a computer that currently stores the Office 97 tips and tricks for a larger, faster computer. The new computer will require a new IP address, but the same domain name used for the old computer can be used for the new computer. Because existing users to the site continue to locate the computer using the domain name, they are unaffected by a change in IP address. DNS portability is one of the advantages of having an Internet domain name as well as a location IP number.

E-Mail Names

When you want to send and receive e-mail across the Internet, your computer *must* have an IP address so that you other computers on the Net can locate you. If you are connecting through your company's LAN or a service provider, you, as an individual, may not know the IP address associated with your connection to the Internet. And, even if you knew your IP, you would probably not want to give out and be identified by a difficult-to-remember series of numbers.

To eliminate any IP confusion, your company or your service provider will give you a domain (text) address to use at their organization called an *e-mail address*. The e-mail address consists of:

```
name@second-level.top-level
```

For example:

```
LSloan@crtinc.com
```

Your company or service provider will handle the IP number problem themselves, using mail servers or temporary IP addresses so that you are able to give out your e-mail domain name and not an IP address number. The mail software in TCP/IP manages the mapping of an e-mail domain name to an organization domain name and IP addresses.

What Is the World Wide Web?

Because of its glamorous interface and easy navigational methods, one of the most popular parts of the Internet is the World Wide Web, which is really a term for a system of documents that can be stored, retrieved, and viewed by individuals connected to the Internet. Special software allows a computer requesting Web pages (a client computer, which uses browser software) to talk to the computer storing the pages (the host or server, which uses Web server software).

Web documents are informational pages that can contain text, graphics, color, sound, video, animation, and 3-D graphics. These pages also contain links to other documents that contain more links to yet other documents. The Web's greatest innovation is that when you are seeking information, you do not need to know exactly where the Web information is stored—the hyperlinks take you to different sites you're interested in. A special set of communication rules, called *Hypertext Transport Protocol* (HTTP), make it possible to embed and execute links from one document to another document.

Figure 4.4 displays a popular Web site and its numerous hyperlinks.

The World Wide Web was developed in 1989 by physicists at CERN (European Laboratory for Particle Physics) in Switzerland. The Web communications system they created enabled the researchers to locate one document on the Web and view the document using a special program called a *browser*. The first document could contain links to other remote documents that didn't require the user to enter complicated retrieval commands or know exactly where the document resided.

FIGURE 4.4

CNET is a favorite Web site for hyperlinking to different articles and sites.

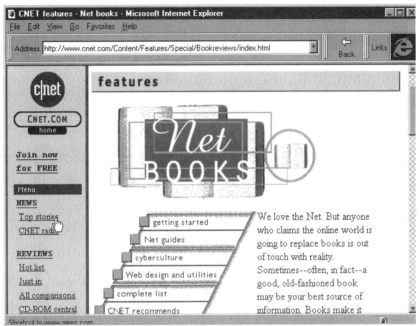

Since those early development days of the first Web pages, sophisticated search engines, such as Yahoo, AltaVista, and Excite, have been created that now allow you to type topics of interest; these engines will then locate specific Web pages containing the topic, or locate Web pages within which you can search further.

The Web is changing the way we interact as people and how business is conducted. The richness of the information you can deliver and receive using the Web cannot be matched by any other single technology, including phones, faxes, or television. The Web can be the library and the librarian, Federal Express, the newspaper delivery person, and the nightly news. The Web has business value, entertainment value, and educational value. With its ease of use, visual excitement, publishing ability, and low cost, the Web is how many of us prefer to communicate.

What Is a Web Page?

A Web page is a page or a collection of pages designed using HTML—Hypertext Markup Language. HTML allows you to use any word processor, text editor, or HTML editor to *code* or *tag* your headings and sentences for special formatting such as bold, italics, numbering, bullets, fancy fonts, and so on. When the browser sees these codes, it knows to display your document with the special formats. Web pages can be viewed by any computer user regardless of their platform (Apple, Windows, UNIX, and so on).

The most important HTML codes are anchor codes that allow you to link Internet addresses to other documents or files. The anchor refers the reader to files that reside on various servers throughout the Internet or to files that may be on the user's local computer network.

HTML also allows you to send documents containing more than just formatted words. The browser software allows helper programs to run so that you can view special graphics, diagrams, sound clips, animation, videos, and virtual reality scenes.

NOTE

When the scientists at CERN were developing the concept of hypertext documents, they created HTML as a variation of an existing markup language called SGML (Standard Generalized Markup Language). SGML is a complex markup language that is used extensively by the government in their publications.

Home Page

A *home page* is the first HTML page that a person or organization presents when you visit their site. The home page is a "Welcome to my site" page that describes the purpose of the site and generally allows you to click onto links that will take you to other parts of the site. The home page can be the only page that makes up a Web site or can be the first page of a collection of interconnected pages.

Home pages are generally quite attractive, as they must invite and entice the Web "surfer" into spending more time at the site. Usually there is a large graphic or a series of graphical buttons that links the viewer to the different components of the site. Many corporations' sites sell their products through their Web sites, so a handsome presentation is important to entice viewers to buy their goods. One of the interesting features of the Internet culture is that you must "give" in order to "get." Many companies will not blatantly "sell" to you on their home page; instead, they'll reel you in through attractive and interesting content, encouraging you to click further until you reach the "pitch."

Figure 4.5 shows the home page of Jazz Online, where you can read articles about jazz in America, listen to new artists, and, of course, purchase jazz recordings online (`http://www.jazzonline.com`).

To visit a Web site, you must be connected to the Internet and be using browser software to view and click on links to other HTML documents. Each time you start your Internet session and launch your browser, the home page for the company that

FIGURE 4.5

With thousands of Web sites to see, the home page must capture the attention of the Web surfer.

created the browser appears. So, for Internet Explorer, you will automatically be taken to Microsoft's home page; if you are using Netscape Navigator as your browser, the home page for Netscape will appear. You can change these settings on your browser, so that any home page you designate appears when you launch your browser.

HTML Tags

The key to HTML is in the *tags*, keywords enclosed in angle brackets that indicate what kind of content is going to be shown. Tags are used to indicate how text should be formatted (bold, italic, underline, font size, and so on) and whether text should be displayed as a table or list, as well as to designate hyperlinked text and graphics.

A simple example of HTML coding would be a large heading at the top of a home page, such as "ABC COMPANY HOME PAGE" enclosed in a heading tag. It would look something like this:

```
<H1>ABC COMPANY HOME PAGE</H1>
```

<H1> is the tag for a Level 1 heading, which is the largest heading. HTML also has level 2, 3, 4, 5, and 6 headings, corresponding to smaller and smaller font sizes.

Every tag must have a beginning and end tag. The </H1> marks the end of the heading 1 tag. The forward slash in front of the letters H1 indicate the end tag.

Browsers

In their source (raw) HTML coded form, HTML documents look like a bunch of words enclosed in angle brackets. It is necessary, therefore, that some type of software translate the HTML coding language into an attractive document by displaying the fonts and graphics, playing the sound files, and showing animation. This type of software is called a browser program.

With your browser, you'll see a beautiful and graphical page, not HTML coding. The Jazz Online Web page and it's source code are shown in Figure 4.6

FIGURE 4.6

The hyper-text markup language is transformed when seen through browser software.

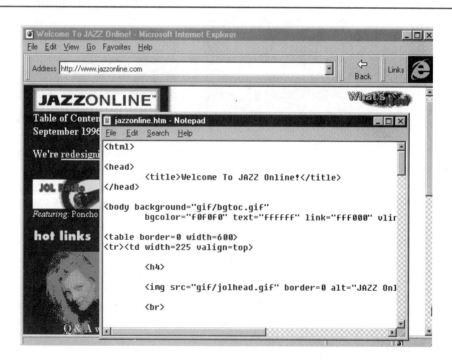

A browser does more than translate the HTML codes, however. All browsers let you store frequently requested Web site URLs and select them from a categorized list. And you can guide movement forward and backward between hypertext pages. A Stop button is generally available for canceling the loading of a Web page. The browser is also responsible for managing security issues, supporting other Internet applications, and locating and starting "helper" programs such as those used to process sound, video, or virtual reality viewing.

The first browsers were text-only browsers and did not have the windows-like interface we are now accustomed to. When an employee at the National Center for Supercomputing Applications (NCSA), Marc Andreessen, created the first graphical browser, Mosaic, he could not have foreseen the success of his next creation— Netscape Navigator, now one of the most widely used browsers on the Internet. The most popular browser programs today are Netscape Navigator, Microsoft Internet Explorer, and NCSA's Mosaic. Other browsers are available, but most users view the Web through one of these three. Because of their ability to allow users of different systems to view the same documents, browsers are quickly being considered the new operating systems of the Internet.

Uniform Resource Locators (URLs)

Because Web pages reside on host computers throughout the Internet, to locate a particular page you must know the domain name for the host computer, and the file name(s) for the page(s) you want. It will also be necessary to designate what transport protocol the Web server should use when retrieving the page. Hypertext protocol (HTTP) or file transfer (FTP or FILE) are the most common protocols you will use when retrieving Web pages.

The full address for a Web document is called its Uniform Resource Locator (URL). The information after the double slash (//) in a URL is known as the FQDN or Fully Qualified Domain Name. A typical URL looks like this:

```
http://www.crtinc.com/training/courses.html
```

This URL can be broken down into the following parts:

```
http://
```

Hypertext Transport Protocol. HTTP represents the rules for retrieving a hypertext document. Note the protocol is always followed by a colon and a double slash.

```
www
```

A subdomain of the server that stores the pages (World Wide Web).

```
.crtinc
```

The organization or company name that is a second-level domain name. This is the domain name that is registered with the InterNIC.

`.com`

A top-level domain name that means the domain is a commercial business (see the earlier section, "Domain Names," for further explanation).

`/training`

The directory on the server that contains the Web page(s).

`/courses.html`

The name of the actual Web page document to be retrieved. It is always the last part of the URL.

NOTE
When no filename is shown at the end of a URL address, yet a page appears on the screen, it means that the Web server automatically loaded a document named `index.html`. Home pages are generally given this default name.

Internet Explorer

As a user of Office 97, you have a browser that comes with the Office 97 suite: Microsoft Internet Explorer. To launch Internet Explorer, you need to be connected to the Internet using either the services of an independent Internet provider—an online service such as Microsoft Network or AOL—or through a local area network (LAN) connection to the Internet.

You may have files on your computer that end with an extension of *.htm. When you double-click on such a file, Windows 95 associates the file type of *.htm with the Internet Explorer program. Windows loads the browser first and then the HTML page so that the Explorer browser can correctly display the HTML codes within the file.

In Office 97, Internet Explorer is accessible from each application from the Web toolbar. Click on the Search the Web button to launch the Internet Explorer; you will automatically be taken to Microsoft Corporation's home page. Explorer will also launch if you double-click on a hypertext link URL within a document. Figure 4.7 shows the enhancements Microsoft is making to Internet Explorer. (You can learn more about Internet Explorer in Chapter 50.)

Web Servers

A computer that is designated to store and display Web pages is called a *Web server*. A Web server uses special software to "serve" the *clients* (other computers) who dial its IP address to access files and/or Web pages. To make your Web pages accessible to other computers on the Internet, you must "upload" them to a Web server using that Web server's software.

FIGURE 4.7

The power is in the Internet Explorer Browser!

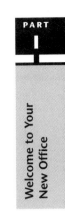

A Web server does more than simply distribute Web pages. For example, there are special types of Web pages that prompt users for information via a form. The information obtained from these forms is stored on the Web server; and special programs on the server handle the stored information.

Many independent Internet service providers allow you to store your home page on their Web servers, and they will perform the upload procedures required. You need only create the Web pages. In other cases when you want your Web pages placed on your corporate Web server, you must work with a Webmaster—an individual skilled in the network management of Web servers and Web pages. Chapter 49 shows you how to create Web pages.

Intranets

HTML and general hypertext pages are now being designed and used internally by corporations to store their corporate information (policy manuals, announcement, benefits packages, and so on) in a graphical and user-friendly method.

A new buzzword, *intranet*, has been coined to describe the use of linked pages on a corporate network. A corporation may set up their intranet so that some of their pages may be accessed from anyone on the Internet, but other pages will have passwords so that only employees can access them. These types of intranets install all of the TCP/IP protocols and Internet connections.

Other corporate intranets cannot be accessed by outside computers. Their HTML or hyperlinked pages reside on a normal network computer and not on a Web server. Only the other employees on the network can view these pages. This type of intranet is used for *workgroup* interactivity and is becoming one of the most popular uses for HTML hypertext documents and browsers. Web pages can be created using any text editor (such as Notepad that comes with Windows). The cost of the browser ranges from free (Internet Explorer) to approximately fifty dollars (Netscape Navigator). Many corporations are exploring workgroup intranets because they don't require actual connection to the Internet, yet they provide an excellent and inexpensive hypertext document management system.

Your Office Links to the World

The most obvious indicators of a shared Internet capability among the Office applications are the two special buttons on the Standard toolbars in all of the applications. The two buttons allow you to insert a hyperlink into an application's data or display a full-blown Web toolbar.

Microsoft Office 97 has taken full advantage of the Web's HTTP protocols and the fact that hyperlinked publications can be built and viewed on local networked workgroups as well as on the Internet. Even if you work on stand-alone computers, you can use all of the hyperlink and Web features available in each of the Office applications and its browser, Internet Explorer.

Each of the five Office 97 applications—Word, Excel, PowerPoint, Access, and Outlook—is capable of creating hypertext links, accessing Internet-based documents, creating Web pages and navigating through hypertext pages.

Inserting Hyperlinks

The Insert Hyperlink command, a button on each application's Standard toolbar, allows you to reference (link) to the addresses of other Office files residing on your local computer or network, as well as to the addresses of documents at remote sites on other computers.

Hyperlinking is a concept invented in the late 1960s by computer scientist Ted Nelson in his attempt to create new ways for exploring information. For example, while reading a document, he wanted the reader to be able to click on a highlighted word or phrase that was linked to another document. When the other document opened, additional information would be available about the meaning or purpose of the hyperlink word. Once the additional information had been opened, the reader could then click a button and return back to the original document.

When using hyperlinks, you are not limited to documents on your computer or local area network; links can reference the addresses (URLs) of documents located on other computers. The creators of the World Wide Web saw the benefits to this concept and used it as the basis for their Web document system—documents that link to other documents that link to other documents from computer to computer across the Internet. See Chapter 48 to learn about using hyperlinks.

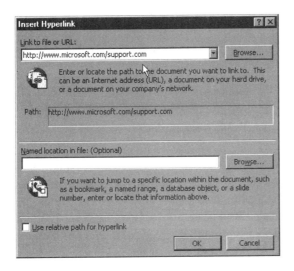

Creating Web Pages

Web pages are informational documents, coded in a special language, that contain hyperlink references to other files.

You can create your own Web pages using a special Web page editor program or an ASCII text editor as simple as Notepad. With the Web page creation features now in Office 97, you can click on a button, and the Web Page Wizard will walk you through the process of creating exciting personal or corporate pages that can be accessed by millions of users of the Internet. See Chapter 49 for the details of creating pages.

The Web Page Wizard is only one method for creating a Web page. If you need to create a Web page from existing data, it is not necessary to code the data using the Hypertext Markup Language (HTML). Every Office 97 program allows you to save your work with HTML formatting by choosing File ➢ Save As HTML (see Chapter 50). Corporate spreadsheet data, database names, policy manuals, and presentations can all become instant Web pages and sent to the Webmaster for uploading to the Web server computer.

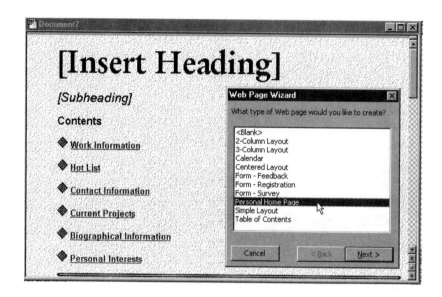

If you wish to code HTML pages yourself, Word 97 comes equipped with a Web template style so that you can create your own pages from scratch, yet have all of Word's powerful word processing features available to you. It is tedious and time-consuming to create your own HTML coded Web pages from scratch, however. It is much easier to use the Web Page Wizard to create your initial pages and then make changes to the HTML codes as necessary. Viewing and editing the Wizard's HTML codes from within Word allows you to add tags that are not part of the Web Page Wizard's programming. Choose View ➤ HTML Source to view and edit the source code (see Figure 4.8)

Navigating Hypertext Documents

For navigating in a hypertext world, each Office 97 application offers a Web toolbar with buttons that allow you to quickly move back and forth between hyperlinked documents, start Internet Explorer, set the default Start page for Explorer, search the Web, store your Favorite Web sites, and open a history address list of the most recently used URLs. The Go button on the Web toolbar displays a menu that groups all of the Web toolbar buttons. Part Seven describes how to utilize the toolbar while creating hyperlinks, Web pages, and using the Internet to access pages.

FIGURE 4.8

When you open an HTML page in Word, you can view and edit the source code.

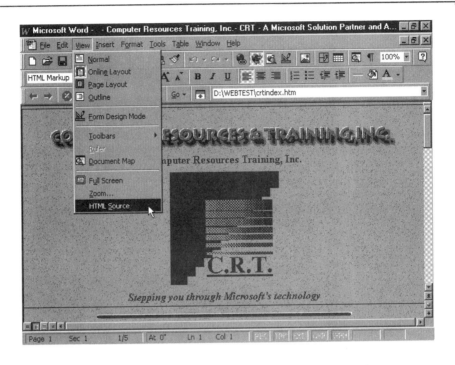

Welcome to Your New Office

Exploring Office: Hyperlinks and the Internet

Here is a quick breakdown of most of the hyperlink and Internet features now within the Office suite:

- A method for inserting *hyperlink references.* You can insert these links into the data of any Office application. The inserted linked references allow you to jump to other Office documents, pages, or objects, as well as to other World Wide Web pages on other computers. See Chapter 48 for a detailed discussion of hyperlink anchors. You do not have to be on the Internet to use hyperlinks in Office documents. For example, you could create a Word document with hyperlinks to both a cell in an Excel spreadsheet and an Access database, as long as all three are on the same hard disk or network file server.
- Access to Microsoft Corporation's Web site on the Help menu, as illustrated in Figure 4.9.
- The ability to store URLs to documents on the World Wide Web, which can then be opened by using the Open dialog box (File ➤ Open). See chapter 48 for how store and access your Favorite URLs.

FIGURE 4.9

On each application's Help menu there is an Internet link to Microsoft Corporation for online freebies and support.

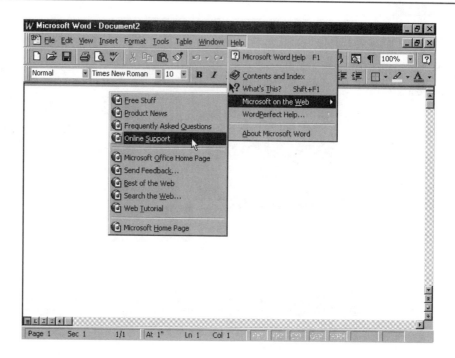

- A Web toolbar, which supports the protocols needed for connection to Web sites (HTTP), other computers' data (FTP), and your own internal Web pages. Protocols are rules or standards designed to ease the complex process of enabling computers of different makes and models to communicate.

NOTE

All of the features listed here will be explained in depth in Part Seven. Chapter 48 describes the Hyperlink command; Chapter 49 takes you through the steps of creating a Web page; and Chapter 50 tells you how to save data as HTML in each Office 97 application.

- A method for saving the application's data in HTML format—the format needed to display information on the World Wide Web. Chapter 49 takes you through the steps for creating Web pages.
- Access to Microsoft's browser, Internet Explorer 3.0, which is included with the Office 97 CD installation. A browser is the program that allows you to locate and connect to Web pages and to view HTML codes as graphical pages. The browser can launch helper applications so that you can hear sound or view animation on the page.

PART II

Communicating
with Word

- **Create Polished and Professional Documents**

- **Use Special Effects on Text**

- **Store Frequently Typed Text**

- **Draw Table Forms**

- **Embed Hyperlinks to Files**

- **Create Reusable Documents**

- **Automate with Mail Merge**

- **Create Web Pages**

- **Insert Data from Office 97 Programs**

Chapter

5

The Road Map

FEATURING

The Road Map

Word 97, Microsoft's state-of-the-art word processing program, encompasses a vast territory of word processing capabilities. Whether you want to create a one-page letter, a hundred-page report, link Excel numbers and charts to a proposal, design a Web page for your company's Internet or intranet Web site, or simultaneously work on a document with another person, this program has it all.

What Word Can Do

Word 97 is an application program that allows you to create and type letters, reports, memos, proposals, newsletters, brochures, graphic presentations, Web pages, tables, form letters—virtually all the communication-related documents commonly found in today's businesses.

The sheer variety of document types is impressive, and so is the power "under the hood." Word's powerful AutoText and AutoCorrect features allow you to store text—from a few words to whole documents—that can be reused from document to document.

Word's built-in IntelliSense technology contains "artificial intelligence" programming that can, for example, predict the type of formatting you wish in a document.

Suppose you begin to manually number lines of text: Word sees this numbered text and automatically begins incrementing the numbering on subsequent lines. You do not have to continue typing the numbers for the remaining lines of text.

Another powerful feature is Microsoft's professionally predesigned forms called *document templates*. These templates include memo forms, résumés, brochure layouts, newsletters, proposals, press releases, and report layouts. All you need to do is compose your thoughts and not worry about how your document will look.

What's New in Word 97

Word 97 won't disappoint new users and upgraders hoping for new and innovative features in this next iteration of Microsoft's premier word processing program. Word 97 includes several powerful new features, including hyperlinking, Web page design, free-form table draw, document mapping, advanced document navigation, and artistic AutoShapes. A new Help feature, the Office Assistant, provides tips and tricks as you work; Microsoft also provides a link to their Web page for more online support. The sections that follow provide an overview of many of Word 97's new and interesting features.

Internet

In Word 97, the possibilities for powerful document management have jumped exponentially. Word now includes features that allow you to convert documents into a format that can be viewed on the Internet—HyperText Markup Language (HTML). A complete Web toolbar is provided, along with various colored backgrounds that can be used to design beautiful Web pages. You also can insert hypertext links that link your document to existing Web pages.

You can go to Microsoft's Web site, listed in the Help menu, for online support, as well as to obtain additional clip art and Web page design tips and tricks (see Figure 5.1). See Part Seven for full coverage of all the new Internet features in Word 97.

Draw Table

Microsoft has given a new twist to Word's table features by adding a free-form line draw capability. In free-form "pencil" mode, you can draw or erase your own table lines, thicken and shadow the lines, and split and merge cells in ways you never thought possible. Custom forms and unusual table layouts can be created in minutes with this new feature (see Figure 5.2). See Chapter 11 for full coverage of the Draw Table feature.

FIGURE 5.1

*Word's Help
menu lists
Microsoft's Web
site, where free
stuff and online
support are
available.*

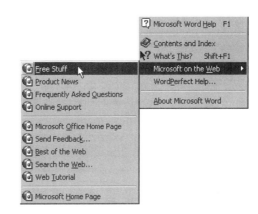

FIGURE 5.2

*The new Draw
Table feature is
great for cus-
tom table and
form layouts.*

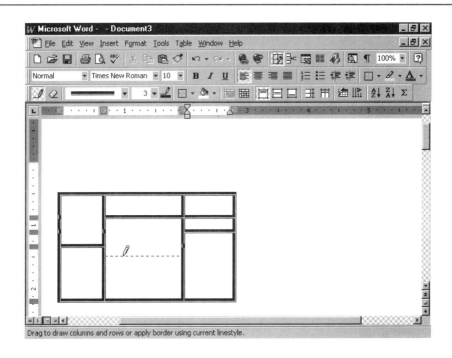

AutoShapes

Other new drawing tools have been added to Word under the AutoShapes category. Specifically, you will find 32 different shapes, 28 types of arrows, 28 flowchart diagram shapes, 16 stars and banners, and 20 callouts (see Figure 5.3). If this weren't enough, you can add 3-D perspective, drop shadows, stretch, skew, and type text on these new objects. Many desktop publishing experts will be asking themselves whether they need to invest in a dedicated graphics program after seeing some of the accessible drawing features within Word 97. See Chapter 11 for coverage of this new feature.

FIGURE 5.3

The variety of graphical shapes available in Word 97 is truly impressive.

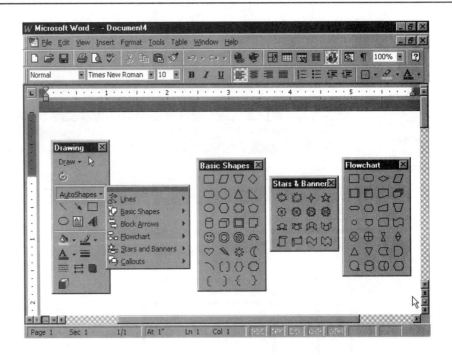

Office Assistant

Along with the other products in the Office 97 suite, Word 97 contains the next evolution of Microsoft's famous lightbulb screen tips: its new *Office Assistant*. The Office Assistant is an animated character that helps you with questions and suggests tips and tricks. There are a variety of animated characters, but the initial Office Assistant that greets you is Clippit (see Figure 5.4). Clippit is a paper clip (what else!) that appears in its own window and "grooves"—dances from side to side, glances at you, writes down notes, and generally watches your every keystroke. Clippit blinks, winks, and gyrates while giving you helpful tips as you work. It's so silly you wonder if Bill Gates saw this feature before the programming team put it out to the public. Chapter 3 describes the Office Assistant help feature for all of the Office suite.

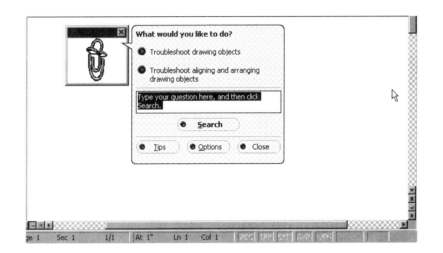

FIGURE 5.4

Office Assistants are animated characters offering "cool" screen tips as you work.

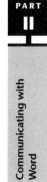

PART

II

Communicating with
Word

Document Map

Another new feature, the Document Map, is a great help to those of you who work with long documents that contain headings. A vertically split screen displays a document's headings on the left and the document text on the right (see Figure 5.5). You can scroll to view the headings contained in the document, and when you click on a heading, you are launched to the location in the document where that heading appears. No more scrolling or looking through pages, hoping to get close to the text you need to work on. See Chapter 10 for coverage of this new feature.

Sticky Notes

Sticky-type notes are now available when inserting a Comment into your text. The Comment command was a feature in previous versions of Word, but it was not very useful because of the difficulty seeing which text had comments and what the comments said. In Word 97, commented words are indicated with a light yellow highlight. As you pause the mouse over the yellow highlighted area, a sticky note pops up to display the name of the author and the text of the comment (see Figure 5.6). With so many users moving to the Office 97 suite of products, you will have a vast universe of other Word 97 users with whom to share commented text. See Chapter 12 for coverage of this new feature.

FIGURE 5.5

The new Document Map feature allows you to jump to specific headings in your document.

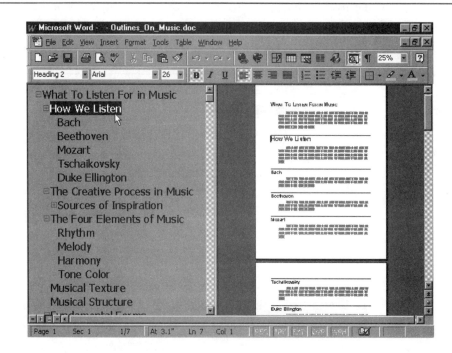

FIGURE 5.6

Inserted comments can be viewed as pop-up notes.

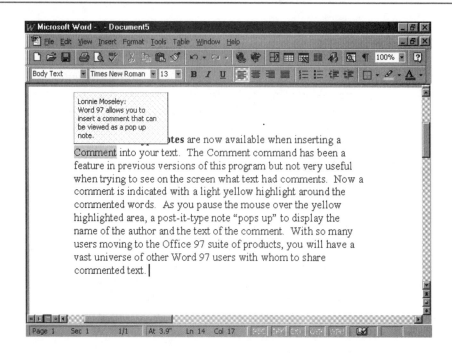

Fancy Fonts and Text Animation

If you thought you had done as much as could be done with fonts and typefaces, Microsoft has stunned you again by adding four new font flavors: embossed, engraved, shadow, and outlined text (see Figure 5.7). Even more impressive, you'll notice in the Format ➤ Font menu that you can also animate your text with Blinking Background, Shimmer, Sparkle Text, and Las Vegas Lights, to name a few. You may not know exactly what you are going to use these for—yet—but you'll have fun experimenting with these new text animation styles. See Chapter 8 for coverage of these new features.

FIGURE 5.7

New font styles will enhance the text in your documents and Web pages.

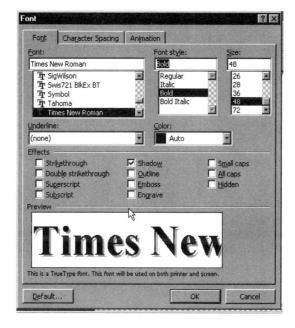

PART

II

Communicating with Word

Page Borders

For those of you who begged Microsoft for a way to place a border around the page, you'll be pleased to know that there are now Page Border styles in addition to the traditional paragraph and table border styles (see Figure 5.8). Pages can be bordered in 3-D, shadow, and graphic art styles. (By the way, Word also has a new 3-D paragraph border style for making that really dramatic impact on your readers.) See Chapter 11 for coverage of this new feature.

FIGURE 5.8

It takes seconds to apply a page border—a long-time wish list feature.

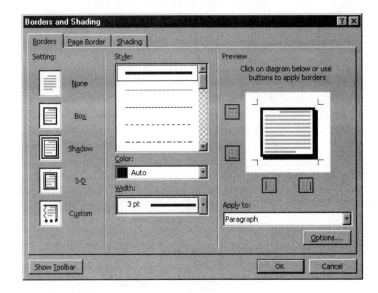

Drop-Down Menus

Word's menu design has changed a bit: menu items in Word 97 indicate their associated toolbar icons so that new users will be able to identify toolbar icons more easily (see Figure 5.9). See Chapter 13 for full coverage of this new feature.

One addition you may find unusual is the animation options for the menus. If you set a menu animation option, menus will "unfold" or drop like "slides" when you click on a main menu item. After a few minutes of watching menus unfold and slide, a pressure begins to form in the middle of your forehead, accompanied by a slight sense of vertigo. Be careful.

Toolbars

You could always make yourself laugh by displaying all the toolbars at one time on the screen in the previous versions of Word because there were so many (there were nine toolbars in those versions). There are *eighteen* toolbars in Word 97—so many that there is a toolbar that consolidates features from the other toolbars (see Figure 5.10). And, oh yes, you can still create your own customized toolbars.

FIGURE 5.9

New users will find it helpful that menu items are shown with their associated tool-bar buttons.

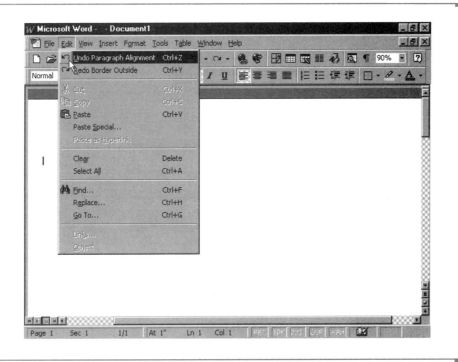

FIGURE 5.10

Word 97 includes a whopping eighteen toolbars (all of which are not shown).

Jump-Start into Word 97

The following sections summarize the actions and functions needed to produce a document—giving you a jump-start into Word 97.

Starting Word

You must launch or start Word before you can begin to type a letter or any other kind of document. There are a number of ways to start the Word program; the steps listed below launch Word from the Start button on the Windows 95 Taskbar.

1. Click on the Start button on the Taskbar.
2. Move the mouse up to the Programs item. A submenu will open.
3. Move to the Microsoft Word item, as shown in Figure 5.11. (The Word item may be within an Office 97 or other Office folder depending upon your installation selections).

FIGURE 5.11

Starting Word from the Start button on the Taskbar

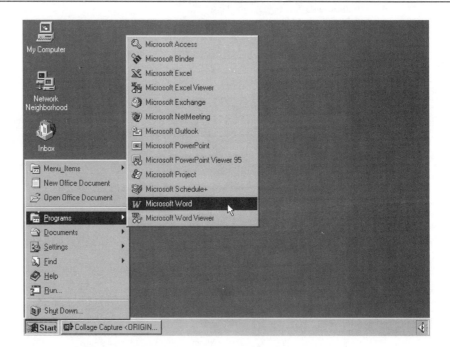

Starting a New Document

To begin typing a new document, you must have a blank page on which to put down your thoughts. Here are the steps for launching a new document:

1. When you first launch Word, a blank screen will appear, ready for you to begin typing. If you do not see a blank, white typing screen, choose File ➢ New from the menu bar to start a new document. The New dialog box will appear. Click on the General tab and double-click on the Blank Document icon. A blank typing screen

will appear. This screen represents an $8\frac{1}{2}$-by-11-inch piece of paper with left and right margins of $1\frac{1}{4}$ inches and top and bottom margins of 1 inch.

2. Look around the screen to get your bearings. Pause the mouse for a few seconds over each button that appears on the top rows of the screen. A tip shows what each button does.

3. Begin typing. When you reach the right margin, the text will automatically wrap around to the next line. Press the Enter key only when you have finished typing a paragraph of information or at the ends of short lines of address information.

Figure 5.12 shows the toolbars and the typing area with sample lines of typing.

Correcting Your Document

Corrections are a necessary part of creating and editing documents. Word provides excellent correcting methods and tools. The most common of these methods are listed below.

- Use the Backspace key (located above the Enter key) to back over your typos immediately after you make them. Do not use the Backspace key to back over a whole line of good typing just to correct a few letters.
- Click the mouse where you find typos. Then use the Delete key (located to the right of the Enter key) and/or the Backspace key to remove the typos. (The Backspace key deletes the character to the left of the insertion point, and the Delete key deletes the character to the right.) Click and drag the mouse (*select*) across and/or down multiple words or lines and then press the Delete key to remove the highlighted block.

Enhancing Your Work

You will want to give emphasis to particular words by using the bold, italic, or underline formatting features. You may also want to center a line of text as you are typing. The fastest method for enhancing and aligning text is to use the commands on the Formatting toolbar. This is the toolbar that shows the capital B, I, and U (bold, italic, underline). If you do not see this toolbar, choose View ➤ Toolbars and click on the checkbox next to Formatting or right-click anywhere in the toolbar area and select Formatting from the pop-up menu.

- To add bold, italic, or underline formatting, select the word or words to be formatted. Click on the appropriate toolbar button to add the desired format. To remove the formatting, click on the same button. This on and off effect is called a *toggle*.
- To center a line of text, select the text and click on the Center button (the button with the centered lines next to the bold, italic, and underline buttons). To return the text to the left margin, click on the left alignment button.

Communicating with Word

FIGURE 5.12

A Word screen with sample typing

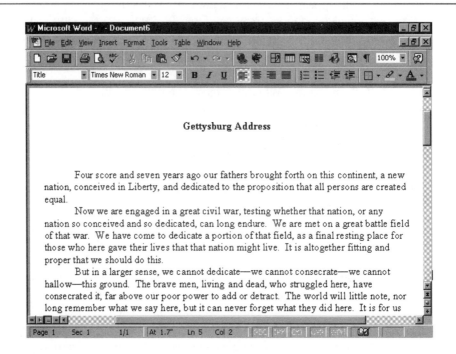

Below you'll see the Formatting toolbar used to change the style, typeface, point size, formats and alignments, bullets, numbering, and indentation. Bold, italics, and underline are the most frequently used text formats.

Undoing Problems

Using the Undo feature, you can reverse the last action you performed in a document. When you perform an unintended action, choose Edit ➤ Undo, Ctrl+Z (hold down the Ctrl key and tap the letter Z), or click on the Undo button on the Standard toolbar to activate the Undo feature. Repeat as many times as necessary to undo up to 99 of your previous actions.

NOTE

If you close a file without saving, you can't undo it. You also can't undo it if you accidentally save over a file (overwrite an original file).

Saving Your Work

Many times it is necessary to store a permanent copy of your work. For example, a document you are modifying will disappear from the computer's memory when the computer is shut down. You must, therefore, manually store or save your work on a disk. This disk can be the hard disk that resides inside your computer, or a small disk you insert into your computer's disk drive. If you are a member of a workgroup on a network, the drive you save your work on (the network drive) won't be near you at all. Regardless of the medium, save your work as often as you can to avoid losing data through accidents and power loss. Save at any point at any time.

1. Choose File ➢ Save or click on the Save button on the Standard Toolbar. The Save As dialog box (shown below) will appear.

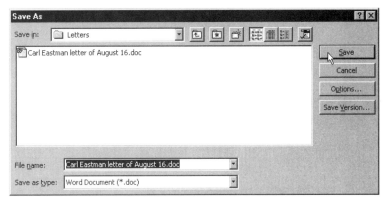

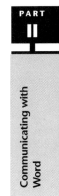

PART
II

Communicating with Word

2. Type a name for your document. You are allowed to use spaces, periods, and numbers, as well as letters. You can have a maximum of 250 characters in the name.

You only need to name a document the first time you save it. When you choose File ➢ Save thereafter, Word automatically saves without asking for a name.

Backing Up Your Work

You may want an additional copy of each of your documents. The Always Create Backup Copy option tells Word to save a second copy of everything you do. Although having a backup is a safeguard, it does take up twice the disk space because Word is keeping two copies of every document. For mission-critical work, however, it is highly recommended to create backup copies. To start creating backup copies, follow these steps:

1. Choose Tools ➢ Options from the menu bar.

2. Click on the Save tab (shown below) and check the Always Create Backup Copy option (the Allow Fast Saves checkbox will clear itself). Whenever you save, a backup will be created.

3. Click on OK.

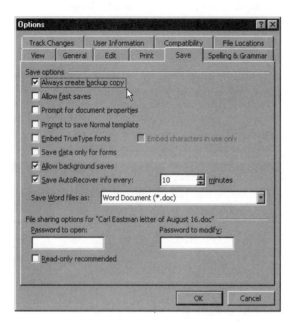

Spell-Checking Your Work

Word has designed a unique feature into its spell-checking command: If you choose Tools ➤ Options ➤ Spelling & Grammar and select Check Spelling as You Type, Word will automatically check your spelling as you are typing. When an incorrect word (or a word not in Word's dictionary, such as the name of a person or a company) is typed, Word will immediately underline the word with a wavy red line.

You can activate the Speller's suggested word list by right-clicking on the underlined word (or pressing Shift+F10) or double-clicking on the Speller icon in the Status bar. Select the correct spelling with either mouse button, or press the down arrows if you are using the keyboard method. If no possible spelling suggestions are shown, press Esc and edit the word on-screen yourself, or select the Spelling option from the bottom of the pop-up dialog box and use the Not in Dictionary area to edit the word.

If the word you type is not a misspelled word but is being flagged because it is not in the dictionary, right-click on the word and choose Ignore All. The wavy red line disappears from underneath the word, and future occurrences of this word will not be flagged.

Even though Word does a great job of checking as you type, it is still a good idea to spell-check once again after you have finished typing your entire document:

1. Go to the top of your document. Save your work with File ➤ Save (to ensure you do not lose your work during spell-checking).
2. Choose Tools ➤ Spelling and Grammar or press F7.
3. When the spelling checker starts, notice the words it stops on. If a word is correct, click on the Ignore All option from the Spelling and Grammar dialog box (shown in Figure 5.13). If a word is not correct, and you see the correct spelling in the Suggestions box, click on the correct spelling and choose the Change option or double-click on the desired spelling in the Suggestions box.
4. If the word is not correct and you do not see the correct spelling in the Suggestions box, click outside of the dialog box onto the Word in the document. Correct the word and then click on the Resume button to continue spell-checking the rest of your document. You can also make changes in the Not In Dictionary box and then click on the Change button.

PART

II

Communicating with Word

FIGURE 5.13

You can easily correct typos using the spell-checking feature.

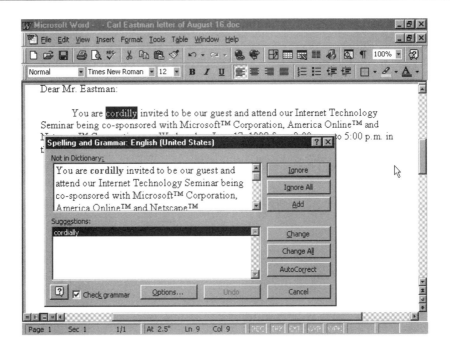

Previewing and Printing Your Work

Rarely does the first printing of a document meet your expectations. You can reduce the number of printings, however, by previewing a document before you print it:

1. Choose File ➤ Print Preview. Your document will appear as a small page.

- You can edit the page. For instance, as long as the Magnifier button is toggled off, you can insert additional blank lines by pressing the Enter key multiple times, or remove lines by pressing the Delete key multiple times.
- You can change the viewing percentage to a larger size, perhaps to 50 percent, so you can fully proof the screen.
- If your document runs over a couple of lines to the second page and you want your work to fit on one page, click on the Shrink to Fit button on the Preview toolbar to force the document to one page.

2. When everything looks fine, click on the Print button on the toolbar or press Ctrl+P to send the work to the printer. Click on the Close button to return to Normal view.

Figure 5.14 shows the Print Preview screen and toolbar buttons.

FIGURE 5.14

The Print Pre-view screen shows how your document will look before it is printed. Click on the screen to increase the magnification.

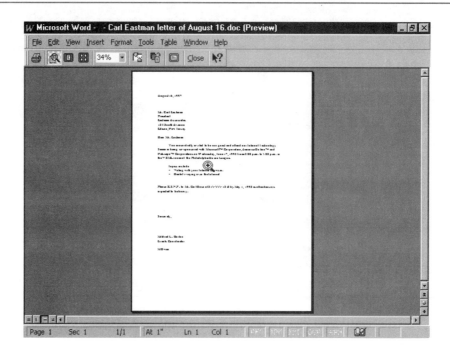

Printing an Envelope for Your Work

If you have completed a letter, you may wish to print the address on an envelope. Most laser-jet and desk-jet printers will allow you to place an envelope on top of the paper tray. The feeder on these printers has been programmed to take the envelope when printing the address. To print an envelope:

1. Select the entire address of the person to whom the letter is being sent.
2. Choose Tools ➤ Envelopes and Labels. The top part of the dialog box shows the recipient's address. The bottom half of the window shows the return address. You can click on Omit and choose not to have a return address for envelopes that already have a preprinted return logo.
3. Position the envelope in the printer and click on the Print button on the Envelopes and Labels dialog box (shown below). If the return address is the default return address to be used for the next envelope printing, choose Yes from the message box that appears. The envelope will print. Make sure you save your work again (choose File ➤ Save or press Ctrl+S).

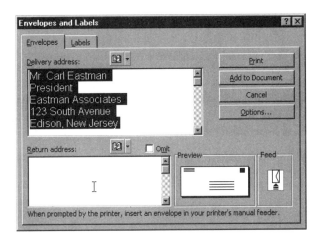

Closing/Clearing Your Work from the Screen

When you have completed a document or have finished working on a document, you will want to clear it from the screen. This is called *closing* the document:

1. Save your work.
2. Choose File ➤ Close. If you have already saved your work, your file will close. If you have not saved your work, you will be reminded to do so; then, if you want to save your work, choose Yes and, if prompted for a filename, type in a name for your document (your name can be a maximum of 255 characters and can include

spaces). The dialog box below shows a message similar to the one you will see if you have not saved your work before closing the file.

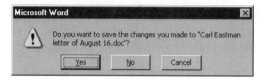

Opening an Existing Document

When you have saved and closed your work, you may need to reopen the document back into the computer's memory in order to make additional changes.

You can open as many different documents as your memory will allow. The normal method for opening a file is to choose File ➤ Open from the menu bar. Another method is to choose File from the menu bar and look at the end of the File menu for the list of the last four documents that were opened. (You can set this number up to nine; see Chapter 9.)

A third method is to use the Start button to view the Documents folder so you can see the last fifteen documents that were created using any program (Excel, Lotus, Word, WordPerfect, PowerPoint, Access, and so on). Figures 5.15, 5.16, and 5.17 show the different ways you can open an existing document.

1. Choose File ➤ Open or press Ctrl+O or click the Open button on the Standard Toolbar to see the list of files on your disk.
2. Find the name of your file and double-click to open or click once and choose the Open button.

   or

1. Choose File from the menu bar.
2. Look for your file at the bottom of the File menu. You will see the last four documents created in Word.
3. Click on the name of your file.

   or

1. Click on the Start button on the Taskbar.
2. Choose the Documents folder to see a list of the last fifteen documents you were working on among all programs.
3. Click on the name of the document.

FIGURE 5.15

The File ➤ Open option is the most common method of opening stored documents.

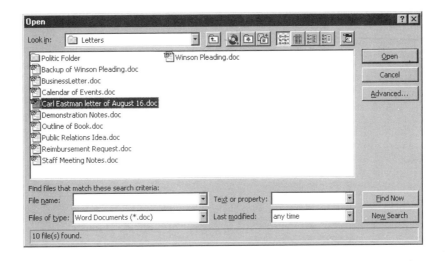

FIGURE 5.16

Use the File menu to see a list of the last four files you were working on in Word.

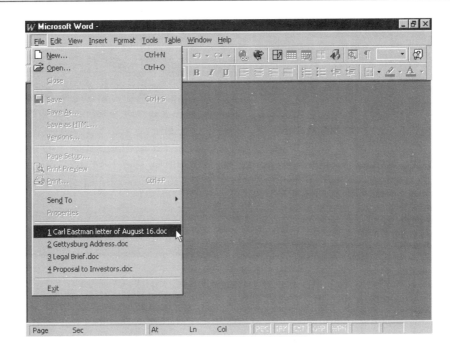

FIGURE 5.17

Windows 95
remembers the
last fifteen
documents you
were working
on among all
programs.

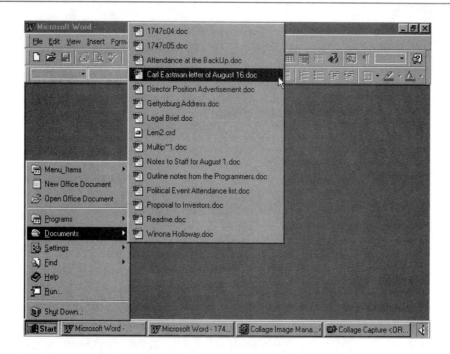

Switching between Multiple Open Documents

Word allows you to open multiple documents into memory. You can switch to any
other open document by choosing Window on the menu bar. A list of the open documents will appear. Click on the document you wish to make active. To close these documents, switch to each one and choose File ➤ Close (make sure you save your work
when prompted), or hold down the Shift key before clicking on the File menu, and
select Close All. Figure 5.18 shows the drop-down list of open documents.

NOTE

Press Ctrl+F6 to cycle through each document currently open in memory.

What Dedicated Word Processors Need to Know

Individuals who come to Word with years of experience working with other word processing programs bring with them concepts and techniques inherited from the other
systems they used. There is nothing more frustrating than attempting to use another

You can have multiple documents open and switch between them using the Window menu option.

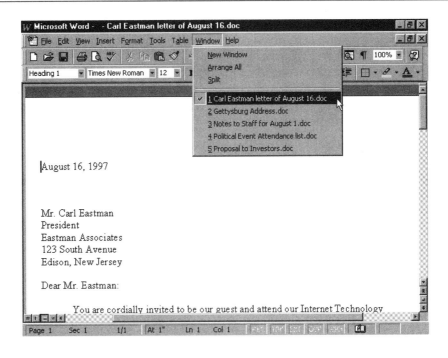

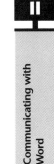

word processor's strategy on a new word processing program only to find that the two programs are based on very different methods for accomplishing the same tasks. The following sections are tips for current word processor users and new users (although new users don't bring as many preconceptions to Word) about the premises Word operates under.

Paragraph-Based Formatting

Word 97 uses paragraph-based formatting rather than page-based formatting. In other words, you can't position your insertion point just anywhere on a page, issue a formatting command, and expect Word to format the rest of the page or document.

If your insertion point is in a paragraph, only that paragraph will be affected by a formatting command. If you want to reformat an entire set of paragraphs, you must first select (highlight) them and then issue the commands. You can tell where a paragraph ends by its paragraph marker; click on the Show/Hide Paragraph symbol (shown at left) to see the paragraph (hard return) markers.

An example of paragraph-based formatting is the spacing command. Place the insertion point into any paragraph and press Ctrl+2 to activate double-spacing. Only the paragraph in which the insertion point resides will be double-spaced. If there are multiple paragraphs to be double-spaced, select all the paragraphs first, then press Ctrl+2. Ctrl+1 returns you to single-spacing.

Copying Paragraph Formats

An important fact to remember about Word's paragraph-based formatting is that each paragraph symbol at the end of a series of typed lines contains the "genetic code" of the entire paragraph (the formats, styles, and alignments, and so on).

You can copy one paragraph symbol to another paragraph using the Format Painter button on the Standard toolbar, and Word will copy the source paragraph's genetic code to the target paragraph. You will need to do this when one paragraph is correctly formatted and another paragraph has gone haywire. Simply copy the paragraph symbol (using the Format Painter button) of the good paragraph over the paragraph symbol of the incorrectly formatted paragraph. The genetic code will be copied and the target paragraph will appear identical to the source in paragraph formats.

Tabs

To change tabs for text that is already typed, you must first select (highlight) the text that has been tabbed. You can then change the tabs by dragging the tab-setting markers that are displayed on the ruler.

Indenting

Word's Increase Indent button on the Formatting toolbar is considered a temporary left margin indent. All text indents from the left margin and stays indented until you press the Decrease Indent button. If you wish to create a hanging indent for numbered paragraphs, use Word's numbering button on the Formatting toolbar. The numbering feature is a natural hanging indent. If you want to have a blank line between the numbered paragraphs, press Shift+Enter instead of Enter to produce a blank line without numbers.

For multilevel numbering, however, choose Format ➤ Bullets and Numbering, and in the dialog box that appears, select Outline Numbered. You can indent and outdent levels in your outline by pressing Shift+Alt+→ or Shift+Alt+←.

Styles

Default fonts, point sizes, and alignments (left, right, center, full) are held within a style. On the Formatting toolbar, there is a drop-down list box with the word "Normal" in it. Normal is the style Word uses for a simple business style. If you click on the drop-down list arrow to the right of the word "Normal," you will see a number of other styles. If you hold down Shift and click on the drop-down list arrow, you will see a list of all of the other styles contained in the program. A list of styles is displayed at left.

When you click anywhere in a paragraph and choose another style, Word will change the paragraph's style to what you selected. If you want multiple paragraphs to receive the new style, select all of the paragraphs to be changed and then choose the new style.

Sections

Word documents can be divided into *sections*. You insert *breaks* into a document to create your own sections (choose Insert ➤ Break ➤ Section Breaks). You can create a section that has very different margins than another section, or you may wish to have different sets of headers and footers for different sections of your document.

Starting a new section on the same page is frequently used in documents where you need multiple-column layouts on one page. For example, imagine a newsletter that requires three columns in the top part of the page and two columns in the bottom part of the page. You would use the Section Break feature to control where the different layout begins.

Next Page section breaks are used when you must start a group of pages with a new page number. For example, let's say the first five pages of a document are preface pages numbered with lowercase Roman numerals, but you want the pages after the sixth page to be numbered starting with the Arabic numeral 1. To do this, insert a Next Page section break to create a new next page. On the new page, choose Insert ➤ Page Numbers ➤ Format and assign "1" as the new Start At number.

One thing to remember when you insert a Next Page section break is that you must delete any existing page breaks, otherwise you will have a section break and a page break. Go to Normal view (View ➤ Normal View) to see if you have both a page break and a section break. Click on the page break and press the Delete key to remove it. You only need the section break to separate one page from the other.

PART

II

Communicating with
Word

Multiple Documents

Word allows you to open as many documents as your computer memory allows and then view them through the Window option on the menu bar. You can switch back and forth between multiple documents by pressing Ctrl+F6 or by choosing a document from the list of open documents you see when you click on Window on the menu bar.

You can arrange to view multiple documents all at once by choosing Window➤Arrange All. To return an open document to a full screen, click on the Maximize button to the right of the title bar.

Chapter

6

The Launch and Tour

Chapter

6

The Launch and Tour

Windows 95 offers many ways to start your applications. One way you can launch Word is from the Programs menu on the Start menu. Another is to select a Word-created document from the Documents menu on the Start menu. Or you can place a Word shortcut reference in the StartUp folder so that Word starts automatically whenever Windows 95 starts.

In this chapter you will be presented with some of the ways you can start the Word program. There will also be a tour of Word's screen layout, important points, and special features you might not immediately recognize from their pictures on the toolbars.

Starting Word through the Start Button

Whether you are viewing the Desktop or working in another program, you can easily start Word (or any other program) by clicking on the Start button and choosing the program you want from the Programs submenu. Figure 6.1 shows items in the Programs submenu.

FIGURE 6.1

*Windows 95
Start button and
menu system*

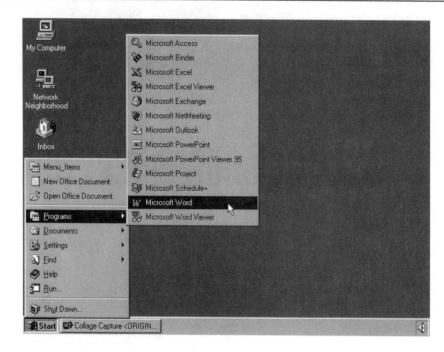

To locate and start Word:

1. Click on the Start button.
2. In the menu that appears, slide the mouse up to the Programs item. Another menu will appear.
3. In this submenu, click on the Microsoft Word icon. Depending upon your installation, the Microsoft Word icon may be within an Office 97 or other Office folder. The icon is a light blue W.

Starting Word with a Document

On the Start button menu you will find a Documents folder. Point to this item to see the names of the 15 most recent documents you created or opened using Windows 95. Documents listed here are files created from any Windows program (Word, Excel, Lotus, WordPerfect, PowerPoint, and so on). This feature allows you to quickly start both the program and a file you were recently working on. If you click on a document that you created using Word, for example, Word will launch, and the document will open. Figure 6.2 shows an example of a Documents folder's contents.

FIGURE 6.2

The Documents folder on the Start menu

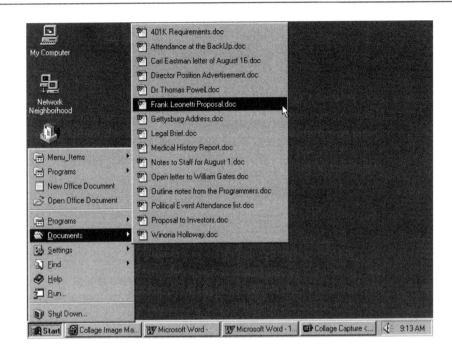

Starting Word Automatically When Windows 95 Starts

If Word is the main Windows program you use, you may want Word to start automatically when Windows 95 starts. Follow these steps to place the Word program shortcut in your StartUp folder. This placement will tell Windows 95 to launch Word after the system files have loaded into memory.

1. Click on the Start button.
2. On the Start menu, point to the Settings item. A submenu appears. On this menu, click on the Taskbar item. You can also right-click on the Taskbar and select Properties from the pop-up menu.
3. When the Taskbar Properties dialog box appears, click on the Start Menu Programs tab at the top of the dialog box.
4. Click on the Add button in the Start Menu Programs tab dialog box to start the Create Shortcut Wizard.

PART

II

Communicating with Word

5. You will be prompted for the name of the program you wish to create a shortcut to. This is called the command line for the program. Click on the Browse button, and search on drive C for the Windows folder. Double-click on the Windows folder.

6. From within the Windows folder, double-click on the Start Menu folder, then double-click on the Programs folder. Double-click on the Microsoft Word icon. (This icon may be within another folder, such as an Office 97 folder, depending on your installation.)

NOTE

You may have to change to another drive in the Browse window in order to find the folder containing the Office programs, depending upon what drive letter was given when Office was originally installed.

7. You will be returned to the Create Shortcut Wizard, and the command line option will be filled in with the address (path) of the Word program/shortcut link file. Click on the Next button at the bottom of the dialog box.

8. You will be asked for the folder you want the shortcut placed in. Scroll to the StartUp folder in the Programs folder of the Start Menu, then click on the StartUp folder. Click on the Next button.

9. When asked for a title for the program, use the default title suggested in the text box. Click on the Finish button, then click on the OK button.

To find out if you successfully performed the steps, click on the Start button on the Taskbar and then point to the Programs folder, as shown in Figure 6.3. Point to the StartUp menu item to see the names of the programs that will start automatically when Windows 95 starts. Microsoft Word should be one of the start-up programs.

FIGURE 6.3

From the Start button, go to the Programs menu, then to the StartUp menu to display all the programs that will start automatically whenever Windows 95 starts.

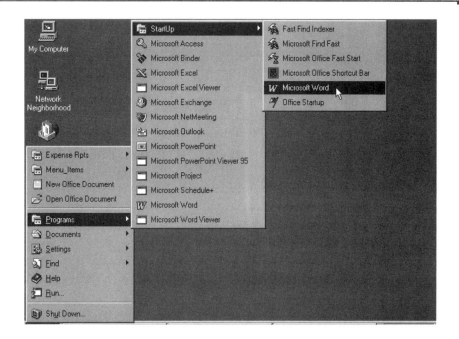

A Tour of the Word Screen

The Word screen/window contains a variety of objects. We'll describe Word's default appearance here.

To see the screen more or less as shown in Figure 6.4, click on the New button (the first button on the left) on the strip of buttons identified in the figure as the Standard toolbar (the first strip of buttons across the top of the Word screen).

Starting at the top of the window are four rows of objects: *title bar*, *menu bar*, *Standard toolbar*, and *Formatting toolbar*. Depending on your View menu settings, you may also see a *ruler* below the toolbars. Below these upper rows is the *typing area*, which may show a *scroll bar* along the right side and across the bottom. Within the typing area is the *Office Assistant* box displaying an animated character of a paper clip. Below the typing area is the *Status bar*. All of these items will be described in the following paragraphs, and are identified in Figure 6.4.

FIGURE 6.4

The elements of the Word screen

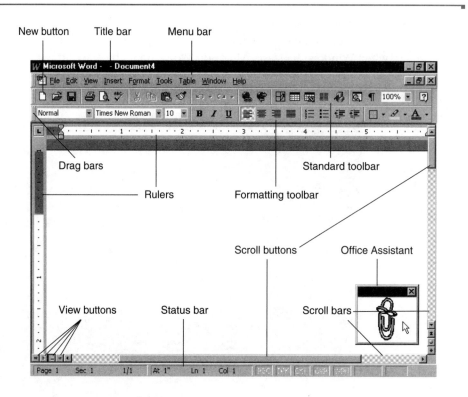

NOTE

If you do not see the toolbars (the two strips of buttons along the top of the Word window) as shown in Figure 6.4, select View ➤ Toolbars from the menu bar. Make sure there is a checkmark beside the toolbars named Standard and Formatting. (If the checkmark is not present, click on the toolbar names.) Similarly, if you don't see the ruler as shown in Figure 6.4, select View ➤ Ruler.

Title Bar

The title bar is common to all Windows programs; it displays the name of the program in which you are working, for example, "Microsoft Word." The bar also displays the name under which you registered the software. If the next word is "Document" followed by a number, what you see in the window represents a new, unsaved document. Once you save the document, you can give it a more descriptive name than Document1 or Document2.

Menu Bar

The menu bar displays the names of the *menus* (lists of commands) in Word. You can activate a menu by clicking on its name with the mouse, which drops down a list of commands. Click on a command to initiate it. (If some of the commands appear only dimly, they are not currently enabled. Different software circumstances cause command items to be enabled.)

For typists who prefer using keyboard commands rather than the mouse, there are key combinations for activating each menu bar item: hold down the Alt key and press the letter that is underscored. For example, Alt+F will activate the File menu, and Alt+O will activate the Format menu.

Once the menu is activated, any of the menu's commands that have underscored letters can then be activated by pressing the underscored letter—it is not necessary to hold down the Alt key when you press a command's underscored letter.

 **WARNING**

Using the keyboard to initiate a menu command is slightly different from using it to activate an option in a dialog box. While a menu command that contains an underscored letter can be initiated simply by typing that letter, a dialog box option that contains an underscored letter requires you to press Alt along with the underscored letter. (If you type the letter without pressing the Alt key, Word will think that you are entering text—for example, a filename—into a text box in the dialog box.)

Toolbars

There are eighteen toolbars that are standard with Microsoft Word 97; the previous version of Word had nine different toolbars. You can also create your own toolbars and populate them with the buttons of your choice. Other toolbars may appear automatically in certain situations (for example, when you are using Print Preview mode or Outline view or when creating a Header or Footer.)

When you slide the mouse over the menu and the toolbars, the buttons on the toolbars become visible—that is, they form visible button boundaries. When the mouse is pulled away from the toolbars, the button effect disappears.

Default Toolbars

The Standard toolbar (the first strip of buttons in Figure 6.4) is relatively consistent across all of the Office programs, which is to say that most of the buttons you see in this toolbar when you're working in Word will also appear when you're working in Excel or PowerPoint. The Standard toolbar contains buttons that represent functions that are common to many of the Office programs. For example, clicking on the Printer button will quickly print a copy of the entire current document.

The Formatting toolbar (the strip that includes the buttons lettered B, I, U—for bold, italic, underline) is also consistent across all of the Office applications. The Formatting toolbar contains buttons that represent common actions for changing the appearance of your work.

Moving Toolbars and Menu Bars

You can move the toolbars and menu bars to different positions on the screen. If you move a bar to the top, bottom, left, or right side of the screen, the bar "docks" itself at that position. You can also move a bar so that it "floats" in the middle of the screen.

Before you move a toolbar, notice the two thin vertical lines—called *drag bars*—on the left side of the toolbar (see Figure 6.4). To move the toolbar, click and drag on these drag lines, and pull the toolbar down into the middle of the screen. This a *floating* toolbar. To reposition the toolbar where it was last docked, double-click on the blue title bar at the top of the toolbar. It will redock into its last docked position.

Command Icons

Some of the toolbar buttons are also displayed as icons next to the text of their associated menu command items. Click on the File, Edit, View, Format, or Tools menu items and look at the text of the commands and notice the button icons that appear next to many of the commands. You will quickly become proficient with the toolbar buttons because of this association between menu commands and toolbar button icons.

ScreenTips

When you pause the mouse for a couple of seconds over any toolbar button, you will see a yellow pop-up note telling you the meaning of the button. This pop-up note is called a *ScreenTip* and each button on every toolbar is described by a ScreenTip.

To see how ScreenTips work, look at the Formatting toolbar at the four buttons that look like scratch marks. These buttons represent the different text alignments (left-justified, centered, right-justified, and full justification). Notice that the left-alignment button appears "pushed in" or recessed. A pushed in or recessed button lets you know that the format is already applied. Pause the mouse over this button and you will also see the ScreenTip associated with the button.

Paragraph alignment buttons—left, center, right, and full justification

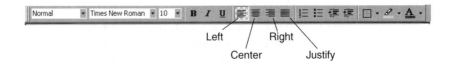

Turning on ScreenTips

If you do not see the yellow pop-up note when you hold the mouse over a toolbar button, this option may be turned off. Turn the option on by doing the following:

1. Choose View ➢ Toolbars ➢ Customize.
2. When the Customize dialog box appears, click on the Options tab at the top of the box.
3. Check Show ScreenTips on Toolbars.
4. Click on the Close button at the bottom of the dialog box.

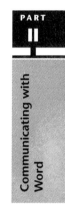

The Ruler

The ruler displays a horizontal scale that reflects the width of your typing area; it is invaluable when you want to quickly set tabs, margins, and indents. If you do not see the ruler, select View ➢ Ruler. Figure 6.6 shows a typical ruler in Page Layout view (choose View ➢ Page Layout to simulate Figure 6.6).

Quick Tab Sets

To quickly set a tab, click the mouse on the ruler. The default tab set is a left tab. You can "pull off" tabs you have set by dragging them down from the ruler: Click and hold down the mouse on a tab set, and a vertical line will appear. You can then drag the tab to another position on the ruler.

FIGURE 6.6

This ruler shows a left margin at 0" and a tab set at 1"

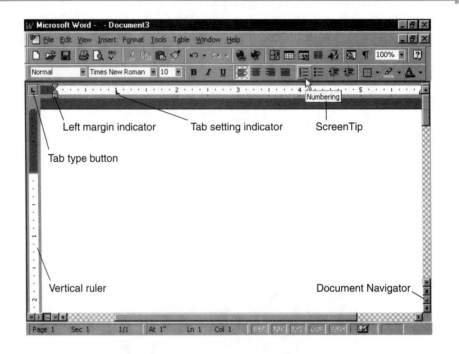

When you pause the mouse over a tab set, a ScreenTip will appear telling you what type of tab it is. To change the type of tab from a left tab to a right, center, or decimal tab, click on the L-shaped icon on the left side of the ruler; this is the tab type button. The icon will change as the tab type changes to center, right, decimal, then back to left. When you have the new tab type you want, click on the ruler at the point where you want to place the tab; a new tab will be set at that position with the icon reflecting the type of tab you chose. See Figure 6.6 for the tab type button.

NOTE

To see both the horizontal and vertical rulers, make sure that you are in Page Layout view (select View ➢ Page Layout). Normal view shows only the horizontal ruler when View ➢ Ruler is selected.

The Typing Area

The open area below the rulers and toolbars is the writing or typing area. This is your "piece of paper" on which you type and place your thoughts, procedures, tasks, graphics, and so on. If the ruler is showing, you can make the area somewhat larger by getting rid of the ruler. From the menu bar, select View ➢ Ruler to turn off the ruler.

You can begin typing immediately in the typing area. Do not press the Enter key at the end of each line, as Word allows the text to automatically wrap to the next line. If you wish to make corrections, press the Backspace key (above the Enter key). You can also drag the mouse over text to select (highlight) it. If you are new to typing in a word processing program, see Chapter 5.

Typing Screen Objects

There are certain objects that are a permanent part of the typing area. For instance, the insertion point and some version of the mouse pointer are always visible. The end-of-document marker (an underline character) is only visible at the end of the document when you are in Normal view (View ➤ Normal). Figures 6.7 and 6.8 show the typing area with a simple sentence typed in both the Normal and the Page Layout views.

PART

II

Communicating with Word

Normal view with a simple sentence typed

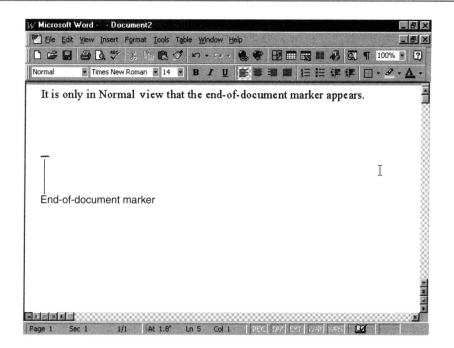

Insertion Point

The black vertical blinking line, or *insertion point*, that is initially at the top left side of the typing area is the guide for your typing—it indicates the place where your typing is inserted into the document. As you type, the blinking line continuously moves along.

FIGURE 6.8

Page Layout view with a simple sentence typed

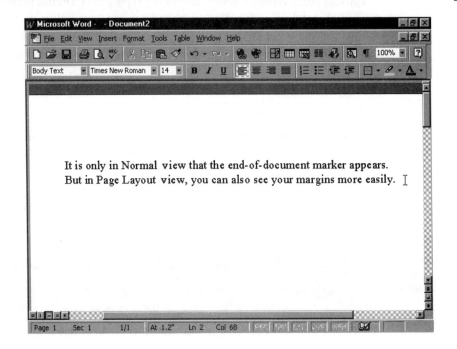

When you press the up, down, left, or right arrows on your keyboard, the insertion point moves accordingly, one character or line at a time in the typing area. Note that you cannot move the insertion point or the arrows to areas of the screen where there is not preexisting typing. You must have typed characters on the screen first, or inserted blank lines, before you can move the insertion point or the arrows.

NOTE

The insertion point is also commonly referred to as the *cursor*.

Mouse Pointer

When you move the mouse around in Word's typing area, the mouse pointer is in the shape of a thin I-beam. (You can see it at the end of the typed line in Figure 6.8.) As you move the mouse near the menu line and toolbars (or anywhere outside of the typing area), the mouse pointer becomes a white pointing arrow.

Move the mouse pointer to some existing piece of text and click the mouse. This action will bring the insertion point to that spot in the text.

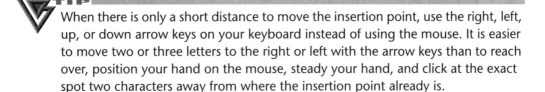

When there is only a short distance to move the insertion point, use the right, left, up, or down arrow keys on your keyboard instead of using the mouse. It is easier to move two or three letters to the right or left with the arrow keys than to reach over, position your hand on the mouse, steady your hand, and click at the exact spot two characters away from where the insertion point already is.

End-of-Document Marker

The horizontal line situated like a short underline at the end of the document is seen only when Word is in Normal view, as shown in Figure 6.7. As its name makes clear, the end-of-document marker lets you know where the end of the document occurs. It stays below your typing as you go, and remains at the very end of the document when you are finished typing.

If you wish to put the document in Normal view, choose View ➤ Normal from the menu. Page Layout view is better, however, for viewing your margins and page dimensions. Most of the work in this book will be done with the document view in Page Layout.

Vertical Scrolls

The typing area is bordered on the right side by the vertical scroll bar with a scroll button and arrows. The single down arrow scrolls through the document line by line. The double down arrow, however, allows you to move to the top of the next page. The double up arrow allows you to move to the top of the previous page. You can also drag the vertical scroll button up and down the scroll bar to move up and down through the document.

Horizontal Scrolls

The first bar along the bottom of the typing area is the horizontal scroll bar. Use the left and right arrow buttons on this bar to see text that is off the right or left side of the screen. The position of the bar or button in the middle of the scroll bar represents where the screen is in relation to the left and right margins of the document. To scroll horizontally, drag the button to the left or right margins. (You'll find that you have to use this horizontal scroll button to reset your view after you have performed an indent.)

PART

II

Communicating with
Word

Document Navigator

When you need to move to objects that are not single pages—such as text in a document, footnotes, multiple pages, and so on—use the *Document Navigator* to choose what object you wish to move to. The Document Navigator box is activated when you click on the tiny 3-D ball that sits between the double up and down arrows on the vertical scroll bar (see Figure 6.6).

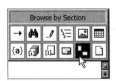

The Document Navigator offers twelve ways for you to go to or search for different types of objects in a document: Go To, Find Text, Browse by Edits, Browse by Heading, Browse by Graphic, Browse by Table, Browse by Field, Browse by Endnote, Browse by Footnote, Browse by Comment, Browse by Section, and Browse by Page.

View Buttons

To the left side of the horizontal scroll arrow at the bottom of the screen are buttons for the four document views: Normal, Online Layout, Page Layout, and Outline.

Normal view allows you to see your document in a traditional word processing fashion. No real margins are shown, page and section breaks appear as a dashed line across the screen, and there is no promise that you are seeing an actual graphic representation of how the page will look when printed. Because there is no memory taken up to show you a graphical representation, Normal view used to provide for faster scrolling than Page Layout view until fast 486 and Pentium machines came along. Page Layout is now the better view to use.

Online Layout view makes online reading easier. Whether you are looking at a Web page or want to see your own pages more clearly, the Online Layout view makes text appear larger and wraps text to fit the window, rather than wrap text the way it would actually print.

Online Layout view includes a resizable navigation pane—called the *Document Map*—that shows the outline view of the document's structure. If the Document Map is not visible, select View ➤ Document Map. Note that when you are in Online Layout view, the View buttons are no longer visible. To change back to Page Layout view, choose View ➤ Page Layout from the menu.

The *Page Layout* view button changes the screen to a graphical representation of your document, more or less as it will appear when printed. Margins and page breaks are more obvious in Page Layout view than in Normal view. At a zoom setting of 75% or less (select View ➤ Zoom or click on the arrow next to the Zoom box on the Standard toolbar), you can see both the right and left edges of a standard $8\frac{1}{2}$-by-11 inch page. In addition, while in Page Layout view, you can choose View ➤ Zoom ➤ Many Pages and drag the mouse over the tiny PC next to the Many Pages option. Word will display many tiny pages of your document simultaneously.

NOTE

Word will actually alert you that you cannot perform certain commands unless your document is in Page Layout view, and will ask permission to switch you over to this view. Other times, Word will automatically switch you to Page Layout mode (for example, when you start working with headers and footers).

PART

II

Communicating with Word

Outline view is used to create or view documents as outlines, which lets you choose how many levels of content you want to display. You can use Outline view to show only the headings in a document so that you can see at a glance how the document is organized. By clicking the plus or minus buttons next to each heading level, you can show or hide the subheads and/or the regular text. One attractive way to use outlines is to open them in PowerPoint to be shown as slides.

Status Bar

At the bottom of the typing area, below the horizontal scroll bar, is a Status bar that displays information about the current page number, the position of the insertion point, and the status of certain settings. If the Status bar is not showing, choose Tools ➤ Options and click the View tab. Then, in the Window area, check the Status bar option.

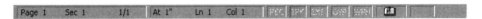

TIP

Double-click on the gray area of the Status bar as a shortcut for activating the Go To page command. This brings up a dialog box, which has a Go To tab. Type in a specific page number and press Enter. The insertion point will move to the top of the page you specified. Tap the Esc key to remove the dialog box.

The Status bar is divided into three sections:

- The left portion of the bar shows the page number of the current screen, the section number, and the page number as a fraction of the total number of pages in the document (for example, 1/12 for page 1 of 12).
- When the insertion point is on the current screen, the middle portion of the bar shows its vertical position on the page as measured in inches as well as in lines, and its horizontal position as measured in columns. These readings can be quite helpful when you are trying to place characters or other elements very precisely, as when you are working with tables or graphics.
- The right side of the bar contains abbreviations for settings that you can turn on and off by double-clicking the mouse on them. Table 6.1 provides the meaning of each of the Status bar's abbreviations.

TABLE 6.1: STATUS BAR ABBREVIATIONS

Abbreviation	Explanation
REC	Macro record on/off. Turns macro recording on and off. Macros are short programs you can create by recording steps you perform frequently while working in Word.
TRK	Track changes on/off. Turns on and off the colored marking of revisions that are made during the editing of a document. When you right-click this option, a pop-up menu appears.
EXT	Extend selection on/off. When EXT is displayed, everything between the current location of the insertion point and the point where you turn off the EXT indicator will be highlighted (selected). Double-click again on the EXT indicator, or press the Esc key, to turn off the EXT feature, leaving the selection on-screen, ready to be moved, copied, or deleted.
OVR	Overtype on/off. Turns on and off the ability to type over text, in effect replacing text a character at a time alongside the insertion point (rather than the default of inserting text without destroying the text alongside it). Works the same as the Insert key on the keyboard.

Continued ▶

TABLE 6.1: STATUS BAR ABBREVIATIONS (CONTINUED)	
Abbreviation	**Explanation**
WP/WPH/WPN	WordPerfect keystrokes, WordPerfect Help, WordPerfect navigation keystrokes. When you double-click on these options, users who are migrating to Word from WordPerfect can use WordPerfect keystrokes to perform many Word tasks, to provide WordPerfect Help (identifying equivalent keystrokes in Word), or to just let you use WordPerfect navigation (cursor-movement) keys. You can uncheck the Help and Navigation keys in this dialog box to turn off the automatic WordPerfect keystrokes and Help.

Spelling and Grammar Status

The Spelling and Grammar Status indicator icon is an open book with a red X on the right side; the book becomes animated with a pencil moving across the page when you begin typing. The spelling and grammar checkers check for misspelled words (red wavy lines will appear underneath misspelled words) or grammatical errors (green wavy lines will appear underneath grammatical errors).

When you see red or green wavy lines under your words, double-click the book on the status bar. Word will move to the word, and a pop-up list will appear displaying either suggestions for correct spellings or suggestions for grammatical corrections. You can then choose or ignore the spelling or the grammar suggestions.

If you prefer not to have Word check your grammar as you type, turn off this option by choosing Tools ➤ Options and click the Spelling & Grammar tab. In the Grammar section, uncheck the option *Check grammar as you type*.

Background Save

The rightmost section of the Status bar (next to the Spell and Grammar Status indicator) has no text or icons, but if you pause the mouse over this blank area, you will see a ScreenTip that says "Background Save." If you have the Allow Background Saves setting checked in the Tools ➤ Options ➤ Save tab, you will see a pulsing disk whenever you save your document.

The Background Save is only obvious if you are saving a long document that takes a number of seconds to save. In previous versions, a user saving a long document would have to wait out the duration of the save, as indicated by the blue progress bar on the status bar. With the Background Save feature, you are able to type and perform other actions in Word while the save is happening.

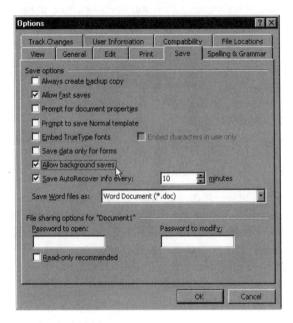

The Taskbar

Although technically not part of the Word screen, you can't miss the importance of the Windows 95 *Taskbar*, which by default remains on the screen whenever Windows 95 is running. (You can override this default behavior by selecting Auto Hide as one of the Taskbar Property options. With Auto Hide on, the Taskbar only appears when you bring the mouse pointer to its hidden location.) The Taskbar displays the Start button and other buttons for any application programs that are currently open in memory. You can click on the Start button to find another program to start while you are in Word, or click on another Taskbar button to switch to a program that is already open.

NOTE

The Windows 95 Taskbar and Start button are described more fully in Chapter 2.

Changing the Date and Time

When you save your work, Word date-stamps your document. For this reason, you will probably want to synchronize your computer's clock to the correct date and time so that your documents are saved with the correct information. You can view the dates and times when you created and last revised a document by selecting File ➤ Properties ➤ Statistics from the Word menu bar.

The time is displayed on the far right side of the Taskbar. To view the date, let the mouse pointer linger on the time in the Taskbar; Windows 95 will display the current date. To change the date and time, double-click on the time readout in the Taskbar; the Date/Time Properties dialog box will open, displaying a calendar and a combination analog/digital clock (see Figure 6.9). Drag the mouse over the hours or minutes of the time and change them as necessary. To change the month or year, click the spinner buttons next to the month and year boxes. To change the date, click on the correct date on the calendar layout.

Communicating with
Word

FIGURE 6.9

*The Windows 95
Date/Time Prop-
erties dialog box*

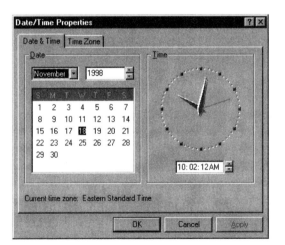

Templates and Magical Wizards

Word contains a number of predesigned documents called *templates* that you can use as the basis for your documents. The templates include fax forms, memos, newsletters, Web pages, legal pleadings, letters, and mailing labels. Word may set the specific margins, point size, typeface, indentations, and even graphics for each of these types of documents. You can enter your own text into the example documents without being concerned with setting up the layout and formatting. Word has completely managed the details so that you can concentrate on typing out your thoughts.

Some of the templates are programmed to walk you through the steps of creating your document. These step-by-step programs are called *Wizards*. Word offers Wizards in a number of template categories including Other Documents, Publications, Memos, Letters & Faxes, and Web Pages.

When you create a new document, the default template is the predesigned Normal template: the margins on the left and right are set at 1.25 inches, the top and bottom margins at 1 inch; the tab stops are set every $\frac{1}{2}$ inch, and the page is laid out in a portrait orientation (as opposed to a landscape orientation). These settings are nothing fancy, as this template is intended to serve as a generic layout. To choose a template:

1. Choose File ➤ New from the menu bar.

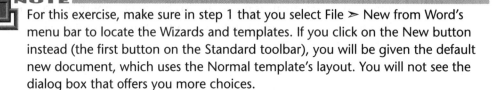

NOTE For this exercise, make sure in step 1 that you select File ➤ New from Word's menu bar to locate the Wizards and templates. If you click on the New button instead (the first button on the Standard toolbar), you will be given the default new document, which uses the Normal template's layout. You will not see the dialog box that offers you more choices.

2. Click on each tab in the New dialog box to familiarize yourself with what is available in each category. When you click on one of the templates or Wizards, a sample document will appear in the Preview portion of the dialog box in the lower right corner of the dialog box.

3. Double-click on any document with a magic wand across the document icon. These are the Wizard templates mentioned above that will help you design your document. (Remember, you can always choose File ➤ Close to close the template without saving after you have looked at the design.) If you like the design, go ahead and use it as the basis for a document and save your work as you would normally (select File ➤ Save and name the document as you wish).

Figure 6.10 shows the Letters & Faxes category of templates, which contains a number of Wizards to try.

If you cannot find the template or the Wizard you want to use, do any one of the following:

- Rerun Setup, and click the Custom button to install additional files.
- Go to the Microsoft Office Web Site and download free templates and Wizards. On the Help menu, point to Microsoft on the Web, and then click Free Stuff.
- If you installed Microsoft Word from a CD-ROM, insert the disk and double-click on the ValuPack folder to see what other templates and Wizards are available. Copy the files you want to the Templates subfolder in the Microsoft Office folder.

FIGURE 6.10

Word provides a variety of Wizard templates that take you step-by-step through the document process.

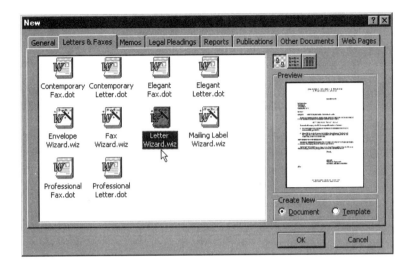

Other Useful Features and Commands

Word includes many features that are not obvious from the pictures on their buttons or their menu descriptions, but which nonetheless provide capabilities you may need during your work with the program. In this section, we'll show you some of these more subtle capabilities of Word. You can:

- Select the entire document: To select (highlight/block off) the entire document quickly, press Ctrl+A. You'll also find this command in the Edit menu.
- Display a document's hard returns, tabs, and spaces: Click on the paragraph symbol button on the right end of the Standard toolbar. The keystroke combination is Ctrl+Shift+8.
- E-mail the document on the screen: Choose File ➢ SendTo ➢ Mail Recipient.
- Save a file without the .doc extension: Put the filename in quotes when you save the file; for example, "Letter.Jun".
- Undo the last 99 actions performed on a document: Press Ctrl+Z or click on the Undo button on the Standard Toolbar to reverse up to the last 99 actions. If you undo too many actions, press Ctrl+Y to "redo your undo" or press the Redo button on the Standard toolbar.
- Use the AutoComplete feature: Press Enter when Word suggests phrases while you are typing. For example, begin typing the current month's date, and a yellow pop-up tip will appear with the complete spelling of the month's name. Press Enter to have Word automatically complete the word for you. The list of AutoComplete words is in the Insert ➢ AutoText menu.

Communicating with Word

- Insert common phrases into your text: Show the AutoText toolbar that lists pre-typed phrases and words that you can then insert into your document. Choose View ➤ Toolbars and check AutoText.
- Get online help from Microsoft: Make sure you are connected to the Internet while using Word 97. Choose Help ➤ Microsoft on the Web ➤ Online Support. The Microsoft site will launch and you can view the online support questions and answers.
- Design your own table or form: The Tables and Borders button (icon with a pencil on grid lines) allows you to free-form draw and erase your own table layouts.
- Use multilevel numbering: If you need to number in an outline form, choose Format ➤ Bullets and Numbering ➤ Outline Numbered to create indented numbering structures.

Chapter

7

Sharpening Your Word Skills

Chapter 7

Sharpening Your Word Skills

Word 97 offers you a tremendous number of features that allow you to quickly create documents and make them look professionally designed. Although you will have to know more commands and features to create a 30-page report than you will to create a simple letter, you'll find that there are tasks you perform in almost *every* document. These include:

- Deciding document layout
- Typing/editing
- Saving often
- Formatting to enhance appearance
- Checking text
- Printing
- Customizing the environment for future work

In this chapter, you'll learn the basic skills you'll need to create documents in Word and the considerations you must bring to each document you create.

Word's Document Defaults

New documents in Word have predefined settings called *defaults,* which differ depending on the type of document you are working with. If you pick one of the predesigned documents (called *templates*) from the New dialog box (File ➤ New), your margins, spacing, and other settings will be quite different from the settings for a document created with the Normal template. The list below displays the default settings for the Normal (Blank Document) template.

Paper size	$8\frac{1}{2} \times 11"$
Orientation	Portrait
Top margin	1"
Bottom margin	1"
Left margin	1.25"
Right margin	1.25"
Alignment	Left-aligned text
Page numbering	None
Sections	One
Tabs	Set every half inch
Typeface	Times New Roman (depends on printer type)
Point size	10 points (depends on printer type)
Paper bin	Upper tray in printer (if printer has multiple trays)

Starting a New Document

When you begin a new document in Word, a blank page appears with the generic name Document# (as in Document2) in the title bar. This is how Word refers to the document until you save your work with a more specific name.

You then need to decide what kind of document you are creating. Is it a single- or multiple-page letter or memo? Is it a report or proposal? Does your letterhead paper require a certain margin width at the left side or at the top? Will the document be laid out sideways (landscape)? Does the document require page numbers? What about repeating text at the top or bottom of each page (headers or footers)?

Word makes it very easy to modify page settings. Table 7.1 lists the menu commands used to change the page settings of a document.

TIP

It is a good idea to change these settings before you begin typing, because they could drastically affect the appearance of the document. For example, if you create a table in portrait mode and then change the paper size to landscape, the tables will probably need to be adjusted to fit the new paper size.

TABLE 7.1: MODIFYING PAGE SETTINGS

To ...	Choose...
Adjust margins	File ➢ Page Setup ➢ Margins
Adjust paper size	File ➢ Page Setup ➢ Paper Size
View the margins and/or page breaks	View ➢ Page Layout. This view displays the document as it will look when printed. To see the margins more clearly, adjust the zoom to 50% or Whole Page.
View the document using different page sizes	View ➢ Zoom ➢ 75%. To see a whole page in Page Layout view, choose Whole Page (it will be difficult to type in this small view).
Add page numbers	Insert ➢ Page Numbers. If you don't want to have a page number on the first page, click on the Show Number on First Page checkbox to uncheck this feature.
Add headers and footers	View ➢ Header and Footer. To add text that appears on the top of every page, start typing in the Header area. To add text that appears on the bottom of every page, click on the *Switch between Header and Footer* button, and start typing in the Footer area.
Turn on AutoRecovery to have Word automatically save your document every so many minutes.	Tools ➢ Options ➢ Save, then check AutoRecovery Info Every *x* Minutes.

PART

II

Communicating with Word

Getting Around the Document

It is important to learn to move around in a document quickly and efficiently so you can concentrate on your thoughts and not on the mechanics of the software. Word has a number of mouse and keyboard "moves" that you will find helpful and interesting to use. Users are often tempted to use the mouse constantly, even to move short distances; however, in some cases you can move short distances more efficiently using keyboard combinations.

Vertical Scroll Bar

To move through a document several pages at a time, use the mouse to drag the scroll box (or *slide*) up or down the vertical scroll bar on the right side of the screen; Word will show you the page number you are on as you slide. Clicking in the empty vertical space above or below the scroll box moves you up or down one screen. Look at your Status bar to see what page you are on.

When looking at the right side of the screen, you will see two sets of up and down arrows on the vertical scroll bar. Clicking on the single down arrow will move you down one line at a time (although it is quicker to tap the keyboard's down arrow). The double up and down arrows move you to the previous page and the next page, respectively.

Document Navigator

Word's Document Navigator feature is activated by clicking on the tiny 3-D button located on the bottom of the vertical scroll bar (see below).

The Document Navigator allows you to move around a document in different ways. You can also use the double up and down arrows located above and below the Document Navigator button to move to the Next or Previous occurrences of an object.

The browse methods on the Document Navigator include:

- Go To method
- Find and Replace method

The browse objects on the Document Navigator include:

- Edits—pointer moves to the next and previous three edits
- Headings—pointer moves to the next and previous headings
- Graphics—pointer moves to the next and previous graphics
- Tables—pointer moves to the next and previous tables
- Fields—pointer moves to the next and previous fields
- Endnotes—pointer moves to the next and previous endnotes
- Footnotes—pointer moves to the next and previous footnotes
- Comments—pointer moves to the next and previous comments
- Sections—pointer moves to the next and previous sections
- Pages—pointer moves to the next and previous pages

Document Map

Microsoft has invented a navigation tool in Word that helps you move easily through long documents like reports, proposals, and long tables. Using a document's headings as navigation points, the Document Map splits the screen so that you see your document on the right and any headings on the left. You can quickly jump to a location in the document by clicking on a heading instead of scrolling and looking through the text. To use this navigation tool:

1. Open a document that has heading styles.
2. Click on the Document Map icon on the Standard Toolbar or choose View ➤ Document map. See Figure 7.1.
3. The screen splits to display the headings on the left and the document text on the right.
4. Click on any heading on the left and you will be moved to the corresponding section in the text.
5. To remove the split, double-click on the vertical line separating the left side from the right side.
6. To return to Page Layout view, choose View ➤ Page Layout from the menu.

The Insertion Point

The blinking vertical line that sits at the beginning of a new document is a guide for your typing; it is called the *insertion point*. The insertion point remains in a document at all times. It is called the *cursor* in many other programs.

To position the insertion point so you can make a change or add or delete words, click the primary mouse button (usually the left mouse button) on the screen at the

Communicating with Word

FIGURE 7.1

The Document Map allows you to navigate quite effectively in long documents that contain heading styles.

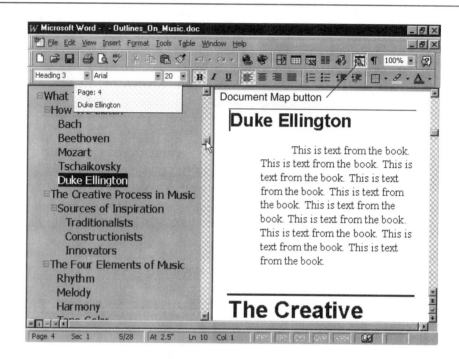

point where you want to make the change. You can also press the up, down, left, or right arrow keys to move the insertion point, instead of using the mouse (see Table 7.2).

When the insertion point is to the left of a letter, think of the insertion point as being "in front of" that letter; any new text you type will be inserted to the left of that letter. If you press the Delete key, Word will delete the letter that is to the right of the insertion point.

Repositioning the Insertion Point

You can quickly reposition the insertion point using either the mouse or the keyboard. There are times when it is more efficient to use the keyboard than to use the mouse. For instance, it takes less time to press the left arrow key than it does to use the mouse to move the insertion point one letter to the left. It is also more efficient to use the Home and End keys (rather than the mouse) to move the insertion point to the beginning or the end of a line. The mouse, however, is far more efficient when moving the insertion point to a specific spot on the screen that is some distance away.

Tables 7.2 and 7.3 show you some of the ways you can move around in your document using the keyboard and the mouse, respectively.

TABLE 7.2: POSITIONING THE INSERTION POINT USING THE KEYBOARD

Keyboard Combinations	Where the Insertion Point Is Repositioned...
Home	Beginning of the line
End	End of the line
Up, down, left, right arrow keys	Lines up or down or characters left or right
Ctrl+← or Ctrl+→	Words right or left
Ctrl+↑ or Ctrl+↓	Paragraphs up or down
PgUp or PgDn	Screens up or down
Ctrl+Alt+PgUp or Ctrl+Alt+PgDn	Previous pages or next pages
Ctrl+Home	Top of document
Ctrl+End	End of document
Ctrl+F and type a word	The word that was found
Ctrl+G, or F5, and type a page number	Top of that page
Shift+F5	Previous locations where edits occurred (up to three)

TABLE 7.3: MOVING AROUND USING THE MOUSE

Feature	Allows You To
Vertical scroll arrows	Move up and down a line at a time
Vertical Scroll box	Move to any point in the document by dragging the vertical scroll box to a proportional point on the scroll bar. For example, if in a 30-page report you drag the vertical scroll box to the middle of the bar, you will be positioned at page 15.
Vertical double up and down arrows	Move to the previous and next pages
Vertical scroll box	Slide up or down to see the page number
Document Navigator	Move to an object you specify in the Browse Object box.

Quick Word Processing Tips

Users of word processing programs know that there are concepts you should learn sooner rather than later. The next sections discuss the most common word processing concepts you should know regardless of your of Word skill level.

NOTE
General business typing information can be best gleaned from someone with a background in generating office documents. If you are not a touch typist, you may want to increase your typing speed by purchasing a typing program. If you have no experience at all in typing documents, you may want to speak with a typist or someone who creates electronic documents to get a sense of the issues involved with typing.

Word Wrap

You can start typing a document as you would with a typewriter or any other word processor. Unlike with a typewriter, however, you do not press Enter at the end of each line. Continue to let your text wrap around until you are ready to start a new paragraph. Press the Enter key at the end of short typed lines, such as those found on the address of a letter or on a list of items.

Wrapping Words Together

If you want to make sure that two words (such as someone's first and last names) always wrap to the next line together, put a *nonbreaking space* between them. The keyboard combination for a nonbreaking space is Ctrl+Shift+spacebar. For example, many word processing users find that dates will invariably break between the month and the day or the day and the year. Press Ctrl+Shift+spacebar between the month and the day, and again between the day and the year, instead of typing a regular space; this date will now wrap as a whole in the document.

Justifying Text

Word uses a mathematical algorithm to decide whether a word can fit at the end of a line or should wrap to the next line. The right margins of your text where the wrap occurs will look "ragged," depending upon the length of the words in each line. This is correct, but if you do not like the look of a ragged right margin, click on the Justify button on the Formatting toolbar (or press Ctrl+J) to make the text "square" off at the right margin.

Centering Text

Use the Center button on the Formatting toolbar, or press Ctrl+E, (think "even" between the margins) to center a line, then type your text and press Enter. To return the text to the left margin, place the insertion point in the line, and click on the left alignment button on the toolbar or press Ctrl+L. You cannot type text at the left align and center the same line at the same time. Use the Tab key if you must have multiple headings on a single line with different alignments. See Chapter 8 for a full discussion of line alignments.

Spacebar and Tabs

Use the spacebar as a separator for your words and sentences. Don't use the spacebar to move the insertion point across a line of text—known as "spacing across a line." The spacebar method works on a typewriter as a way of moving across a line, but it doesn't work in word processing; if you use the spacebar to move around, Word will make additional spaces, which you'll then have to delete.

Avoid using the spacebar to create columns of text; use the Tab key instead. Text that has been separated by more than a couple of spaces tends not to align correctly when printed.

TIP

Use the Table feature (Table ➢ Insert Table) if you want to designate a specific number of columns and rows in which to type your columnar text.

Paragraph Markers

You may find it easier to type when you can see the returns, spaces, and tabs in your document. If so, click on the Show/Hide ¶ button on the Standard toolbar to display the marks. Click on the symbol again to hide them.

TIP

The Caps Lock key can be a source of frustration if you accidentally hit it when typing. When Caps Lock is on (look for the indicator light on your keyboard), any text you type regularly will be uppercase, and text you type with the Shift key held down will be lowercase. If you inadvertently type a bit of text with Caps Lock on, select the text and choose Format ➢ Change Case ➢ tOGGLE cASE to change the case back to normal.

PART

II

Communicating with Word

Selecting (Highlighting) Text

When you want Word to change the formatting for particular characters, words, lines, sentences, paragraphs, or pages, you must show the computer the specific text you are referring to by selecting it. Selecting text is also called *highlighting* or *blocking*. You can use the mouse or the keyboard to select text.

WARNING

When text is selected, it is vulnerable to deletion. Selected text can be easily replaced by other characters by tapping any key on the keyboard. For example, if you select a page of text and inadvertently tap the spacebar, Word will replace the selected page with a space! (If this happens, immediately click the Undo button, press Ctrl+Z, or choose Edit ➤ Undo.) Try not to keep text selected after you have performed an operation on it. Click the mouse anywhere on the screen to deselect the text.

Selection Bar

There is an invisible area on the left side of a line of text called the *selection bar*. You can "see" this area only by noticing how the mouse pointer changes from an I-beam to a left arrow. Sweep your mouse slowly to the left side of a line of typed text and watch it change from an I-beam to a left arrow. When it changes, click the mouse button to select a line of text.

Once a line is selected, drag down to select multiple lines. Double-click in the selection bar area to select a paragraph. In Figure 7.2, you can see that the mouse pointer has changed from an I-beam to an arrow and is pointing to a line of text.

Mouse Techniques

You can use the following techniques to select text with the mouse:

- Select characters by dragging the mouse over the characters.
- Select a line by moving the mouse to the left side of the line until the I-beam turns into an arrow, then click once or drag the mouse across the entire line.
- Select a word by double-clicking on it, or by merely clicking into the middle of the word. (To apply formatting to a single word, it is not necessary to have the whole word selected. As long as the insertion point is in the word, Word will know you want the formatting action to apply to the word.)

FIGURE 7.2

The selection bar is an invisible area on the left side of a screen of text. Click once to select a single line of text.

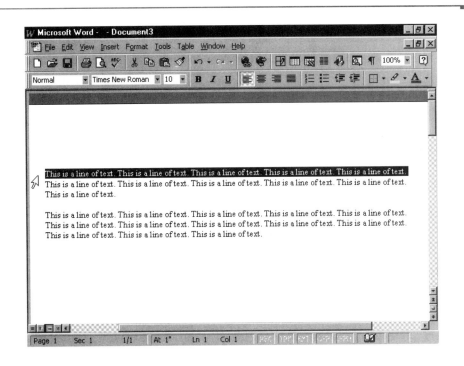

PART

II

Communicating with Word

- Select a sentence by holding down the Ctrl key and clicking anywhere in the sentence.
- Select a paragraph by triple-clicking within the paragraph or double-clicking in the selection bar next to the left of the paragraph.
- Select a page by pressing the mouse button and dragging down the page.
- Select the entire document by pressing the keyboard combination of Ctrl+A or using the mouse and triple-clicking in the selection bar area.
- Select a rectangular area by holding down the Alt key and dragging the mouse pointer across and down the text in a rectangle. Figure 7.3 displays text selected using the Alt key.

Keyboard Techniques

You can use the following techniques to select text with the Shift key:

- Select multiple characters one at a time by holding down the Shift key and pressing the right (→) or left (←) arrows repeatedly.
- Select whole words by holding down the Shift key and pressing Ctrl+← or Ctrl+→ repeatedly.

FIGURE 7.3

You can make a rectangular text selection by holding down the Alt key while you click and drag.

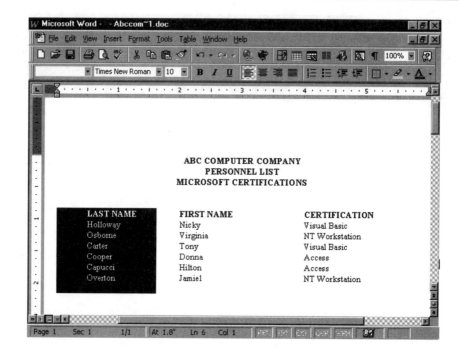

- Select a whole line by holding down the Shift key and pressing the End key.
- Select multiple lines by holding down the Shift key and pressing the ↑ or ↓ arrow.
- Select multiple paragraphs by holding down the Shift key and pressing Ctrl+↑ or Ctrl+↓.
- Select multiple screens by holding down the Shift key and pressing PgUp or PgDn.
- Select the entire document by pressing Ctrl+A or Ctrl+5 (on the number pad).

F8 Key Techniques

The F8 key is an interesting selection key. It functions in a similar way to the block key (F12 or Alt+F4 key) in WordPerfect for DOS. The F8 key selects a unit of text each time you press it. After you highlight text by pressing F8, you can then press a single character, such as a period or a dash or a letter, and the highlight (selection) will jump to the first occurrence of this character. Table 7.4 is a reference guide for effectively using the F8 key.

TABLE 7.4: THE F8 KEY REFERENCE GUIDE

F8 Key Combination	Selection
Press F8 once	Turns on the F8 selector
Press F8 again	Word
Press F8 a third time	Sentence
Press F8 a fourth time	Paragraph
Press F8 a fifth time	Entire document
Press a period	Highlights all text to the right of the selection up to the first period
Press any letter/character	Highlights all text up to that letter/character
Press Esc	Turns off F8, but selection remains
Click the mouse or tap an arrow key	Turns off F8, but selection remains, up to where you clicked the mouse
Press Esc and click the mouse or tap an arrow key	Highlight goes away (selection is no longer active)

Copying and Moving Text

Part of the editing process is copying or moving text to other sections of your document. You can use the copy and cut commands to avoid retyping text in your document.

When you copy or cut text, the text is stored in an area of memory called the Clipboard and can be *pasted* back into the document or into any other document. Word only remembers the last text you copied or cut.

Copy and Cut Text Methods

All Windows programs use the same menu and keyboard commands for copying and moving text:

1. Highlight (select) the text first by dragging the mouse or using the shift and arrows keys.

2. Choose Edit ➤ Copy to copy the selected text, or Edit ➤ Cut to move the selected text. You can also click on the Copy or Cut buttons on the Standard Toolbar, or press Ctrl+C (copy) or Ctrl+X (cut).

3. Reposition the insertion point at the location where you want to insert the copied or cut text.

4. Choose Edit ➤ Paste to paste (retrieve) the text from the Clipboard. You can also click on the Paste button on the Standard Toolbar, or press Ctrl+V (paste).

Once you have copied or moved text onto the Clipboard, you can paste the same text again and again until you copy or cut another selection.

Shortcut Menu Method

You can also copy, cut, and paste text by clicking the secondary mouse button in a document and choosing these commands from the shortcut menu that pops up. (The secondary mouse button is the one you *don't* normally click—usually the right button.) The procedure for using the Copy, Cut, and Paste commands in the shortcut menu is as follows:

1. Select the text to be copied or cut.

2. Keep your pointer on the selected text and click the secondary mouse button (*right-click*).

3. Choose Copy or Cut from the menu that pops up.

4. Reposition your insertion point at the location you want to copy or move the text to. Right-click and choose Paste from the shortcut menu.

Drag-and-Drop Method

The drag-and-drop method for copying, cutting, and pasting doesn't use the Clipboard. (You can activate or deactivate this feature by choosing Tools ➤ Options ➤ Edit on the menu bar.) To move text using drag-and-drop, select the text to be cut, click on the selected text, and drag the selected text to the new location. You will see a small, gray outline box attached to your cursor as you drag the text. When you release the mouse button, the text will be moved from its original location to the new location.

To copy the text instead of moving it, hold down the Ctrl key as you drag. You will see a small, gray outline box with a plus sign attached to the cursor as you drag the copy to its new location.

WARNING

Drag-and-drop can be unwieldy, because the mouse moves very quickly when you drag text around. Often you will find yourself running past the location where you are trying to drop off the text. If drag-and-drop does not go well, immediately press the Undo key to return the document to its previous state; then, use the other methods for copying and cutting text that you learned in the previous sections.

 MASTERING THE OPPORTUNITIES

PART

II

Communicating with Word

Copying Data to Other Applications

If you want to integrate data among the multiple Office 97 programs, you must understand the role of the Clipboard. The Clipboard is the part of memory that stores the last selection of text you copied or cut. When you copy or cut a new selection, the previous selection is over-written in the Clipboard.

Once a selection is on the Clipboard, it is available to other Windows programs. You can start another program and paste or "paste special" the contents of the Clipboard. For example, to copy data from Excel to Word:

1. Select a range of cells in Excel to be copied.
2. Click on the Copy button on the Standard toolbar or press Ctrl+C.
3. Start Word from the Start button or switch to Word if it is already launched.
4. Click on the location in the Word document where you want to paste the copy.

5. Click on the Paste button on Word's Standard toolbar or press Ctrl+V.

If you want the Excel data to be linked into the Word document, choose Edit ➤ Paste Special. Click on the Paste Link option and choose Microsoft Excel 8.0 Excel Workbook Object. Now every time you change the data in Excel, it will be changed in the Word document.

To copy data from Word to Excel:

1. Select the Word table or text to be copied.
2. Click on the Copy button on the Standard toolbar or press Ctrl+C.
3. Start Excel from the Start button on the Taskbar or switch to Excel if it is already in memory.
4. Click on the location in Excel where the Word text copy will be inserted.
5. Click on the Paste button on Excel's Standard toolbar or press Ctrl+V.

If you choose Edit ➤ Paste Special, you can link the copied text to the original Word selection. Then, when you make changes in the data in Word, they will appear in Excel.

The methods described for correcting, editing, cutting, and pasting are listed for quick reference in Table 7.5.

TABLE 7.5: EDITING REFERENCE GUIDE

To...	Method
Insert text	Click on location for new text, then begin typing
Replace text	Select text to be replaced, then type new text
Delete previous letter(s)	Press Backspace
Delete previous word(s)	Press Ctrl+Backspace
Delete the next letter(s)	Press Delete
Delete the next word(s)	Press Ctrl+Delete
Delete multiple words	Select text, then press Delete
Delete a sentence	Ctrl+click in sentence, then press Delete
Delete a paragraph	Triple-click in paragraph, then press Delete
Delete a page	Select page (click and drag), then press Delete
Copy text	Select text, press Ctrl+C or click on the Copy button, reposition, then paste by pressing Ctrl+V or clicking on the Paste button
Move text	Select text, press Ctrl+X or click on the Cut button, reposition, then paste by pressing Ctrl+V or clicking on the Paste button

Correcting Text

You can easily correct text and proof your work using Word. There are a number of strategies and techniques for correcting typos and making changes quickly as you type in Word documents.

Manually Correcting As You Type

When you are typing a line of text and you make a typo, the automatic spelling checker will alert you with a wavy red line under the typo. The easiest way to correct the word is to immediately press the Backspace key to back over the typo, or press Ctrl+Backspace to back over the entire word. Do not tap the left arrow and then press Delete; that takes too many keystrokes.

Undo

Use the Undo feature (Edit ➤ Undo) to immediately reverse a typo. Be careful—it might undo the entire line you just typed. If you "undo" too much, press Ctrl+Y to redo the undo. The Undo feature remembers the last 99 actions you performed on a document; repeatedly click the Undo button, or press Ctrl+Z, to reverse your last 99 actions.

Redo

The Undo feature can reverse up to ninety-nine actions. Press Ctrl+Y to bring back your last Undo or click on the Redo button on the Standard toolbar.

If you click on the drop-down list arrow next to the Undo button, you will see the list of previous Undo actions. If you click on the drop-down list arrow next to the Redo button, you will see the actions you can do again.

Automatically Correcting As You Go Along

If there are specific typos that you always make, such as *don;t* when you mean to type *don't*, nine times out of ten, Word has been programmed via its AutoCorrect command to recognize the typo and will automatically correct the typo for you. There are times, however, when your particular brand of typo will not be programmed into Word. You can add your own typos to the AutoCorrect list so it will automatically change your typos as you type.

To add your typos to Word's powerful and flexible AutoCorrect list, follow these steps:

1. Choose Tools ➤ AutoCorrect.
2. In the Replace box (where the insertion point is blinking), type the typo that Word should look out for in the future.
3. Press Tab or click in the With box and type the correct spelling.
4. Click on Add on the right side of the AutoCorrect dialog box.
5. Click on OK.

Now, when you make that particular typo, Word will automatically change it to the correct spelling after you have pressed the spacebar or the Enter key. You will have more fun with AutoCorrect in Chapter 12.

PART

II

Communicating with Word

Inserting a Page Break

Word automatically creates new pages as you type. But you will sometimes need to create a new page manually. This occurs frequently in long reports when you must end one part and start a new part on another page.

Click at the beginning or end of the line where the new page is to start and press Ctrl+Enter or choose Insert ➤ Break ➤ Page Break ➤ OK. A new page break will appear. If you change your mind and don't want a page break, press Backspace to delete it. Remember you can also press Ctrl+Z or Edit ➤ Undo or click on the Undo icon on the Standard toolbar if the action was just performed.

In Page Layout view (View ➤ Page Layout), you can easily see different sized pages by changing the zoom control (the 100% in the upper right corner of the Standard toolbar) to Whole Page or Two Pages or 25%.

Deleting Pages

You can delete a page of typed text by dragging the mouse over the typed text on the page and pressing the Delete key (remember the Undo button reverses this action).

If there is a blank page you wish to remove, click on the blank page and press the Backspace key until you "back" the blank page up into the previous typed page. If that doesn't work, it means that there are blank lines on the page that you must highlight and delete just as you would delete typed text. Click on the Show/Hide ¶ button (next to the zoom control box) to turn paragraph symbols on; you will then be able to see the blank lines. Click on the same button to turn off the viewing of the paragraph symbols.

Another technique used to delete blank pages is to change to Normal view (View ➤ Normal) and look for the dotted Page Break line. Click on the line and press the Delete key on the keyboard.

Typing over Text

To type over existing text, tap the Insert key so that OVR (for Overstrike mode) appears in black on the left side of the Status bar. Keep in mind that typing over existing text (using Overstrike rather than Insert mode) is risky business because you must watch the screen carefully to make sure that you only type over text you want to delete. We recommend that you delete your old text and add your new text in Insert mode, rather than turning on the Overstrike option. You can toggle between Insert and Overstrike modes by tapping the Insert key.

If you find that you are inadvertently typing over text instead of inserting the text, look at the bottom of the screen on the Status bar at the white letters on the right-hand side. If the letters OVR are black, it means that you have overtype mode on by accident. Press the Insert key on your keyboard or double-click on the OVR letters so that overtype is turned off (white letters instead of black letters).

Replacing Text

To replace text, you must select the lines or word(s) you wish to replace, then type your new text. The selected text will be replaced by the new typing. By specifically selecting the text you wish to type over, you control what will be replaced in your document.

Do not sit with selected text on the screen. Click on the screen anywhere to deselect text.

Checking Spelling and Grammar

The Spelling and Grammar features (choose Tools ➢ Spelling & Grammar, or press F7) electronically check your document for misspellings, irregular case problems, and grammatical problems.

Word also has an automatic spelling and grammar checker that is turned on when you begin Word. The automatic spelling checker will underline any misspelled words with a wavy, red line as you type. The grammar checker will underline any grammatical consideration with a wavy, green line.

Initiating Automatic Spelling and Grammar Checking

If this feature is not turned on, but you would like your spelling and grammar to be checked automatically as you type, follow these steps:

1. Choose Tools ➢ Options.
2. Click on the Spelling & Grammar tab.
3. In the Spelling section, check the first box to activate the *Check spelling as you type* option. In the Grammar section at the bottom, check the first box to activate the *Check grammar as you type* option.
4. Click on OK.

Once the Spelling section is activated, the spelling checker will place a wavy, red line under words *not* in its dictionary. This does not always mean that the word it stops on is incorrectly spelled. It only means that the word is not in the dictionary.

Many proper names, street names, company names, and company-specific words are not in the dictionary. During a formal spelling and grammar check, you can choose to ignore words, change words to other spellings, or add words to the custom dictionary (so when you use those words in future sentences, Word will know they are correct).

NOTE
Homophone problems such as using *for* instead of *four* or *their* instead of *there* will not be picked up by the spelling checker. Homophone problems are spotted by the grammar checker.

PART

II

Communicating with Word

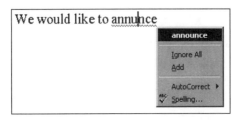

If Word alerts you that a word is misspelled and you are not sure of the correct spelling, you right-click on the underlined word and look at the suggestions. Click on the correct spelling to automatically correct the word. If the correct spelling is not listed, click anywhere in the document to get rid of the shortcut menu, backspace over the word, and try again with another spelling to see if you get attacked again by the wavy, red underline. Here you'll see the automatic-spell-checker shortcut menu with a suggested correct spelling.

Spell-Checking

Some Word users turn off the automatic spell- and grammar-checking options, preferring instead to check the document when they are done creating it. Using the Spelling and Grammar button on the Standard toolbar, you can check the spelling and grammar of some or all of the text in your document:

1. Select the text to be spell-checked (for partial document checking) or start with the insertion point at the top of the document (really, you can start anywhere in the document and the spell checker will wrap around).
2. Press F7 or choose Tools ➣ Spelling and Grammar to activate the spelling and grammar checkers.

If there are no typos or grammar problems, you will not see the Spell Check dialog box. Instead, Word will display a message telling you that the spelling and grammar check is complete, as shown at left.

Changing or Ignoring Incorrect Words

When Word finds text that is not in either its own dictionary or the added custom dictionaries, it will stop on the word and offer you options for handling the problem.

Type the following sentence on a blank line, misspellings and all (ignore the wavy red underlining):

This is a hapy evnt for Bob Ziegler, his fmily, and the entire Bromberg community.

Next, start the spelling checker by clicking on the Spelling & Grammar button on the Standard toolbar, or by pressing F7. Figure 7.4 shows the Spelling and Grammar dialog box displaying the first typo in the sentence.

FIGURE 7.4

The spelling checker suggests spellings for your words.

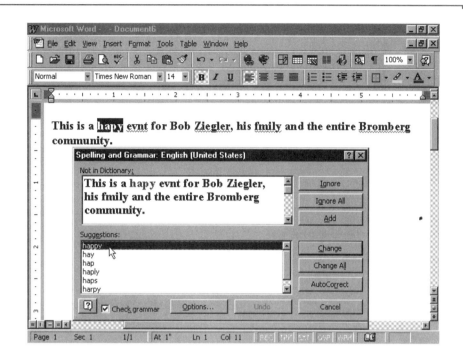

Word, of course, correctly identifies the first typo, *hapy,* as not being in its dictionaries and displays a list of suggestions for the correct spelling. Because Word's first suggestion is the correct one, you do not have to type the correction yourself. Click on the Change button, and Word will automatically change the spelling to the highlighted suggestion. Word then goes to the next problem word, *evnt,* which you can now change to *event.*

When Word gets to *Bob Ziegler,* it stops because *Ziegler* is not in Word's dictionaries; Word will not have any suggestions for you either. To tell Word that *Ziegler* is correct and to ignore the fact that the word is not in its dictionaries, click on Ignore. Word moves on to the next word.

TIP

If a word that is not in Word's dictionaries but is correct occurs repeatedly in a document, choose Ignore All so Word will not stop each time it encounters this word in this document.

PART

II

Communicating with Word

Adding an AutoCorrect Entry during Spell-Checking

At this point in the exercise, spell check has stopped on *fmily*. Now suppose the word *fmily* is a common typo you make, and you see it all the time when you are spell-checking documents. You will want to tell Word to make this typo an AutoCorrect option so when you type *fmily* in future documents, Word automatically corrects it the minute you make the typo.

Highlight the correct spelling, *family,* in the Suggestions box. Then, click on the AutoCorrect button. Word adds the typo and the correct spelling to its list of Auto-Correct words and moves on to the next word. We will manage the next word by adding it to the custom dictionary.

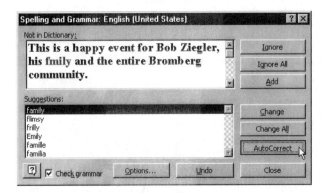

The Custom Dictionary

Many words—such as proper names, business acronyms, or technical, medical, or legal terms—may not be in Word's dictionary. Although you cannot make changes to Word's dictionary, you can add to and edit words in the custom dictionary.

During the installation process, a dictionary is created for you to add your own words to. The default name of this dictionary is Custom.dic, and it resides in the C:\Program Files\Common Files\Microsoft Shared\Proof folder of your hard disk or network drive. These are folders that all of the Office products share.

Adding Words to the Custom Dictionary

The next problem word in our example sentence is *Bromberg*. Because it's the name of a town that is frequently referenced in correspondence, you will want to add this to Custom.dic by clicking on the Add button on the Spelling and Grammar dialog box.

Here are the general steps for adding a word to the custom dictionary:

1. Activate the spelling and grammar checker (press F7, or click on the Spelling button, or choose Tools ➤ Spelling & Grammar).

2. When Word pauses on a word that is not in its dictionary that you think should be part of the custom dictionary (right now it should be stopped on *Bromberg*), click on the Add button on the right side of the dialog box.

3. Repeat the previous step for as many words as you wish to add. If you inadvertently add a word, you can edit the custom dictionary later and remove the word, as explained below.

Removing Words from the Custom Dictionary

To remove words from the custom dictionary:

1. Choose Tools ➤ Options. The Options dialog box appears.
2. Choose the Spelling & Grammar tab.
3. In the middle of the dialog box, to the right side, click on the button that says "Dictionaries."
4. When the dictionary(s) appear, CUSTOM.DIC will be selected, because the custom dictionary is currently open in memory and being used in conjunction with Word's proprietary dictionary.

5. Click on the Edit button at the bottom of the dialog box. (Do not choose the Remove button.)

6. Word shows the contents of the custom dictionary in a document. Scroll down and look at the words. The word *Bromberg* should now be in your custom dictionary, but the other items will be unique to your work. Delete or edit the words you do not wish to have in the dictionary just as you would any text in Word.

7. Double-click on *Bromberg* and press Delete.

8. Save the custom dictionary. Click on the Save button on the Standard toolbar or choose File ➣ Save from the menu. Word will save over the previous version of the dictionary.

9. Choose File ➣ Close to return to your document.

WARNING

After editing the custom dictionary, it is necessary to return to the Tools ➣ Options ➣ Spelling & Grammar tab and check the option *Check spelling as you type* again; Word turns off this option when the custom dictionary is being edited.

Creating New Dictionaries

You can create additional dictionaries (as many as you want) to store words that you may want to group together, such as legal or computer terms. You create these new dictionaries for Word to reference when spell-checking your documents.

The steps for creating your own custom dictionary are easy to follow; Word has made this multi-dictionary feature the best among all the word processing programs.

1. Choose Tools ➣ Options to open the Options dialog box.

2. Click on the Spelling & Grammar tab.

3. In the middle of the dialog box, to the right side, click on the button that says "Dictionaries." The Custom Dictionaries dialog box will appear.

4. Click on the New button. The Create Custom Dictionary dialog box will open, displaying the folder where all of the dictionaries are filed.

5. At the bottom of the Create Custom Dictionary dialog box, the entry *.dic is selected. Type a name for your dictionary (for example, **MEDICAL WORDS**). Click on Save. Word adds the .dic extension to the name so it knows this is a dictionary file.

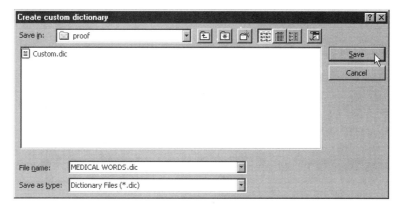

6. Make sure that your new dictionary is checked in the Custom Dictionaries dialog box so Word knows to use it, as well as Custom.dic, during spelling checks. Click on OK until you return to document window. The Custom Dictionaries dialog box below shows three custom dictionaries.

Adding Words to a New Dictionary

You can add words to your new dictionary just as you did to the Custom dictionary:

1. Choose Tools ➢ Options. The Options dialog box will appear.

2. Choose the Spelling & Grammar tab.

3. Click on the button that says "Dictionaries."

4. When the dictionaries appear, select MEDICAL WORDS.Dic or whatever new dictionary name you used in the previous exercise.

5. Click on the Edit button at the bottom of the dialog box. Word shows the contents of the custom dictionary like a document. Right now it is a blank screen.

6. Type the words to be included in your new custom dictionary. Press the Enter key after each entry.

7. Click on the Save button on the Standard toolbar or choose File ➢ Save from the menu. Word will save your dictionary text.

8. Choose File ➢ Close to return to your document.

Adding Words to AutoCorrect

Although Word has created a list of the common typos that are made during word processing sessions, the typos Word already knows about may not be the ones you make. You can easily add your own typos and their corrections without spell-checking:

1. Choose Tools ➢ AutoCorrect. The insertion point will be blinking in the Replace box, which is where you will type the typo.

2. Type **itinery**.

3. Press the Tab key to move to the With box. Here you will tell the program the word it should replace *itinery* with.

4. Type **itinerary**.

5. Click on the Add button on the lower right side of the dialog box.

6. Click on OK.

7. Test your typo. On a blank line, type the incorrect spelling **itinery**. Tap the spacebar or press Enter; Word automatically corrects the typo. Figure 7.5 shows the entry in the AutoCorrect dialog box.

FIGURE 7.5

The Auto-Correct list of replacement words

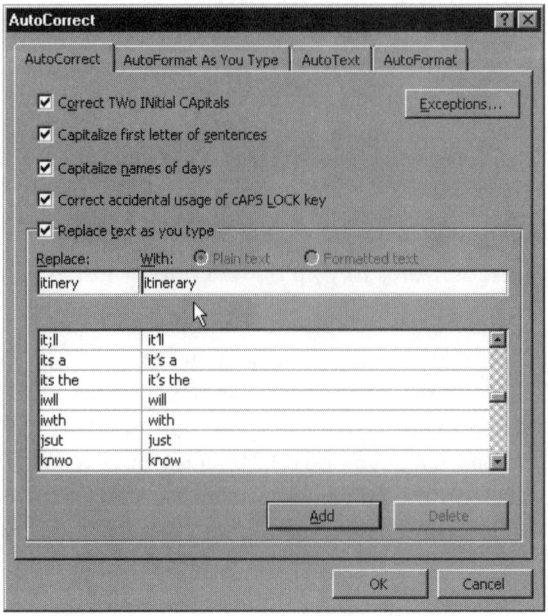

In Chapter 12, you will be given more invaluable uses for the AutoCorrect as well as the AutoText features. Right now, add in as many typos as you can think of.

The entries you make in AutoCorrect are shared by the rest of the Office products, so typos you add to the AutoCorrect list in Word will automatically be corrected when you make them in the other Office programs.

The Thesaurus

Effective writing means finding words that express your meaning and thoughts precisely. To help you with this, Word's built-in thesaurus provides multiple synonyms for 90 percent of the words you will use in writing. When Word displays a list of synonyms, you can easily replace a word in your document with one of them.

To use the Thesaurus, click on any word and choose Tools ➤ Language ➤ Thesaurus, or press Shift+F7. The word you're looking up will appear on the left side of the Thesaurus dialog box in the Looked Up box. Below that, in the Meanings list, you'll see a short definition of the word, the part of speech, and sometimes the antonyms for the word. In the right side of the dialog box, you'll see the suggested synonyms for that word. If one of those synonyms is the word you want, click on it once and then click on the Replace button. If you change your mind and don't want to use any of the suggested synonyms, click on the Cancel button.

Below you'll see the list of synonyms for the word *conceived*, used in the first sentence of the Gettysburg Address.

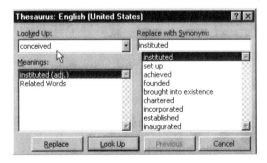

If you double-click on one of the synonyms or click on the Lookup button in the right side of the Thesaurus dialog box, it will become the Looked Up word, and more synonyms and meanings will appear. To move back through words that were selected, click on the Previous button at the bottom of the dialog box.

To return to the list of synonyms for the first word you were using, click on the drop-down arrow next to the Looked Up box, and you will see all of the words you looked through in that session.

PART

II

Communicating with
Word

The Grammar Checker

If you are concerned about the readability of your document or want Word to check for correct word usage, you will find the grammar checker to be helpful but not always accurate.

Word's grammar checker uses rules to identify problems in your writing, such as passive verbs, pronoun errors, possessive noun errors, problems with homophones (like *there* and *their*), double negatives, and even political incorrectness.

Figure 7.6 shows the result of grammar-checking a sentence in the Gettysburg Address. The grammar checker has flagged a sentence in the address for being "too long." There seems to be a standoff between Abe Lincoln and Microsoft's Office Assistant on this grammatical consideration.

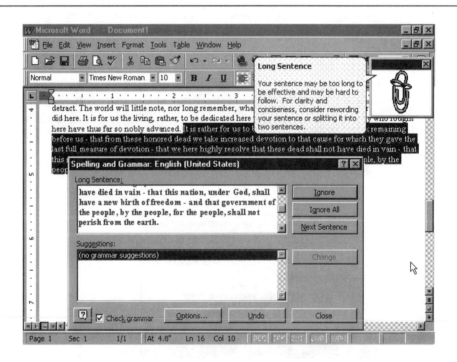

Grammar-checking will occur with spell-checking, unless you turn off this option by choosing Tools ➤ Options, clicking on the Spelling & Grammar tab, and unchecking the *Check grammar with spelling* option. The grammar checker will stop on the first word or sentence that is programmed for grammatical consideration. You can read what the Office Assistant has to say about the grammar and then make changes or go on with your life.

Readability Statistics

When the grammar checker has finished checking your document, the Statistics dialog box will appear, giving you some readability statistics to ponder, including the number of words, sentences, and paragraphs in your document and the grade level the writing is appropriate for. After you have read the statistics, press Esc, click on the X in the upper right corner of the dialog box, or simply click on OK to remove the dialog box. If you do not see the readability statistics, select Tools ➤ Options ➤ Spelling & Grammar and make sure that *Show readability statistics* is checked.

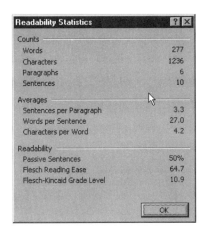

Chapter

8

Enhancing a Document's Appearance

Enhancing a Document's Appearance

E nhancing a document's appearance is Word's specialty. Word's formatting features allow you to create beautiful documents without doing much more than typing the headings and text—Word will do the rest. Word offers a tremendous amount of formatting options: multiple typefaces and point sizes (depending on your printer); easy-to-apply character font styles, such as bold, italic, and single and double underline; and paragraph formats such as alignment (centering, justifying, etc.), spacing, and indentation.

NOTE

Word also provides features that take you into the realm of desktop publishing, allowing you to create everything from fancy tables to multiple-column news-letters. These features are covered in Chapter 11.

Understanding Formatting in Word

Word's formatting techniques depend on whether you are formatting characters or paragraphs or pages. This chapter focuses on character and paragraph formatting. Formats you'll apply to characters include font, font size, and font styles; formats you'll apply to paragraphs include alignment, spacing, indentation, and tabs. Page formats—also considered page layouts—include borders, margins, page orientation, headers and footers. Chapter 9 discusses page formats in detail.

You can apply the most common text formats from the Formatting toolbar:

Keyboard shortcuts are also available for some formats. The Font dialog box offers the standard character formats, as well as other options, such as colors for your text, special effects, and text animation. The Paragraph dialog box contains the paragraph formats, including indent, spacing, and alignment choices.

When you want to apply a format to text that is already typed, you must select the text first and then apply the format. Use all of your selection shortcuts—double-clicking to select an entire word, Ctrl+clicking to select a sentence, using the selection bar to select a line, and so on.

You can also turn on the formats before you type, so that as you type, the formatting will be applied. For example, if you press Ctrl+B to turn on bold type, any text you type will be bold until you tap Ctrl+B again to turn off this type style.

Some formatting is turned on and off using the same commands; for example, you use the same toolbar buttons to apply the bold, italics, and underline character formats as you do to remove them. But some formats (particularly paragraph and page formats) are turned on and off using different commands. For example, you click on one button to increase the indent on a paragraph, but click on another button to decrease the indent.

Changing Character Formats

You will find that character formatting is what you will do most. The basic formats to apply to characters include font, point size, and type styles like bold, italics, and underline. The Formatting toolbar and the Font dialog box contain the most common font formats, as well as other formatting options, such as colors for your text, special effects, and animation.

To change character formatting, select (drag the mouse across) a series of multiple characters. Then, click a format button on the Formatting toolbar to *apply* the format. You can remove the formatting by clicking the same button again. Keyboard shortcuts are also available for many character formats: Select the text you want to format, then press Ctrl+B (bold), Ctrl+I (italic), or Ctrl+U (underline). See Table 8.1 later in this chapter for additional keyboard shortcuts.

NOTE

Fonts applied to selected characters don't affect the entire paragraph (unless you select an entire paragraph). For example, when you bold a word within a paragraph (by, for example, selecting the word and then pressing Ctrl+B), the entire paragraph does not become bold.

You can also turn on formatting before you begin typing: Turn on the formatting you want (through the Formatting toolbar, the Font dialog box, or a keyboard shortcut), and begin typing. The new text will appear in the new format you chose. When you finish typing the text you want to be in that format, turn off the formatting.

The Font dialog box contains all of your character formatting options. To get to the Font dialog box (shown in Figure 8.1), choose Format ➤ Font, or *right-click* the mouse on the text and choose Font from the shortcut menu. You can also press Ctrl+D to activate the Font dialog box. In this dialog box, you'll find three tabs: Font, Character Spacing, and Animation.

On the Font tab, there are various areas of formatting options. The most common options are within these areas: Font, Font Style, and Size. (These options are also available on the Formatting toolbar.) You'll also find different flavors of underline and a Color list box that allows you to change text color. In the Effects area, You can select special text styles, including Strikethrough, Double Strikethrough, Superscript, Subscript, Shadow, Outline, Emboss and Engrave, Small Caps, All Caps, and Hidden.

PART II

Communicating with Word

FIGURE 8.1

The Font dialog box contains all the character formatting options.

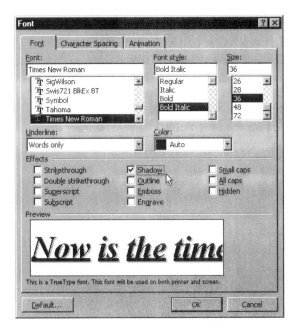

The Preview section in the bottom of the Font dialog box shows how the changes you make to the available options will affect your text, so you can experiment with character formatting before making a final selection.

Changing the Font

A *font* (or *typeface*) refers to a family of letters of a particular design. The font gives the reader their first impression of what they are about to read. The fonts you choose will depend on the audience for your document—for example, you probably wouldn't pick the same font for a newsletter as you would for a serious proposal. The most common business fonts used with Microsoft Word are Times New Roman, Arial, and Courier. It is fun to experiment with other fonts, as well.

You can change the font for your entire document or for selected text. First, either select the entire document by pressing Ctrl+A, or select a specific text area by dragging the mouse over the text to be formatted. Then do one of the following:

- Choose Format ➤ Font. In the Font dialog box that appears, choose the font you want from the Font list. The Preview box will reflect your choice.
- Choose a font from the Formatting toolbar by clicking the drop-down arrow next to the Font list box, then selecting a font from the drop-down list. (The fonts available to you may depend on the type of printer you have.)

The shortcut key combination Shift+Ctrl+F also activates the Font list box on the Formatting toolbar. Press Shift+Ctrl+F, then press Alt+↓ to display the drop-down list of available fonts. Continue pressing the down arrow to move down the list.

Changing the Font Size

The size of a font is measured in *points*. There are 72 points in 1 inch. The larger the font, the more easily your reader's eye will be drawn to lines of text in that font size. For instance, dramatic headlines on newspapers can be as large as 216 points, or 3 inches high.

Normal business letters use font sizes between 9 and 12 points. Fonts between 13 and 18 points are used for subheadings in the text of a business document like a proposal or report. Business brochures use 18 to 24 points for their headings and between 13 and 16 points for the body text. Experiment with different typeface and font sizes, and let other people look at a draft of your document to get their initial impressions of what they are reading.

You can change the font size for your entire document or for selected text. First, either select the entire document by pressing Ctrl+A, or select a specific text area by dragging the mouse over the text to be formatted. Then do one of the following:

- Choose Format ➤ Font. In the Font dialog box that appears, choose a font size from the Size list. The Preview box will reflect your choice.
- Choose a font size from the Formatting toolbar by clicking the arrow next to the Font Size list box, then selecting a font size from the drop-down list. (The font sizes that are available to you may depend on the type of printer you have.)

You can change the font size quickly by pressing the shortcut key combination Shift+Ctrl+P (thus activating the Font Size list box on the Formatting toolbar), and then pressing Alt+↓ to display the drop-down list of font sizes.

You can change the sizes displayed in the Size list within the Font dialog box and the Font Size list on the Formatting toolbar to other sizes not shown in the lists. To apply a font size that is not in the Font Size list, drag over a size that is in the top of the list box, type the size you want, and press Enter. See Figure 8.2 for examples of different point sizes.

FIGURE 8.2

You can apply different point sizes to text in your documents.

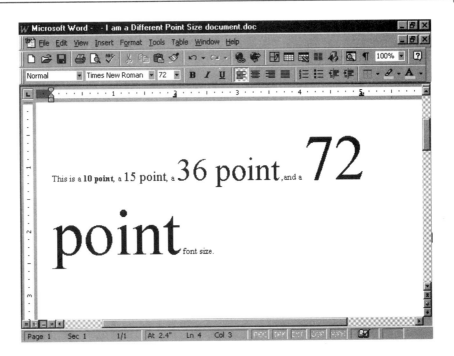

Changing the Font Style

The three most common character formats in most documents are bold, italic, and underline. There are several methods for selecting these font styles. First, select the text you want to change to bold, italic, or underline; then do one of the following:

- Display the Font dialog box (Format ➤ Font) and select bold, italic, or a combination of both from the Font Style area. For Underline, click on the drop-down arrow next to the Underline list box to see a list of various underline styles.
- Click on the B, I, or U buttons (for bold, italic, and underline, respectively) on the Formatting toolbar.
- Press Ctrl+B for bold, Ctrl+I for italic, or Ctrl+U for underline. These key combinations are as easy to use as the buttons on the Formatting toolbar. Table 8.1 lists character and paragraph formats that have shortcut key combinations.

TIP

If you are applying a font style to a single word, you do not need to drag across or double-click on the word. Put the insertion point into the *middle* of the word and then apply the format. The entire word will be formatted.

You can apply multiple font styles at once. For example, to apply all bold, italic, *and* underline, select your text, then click on all three toolbar buttons (B, I, and U) or press the three keyboard shortcuts for these styles.

TABLE 8.1: CHARACTER FORMATTING SHORTCUTS

Format	Keyboard Shortcut
Bold	Ctrl+B
Italic	Ctrl+I
Underline	Ctrl+U
Words-only underline	Shift+Ctrl+W
Double continuous underline	Shift+Ctrl+D
Font typeface change	Shift+Ctrl+F
Font point size change	Shift+Ctrl+P
Increase the font size to the next size	Shift+Ctrl+ > (greater than sign)

Continued ▶

TABLE 8.1: CHARACTER FORMATTING SHORTCUTS (CONTINUED)	
Format	**Keyboard Shortcut**
Decrease the font size to the next size	Shift+Ctrl+< (less than sign)
Uppercase, proper case, lowercase	Shift+F3 (press repeatedly to see all 3)
Subscript text	Ctrl+=
Superscript text	Shift+Ctrl+=

Underline Styles

The normal underline style is a single, continuous line. You can also choose several types of underline style from the Font dialog box:

1. Select your text.
2. Choose Format ➢ Font from the menu bar or press Ctrl+D.
3. On the left side of the dialog box, the Underline drop-down list lists the different underline styles you can apply to text. Choose an underline style, and look at the Preview area to see if you like it. Select the style you like, and close the dialog box.

NOTE
You can press Shift+Ctrl+W for noncontinuous word underlining, instead of going through the format menu.

To create underlines that spread across a page—for example, signature block lines—click on the Underline button or press Ctrl+U and then press the Tab key repeatedly. Make sure you press Ctrl+U or click on the underline button to turn off the underline feature when you've finished. If you type on these lines, you will extend the underline to the right. Delete the unwanted underlines.

Applying Effects to Text

Microsoft has added features to Office 97 that allow documents to easily become great-looking Web pages, including four new text effects in Word 97 that you can apply to text:

- Shadow
- Outline
- Emboss
- Engrave

These effects are found in the Effects area of the Font dialog box. The Shadow and Outline effects can be applied concurrently to text. The other effects, Emboss and Engrave, can only be applied individually.

Other effects you can apply to text in Word 97 include:

- Strikethrough
- Double Strikethrough
- Superscript
- Subscript
- Small Caps
- All Caps
- Hidden

The effects Strikethrough and Double Strikethrough are very popular in the legal community; they are used to represent text that has been changed or deleted. The reader can still view the original text through the strikethrough, and therefore knows exactly what was deleted or changed.

Superscript and Subscript are two very common effects used in the scientific and mathematics community. Superscript text is raised text in a smaller font size. The degree symbol (as in 90^0) is a familiar superscript character. Subscript text is dropped text in a smaller font size. Chemical compounds (as in H_2O) frequently require subscript characters.

Although you can apply the superscript and subscript formats in the Font dialog box, the keyboard combinations for both are faster. To format text as superscript, either select the text or position the pointer at the location where you are going to type a superscript character and press Shift+Ctrl+=. The selected text or the next character you type will be raised. To turn off or remove the superscript, repeat the same keystroke combination you used to turn on superscript.

To format text as subscript, either select the text or position the pointer at the location where you are going to type a subscript character and press Ctrl+=. The selected text or the next character you type will be dropped. To turn off or remove the subscript, repeat the same keystroke combination you used to turn on subscript.

Small Caps is a nice effect for brochure heading text. Lowercase letters are formatted as uppercase letters but in a reduced font size. The effect is that of an all caps heading, but the capitalization is still apparent.

All Caps is the same effect produced when typing with the Caps Lock turned on. Choose this option from the Font dialog box to quickly apply all caps to selected text. The keyboard combination for applying lowercase, uppercase, and proper case is Shift+F3. Select your text and press Shift+F3 repeatedly to cycle you through these three capitalization effects.

The Hidden effect prevents text from being displayed or hidden. To hide text, select it, choose Format ➤ Font, and check Hidden. To display the hidden text in a document, select Tools ➤ Options ➤ View, check the Hidden Text option, and click on OK; the text that had been hidden will be displayed with a light gray dashed underline. To remove the Hidden effect, select the text and go back into the Font menu (Format ➤ Font) and uncheck Hidden.

Applying Animation to Text

With the advent of hyperlinked documents and graphically exciting Web pages, documents are now expected to entertain, grab the reader's interest, focus the reader's attention on specific text, and quickly communicate a message. One way to do this is through text animation.

Animated text guarantees that a message will be seen (if not read). Special-purpose documents—such as marketing materials, training manuals, sales and product brochures, and announcements—can all benefit from animated text.

You can add animation to documents you create in Word 97. In Word documents, animated text is immediately visible and does not require that the reader place the mouse over the text.

To apply animation to text, select the text you want to animate. Then:

1. Choose Format ➤ Font from the menu bar, or right-click the mouse on the text and choose Font from the shortcut menu, or press Ctrl+D.
2. Click on the Animation tab at the top of the dialog box
3. Select one of the animation effect styles. The Preview box at the bottom of the screen will show how the animation effect will look. Figure 8.3 shows the Sparkle Text animation effect applied to a word. (If you wish to switch back to see the other font properties, click the Font tab at the top of the dialog box.)
4. Click on the OK button to apply the effect.

NOTE
Animated text styles do not print to a printer.

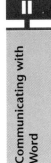

PART

II

Communicating with Word

You can choose animated effects for your text in the Animation page of the Font dialog box.

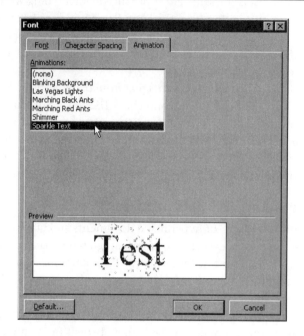

Setting a New Default Font

The default font size in Word, 10 pt., is considered by many business typists as too small. You can easily change the default font size (and all the other font settings) by setting a new default font:

1. Choose Format ➤ Font from the menu bar.
2. Select the font, style, and size you wish to be your default font.
3. Click on the Default button at the bottom left side of the Font dialog box. When Word asks you to confirm the change, choose Yes.

All new documents using the Normal template (the default blank document in Word) will reflect this change. The new font and point size will not affect documents you have already typed and stored on the disk.

Highlighting Your Text

You can apply color to text using Word's highlighting feature, which allows you mark text as you might with a yellow highlighter marker in a book or manual. This is a great feature in a workgroup environment where you route a document to other individuals. Highlighted words can be used as discussion points. Even if you are in a single PC environment, you can use the highlight feature to dramatically emphasize words in a printed document or use highlighting as on-screen reminders for yourself.

You can choose from fifteen colors and the None option which removes or turns off the highlight. Highlighting will show on the screen and when printed; if you don't have a color printer, the different highlight colors will print in different shades of gray. Yellow highlight produces the lightest printable shade of gray. The highlight color drop-down list is shown in Figure 8.4.

PART

II

Communicating with Word

FIGURE 8.4

Choosing a highlight from a floating Formatting toolbar

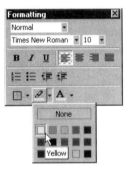

NOTE

Your document must contain text in order to apply a highlight; unlike other formats that can be turned on before typing, the highlighter can only be applied to existing text.

Follow these steps to use the highlight feature:

1. Select a highlighting color:

- To select the default highlight color of yellow, click on the yellow highlight marker button on the Formatting toolbar. If the default is not the yellow highlight marker, see below for how to select another color.
- To select a highlight color other than the default, click on the drop-down arrow to the right of the highlight marker button on the Formatting toolbar and click on another color (see Figure 8.4).

2. Pause the mouse over the line of type to be highlighted. Notice that the I-beam cursor now has an animated marker symbol with it.

3. Click and drag across the word(s) you want to highlight.

To turn off the highlight feature, press Esc or click on the highlight marker button on the Formatting toolbar again. Note that if you drag across highlighted text with the same color, the highlight removes itself.

Changing Paragraph Formats

Paragraph formats—such as centering, indentation, spacing, bullets, numbering, and tab stops—are applied to paragraphs rather than to individual characters. For example, you cannot center one word within a paragraph of words without centering the entire paragraph. This is in contrast to character formats, which you can apply to selected characters or words without affecting the other text in the paragraph.

When you apply formatting to a single typed paragraph, it is not necessary to select the paragraph first. Click the mouse in any part of the paragraph and then apply the paragraph formatting. For example, to apply double-spacing to a paragraph, click the mouse in any part of the paragraph and press Ctrl+2. The entire paragraph will be double-spaced. If you wish to apply paragraph formats to multiple paragraphs, you must select all of the paragraphs before applying the paragraph format.

A paragraph is defined as any amount of text that ends with a paragraph mark. You can click on the Show/Hide ¶ button on the Standard toolbar (or use the keyboard shortcut Ctrl+Shift+8) to see where the paragraph marks are in your document.

Adjusting the Alignment

In Word, you can center, right-align, left-align, and justify text. Figure 8.5 shows examples of all four text-alignment positions. The default text alignment is left; when a line of text word wraps to the next line or when you press the Enter key yourself, the insertion point returns to the left margin (unless an indent is set).

You can set these alignments by pressing their shortcut keys—Ctrl+L (left align), Ctrl+E (center), Ctrl+R (right align), Ctrl+J (justify); or by using the four alignment buttons on the Formatting toolbar:

You can also select alignments, as well as the other paragraph formats discussed in this chapter, by choosing Format ➤ Paragraph, or by right-clicking and selecting Paragraph from the shortcut menu, to get to the Paragraph dialog box.

FIGURE 8.5

*Word's four text
alignments*

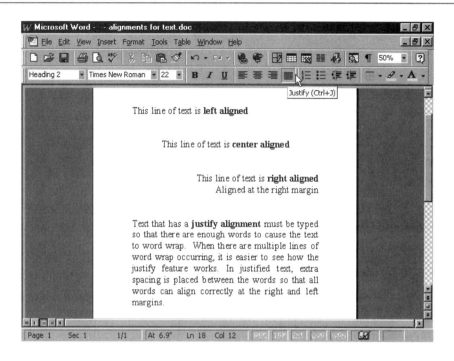

Centering Text

Word's center alignment command centers text between the left and right margins. To center your text:

1. Click in a paragraph of text or position the cursor at a new blank line. Select multiple paragraphs to center all of them at the same time.
2. Click on the Center button on the Formatting toolbar or press Ctrl+E.
3. If you clicked in an existing paragraph of text, it will be centered. If you are typing new text, it will become centered as you type.
4. To return text to left alignment, click on the Align Left button or press Ctrl+L to return to the left margin of the document. (You cannot press Ctrl+E again or click on the center button to turn off the centering. You cannot turn paragraph formatting on and off with the same key.)

TIP

Even if the text does not look centered on the screen, it should print centered on the page. To get a realistic view of the centering, use the File ➢ Print Preview option to see how the document will look when it's printed.

PART

II

Communicating with
Word

Centering Text Vertically on a Page

You can center text vertically on a page, not just horizontally between the margins. For example, you may want to vertically center a title page that only has a few lines of text on it. To center text vertically on a page:

1. Type the lines of text to be vertically centered.
2. Choose File ➢ Page Setup, then select the Layout tab. In the Vertical alignment area, click on the drop-down arrow to see a list of page alignments, then select Center. Click on OK to close the dialog box. The text lines will be centered between the top and bottom margins.

Left-Aligning Text

Left alignment means the text will be aligned at the left margin of the document or the temporary left margin made by an Indent command. The left margin and indent settings of a document determine where the text will align on the left. For example, if your left margin is set at the default of 1.25 inches, the text will line up 1.25 inches from the left edge of the paper. You can change the settings for the left margin by choosing File ➢ Page Setup ➢ Margins.

Because left alignment is the default alignment, it is only necessary to tell Word when you want to return to left alignment from another alignment (centered, right-aligned, or justified). To switch back to left-aligned text:

1. Click in an existing paragraph or position the cursor at a blank line.
2. Click on the Align Left button on the Formatting toolbar or press Ctrl+L.
3. If you clicked in an existing paragraph of text, it will be left-aligned. If you are typing new text, it will become left-aligned as you type.

Right-Aligning Text

When you choose right alignment, the right side of each line of text will align with the right margin; the left side of the text will not be aligned. To right-align text:

1. Click in an existing paragraph or position the cursor at a blank line.
2. Click on the Align Right button on the Formatting toolbar or press Ctrl+R.
3. If you clicked in an existing paragraph of text, it will be right-aligned. If you are typing new text, it will become right-aligned as you type.

To return text to left alignment, click the Align Left button or press Ctrl+L.

Justifying Text

Word's Justify format aligns both the left and right side of text along the left and right margins. This alignment gives your text a typeset look, similar to the text lines on a newspaper, where the text is squared off. Justification only works correctly with word-wrapped lines.

NOTE

Keep in mind that justified text has a professional but somewhat static appearance. It is generally easier to read text that is not justified.

To justify text:

1. Click anywhere in a paragraph that should be justified or select multiple paragraphs to justify.
2. Click on the Justify button on the Formatting toolbar or press Ctrl+J. The left and right sides of the text will align with the margins.

To return to left alignment, click on the Align Left button on the Formatting toolbar or press Ctrl+L.

Changing Paragraph Spacing

Single-spacing is the default spacing when you begin new documents in Word. You can use keyboard shortcuts and quickly change the spacing between lines in a paragraph of text to double-spacing (Ctrl+2) or one-and-one-half-spacing (Ctrl+5). For other spacing increments, choose Format ➤ Paragraph to open the Paragraph dialog box. Then, click on the Indents and Spacing tab and adjust the Line Spacing option.

The size of the spaces between lines in your document depends on the point size of your text. When you change the point size of your text, the size of the spacing between lines changes accordingly.

Changing Spacing Using Keyboard Shortcuts

The keyboard shortcuts are the easiest way to set new spacing increments:

1. Click into any part of a single paragraph. If multiple paragraphs are involved, select the paragraphs.
2. Press Ctrl+2 for double-spacing, press Ctrl+5 for one-and-one-half-spacing, or press Ctrl+1 for single-spacing. (See Table 8.2 later in this chapter for more keyboard shortcut combinations).

Changing Spacing Using the Paragraph Dialog Box

There are no keyboard shortcuts for certain spacing increments. It is necessary to go the Paragraph dialog box to set, for example, triple spacing:

1. Choose Format ➤ Paragraph. The Paragraph dialog box will appear.
2. Click on the Indents and Spacing tab.
3. Click on the drop-down arrow next to the Line Spacing list and choose Multiple.

PART

II

Communicating with
Word

4. When you choose Multiple, the default number of spaces between lines is 3. Type in a different number if you wish (2.5, 3.5, 4, and so on). The Preview box shows what your new spacing will look like. Figure 8.6 shows the Line Spacing options on the Indents and Spacing tab of the Paragraph dialog box.

FIGURE 8.6

The Multiple option allows you to designate your own spacing increments.

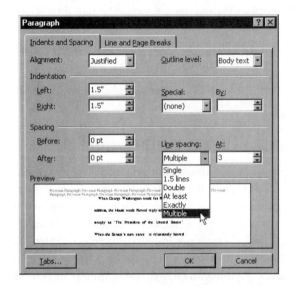

> **TIP**
>
> When you create your own custom toolbar (see Chapter 13), you can add a spacing button to the toolbar that will give you a third method for changing the spacing in a document.

Indenting Paragraphs

If you want to indent text at the beginning of a paragraph, you can press the Tab key before you start typing. A tab will push the first line of the paragraph in by one tab stop (one-half inch, by default). Using the Tab key to indent is preferable to using the spacebar. A tabbed paragraph, however, is not considered an indented paragraph.

Word's Indent commands offer you a number of special types of indents that are more flexible than using tabs or changing the margins. Figure 8.7 shows paragraphs indented in three different ways: tabbed, indented, and hanging-indented.

FIGURE 8.7

Tabbed, indented, and hanging-indented paragraphs

Our American Government

What form of government do we have in the United States? (TAB PARAGRAPH)

The United States, under its Constitution, is a Federal, democratic republic, an indivisible union of 50 sovereign States. With the exception of town meetings, a form of pure democracy, we have at the local, state, and national levels a government which is "democratic" because the people govern themselves; "representative" because the people choose elected delegates by free and secret ballot; and "republican" because government derives its power from the will of the people.

What form of government do we have in the United States? (INDENTED PARAGRAPH)

The United States, under its Constitution, is a Federal, democratic republic, an indivisible union of 50 sovereign States. With the exception of town meetings, a form of pure democracy, we have at the local, state, and national levels a government which is "democratic" because the people govern themselves; "representative" because the people choose elected delegates by free and secret ballot; and "republican" because government derives its power from the will of the people.

What form of government do we have in the United States? (HANGING INDENT)

The United States, under its Constitution, is a Federal, democratic republic, an indivisible union of 50 sovereign States. With the exception of town meetings, a form of pure democracy, we have at the local, state, and national levels a government which is "democratic" because the people govern themselves; "representative" because the people choose elected delegates by free and secret ballot; and "republican" because government derives its power from the will of the people.

To set indents, you can click on the Formatting toolbar buttons, press key combinations, or directly drag the indent markers on the ruler. You can also set indents through the Paragraph dialog box, in the Indentation area on the Indents and Spacing tab. The following sections describe the various types of indents available in Word and how to set them.

It is recommended that you display the ruler so that you can see the indentation markers on the ruler while you are experimenting with these features. To display the ruler, choose View ➤ Ruler from the menu bar. If the option is not available to you, make sure you are in Page Layout or Normal view (View ➤ Page Layout or View ➤ Normal).

WARNING

Do not press the Enter key at the end of a line and then press the Tab key in order to produce an indented paragraph. Use the Increase Indent and Decrease Indent buttons at the end of the Formatting toolbar to indent text in and out from the left margin. Using the Tab key on each line will cause editing problems, because text inserted later on will produce large tab gaps between words. You will need to find and delete the gaps manually with the Delete key.

PART
II

Communicating with Word

MASTERING THE OPPORTUNITIES

Saving a Style

Sometimes you will find that you frequently apply a certain combination of character formats over and over in a document. Word's Style feature allows you to save a set of formats with a unique name so they can be reapplied easily. For example, suppose you are working in a document that contains a series of questions that must be formatted with a 14-point font size, bold, italics, and underline font styles, and indented text. You will want to create a style for this collection of formatting that you want to reuse:

1. Select a paragraph of text and apply this formatting: 14-point font size, bold, italics, and underline font styles, and indented text.
2. Click anywhere in the paragraph and press Shift+Ctrl+S.
3. The word "Normal" (the default style) will be selected in the list box on the left end of the Formatting toolbar. This is the Style list box.
4. Type a name for your style—for example, **Q&A**—and press Enter. The paragraph's collection of formats is now saved under the single name of Q&A.

To apply the new Q&A style to other paragraphs of text:

1. Click into any paragraph that should receive the Q&A style.
2. Press Shift+Ctrl+S and type **Q&A**, or click the drop-down arrow next to the Style list box and click on Q&A. Then, press Enter. Your paragraph will receive all the style combinations at one time.
3. Repeat these steps for each paragraph you want to apply the Q&A style to, or select a group of paragraphs and repeat step 2.

Increasing and Decreasing Indents

You may need to produce documents in which entire paragraphs are indented from the normal left margin. You can set a temporary left margin by using the Increase Indent button on the Formatting toolbar, and remove the indent by clicking on the Decrease Indent button.

To increase the indentation of a paragraph:

1. Click into or select the paragraph(s) that should be indented.

2. Click on the Increase Indent button or press Ctrl+M for each indent increment (see Table 8.2 for more keyboard shortcut combinations). The paragraph moves in one-half inch for each press of the indent button. All the lines in the paragraph will be indented.

To decrease the indentation of a paragraph, click on the Decrease Indent button or press Shift+Ctrl+M for each indent decrement.

TABLE 8.2: PARAGRAPH FORMATTING SHORTCUTS

Format	Keyboard Shortcut
Center text	Ctrl+E
Left align text	Ctrl+L
Right align text	Ctrl+R
Justify text	Ctrl+J
Single spacing	Ctrl+1
Double spacing	Ctrl+2
One and a half spacing	Ctrl+5
Indent—increase	Ctrl+M
Indent—decrease	Shift+Ctrl+M
Hanging indent—increase	Ctrl+T
Hanging indent—decrease	Shift+Ctrl+T
Apply bullets	Shift+Ctrl+L
Remove all paragraph formatting	Ctrl+Q
Undo the last actions (up to 99)	Ctrl+Z

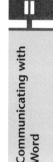

PART
II

Communicating with Word

Creating Hanging Indents

Hanging indents use an indented left margin for the word-wrapped lines but not for the first line of the paragraph, which is flush with the left margin.

Before you begin typing a paragraph that you want to have a hanging indent, press the keyboard shortcut Ctrl+T. As you type, each wrapped line of text will be indented one-half inch. Remember, the first line stays flush with the left margin. When you have finished typing the paragraph, press the Enter key to position on a blank line and then press Shift+Ctrl+T to remove the hanging indent.

If you prefer to use the menu to set a hanging indent:

1. Choose Format ➢ Paragraph. The Paragraph dialog box will appear.
2. In the Indentation section of the Indents and Spacing tab, look to the right side of the dialog box at the Special option. Click the drop-down arrow and choose Hanging. The default By setting will be .5".
3. Change the hanging indent setting to the desired number of inches.

Formatting a Two-Column Hanging Indent

You can also use Word's hanging-indent format to produce simple but effective two-column layouts (see Figure 8.8 to understand where the example is headed):

1. Display the ruler (View ➤ Ruler). It is helpful to have the ruler on the first couple of times you use the indent feature with Word so that you can fully understand—and therefore control—the indent operation.
2. Type the first column of text. In this example it is the name **Anita Ober**.
3. Press Tab once. (Don't worry that the tab does not go over far enough; the Ctrl+T keypress in the next step will fix this.)
4. Press Ctrl+T six times. The bottom indent marker will position itself at 3" on the ruler.
5. Begin typing the second column of text. When the line wraps down to the next one, the text correctly indents.
6. Press Enter only when you've finished typing the paragraph.
7. Type the first line of your next paragraph. In this example, it is **Douglas Barton**.
8. Press Tab once. The insertion point is automatically positioned at 3". You do not need to press Ctrl+T again. Remember, every new paragraph will have its wrapped lines start at 3" unless you press Shift+Ctrl+T to turn off the hanging indent.

Figure 8.8 shows an example of a two-column format using the hanging-indent feature. Note on the ruler the position of the triangular indent symbol on the *bottom*—it represents the indent for the lines after the first line and is at the 3" mark. The top triangular indent represents the first line, which is at the left margin. The next section describes the indent markers on the ruler.

Setting Left and Right Indents

Left and right indents (sometimes called *double* indents) are activated in the Indents and Spacing tab of the Paragraph dialog box. Double indents are often used for long quotes that must be indented on both sides. Figure 8.9 shows a paragraph that has a left indentation of 1.5 inches and a right indentation of 1.5 inches.

To set left and right indents:

1. Choose Format ➤ Paragraph. Click on the Indents and Spacing of the resultant Paragraph dialog box.
2. Change the values for the left and right indents in the Indentation section of the Paragraph dialog box (see Figure 8.6) to 1.5" and 1.5", respectively.
3. Click OK. When you return to the writing area, there is a different (temporary) left margin. Begin typing lines of text that will wrap around. Notice how the line wraps at the new "shorter" right margin.

FIGURE 8.8

A simple two-column format created by using the hanging indent feature

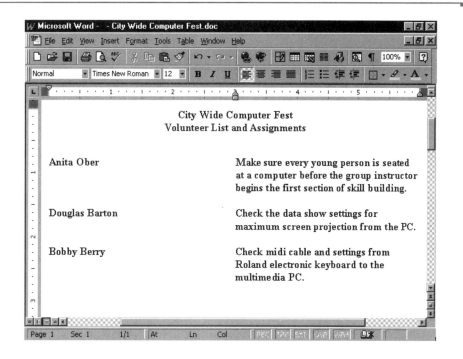

FIGURE 8.9

Text formatted with indents on the left and right

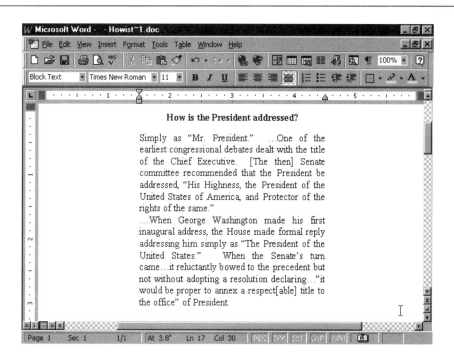

Now look at the ruler (View ➤ Ruler) and notice where the triangular indent markers appear. The left margin markers on the ruler indicate that the left margin indentation will be at 1.5". The right margin marker shows that the word wrap will occur at 4.5" (normally the right margin is at the 6" mark). See the next section to learn how to set a double indent by dragging the markers on the ruler.

Using Indent Markers on the Ruler

The indent markers are normally positioned at the beginning (left indent) and end (right indent) of the ruler. The top left indent marker represents the first line of typing of a paragraph. The bottom left indent marker is divided into two parts: the triangle part (hanging indent) and the square part (left indent). Pause the mouse over the parts of the left indent markers and a ScreenTip will appear naming the parts. When you indent text, these markers move to show you where the indentations will occur in a paragraph(s).

Increase and Decrease Indent Markers - Clicking on the Increase or Decrease Indent button on the Formatting toolbar, or pressing Ctrl+M (increase) or Shift+Ctrl+M (decrease), causes the left markers to move together. This arrangement indicates that the first line and the wrapped lines of a paragraph will both be at a new setting.

Hanging Indent Marker - The hanging indent operation (Ctrl+T to increase or Shift+Ctrl+T to decrease) causes the bottom indent marker to move to the next tab stop and the top indent marker to stay at the left margin. This arrangement indicates that the first line of the paragraph will remain at the left margin (hang back), and the wrapped lines will become indented. Here is a hanging indent setting on the ruler:

Double Indent Markers - To indent a paragraph on the left and the right side, drag the left indent marker forward to a desired position (for example, 1.5"). Drag the right indent marker (at the right margin) backward to a desired position (for example, 4.5").

Indent Marker Problems

When you use the mouse to drag the indent markers on the ruler when changing the indent position (rather than using the Paragraph dialog box menu or the keyboard shortcuts or toolbar buttons), you can easily get the markers out of alignment, causing text to wrap erratically. The mouse can be unwieldy when sliding the indent markers, and the top and bottom of the indents can separate. When this happens, do not try to further manipulate the indent markers using the ruler. Instead, use the menus to get the paragraph(s) back to normal.

If you need to fix the indentation of a paragraph(s), position in or select the paragraph(s) and then choose Format ➤

Paragraph. Click on the Indents and Spacing tab in the resultant dialog box. Make sure that the left indentation and the right indentation settings are set to 0". Across from the right indentation setting is the Special option. Make sure that the setting says None.

These settings will bring your paragraph(s) back to a normal left and right margin without indentation and you can start again. Many times, it easier to drag the right margin marker than it is to manage the two left margin markers.

You can use the Format Painter, described in the next section, to copy formats (including indentation) from one paragraph to another.

Assigning Outline Levels to Paragraphs

In the Paragraph dialog box, there is an Outline Level option that allows you to assign up to nine outline levels to text without changing the appearance of the text. You may want to use this option if you are working with text that maintains a topic and sub-topic flow—for example, organized topical text found in proposals, dissertations, long reports, or business plans.

You do not see the result of assigning outline levels until you change your view from Normal or Page Layout to Outline view (View ➤ Outline, or click on the Outline View button at the lower left corner of the screen). In Outline view, the higher the outline level a paragraph is assigned, the further to the right the paragraph is indented. The Body Text outline level displays the paragraph without indentation.

In Outline view, paragraphs that have outline levels assigned to them are displayed with plus and minus signs to their left, which indicate whether or not there are sub-paragraphs underneath a particular paragraph. In addition, the level numbers are shown on the Outline toolbar. Click on the number associated with the level of indentation you wish to see.

NOTE
The Outline Level option in the Paragraph dialog box is not available once you switch to Outline view, because it is no longer necessary to use this feature to further assign paragraph outline levels. Rather, you can just click the number on the Outline toolbar associated with the level of indentation you want.

Copying Formats with Format Painter

Word has a unique feature that allows you to copy the formats of characters or paragraphs and apply these formats to other locations—the Format Painter.

Once you have formatted a series of characters or a paragraph, you can easily copy these formats to other characters or paragraphs. This is helpful because you won't need to remember which formats (font, point size, and so on) you applied to a character(s) or paragraph. You can then create documents that have a more consistent look to them.

Imagine that you have bolded, underlined, and small-capped a word. You want the same formats applied to another word without performing the keystrokes to format it again. Or suppose you have a heading that is in a special typeface and font size, and is bold, italic, and centered. The next two headings in your document should have the same formats, but you don't wish to create a style because you will never use this heading format again. This is when you would use the Format Painter. The Format Painter can copy formats applied to both characters and paragraphs.

To copy a format, follow these steps:

1. Click in the word that already has the character formats you want to copy or in the paragraph that already has the paragraph formats you want to copy.
2. Click (for a one-time copy) or double-click (for multiple copies) on the Format Painter button on the Standard toolbar.

When you hover the mouse back onto the screen, the I-beam cursor now also shows an animated paintbrush.

3. Click once on the word to receive the format copy or drag the mouse over the multiple words or lines that should receive the format copy.
4. Turn off the Format Painter by clicking on the Format Painter button again or by pressing the Esc key.

You can use the Format Painter to copy all formats: character and paragraph formats and even the tab settings that you will learn about in the next section can be copied to different paragraphs using the Format Painter.

Setting Tabs

Setting tab stops has been the traditional method for lining up columnar, multiple lines of text on a typewriter. You can still use tabs to do this in Word, too, although Word also provides both column and table features as additional methods for you to produce tabular formats. Tabs do not allow you the full flexibility you can have with tables. For example, you cannot insert text into one tabbed column without affecting the alignment of all the tabbed columns, as you can with tables. Tabs are recommended for the initial space indentation on the first line of a paragraph and for simple row and column typing. For more complex formatting, use columns or tables, which are discussed in Chapter 11.

Tab Types

Word offers five types of tab stop alignments: left, center, right, decimal, and bar. Make sure that the ruler is on in order to see the tab settings (View ➤ Ruler).

- The default tabs are left tabs; left tabs are preset at an increment of every half an inch. When you press the Tab key, the insertion point jumps to the first tab stop, and the left side of the text lines up at the tab stop.
- Center tabs cause the text to be centered on either side of the tab stop.
- Right tabs cause the right side of the text to line up at the tab stop.
- Decimal tabs allows you to line up numbers on their decimal points.
- Bar tabs are a special type of tab stop. A vertical bar appears at a bar tab stop, giving an effect similar to border lines in a table, as shown in Figure 8.10.

You can set a bar tab in the Alignment section of the Tabs dialog box (Format ➤ Tabs). You cannot set the bar tab on the Ruler, but once a bar tab is set through the Tabs dialog box, a small, vertical line appears on the ruler at the position where the bar tab was set. A vertical bar also appears in the typing area at the position where the bar tab was set. Each time you press the Enter key, a new vertical bar appears on the next line ready for you to type your text.

NOTE

The tabs in Word 97 are *relative to the margin,* in that they are set from the left margin of your document. For example, if your left margin is set at the default 1.25 inches, a tab at the 2" mark is 2 inches from the left margin. The tab is actually 3.25 inches from the left edge of the piece of paper.

FIGURE 8.10

Bar tabs create vertical bars.

ABC COMPUTER COMPANY
PERSONNEL LIST
MICROSOFT CERTIFICATIONS

LAST NAME	FIRST NAME	CERTIFICATION
Holloway	Nicky	Visual Basic
Osborne	Virginia	NT Workstation
Carter	Tony	Visual Basic
Cooper	Donna	Access
Capucci	Hilton	Access
Overton	Jamiel	NT Workstation

Word also allows you to set leaders for your tabs. Leaders are strings of characters (dots, dashes, underlines) that help the reader's eye move across a tabbed line of text or numbers. When you set a tab (left, right, center, or decimal tab), you can also give that tab setting a leader attribute of dots, dashes, underline, or none. The default attribute is none (for no leader). Figure 8.11 shows a document that includes dotted tab leaders.

FIGURE 8.11

Tab leaders help guide the reader's eye.

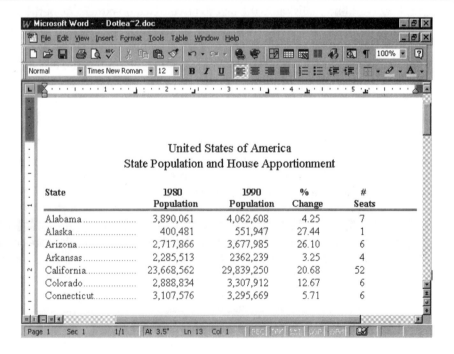

Setting New Default Tabs

View the ruler (View ➤ Ruler) and notice the small tick marks at every half an inch:

Word sets the default tabs at every half inch so that you do not need to use the space-bar to move across a line. Always use the Tab key instead of the spacebar to line up your columnar work (or use Word's column and table features, described in Chapter 11). However, you may want to change the default tabs to a different tab increment because of your document's specific text alignment requirements. A common default tab set is for every inch instead of every half inch.

To change the default tabs to another increment:

1. Choose Format ➤ Tabs to view the Tabs dialog box. Notice the Default Tab Stops text box at the top right corner of the dialog box.

2. Change the default from .5" to any other increment by typing a new increment or clicking the up/down spinner buttons. You can set default tab settings as low as every .01" and as high as every 22".

3. Click on OK to save your changes.

TIP

The Tabs dialog box can also be accessed from the Paragraph dialog box by clicking on the Tabs button in the lower left corner of the dialog box.

Setting Multiple Tab Stops

Word allows you to set tabs using either the Tabs dialog box or by clicking on the ruler. In this section, we will go through the steps for creating the sample shown in Figure 8.12. Setting tabs on the ruler is discussed a little later in the chapter.

To create the sample document, follow these steps:

1. Position the cursor on a blank line and choose Format ➤ Tabs. The Tabs dialog box will appear.

2. Type the number **2** in the Tab Stop Position text box. This sets a tab stop at 2".

3. Click on the Right radio button in the Alignment section.

4. Click on the Set button on the left side of the dialog box. Do not click on OK yet.

5. In the Tab Stop Position again, type the number **5** to set a tab stop at 5" (You will be typing over the previous setting of 2".)

6. Click on the Decimal radio button.

7. In the Leader section, click on the radio button next to #2 (the dotted leader).

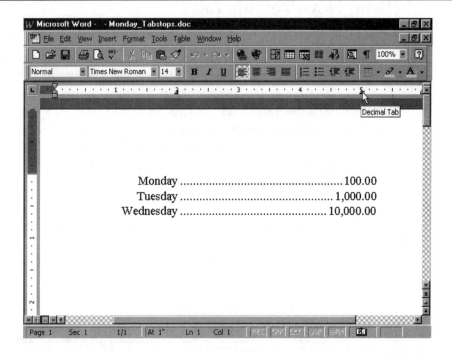

FIGURE 8.12

Two tab sets and a dot leader can produce visually interesting text alignments that are difficult to create using the Table feature.

8. Now click on the Set button on the left side of the dialog box.

9. Click on OK. Look at the ruler (View ➤ Ruler) and notice the two tab stops on the ruler. If you pause the mouse at the two stops, you will see a ScreenTip describing the type of tab set.

 TIP

To get to the Format ➤ Tabs dialog box quickly, use the right mouse button and double-click on the ruler at an existing tab set.

When you've completed the steps above, you will have created tab stops at 2" and 5". The tab stop at 2" is a right-aligned tab and the tab stop at 5" is a decimal-aligned, dot leader tab stop.

1. When you return to the document, press the Tab key once and then type the word **Monday**.

2. Press the Tab key again to jump to the tap stop at 5". Notice the dots leading over to this tab stop.

3. Type **100.00** and press the Enter key.

4. On the second line, press the Tab key and then type **Tuesday**. Press Tab again and then type **1,000.00**. Press the Enter key.

5. On the third line, press the Tab key and then type **Wednesday**. Press Tab again and then type **10,000.00**. Press the Enter key.

Figure 8.12 shows the completed example.

Setting Tabs Using the Ruler

In the previous example, you set custom tabs through the Tabs dialog box. You can also set tabs directly on the ruler. Follow these steps:

1. Make sure that the ruler is displayed (View ➤ Ruler).

2. Change the type of tab to right-aligned by clicking on the L-shaped tab symbol on the left end of the ruler. Repeatedly click on this symbol to cycle through the four tab marker symbols. Find the one that looks like a backwards L (for a right-aligned tab).

3. Click on a point on the ruler where you want to set this right-aligned tab; for this example, click on the ruler below the 2." number. A small right angle tab symbol will appear.

4. Now change the type of tab to decimal-aligned by clicking on the current tab symbol on the left end of the ruler. You should only need to click once on this symbol to find the decimal-aligned symbol which looks like an upside down T with a dot.

5. Click on the ruler below the 5" mark. The decimal alignment symbol is set at this point.

6. Add the dot leader to the decimal-aligned tab by pointing to the decimal alignment symbol and double-clicking with the *right* mouse button. The Tabs dialog box appears.

7. In the Tab Stop Position list of current tabs on the left side, click on the 5" decimal tab. The option button for decimal tab appears in the Alignment area.

8. Below the Alignment area is the Leader area. Click on the second dot leader option. Click on the Set button at the bottom of the dialog box and click on OK. The ruler displays the two tab sets.

The dot leader effect is not obvious on the ruler until you press the Tab key and type text. Tab once to the first tab stop at 2". Type some text and tab again to produce the dots leading over to the decimal-aligned tab stop at 5".

PART

II

Communicating with Word

If you want to set a different type of tab, first change the tab type symbol on the furthest left side of the ruler (at the left corner of the ruler). Click on this symbol to cycle through the four possible tab marker symbols:

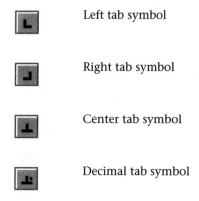

Left tab symbol

Right tab symbol

Center tab symbol

Decimal tab symbol

Moving Tabs

There will be times when you create a tabbed document, and then decide you want to move the tab stops. Using the ruler, you can easily drag the tab stops back and forth. The trick is to select the lines of text that are currently using this tab stop before you drag the tab set markers. Then, click on the symbol for the tab stop you want to move and drag it to the left or the right to reposition it. Make sure you keep a steady hand as you are dragging. If you inadvertently drag the tab stop off the ruler, make sure your text lines are still selected and go back into the Tabs dialog box (Format ➤ Tabs) to set the tab again.

Clearing Tabs

To clear specific tab stops:

1. Select the tabbed text lines (if you have pre-typed information).
2. Choose Format ➤ Tabs. The Tabs dialog box will appear.
3. In the Tab Stop Position list box, click on the tab stop you want to clear, then click on the Clear button at the bottom of the dialog box. If you click on Clear All by mistake, click on the Cancel button and start all over again. Repeat this step for each tab stop you want to clear. Click on OK to signal you have finished.

Clear All is the button to use when you want to remove all of your custom tabs. When you choose Clear All, the default tab stops are restored.

Clearing Tabs from the Ruler

You can also clear tabs using the ruler:

1. Make sure the ruler is showing (View ➤ Ruler).
2. Drag the tab stop you want to clear off of the ruler by clicking the tab symbol and dragging the symbol off of the ruler. The tab symbol (and setting) will disappear.

If you inadvertently pull off the wrong tab setting, click on the Undo button on the Standard toolbar or press Ctrl+Z. To reset a tab setting, click on the ruler at the number where you want the tab to appear and the tab is set again.

PART

II

Communicating with
Word

Chapter

9

Page Views and Page Formats

Page Views and Page Formats

I n Word, you have the ability to work with your documents in various *views,* which give you different perspectives of your document. Word offers seven unique views: Normal, Page Layout, Online Layout, Outline, Print Preview, Master Document, and Full Screen. Each view has different advantages.

Page formats are formats that control entire document pages, not just characters or paragraphs. For example, headers and footers are types of page formats: when you create a header or footer, it sits at the top or bottom of every page that you designate. Page formats also include numbering, margins, page orientation, and paper size.

Changing Your View

 You can use toolbar buttons and keyboard shortcuts to change views. Five of the views are represented on the screen with toolbar buttons. Normal, Page Layout, Online Layout, and Outline views have icons on the horizontal scroll bar near the bottom of the screen.

 The Print Preview button is located next to the printer button on the Standard toolbar.

You can also use menu commands to change to another view. The Print Preview command is listed on the File menu; the other four views, plus the Master Document and Full Screen commands, are listed on the View menu.

Normal View: An All-Purpose Typing View

Normal view, the default view, allows you to type, format, and edit your work. In this view, you can see all character formats (such as bolded text and font size changes) and all paragraph formats (such as indents, tabs, and alignments). Tables (discussed in Chapter 11) are visible and print as shown.

Normal view, however, is not a graphical view. Specific page formats, such as margins, page numbering, headers and footers, and whole page zoom, are not available in Normal view. Multiple columns (covered in Chapter 11) are displayed as a single strip of text, not as multiple columns. You must switch to Page Layout view or Print Preview to see more accurately how your document will look when printed.

One of the advantages of Normal view used to be that the screen scrolled faster while in Normal view than it did in Page Layout view, but with the advent of the 486 and Pentium computers, this is no longer a problem. Normal view does allow you to see much more of your text than Page Layout view, making documents easier to edit. Figure 9.1 shows a 12-page document at a 25% zoom in Normal view and at the same 25% zoom in Page Layout view.

To switch to Normal view, use one of these methods:

- Choose View ➤ Normal.
- Click on the Normal View button on the horizontal scroll bar.
- Use the keyboard shortcut Alt+Ctrl+N.

Page Layout View: A Graphical View

Page Layout view is the WYSIWYG ("what you see is what you get") view of your document. Page Layout view is the preferred typing view, because it gives you a sense of how your document is laying out on the page. Margins, page breaks, headers, footers, page numbering, and graphics are visible in Page Layout view.

An additional advantage of Page Layout view is that it allows you to view your pages in whole page magnifications. And it allows you to change the magnification (zoom control) to 10% or 15% and view up to 18 to 21 pages at a time—an excellent method for finding blank pages, seeing where graphics will fall, investigating hanging lines, and checking for other problems. Figure 9.1 shows a multiple-page document in Page Layout view.

PART

II

Communicating with Word

FIGURE 9.1

Normal view versus Page Layout view of a multiple-page document

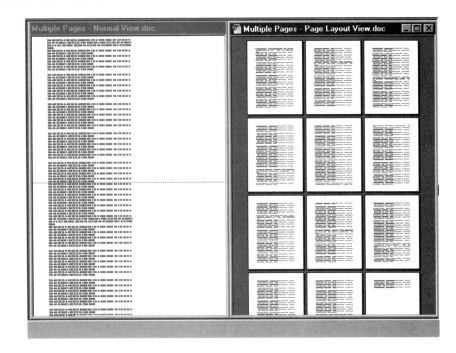

To switch to Page Layout view, use one of these methods:

- Choose View ➤ Page Layout.
- Click on the Page Layout View button on the horizontal scroll bar.
- Use the keyboard shortcut Alt+Ctrl+P.

Online Layout View: An E-View

The Online Layout view is the optimum view for reading documents on your computer screen. Text is more legible in this view because of its shorter, fixed-width lines, increased type size, and increased space between lines. This view hides many page layout elements, such as margins, headers, and footers.

Figure 9.2 shows the same document in Online Layout view and Page Layout view.

To switch to Online Layout view, use one of these methods:

- Choose View ➤ Online Layout.
- Click on the Online Layout View button on the horizontal scroll bar.

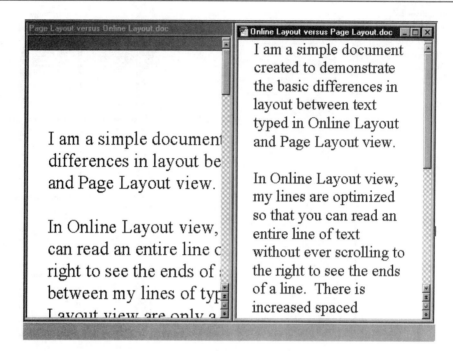

When you switch to Online Layout view, the Document Map sometimes appears in a separate pane; you can use the Document Map to navigate around your online document. If the Document Map doesn't appear, click on the Document Map button on the Standard toolbar.

Many times, you won't have any headings in your document and the Document Map shows nothing. To remove the pane, click the Document Map button on the Standard toolbar (near the 100% zoom control). See Chapter 7 for a fuller discussion of the Document Map.

Outline View: An Organizational Tool

Organizing your thoughts and information into indented headings has long been encouraged by teachers, writers, and project managers. Word's Outline view allows you to indent and outdent the headings and subheadings of your document—up to eight levels. Outline view also makes it easy to reorganize documents by allowing you to copy or move entire sections of text up and down levels.

When working with your text in Outline view, pressing Tab or Shift+Tab allows you to indent and outdent the headings of your document. Word displays a plus sign next to headings and subheadings that contain indented subheadings or text beneath them. A minus sign is shown next to headings and subheadings that do not contain indented subheadings or text beneath them.

To switch to Outline view, use one of these methods:

- Choose View ➢ Outline.
- Click on the Outline View button on the horizontal scroll bar.
- Use the keyboard shortcut Alt+Ctrl+O.

To indent a heading, click on the heading, then press the Tab key or click on the green right arrow on the Outline toolbar. To outdent (return to a previous level), press Shift+Tab or click on the green left arrow on the Outline toolbar. The heading styles correspond to the Heading 1, Heading 2, Heading 3, … styles of the Normal template.

To collapse a heading so that the indented subheadings are not showing, double-click on the plus sign to the left of the heading. The indented subheadings will disappear. Double-click on the plus sign again to make the indented subheadings visible.

 NOTE Documents created in Outline view using Word's default style headings are already in a format that can be used to create slides in PowerPoint.

You can also assign a numbering style to the headings in Outline view. Select the outlined text, then select Format ➢ Bullets and Numbering ➢ Outline Numbered to try out numbering styles. You can also customize the Outline numbering style. Figure 9.3 shows an Outline view with a common outlining style.

 NOTE You can use the Document Map to view any document that was created using the Heading styles. This split pane view shows the Outline view on the left and your document on the right.

Print Preview: A View of the Printed Document

Print Preview gives you an accurate picture of how your document will print to the printer. It is similar to Page Layout view. An advantage is that Print Preview has its own toolbar, and it allows you to easily view multiple pages and change the magnification of the screen. You can also edit your document in Print Preview mode. Figure 9.4 shows a document in this view.

PART

II

Communicating with Word

FIGURE 9.3

You can double click on the plus and minus signs in Outline view to collapse and expand levels.

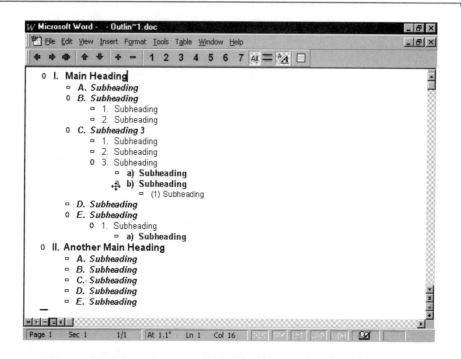

FIGURE 9.4

Print Preview shows multiple pages of your document and allows you to edit them.

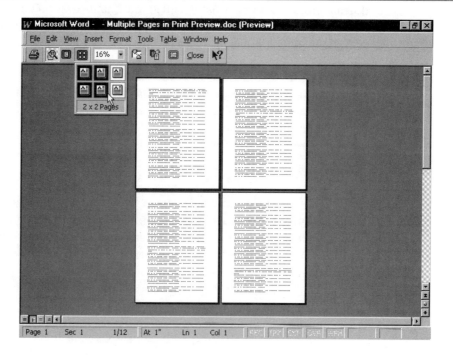

Use one of these methods to switch to Print Preview:

- Choose File ➢ Print Preview.
- Click on the Print Preview button on the Standard toolbar.
- Press Ctrl+F2.

While in Print Preview, you can perform many of the same actions that are available to you in Page Layout or Normal view. You can change the zoom control, the document's margins, and format text. You can also edit, move, and copy text. An option that is unique to Print Preview is the ability to shrink a document to fit on one less page. Many of the Print Preview options are available through the Print Preview toolbar, described in the next section.

Using the Print Preview Toolbar

PART
II

Communicating with
Word

When you click on the Print button on the Print Preview toolbar, Word immediately prints one copy of your entire document with the default options (the Print dialog box will not be displayed). If you want to print more than one copy, or want to print specific pages, press Ctrl+P or choose File ➢ Print to make choices in the Print dialog box.

When the Magnifier button is depressed, the view toggles between small page and 100% magnification. When you first start Print Preview, your document is shown in full page view (approximately 30% magnification on monitors with 640×480 pixel concentration; 55% on 1024×768 monitors). With the magnifier button depressed, pause the mouse over the page of text, and the mouse pointer turns into a magnifying glass with a plus sign, which means you can increase the magnification. Click on the mouse button once, and the magnification increases to 100%. The magnifying glass will then show a minus sign, which means you can decrease the magnification.

The One Page button shows a single page at a time. You will see whatever page your pointer was on in Normal or Page Layout view. Use the vertical scroll bar or press the PgUp and PgDn keys to move backward and forward through the pages of your document, one page at a time.

The Multiple Pages button allows you to decide how many pages you wish to see at one time (reduced magnification, of course). The maximum number of pages you can view depends on the resolution of your monitor. On computers with SVGA (Super Video Graphic Adapter), sometimes known as high-resolution, monitors, you can see up to 21 pages at a time. VGA monitors let you see a minimum of 12 pages. Click on the Multiple Pages button, and drag the mouse down and over the number of pages to be shown at one time; when you release the mouse button, you will see a display of miniature pages.

The zoom control drop-down list (to the right of the Multiple Pages button) functions the same in Print Preview as it does in the other views. You can click on the drop-down list arrow on the right side of the zoom control box and choose from the different zoom percentages, or you can type in a zoom percentage.

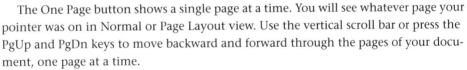

The View Ruler button allows you to toggle the display of the horizontal and vertical rulers on and off; these rulers allow you to see margin and tab stop settings. You can also turn the ruler on and off by choosing View ➢ Ruler.

If the last page of your document has only a few lines of text, you can click on the Shrink to Fit button. This tells Word to try to shrink the document so that the lines of text stuck on a page by themselves fit on the previous page. Sometimes you can do a better job yourself by changing the left and right margins to fit more text on a line or by changing the font size.

Full Screen view is a toggle button that switches between a screen with the menu bar and the ruler (if you have the ruler turned on) and one without. The Print Preview toolbar will always remain on the screen.

To return to the view you were in before you chose Print Preview, click on the Close button on the Print Preview toolbar. You can also click on one of the view buttons at the bottom of the screen to change to Normal, Online Layout, Page Layout, or Outline view. If you choose File ➢ Close, you will close your document, not just exit Print Preview.

When you click on the Help button, the mouse pointer turns into a question mark. Point to any text, and the paragraph and font formatting information box will appear, telling you which formats have been applied to the text. If you click on any screen element, such as the horizontal ruler, you will see help information explaining that element.

Editing in Print Preview

You can type in Print Preview at any time. The typing will appear where your pointer was positioned in the document before you switched to Print Preview. To start typing elsewhere in the document, make sure you are viewing at 100% magnification, then click on the Magnifier button on the Print Preview toolbar (so that it does not appear pushed down). The mouse turns into an I-beam. Click anywhere on your document screen to reposition the insertion point. You can use this method to type additional text or edit the text on the page.

Now that you are in full edit mode, you may want to use your Standard or Formatting toolbars. Right-click in the toolbar area and select the Standard or Formatting toolbar from the pop-up menu. When you have finished editing, click on the Magnifier button again to return the mouse pointer to a magnifying glass that toggles between magnifications.

Changing Top and Bottom Margins in Print Preview

You can change the page margins while in Print Preview view. Make sure you display the ruler (by clicking on the View Ruler button on the Print Preview toolbar or by choosing View ➢ Ruler). Then, to change the top or bottom margin:

1. Move your mouse to the ruler on the left side of your screen. If you hover at the point where the gray and white sections intersect at the top of the ruler, you will see the two-headed top margin arrow appear. If you hover at the point where the gray and white sections intersect at the bottom of the ruler, you will see the two-headed bottom margin arrow appear.

2. Drag the top or bottom margin up or down.

Figure 9.5 shows how the top margin of a document can be adjusted in Print Preview.

FIGURE 9.5

You can use the Print Preview ruler to change the top and bottom margins of your document.

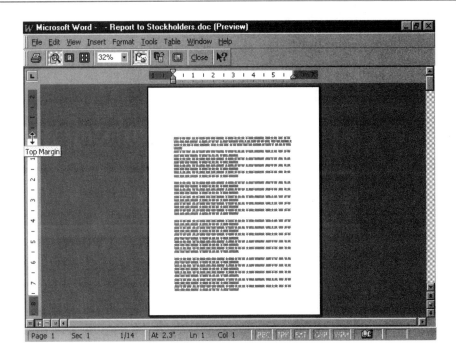

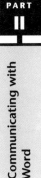

PART

II

Communicating with Word

Changing Left and Right Margins in Print Preview

To change the left or right margin of a document in Print Preview mode:

1. Move your mouse to the ruler on the top of the screen. If you hover at the point where the gray and white sections intersect on the left side of the ruler between the indent buttons, you will see the two-headed left margin arrow appear. If you hover at the point where the gray and white sections intersect on the right side of the ruler, you will see the two-headed right margin arrow appear.

2. Drag the left or right margin to the desired width. Do not drag the indent markers.

Figure 9.6 shows how the left margin of a document can be adjusted in Print Preview.

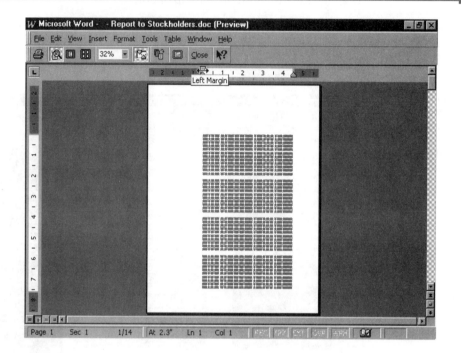

Full Screen View: A View without Obstructions

You can remove the menu bar, toolbars, rulers, and other screen elements by choosing the Full Screen command (View ➤ Full Screen). Word will show you a screen with only your text in it. This view is useful when you want to see as much text as possible, such as during proofreading.

Once you are in Full Screen view, you can easily toggle it back off. At the bottom of the screen, you'll see a Full Screen toolbar with one button on it, the Close Full Screen button. When you click on the Close Full Screen button, all the screen elements will return. You can also put the mouse to the very top of the screen to make the menu bar reappear; then, choose View ➤ Full Screen again to toggle Full Screen view off. You can also press the Esc key to get rid of Full Screen.

Because you cannot access the toolbars in Full Screen view, you'll need to issue commands in other ways. You can right-click to use the shortcut menus or use the keyboard shortcut keys (such as Ctrl+B for bold, and Ctrl+E for centering text). See Chapter 8, Tables 8.1 and 8.2, for a list of formatting keyboard combinations.

Master Document View:
Keeping Track of Subdocuments

Word's Master Document feature helps you organize long documents by separating them into separate document parts, or *subdocuments*. Each subdocument is saved in its own file. Use this feature to create a consistent format, and to have the page numbering, index, cross references, and table of contents apply across all the subdocuments.

To change to this view, choose View ➤ Master Document. The Master Document view is similar to the Outline view. Outlining, however, works with a single document; Master Document view lets you create different files from your outline.

Although the Master Document feature is beyond the scope of this book, you can use Word's Office Assistant (press F1) to get additional information on creating Master Documents. Figure 9.7 shows the Office Assistant going "crazy" when asked about Master Documents. There is very good step-by-step information in the Help regarding Master Documents.

PART

II

Communicating with Word

Magnification: Zoom Control in Any View

In all Word views, you can change the magnification of the screen from as large as a 500% magnification to as small as 10% magnification. You can type in your own magnifications in addition to the increments listed in the zoom control box. To change the zoom control:

1. Click on the drop-down arrow on the zoom control box at the end of the Standard toolbar.
2. Choose a different zoom from the list. If you are in Page Layout view (View ➢ Page Layout), you will see zoom options for Page Width, Whole Page, and Two Pages.

The zoom control does not affect the way the document will print, and it does not change the font size—it is only for viewing purposes. When your eyes are extremely tired, it is better to change to a higher zoom while working on your document. Figure 9.8 shows a document zoomed to 500%.

Magnification, or zoom control, is available for all of the views: Normal, Online Layout, Page Layout, Outline, and Print Preview. The Page Layout and Print Preview views allow for reduced magnifications to display small and multiple pages on the same screen (commonly called *thumbnails*). While in Page Layout view, change the zoom control to 10% to see your pages as thumbnails.

Change to a higher zoom when your eyes are tired. The zoom does not affect the way the document will print.

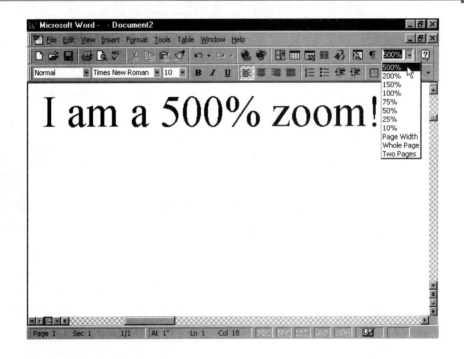

Remember, the zoom control magnifications are different from view to view. Normal and Online Layout views cannot display whole pages, while Page Layout and Print Preview views can.

MASTERING THE OPPORTUNITIES

Viewing Multiple Documents

As you are working with Word, you will often need to work with more than one document open in memory. Switching between multiple documents is as simple as pressing Ctrl+F6 or choosing Window from the menu bar and selecting the other document. But if you have many multiple document management tasks, you may want to see two documents on the screen *at the same time*. Here are the steps to see two or more open documents stacked horizontally on the screen:

1. Open the two documents you want to view at the same time.
2. Choose Window ➢ Arrange All. The screen will be split horizontally into two windows.

Horizontal arrangements are not always the best document view. In some cases, vertical arrangements would be better for document viewing—for example, if you

want to view multiple documents side-by-side. You must size and position the windows manually in order to see multiple documents side by side. Follow these steps:

1. Open each document.
2. Choose Window ➢ Arrange All. The documents will be stacked horizontally, one on top of the other.
3. Drag the lower right corner of one of the windows and pull to the left to form a rectangle. Repeat this step for the other windows.
4. Move the windows by dragging the title bars so as to position the windows side-by-side.
5. To move from one document window to the next, press Ctrl+F6 or click on the title bar of the document window you want to activate.

For an example of this, see Figure 9.2, which shows two documents open side-by-side on the screen.

Formatting Pages in Word

Formatting pages can mean changing the margins, paper size, or orientation (landscape or portrait). You may need to center text vertically on a page, insert new pages, number existing pages, or use headers and footers on multiple pages. You may need to have different page numbers in different sections. All of these formats involve the entire page rather than just characters or paragraphs of text. Word's page formatting commands are plentiful and can be applied before or after you have created your document. The following sections focus on the most frequently used page formats.

Setting Margins

Setting the margins for your documents is a fundamental feature of any word processing program. In Word, this is one of the easiest tasks to perform.

Word's default margins are 1-inch top and bottom margins and 1.25-inch left and right margins. You can change any of these margins to suit your documents.

TIP

If you print on letterhead paper, its logo placement determines what types of margin widths you need. With a ruler, measure from the top of the paper to where the text should begin. Measure from the left edge how many inches your text needs to "come in" on the left. Use these measurements when setting the margins in Word. If you will print to this paper most of the time, you can make these margins the new default settings.

Changing Margins for the Entire Document

Position the pointer anywhere in your document when you are going to make global margin changes. Then perform the following steps:

1. Choose File ➤ Page Setup.
2. When the Page Setup dialog box appears, make sure the Margins tab is selected.
3. Change the top, bottom, left, and right margins as desired: type the new margin settings, or click the spinner buttons to have Word enter the settings for you. Margins are measured in inches. Note that you cannot reduce the margins to zero in many cases because of printer restrictions; some printers require a minimum margin width of .25 inch.
4. At the bottom of the dialog box, make sure that the Apply To option is set to Whole Document.

Click on OK to return to your document. If you are not happy with the results, click on the Undo button on the Standard toolbar or press Ctrl+Z and start again.

TIP

If you find that you are changing the margin settings for 80 percent of your documents, click on the Default button at the bottom of the Margins tab in the Page Setup dialog box to change the default margin settings. Each new document you start will have these margins.

Changing Margins from This Point Forward

To change the margins from a certain page forward in a document:

1. Position the pointer at the top of the page where you want the new margins to take effect.
2. Choose File ➤ Page Setup, and make sure the Margins tab is selected. Change the margins to the dimensions you need for your work. Figure 9.9 shows the Margins page in the Page Setup dialog box.
3. Click on the drop-down arrow next to the Apply To list box, and change the option to This Point Forward.
4. Click on OK. If you are not happy with the results, click on the Undo button on the Standard toolbar or press Ctrl+Z and start again.

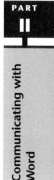

FIGURE 9.9

Change the dimensions of the margins and see the results immediately in the Preview box on the Margins page in the Page Setup dialog box.

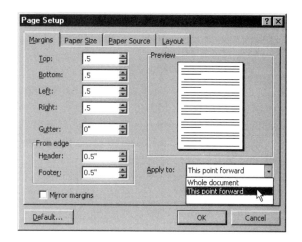

Changing Margins for Selected Text

The Selected Text option in the Apply To drop-down list is available only if you have text selected in the document. To give different margin settings to specific selected pages:

1. Select the multiple pages of text that will have different margins.
2. Choose File ➤ Page Setup and click on the Margins tab at the top of the dialog box, if it is not already selected.
3. Change the margin settings as desired.

4. Make sure the Apply To option at the bottom of the dialog box is set to Selected Text. Word will create multiple section breaks before and after these selected pages so that it knows that the margin settings are different for these pages. (In Normal view, you can see the section break lines.)

5. Click on OK. If you are not happy with the results, click on the Undo button or press Ctrl+Z and start again.

NOTE
You cannot set different margins on the same page. Use the left and right indent options in the Paragraph dialog box (Format ➤ Paragraph) to create temporary left and right margins for selected text at different locations, as described in Chapter 8.

Setting Landscape or Portrait Orientation

Word's Paper Size command in the Page Setup dialog box allows you to change a page's orientation (to landscape or portrait) and to change the size of your paper (standard, legal, and so on).

Your printer, however, controls whether a document image can be rotated to print landscape (sideways) or can handle legal size paper. Laser and ink-jet printers offer the greatest amount of flexibility in handling different paper sizes and orientations. Dot-matrix printers may require that you place the paper in sideways before printing a page that has a landscape orientation.

To change the paper orientation:

1. Position the pointer at the top of the page on which you wish the change to take effect if you are changing the orientation from a particular page forward.

2. Choose File ➤ Page Setup and click on the Paper Size tab. Figure 9.10 shows this page in the Page Setup dialog box.

3. In the Orientation area at the bottom of the dialog box, the capital *A* shows the current orientation setting. Click on the radio button to the right of the capital *A* for either landscape or portrait orientation. The Preview changes to reflect the orientation you chose.

4. The Apply To option lets you choose whether the Whole Document or only from This Point Forward will have the different orientation. Depending on your text selection, the options Selected Text, This Section, and Selected Sections may appear in the drop-down list.

5. Click on OK to close the Page Setup dialog box.

FIGURE 9.10

Change the page orientation in the Paper Size page of the Page Setup dialog box.

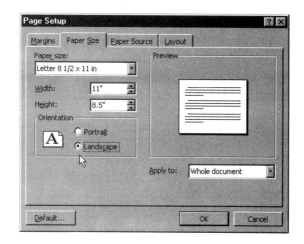

Multiple Orientations in a Document

You can mix orientations in a document, with some pages in portrait and others in landscape orientation. Word will insert section breaks above and below the pages that have a different orientation.

If you have already typed your text and discover you need multiple orientations in the same document—for example, pages 1 through 3 should be portrait, pages 4 through 6 should be landscape, and then pages 7 and 8 should be portrait—you can select specific pages and then change the orientation for those pages. Here are the steps for setting multiple orientations:

1. Switch to Page Layout view (View ➢ Page Layout) and set the zoom control box to approximately 15% so you can see miniature pages (you can type in your own zoom percentages).

2. Select the group of multiple pages to receive the different orientation.

3. Choose File ➢ Page Setup, and click on the Paper Size tab. Then, click on the Orientation option you need for that group of selected pages.

4. Make sure the Apply To option is set to Selected Text, and then click OK. Repeat these steps for every group of pages you want to change the orientation of.

If you do not get the results you desire, immediately click on the Undo button on the Standard toolbar or press Ctrl+Z. Try again. Figure 9.11 shows how multiple orientations in the same document appear in Page Layout view.

PART

II

Communicating with Word

A document with groups of pages set to different orientations.

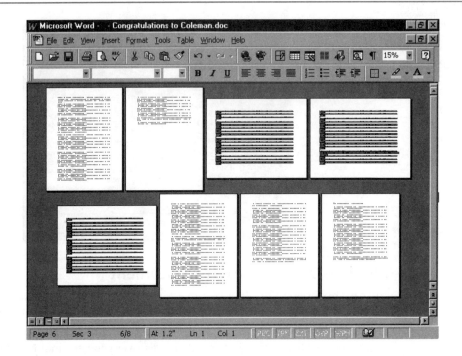

Setting Paper Size

Your printer also determines the paper sizes you can print. To change the paper size, choose File ➤ Page Setup, and click on the Paper Size tab. The Paper Size option defaults to Letter $8\frac{1}{2} \times 11$ inches (see Figure 9.10).

Word 97 provides preset paper sizes other than $8\frac{1}{2} \times 11$ and $8\frac{1}{2} \times 14$ (legal paper). For example, the $9\frac{1}{2} \times 4\frac{1}{8}$ size is popular for printing letter envelopes. You can choose other paper sizes as well as specify your own custom page sizes.

Setting Up, Creating, and Printing Envelopes

When you choose an Envelope paper size from the Paper Size tab, the orientation for the envelope is still portrait. You must choose landscape to have the envelope rotate its orientation. Figure 9.12 shows the settings for envelope printing.

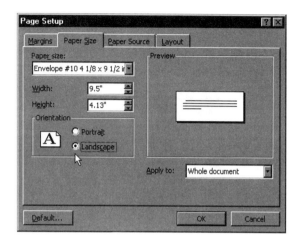

Setting Envelope Margins

You may also want to change the margins of the envelope so that your text will appear on the envelope at the proper locations. Envelopes that already have a return address printed on them need only the delivery address. In general, business envelopes have a top margin of 2 inches and a left margin of 4 inches. The bottom and left margins are .25 inch.

To change the margins on an envelope, choose File ➤ Page Setup ➤ Margins tab (or if you are already in the Page Setup dialog box, click on the Margins tab) and change the margins to suit the envelope format.

Creating Envelope Text

When you return to the view you were working in after you set up the envelope page format, the insertion point will be at the proper location for you to begin typing. To see a graphical representation of the envelope paper size, switch to Page Layout view (View ➤ Page Layout) and change the zoom control to Whole Page.

An easier way to create an envelope is to let Word do it for you. Word will create an envelope for you automatically using the inside address that you typed on a letter as the address on the envelope. Follow these steps to have Word quickly create an envelope from pretyped information:

1. Type a letter, including the address of the person to whom the letter is going.

2. When you have finished typing the letter, select the inside address.

3. Choose Tools ➤ Envelopes and Labels. The Envelopes and Labels dialog box appears with the address from the letter selected in the Delivery Address text area, as shown in Figure 9.13.

FIGURE 9.13

Word can quickly create an envelope from address information in your letter.

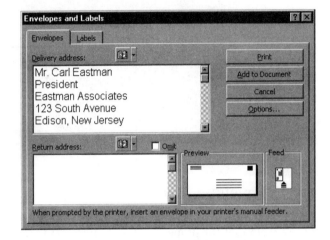

4. If you do not wish to use the Return Address shown at the bottom of the dialog box (perhaps because the envelope already has a preprinted return address), click on the Omit checkbox above the Return address area. You can also delete the Return address if shown and type a new one.

5. If you need to change the address, first click the mouse on the line where you wish to make a change. Note that if you start typing on the address line, the entire address will be overwritten because it is selected. Remember to click the mouse first before typing on the address line, unless you want to replace the entire address.

6. Once everything looks correct, click on the Print button on the right side of the dialog box to signal to Word to print only the envelope. Make sure that you feed the envelope according to the small Feed diagram shown in the lower right corner of the dialog box.

7. If you would like to add the envelope to your document to save it, click on the Add to Document button on the right side of the dialog box.

NOTE

The Options button on the Envelopes tab of the Envelopes and Labels dialog box offers you choices for changing the envelope size, delivery point bar-code, font, and position of the delivery and return addresses.

Centering Text on a Page

Centering words *on a line* (between the left and right margins) takes one click of the mouse or the keypress Ctrl+E. However, when you need to have text centered between the top and bottom margins, such as for a title page or report cover page, there are a few more actions involved.

The traditional method for centering has been to add returns (press the Enter key) in order to "shove" the text down. Usually, part of the text disappears onto the next page, and then you must delete the extra returns. Word solves this problem with its Vertical Alignment feature, which centers text on a page between the top and bottom margins. Use the following steps to apply this feature:

1. Type your lines of text at the top of a page. Click on the Center button on the Standard toolbar or press Ctrl+E to center your words on the line.
2. Choose File ➢ Page Setup, and click on the Layout tab. This page is shown in Figure 9.14. Notice the Vertical Alignment section near the lower left side of the dialog box. The default setting is Top (text begins at the top of the page normally).

PART

II

Communicating with Word

FIGURE 9.14

Use the Vertical Alignment setting in the Layout page of the Page Setup dialog box to center text on a page vertically.

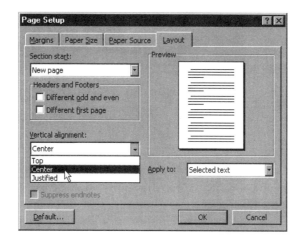

3. Click on the drop-down arrow to the right of the current alignment and choose Center.
4. Make sure the Apply To option says "Selected Text."
5. Click on OK. Your selection of text will be centered between the top and bottom margins on a new page.

Numbering Pages

For multiple-page documents, Word provides a page numbering feature, so you don't need to type in the page numbers yourself. Word has a myriad of page numbering options that allow you to choose different positions and formats for page numbers.

If you have a typed document that only has one section, it does not matter where you position the insertion point to start the page numbering. The page numbering always starts on the first page (although you can tell Word to not show the number on that page). To place page numbers on all the pages of a document:

1. Switch to Page Layout view (View ➤ Page Layout).
2. Choose Insert ➤ Page Numbers. Figure 9.15 shows the Page Numbers dialog box.
3. In the Position list box, choose whether you want the numbering at the top or bottom of the page. In Figure 9.15, the position is set for the top of the page.
4. In the Alignment list box, select whether you want the numbering on the left side, center, right side, inside, or outside. In Figure 9.15 the page numbering is set for the center of the page.
5. Click on the OK button to close the dialog box.

FIGURE 9.15

Page numbers can be inserted at the top or bottom of pages, with left, right, centered, inside, or outside alignment.

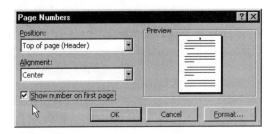

If you chose the settings in Figure 9.15, the page numbers will appear in a light gray background at the top center of your document. If you double-click on the page number, you will be switched into the Headers and Footers view, and a special toolbar will appear. Click on the Close button on this toolbar to get out of Headers and Footers view. Headers and Footers are discussed later in this chapter.

Suppressing Page Numbering

If you do not want the page number to appear on the first page, but the second page should start with the number 2, uncheck *Show number on first page* in the Page Numbers dialog box. You can perform this action before or after your insert page numbers.

Changing the Start Value

You can change the Start At value in the Page Number Format dialog box to have the page numbering begin with whatever number you like. For example, you probably would not want numbering to begin on the title page of a report. If you merely suppress the page number from showing on the title page, the next page will print with the number 2 because Word considers the title page as page 1. Instead, follow these steps:

1. Uncheck *Show number on first page* in the Page Numbers dialog box.
2. Click on the Format button at the bottom of the Page Numbers dialog box.
3. At the bottom of the Page Number Format dialog box, click on the Start At option and type **0** (zero). The 0 will not show on the title page because you unchecked the option; but a page number will show on the second page, and it will be the number 1.
4. Click on the OK button on the Page Number Format dialog box.
5. Click on the OK button on the Page Numbers dialog box. See Figure 9.16 for the dialog box settings.

When you return to the document, look at the top center of the page. The "first" page, which is the title page, will not show a number. The second page, which is where the report begins, shows the number 1 for the page number. Each page thereafter will be numbered sequentially.

PART

II

Communicating with Word

FIGURE 9.16

You can start page numbering with any number.

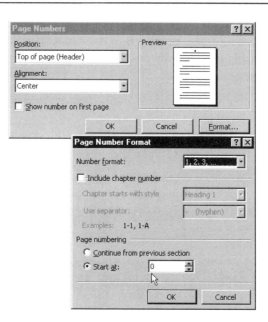

Deleting Page Numbering

Once you have turned on page numbering, it seems difficult to remove the numbering. Remember that the Undo button is ideal in a situation where you want to reverse the action you have just performed. However, the Undo button does you no good if you have inherited someone else's document or you decide down the road that there should be page numbering in another position (bottom instead of top, for example). Then you need to delete the current numbering.

You can delete the numbering and start again, but it will require that you work with the header and footer features of Word. If your page number is at the bottom of the page, it is in the footer. If it is at the top of the page, it is placed in the header. The next section goes into more depth about working with headers and footers. For now, let's get rid of the page numbers:

1. Change to Page Layout view (View ➤ Page Layout) if you are not already in this view.
2. Choose View ➤ Header and Footer from the menu bar. A new toolbar appears labeled Header and Footer. The header is shown first. If you can see your page number immediately, skip to step 4.
3. If you do not see your page number, it may be suppressed until further into the document, or it may be in the Footer instead of the Header. To find it, do one of these things:

   - If your page number is in the Footer, click on the Switch Between Header and Footer button in the Header and Footer toolbar or press the down arrow key to move to the Footer.
   - If your page number is in the Header but you don't see it, it may be suppressed and not showing on the first page. Click on the Show Next button to display the next Header.

4. When you see the page number, pause the mouse over the number and the mouse will turn into a four-headed arrow.
5. Click on the page number when the mouse is a four-headed arrow. Object markers will display in a rectangular box around the number; the number will turn gray and be selected.

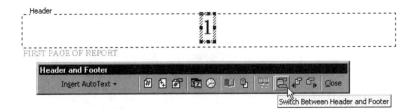

6. Press the Delete key on your keyboard to delete the number. It will disappear from all pages within that section of the document.

TIP

When you use Edit ➤ Select All or press Ctrl+A in a header or footer and then press the Delete key, *all* of the information in all the document's headers or footers will be deleted.

Repeating Information in Headers and Footers

Headers and footers are word processing holding areas for repetitive information that must appear either in the top margin (header) or in the bottom margin (footer) of every page of your document. You can format and align text, add page numbers, insert the current date or time, and show graphics, clip art, or lines within the boundaries of headers and footers.

Word also gives you the ability to have different headers and footers for different sections of your document. You must insert a section break to designate different headers and footers for the new section.

When you choose headers and footers (View ➤ Header and Footer), Word switches to Page Layout view automatically. The insertion point is placed in the dashed outlined area of the header. A special Header and Footer toolbar appears:

Creating a Header or Footer

As an example, suppose that you want to create a header that repeats the name of a corporation and the page number on every page of a document except for the first page. The corporate name will be on the left side of the header, the words *Draft Report* will be centered, and the page number will be right-aligned. The page numbering will begin at 100 (because the previous sections are being done by other individuals).

NOTE

Although we are putting this information in a header, you can follow the same procedure for a footer.

Adding Text to a Header or Footer

First, you will want to add the text to your header (or footer):

1. Choose View ➤ Header and Footer. If you are in Normal view, you will be switched to Page Layout view, and the insertion point will be on the left side of the Header box. If you wish to create a footer instead of a header, click on the Switch Between Header and Footer button on the toolbar or press the down arrow key to move to the Footer box.

2. Type **ABC Corporation**. You can change the font, font size, and font style as you wish.

3. Press the Tab key. The insertion pointer will jump to the center of the header.

4. Type **Draft Report**. The text centers as you type.

Placing Page Numbers in a Header or Footer

Next, you will want to format the page numbering:

1. Position the insertion point where you want the page number. To continue with the above example, press the Tab key to move to the insertion point to the right side of the Header (or Footer) box.

2. Type the word **Page** and format it just as you did for the company name. Press the spacebar to add a space before inserting the page number.

3. Click on the Insert Page Number button on the Header and Footer toolbar or press the Alt+Shift+P key combination. The page number will appear. (For now, the page numbering will start with 1; you will change it to 100 in the next step.) Leave the insertion point right where it is.

4. Click on the Format Page Number button in the Headers and Footers toolbar. The Page Number Format dialog box will appear. Click on the Start At radio button and type the number **100**.

5. Click on OK. The first page number of your document will now be 100. If you want the page numbers bolded and the same point size as your other text, drag the mouse over the number 100 to select it, and apply the formatting as you wish.

6. Click on Close to return to your document.

When you return to the typing area, move to subsequent pages to see the header with the appropriate page numbers. Create multiple page breaks (press Ctrl+Enter a couple of times), to force page breaks so that you can simulate multiple pages for this example. Notice the sequential movement of the numbers in the header.

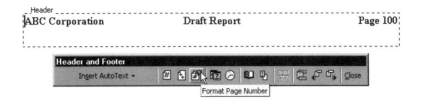

Editing Headers or Footers

To change an existing header or footer, choose View ➤ Header and Footer. If you don't see your header or footer, click on the Show Next button on the Header and Footer toolbar to move to the next header or footer, or click on Switch Between Header and Footer button on the toolbar. You can then edit the header or footer text. To delete a header or footer, select all of the text within the header or footer and press the Delete key. You cannot remove the Header and Footer dashed box—only the information within it.

To delete headers or footers in all sections, position the insertion point in the header or footer and press Ctrl+A, or select Edit ➤ Select All. Press the Delete key. All the headers or footers in the document will be deleted.

When you've finished editing your headers or footers, click the on Close button on the toolbar.

> **TIP**
>
> When in Page Layout view, you can double-click on the light gray header or footer that appears in the background of the document. This action will display the Header and Footer typing area and toolbar.

Inserting AutoText into a Header or Footer

Word has added a new feature to its Header and Footer toolbar: Insert AutoText. Using the Insert AutoText feature, you can insert document information items into a header or footer, such as the date and time that a document was created, the name of the file, the last creation date, or the word "Confidential." The AutoText options are listed in Table 9.1.

To Insert an AutoText item into a header or footer:

1. Choose View ➤ Header and Footer. (Switch to the footer, if desired.)

2. On the Header and Footer toolbar, click on the Insert AutoText button. Figure 9.17 shows the text options available from the AutoText menu.

3. Select an option. It will be inserted into your Header or your Footer. To delete the inserted text, drag the mouse over the text and press the Delete key. See Table 9.1 for a description of each AutoText option.

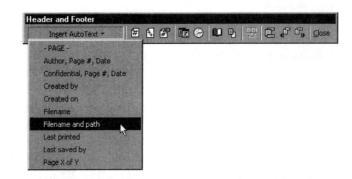

FIGURE 9.17

You can insert an AutoText entry into a header or footer by clicking on the Insert Auto-Text button on the Header and Footer toolbar.

TABLE 9.1: AUTOTEXT OPTIONS FOR HEADERS AND FOOTERS

Insert AutoText Option	Description
- PAGE -	Places the page number in the center of the header or footer and puts dashes on either side of the number.
Author, Page #, Date	Places the author's name on the left side, centers the page number, and places the current date on the right side. Note that the author name is taken from the User Info page of the Options dialog box (Tools ➤ Options).
Confidential, Page #, Date	Places the word "Confidential" on the left side of the header or footer, centers the page number, and places the current date on the right side.
Created By	Places the author's name after the words "Created by" on the left side of the header or footer.
Created On	Places the create date and time after the words "Created on" on the left side of the header or footer.

Continued ▌▶

TABLE 9.1: AUTOTEXT OPTIONS FOR HEADERS AND FOOTERS (CONTINUED)	
Insert AutoText Option	**Description**
Filename	Places the name of the file on the left side of the header or footer.
Filename and Path	Places the name of the file and its full path—for example, H:\Angela\Memos\FileName.
Last Printed	Places the date and time after the words "Last printed" on the left side of the header or footer.
Last Saved By	Places the author's name after the words "Last saved by" on the left side of the header or footer.
Page X of Y	Places the word "Page" and the current page number, followed by the word "of" and the last page number in the left side of the header or footer.

MASTERING TROUBLESHOOTING

Updating AutoText Information

AutoText entries that you insert into your header or footer often won't be updated automatically. For example, say you insert the Filename (or the Filename and Path) AutoText option into a header or footer to display the name of your document. If you change your document's filename, Word will not update the information in the header or footer until you reopen the document. In cases like this, you may wish to update fields right away, without having to close and reopen the document. To do this, you will have to manually perform the keystrokes to update the information:

1. Go to the header or footer by choosing View ➢ Header and Footer, or by double-clicking on the gray background of the header or footer.
2. Once in the header or footer area, press Ctrl+A to select all.
3. Press F9 to update the document information in the header or footer. Page numbering and other document information will be updated.

Inserting and Deleting Pages in a Document

When you are typing along and reach the bottom of a page in a Word document, a page break will be inserted and a new page will be created automatically. The paper size will determine where automatic page breaks occur.

If you wish to end one page and start another before the natural page break, you should not press the Enter key repeatedly in order to move to the next page. Instead, you can insert a page break at any place on the page by pressing Ctrl+Enter or selecting Insert ➣ Break ➣ Page.

Inserting a Page Break

There are two methods for creating a page break. Remember to position the insertion point at the line where the page should end. Then do one of the following:

- Choose Insert ➣ Break ➣ Page Break. Click on OK.
- Use the keyboard shortcut that all experienced Word users use to manually break the page: Ctrl+Enter.

When you look at the document, a page break will have been inserted, and the insertion point will be on a new blank page. If you inadvertently created the break, press the Backspace key to remove the break or press the Undo button on the Standard toolbar.

In Normal view, a page break appears as a line across the screen with the words "Page Break" in the middle of it, as shown in Figure 9.18. In Page Layout view, a page break appears as a gray area, showing the separation between the pages.

Inserting Blank Pages

If you have existing text in your document and you wish to insert a blank page between two pages of text, position the insertion at the top of the second page and press Ctrl+Enter twice. For example, suppose you wish to insert a blank page between pages 4 and 5. Position the pointer at the top of page 5 and press Ctrl+Enter twice.

Deleting a Blank Page

If you find a blank page in your document, it is probably caused by two consecutive page breaks. The easiest way to delete blank pages is to find and remove the extra page break indicator in the document. To do this In Normal view, click on the page break line and press Delete.

FIGURE 9.18

The page break
indicator in
Normal view

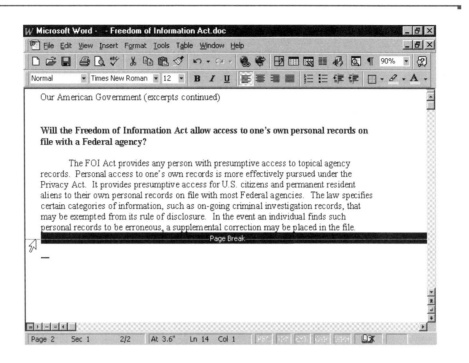

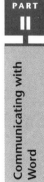

To delete a page break in Page Layout view, click on the Show/Hide ¶ button at the end of the Standard toolbar (or press Ctrl+Shift+8) to show the nonprinting characters of the document. Then, double-click on the page break line and press the Delete key to remove the page break.

Deleting Pages of Text

To delete a page that contains text, drag the mouse over the text to select it and press the Delete key. If you are left with a blank page, see the above section for deleting blank pages in a document.

Chapter

10

Managing and Printing Your Files from Word

FEATURING

Chapter 10

Managing and Printing Your Files from Word

This chapter describes how to use the file and print features of Word. File and print operations are essential components of any document management process.

Basic file operations include saving, closing, opening, finding, deleting, renaming, and copying files. Advanced file operations include inserting (combining) multiple files, setting the AutoRecover intervals, making automatic backups and saving versions of your documents, and sharing documents for multiuser editing.

Word's printing options include printing selected pages and multiple copies, and managing multiple paper bins.

Starting a New File in Word

When you first launch Word, a fresh document is started for you. From this point, you can begin working with the new document, or choose File ➤ Open to load a previously saved document.

To start a new document (file) with either the standard defaults or any of the preformatted document templates, choose File ➤ New from the menu bar. Figure 10.1 shows the tabbed New dialog box; each tab contains a different category of documents.

FIGURE 10.1

The New dialog box lists the template categories for Word.

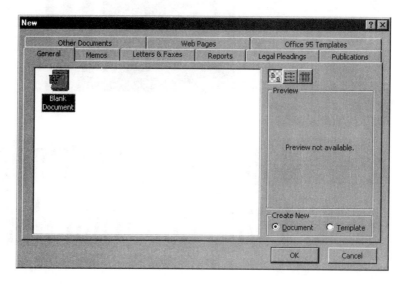

Starting a "Normal" Document

To start a new document with default settings, go to the New dialog box (File ➤ New), click on the General tab, and double-click on the Blank Document icon. This document will have the following default settings:

- Left and right margins of 1.25 inches
- Top and bottom margins of 1 inch
- Tab stops set every .5 inch
- Paper size of $8\frac{1}{2} \times 11$ inches
- Portrait orientation
- Times New Roman typeface (depends on your default printer settings)
- Font size of 10 points

When you start a new document by clicking the Blank Document icon, you are actually using something called the Normal template. (You can, however, base your document on other kinds of templates, as described in the next section.) If you know that you want to use the default Normal template, you can save yourself a few steps by clicking the first (New) button on the Standard toolbar; Word will quickly give you a fresh document page on which to type. You can also use the keyboard combination Ctrl+N to start a new document.

Starting a Document Using a Template Wizard

In addition to the Normal template, Word supplies a number of other templates, which are divided into eight categories:

- General
- Publications
- Other Documents
- Memos
- Reports
- Letters & Faxes
- Legal Pleadings
- Web Pages

The General category contains the Blank Document template, with the default settings described in the previous section. The Publications and Other Documents categories include some interesting templates that help you create normally complex documents in a snap.

NOTE

You can create your own templates by saving documents as templates (see Chapter 12), or by modifying one of Word's templates (see Chapter 13).

Word also includes a special type of template called a *Wizard*, which helps you to develop your document by following a series of steps and questions. If you are not familiar with business letter layouts, for example, you can use the Letter Wizard to create a new letter:

1. Choose File ➢ New.
2. Click on the Letters & Faxes tab. This page lists a number of Template Wizards.
3. Double-click the Letter Wizard icon. (This particular Wizard can also be started by selecting Tools ➢ Letter Wizard)
4. The Office Assistant pops up and asks you what it is you would like to do—write a letter to an individual or to a group of people on a mailing list. Select Send One Letter.
5. Step 1 of the Letter Wizard, shown in Figure 10.2, presents you with a multi-tabbed dialog box that you should use to fill in the details of your letter. At this point, you should check the Date Line box and leave the current date; select Professional Letter from the Page Design combo box; select Full Block as the Letter Style; and then click on Next.

FIGURE 10.2

The Letter Wizard prompts you through the steps of creating a letter.

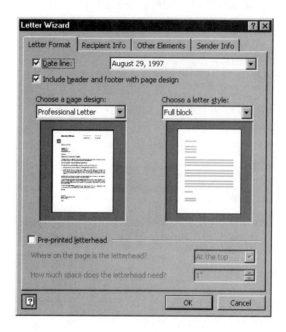

6. For Step 2, enter the address of the person the letter is going to and select a Formal Salutation. Click on Next.

7. Leave the fields on the Other Elements tab for Step 3 blank, and click on Next.

8. Step 4 places you on the Sender Info tab. Enter your address information and what you want as a closing.

9. Click on Finish. A new document will be generated according to your specifications; you can then enter the body of the letter. The Office Assistant will also ask if there is anything else you would like to do, like create an envelope or mailing label for the letter.

> **NOTE**
>
> Choose Tools ➤ Options and click on the User Info tab to set the Mailing Address you want to appear as the return address whenever you use the envelope feature.

10. When you've finished typing your letter, do not forget to save your work (File ➤ Save).

Saving Your Work

You should periodically tell Word to save a copy of your document onto a more permanent medium (hard disk, floppy disk, network drive, or tape drive). The document you see when you are typing is a reflection of what is in the computer's memory. If you turn off the computer or experience electrical problems while you are creating your document (and you have not told Word to save your work), you will lose the valuable effort you have made, because the computer's memory will be cleared.

One way to ensure that you keep a copy of your work is to frequently save to disk what you have done so far. You can also protect yourself from electrical problems by requesting an automatic save every couple of minutes. If your computer shuts down before you have saved your file, you can recover the last document on which you were working.

Naming and Saving Files to Disk

You can save your work at any point while you are typing or editing by choosing File ➤ Save from the menu bar. You should save your work frequently.

When you save your work the first time, you must name the document. The name of your document can be up to 250 characters long and can contain spaces and periods. However, if you think that you might be sharing documents with other individuals who are using previous versions of Word that do not support long filenames, you should restrict your name to eight characters only, without spaces or periods.

To save and name your document the first time, follow these steps:

1. Your pointer can be anywhere in the document. Choose File ➤ Save from the menu bar. The Save As dialog box will appear. At the bottom of the dialog box is a text area designated for the filename.
2. Word displays the first few words of the text in your document as a suggested name for your file. If you do not want the suggested name, type over it with another name that is more suitable for the document. As noted, you can enter up to 250 characters and can include spaces and periods. Figure 10.3 shows a completed Save As dialog box.
3. After you have typed the name of your document, click on the Save button on the right side of the dialog box.

When you return to your document, the name you assigned to it will appear in the document's title bar at the top of the Word screen.

After you have named and saved your document the first time, you will not need to designate the name again for subsequent saves.

FIGURE 10.3

Word allows filenames up to 250 characters with spaces and periods in the name.

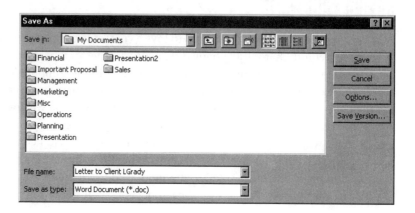

When you save a new document, be careful not to give it the same name as another document, unless you want to replace the existing file with the new one. Word will write over the previous document with that name. Fortunately, Word will prompt you to confirm the replacement.

It is recommended that you save your work again and again as you are creating and editing your document. Saving frequently serves two purposes:

- You have a stored copy of your latest changes if there is any electrical problem (or human error) in your office and the computer's power is turned off. If there is such a problem, you can restart the computer and open the document you were working on with its most recent edits.
- You have a stored copy on disk in case you "mess up" the copy of the document on the screen. You can always close the copy of the document on the screen—without saving—and use File ➢ Open to go back to the last saved copy.

You will never see multiple saved copies of the same document within the same folder. Because Word replaces your last saved file with the most recently saved file, you will see only one copy of your document (with the same name) in a folder.

Word provides a toolbar button to allow you to quickly perform saves. Click on the button with the image of a diskette on the Standard toolbar (third button in from the left).

If you have already named and saved your work, Word will simply replace your old saved version with the new version on the screen. No message will appear on the screen to tell you that the save was completed. You can, however, look down at the Status bar at the bottom of the screen, where you should see the horizontal blue box, showing the saving action "thermometer-style." If your document is short, the action is very quick.

You can also use the keyboard combination Ctrl+S to save your work. Again, you will see the horizontal blue box with the thermometer-style saving indicator at the bottom of the screen.

WARNING

If you plan on saving a document for someone with an earlier version of Word on their computer, keep in mind that previous versions of Word cannot read Word 97 documents without a special filter. This filter is available with Office 97 or on Microsoft's Web site. If the recipient of your document does not have this filter, you will need to save the file in the format of Word that they are using. Choose File ➢ Save As; in the Save as Type text area, click on the drop-down arrow and select Word 6.0 - 7.0.

Making Quick Copies of Files with Save As

Each time you choose File ➢ Save (or use the Save toolbar button or press Ctrl+S) after you've named a file, Word remembers the document's name and immediately saves over your old version with the latest version of your document.

If you want to edit a document, but don't want to save over the original, unedited version of the document, you should make a copy of the document or use the new Versions feature (discussed in the next section). To make a copy of your document and work on the copy, choose File ➢ Save As or press the shortcut key, F12. In the Save As dialog box that appears, enter a new name for your document. When you return to the document, you will see the new name in the title bar. This is the copy you are working on; the original file is still on the disk. (You can open the original file by choosing File ➢ Open and selecting the original filename.)

Keeping Track of Versions

This newest version of Word will allow you to save multiple versions of a document *without* maintaining multiple copies of the file under different names. Each time you save a document, the changes of that version will be stored with your document;

Word can then roll back a particular version of your document, in case you want to review what the document was like before you or another user modified it.

In order to save multiple versions of a document without changing the filename each time, select File ➤ Versions from the menu bar. The Versions in *X* dialog box will appear. To save the current version, click on the Save Now button. Word will prompt you for any special comments regarding the version; type your notes, and click OK. This version is not saved as a separate file; rather, the changes are stored with the current file.

You can also access the Save Version option from the right side of the Save As dialog box which is seen when you choose File ➤ Save or File ➤ Save As. When the Save Version comments box appears, type your notes about this particular version you are saving.

If you have saved multiple versions of a document, you will see a listing of the date and time these versions were saved in the Versions dialog box accessed from the File menu. In this dialog box, you can open a specific version, delete previous versions, and review version comments. You can also check the *Automatically save a version on close* option so that whenever you close the file, Word creates a new version automatically.

Saving Your Work Automatically

The AutoRecover command tells Word to automatically save your work at specific intervals. AutoRecover does not make a copy of your file that you can see on the disk. Rather, at regular intervals, Word automatically saves a special copy to be used in case of an emergency. If your computer crashes and doesn't allow you to properly exit Word, the last saved versions of any documents that were open and being automatically saved will be "recovered" when you restart Word after restarting the computer.

Keeping an automatic save interval set is good protection for your work. You can set the automatic save interval (the number of minutes between saves) by choosing Tools ➤ Options, and clicking on the Save tab. The default setting for AutoRecover is every 10 minutes. To set a different interval for the automatic save, follow these steps:

1. Choose Tools ➤ Options, and click on the Save tab. You'll see the page shown in Figure 10.4. Notice the Save AutoRecover Info Every checkbox at the bottom of the list of Save Options.
2. Click on the spinner buttons next to the current interval to increase or decrease the number of minutes between automatic saves. If you think you need more protection than the default of every 10 minutes, set a more frequent interval. On the other hand, for large documents, frequent AutoRecover interruptions can be time-consuming, so you may want to set a less frequent interval.
3. Click on OK to close the Options dialog box and save your changes.

FIGURE 10.4

Setting an AutoRecover interval is important for those times when the computer shuts down or locks up, and you cannot save your document.

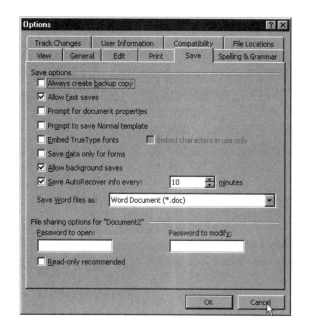

PART

II

Communicating with Word

Recovering an Automatically Saved File

If you set an interval for the automatic save, Word will save your document for you according to this interval. If your computer shuts down, you can recover the Auto-Recover version. When you restart your computer and start a new Word session, the last automatically saved version will immediately be recovered. There is no special command to issue

Now, take a look at the recovered document and see how current you think it is. You, of course, should have been saving all along (with File ➤ Save, the Save button on the toolbar, or Ctrl+S), and your own saved version should be very current. If you think that your own saved version is more current than Word's automatically saved version, choose File ➤ Save As to save Word's "recovered" file under another name (to keep it just in case). Then, choose File ➤ Open to choose the last version of the file you saved.

WARNING

If you exit Word or close your file, and you forget to save your document, you cannot recover the automatically saved version. Word keeps this special saved version only if you must reboot or restart the computer and you are not able to exit Word using the normal method of File ➤ Exit. If you exited or closed normally, Word throws away the automatically saved version.

MASTERING TROUBLESHOOTING

Last Resort for Saving Changes if Word Will Not Let You Save

Word has been known—when working with very large documents that contain numerous objects like pictures and drawings—to refuse to save your document, citing insufficient disk space even though there is plenty. Although this does not happen often, when it happens to you after you worked for over an hour without saving a copy of your document, you will care that it decided to happen *now*.

If you close a document without saving your changes (because Word won't let you), you will lose your changes. A last resort is to do the one thing that everyone has always told you not to do—turn your machine off without shutting down!

Although this is not a recommended habit to get into, in this case it simulates Word, or your computer, crashing. Word won't get a chance to delete the AutoSave files. If you turn your computer back on and launch Word, it will find the files still on the hard drive and attempt to open them up and ask you if you want to recover them.

Remember that these files are not the ones you were working on, but a second copy Word was saving on its own in case the computer crashed before you could save your files. This means that although you were unable to save your copy of the document, Word may have been able to save its AutoSave copy. While you may not be able to recover all of your changes, you should have the changes up until the last time Word did an AutoSave.

Closing a File

When you have finished working with your document and want to remove it from the screen, you can close the document by selecting File ➢ Close. If you have not performed a recent save, the message box shown below will appear, asking if you wish to save your work:

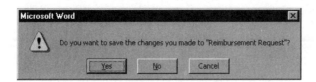

This prompt is a built-in safeguard, which allows you to perform a last-minute save before closing the document.

WARNING

If you save and close a document residing on a floppy disk, make sure that you allow Word to fully close the document before pulling the diskette from the floppy disk drive. Files can become corrupted and unreadable if Word does not fully close the document before the diskette is removed.

Opening Saved Files

You can open a saved file in Word directly from the Desktop or from within Word. You can also tell Word what information to display in the list of saved files.

Word's shortcuts let you open your most recently used files from the File menu or store frequently used files in a Favorites folder. You can easily open multiple documents at once and switch between them.

Opening a Saved File from the Desktop

You can open a document from the Windows 95 Desktop, whether Word is launched or not. The Documents folder, activated from the Start menu, lists the last 15 documents you saved. If you work fairly exclusively with Word, you will see the last 15 files you were working on listed there (as compared with Word's File menu, which lists between 4 and 9 of the most recently used files).

TIP

The list in the Documents folder can include saved filenames from all of your programs—Excel, PowerPoint, Access, and so on—as well as Word. When you click on a file in this list, the program that was used to create that document launches with the document in tow.

Follow these steps to open a document from the Desktop:

1. Click on the Start button on the Taskbar.
2. Choose the Documents option on the Start menu. The last 15 documents that you created, saved, or just opened will be listed.
3. Click once on the document file you wish to be loaded into memory.

Note that you cannot load multiple files at the same time. However, you can click on the Start button and choose the Documents option again to continue to load more document files into memory.

PART

II

Communicating with Word

Opening a Saved File within Word

Within Word, you can see a list of your files on disk and select the files you wish to load into memory: Choose File ➤ Open, or press Ctrl+O, or click on the Open button on the Standard toolbar. The Open dialog box will appear. In it, Word shows you the names of files you have stored, listed in alphabetical order (see Figure 10.5). Word documents have a blue letter W next to them.

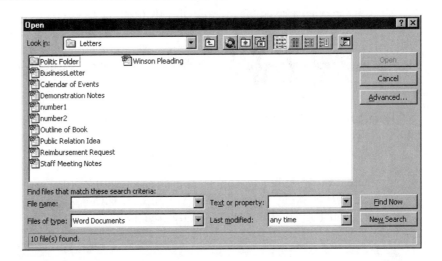

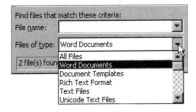

By default, the file list shows only Word files, but you can choose to see files of a different type. At the bottom of the Open dialog box, click on the drop-down arrow next to the Files of Type box. From the list that appears, choose another file type (the All Files option shows every file in your folder, even if the file is a proprietary one that only Word understands).

After you select a different file type, the file list will show the files of this type.

Next, double-click on the name of the file you wish to open. Alternatively, click once on the filename and then click on the Open button on the right side of the dialog box. Word will open the file and place you in the Word typing area on the first page of the document. Press Shift+F5 to return to the location where you were editing or typing when you last saved the file

When you open a file, Word places the insertion point at the top of the file and not at the spot where you last typed or edited. Press Shift+F5 (GoBack) to return to the location of your last edit. While working in a document, you can repeatedly press Shift+F5 and cycle through the three most recent edits performed on the document.

Displaying and Sorting File Details

In the Open and Save As dialog boxes, you can tell Word to show details about the files in your file list and rearrange their sort order. For example, in addition to their full filenames, you may want to see when your files were created or how large your files are. You may also want to sort your file list by date from the oldest files to the most recent, or vice versa.

At the top right corner of the Open dialog box, you'll see a number of buttons. Some of these buttons control how the files in the list will be displayed. Place the mouse over the buttons and read the ScreenTips until you find the button called Details. Click on the Details button. The file list area will change to display columns with the headings Name, Size, Type, and Modified, as shown in Figure 10.6. When you click on a particular column heading, the list of files is sorted in ascending order according to the column heading. Click the column heading again and the files are sorted in descending order.

To widen a column, place the mouse at the top of the column, at the divider line between the column heading names. When the mouse turns into a small black cross, double-click. The column will automatically adjust to fit the widest entry.

You can choose a sorting order for your file list as follows:

- Click on the Name column heading to sort by filenames.
- Click on the Size column heading to sort by file sizes.
- Click on the Type column heading to sort by file types.
- Click on the Modified column heading to sort files by the dates the files were modified.

You can toggle between ascending and descending order for each sort category by clicking on the column heading again.

PART

II

Communicating with
Word

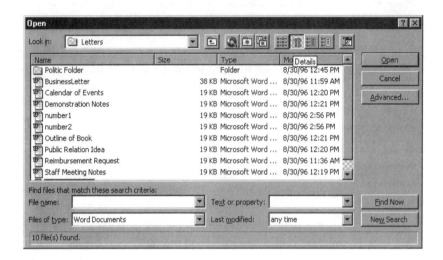

Selecting from the List of Recently Used Files

At the bottom of the File menu, Word displays, by default, the names of the last four to nine files that were opened. You can increase or decrease the number of documents listed on the File menu by choosing Tools ➤ Options, and clicking on the General tab. Click on the spinner button next to the Recently Used File List number to change the number of files you wish to be shown on the File menu's list. You can choose to display up to nine recently used file names.

Finding Files

When you cannot remember the exact name of a file, but you remember a few words that may be in the filename, use the Find Now button in the Open dialog box. Word will search through the list of files in the current folder for your particular file.

One of the best aspects of the Find Now command is that you can enter any amount of characters from the filename that you want to find. For example, you can type the letters **att** to find a file that has a full name of Political Event Attendance List. Word will locate this file, even though the letters you entered are in the word *Attendance*, the third word in the filename.

Follow these steps to find files:

1. Choose File ➤ Open to see a list of your files.

2. In the File Name text box at the bottom of the screen, type in any amount of characters you remember in the name. You can type uppercase or lowercase characters (the search is not case sensitive).

3. Press the Enter key, or click on the Find Now button in the lower right corner of the dialog box. Word will display a list of files matching the characters you typed (if any matches were found), as shown in Figure 10.7.

4. Once you have located your file, double-click on the filename, or click once and then click on the Open button.

5. To clear the list, click on the New Search button below the Find Now button in the Open dialog box. The dialog box will list all the files again.

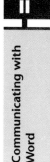

FIGURE 10.7

You can type in some of the characters in a filename to have Word search for all files that have those characters in it.

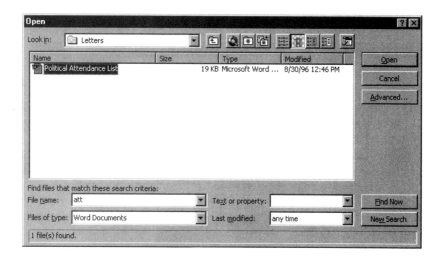

Word remembers the searches that you perform in the Open dialog box (File ➤ Open). When you want to perform the same search again, instead of typing in your filename characters, click the drop-down list arrow next to the File Name text box and select the search you performed previously.

Working with Favorites

You can place shortcuts to documents or folders that you use over and over into a Favorites folder. The Favorites folder eliminates the chore of searching among hundreds of files for your most frequently used Word documents. You set up this folder using the shortcut feature in Windows 95.

Advanced Find Options

While the bottom of the File Open dialog box provides search capabilities sufficient for a local search within the current folder, the Advanced Find dialog box contains very powerful options that allow you to search entire drives, not just a single folder.

In the Define More Criteria area of the dialog box, choose a property, a condition, and a value for the condition to form a criteria statement; then, click on Add to List to include the criteria with your current search.

You can also specify where you want Word to search by entering a location into the Look In list box. If you want to search the subfolders of the location you specified in the Look In list box, check the Search Subfolders checkbox.

You will also want to decide whether you want Word to check for all word forms or be case sensitive. The checkboxes for these options are directly below the list of criteria for your current search. If you choose to Match All Word Forms, Word will look for all the forms of the word within the document; for example, if you specify the word *write* Word will look for *written, wrote, writes,* and so on. If you

choose Match Case, Word will look for only those words that match the case of the word exactly as you typed it; for example, if you are searching for *write,* then *Write* will not be found.

To perform your search, click on the Find Now button. This will return you to the Open dialog box as Word searches for your request. The Find Now button in the Open dialog box changes to a Stop button while it searches.

If you chose to search subfolders and the search is successful, you will see cascading folders to show which files whose names or text match your search criteria. You can now choose which file it is that you want to open.

One quick hint here: once you have the initial Advanced Find criteria set, including whether you want to search subfolders, you can modify the options at the bottom of the Open dialog box while still retaining the advanced criteria. For example, if you click on Search Subfolders in the Advanced Find dialog box, and then return to the Open dialog box, all of your searches will include subfolders until you say otherwise by clicking on New Search.

Continued

◀ MASTERING THE OPPORTUNITIES CONTINUED

Advanced Find

Find files that match these criteria

File name **includes** ord.
Files of type **is** Word Documents.
Contents **includes the words** write.

☐ Match all word forms   [Delete]   [New Search]
☑ Match case

Define more criteria

                                            [Add to List]
⦿ And   Property: Condition: Value:
○ Or   [Contents   ▾] [includes words ▾] [   ]

Look in: [C:\   ▾]   ☑ Search subfolders

[Find Now]   [Cancel]   [Save Search...]   [Open Search...]

The Favorites buttons are at the top of the Open dialog box. The Add to Favorites button allows you to add selected files to the Favorites folder, and the Look in Favorites button allows you to see what is in the Favorites folder.

▼ TIP

If you want to place multiple folders in your Favorites folder, select them all at once by Shift+clicking, then click on Add to Favorites. All of the folder shortcuts will be listed in the Favorites folder.

You will want to store the names of files you use frequently in the Favorites folder. This is the place to keep minutes that are revised each month or weekly reports in which a few items change from one week to the next.

To add documents to the Favorites folder, follow these steps:

1. Choose File ➤ Open.

2. Select the files you wish to place in your Favorites folder. To select multiple, non-contiguous files, hold down the Ctrl key and then click on each filename. To select a contiguous group of files, click once on the first file, hold down the Shift key, and click once on the last file.

3. Click on the Add to Favorites button at the top of the dialog box.

4. When the submenu appears, click on the second option, Add Selected Items to Favorites.

5. Click on the Look in Favorites button (to the left of the Add to Favorites button). You will see the names of the files and folders in the Favorites folder, as shown in Figure 10.8.

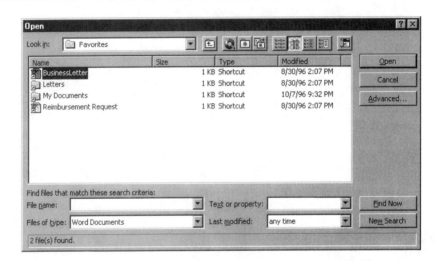

 TIP

From the list of the Favorites folder files, you can click on the Look in Favorites button (it will now be called the Return To button) to toggle back to the folder you were working in.

Look at the Word icon to the left of the name of one of the files you placed in your Favorites folder. You will see that the icon has a tiny, curved arrow at the lower left corner. This arrow means that you have created a *shortcut* to your original document.

What does that mean? Well, the shortcut for your document in the Favorites folder is merely a pointer to your original file—you are not working with two different copies of the same file. You can still open the document in your regular Open dialog box. If you make changes and save them, the changes will be there the next time you open the file, whether you open the file through the shortcut in the Favorites folder, or from the folder where the actual file is stored.

NOTE

Of course, you can set up your own folders to organize your Word documents. To learn how to create your own folders, see Chapter 4.

Deleting a Favorite Shortcut

When one of the files in your Favorites folder is no longer a "favorite," you can remove its shortcut. Choose File ➤ Open and click on the Look in Favorites button at the top of the dialog box. Click on the shortcut associated with your filename, and press the Delete key on the keyboard. Word will ask if you are sure that you want to remove this shortcut. Notice that the deleted shortcut file will be sent to the Recycle Bin. This means you can still retrieve it, as explained later in this chapter.

When you delete a shortcut associated with a filename, your original file is not deleted. Click on the Look in Favorites button (now the Return To button) to toggle back to your normal file list, and you will still see your original file.

If you delete the original file in your regular documents folder but leave the shortcut in the Favorites folder, the shortcut will no longer have a correct pointer to the original file. If you choose to open a shortcut file that points to a deleted or moved original file, Word searches but comes up empty-handed, telling you that it was unable to locate the file.

The Internet Button

You can start Internet Explorer by selecting the Search the Web button at the top of the Open dialog box. The Internet Explorer launches. If you are on a network connected to the Internet, Microsoft's home page is contacted. If you are connected via a dial-up, you will be asked for your password. Once you fill it in, you'll be connected with Microsoft's home page.

Opening Multiple Files

You can open multiple files into memory one at a time, by continuing to choose File ➤ Open and double-clicking on a different filename each time. However, there is another, easier way to open multiple files.

When you choose File ➤ Open, you can select contiguous (all together) and non-contiguous (in any order) file groups to open at the same time, as follows:

- To select a contiguous group of files, click once on the first file, hold down the Shift key, and click once on the last filename in the group.
- To select noncontiguous groups, hold down the Ctrl key and click once (don't double-click) on each file you wish to open.

PART

II

Communicating with Word

Figure 10.9 shows an example of multiple files selected in the Open dialog box.

FIGURE 10.9

You can select
multiple files
and open them
all at once.

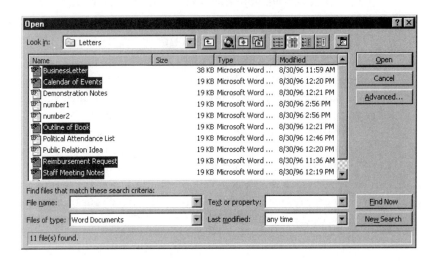

When you have selected the multiple files, click on the Open button on the right side of the Open dialog box. All of the files will open at one time. Click on the Window command on the menu bar to see a list of the different files open in memory.

The only limitation on how many files you can have open at the same time is the amount of memory your computer has available. Each program and document file open in memory takes up a different amount of memory. Word will alert you when it has run out of memory and ask you to close some of your files.

Switching between Multiple Open Files

If you have several files open at the same time, you will want to switch between them so that you can edit or read their contents. You can select a window from the Window menu's list of the files currently open in memory. Press the number associated with the file, or just click on it, to make it the active window.

A quicker way to cycle through each of your open files is to use the shortcut keyboard combination Ctrl+F6.

Closing Multiple Files

When you have a number of files open in memory, it can be tedious to close each one separately with the File ➢ Close option. Word has a hidden shortcut that you can use to close all files open in memory. Just like with the regular File ➢ Close command, Word will ask you if you need to save any files that you may have forgotten to save.

When you have multiple files open in memory, you can easily copy text from one open document to another. Switch to the document that has the information you want to copy. Select the text to be copied and press Ctrl+C. Switch to the other document that should receive the copy. Position the insertion point where the copy should be inserted and press Ctrl+V.

This hidden shortcut requires that you use the mouse. It does not work with the keyboard method of closing files. Follow these steps to close all open files:

1. Hold down the Shift key.
2. With the Shift key still down, click the mouse on the File menu in the menu bar. The Close option is no longer listed. Instead, a new option, Close All, is displayed.
3. Choose Close All, and Word will automatically close the files. If any file has been changed but not saved when you issue this command, Word will give you a chance to save it before closing that file.

When all the files are closed, you will see the blank Word screen. From there, you can open a new or existing file or exit Word.

Renaming a File

If you do not like the name you designated for a document and have come up with a better name for it, you can rename the file without making a copy of the document.

First, Choose File ➤ Open to see the list of filenames in the Open dialog box. Click once on the name of the file you wish to rename to select it. Pause, and then click once again. Do not perform a rapid double-click, as this would open the file into memory.

After you have clicked twice, an outline box will appear around the entire filename, and the name will be selected. You can type over the entire selected name with a new name, or select individual characters and change them to something new. For example, Figure 10.10 shows a file being renamed. In this example, the word *Idea* is selected so that it can be typed over.

Press the Enter key after you have renamed the document. The screen will flash and redisplay with the new name. If you do not want to open the file, you can click on the Cancel button. The file will maintain its new name.

You can also rename a file by right-clicking the mouse on the filename and choosing Rename from the pop-up shortcut menu.

FIGURE 10.10

Word makes it easy to rename a file. In the Open dialog box, click twice on the file-name, pausing between clicks. An outline box appears around the filename to let you change the name.

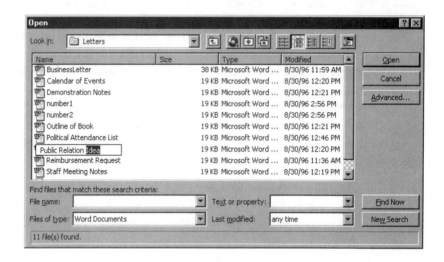

Making Backup Copies Automatically

You can customize Word so that you get an automatic backup of every document you create. Then, every time *you* save your work (not each time Word performs an automatic save), Word will make another copy of your document. The automatic backup feature is the ultimate in word processing insurance, but it is also very costly in disk space.

If you choose to have backup copies created for every document you save, your hard disk storage space will fill up more quickly than if you weren't using this feature—so use the backup feature judiciously. If you are working on an extremely important document and you must protect yourself at all costs, turn on the automatic backup feature. When you working with less critical documents, make sure automatic backup is turned off. Remember, you must continuously save your document as you are working on it, if you want the automatic backup to reflect the most current edits.

Turning on Automatic Backup

Follow these steps to set the automatic backup feature:

1. Choose Tools ➤ Options, and click on the Save tab.
2. Click on the first checkbox option, Always Create Backup Copy. Word will remove the check next to Allow Fast Saves, because the backup save requires a complete save.
3. Click on OK. You will be returned to your document area.

4. You must close Word and restart the program to activate the new setting for the automatic backup option. If you don't need a backup right after you have set the option, you can continue to work in Word. The next time you start the Word program, the automatic backup option will be on.

With the backup option set, whenever you create and save any document, a copy of your work will be made. The filename for this copy will have the words *Backup of* in front of it. For example, the copy of a file named REPORT97 will be named Backup of REPORT97. As long as the backup option is set, Word will duplicate each of the documents you save.

The extension for Word's backup files is .wbk—an extension you may or may not see in the file list, depending on your Windows settings.

Opening a Backup Copy

After you have turned on the automatic backup feature as described in the previous section, you can open (retrieve) the backup copies Word has made of your documents. To see these files in the Open dialog box, follow these steps:

1. Choose File ➤ Open.

2. In the File Name text box, type **Backup of**.

3. At the bottom of the Open dialog box, select All Files in the File Name list box and press Enter.

Word will now list the names of all of your backup files in the current folder, as shown in Figure 10.11. Notice the special icon to the left of the filename designating that this is a backup copy of the original file.

TIP

You can also see the backup files without changing to the All Files type. Let the Files of Type option remain Word Documents. In the File Name text area, type ***.wbk** and press Enter. Word will show you all of the backup files.

Deleting Files

Files that have served their purpose and no longer need to be stored should be deleted so that you can maintain adequate disk space, and because extraneous files obscure the list of current and relevant files.

To delete a file from the Open dialog box file list, click once on the file to be deleted. Press the Delete key on your keyboard, or click the right (secondary) mouse button and choose the Delete command from the shortcut menu (you can click on the

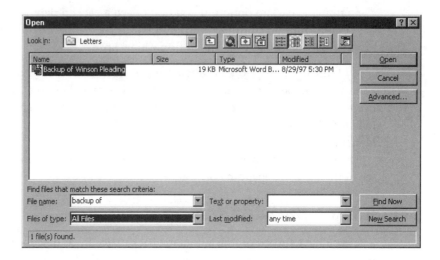

word Delete with either mouse button). You will see the Confirm File Delete message box. Click the on Yes button to send the deleted file to the Recycle Bin.

 TIP

If you are absolutely sure that you will never need a file again, you can bypass the Recycle Bin option when you delete a file from the Open dialog box. When you select a file(s) to be deleted, hold down the Shift key and then press the Delete key. Word will ask you if you want to truly delete the file(s)—not whether you want the file(s) sent to the Recycle Bin.

Deleting Multiple Files

You can select multiple files for deletion in the Open dialog box. Use the Windows Shift+click or Ctrl+click techniques. As when you choose multiple files to open, the Shift+click method selects contiguous files (multiple files in a row), and Ctrl+clicking selects noncontiguous files (multiple files not in a row). To deselect individual files in the noncontiguous list, hold down Ctrl and click on the filenames again.

After you have selected the multiple files, press the Delete key on the keyboard or pause the mouse over any selected file and right-click. Choose the Delete command from the shortcut menu. After you choose Delete, the Confirm File Delete message box appears, just as it does for single files.

Restoring Deleted Files

If you wish to restore a file that was deleted and sent to the Recycle Bin, you must activate the Recycle Bin. Follow these steps to restore deleted files:

1. Double-click on the Recycle Bin icon on the Desktop to open the Recycle Bin window. This window lists the names of the files that were sent to the Recycle Bin.
2. To rearrange this list, click on the column headings by which you wish to sort the files (Name, Original Location, Date Deleted, Type, or Size).
3. Click on the name of the file to be restored to select it and choose File ➤ Restore. You can also right-click on the filename and choose Restore from the shortcut menu shown in Figure 10.12. The name will disappear from the Recycle Bin list.
4. Repeat step 3 for each file you want to restore.
5. Close the Recycle Bin window. The restored files will once again be listed in Word's Open dialog box.

PART

II

Communicating with Word

The Recycle Bin shows the list of deleted files. Use the Restore command to "undelete" files.

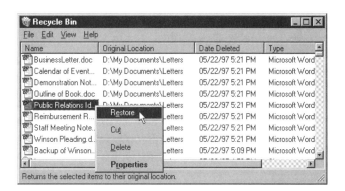

NOTE

The Recycle Bin retains all of the files you have deleted in each application, even after you turn off the computer. You must occasionally empty (clean out) the Recycle Bin, because the deleted files take up hard disk space.

Combining Files Using the Insert Command

You can combine files by inserting one into another. For example, you may have a set of paragraphs that you usually need to insert into the middle of a monthly report. If you have typed these paragraphs and saved them by themselves in a separate file, you can insert this file into your report. You may also need to combine files when others have worked independently on sections of a report, and you need to combine their sections with yours.

When you choose Insert ➤ File to combine multiple files, the inserted file is actually a copy of the file's contents. You are not removing any files from the disk.

You can also use the Insert ➤ File command to insert just a part of another Word document. First you must select the part and give it a bookmark name in Word (Insert ➤ Bookmark).

Follow these steps to combine files:

1. Make sure you have the original document on the screen. This will be the main document into which other documents will be inserted.
2. Position the insertion point at the exact location where you want the other file to be inserted.
3. Choose Insert ➤ File. The Insert File dialog box appears.
4. In the Range text area, you can type in a bookmark to insert the text specified by the bookmark or range name.
5. In the File Name text area, type the name of the file to be inserted and click on OK, or double-click on the filename that you see in the list of files. The entire new file or the bookmarked section of the file is inserted into the document.
6. Tap the PgUp key to see all of the inserted text.

TIP

The AutoText feature in Word allows you store frequently used paragraphs, pages, tables, graphics, and clip art. If you need to insert the same text on a routine basis, consider using this feature, which is described in Chapter 12.

Printing Your Documents

Word lets you see on screen how your printed document will look. When you're ready to print to the printer, you can display the Print dialog box and choose a different printer, select specific pages to print, and print multiple copies. If necessary, you can usually cancel a print job that is in progress.

Printing to the Screen

Before printing your document to the printer, you may want to preview it with Word's Print Preview feature. Choose File ➤ Print Preview or click on the Print Preview button on the Standard toolbar (the button to the right of the printer button) to see a representation of how your document will print. Print Preview is another view within Word, just like the Page Layout, Normal, and Outline views.

Although you are not required to view your document in Print Preview before actually printing your work, it can be a time and paper saver. You can see how the document will print before you expend time, effort, and paper on a print job that turns out to have problems, such as blank pages or too much spacing between some paragraphs. You can edit the document or print it directly from the Print Preview screen, or return to another view before printing. See Chapter 9 for more information about working in Print Preview.

Printing to a Printer

The successful printing of your document to a printer requires that your printer(s) are correctly installed.

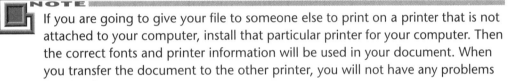

NOTE
If you are going to give your file to someone else to print on a printer that is not attached to your computer, install that particular printer for your computer. Then the correct fonts and printer information will be used in your document. When you transfer the document to the other printer, you will not have any problems printing it.

To print to the printer, use one of these methods:

- Choose File ➤ Print.
- Click on the Print button on the Standard toolbar.
- Press the keyboard shortcut Ctrl+P.
- From the Open dialog box, click the right mouse button on the file and select Print from the shortcut menu.

Both the menu (File ➤ Print) and the shortcut (Ctrl+P) bring up the Print dialog box, shown in Figure 10.13. Here you can specify the number of copies and tell Word that you want to print just specific pages. Clicking on the Print button on the Standard toolbar or printing a file from the Open dialog box, however, sends one copy of your entire document to the printer immediately, according to the default settings, without showing the Print dialog box.

Selecting a Different Printer

If you use only one printer, it is not necessary to choose a printer each time you start Word. But if you can use multiple printers (such as different network printers), you must first select your printer from the Print dialog box. Click the drop-down list arrow next to the Name text box and choose the name of another printer. When you click on OK, the document will print to the selected printer.

FIGURE 10.13

The Print dialog box allows you to specify printing parameters.

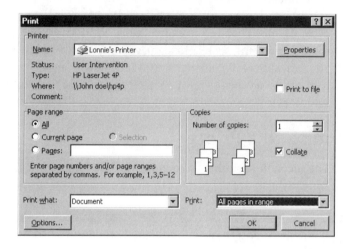

Printing All Pages

The default page range setting is to print all pages in the document. This option is immediately activated when you click on the Print button on the Standard toolbar. When you choose File ➢ Print or press Ctrl+P, the Print dialog box allows you to see the actual setting and change it to current page or multiple pages.

Printing Selected Pages

You may need to reprint one page or print a range of pages rather than the whole document. Word gives you the ability to print multiple pages, single pages, a range of pages, or pages you have selected with the mouse.

In the Page Range area of the Print dialog box, All is selected by default. Word will print all of the pages of your document unless you specify one of the other options.

To print the current page, make sure your insertion point is on the page you want to print. For example, if you only want to reprint page 16, click the mouse anywhere on page 16 before you choose File ➢ Print. In the Print dialog box, click on the radio button next to Current Page to tell Word that only the page that has the insertion point should be printed. Then click OK. Only page 16 will be printed.

To print multiple selected pages, click on the radio button next to the Pages option and type in the page range you wish to print. Noncontiguous pages should be separated by commas (for example, 4,11,13,16). A range of pages is designated with a dash (for example, 8-14). You can mix and match multiple pages with a range of pages. For example, you can specify that Word print pages 5, 8, 12-16.

Sometimes, you may want to print a selection, such as text that starts in the middle of page 5 and continues three-quarters of the way through page 7. Drag the mouse and select these pages and then choose File ➢ Print. Click on the radio button next to the Selection option. Click on OK to print just your selection.

Printing and Collating Multiple Copies

To the right of the Page Range option in the Print dialog box is an option for printing multiple copies of your documents. There is no limit to the number of printed copies that can be produced. You can use this option whether you are printing all pages, selected pages, or page ranges.

By default, Word checks the Collate option. This option tells Word to print all the pages in one copy of a document before printing the pages in the next copy. For example, if you choose to print three copies of a five-page report, Word prints all five pages, then prints all five pages again, and then prints all five pages of the final copy. If the Collate option is not on, Word would print three copies of page one and then three copies of page two, and so on.

Printing Objects Other than Documents

In the Print What drop-down list box, you can specify objects other than documents to print. You can also print the following:

- Document properties
- Comments
- Styles
- AutoText entries
- Key assignments

The most common objects to print are the document properties, comments, and AutoText entries.

Document properties are the information contained in the categories of the tab off of the File menu. The selected fields that are printed from these document categories are Filename, Directory, Template, Title, Subject, Author, Keywords, Comments, Creation Date, Change Number, Last Saved On, Last Saved By, Total Editing Time, Last Printed On, and As of Last Complete Printing: Number of Pages, Number of Words, Number of Characters.

Because it is hard to read all of the comments placed into a document, the ability to print all the comments in a document is a plus. The page number, the initials of the Reviewer, and the comment itself print one after another down tne page.

If you have stored an unlimited number of AutoText entries, trying to remember what you have stored can be a chore. Thus, you may want to print the list of AutoText entries. The entries print in alphabetical order; the unique identifying name is displayed first, followed by the entry itself.

Printing Odd or Even Pages

In the Print dialog box, you can also designate the printing of Odd or Even pages for the range of pages specified to be printed. For example, if you specified printing pages 4–6 out of a 10-page document, you can specify whether all of these pages should print or whether odd or even pages of this range should print.

Printing to a File

When you wish to print a document using another printer that is not connected to your computer or network, use the Print to File option on the Print dialog box. Word will save the file in the appropriate printer language of the printer you specify in the Print to File name box. Word users who send their files to a service bureau for special typesetting might save the file using a Postscript printer even though that printer is not at their computer. When the service bureau gets the file, they can print the file using a Postscript printer. Word does not have to be installed in order to print the file.

To print to a file, choose File ➢ Print. When the Print dialog box appears, check the Print to File box on the right side of the dialog box. In the Name box, choose the printer that will be used to print the document (this doesn't have to be the printer that is currently connected to the computer), then click OK. In the Print to File dialog box, specify a name for the file in the File Name text box at the bottom, then click OK. This file can now be printed with the printer name you used in the Print to File name box. The file is saved with a .prn file extension.

Printing from Multiple Trays

If you have a printer that supports dual printing trays Word has options that allow you to specify which tray to use for printing letterhead and second sheets. Follow these steps to designate your printing trays:

1. Make sure that the printer Name in the Print dialog box is set to the printer that supports dual trays; otherwise, you will not see the correct settings for your printer. For example, if you have two printers you can print to, change to the one with multiple trays before specifying changes in the Paper Source tab of the Page Setup dialog box.
2. Choose File ➢ Page Setup, and click on the Paper Source tab (shown in Figure 10.14). This page lists options for the sources of First Page and Other Pages.
3. Select which tray will hold your First Page letterhead.
4. For Other Pages, select the appropriate tray (usually Lower Tray).
5. Click on OK.

FIGURE 10.14

Word allows you to use printers with multiple paper trays for letter-head and second sheets.

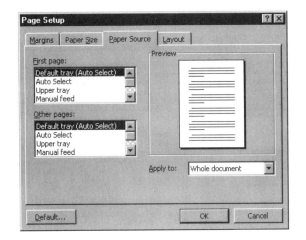

Stopping the Printer

There will be occasions when you may need to stop a print run before it is completed. If the print run is between one and five pages, don't bother trying to stop the printer, particularly if it is a laser printer. By the time you reach the option that tells the computer to stop sending the pages to the printer, the entire print job will already have been sent.

Stopping the printer requires that you stop the computer from sending the data to the printer. When you issue a print job, Word begins to send the pages of your document to the printer's buffer (memory area). On the right side of the Status bar, you can see a small printer icon flashing the pages that are being sent. Immediately begin double-clicking this printer icon to cancel the current print job. The printer may continue to print a few more pages, but you will have effectively stopped the computer from sending additional pages.

WARNING

It is not a good idea to turn off the printer in the middle of printing, because doing this can cause paper jams.

Canceling Printing from Windows

When the printer is printing, you will see a printer icon on the Taskbar, next to the time (not flashing). This icon means that the printer has the job and is now getting ready to print.

PART

II

Communicating with Word

Double-click on the printer icon on the Taskbar, and the Print window will appear with the name of your job in the window, as shown below. If your document job name does not appear, it means that the printer has already sent the entire document through its memory to the printer. You cannot cancel the job.

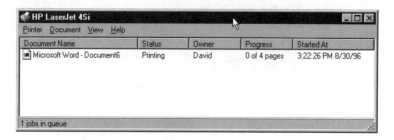

If you see the name of your job, click on that name and choose Document ➤ Cancel Printing from the Print menu bar. In a few seconds, the printer will begin deleting the print job (a few pages left in the print buffer will still print).

Chapter

11

Special Formats and Styles

Chapter 11

Special Formats and Styles

When word processing software first started to become widely available, users were limited to basic fonts, which could not be scaled to various sizes and could only represent basic alphanumeric characters. Even the simplest desktop publishing work needed to be sent out to a printer for the professionals to handle from start to finish.

Today, with Microsoft Word, you can generate most of your desktop publishing originals right from your desktop. Although most users do not need the full arsenal of Word publishing tools, you will find some special formatting layouts and tools extremely helpful.

WARNING

When you're using the formatting features of Word, it is very easy to get carried away with all of the options. Try to remember while you are formatting your document that more is not always better. Definitely use the tools, just not all at one time.

Adding Borders and Shading

One basic yet effective formatting option in Word is the ability to apply borders and shading to parts of your document. Borders and shading are generally used in conjunction with either paragraphs or tables; but new in Word 97 is the page border feature—a long awaited addition to the borders menu. Other objects in Word, such as frames and pictures, can also have formatted borders.

Here are the general steps to apply border formatting:

1. Click into the paragraph or onto the page to receive the borders.
2. Choose Format ➢ Borders and Shading from the menu bar. The dialog box shown in Figure 11.1 will appear. This dialog box has three tabs: Borders, Page Border, and Shading.
3. Click on a tab and choose the Border style you prefer.
4. Click on OK.

FIGURE 11.1

The Borders and Shading dialog box is displayed by choosing Format ➢ Borders and Shading.

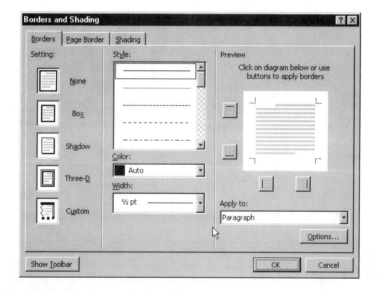

Paragraph and Table Borders

Word supplies some preset paragraph and table border options. These border options depend on what you selected before accessing the Borders and Shading dialog box. If the insertion point is within a paragraph, or multiple paragraphs are selected, the border options that appear in the Setting area of the dialog box will be None, Box, Shadow, Three-D, and Custom. If the insertion point is in a cell of a table, or multiple cells are selected, the options will be None, Box, All, Grid, and Custom.

Figure 11.2 shows both a paragraph formatted with the 3-D border option, and a table formatted with the Grid option.

FIGURE 11.2

A paragraph and table formatted with different Border options

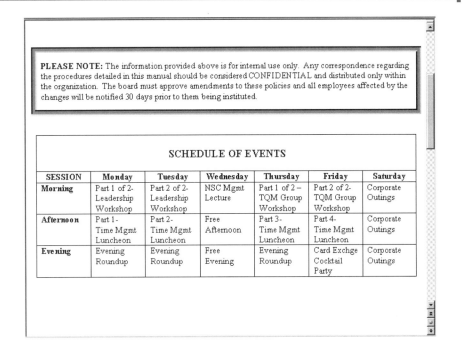

PLEASE NOTE: The information provided above is for internal use only. Any correspondence regarding the procedures detailed in this manual should be considered CONFIDENTIAL and distributed only within the organization. The board must approve amendments to these policies and all employees affected by the changes will be notified 30 days prior to them being instituted.

SCHEDULE OF EVENTS

SESSION	Monday	Tuesday	Wednesday	Thursday	Friday	Saturday
Morning	Part 1 of 2- Leadership Workshop	Part 2 of 2- Leadership Workshop	NSC Mgmt Lecture	Part 1 of 2 – TQM Group Workshop	Part 2 of 2- TQM Group Workshop	Corporate Outings
Afternoon	Part 1- Time Mgmt Luncheon	Part 2- Time Mgmt Luncheon	Free Afternoon	Part 3- Time Mgmt Luncheon	Part 4- Time Mgmt Luncheon	Corporate Outings
Evening	Evening Roundup	Evening Roundup	Free Evening	Evening Roundup	Card Exchge Cocktail Party	Corporate Outings

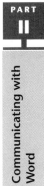

When you're formatting borders, however, you do not need to restrict yourself to the preset border styles. The last style, Custom, works with the Border preview shown on the right side of the dialog box. You can click on the buttons around the Preview area to turn on and off the different border lines. When you use the buttons around the Preview area, the Custom button at the bottom of the Setting area is selected.

Customizing Table Borders

Tables created in Word 97 are automatically formatted with $\frac{1}{2}$-point border grid lines throughout the table (these border lines will be printed). The steps below show how to format the table shown in Figure 11.3. To customize the borders so that lines show only between the columns, we used use the Custom border feature. (This example demonstrates how borders can be used to enhance a table; creating tables in Word is discussed later in this chapter.)

1. Insert a table into your document by selecting Table ➤ Insert Table.
2. Change the Number of Columns to 5 and the Number of Rows to 3. Then choose OK.
3. Grid lines are automatically applied to the Table.
4. Choose Format ➤ Borders and Shading.
5. In the Borders Preview section of the Borders and Shading dialog box, click each of the three horizontal line buttons on the left side of the Preview area. The horizontal lines disappear from the preview sample.
6. Choose OK. Your table should look like the one shown in Figure 11.3.

FIGURE 11.3

Table formatted with the horizontal lines of the grid removed.

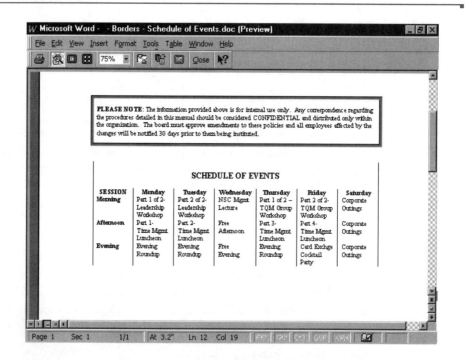

Formatting the borders of tables is a great way to reproduce the appearance of paper forms in Word. By selecting various groups of cells within a table and applying different borders, you can achieve quite effective results.

Removing Table Borders

If you prefer not to have any printed border lines in your table, remove them by selecting Format ➤ Borders and Shading from the menu bar. Make sure the Borders page is selected, click on the None box, and then click on OK at the bottom of the dialog box.

When you return to your table, there will only be the light gray lines showing you where the table's cell boundaries are. These lines do not print.

Page Borders

You can use the new page borders option to apply border lines around an entire page. The border settings are None, Box, Shadow, Three-D, and Custom. Page borders can be applied to:

- Whole Document
- This Section
- This Section - First Page Only
- This Section - All Except First Page

From a simple thin-line Box border style or to a dramatic thick-line Shadow border style, you can create interesting pages with very little effort.

To apply a page border to the whole document:

1. The insertion point can be on any page. Choose Format ➤ Borders and Shading from the menu bar.
2. Click on the Page Border tab at the top of the dialog box.
3. Choose from among the preset styles on the left.
4. Change the line style width.
5. Use the Preview area to see how you like the effect.
6. Click on OK when you have finished.

Figure 11.4 shows a page bordered by a Shadow style with a 6-point line style. As with a paragraph or a table, you can customize the page border lines so that the lines are applied only to the top, bottom, left, right, or any combination of these positions. Use the Preview buttons to isolate the border lines you wish to appear.

Art Borders

In addition to the preset styles available for page borders, you can also choose an art style border. Figure 11.5 shows the Page Border dialog box with a preview of an art deco border style. With the ability to chose from more than 160 different art styles that range from strawberry shortcakes to sophisticated beveled boxes, document creation has never been more exciting.

FIGURE 11.4

A Shadow style page border gets instant attention for your documents.

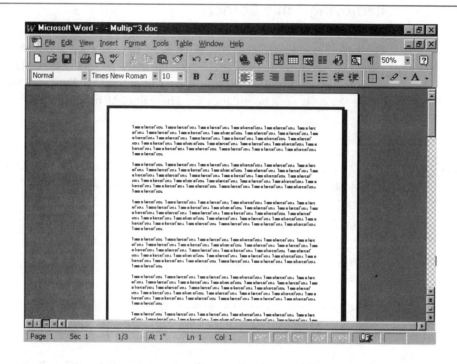

FIGURE 11.5

There is little excuse for boring documents using Word's new page border art styles.

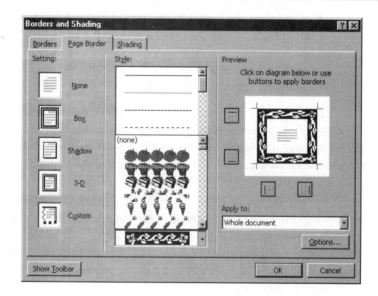

Shading Paragraphs

Another effective method of bringing attention to sections of your document is to format the interior of paragraphs or table selections with shading. Used in the right places, shading can help turn a bland document into a polished piece.

Select the paragraph or table cells you want to shade, and then choose Format ➤ Borders and Shading, and click on the Shading tab to see the options. The Shading tab of this dialog box is shown in Figure 11.6.

FIGURE 11.6

*The Shading
page of the
Borders and
Shading
dialog box*

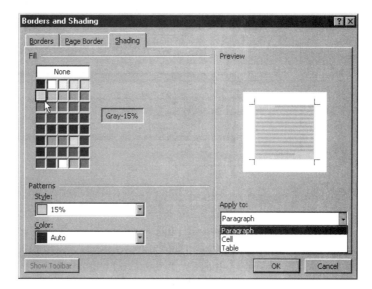

You can select from the palette of Fill options, which range from None through various percentages of gray and also colors. You can also choose patterns from the Patterns Style or Patterns Color list boxes at the bottom of the dialog box.

If you want to have the effect of reverse printing (white text on black background), select the Solid Pattern Style (100% shading). This is a helpful technique for bringing crucial text to the attention of a reader. Shading percents over 75% all result in this reversed print. Figure 11.7 shows examples of shading, including the Solid (100%) and 20% options and a table with shading and borders.

FIGURE 11.7

A few examples
of Word's
shading
formats

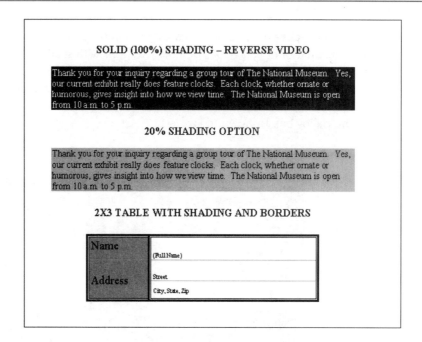

Using the Tables and Borders Toolbar

Working with a document that has multiple border and shading formats could require many trips to the menu and dialog box to get to your formatting options. An alternative is to use Word's Tables and Borders toolbar. Like the other toolbars, the Tables and Borders toolbar is available through the Toolbars dialog box (View ➤ Toolbars). You can toggle the display of the Tables and Borders toolbar (shown below) on and off, by clicking on the Tables and Borders button on the Standard toolbar.

Using the Tables and Borders toolbar, you can access just about all of the options in the Borders and Shading dialog box. (The exceptions are shadowed borders and the distance your borders are from the text.) There are additional features on the toolbar that allow you to create and manipulate free-form table design. These options will be covered later in this chapter.

TIP

If you only wish to add or change borders, click on the Outside Borders button on the Formatting toolbar

The buttons on the Tables and Borders toolbar allow you to do the following (from left to right):

- Draw a table
- Erase table lines
- Change the line style
- Change the line weight
- Draw a free-form border box using colors
- Place borders on selected objects (paragraphs, tables, cells)
- Apply a shading color
- Merge cells and split cells
- Align text in a cell (top, center, bottom)
- Distribute rows and columns evenly
- Format and change text direction
- Sort ascending or descending
- Automatically sum rows and columns of numbers

Placing Tables in Your Documents

Tables allow users to easily line up text or numbers, as well as emphasize information by applying border formats to the rows and columns. Word has an entire menu devoted to tables that offers many options for creating, formatting, and editing your tables.

Creating Simple Tables

To create a simple table, select Table ➤ Insert Table; the Insert Table dialog box will appear. Specify the number of columns and the number of rows you want in your table. (You can always add or delete rows or columns later.) Click on OK when you're done. The dialog box will close, and a table will be inserted into your document.

When your table is inserted, your insertion point will be in the top left cell of the table. Printable border lines appear around each cell of the table. If you start typing, information will go in that cell. To move from one cell to another, use the arrow keys, the Tab and Shift+Tab keys, or click the mouse in the cell you want to move to.

As an example, we will insert a table and enter some information into its cells. Follow these steps:

1. Start a new document and select Table ➤ Insert Table.
2. Specify 5 columns by 5 rows and click OK. Your table will be inserted into your document, as shown in Figure 11.8.

Communicating with Word

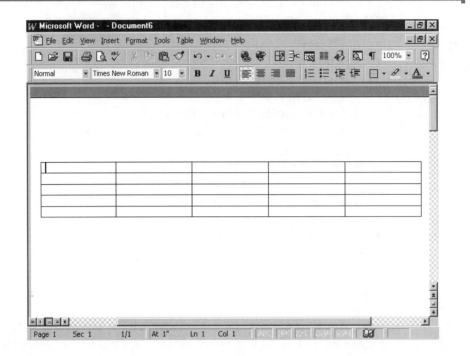

3. Starting in the top left cell, type the following words, following each with a press of the Tab key: **SALESPERSON**, **EAST**, **WEST**, **NORTH**, **SOUTH**. When you're done, your insertion point should be in the first column of the second row.

4. Type the following names into your table, following each with a press of the down arrow key: **Dann**, **Scheeler**, **Wixted**, **Wright**.

5. With your mouse, click in the second cell in the second column.

6. In the second through fifth rows of the second column, type the numbers **100**, **200**, **300**, **400**.

7. Place your mouse in the cell with "100" in it so the pointer turns into an I-beam. Then, click and drag your mouse to select the second through fifth cells of the second column.

8. Select Edit ➢ Copy, or right-click in your selection and select Copy from the shortcut menu. Place your insertion point in the second cell of the third column, and select Edit ➢ Paste Cells, or right-click and select Paste Cells from the shortcut menu.

9. Paste the copy again for the fourth and fifth columns by either choosing Paste Cells from the Edit menu, or using the right mouse button and choosing Paste Cells from the shortcut menu (shown in Figure 11.9).

TABLE 11.1: SELECTION AND MOVEMENT TECHNIQUES IN A TABLE (CONTINUED)

Action	Techniques
General movement	Use the arrow keys to move up, down, left, or right. If there is text in a cell, use the movement keys shown below.
Move to next cell	Tab key
Move to previous cell	Shift+Tab
Move to the end of the row	Alt+End
Move to the beginning of the row	Alt+Home
Move to the top of the column	Alt+Page Up
Move to the bottom of the column	Alt+Page Down
Move to the first cell in a table	Two shortcuts are required: Press Alt+Home to go to the beginning of the row. Then press Alt+PgUp to go to the top of the column. Your pointer will be in the first column, first row.
Move to the last cell in a table	Two shortcuts are required: Press Alt+End to go to the end of the row. Then Press Alt+PgDn to go to the bottom of the column. Your pointer will be in the last column, last row.
Tab within a table cell	Press Ctrl+Tab. (Pressing Tab moves you to the next cell.)
Set a decimal tab in a cell	Use the Tabs dialog box (Format ➤ Tabs) and set a decimal tab for the table column.

Sizing Your Tables

The data that you want to put into a table may not fit into the cell space provided. Your data may wrap around the cell if it is too long, or your table may look lopsided if there is not enough data to fill the space. To improve the appearance of your table, you can resize the width and the height of the cells.

Sizing Columns

One way to size table columns is to place the mouse pointer over the column divider line to the right of the column that you want to resize. The insertion point will change to a double-headed arrow. Click and drag to the left to decrease the column width, or click and drag to the right to increase the column width. If you double-click when the double-headed arrow appears, Word will automatically adjust the column width to accommodate the widest entry in the column.

To enter a precise column width, use the Cell Height and Width feature from the Table menu:

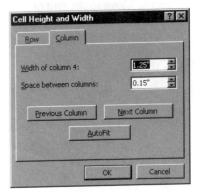

1. Click into the column you want to widen.
2. Select Table ➤ Cell Height and Width from the menu bar. The Cell Height and Width dialog box will appear.
3. Select the Column tab, and in the Width of Column # text area, type the width you want, or click on the spinner buttons to increase and/or decrease the column widths.
4. Click on the OK button.

To enter a precise column width for multiple columns, drag the mouse over the columns to be widened and then choose Tables ➤ Cell Height and Width, and click on the Column Tab. Set the precise width to change all the selected columns.

NOTE You can make all the columns evenly spaced by selecting the table (using one of the selection techniques in Table 11.1) and choosing Tables ➤ Cell Height and Width, and selecting the Column tab. Click the down spinner button next to Width of Column until the Auto option appears. All the columns will be evenly spaced.

Sizing Rows

You can now size the height of rows in Word—just as you can with a spreadsheet like Excel or Lotus. You no longer need to press the Enter key multiple times within a cell in order to enlarge it. Instead, you can drag the horizontal row line up or down to size a row.

To widen or shorten a row, place the mouse pointer over the border or grid line that separates one row from another. The insertion point will change to a double-headed arrow. Click and drag up to decrease the row height or drag down to increase the row height. If you don't like the results, press Ctrl+Z, or click the Undo button on the Standard toolbar.

> **NOTE**
>
> To make all rows in a table evenly spaced, select the rows, then choose Table ➤ Cell Height and Width and click on the Row tab. Click on the drop-down arrow next to Height of Rows, and choose Auto from the list.

Adding and Deleting Rows and Columns

Your initial estimate of the size of a table may not always be accurate. It's easy to add rows or columns as you need them or delete ones that you don't need.

Inserting Rows

When you reach the last cell in your table, press the Tab key. Word will automatically add another row. If you need to add a row somewhere in the middle of the table, it requires just a couple more steps.

To insert a row between other rows in a table, place your insertion point in the row that you want the new row to appear above and do any one of the following:

- Select Table ➤ Insert Rows. You new row will be inserted.
- Click on the Insert Rows button on the Standard Toolbar.
- Right-click the mouse and choose Insert ➤ Rows from the pop-up menu.

Deleting Rows

To delete a row in the table, place your insertion point in the row you want to delete and do any one of the following:

- Press Ctrl+X or click on the Cut button on the Standard toolbar.
- Select Table ➤ Delete Rows. If you change your mind, press Ctrl+Z or click on the Undo button on the Standard Toolbar.
- Right-click and choose Delete Cells from the menu. When the submenu appears, choose Delete Entire Row. If you select the entire row first instead of clicking in a cell, you will see the Delete Rows option right away in the pop-up menu.

Inserting Columns

Inserting and deleting columns is very similar to inserting and deleting rows. Columns are more easily inserted between other columns than at the end of the table. To insert a column between columns:

1. Select the entire column that you want the new column to appear to the left of.

PART

II

Communicating with Word

2. Choose Table ➤ Insert Columns or click on the Insert Columns button on the Standard toolbar. Note the menu item and the icon only appear if a column in a table is selected as shown in Figure 11.10.

To insert multiple columns, select the multiple columns, then choose Table ➤ Insert Columns, or click on the Insert Columns button on the Standard toolbar.

FIGURE 11.10

You must select a column first before you see the Insert Columns icon on the Standard toolbar.

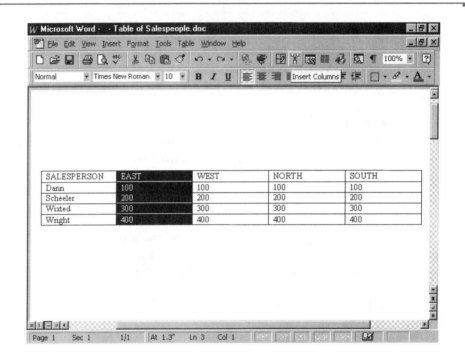

Inserting Columns at the End of the Table

Inserting a column at the end of a table is not as easy as inserting a column between other columns. Experienced users at Vickers Inc., a firm in Glenolden, PA., developed a technique that uses the Split Cells command to add a column at the end of a table:

1. Select the last (far right) column in the table—make sure the entire column is selected.

2. Choose Table ➤ Split Cells.

3. When the Split Cells dialog box appears, it is important to uncheck the Merge Cells Before Split option; leave all the other settings as they are.

4. Click on OK.

5. The new column will be of a different width than the others. To distribute the widths evenly, select the entire table using one of the selection techniques described in Table 11.1 Right-click the mouse on the selected table and choose Distribute Columns Evenly from the pop-up menu (see Figure 11.11).

FIGURE 11.11

You may need to evenly distribute the width of all columns after inserting a new column.

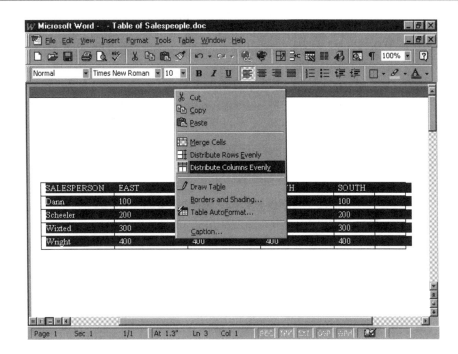

PART

II

Communicating with
Word

Deleting Columns

To delete a column(s), select the column(s), then choose Table ➤ Delete Columns, or right-click and chose Delete Columns from the pop-up menu. You can also use the Cut command on the selected column(s): press Ctrl+Z or click on the Cut button on the Standard toolbar

Formatting Your Tables

You can apply formatting to the borders and interiors of a table's cells to add to its presentation power. The first choice you need to make is whether you want to do the bulk of the formatting manually or allow Word's Table AutoFormat feature to take most of the work off of your hands.

Formatting Table Headings

You will probably want to format your table's row and column headings to make them stand out (for instance, making them centered, bold, underlined, or italicized, or increasing the font size). To format row headings:

1. Select the entire row of headings.

2. Apply an alignment by clicking one of the alignment buttons on the Formatting toolbar or using a keyboard shortcut: center (Ctrl+E), right (Ctrl+R), left (Ctrl+L).

3. Apply character formats by clicking the formatting buttons on the toolbar or using the keyboard shortcuts: bold (Ctrl+B), italic (Ctrl+I), underline (Ctrl+U).

4. Apply point size changes by clicking the drop-down arrow next to the Font Size list box on the Formatting toolbar and selecting a different size; or press Shift+Ctrl+P, type a new point size, and press Enter.

5. If the formatting causes the text to wrap in the cell, widen the column by dragging the vertical line to the right of the column to the right (see the "Sizing Columns" section, above).

Repeating Table Headings across Pages

In a large table that flows across multiple pages, the headings that you designed at the top of the table on one page do not repeat at the top of each subsequent page, unless you issue a special command. Follow these steps to make your table headings repeat across multiple pages:

1. Select the rows that contain the headings (make sure the first row is one of them).

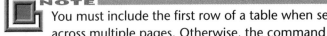

NOTE You must include the first row of a table when selecting headings to be repeated across multiple pages. Otherwise, the command will not work.

2. Choose Table ➤ Headings from the menu bar. If your table already crosses a page, go to the top of the next page, and you will see the repeated headings. If you have not typed enough to have a table cross to the next page, continue typing, and when the page break appears, the headings that you selected will appear again at the top of the next page.

You cannot edit the headings that appear on the subsequent pages—only the original headings at the top of the table can be changed. When you make changes to the original headings at the top of the table, all the subsequent page headings will reflect these changes.

Manually Formatting a Table

Manual formatting leaves the formatting of a table completely up to you. You will need to decide which cells to select and how to format them. The procedure you follow to format a table or parts of a table is the same as formatting text: select the cells you want to format and choose the format(s) you want to apply.

As explained earlier in this chapter, the options in the Format ➤ Borders and Shading dialog box can be applied to your tables. When working with tables, you will also want to take advantage of the regular paragraph and font formatting that you can apply to the contents of cells.

You can format the contents of cells within a table individually from one another. For example, some cells can have the text inside of them centered, while others contain left-aligned text. When applying this type of paragraph or font formatting, either select the specific text in the cell that you want to format or, if you want a paragraph or font format applied to all the text within a cell(s), select the cell or cells you want to be affected.

Using the Table AutoFormat Feature

You can apply one of a number of preset table formats by choosing Table ➤ Table AutoFormat. You only need to select the style, and Word will do the rest to the active table (the table in which the insertion point resides).

To see how Table AutoFormat works, place your insertion point into the table we created earlier in this chapter, insert a new table, or open an existing table that you have already created. Then select Table ➤ Table AutoFormat to open the dialog box shown in Figure 11.12.

PART

II

Communicating with Word

FIGURE 11.12

The Table Auto-Format dialog box includes a variety of pre-defined formats.

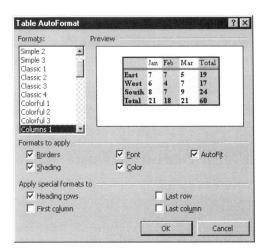

The Formats box in the top left corner of the Table AutoFormat dialog box lists the available preset table formats that you can choose from. Click once on the various formats listed and notice how the Preview on the right changes.

The Formats to Apply area of this dialog box allows you to select or deselect the particular options that you want or do not want Word to apply, based on the preset format you selected. If you don't want the font in your table to be changed, or the columns to be AutoFit, for example, deselect the appropriate option.

The Apply Special Formats To area gives you the chance to specify which parts of your table should or should not be formatted so that attention is brought to them (or directed away from them). For example, some of the preset table formats, such as Colorful 1, 2, and 3, apply special formatting to the first column *and* to the headings row. However, in a particular table, you may want the format to be applied to the first column only. The ability to check and uncheck the different parts of a preset AutoFormat gives an additional flexibility to an already powerful feature.

Let's format the Salesperson table that you created earlier. Open the Salesperson file and position the insertion point in any cell of the table. Select Table ➤ AutoFormat, then choose the Columns 1 format option and click on OK. When you return to the document, you see that the table has been formatted with yellow and gray shading.

Also notice that the table's columns have decreased in width. This is because the AutoFit button was checked at the bottom of the Table AutoFormat dialog box. If you do not want your columns to automatically fit to the entries in a column, uncheck this option. For now, you can press Ctrl+Z or click on the Undo button on the Standard toolbar to reverse the formatting and return to the table to normal. Try another formatting option.

SALESPERSON	EAST	WEST	NORTH	SOUTH
Dann	100	100	100	100
Scheeler	200	200	200	200
Wixted	300	300	300	300
Wright	400	400	400	400

If the formatting doesn't meet your expectations, you can remove the formatting by selecting the table and choosing Table ➤ Table AutoFormat again. Choose the first option in the list, None, and then choose OK. Your table will be returned to the way it was before you formatted it.

Aligning Numbers in a Table

Tables are perfect for typing columns of numbers and performing mathematical calculations. To type numbers into a table, insert a table into a document (Table ➤ Insert Table) and type the numbers into the cells of the table. To align numbers to the right, choose the right alignment button on the Formatting toolbar or press Ctrl+R.

To align the numbers on the decimal point, you must set a decimal tab in the column. To set a decimal tab:

1. Make sure that the Ruler is on (View ≻ Ruler).
2. Select the entire column for which you want to set a decimal tab.
3. Click on the ruler on the tab set number where you want the tab. You will see a tiny L-shaped icon that represents the default left tab set.
4. Double-click on this small symbol and the Tabs dialog box will appear.
5. Click on the Decimal radio button, then click on the Set button at the bottom of the dialog box. Click on OK to return to the table.
6. The decimal alignment is evident in the column where the insertion point is positioned. Begin typing your numbers.
7. To remove the decimal tab, select the column again and drag the small decimal tab symbol off of the ruler.

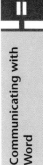

PART

II

Communicating with Word

NOTE

If you are working almost exclusively with numbers and mathematical calculations, you should be using Microsoft Excel instead of Word. You can copy and/or link an existing Excel spreadsheet into your Word document, or you can embed an Excel object into a Word document. See Chapter 14 to learn how to copy and link an existing Excel spreadsheet into a Word document.

Adding Numbers in a Table

Using the AutoSum button, located at the end of the Tables and Borders toolbar, you can quickly add up columns and rows of numbers.

1. Position the insertion point in a blank cell at the bottom of a column of numbers or in a blank cell at the end of a row.
2. Click on the AutoSum button.
3. All of the numbers above the insertion point (in the case of the column), or all the numbers to the left of the insertion point (in the case of the row) are summed. You may want to click on the right alignment button or press Ctrl+R to align the answer in the cell

SALESPERSON	EAST	WEST	NORTH	SOUTH	TOTALS
Dann	100	100	100	100	400
Scheeler	200	200	200	200	
Wixted	300	300	300	300	
Wright	400	400	400	400	
TOTALS	1000				

WARNING

There is no easy way to assign a dollar sign ($) format to columns of numbers in Word tables. If you place a formula into a cell (Table ➤ Formula), you can then apply a number format to that cell only (Table ➤ Formula ➤ Number Format). For cells that don't have formulas—just numbers you typed yourself—you must type the dollar sign for each number in the cell.

Designing Complex Tables

You can design your own table layout using the Tables and Borders toolbar. You can create a table of any size, draw and erase table cell borders, and change the color of any of the borders.

To create a more complex, free-form table:

1. Make sure the Tables and Borders toolbar is active. If not, select View ➤ Toolbars and click on the Tables and Borders option.
2. Click on the drop-down arrow next to the Line Style box on the Tables and Borders toolbar (third option from the left).
3. From the list that appears, select a thick double black line (near the end of the list).

4. Click on the Draw Table button. When you move the mouse pointer over the typing area, it changes to a pencil.
5. Drag a rectangular box about 4 inches wide and 3 inches deep.
6. Begin drawing vertical lines from the top to the bottom of the box. Then draw horizontal lines to complete your table.
7. To turn off Table Draw, click on the Table Draw button again. You can then begin typing in the table.

Once the table has been drawn, you can:

- Erase lines (click on the Eraser button)
- Type text and/or draw more lines
- Rotate text (click on the Change Text Direction button)
- Add borders and shading

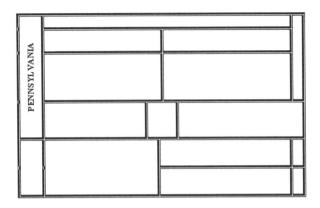

- Shorten and widen columns and rows
- Insert and delete rows and columns
- Merge and split cells (click on the merge or split buttons)
- AutoFormat the table (choose Table ➣ Table AutoFormat)
- Fill cells with color

 MASTERING THE OPPORTUNITIES

Rotating Text in a Complex Table

Word tables can now be more complex in their layout and design. The Table Draw feature, combined with the Split Cells and Merge Cells commands on the Table menu, allow you to design beautiful forms and creative table layouts.

To enhance your table, you can apply different line styles, widths, shading, and fill patterns to table cells, as well as different border colors. You can also rotate text within a cell.

Rotated text is used in cells where the column width doesn't accommodate horizontal text. You can rotate the text on three sides of the cell: top (regular), right-side

(rotated), and left-side (rotated); upside-down rotation is not supported.

 Click on the Change Text Direction button on the Tables and Borders toolbar repeatedly to cycle through the rotations. When you rotate the text, the buttons on the formatting toolbar are rotated so that they appear in the same direction as the rotated text.

Experiment with changing the direction of text in a cell: Use the Table Draw icon to draw a single table cell. Type a word into the cell. Click on the Change Text Direction button to rotate the word. (If the toolbar is not showing, select View ➣ Toolbars ➣ Tables and Borders).

PART

II

Communicating with Word

Using Newspaper Columns

In Word, when you want to type text in columns, you can use tabs, Word's Table feature, or Word's Columns feature. Tabbed columns are sufficient if there are only one- and two-word items in each column. Tabbed text cannot "wrap" around within the column, and inserting additional words on a tabbed row is difficult, because sometimes the addition will push the text to the next tab stop.

Word's Table feature, described in the previous sections, allows you to type text that wraps in a single column. You can then move to the next column and type text that wraps independently from the first column. Tables allow for easy-to-read parallel columns and are the preferred layout for reports and proposals.

Columns allow you to type text in a newspaper or "snake" style. All the text moves vertically down the page until it hits the page break, and then it snakes up to the next column to continue down vertically until it hits the page break, and so on. This pattern continues according to the number of columns you defined. Newspapers, newsletters, brochures, and magazines use this style of text layout. Figure 11.13 shows the Column dialog box with its different column choices.

FIGURE 11.13

The Columns feature in Word allows you to create newspaper-style columns.

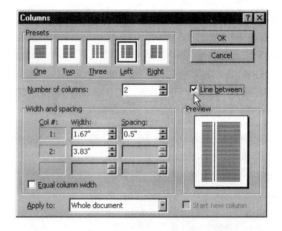

Word's Columns feature allows you to create up to 45 columns, define different column layouts on the same page, and quickly draw lines or rules between the columnsBy default, the columns are of equal width, but you can define a different width for each column. Word also allows you to define columns before or after text is typed in the document.

Follow these steps to create columns in your document:

1. Position the insertion point where the columns should begin. If you want to include a heading that spans across all the columns at the top of the page or section, type this heading first before defining columns. You can also select existing text to be formatted as columns.

2. Choose Format ➣ Columns.

3. In the Presets area, select the type of column layout you prefer (the default is one column). The first three layouts are for equally spaced columns; the last two will produce unequal columns. You can add columns in the Number of Columns box, and change the width of each column in the Width and Spacing area. Word will show you a preview of how the columns will look.

4. To add a line or a rule between the columns, check the Line Between option, which is above the Preview area.

5. Column layouts can apply to selected text, to the whole document, or from a particular point forward in the document. In the Apply To drop-down list box at the bottom of the dialog box, choose the appropriate setting.

6. After making your selections, click on OK.

Creating Bulleted and Numbered Lists

Bulleted lists and numbered lists are often used to bring main points to a reader's attention. With Word, creating either a bulleted or numbered list has become as easy as clicking on a toolbar button.

Adding Numbers or Bullets As You Go

When you are ready to begin typing a list, you can choose to have that list be either numbered or bulleted. On the Formatting toolbar, the Numbering and Bullets buttons are the sixth and seventh buttons from the right.

Here is the procedure for turning on either a numbered or bulleted list format:

1. Position your insertion point on the line where you want to begin your list.

2. Click on the Numbering or the Bullets button on the Formatting toolbar. You will see either a number 1 or a bullet in your text.

3. Type the first line of your list and press Enter. A number 2 or another bullet will appear, ready for you to type your second line.

4. Repeat step 3 for each item in your list.

5. Press Enter on the last line of your list.

6. To end the numbering or bullets style, press Enter without entering text on the new line.

If you want a blank line between each numbered or bulleted line, press Shift+Enter at the end of the line; then press Enter. For each line, repeat this pattern of Shift+Enter (blank) then Enter (new number or bullet). If you want to remove a number or bullet from a line, press the Backspace key.

Adding Numbering and Bullets with AutoFormat

With Word's AutoFormat feature, you can get a numbered or bulleted list automatically as you type by beginning a line with a number or an asterisk. When you press the Enter key at the end of the line with the number or asterisk, AutoFormat picks up the formatting for the next line. In the case of a number, the next sequential number appears for each subsequent line. For bullets, the asterisk is converted to the default bullet style and appears each time you press the Enter key. To start automatic numbering:

1. At the beginning of a line, type **1**.
2. Press the spacebar or the Tab key to put some space between the number and the text you are going to type.
3. Type some text on the line.
4. After you type your text on that first line, press the Enter key. Word will automatically begin the next line with the number 2, and so forth.

Make sure you type some text on the line before you press the Enter key. If you only type a number or asterisk and then press the Enter key, Word will not automatically number the next line.

To create a numbered list down the left side of a document without typing any text, use the line-numbering feature instead of the numbering feature. Choose File ➢ Page Setup ➢ Layout, and click on the Line Numbers button. In the Line Numbers dialog box that appears, click on the Add Line Numbering button, and choose the Numbering option you want. Click OK, then OK again. When you return to the document, the first number appears; press the Enter key for as many numbers you want.

Formatting Existing Text as a List

Forethought is a wonderful thing. The problem is that many of us simply don't have it when we are rushing to get a document ready. Fortunately, as with all Word formatting options, you can apply a numbered or bulleted list format after the fact. Here's a simple example to demonstrate:

1. Type the following four words into your document, pressing Enter after each one: **Top**, **Bottom**, **Left**, **Right**.
2. Select the four lines.
3. Click on the Bullets button on the Formatting toolbar. Your list should now be bulleted and look like this:

   - Top
   - Bottom
   - Left
   - Right

4. Select the text again, but this time click on the Numbering button on the Formatting toolbar to change the bullets to numbers.

   1. Top
   2. Bottom
   3. Left
   4. Right

Stopping and Resuming a List Format

When you are using a bulleted or numbered format in your document, you may want to interrupt your list to add supporting text or graphics. To do this, you must turn off the bullets or numbering, add the supporting text or graphics, and then restart the bullets or numbering. Restarting bullets is easy—you simply click on the Bullets button again. Restarting numbers takes a few more steps.

If your document already contains a formatted list, and you want to add blank lines within it—in order to insert a chart, diagram, or other information—position your insertion point at the end of the line right before the lines to be added and press the Enter key.

In our example above, suppose you wanted to add some blank lines between "Bottom" and "Left," so that you could insert additional words that did not need to be formatted or numbered. Follow these steps:

1. Position the insertion point at the end of the word "Bottom."
2. Press Enter. The next line is blank, but still has a number on it (see the "Before" side of Figure 11.14).
3. Press the Backspace key to remove the number.
4. Press Enter again to give yourself another blank line. You can now add additional text in this area. Word automatically numbers the rows after the inserted text, as shown in the "After" side of Figure 11.14.

FIGURE 11.14

Adding text in the middle of a formatted list

BEFORE	AFTER
1. TOP	1. TOP
2. BOTTOM(press Enter here)	2. BOTTOM
3. (press Backspace here)	
4. LEFT	I am text inserted between two lines. Notice that the numbers are still sequential.
5. RIGHT	
	3. LEFT
	4. RIGHT

Changing Bullet Styles

Naturally, you will want to know if you can change the style of the bullet Word adds to your bulleted lists. The answer is yes.

To modify a bullet, select Format ➤ Bullets and Numbering, and click on the Bulleted tab, or right-click in a bulleted list and select Bullets and Numbering from the shortcut menu. The Bulleted page of the Bullets and Numbering dialog box is shown in Figure 11.15.

FIGURE 11.15

The Bullets and Numbering dialog box

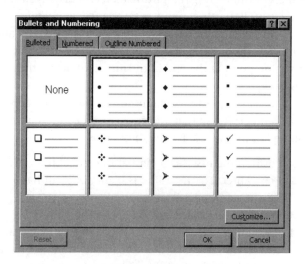

The Bulleted page offers seven preset styles of bullets. If one of these will do the job, all you need to do is click on its preview and then click OK. If you want even more choices of bullet types to choose from, or need to change one of the preset bullets, click on the Customize button. The Customize button is only available if you have a bullet style selected (not the None option). When you click the Customize option, you will see the Customize Bulleted List dialog box.

This dialog box lets you change the bullet character. Select the Font button and you will be able to change the bullet's font, point size, color, and position. You can even add blinking and shimmering bullets to your text, by clicking on the animation tab in the Font dialog box.

You can also change the distance from the left side of the page to the bullet (in the Bullet Position area) or change the distance between the text and the bullet (in the Text Position area). Bullets are formatted with hanging indents, which means that the bullet hangs back at the left margin and the text (when it wraps) indents each line.

You can follow these steps to begin a list with a custom bullet:

1. Place your insertion point on a blank line.
2. Choose Format ➤ Bullets and Numbering, and click on the Bulleted tab, if it is not selected already.
3. Click on some bullet style, even if it is not the one you ultimately want, so that the Customize button can become available. Do not select the None option (the default).
4. Click on the Customize button in the lower right corner.
5. In the Customize Bulleted List dialog box, click on the Bullet button. The Symbol dialog box, which contains many types of bullet styles, will open. You can choose sets in the list box at the top of the Symbol dialog box; the Symbol set and the Wingdings set contain the most popular types of bullets.
6. Click on the different pictures in the grid; the pictures will "zoom out" so you can get a better view of them. Hold down the mouse and move it along the rows of pictures until you see the one you want. Click on OK.
7. You will be returned to the Customize Bulleted List dialog box, where you can now either accept the new bullet with its default properties or modify its font options.
8. Once everything is the way you want it, click on OK. The line you were on will now be formatted with your chosen bullet.
9. Type the lines of your list until you get to the last line. On the last line, backspace over the bullet to get rid of the leftover bullet.

Here's an example of a list with a custom bullet:

- ☯ Simplicity brings more happiness than complexity
- ☯ Learn to be silent
- ☯ Perfect kindness acts without thinking of kindness

PART

II

Communicating with Word

NOTE

You can use basically the same steps as above to modify the bullets in an existing list. Select the list first (the bullets will not appear to be selected, but they are) and work through the dialog boxes as described in this section.

MASTERING TROUBLESHOOTING

Lining up Numbers

If you type a numbered list, and the numbers exceed the number 9, the two-digit numbers will not line up on the right side of the numbers. The default alignment for the numbers in numbered lists is left-aligned, but for two-digit numbers to line up, you should change the alignment of the numbers to right.

1. Choose Format ➤ Bullets and Numbering, and click on the Numbered tab.
2. Click on the desired number style (anything but None) in order for the Customize option to be available.
3. Click on the Customize button in the lower right side of the box.

4. In the Customize Numbered List dialog box, click on the Number Position at the bottom of the dialog box.
5. Select Right Alignment and click on OK.
6. When you return to the document typing screen, the first number appears. Type your text and press Enter. The next number appears. Continue typing until you reach two-digit numbers. The numbers above align on the right side.

If you have numbered text already typed, select all the text first and then change the settings described in the steps above.

Changing Your Numbering Scheme

In some cases, Arabic numerals (1, 2, 3) may not make the grade as a numbering style. You might prefer a lettering style (A, B, C) or Roman numerals for your list. You can choose a different numbering style in much the same way that you can select different bullet styles.

To change the numbering style, choose Format ➤ Bullets and Numbering, and click on the Numbered tab. The Numbered tab page allows you to choose from seven preselected numbering options. The Customize button on this page will take you to the Customize Numbered List dialog box, shown in Figure 11.16. The options here let you specify text before and after the number, various numbering schemes, that number to start at, and the number's position.

FIGURE 11.16

The Customize Numbered List dialog box lets you customize your numbered list format.

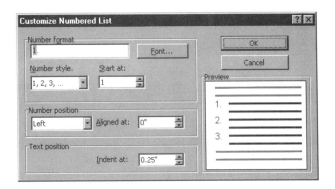

As an example, we will create a numbered list format with the word *PHASE* before each number and the characters ---> after each number. Follow these steps:

1. Place your insertion point on a blank line and select Format ➤ Bullets and Numbering, and click on the Numbered tab.
2. Click on any numbering preview except for None.
3. Click on the Customize button.
4. In the Number Format box, click in front of the sample of the number, type **PHASE**, and press the spacebar.
5. Look at the preview sample in the lower right corner to have a sense of what is going on with the added text.
6. Click after the number sample and backspace over the period. Type ---> (three dashes and a greater-than sign). Look at the preview again.
7. When you have finished customizing, click on OK. The line you were on will now have "PHASE 1--->" on it.
8. Type the lines of your list until you get to the last line, and then press Backspace to remove the extra custom number.

Here's an example of a numbered list formatted as described in the steps above:

```
PHASE 1---> Database Design
PHASE 2---> Non-Functional GUI designed
PHASE 3---> Customer authorization to proceed
PHASE 4---> Functionality put behind GUI
PHASE 5---> In house Testing
PHASE 6---> Beta Testing
PHASE 7---> Installation
PHASE 8---> Support
```

PART

II

Communicating with Word

When You Need More Details: Outline Numbered Lists

There will be times that you need to include multiple-level lists in your documents, in order to provide more details about what you are trying to say. When you need to show levels of details in your lists, use Word's improved Outline Numbered feature.

To see your options, choose Format ➤ Bullets and Numbering, and click on the Outline Numbered tab. This page of the Bullets and Numbering dialog box, shown in Figure 11.17, offers seven preset formats, along with a Customize button that allows you to specify a custom outline numbered list format. To make the Customize option available, click first on any one of the outline numbered styles.

FIGURE 11.17

You can create a multilevel list through the Outline Numbered tab page of the Bullets and Numbering dialog box.

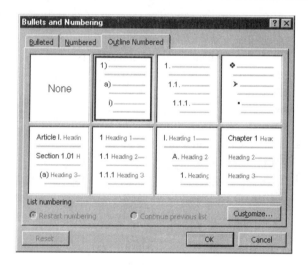

After you select one of the outline numbered formats, your list will be formatted so that each time you press the Tab key at the beginning of a line, it will be demoted (indented) one level. To promote (outdent) a line, press Shift+Tab.

Follow these steps to get a feel for creating outline numbered lists:

1. Place your insertion point on a blank line and select Format ➤ Bullets and Numbering, and click on the Outline Numbered tab, or right-click and select Bullets and Numbering from the shortcut menu.
2. Click on the first outline numbered option in the top row next to the None option, then click on OK.
3. The Roman numeral I appears. Type some text and press Enter. The next line appears with the Roman numeral II.

4. Type additional text and press Enter. On the next line, press the Tab key to demote (indent) the text. The letter A appears. Type some text and press Enter.

5. Press Shift+Tab to promote or outdent the text. There are nine levels of numbered indentation.

Experiment with the promote and demote (Tab and Shift+Tab) commands. Here's an example of the different multilevel outline numbered levels:

```
I.    This is a level 1
II.   This is a level 1
   A. This is a level 2
   B. This is a level 2
   C. This is a level 2
      1. This is level 3
      2. This is level 3
         a. This is level 4
         b. This is level 4
            (a)   This is level 5
            (b)   This is level 5
              (i) This is level 6
              (ii) This is level 6
                 1. This is level 7
                 2. This is level 7
                    a. This is level 8
                    b. This is level 8
                       i.  This is level 9
                       ii. This is level 9
```

Adding Formatting with Styles

When you are working with documents, especially long documents, formatting your text with multiple levels of headings and various formats for different parts of your body text can become tedious. Word assists in making formatting text in your documents more efficient by providing built-in styles, and allowing you to create custom styles of your own.

In Word, a style is a collection of formatting options labeled with one name. Styles define all aspects of formatting—from the font and point size of the text to paragraph formatting, such as alignment, line spacing, borders, and tab stops.

Word's Built-in Styles

Even if you are not aware of it, you are always working with styles in Word. The Normal style is the default, and it is the style that all other styles are based upon.

The first item on your Formatting toolbar is a combo box that identifies the current style that you are using. If you do nothing with styles, the combo box will show that you are using the Normal style.

The Normal style uses 10-point Times New Roman, single-spacing, left-aligned paragraphs, and other default format settings that you can view in the Modify Style dialog box. To see this dialog box, select Format ➤ Style and click on the Modify button. In the Modify Style dialog box, click on the Format button to see the different categories of formats that a style contains. Figure 11.18 shows the Modify Style dialog box with the Format list for the Normal style.

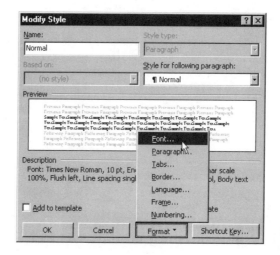

In addition to the Normal style, Word comes with a number of other built-in styles that help you format your document, including nine levels of heading styles. Here is a quick example to give you an idea of how styles in general, and the heading styles in particular, help you format your documents:

1. Start a new document in Word.
2. Click on the Style list box on the Formatting toolbar, and select Heading 1 or press Ctrl+Alt+1.
3. In your document, type **Heading 1** and press Enter.
4. Click on the Style list box again, and select Heading 2 or press Ctrl+Alt+2.
5. In your document, type **Heading 2** and press Enter.
6. Click on the Style list box a third time and select Heading 3 or press Ctrl+Alt+3.
7. In your document, type **Heading 3** and press Enter.

Although you can only see three heading styles when you click on the Style list box on the Formatting toolbar, six other heading levels are available. A quick way to access the other heading styles, and all the other built-in styles as well, is by holding down the Shift key while clicking on the Style list box drop-down arrow.

Defining Your Own Styles

One of the biggest benefits of Windows and programs like Word is that they are customizable; no two people need to use them in the same way. The styles that come with Word are by no means meant to be the "be all and end all" in styles. You can create your own styles to fit your needs.

For example, suppose that you need a heading style that is in 20-point bold Arial font, is centered, and always has a border around it. You could create it by following these steps:

1. Start a new document in Word.
2. Select Format ➤ Style.
3. In the Style dialog box, click on the New button to open the New Style dialog box.
4. In the Name text box, type **MY STYLE** (do not press Enter).
5. Click on the Format button and select Font from the list.
6. In the Font dialog box, choose Times New Roman for Font, Bold for Font Style, and 20 for Size. Leave the other options as they are and click on OK.
7. Click on the Format button and choose Paragraph from the list.
8. Click on the Alignment list box.
9. Select Centered from the list, and then click on OK.
10. Click on the Format button and choose Border from the list.
11. In the Presets area, select the Box option. In the Style area, scroll until you find a double line, then select the double line style. Click on OK.
12. Click on OK in the New Style dialog box.
13. Click on the Close button in the Style dialog box. Your style is now available to this document.
14. Type **THIS IS MY STYLE** on the first line (do not press Enter).
15. Click on the Style list box on the Formatting toolbar and look for the MY STYLE style.
16. Select your style. Your screen should look like the one shown in Figure 11.19.

FIGURE 11.19

Your new style applied to the first paragraph

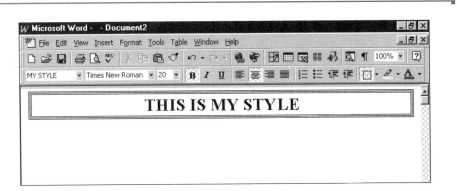

If you now press Enter, you will see that the style is carried forward to the next paragraph. If you want to go back to the Normal style or another style, you can select it from the Style list box on the Formatting toolbar.

If you want the Normal style to start automatically following your new style, you can specify the Style for the Following Paragraph as part of your style settings. Choose Format ➢ Style, select your style, and click on the Modify button. In the Modify Style dialog box, change the setting for the Style for Following Paragraph option to Normal, if it is not already selected.

At this point, MY STYLE will be available only in the current document. If you want to make the style available in all of your documents, click on the Add to Template checkbox in the bottom left corner of the Modify Style dialog box for MY STYLE. Click on OK and then click on the Close button.

If you no longer need a style you created, you can delete it. However, you cannot delete Word's built-in styles. To delete a style such as MY STYLE, select Format ➢ Style, select your style, and click on the Delete button. Close the Style dialog box when you've finished.

Instead of using the dialog boxes to create a style, you can create a style by example. To create a style by example, format a paragraph in your document, and then select the paragraph. Next, click in the Style list box on the Formatting toolbar. Type the name of the new style over the name that appears in the text box and press Enter. Your new style is now available in your document.

TIP

If you have a set of formats that you want to use a couple of times, but you do not want to go through the process of setting up a style, you can use the Format Painter button (the one with a paintbrush) on the Standard toolbar. The Format Painter allows you to take all of the formatting from one paragraph and apply the format to another paragraph. See Chapter 7 for details.

Seeing Styles in a Document

If you wish to view all of the styles being used in your document without placing your insertion point in different paragraphs, select Tools ➢ Options, and click on the View tab. At the bottom of the dialog box, increase the size of the Style Area Width to 1" and click on OK. Your style names will be listed along the left side of your screen, similar to Figure 11.20.

To widen or shorten the Style Area Width, place the mouse over the vertical line that separates the Style Area from your document. When the two-headed arrow appears, click and hold down the mouse and drag the vertical line to the right or left. To close up the Style Area without going back into the Options dialog box, drag the vertical line back to the left margin.

You can view the
styles in your
document in
the Style Area.

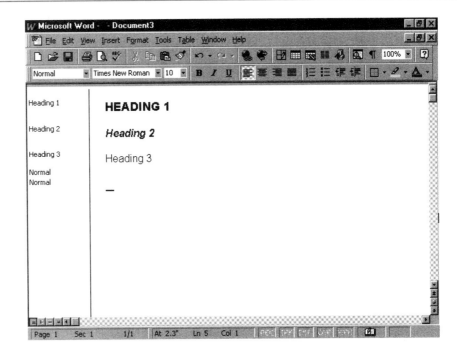

PART

II

Communicating with
Word

Chapter

12

Word's Reusability Features—Never Type Again!

12

Word's Reusability Features—
Never Type Again!

Word has wonderful tools that you can use to reduce or eliminate the retyping of words, phrases, or even whole documents. Which tool is the best one to use depends on what you are trying to accomplish. The tools we are going to explore in this chapter are AutoComplete, Auto-Text, AutoCorrect (for more than just fixing spelling errors), Find and Replace, In-Place Comments, Word's renowned templates, and Mail Merge.

The AutoComplete feature is an implementation of Microsoft's IntelliSense and is a series of pop-up suggestions that appear while you are typing. You can use these suggestions to complete your phrase or word.

The AutoText and AutoCorrect tools allow you to store frequently used text as part of the global template in Word; you can then activate the text instantly by typing a few characters.

The Find and Replace function allows you to search through a document looking for specific characters or words, and, if requested, replace them with other characters or words you specify. You can search for words and phrases, as well as special characters (such as page breaks and paragraph symbols) and formatting.

In-Place Comments allow you to add comments to text and see the comment as a pop-up note in your text. Although this is not a specific feature for reusing text, it is a time-saver when you receive a commented document from your boss or colleagues. Specific instructions and notes can be inserted into the document and appear as lightly yellow highlights over the commented text. When you pause the mouse at the commented text, a pop-up note displays the instruction or comment.

Word bases all documents on templates. Templates are predesigned and preformatted documents that you can use for your work. When you choose a new, blank document screen, Word has served you up the Normal template. There are many other templates, such as the Newsletter Wizard template and Fax templates, which you can access by choosing File ➤ New from the menu bar. But you can also design your own templates and use them again and again.

Mail merge has long been a word processing tool used to automate periodic mailings—such as letters, invitations, or newsletters—to many individuals. You don't need to rekey the address and personalized information from mailing to mailing.

AutoComplete

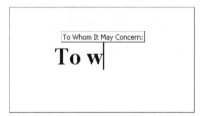

You may have already encountered the Auto-Complete feature—small, yellow ScreenTip messages that pop-up as you type, anticipating your next word or phrase. For example, after you type the first three letters of a phrase that is stored as an AutoText entry (you'll learn how to create AutoText later in this chapter), Word will suggest the rest of the phrase. When you see the suggested pop-up phrase, press the Enter key or press F3 to have Word complete the phrase for you. To reject the suggestion, just keep typing and the suggestion goes away.

AutoComplete provides suggestions for both preprogrammed items and AutoText items you create. Here are the items that are automatically completed:

- The current date
- A day of the week
- A month of the year
- Your name
- AutoText entries

For example, if you type **Dec**, AutoComplete will suggest "December"; press the Enter key or press F3 to take the suggestion. If you are a very fast typist, you may never see AutoComplete suggestions—you will have completely typed a phrase before Word can offer to finish it for you.

AutoComplete uses the text of the AutoText feature. Microsoft created a few frequently typed phrases so that there would be some existing AutoComplete items (see Figure 12.1).

FIGURE 12.1

The AutoText feature contains a list of frequently typed words and phrases that are used as AutoComplete entries.

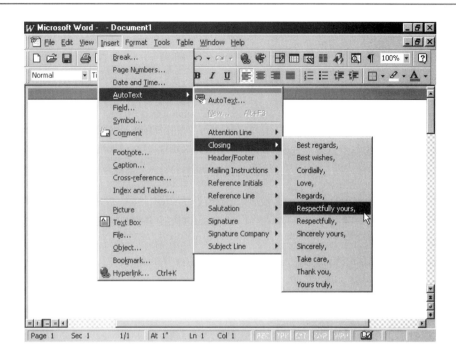

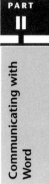

To turn the AutoComplete feature on or off:

1. Select Insert ➢ AutoText ➢ AutoText.

2. Check or uncheck the *Show AutoComplete tip for AutoText and dates* option on the AutoText tab.

3. Click on OK.

AutoText is a feature that allows you to store frequently used words or phrases. When you store this text, you must assign a name (usually an abbreviation) to represent the boilerplate text. This abbreviation must be at least three or more characters so that it can also be used as an AutoComplete item. AutoText is covered in the next section.

To get the most out of AutoComplete, you should store your frequently used text as AutoText.

An AutoComplete suggestion won't be offered until you type the first three letters of a phrase. But if you have stored as AutoText two or more phrases that start with the same three letters, AutoComplete won't offer a suggestion until you type enough for it to recognize which phrase you are typing. For example, if you have stored the phrases Your consideration is greatly appreciated and Your attention to this matter is appreciated as AutoText entries, you will need to type Your plus the first letter of the next word before AutoComplete will be able to suggest the correct text.

To solve this problem, you can also assign unique three-character abbreviations to phrases that start with the same letters. For example, you could assign the abbreviations *yca* and *yaa* to the phrases given above.

Creating AutoText Entries

The AutoText feature in Word 97 is easier and more fun to use than in any other version of Word. Using this feature, you can select and store frequently typed text. An AutoText name, made up of the first couple of words of the text, will be assigned to the stored text. You can change this name to a shorter, abbreviated name—as long as the abbreviation is a minimum of three characters. For example, the phrase *Thank you for your consideration in this matter* can be stored as *Thank you* or as an abbreviation such as *tcm*. The maximum length for an AutoText name is 32 characters.

There are a number of methods for quickly retrieving stored text from AutoText:

- AutoComplete—type the first three characters of an AutoText entry, and a Screen-Tip appears; press Enter or F3 to insert the stored text.
- Choose Insert ➢ AutoText from the menu, select a category (such as Closing) from the submenu, and then select the stored text from the next drop-down menu of stored items.
- Display the AutoText toolbar. When you click the toolbar button, a list of AutoText entries are displayed. Select a stored item.

AutoText entries can also be printed, so that you can have a printed log of the entries you have stored. Open the Print dialog box (File ➢ Print), click on the arrow next to the Print What box, and then choose AutoText Entries (as shown in Figure 12.2). Click on the OK button to print the AutoText entries.

Storing and Retrieving an AutoText Entry

You can store virtually any amount of text and other items as AutoText—phrases, paragraphs, pages, graphics, tables, and so on. To store an AutoText item, select (drag the mouse over) the text you want to store, and choose Insert ➢ AutoText ➢ New or press Alt+F3. The Create AutoText input box will appear, and Word will suggest a name for the entry taken from some of the words or characters of the selected text. You can type a shorter name, if you wish, than what Word is recommending.

TIP

AutoText names can contain any words and numbers, and can include spaces. Thus, an entry name of *Briefing Pg23* is acceptable. We recommend, however, that you keep the name short, so that you only have to type a few letters to activate your AutoText entry.

FIGURE 12.2

You can print the list of stored AutoText entries from the Print dialog box.

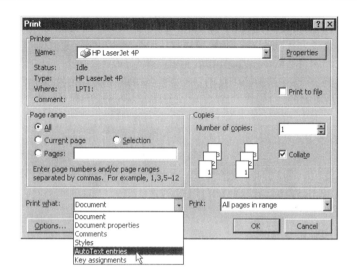

Communicating with Word

Suppose that there is a paragraph that you use often in your documents. You want to store this paragraph as an AutoText entry so that you can reuse it by typing a few letters. The following steps demonstrate the process:

1. In a blank area, type the following paragraph:

Once again, thank you for inquiring about Dalton Industries. You are cordially invited to attend our weekly Wednesday free tour of the manufacturing plant. Tours of the plant begin promptly at 10:00 a.m. and end at 12:00 p.m. We ask that you register no later than Tuesday at 3:00 p.m. to insure that there is room for your group. Please call Kia Darling at 612-111-1111 to register your attendees.

2. Spell-check the paragraph (press F7 or click on the Spelling & Grammar button on the Standard toolbar) and correct any typing errors.

3. Select the text of the paragraph (drag the mouse over the lines of text).

4. Press Alt+F3 or choose Insert ➤ AutoText ➤ New.

5. When the Create AutoText input box appears, type over the suggested name with the word **tour**, as shown in Figure 12.3, then click OK. The entry has been stored.

To retrieve the AutoText entry, position the insertion point where you want the stored text to appear. Type **tou** (the first three characters of *tour*, the name of this AutoText entry); the AutoComplete ScreenTip appears displaying the beginning of the paragraph associated with the abbreviation. Press Enter or F3 to accept the suggestion. The entire paragraph of text will be inserted.

FIGURE 12.3

Typing a new name for an AutoText entry in the Create AutoText input box.

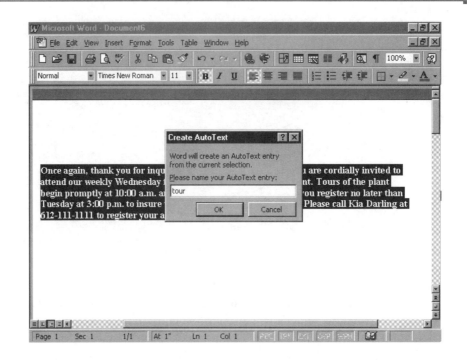

If you wish to retrieve the text the long way, choose Insert ➤ AutoText, and pick the AutoText entry from the drop-down list.

Creating an AutoText Letter Closing

As you work with the AutoText feature, you will begin to store more and more frequently typed text items. Among the most commonly stored items are letter closings. The exercise below details the steps required to store two letter closings. One letter closing is the formal name of a company president and another closing is the informal name of the president.

1. On a blank screen, type the following letter closing:

Very Truly Yours,

Dr. Norman Spencer

President

Enclosure

2. Select the entire closing (drag the mouse over the text to select it).
3. Press Alt+F3 or Choose Insert ➤ AutoText ➤ New.
4. When the Create AutoText dialog box appears, create an abbreviated name instead of using the default name provided by Word. Type **NS1** (don't worry about upper- or lowercase, it can be either).
5. Press Enter or click on OK to finish creating the AutoText.
6. Test this version of the closing by retrieving it. Remember there are two easy methods for retrieving an AutoText entry into your document. Slowly type the first three characters of the abbreviated name, and the AutoText ScreenTip will appear. Press the Enter key or F3 to accept it. Or you can type the actual abbreviated name and press F3 to retrieve the AutoText into the document.

You are now going to create the second closing for Dr. Spencer, but you will use a more informal name.

1. In the closing you retrieved in the previous exercise, change the name from *Dr. Norman Spencer* to *Norm.*
2. Select the entire text of the closing again and press Alt+F3 or choose Insert ➤ AutoText ➤ New.
3. When the Create AutoText dialog box appears, create the abbreviated name of **NS2.**
4. Click on OK.
5. Test the retrieval of the second closing by slowly typing the letters **NS2** and watching for the AutoComplete ScreenTip to appear. Press the Enter key. You can also type the abbreviated name and press F3 to retrieve the closing.

Remember, you should retrieve the AutoText entry at the exact spot you need to have the text appear in the document. We expanded the text on a blank screen to see how this feature works. In reality, you should type the AutoText abbreviated name at the exact position in the document to retrieve the text at the end of a letter, where you would expect to see a closing.

If you want to delete these test AutoText entries, choose Insert ➢ AutoText ➢ Auto-Text. Find the NS1 entry in the list, click on it, and click on the Delete button. Repeat this procedure for the NS2 entry.

AutoText and WordPerfect Help Key Conflict

If you have Word set up to use the WordPerfect Help key, pressing F3 will not retrieve an AutoText entry; instead, F3 activates the WordPerfect Help dialog box.

If you want to turn off the WordPerfect Help option, select Help ➢ WordPerfect Help, and click on the Options button in the Help for WordPerfect Users dialog box. Uncheck *Help for WordPerfect users* and *Navigation keys for WordPerfect users,* if you do not want any WordPerfect keyboard combinations to work. Click on OK and then Close. Another way to turn off the WordPerfect Help is through the Options dialog box. Choose Tools ➢ Options ➢ General tab, and deselect the *Help for WordPerfect users* and *Navigation keys for WordPerfect users* options.

If you wish to keep WordPerfect Help turned on, remember to press Enter (and not F3) to insert an AutoText entry.

Changing or Deleting an AutoText Entry

To change an AutoText entry, you must redefine it by editing it and then saving it under the same name:

1. Type or expand the AutoText entry into a document.
2. Make your editorial changes.
3. Select the entry and press Alt+F3. The Create AutoText dialog box appears.
4. Type the same name you used before for that entry.
5. Word will see ask if you wish to redefine the AutoText entry. Click on the Yes button. The entry has been redefined.

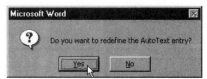

To permanently delete an AutoText entry from storage, choose Insert ➢ AutoText ➢ AutoText. In the dialog box, find the entry you wish to delete, and then click on the Delete button on the right side of the dialog box. Unfortunately, you will not be asked to confirm the deletion—Word swiftly removes the entry and does not offer a Cancel button. (Of course, if you inadvertently delete an AutoText entry, you can find the text in another document and store it again.

> **TIP**
>
> The AutoText command has its own toolbar that lists the AutoText entries you've made. Choose View ➤ Toolbars and click on the AutoText option. When the Auto-Text toolbar appears, click on the middle button to display the list of entries. Select your entry from the list.

Using AutoCorrect to Correct Typos

Word will automatically correct some typos as you type them. This automatic correction is different from the spelling check function, which displays a wavy red line underneath a word that is misspelled, but doesn't fix it for you. If you are not watching carefully, you will not realize that Word is helping you out by automatically correcting some of your words.

To see AutoCorrect in action, type **You adn me** and press the spacebar. Word will automatically change *adn* to *and*.

AutoCorrect entries are activated by typing the entry name and pressing the spacebar, the Enter key, or the Tab key. Choose Tools ➤ AutoCorrect to display a dialog box that includes an extensive list of common typing errors that Word is programmed to change. You can remove entries from this list or add your own errors.

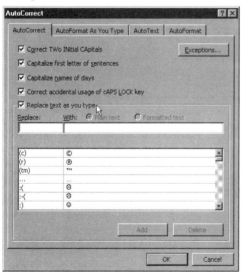

If you do not want Word to automatically correct any errors at all, you can turn off the AutoCorrect feature. Choose Tools ➤ AutoCorrect and remove the check in the *Replace text as you type* checkbox. The other checkboxes in the AutoCorrect dialog box let you disable rules for automatic corrections.

Defining AutoCorrect Exceptions

When AutoCorrect is on, Word will try to do you a favor by capitalizing the first letter of any word that follows a period, because it thinks that a word that follows a period must be the beginning of a sentence.

Word's AutoCorrect feature maintains a list of exceptions to its rules for capitalizing the first letter. If Word keeps annoying you by, for example, capitalizing the word after an abbreviated term you use often, you might want to select Tools ➢ AutoCorrect and remove the check next to the *Capitalize first letter of sentences* checkbox to turn off this rule. An alternative is to leave the rule checked, but add the abbreviation to the Exceptions list; thereafter, Word will leave the word that follows it as you typed it.

Choose Tools ➢ AutoCorrect and click on the Exceptions button to see the AutoCorrect Exceptions dialog box. Click on the First Letter tab. The dialog box lists words that end in a period that AutoCorrect should not capitalize after, as shown in Figure 12.4. Add any special words you want to this list by clicking on the Add button. Delete words from the list by clicking once on the word and clicking on the Delete button. You can follow the same procedure to add or remove exceptions to the rule about not allowing two capitalized letters followed by lowercase ones. Click on the INitial CAps tab to change those exceptions.

FIGURE 12.4

You can add or remove terms that are exceptions to Auto-Correct's rules.

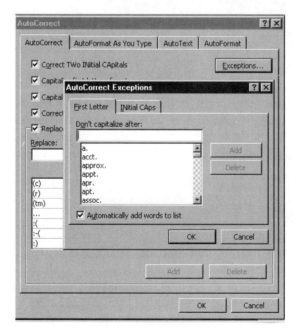

> **TIP**
>
> The Automatically Add Words to List checkbox in the AutoCorrect Exceptions dialog box allows you to add words to the list of exceptions "on the fly." When Word automatically corrects a word that you don't want it to change, press Backspace and type over the correction. Word will then add that word to the AutoCorrect Exceptions list. The next time you use that word, Word will not correct it.

Finding and Replacing Text and Formats

As with most quality word processing programs, Word gives you the ability to find specific words or phrases in your document (Edit ➢ Find). The Find dialog box includes a Replace tab so that you can both find and replace text. (This feature is sometimes called Search and Replace in other word processing programs.)

The Find and Replace dialog box also contains the Go To tab (Ctrl+G), which jumps to specific pages or sections. The find feature allows you to specify the particular word or phrase without knowing the page number(s) on which this text resides.

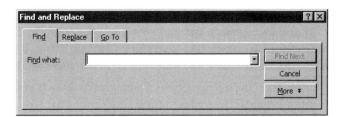

As an example of using the Find and Replace feature, suppose that you type the name Mr. John W. Smith at least four to five times in a document and then discover that you spelled the name incorrectly—the man's name is Mr. John W. Smythe. You could locate the word, *Smith*, delete it, and then rekey it four to five times. But it's easier to use the Find and Replace feature to find every occurrence of the name *Smith* and replace it with *Smythe*. Using Find and Replace also eliminates typos that can occur when you manually rekey multiple changes.

It is always a good idea to first save your document before you perform a Find and Replace, because the results may not be what you expected. If you save the document immediately before you perform the Find and Replace, you can always call up the previously saved version if things go wrong. The Undo button is also handy when a Find and Replace has gone haywire.

Imagine finding and replacing all occurrences of the word **men** with the word **chaps**. If you do not specify that Word should Find Whole Words Only (one of the options you can set in the Replace tab in the Find and Replace dialog box), Word will find the letters within any word in the document and replace them with the characters you specified. You can end up with the word *women* becoming *wochaps* and *increment* becoming *increchapst*. Thank goodness for the Undo button.

Specifying Search Criteria

The previous section described a Find and Replace requirement that could have come up with unexpected results if the Find Whole Words Only search criteria had not been used. On the Find and Replace dialog box (press Ctrl+F or choose Edit ➢ Find), the More button displays the criteria section. Search criteria allows you to narrow your search, and to find and replace information that is represented by symbols or special characters, such as page breaks and paragraph endings.

The search criteria in Word allows for tremendous flexibility when finding and replacing text and special characters. The checkboxes in the dialog box offer the following options:

Match Case: Finds only the characters that are the same case as the ones in the Find What box and replaces them with the same case as in the Replace With box.

Find Whole Words Only: Finds the whole word rather than the specific characters. For example, if you enter **men** in the Find What box and specify Find Whole Words Only, Word will locate only those characters when they are a word by themselves, and not words with those characters within them, such as incre*men*t.

Use Wildcards: Allows you to specify wildcard symbols (**?** or *****) in the Find What text box. Using wildcards is described a little later in the chapter.

Sounds Like: Finds different spellings of words that sound similar. For example, entering **Here** in the Find What text box will find *hear, hair, hare,* and *heir.*

Find All Word Forms: Finds all grammatical forms of a word. If you search for **sit**, Word will find *sat* and *sitting*. This is an added feature to Word's Find and Replace criteria that is not common to other programs. (This new capability is the result of Microsoft's IntelliSense Technology—a bonus to all Office 97 users.)

The three buttons at the bottom of the dialog box provide more ways to specify the type of Find and Replace operation:

No Formatting: If you specified formatting with the Format button, this option removes it.

Format: You can find different formats (fonts, styles, paragraph alignments, and so on) and replace them with other formats.

Special: You can find and replace special characters, such as manual page breaks, paragraph marks, and tab characters. If Use Wildcards is checked, clicking on the Special button displays a list of symbols for complex search criteria.

The Basics of Finding and Replacing Characters

The general steps for finding and replacing text in Word are as follows:

1. Choose Edit ➤ Replace or press Ctrl+H or click on the Replace tab on the Find and Replace dialog box.
2. In the Find What text box, specify the text or special characters you are looking for in the document.
3. Optionally, check one of the search criteria options (such as Match Case or Find Whole Words Only).
4. If you are looking for special formats or characters, select the Format or Special button at the bottom of the dialog box.
5. In the Replace With text box, specify the text or special characters you are substituting.
6. In the Search box, specify the direction of the search. Click on the drop-down arrow to see your choices: Down, Up, or All. The search will be conducted in the direction you specify, beginning where the insertion point is placed. The Default is All, which means Word will search up and down the document.
7. When you are ready to start the operation, click on the Replace or Replace All button. The Replace button will cause the insertion point to stop at each occurrence; you will then have the opportunity to accept or reject each change by clicking on the Replace button or Find Next button. The Replace All button causes Word to go through the document rapidly, replacing everything at once. Word does not ask you first before making the replacements.
8. When it is finished, Word will display a message showing the number of replacements made in the document.

WARNING

Be careful about choosing Replace All. If you think that there may be occurrences that should not be replaced, use the Replace button instead of the Replace All button.

Finding with Wildcards

When searching for words, you may want to use *wildcards* instead of typing out the entire phrase. Wildcards are special symbols that can be substituted for text. Used correctly, they can help you search for every variation of a word.

To use wildcards, start the Find command (Ctrl+F), then click on the More button so that you can see the Advanced Criteria selections. Check the Use Wildcards checkbox, and then click the Special button at the bottom of the dialog box. You will see the list of complex search criteria symbols. Once you know what a symbol looks like, the next

PART

II

Communicating with Word

time you are using a wildcard, you can type that symbol directly into the Find What box without choosing it from the Special list. Whenever you are using a wildcard, you must check Use Wildcard.

A simple example of using wildcards is to find *Smith, Smythe*, and any other variations of this spelling. You could search for all occurrences of any word that begins with *S*, may have multiple characters after the *S*, and also includes an *h* in the word. The asterisk wildcard is used to represent multiple characters: **S*h**. Figure 12.5 shows the Find dialog box filled in for a wildcard search that will find *Smith, Smythe, Smithsonian*, and any other words that begin with *S* and include an *h*.

FIGURE 12.5

You can use wildcards in your Find What text.

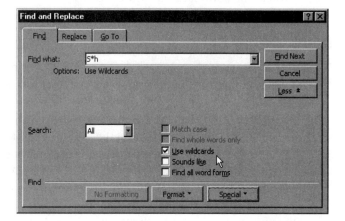

NOTE

Using Find and Replace with wildcard characters can be a little tricky. Remember, if your Replace operation does not give you the results you wanted, immediately click on the Undo button to reverse the last action.

Formatting with Find and Replace

The Find and Replace feature also allows you to find and change character formats and some paragraph formats. For example, suppose that you are typing a long proposal and have referred to a company name several times. Then you discover that the name should always be in bold and italics as part of its company logo copyright. You can use the Find and Replace feature to find the company name and replace it with the same name, but in the bold and italic type styles. Click on the bold and italics buttons on the Formatting toolbar (or press Ctrl+B and Ctrl+I) before you type the name of the company in the Replace With text box. You can also set these formats by clicking on the Format button at the bottom of the dialog box and choosing the Font option.

NOTE

The next time you use the Find and Replace dialog box, the previous information will be shown. You can take off the formatting in the Replace With text box by clicking in this area and selecting the No Formatting button at the bottom of the dialog box.

Word also lets you find and replace special characters, such as tabs, page breaks, and paragraph symbols. Envision a multiple-page report in which each paragraph has the first line tabbed in to indent the paragraphs. For the final draft, however, someone decides to have all the paragraphs flush left. You could go through the entire document, manually moving to each paragraph (Ctrl+↓) and deleting each tab character. An easier way is to use Find and Replace.

To change from tab-indented to left-aligned paragraphs, specify the special character for a tab (**^t**) in the Find What box (by typing it in directly or by selecting it from the list displayed by clicking on the Special drop-down button). Leave the Replace With box blank—to replace the tab with nothing. After you finish the Find and Replace operation, each paragraph's tab character will be removed, and the text will align along the left margin.

TIP

For a complete list of complex search criteria and their meanings, choose Help ➢ Contents and Index. When the Help Topics dialog box appears, click on the Index tab and type in **Finding**. The Finding topic will appear. Look down further to the Finding and Replacing section. Double-click on Search Criteria. In the Topics Found dialog box, double-click on Examples of Search Wildcards. When the list of different wildcard search criteria appears, click on the Options button at the top of the dialog box, and choose Print Topic to print the information as a reference.

Creating In-Place Comments

The In-Place Comments feature allows you to insert a comment into a document; the original text will not change, and the comment will not appear directly in the document. Text that is commented appears with a light yellow highlight; when you place the mouse over the highlight, a pop-up note appears, showing the name of the author and the text of the comment.

Although the In-Place Comment doesn't directly save you typing, these comments can be used for all types of timesaving notes and reminders and can be a valuable communication tool when sharing a document among multiple writers and reviewers.

To create an In-Place Comment:

1. Select the text or place the insertion point into a word that should be commented.
2. Choose Insert ➢ Comment.
3. The selected text will be highlighted in yellow, and the annotated area will open at the bottom of the screen. Your initials as defined in the User Information page of the Options dialog box (Tools ➢ Options ➢ User Information) are shown, and a blank typing area is ready for your comment.
4. Type the text of your comment or insert a sound file (you will need a microphone and a sound card to record your message).
5. When you've finished, click on the small Close button on the toolbar at the top of the Comment typing area.

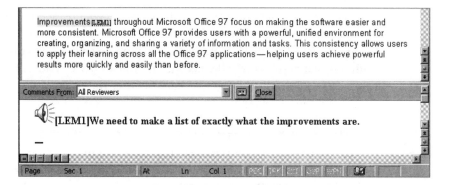

NOTE

When you pass a document among multiple reviewers and get it back with everyone's comments, you will be able to view a specific person's comments or see everyone's comments: In the Comments From list box choose a specific reviewer's name or choose All Reviewers.

Viewing Comments in a Document

Once comments have been placed into a document, a light yellow highlight appears over the text that is selected for comments. You can read the Comment by placing the mouse over the highlighted text. You will first see a comment's icon and then the text of the comment as well as the name of the person who created it.

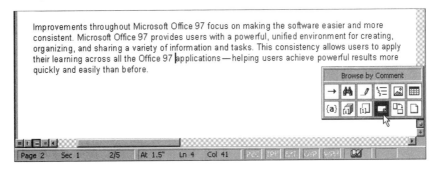

Lonnie Moseley:
We need to make a list of
exactly what the
improvements are.

Improvements throughout Microsoft Office 97 focus on making the software easier and more consistent. Microsoft Office 97 provides users with a powerful, unified environment for creating, organizing, and sharing a variety of information and tasks. This consistency allows users to apply their learning across all the Office 97 applications—helping users achieve powerful results more quickly and easily than before.

Finding Comments in a Document

PART

II

Communicating with Word

Even though the comments are indicated by a light yellow highlight on the commented text, the commented text can be anywhere in the document. In a large document, it will be quite tedious to visually look for all the commented text.

The Go To command (Ctrl+G) or the Document Navigator (small round button below the vertical scroll bar on the far right side of the screen) allows you to sequentially move to each comment in the document.

When you press Ctrl+G, the Go To dialog box will open. Select Comment from the list on the left and click on the Next button. You will be positioned at the next highlighted comment. Place the mouse over the Comment to read the text. Right-click the mouse to edit or delete the comment.

To use the Document Navigator, click on the round button on the vertical scroll bar or press Ctrl+Alt+Home; a panel of objects will appear. Click on the Browse by Comments object, and the insertion point will move to the next comment. To continue to move through the comments in your document, continue clicking on the Document Navigator button, or press Shift+F4 (the Find Again keystroke shortcut) repeatedly.

Editing or Deleting Comments

To edit or delete your own comments:

1. Pause the mouse over the commented text (a light yellow highlight is on text that is commented in the document) and if this is a comment you wish to edit, right-click the mouse on the text. A shortcut pop-up menu appears that includes the commands Edit Comment and Delete Comment.

2. Choose Edit Comment to see your comments and make changes, or choose Delete Comment to delete the comment from the text.

When you edit a comment, the Reviewing toolbar appears below the Formatting toolbar. The Edit Comment button is recessed, an indicator that you are currently in the Comment edit box.

When you delete a comment, there is no confirmation from Word—the comment is immediately deleted. If you inadvertently delete a comment, click on the Undo button or press Ctrl+Z for undo.

 TIP

You can select text in the comments area and change the typeface, font size, formats, and alignments (center, right, left, indent) of the commented text by using the formatting and alignment buttons on the Formatting toolbar. You can also copy a comment in the comments box using the Copy button on the Standard toolbar; you can then paste the comment.

Creating Templates from Documents

The ultimate in reusability of text is to create a template that can form the basis of new documents. You already know about templates. Whenever you choose File ➤ New from the main menu, the Normal template is presented to you as the basis of your next document.

Even though the Normal template does not include text, it does contain certain margin settings, font and typeface defaults, styles, macros, and toolbars. Word saves you time and effort when you create a new document by allowing you to base new documents on templates.

Word provides a number of templates for common types of documents: memos, reports, letters, and newsletters. You can use Word's templates without modification, or you can change them to more closely mirror your business needs. At the simplest level, think of a Word template as a form document. You may have a special memo form that your company prefers. If you create a memo template and store it for continued use, you will no longer need to retype the information that stays the same from memo to memo.

Although it may seem just as easy to open a previously saved document and make changes to it, the danger is that you will overwrite that document or that you will not be able to locate the file containing the previous version of a customized agreement.

When you create a template from the existing document, you can ensure that the document settings are appropriate and the text is correct. Word will store the template in a special subdirectory with its other templates. This avoids the possibility of overwriting or losing the data, because the template is served to you as a copy of the original for you to modify as you wish.

Creating a Template from a Document

The option to create a template from a document is in the File ➢ Save As dialog box. First, open the document you wish to use as the basis for a template. Make the content as generic as possible and perfect the fonts, margin settings, and other formatting.

When the document is ready, choose File ➢ Save As. At the bottom of the Save As dialog box is a Save As Type text box. Click the drop-down arrow and choose Document Template (*.dot). You will be switched to a special Templates subdirectory, which is the area of the disk where Word stores templates. Once within this area, you can double-click on one of the Template subdirectories and save your template into a special category, such as Letters & Faxes or Memos.

In the File Name section at the bottom of the dialog box, type a name for your document template, as shown in the example in Figure 12.6. Finally, click on the Save button on the right side of the dialog box.

PART

II

Communicating with Word

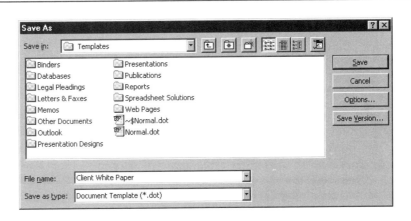

Basing a New Document on a Template

To start a new document based on a document template, choose File ➤ New. Go to the tab that has icons for the category in which you saved your document template and double-click on the template name.

When you choose a template, a *new* document is created. At the top of the screen in the title bar area, you will see the generic document number. Customize or change the document and save it under a different name. You will not be overwriting your original template.

NOTE

Chapter 14 describes how to apply a template design as part of the process of using a Word document to create a PowerPoint slide.

Producing Form Documents with Mail Merge

A common word processing task is to produce periodic mailings to go to a group of individuals. The documents must be customized with the individual's address information and usually other types of personal information, such as a spouse's name or the name of an item the individual purchased.

To produce these types of form documents, you can use Word's Mail Merge feature. Mail Merge requires three types of documents:

- The personalized document or envelope or mailing label, known as the *main document.*
- A list of individuals and their addresses or other specific pieces of information, called the *data source.*
- The result of merging the main document with the data source produces a third document, called the *merge* document. The merge document can be merged to the screen or directly to a printer.

To make the job simple, Word supplies a *Helper* to assist you through the steps of a merge. The Mail Merge Helper helps you to identify the documents for the merge and guides you through the options available to you during each step of the merge process.

WARNING

Don't inadvertently use the Tools ➤ Merge Documents feature for mail merge. This is not the Mail Merge Feature. The Merge Document feature combines comments and changes from multiple reviewers and writers into one document.

Creating the Main Document

The *main document* is the form into which the data information (for example, addresses or billing information) will be merged. The main document is most often a form letter. However, it can also be a mailing label, a postcard, an envelope, a name card, or any other type of document that can fit the categories of your data (such as name, address, account balance, date of appointment, and so on).

Create a simple letter. Insert the date (Insert ➢ Date and Time, select a date format from the Date and Time dialog box, and click on OK) at the top of the letter and then tap the Enter key approximately eight times so that you are ready to type the body of the letter. Do *not* type the inside address. The inside address will come from the categories contained within your data source, which you will create in the next section. Type the body of your letter and then save the letter. Figure 12.7 shows an example of a main document for Mail Merge.

PART

II

Communicating with
Word

FIGURE 12.7

*A main docu-
ment to use
with the Mail
Merge feature.
Notice that the
inside address
is not typed in.*

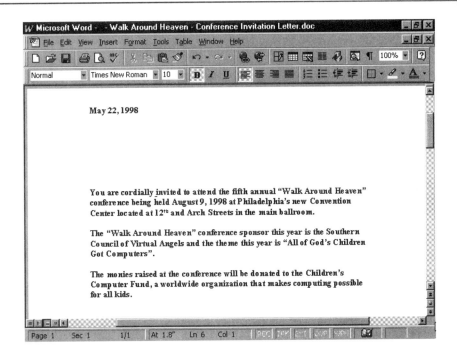

Using the Mail Merge Helper

Now that you have created a main document (letter), you can let the Mail Merge Helper guide you through the steps of what to do with the letter, how to create the data source, and then how to merge the two documents to produce the final merged document.

1. Make sure that the letter you are using as the main document is currently on the screen. Then choose Tools ➤ Mail Merge from the menu bar. Select Mail Merge.
2. In the Mail Merge Helper dialog box, you will begin Step 1 of the mail merge. Click on the Create button.
3. Choose Form Letters from the drop-down list of suggestions. Then, click on the Active Window button, since your main document is already open on the screen. Figure 12.8 shows the Mail Merge Helper screen after finishing Step 1.

FIGURE 12.8

The Mail Merge Helper display after a main document was created

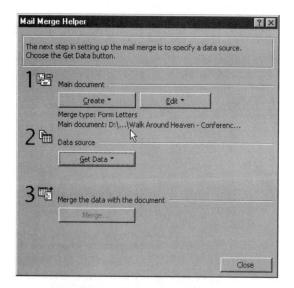

Creating a Data Source

If you do not have an existing database of information, you must create your own data source of the categories (fields) of information that will be inserted into the letter. For example, a Mail Merge letter might require that you have the following categories (fields): Title, First Name, Last Name, Job Title, Company, Address1, Address2, City,

State, Zip, and Salutation. If one of your addressees does not have information for a title or a company, Word will merge only the categories that have information and close up the blank categories.

In the previous section, we left the Mail Merge Helper ready for Step 2, specifying the data source. Proceed as follows:

1. In the Mail Merge Helper dialog box, click on the Get Data button next to Step 2.
2. Choose Create Data Source. The Create Data Source dialog box will appear.

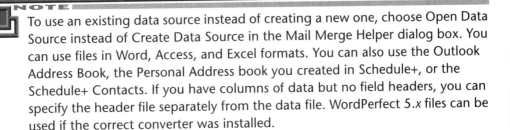

NOTE
To use an existing data source instead of creating a new one, choose Open Data Source instead of Create Data Source in the Mail Merge Helper dialog box. You can use files in Word, Access, and Excel formats. You can also use the Outlook Address Book, the Personal Address book you created in Schedule+, or the Schedule+ Contacts. If you have columns of data but no field headers, you can specify the header file separately from the data file. WordPerfect 5.*x* files can be used if the correct converter was installed.

Word has anticipated that you will need certain fields (categories) in the letter, and it has supplied the most commonly used fields for form letters. These fields are listed on the right side of the Create Data Source dialog box. For our example, we need to add one field that has not been supplied, Salutation, and remove three fields that we don't need: Country, HomePhone, and WorkPhone. Of course, if you actually need these fields in your own form letters, you wouldn't remove them. You can also add any other fields that you may need for this form letter, such as Account Balance or Spouse Name.

1. In the Create Data Source dialog box, click on the field named Country, then click the Remove Field Name button on the left side of the dialog box. Repeat this step again to remove the HomePhone and WorkPhone fields.
2. To add a salutation field, type the name of the field, **Salutation**, in the Field Name text box on the left side of the Create Data Source dialog box (type over any existing data that may be there). Then click on the Add Field Name button.
3. When you have finished, click on the OK button; the Save As dialog box will appear. Word wants you to immediately save the categories you decided should be in your form letter.
4. In the Save As dialog box, type in a name for the data source file that contains these categories. For example, you might name your data source **Invitation List for Conference**.

5. Click on the Save button. The next dialog box wants to know if you want to edit the data source, because this file does not contain any data (names and addresses) yet:

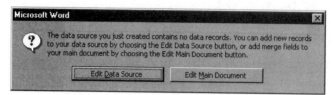

6. To add data to the file, click on the Edit Data Source button. A data form appears with the fields that you designated, as shown in Figure 12.9. Type one piece of information per field on your data form. Once you have completed the field information for each category, the entire group of fields is called a *record*. If you do not have information for a particular field, just leave that field blank. Word will make sure that a blank line does not print for the blank field.

NOTE

To move around in the data form, press the Enter key or the Tab key to move down from field to field. The Shift+Tab key combination moves you up field by field. You can also click the vertical scroll arrows to move up and down and see more fields.

FIGURE 12.9

Word has one of the most attractive data forms for entering database-type information into a word processing program.

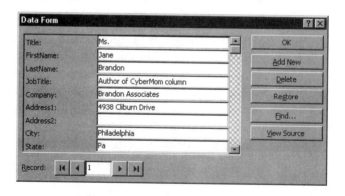

7. Fill in the fields for the first person's record. When you are ready for the next person, click on the Add New button on the right side of the dialog box; you will be presented with a new blank form. You can also press the Enter key after typing the last field's information, and a new blank form will appear automatically.

NOTE

If you inadvertently click on the data form's OK button before you have finished adding your records, you will see the merge letter on which the fields will be placed. Choose Tools ➤ Mail Merge to reactivate the Mail Merge Helper. Click on Step 2's Edit Data Source button. Click on the button displaying the name of your data source. You will be returned to the data form. Also, if you press the View Source button in the Data Form dialog box and see your data in the form of a Word table, click the Window item on the menu bar and switch to your merge letter so that it is active on the screen. Then follow the same steps as described above. You can also click on the Edit Source button on the Mail Merge toolbar, which is displayed when you are in the main document.

PART

II

8. Continue entering the names and addresses of individuals to whom this letter is going.
9. When you have finished, click on the OK button. You will be returned to the merge letter.

After you've created a data source this way, you can always use this list again. The next time you create another merge letter, you can open any existing data source that has the fields you need for your main document (and in the proper format) by choosing Open Data Source, instead of Create Data Source, in Step 2 of the Mail Merge Helper dialog box.

Placing Data Source Fields into the Merge Letter

Although you now have the data source, the merge letter does not have any connection to the data source yet. You must place the fields into the letter where you wish for the information in the fields to appear when the merge has been completed.

To place fields into a form letter, you must have completed both a basic letter and a group of records in a data form. If you have been following along with this example, you have just completed Step 2 of the Mail Merge Helper and entered records into the data form. You are now looking at the merge letter and ready to insert the fields of the data source into the appropriate places on the letter. Follow these steps for placing the appropriate fields into the letter:

1. Click two lines below the date of the letter. This is the line where the inside address fields will be inserted so that Word knows where to display this field information.
2. A new toolbar appears at the top of the screen. If you do not see this toolbar, choose View ➤ Toolbars and put a check in the Mail Merge checkbox.
3. Click on the Insert Merge Field button on the Mail Merge toolbar to see a list of the fields available. Figure 12.10 shows the list of fields from the data source form we created earlier.

Communicating with Word

FIGURE 12.10

The fields designated in the data form are now available to insert into the main document merge letter.

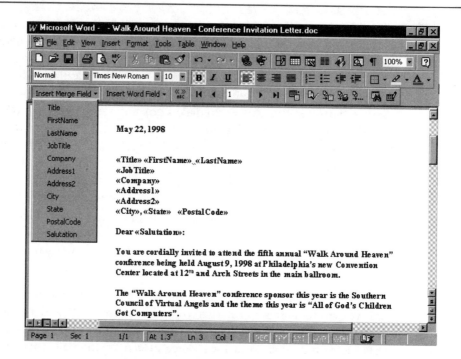

4. Click on the Title field. Word will insert this field into your form letter within double right and left arrows. (During the mail merge, this field name will be replaced with the title of the individual from your data source.) Press the spacebar after the inserted field to insert a space after the title (you don't want the letter to say something like "Mr.JohnBrown").

5. Click on the Insert Merge Field button again and click on the field called First-Name. Press the spacebar to separate this field from the next one.

TIP

If you press Shift+Alt+F, the Insert Merge Field dialog box will appear with the list of field names from the data source. Press the first letter of a field to jump to that particular field. Press the Enter key to drop the field into the document. You must press the Shift+Alt+F combination each time you want to insert a field.

6. Click on the Insert Merge Field button again and click on the field called Last-Name. Press the Enter key to move to the next line.

7. Continue to place the fields. Press the Delete key to remove the extra blank lines until your document looks like the sample shown in Figure 12.10. You must enter all punctuation (spaces, commas, colons, and so on), such as the comma after the City field.

8. After you have entered all of the fields where you wish them to be displayed, save the file again. (If you have not saved previously, create a name for your file.) You are now ready to merge.

NOTE

If you add a field that you do not want on your merge letter, drag the mouse over the field and press the Delete key. The field will be removed from the merge letter, but not from the fields contained on the Insert Merge Field list.

Merging a Letter with a Data Source

You have completed Steps 1 and 2 of the Mail Merge Helper's merge process. You created and saved a main document form letter. Then you created a data source form and entered records that will be merged into the letter. Step 3, the last step within the Mail Merge Helper system, completes the merge by substituting the actual information in the data source form for the field names placed within the main document letter.

If you have been following along with this example, the main document letter is currently on the screen and you have finished inserting merge field names and saving the file. Follow these steps to merge the document and the data:

1. Choose Tools ➤ Mail Merge or click on the Mail Merge Helper button on the Mail Merge toolbar.

2. In the Mail Merge Helper dialog box, within Step 3, click on the Merge button. Figure 12.11 shows the Merge dialog box with the default settings for a mail merge.

PART

II

Communicating with Word

FIGURE 12.11

Word's Merge dialog box includes a setting that prevents blank lines from printing for empty data fields.

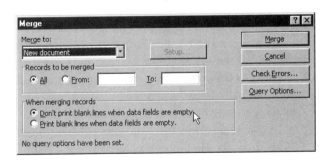

3. The results of your merge can be directed to a printer or to a new document (on-screen copy). You can even merge to electronic mail or fax addresses. To merge to electronic mail, your system must have an MAPI-compatible electronic mail or fax application (such as Microsoft Exchange or Microsoft Mail), and one of the fields in your data source must contain the electronic mail addresses or fax numbers.

4. The default is to direct the merge to a new document so that you can look at the results before printing them. There's no sense in you finding out that there are mistakes in the merge after you have wasted your letterhead and printed a number of these letters.

5. Click on the Merge button on the right side of the dialog box to begin the final merge process.

Inspecting a Merged Document Before Printing

When the final merge step is completed (with the default of merging to a new document on the screen), you will see a new document, called FormLetters1, at the top of the screen (it may say a different number if you have already merged documents).

As you tap the PgDn key and view the completed form letters, you will notice that each record's information from the fields in the data source is in a separate letter (page) and that there is a page break between the letters.

If all looks good, save this merge (although you don't really have to—the original letter and people data file can easily be merged again) and print the merged letter by clicking on the Print button on the Standard toolbar. If you see problems, however, you must be able to identify the source of the problem.

Identifying the Source of a Mail Merge Problem

Experienced mail mergers have a couple of techniques for identifying problems in their mail merge. Unless you can tell which document is causing the problem, you won't know whether to go back to the original merge letter or the data source file. Here are a few common problems that occur during mail merge and some strategies for solving them:

- If a field is missing from each merged letter, the problem is in the original mail merge letter. In the Window menu, select the name of your original letter to make it active on the screen. Examine each field and make sure that you have the correct field in the correct spot. Make your changes and merge the document again (Tools ➤ Mail Merge ➤ Step 3).

- If data is missing from some of the merged letters but not from other merged letters, the problem is within the data source. Make the mail merge letter active on the screen. Then choose Tools , Mail Merge , Step 2 , Edit Data Source, or click on the Edit

Data Source button on the Mail Merge toolbar. Look for the records of the person who had data missing and make sure that you typed the data for that particular field for the person. Click on OK. You will return to the original merge letter. If you have viewed the source for the data—which is really a Word table—and are not able to go back to the main document from the data source, use the Window menu to return to the main document. Merge the document again (Tools , Mail Merge , Step 3).

- If there are typos or the spacing is incorrect on each letter, the problem is in the original letter. In the Window menu, select the name of your original letter and find the location where one field is too close to the text or too close to another field. Make your changes and merge the document again (Tools ➢ Mail Merge ➢ Step 3).

- If only a few letters print out, and you know that there are more people in your data file than names that printed on the merge letters, there is a merge query option that is filtering out some of your records. If for example, you queried during the last merge for records that had CA (California) in the State field, the new merge may still be using the old query. Make sure that the original mail merge letter is on the screen by choosing the letter from the Window menu. Select Tools ➢ Mail Merge ➢ Step 3, but make sure you click on the Query Options button on the right-hand side. If there is a filter set, you can delete the information and merge the letter again.

WARNING

Do not make corrections on the FormLetters1 file. This is the result of the merge of two other files: the main document and the data source document. If you correct the result, the original problem will show up again the next time you merge. You must correct the source of the errors or problems by going back to the main merge letter document first.

Changing the Data Source File without Merging

Your next merge may require that additional names be used, or you may need to make corrections to certain addresses because you received returned mail from the post office. You can add to or update records in your data source file without being involved in the three steps of the mail merge.

When you are not involved in an actual merge process, Word does not make Step 2 active in the Mail Merge Helper dialog box (Tools ➢ Mail Merge). The Helper forces you to create or open a main document before you can use Step 2 and open a previously created data source. You can, however, open the data source file directly and still get to the data form view.

Viewing Your Data in a Word Table

Close any active files that may currently be in memory (make sure that important files are saved). Then, open the data source file through the File ➢ Open dialog box and not through the Tools ➢ Mail Merge menu. The file that appears looks like a Word table, with the fields of your data source listed on the first row of the table as the headings. The actual data that you typed into the data source appears in each subsequent row, but word-wraps in the small widths of the columns. This is how Word stores a data source.

You can add new records right here in the table by clicking into the last column of the last row and pressing the Tab key to start a new row. And you can edit current records—just make sure you type the correct information in the proper field, as designated by each column heading. Figure 12.12 shows data being added to a data source table.

FIGURE 12.12

You can open a data source file directly and add records and make changes to existing records, because the data source file is stored as a Word table.

Dr.	Linda	Powell	Physician	Medical Practice Associates	928 South Street	Phila delp hia	PA	19106
Mr.	Fred	Cooper	Prince of Dimming Light	Pandora Inc.	P.O. Box 499	Phila delp hia	PA	19148
Ms.	Jan	Morgen	Artist in Residence	Picasso Center	527 Breen St.	New York	NY	10000
Rev.	Susan	Greco	Minister	St. Terese	12 Port Street	Phila delp hia	PA	19123
Mr.	Donald	Jones						

You can also delete a record by deleting a row in the table. Click on the row of the record to be deleted and choose Table ➢ Select Row from the menu bar. Then, click on the Cut button on the Standard toolbar or select Table ➢ Delete Rows. The row is immediately deleted. If you make a mistake, click on the Undo button to reverse the action. See Chapter 11 on using the Table feature in Word.

Viewing Your Data in the Data Form

Working with the data source as a Word table gives you tremendous control and allows you to see a number of records at the same time. But you can still use the data form to add, edit, delete, and find records. The convenient form keeps your data organized in a database-type interface.

To place the data form on top of the table, you must first activate Word's Database toolbar. Follow these steps to activate the data form from the Database toolbar:

1. Open the data source file, if you do not already have the file active on the screen. The data source file appears as a Word table when opened by choosing File ➢ Open. Make sure the insertion point is in some cell of the table.

2. Choose View ➤ Toolbars. Put a check in the checkbox next to Database. The Database toolbar will appear below the Formatting toolbar at the top of the screen.

3. Click on the first button—the Data Form button—on the Database toolbar. The Data Form dialog box is superimposed on top of the table, and you can see the information in the table through the data form.

4. Make whatever additions, deletions, or changes you wish. The VCR-type buttons at the bottom of the form move you record-by-record through the database. Use the Find button in the Data Form dialog box to display the Find in Field dialog box and locate a specific piece of information in a field. The Restore button undoes any changes you made to the current data record.

5. Click on the View Source button on the right side of the data form to return to viewing your records in a table.

Using the Database Toolbar

The Database toolbar remains on your screen, even when you are looking at the data in a Word table. You can quickly add and delete records while in the table by choosing the Add New Record or Delete Record buttons. You can perform quick sorts on any column by clicking the mouse into the column on which you want to sort the records and clicking the Sort Ascending button on the Database toolbar to sort in ascending (alphabetical) order. Table 12.1 describes the functions of the buttons on the Database toolbar.

TABLE 12.1: THE DATABASE TOOLBAR BUTTONS

Button	Name	Purpose
	Data Form	Creates a data entry form
	Manage Fields	Adds and removes fields from the database form
	Add New Record	Adds a blank row to a data source table to insert new records
	Delete Record	Deletes the row on which the insertion point is placed
	Sort Ascending	Sorts in low to high order by the column in which the insertion point is placed

Continued ▶

PART

II

Communicating with Word

TABLE 12.1: THE DATABASE TOOLBAR BUTTONS (CONTINUED)

Button	Name	Purpose
	Sort Descending	Sorts in high to low order by the column in which the insertion point is placed
	Insert Database	Inserts information from databases outside Word
	Update Fields	Updates and displays the results of selected fields
	Find Record	Searches for information that may be contained within any field of your database
	Mail Merge Main Document	Switches to a main document set up through the Mail Merge Helper

Printing the Data Source File as a Directory of Names

To print the data source as a directory of names, you must use the Mail Merge feature. Fortunately, Word makes this quick and easy to set up. Word has preprogrammed a mailing label form that can be used for three-across labels. Once the names are merged into the mailing label form, you can print them on regular paper, instead of mailing label stock, to produce a columnar directory. Here are the steps to produce a directory of names:

1. Choose File ➢ Open and bring the data source file to the screen, if it is not there already. The data source file will appear as a Word table. (If the data form is superimposed on the table, click on the View Source button on the right side of the data form so that you can see the data source file as a Word table.)
2. If the Database toolbar is not on the screen, choose View ➢ Toolbars and select Database.
3. Click into the column by which you wish to sort your data (for example, Last-Name, Account Balance, JobTitle, or PostalCode for bulk mailings). After sorting, save the file by clicking on the Save button on the Standard toolbar or press Ctrl+S.

4. Click on the Sort Ascending button on the Database toolbar to sort in ascending order (low to high, or alphabetically) or the Sort Descending button for descending order (high to low).

5. Once the data in the Word table is in the sort order you need for the directory, choose Tools ➤ Mail Merge.

6. Click on the Create button in Step 1 to create a main document that will hold the data records. Choose Mailing Labels, not Catalog. When the confirmation dialog box appears, choose New Main Document (not Active Window), so that Word will create the mailing labels in a new document.

7. In Step 2, click on the Get Data button, and choose Open Data Source. Browse the hard disk until you find your data source (even though it is currently in memory, Mail Merge likes to get the file itself). Select the file and click on Open.

8. Word will alert you that you need to set up the main document for labels. Click on the Set Up Main Document button. The Labels Option dialog box will appear, as shown in Figure 12.13.

PART

II

Communicating with Word

FIGURE 12.13

The Mailing Label main document is an excellent form to use to create a directory of names.

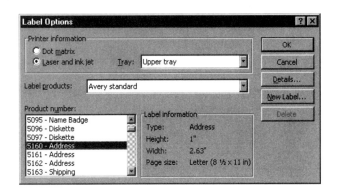

9. For Label Products, choose Avery Standard. In the Product Number list box, click 5160-Address (Avery 5160s are three columns by ten rows deep). Then click OK.

10. The Create Labels dialog box appears. Click on the Insert Merge Field button and insert each of the fields as you would for an inside address. If you make a mistake and insert a field in the wrong order, drag the mouse across the field and delete it. When you've finished placing the fields, click on OK. Figure 12.14 shows a sample label with the data source fields.

11. You are ready to merge the data source records into the mailing label form. Go to Step 3 and click on the Merge button. The Merge dialog box appears.

FIGURE 12.14

You can insert the specific fields that you wish to see printed on the directory.

12. Click on the Merge button on the right side of the Merge dialog box. Word will begin merging the information into the mailing label. Figure 12.15 shows the finished product merged to the screen.

13. Save the results of the mail merge file, if you desire, and click on the Print button on the Standard toolbar to print the mailing label pages.

FIGURE 12.15

Merging to a label form

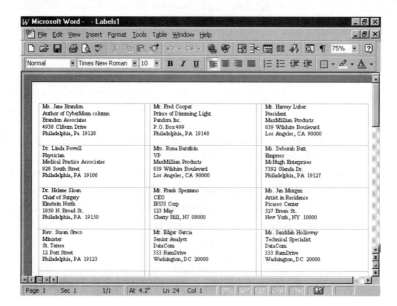

If you need to correct either the main document (mailing label form) or the data source after completing a merge, find the name of the mailing label main document in the Window menu. If you wish to edit the main document, make your changes. Because this is a mailing label main document, any changes you make in one block must be copied to every other block of the mailing label form. If you wish to edit the data source file, however, choose Tools ➢ Mail Merge and select Step 2.

Selecting Specific Records for Merging or Printing

The Query options in Step 3 of the Mail Merge Helper allow you to select specific records from your data source that match a criteria you've set. In other words, if you wish to merge and print letters or create a mailing list directory for individuals from a specific state, you can put the name of the state into the query and merge for those individuals from your data source. The only requirement is that you know the name of the field that contains the information you are looking for.

Many experienced Word users who work extensively with mail merge have learned over time to isolate each unique piece of information into a separate field. In other words, the City, State, Zip information would never be created as one big field but rather three separate fields. By isolating each piece of information, finding specific records is easier.

Adding Fields to a Data Source for Selecting

You will also need to add new fields when you have new information on your customers or employees, or due to government requirements, workplace laws, new marketing categories, and so on. You also may want to change your data source to add additional fields so that you can query for specific records (individuals). Suppose your data source is one big field; all the address information is one field and not broken out into First-Name, LastName, City, State, Zip, and so on. You will not be able to query successfully for a specific piece of information, because there is no specific field you can tell Word to look into.

To add an additional field to your data source so that you can better query, follow these steps:

1. Select File ➢ Open and find the file that contains your data source. You do not have to be involved in a mail merge to work separately with the data source file.
2. When the data source file appears, it is a Word table. Don't worry about narrow columns containing wrapped text. The information for each record will merge correctly.
3. Make the Database toolbar visible. Choose View ➢ Toolbars ➢ Database.

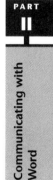

PART

II

Communicating with Word

4. Click on the second button on the toolbar, Manage Fields. (By the way, the first button superimposes the data form on the table so that you can see your record information correctly laid out. You cannot have the data form up, however, and manage the fields at the same time.)

5. When the Manage Fields dialog box appears, type the name of the new field you want for your data source. For this example, type a field called Code1.

6. Click on the Add button below the Field Name box. The new field is placed at the end of the current list of fields and a new column is inserted at the end of the table, as shown in Figure 12.16. When you are finished adding fields, click on the OK button.

FIGURE 12.16

You can create additional fields using the Manage Fields dialog box.

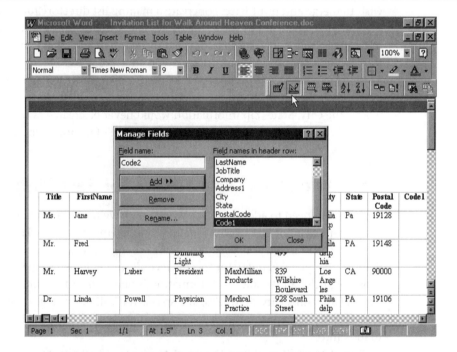

7. Go into the new field(s) you added and type the appropriate information for each record. You can now turn on the data form to make the typing easier. (Click on the first button on the Database toolbar.) Use the code letter A for some of the records, and use B and C for other records, so that you have a few records of each type of code. We will use this information in a later section to query (find and select) records that have the letter A in the Code1 field. Make sure you save the file when you have finished putting in the data. Remember, you can always open the file later and finish typing the information into the new fields.

TIP

If there are fields you would like to delete or rename, click on the field in the list on the right of the Manage Fields dialog box and then choose either Remove or Rename. When you choose Remove, Word will ask you to confirm the removal. If you choose Rename, another dialog box appears asking you for the new name.

Converting a Growing Word Table

As you grow more sophisticated at using a Word table as a database, you may have new ideas for managing data; individuals may begin to ask for reports that are beyond the scope of a mail merge in Word. If your data management tasks begin to increase, tables may become too big to work with comfortably in Word. When this happens, it may be time to look at other tools for management, Excel 97 or Access 97.

If you are continuously adding columns to the data source, you may want to keep the data in Excel. Excel 97 is going to allow you to add more columns than Word will allow. It is quite easy to copy your Word table and have it instantly become an Excel spreadsheet:

1. Select the Word table.
2. Click on the Copy button on the Standard toolbar.
3. Start the Excel program.
4. Click on the Paste button in Excel.
5. Save the Excel file with your table.

If you find that you are doing a good deal of querying of information for different types of mail merge lists or reports, it is time to move to Access 97. Access's report feature is excellent, and the querying ability allows you to ask questions and then save those questions for future queries.

You can still use Word's mail merge feature even though your data resides in Access. The Access table can be the data source during a mail merge (see Part Six on Data Management with Access). Again, it is very easy to take a Word table and have it become an Access table:

1. Use the information above to copy a Word table as an Excel table. Once your Word data is an Excel table, save it.
2. Start Access.
3. Create a new database file (name it anything).
4. Choose File ➢ Get External Data ➢ Import from the Access menu.

5. In the Files of Type text box, choose Microsoft Excel (*.xls).

6. Locate the name of your Excel table copied from Word and double-click on the name.

7. The Access Import Wizard will then take over and walk you through the process (see Figure 12.17).

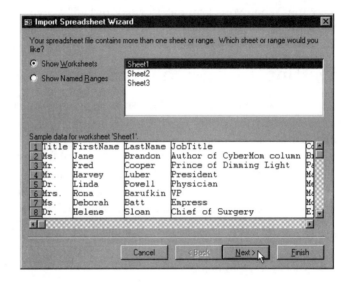

Using the Query Options to Select Records

You've now added fields that may be needed for your query. Your data has been stored into the appropriate program (Word or Excel or Access), and you are ready to query the data source regardless of where the data is stored. To show you how to query to select records, we'll use a label example, because it does not require a pretyped merge letter. You can refer back to the section on creating a merge letter later.

Creating a Name Badge Label

With a query, you can select a particular value (like a state) and print a directory for those records in the data source that match the query value. A colleague can be given a subsection of a list that only deals with their issues. Your coded field may be a sales-person's initials or some other identifier. Name badges for a specific group of individuals can be printed using an Avery label.

Below are the steps to create a query and merge the selected records into a name badge label form. The only prerequisite for this example is that you have an existing data source—either a Word table (see the previous section for how to create a data source), an Excel table, or an Access table. The data source that was used in the previous section is the basis for this exercise.

1. Start with a blank screen.
2. Choose Tools ➢ Mail Merge. The Mail Merge Helper appears, listing the three steps of the merge.
3. In Step 1, click on the Create button in the Main Document area.
4. Choose Mailing Labels from the list and select Active Window from the dialog box.
5. In Step 2, click on the Get Data button and choose Open Data Source.
6. If your data source is a Word document, search for its name and click on Open. If the data source is another type of document (Excel or Access), click on the drop-down arrow next to the Files of Type text box at the bottom of the dialog box and choose the appropriate file type and then click on the Open button.
7. Word will now need to set up your label. Click on the Set Up Main Document button and choose Avery Label 5883 - Name Badge and click on OK.
8. When the Create Labels sample label form appears, click on the Insert Merge Field button, place a few fields onto the label, and click on OK. You will be returned to the Mail Merge Helper. For this example, place the fields Title, FirstName, LastName, JobTitle, Company, and Code1 on the label—not the address fields.

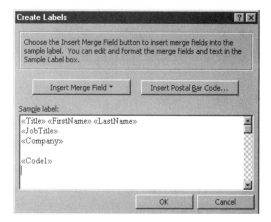

Selecting Specific Records for the Name Badge Label

After you have finished creating the Name Badge label, the Mail Merge Helper reappears, and you are ready for Step 3 to Query and Merge the data. Querying for specific records is a powerful database capability that allows you to set the criteria for the

PART

II

Communicating with Word

records you want to merge. But to specify what you want, you must use the field category names of your data source—for example, STATE. Once you identify the field, then the COMPARISON must be designated—for example, Equal To or Greater Than or Less Than. The third step is to type a VALUE that you are looking for in the data source records—for example STATE=PA. Only those records where the value PA was found in the STATE field will be merged to the main document.

Simple criteria can be set as well as compound criteria, such as STATE=PA AND CODE1=B. Multiple criteria will narrow your record selection. There may have been twenty records in which State = PA, but by adding another criteria of CODE1=B, there are fewer records. This type of criteria is known as an AND statement. Each time you add another layer of criteria, the query is centering to a smaller and smaller group of records.

Compound criteria can also involve OR statements. Take, for example, STATE=PA OR TITLE=PRESIDENT—one criteria has nothing to do with the other. Word interprets the statement OR like the words *and also*. You would like records in which the STATE=PA and you would like records in which the TITLE=PRESIDENT. You will get both groups in your mail merge. There may be some Presidents from PA but that is coincidence.

In this example, you are going to query for records that have the letter A in the Code1 field. You will specify both the Code1 field and the value you are looking for: A.

1. You should be in Step 3 of the Mail Merge Helper. Click on the Merge button.
2. When the Merge dialog box appears, click on the Query Options button in the right side of the box. This is where you will specify your record selection criteria.

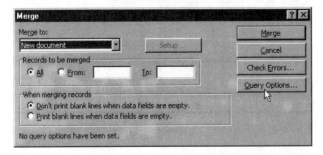

3. The Query Options dialog box appears with the Filter Records tab selected. Click on the drop-down arrow next to the Field list box, and select the field you want to specify a value for. For this example, select the Code1 field.
4. Next to the Field option is the Comparison option. The default is Equal To; let this remain.

NOTE

When you query for specific records, you are also "filtering out" other records that don't match your query. You will sometimes hear the word *filter* used instead of query.

5. In the Compare To text box next to the Comparison option, type the specific value for which you are querying. For this example, type the letter **A**. The Compare To is a value (word, number, or other value) that you want Word to find. If you have a compound query, such as Code1 = A *And* State = PA, use the line that begins with the word *And* to specify the second part of the query. Each *And* line will narrow the amount of records. You can also change the *And* to *Or;* this will increase the amount of records found (see Part 6 on Access for querying concepts).

6. Click on OK when you've finished. You will be returned to the Merge dialog box.

7. Click on the Merge button on the right side of the dialog box to finally merge the records for the Code A people.

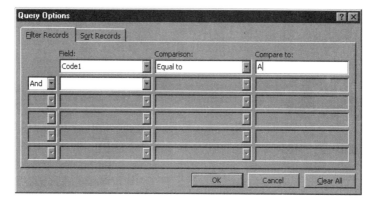

When the merge is completed, you will see which data source records had the value you specified in your query. Word gives a generic name to the document that is the result of the merge, for example, Labels1. (The next time you merge, the number of this merge document will be incremented, so it will be called Labels2).

Merging Again after a Query

If the merge is not correct, you can throw away the result of the merge and merge the information again. But you can only re-merge from your original label form (main document), and that is a file other than the generic merge result document. You must bring the original main document to the active window before merging again.

Select the Window menu, and in the list of documents, choose your original main document (it may not have a saved name). Choose Tools ➤ Mail Merge to select Step 3 (Merge) and select Query Options again to make changes or add additional criteria to your query. Click on OK when you have finished. Then, click on the Merge button to merge the data again.

Chapter

13

Customizing Word

FEATURING

Customizing Word

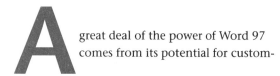

A great deal of the power of Word 97 comes from its potential for customization. With the options available in Word, the user—not the program—is in charge.

Changing even a few of Word's options from their default values can dramatically affect the way a user interacts with the program. While the basic functionality of Word will always remain the same, a user with the knowledge of the available options can make Word a more personal and powerful tool.

Customizing Word's Options

Most of the customization options available in Word can be accessed by choosing Tools ➤ Options from the menu bar, which opens the Options dialog box. The Options dialog box, shown in Figure 13.1, has 10 tabs at the top, each representing a different page of options.

This section provides an overview of the choices available in the Options dialog box. Some of these settings may not be useful to you, but there are quite a few that you will find helpful.

FIGURE 13.1

*Word's Options
dialog box,
accessed by
choosing Tools ➤
Options*

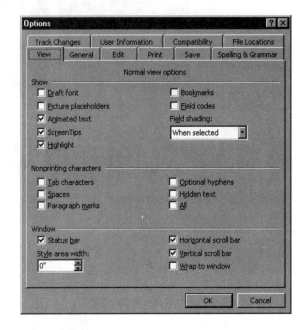

Setting View Options

The first page of interest to most users will be the View page, shown in Figure 13.1. The options on the View page control how Word documents appear on the screen.

The View page gives you different options, depending on which view you are in when you select the Tools ➤ Options menu: Normal, Online, Page Layout or Outline view. We will discuss the Normal view's options, because it holds most of the options you will want to change. Make sure you are in Normal View by selecting View ➤ Normal.

On the View page of the Options dialog box, the checkboxes and drop-down list in the Show area turn on and off the screen display of the features listed. For example, when ScreenTips is checked, you see the ScreenTips when the mouse is placed over a toolbar icon; when it's unchecked, the ScreenTips don't appear.

The checkboxes in the Window area control whether or not you see four of Word's major window components: the Status bar, the Horizontal scroll bar, the Vertical scroll bar, and the Wrap to Window. The Style Area Width option (you must be in Normal view to see this option) is set by default to 0 inches. If you increase the width of the style area, you can see all of the styles that you are using in your document. The style area runs along the left side of the window and is only displayed in Normal view (see Chapter 11 for a discussion of setting the Style Area Width).

The checkboxes in the Nonprinting Characters area of the View page turn on and off the display of nonprinting characters, including tabs, spaces, paragraph marks, optional hyphens, and hidden text. The last checkbox, All, provides a quick way to toggle on an off the display of all such characters.

Setting Save Options

As you learned in Chapter 10, the Save page of the Options dialog box contains the setting for the AutoRecover feature, which is the Save AutoRecover Info Every n Minutes option. The other options you may find useful here are Allow Fast Saves and the File Sharing Password settings.

> **NOTE**
> Remember, when you set the AutoRecover option, Word is saving a copy and not the original document. If you have AutoRecover set for every 15 or 20 minutes, there is a good chance that you have saved a more recent version than what is in the recovered document. See Chapter 10 for more details.

The Allow Fast Saves option tells Word whether you want to save just the changes to your document when you select Save (a *fast save*) or if you want the entire document saved. Fast saves are quicker than normal saves because they save only the changes made to the document since the last time you saved it.

The down side to fast saves is that they take more disk space than normal saves. Microsoft does suggest that if you plan on performing a memory-hungry operation, such as searching for text or compiling an index, you use a full save. You should also think about performing a full save once you have completely finished a document or before you convert a document into another file format.

Fast saves cannot be performed across a network. Also, if you choose Always Create Backup Copy on the Save page, Word will disable Allow Fast saves, because it needs to perform full saves for backups. When the Always Create Backup Copy option is checked, Word automatically creates a backup copy of your file each time you save it. See Chapter 10 for more information about automatic backups.

The File Sharing Options area of the Save page includes a Password to Open, a Password to Modify, and a Read-Only Recommended checkbox. The name of the current document is shown, as these options only apply to the file in the active window. The Password to Open option restricts any access to a file without the specified password. The Password to Modify option requires that a user enter the designated password before being allowed to save changes to the original file. If you check the Read-Only Recommended option, Word suggests to users that they open a file read-only (disallowing any changes).

Setting User Information Options

At first glance, there does not seem to be much to the User Information page of the Options dialog box. However, the User Information page can make your work much easier and more fluid.

The User Information page contains the user name, initials, and mailing address. Word uses this information throughout its operation. The user name is used to define the Author property of documents that you create. The Author property and the user initials are used in the title bar, with Word's Revisions feature, in the Header and Footer AutoText entries, and with In-Place Comments. The mailing address information is used as the default return address for labels and envelopes.

Setting Spelling & Grammar Options

The Spelling & Grammar page of Word's Options dialog box has many useful options regarding the way that Word spells and grammar checks your document. Figure 13.2 shows the Spelling & Grammar page with the default options selected.

FIGURE 13.2

*The Spelling &
Grammar
page of Word's
Options
dialog box*

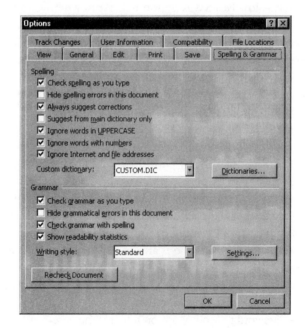

Spelling Options

The first checkbox in the Spelling area turns on the feature that spell-checks your document as you type. When Word finds a misspelled word, it places a wavy red line under it. If you don't want this spell-checking as you go along, uncheck the Check Spelling as You Type checkbox. If you simply don't want to see the red lines until you are ready, check the Hide Spelling Errors in This Document option. Once you are finished with your document and you are ready to see your spelling errors, you can uncheck the option to see the work done by the automatic spelling checker.

Always Suggest Corrections controls whether the Spelling dialog box includes suggestions for correcting an error. Suggest from Main Dictionary Only restricts where the suggestions come from.

The first of the three Ignore checkboxes allows you to instruct the spelling checker to ignore any words that are in all uppercase. This can be a useful feature, as long as you spell everything that is all capitals correctly. You can also instruct the spelling checker to ignore words with numbers in them. If you are working with data that is number intensive, it is frustrating for the spelling checker to stop on each word that contains a number. Ignore Internet and File Addresses is a new option in Word 97. This option tells Word not to spell-check the URL for a Web site or the file location of a hyperlinked document.

Below the list of Spelling options are the Custom Dictionary combo box and the Dictionaries button.

- Custom Dictionary allows you to select which dictionary you want to use during spell-checking. For example, you may have added a medical dictionary or a legal dictionary that you now wish to select.
- The Dictionaries button takes you to a dialog box that allows you to create, edit, and otherwise manipulate custom dictionaries.

WARNING

When you click on the Dictionaries button to edit the contents of a dictionary and then proceed to edit an existing document, the Check Spelling as You Type feature is turned off. Be sure to re-check the option when you want to have automatic spell-checking on again.

Grammar Options

The four grammar options mirror some of the Spelling options. If you turn on the Check Grammar as You Type option, when Word finds a grammatical error in a sentence, it places a wavy green line under the error. If you don't want grammar-checking as you go along, uncheck the Check Grammar as You Type checkbox. If you simply don't want to see the green lines until you are ready, check the Hide Grammatical Errors in This Document option. Once you are finished with your document and you are ready to see your grammar errors, you can uncheck the option and the work done by the automatic grammar checker.

You can separate the grammar-checking from the spell-checking sessions so that they are not performed together by unchecking Check Grammar with Spelling. When you press F7 or click on the Spelling and Grammar icon on the Standard toolbar, both grammar and spelling go into action.

When Word finishes checking spelling and grammar, it can display information about the reading level of the document, including readability scores. Each readability score bases its rating on the average number of syllables per word and words per sentence.

- Flesch Reading Ease score—This score is a rating for your text on a 100-point scale. The higher the score means the easier it is to understand the document. For most standard documents you should aim for a score of approximately 60 to 70.
- Flesch-Kincaid Grade Level score—This score is a rating for text on a U.S. grade-school level. For example, a score of 8.0 means that an eighth grader can understand the document. For most standard documents, you should aim for a score of approximately 7.0 to 8.0. A large document downloaded from Microsoft, which details the new and improved features of Office 97, was sent through the grammar checker and received the Readability statistics in Figure 13.3.

FIGURE 13.3

The Readability statistics dialog box gives you information about the reading level of the document and the audience to which your document is directed.

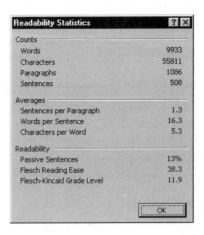

The Writing Style list can be selected if you want to use a different set of rules for grammar-checking. You can change the Writing Style options from Standard to Formal, Technical or Custom. The Settings button in the lower right side of the Grammar area allows you to control what types of grammar problems you want checked by the grammar checker.

Finally, at the bottom of the dialog box, Recheck Document allows you to force a refresh of the automatic spelling and grammar check of the current document.

Setting General Options

The options on the General page of the Options dialog box are, as the name suggests, general—they cover a variety of areas that do not necessarily fit on any of the other pages. Figure 13.4 shows this page of the Options dialog box.

FIGURE 13.4

The General page of Word's Options dialog box

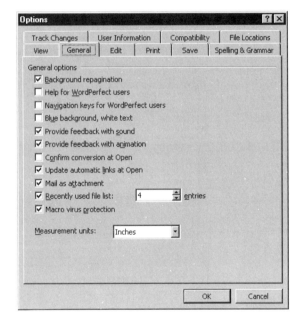

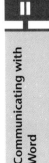

The second and third options in the dialog box, Help for WordPerfect Users and Navigation Keys for WordPerfect Users, provide help for users who are switching from WordPerfect to Word. While these options are helpful for WordPerfect users in the beginning, even the most diehard WordPerfect user will eventually get tired of the constant migration assistance from Word.

Farther down on the list of options is the one to increase the number of your most recently used files that are shown on the File menu. As described in Chapter 10, the number of filenames you can set to appear on the menu ranges from zero to nine.

If you would rather use a measurement other than inches, use the last option on the General page. Measurement Units gives you a choice of units to choose from, including Centimeters, Points, and Picas. The Measurement Units setting affects the numbers on the horizontal ruler and measurements you type in any dialog boxes.

Setting File Locations

The File Locations page specifies the default path for various file types. Knowing where Word retrieves information and places files can be helpful. Figure 13.5 shows the File Locations page with all of the specified paths.

FIGURE 13.5

The File Locations page of the Options dialog box

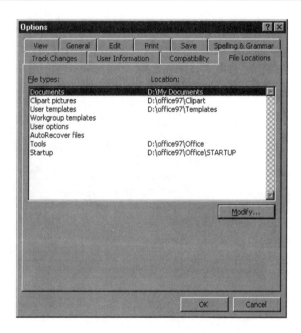

The first file type location is the default setting for documents saved and opened in Word. When Word is installed, a folder called My Documents is created and is used as the default location for your documents. If you want to modify this or any other file location, select the location, click on the Modify button, and set the new path and folder.

When you insert a picture into your document, Word uses, by default, the Microsoft Office ClipArt collection. The path specified for clip art in the File Locations page points to this folder.

Two really important file locations are those for User and Workgroup templates. These two paths tell you where Word retrieves the available templates from when you choose File ➤ New from the menu bar. If Word is installed on a machine that does not reside on a network, chances are that the Workgroup Templates path is blank. If only User Templates has a path, that is where Word gets all of the templates. If you are on a network, templates that everyone has access to are located in the Workgroup Templates path. Check with your network administrator as to where the Workgroup templates are being kept so that this path can be filled in. Templates that are meant just for you (or that you create on your own) are stored in the User Templates path.

If you see a path that is blank, such as the location for AutoRecover Files, it means that the files, if they exist, reside in the default location, which is the main Word folder, generally \MSOffice\Winword. The AutoRecover Files path specifies where you want Word's temporary AutoRecover documents stored while you are editing your main document.

The Startup path specifies files to start when you start Word. If you store documents in the specified folder, Word will open these documents or templates immediately after you launch the program. This is a nice feature if you consistently open certain documents or templates in Word.

Setting Print Options

The Print page of the Options dialog box contains numerous options that will give you more flexibility in printing your documents. Figure 13.6 shows this page of the Options dialog box.

Checking the Draft Output option causes your printer to print your document in draft mode with minimal formatting (if your printer supports this mode). This is ideal when all you need is a hard copy of a document to look at its contents.

The Reverse Print Order option causes your document to print last page first, first page last. Do not select this option if an envelope will be printed, because it will not work correctly.

The Update Fields and Update Links options determine whether your fields and links will be updated right before the document is printed. If you check these options, you won't need to remember to use the Update command to get the most up-to-date information. If you are trying to quickly print a draft with a great number of links and/or fields and the accuracy of the information is not imperative, be sure to have these options unchecked, because updating fields and links takes some time.

Background Printing, if checked, will allow you to return to Word for editing while your document is printing in the background. This option requires more memory and

FIGURE 13.6

*The Print page
of the Options
dialog box*

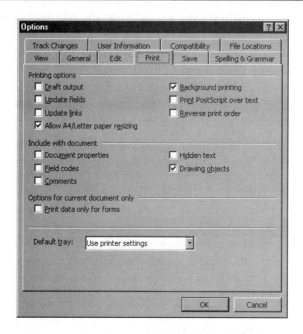

is not as quick as printing in the foreground. If memory or speed is important, you should deselect Background Printing.

The Include with Document area of options on the Print page allows you to choose what will print. The most notable option is Drawing Objects, which lets you turn on or off the printing of drawing objects created in Word. Turning off Drawing Objects in Word while printing will speed up the printing of a document.

Setting Other Options

The Track Changes page of the Options dialog box includes options that are used to customize how revisions are made to documents. The first two groups of options set the method of marking (bold, underline, italic, double underline, hidden, strikethrough, ^, and #) insertions and deletions made to a document protected for revisions. In addition, the color used for changes can be set to different colors for different reviewers. The Changed Formatting area allows you to track whether changes to bold, italic, underline and double underline were done during a revision. The fourth group of options allows you to choose whether you want revised lines to have Outside, Left, or Right borders and what color to make the border.

NOTE

Choose Tools ➤ Track Changes to see the menu options possible. These items allow you to highlight changes, accept or reject changes, or compare documents.

The Edit page of the Options dialog box lets you refine the editing functions of Word. One interesting option is Typing Replaces Selection, which you can turn off to prevent accidental deletion of selections with extraneous keystrokes. For example, if you have a paragraph selected in order to cut or copy it, and you accidentally hit the spacebar, the selection will be replaced by a single space, unless this option on the Edit page is unchecked.

Another option on the Edit page that you might find useful is the option When Selecting, Automatically Select Entire Word. If this option is checked, it causes entire words to be selected when the mouse is used to click and drag selections of text. When the option is not checked, you can click and drag to select parts of words. Smart Cut and Paste deletes extra spaces when you delete an item and inserts extra spaces when you paste an item.

The Compatibility page of the Options dialog box is relevant when you are using Word to work with documents created in other file formats. Once you have the file open, you can select the file format you are working with on the Compatibility page and select your conversion options from the Options list box. If fonts are used in a document that are not on your computer system, the Fonts Substitution feature will map fonts that are on your system for the ones specified in your document.

PART

II

Communicating with Word

NOTE

To see an explanation of any of the options in the Tools ➤ Options dialog box, click on the Help question mark in the top right corner of the window and then click on the option of interest.

Modifying Toolbars

Another area that you can customize in Word is its toolbars. You can do everything from changing the placement of the basic toolbars to creating new toolbars with your own custom buttons.

Moving Toolbars

When Word is first installed, two toolbars appear at the top of the screen: the Standard toolbar and the Formatting toolbar. The first level of customization is the ability to move these toolbars from their default locations.

Moving a toolbar is simple using the *drag bars* Word has placed at the left side of each toolbar. To see how this works, try moving the Formatting toolbar. With your mouse, point to the left side of the Formatting toolbar where there are two raised vertical bars. Click and hold your left mouse button as you drag these bars down into the center of the current document. Your toolbar should now be floating, as shown in Figure 13.7. You can size the toolbar while it is floating in the middle of the screen.

FIGURE 13.7

The Formatting toolbar floating in the middle of the screen

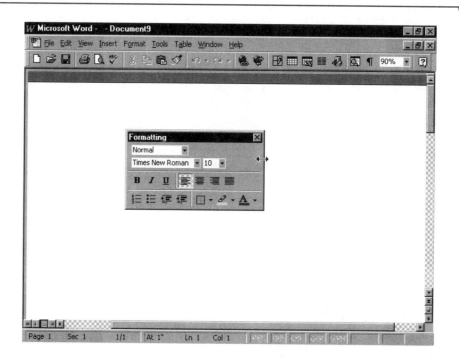

Once the toolbar is floating, you don't see the drag bars. You will now use the title bar to move the toolbar around. Drag the title bar of the toolbar to the right side of the screen so that it docks up against the right side of the document screen. It will lock into place and you will not see the title bar for the toolbar. The vertical drag bars appear at the top of the toolbar.

Some of the buttons invert themselves so that they are readable in a vertical position. The style, typeface and point size buttons are different than they appear when positioned horizontally. You can use the same technique to move the toolbar to the bottom or left side of the screen. This same technique works with all of Word's toolbars.

TIP

To quickly reposition a floating toolbar to its last docked position, double-click the title bar of the toolbar. If it does not dock in the position you want, drag the toolbar by its vertical bars to the correct position. Thereafter, whenever you float the toolbar and double-click it, it will return to that position.

NOTE

If you inadvertently close the toolbar and it no longer appears on the screen, choose View ➢ Toolbars and re-select the toolbar. Then make sure you drag or double-click the toolbar back into its original position.

Creating Your Own Toolbars

Word comes with 18 built-in toolbars. As you've learned in previous chapters, you can turn on and off the display of these toolbars by selecting View ➢ Toolbars from the menu bar. The menu list of toolbars that then appears shows 13 of the 18 possible toolbars. Other toolbars are context sensitive and only appear when certain commands are activated. For example, the Header and Footer toolbar is shown when the View ➢ Headers and Footers command is activated. To see most of the toolbars, choose View ➢ Toolbars ➢ Customize. A Customize dialog box appears with checkmarks beside the toolbars that are currently active.

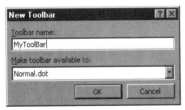

If you want to create your own toolbar, open the New Toolbar dialog box by clicking on the New button on the right side of the Toolbars dialog box. The default name, *Custom1*, is suggested by Word, but you should type a real name for your toolbar and click OK. A tiny new toolbar with no buttons on it appears.

To add buttons to your toolbar, or to any of the other visible toolbars, click and drag the buttons from the Commands tab of the Customize dialog box onto your toolbar. If you drag a button on top of an existing button, the existing button will shift to the right to make room for the new button. If you want to remove a button from a toolbar, you can drag the button off of the toolbar.

PART

II

Communicating with Word

To drag buttons onto your new toolbar:

1. Make sure that your new toolbar is visible (View ➤ Toolbars). Select the name of your toolbar that you created in the previous example.

2. Now, select again View ➤ Toolbars ➤ Customize from the bottom of the toolbars menu. The Customize dialog box appears. If it covers your own toolbar, drag the dialog box out of the way.

3. Click on the Commands tab on the dialog box. On the left are different categories of commands that have buttons associated with them.

4. For this example, you are going to place a Close button on the toolbar. Select the File category on the left.

5. In the Commands list on the right side, click on the Close button and drag the button up to your toolbar. You will see the outline of a button.

6. Drop the button onto your toolbar. Repeat steps 4 to 6, but this time find the Page Setup button farther down in the File category as shown in Figure 13.8.

7. When you have finished adding buttons to your toolbar, click on the Close button on the Customize dialog box.

TIP

If you want to drag a button off of a visible toolbar, you do not need to open the Customize dialog box. Hold down the Alt key, and then click and drag the button you no longer need off the toolbar into your document area.

The Commands tab of the Customize dialog box can also be opened by selecting Tools ➤ Customize from the menu bar. When you pick a category of commands from the Categories list box, the buttons in the selected category will appear on the right. If you want to know what a particular button will do, click on the button and then click on the Description at the bottom of the dialog box.

On the other page of the Customize dialog box, Options, you can choose to show large icons, show ScreenTips on toolbars, and list the keyboard shortcut key (if any) for each button on a toolbar. You can also choose options that animate menus when you select them on the menu bar: In the Menu Animations list box, choose Random, Unfold, or Slide. Unfold causes menus to unfold from the left; Slide causes them to slide down from the top; Random cause menus to either unfold or slide, on a random basis. A strong sense of nausea accompanies the use of these animated options.

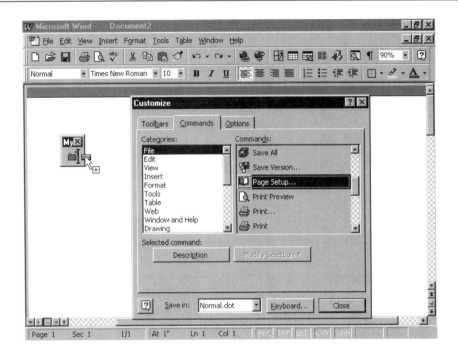

FIGURE 13.8

You can create unlimited personal toolbars populated with buttons.

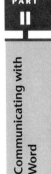

PART

II

Communicating with Word

Modifying Existing Toolbars

Before you can modify a toolbar that comes with Word, the toolbar must be visible. Select View ➤ Toolbars, and choose Customize to see the Customize dialog box (Figure 13.9). Select the Commands tab.

Assigning Word commands to toolbars is an excellent way to customize your working environment within Word. An extension of this ability is adding toolbar buttons that give you direct access to AutoText, fonts, macros, and styles. Figure 13.9 shows the Customize dialog box with these special categories visible in the Categories list.

When you select any of the four categories, the available entries will appear in the list box to the right. Once you have found an item in one of the four categories you want to add, click on it and drag it to the toolbar you want it to be on.

As when you create your own toolbars, drag the new button on top of an existing button, and that button will shift to the right to make room for the new one. To remove a button from a toolbar, click and drag the button off the toolbar.

 TIP

When the Customize dialog box is active, you can right-click on any existing tool-bar button and customize the button by changing the button's image or using text for the button. You can also modify a menu item by right-clicking on the item when the Customize dialog box is active.

You can create special shortcut key combinations for any menu item by selecting the Keyboard button at the bottom of the Keyboard page of the Customize dialog box. You will see many of the same categories as were shown on the Commands tab. If there are existing shortcut keyboard combinations for any item, they are shown when you select a command from the Commands list.

You can change the current keystroke assignments to any combination of Ctrl, Shift, or Alt plus a letter (Alt+Ctrl+K or Ctrl+T, for example). If the keyboard has been heavily customized, use the Reset All button in the Customize dialog box to remove your customized shortcuts and restore the original Word keyboard shortcuts.

Customizing Templates

Templates allow you to have basic text and page formatting available when you want to create new documents. In addition to providing you with the boilerplate text and page formatting, the template can store document-specific styles, AutoText, toolbars, and macros. This way, you avoid filling up your global template (Normal.dot) with items you will only need with certain documents.

Word comes with a number of predesigned templates, which help you with the creation of basic documents (memos, letters, fax cover sheets, calendars, and so on). Some of the templates are actually *Wizards*, which take you through the creation of these documents step by step. These templates store most of the text and all of the AutoText, macros, toolbars, and styles you will need to create the specific document.

Word's built-in templates are definitely useful, but there is no way that the available templates could cover all of the needs of everyone. For this reason, Word allows you to design your own templates to reduce the time necessary to create your specific documents. In Chapter 12, you learned how to create a template from an existing document. The following sections describe how to set up a new template from scratch and how to modify one of Word's predefined templates.

Designing Your Own Template

A Word template is virtually identical to a Word document. The process of creating a fresh new template is also similar to creating a new document.

As an example, we will go through the steps to create a template for memos. We will base this new template on the Normal template (a blank, portrait-orientation page, with 1-inch top and bottom margins and 1.25-inch left and right margins). Follow these steps:

1. Select File ➣ New from the menu bar.
2. On the General page of the New dialog box, select Blank Document.
3. Click on the Create New Template button in the bottom right corner of the dialog box.
4. When your New dialog box looks like the one shown in Figure 13.10, click on OK. After you click on OK, Word opens your new template. Note that the title bar reads *Template1*, not *Document1*. You can now proceed to create your new template with any text, macros, AutoText, styles, and toolbars specific to your template.
5. Change the font size of your text to 14 by clicking on the point size combo box on the Formatting toolbar.
6. Type **MEMO**. Center the text by clicking on the center alignment button on the Formatting toolbar or pressing Ctrl+E.
7. Change the point size to 12 and press Enter twice. Click on the left alignment button on the Formatting toolbar.
8. Type **TO:** and press Enter twice.
9. Type **FROM:** and press Enter twice.
10. Type **RE:** and press Enter twice.
11. Type **DATE:** and press Enter twice. Your template should look like the one shown in Figure 13.11.

PART

II

Communicating with Word

FIGURE 13.10

The New dialog box set to open a new template

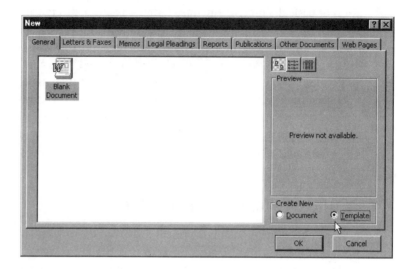

FIGURE 13.11

Creating a memo template

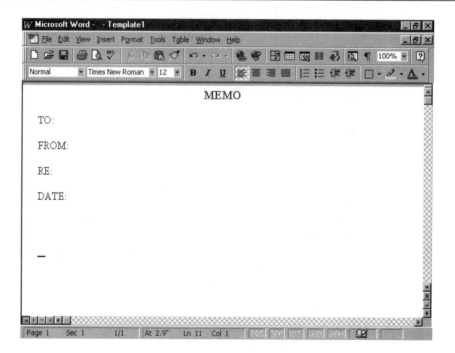

12. To save the template, select File ➤ Save. The Save As dialog box will appear. Because it is a template, Word has taken you into the Templates folder and disabled the ability to change the document type.

WARNING
Remember that the Templates folder that Word opens is specified on the File Locations page of the Tools ➤ Options dialog box. Be certain that when you save a template, you save it in the folder Word opens for you (or in one of the folders contained within that folder). If you do not, Word will not be able to find the template when you select File ➤ New from the menu bar.

13. Change the name of the template in the Save As dialog box to **MY MEMO** and click on the Save button. The title bar of your template should now read *MY MEMO*.

14. Close your template by selecting File ➤ Close from the menu bar.

To create a new document based on your template, choose File ➤ New. You will see MY MEMO as a template option on the General page of the New dialog box, as shown in Figure 13.12. Click on the MY MEMO choice and choose OK. Do not change the Create New option from Document to Template: you do not want to create another template, you want to create a new document based on the template you have already created. When you click on OK, a new document will open with the text that you had in your My Memo template.

TIP
If you will have a number of custom templates that you want to put into a logical group, you can create a new folder under the main Templates folder and store all of your new templates in that folder. When you choose to create a new document, your new folder will appear as a new tab in the New dialog box, as long as it has at least one Word template in it.

Changing Word Templates

You can work with the templates that come with Word in two ways: either you can create a new template based on one of the templates provided with Word and then modify the new template, or you can make changes to an original copy of a Word template.

The New dialog box now contains your new template as an option.

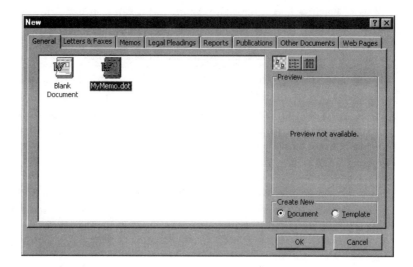

Creating a New Template Based on an Existing Template

Creating a new template based on an existing one is the safest way to modify an existing template. It's safer than modifying the original template because you will still have a copy of the template as it was before you modified it: if you make a mistake, you can return to the original.

To create a new template based on an existing template:

1. Select File ➤ New from the menu bar.
2. In the New dialog box, select the template you want to make a copy of.
3. Click on the Template option button in the lower right corner of the New dialog box and then click OK. The resulting template will be an exact replica of the original; modifications to the new template will not affect the original.

Opening an Existing Template

When you begin to modify the templates themselves, be careful, especially when you are working with the original templates provided with Word. Once you save changes you make to the template, the changes are permanent.

If you do need to make changes to the original, open it as a template by selecting File ➤ Open and changing the Files of Type option to Document Templates. When you find the folder that has the template you want to open, select the template and click on Open. (If you are not sure where your templates are stored, look on the File Locations page of the Tools ➤ Options dialog box, described earlier in this chapter.)

The changes you make to the template will affect how all new documents based on the template will look.

Taking Advantage of Macros

Word's macro language is Word VBA (Visual Basic for Applications). With Word VBA, you can automate many of the procedures you perform in Word on a regular basis. To create Word macros, you can either record the steps with the Macro Recorder or write the macro directly in a code window.

In practice, you will usually combine the techniques of recording and editing of macros. Some commands that you want to use in your macros will be easier to record than write from scratch. You may not be able to record other commands, so you will need to edit your macro code.

The point when most people start needing to edit the code in their macros is the point when they need to get user input. While recording a macro, there is no way to pause for user input. For instance, you may record a macro that inserts specific text and then formats it. When you create the macro, it records the specific text that you typed. When you run the macro, it will always insert the same text. However, you may want to improve the macro by having it prompt the user for the text to insert. To do this, you would need to edit the macro to add code. We will use this scenario for our example in the following sections.

Creating Macros

The majority of macros that you will create will be recorded, at least at the start. To begin recording a macro, select Tools ➤ Macro ➤ Record New Macro from the menu bar. You will see the Macro dialog box, shown in Figure 13.13.

PART

II

Communicating with Word

FIGURE 13.13

The Record Macro dialog box waits for you to name your macro.

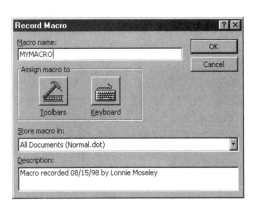

To record a new macro, enter the name you want to give to the macro in the Macro Name text box. You can enter a description of the macro, specify the template in which you want to store the macro and, by using one of two corresponding buttons, assign the macro to a toolbar or to a keyboard shortcut. When you are finished detailing the macro with the Record Macro dialog box, click on OK.

NOTE

Macros can be assigned to the menu bar, shortcut key combinations, and toolbars at any time after you have recorded them. Select Tools ➤ Customize, select the Commands tab, and choose Macros from the category list. Concentrating on making a good recording of your steps should be your primary concern. It is recommended that you wait until after you have successfully recorded your macro to assign it to any of the shortcut options.

When Word begins recording, the Stop Recording toolbar appears. The first button on the toolbar is Stop Recording, the second button on the toolbar is Pause Recording.

After you have turned on the Macro Recorder, remember that every action you take is being recorded. If you make a mistake and then fix the mistake while the recorder is running, then every time you run your macro, Word will make the mistake and then fix it. If you are working on a complicated macro, you may want to practice running through the steps once before you turn on the recorder.

Follow these steps to create a very simple macro that we will modify in the next section:

1. Select Tools ➤ Macro ➤ Record New Macro from the menu bar.
2. In the Record Macro Name text box, type **MYMACRO**. Note the option to store the macro in a specific template and the two buttons that you can use to assign the macro to various shortcuts.
3. Leave the template option as All Documents (Normal.dot) and click on OK without assigning the macro to any shortcuts (this can always be done later by selecting Tools ➤ Customize). The Stop Recording toolbar will appear. On the Formatting toolbar, click on the bold button, the italics button, and the underline button, and change the font size to 24.
4. Type the words **FORMATTED TEXT**.
5. On the Formatting toolbar, click on the bold button, the italics button, and the underline button to turn off these features, and change the font size back to 10.
6. Click on the Stop Recording button on the Stop Recording toolbar.

You have created your first macro. When you run this macro, it will insert the words *FORMATTED TEXT* in a bold, italic, underlined, 24-point font, and then switch to a 10-point plain font.

Editing Macros

The simple macro we created is sufficient if we will always want to enter the same text to be formatted. However, with only a few more steps, we can edit this macro so that it pauses and asks the user for the text to enter.

To edit the macro, follow these steps:

1. Select Tools ➤ Macro ➤ Macros. Click on MYMACRO (the one we recorded earlier in this chapter), and click on Edit.

2. A Microsoft Visual Basic Normal screen appears. The screen is split in half. In the right side of the screen a title bar appears. Click on the maximize button to expand the New Macros screen. Your screen should resemble Figure 13.14.

PART

II

Communicating with Word

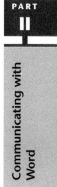

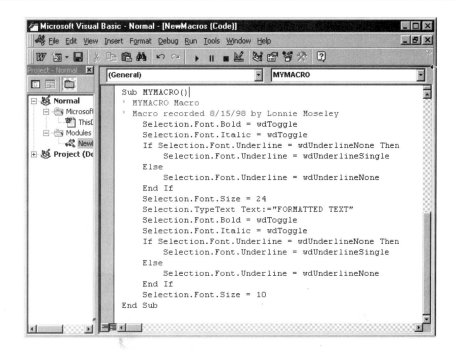

You are looking at the programming involved in turning on bold, italics, underline, point size and typing simple text. Even if you have never seen a line of Word VBA before, you can pick out the specific lines that bold, underline, change point size, and type text.

The line that reads Selection.TypeText Text:="FORMATTED TEXT" is the line that types the text when you run the macro. If you simply modify this line and add one more line of code, you can have the macro ask the user for the text to type instead of typing the same text over and over.

1. Your insertion point should be blinking at the beginning of the first line of code below the green lines of remarks, right in front of the word "Selection." Press the Enter key to add a new line.

2. Type the following on the new line (don't press Enter):

   ```
   MYTEXT$ = InputBox$("WHAT TEXT DO YOU WANT INSERTED")
   ```

3. Change the line that reads *Selection.TypeText Text:="FORMATTED TEXT"* to **Selection.TypeText Text:=MYTEXT$**

4. Look at Figure 13.15 to see an example of how your macro code should look. Select File ➤ Close and Return to Microsoft Word from the menu bar to close the Visual Basic window.

FIGURE 13.15

You can edit the macro recording and change the Visual Basic programming.

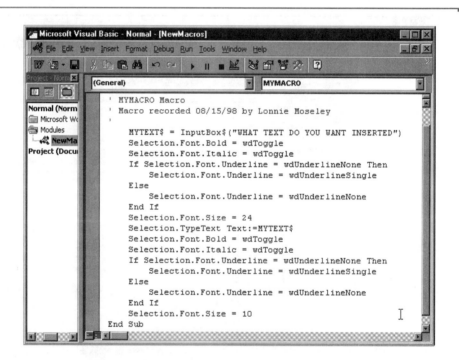

Try running your macro now. Select Tools ➤ Macro ➤ Macros. Choose MYMACRO from the list, and click on Run. You should now be prompted with an input box:

Enter the text you want inserted and click on OK. The text you typed should be inserted into the document from which you ran the macro.

Note that with very little effort, you made a macro much more powerful than it was before, simply by braving the code and making a couple of modifications. Edit the code again (Tools ➤ Macro ➤ Macros) and change the point size to something other than 24 point. Close the Visual Basic programming window and run the macro again.

If you want to learn more about Microsoft Word Visual Basic, refer to Word's online help, select the Index tab, and type **Visual Basic Help**.

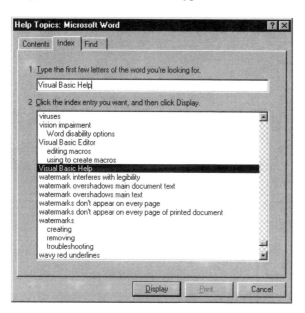

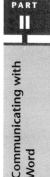

Executing Macros

To run a macro you have created, select Tools ➤ Macro ➤ Macros. You should see your macro in the list box on the left side of the Macros dialog box. Select your macro from the list and click on the Run button.

To copy a macro project item to another template, use the Organizer button located on the right side of the Macros dialog box.

You can assign your macro to run from the toolbar or a shortcut key by using the Customize dialog box. The basic steps for using the Customize dialog box are:

1. Select Tools ➤ Customize.

2. Select Macros from the Categories list on the Commands tab. You will see Normal.NewMacros.MYMACRO in the list on the right.

3. If you are assigning a macro to the toolbar, click and drag the macro name from the Macros list on the right onto a toolbar. The button shows the name of the macro, not an image.

4. Point to the button and right-click the mouse on the macro name button.

5. Move to the item Change Button Image. Select a picture to assign to the macro. Click on the Close button.

This chapter described how to customize some of Word's features to make it more personalized and efficient in your user environment. The next chapter, the last one in this part, shows you how you can integrate your work in Word with the other Microsoft Office applications.

Chapter

14

Office Connections—
Pulling a Proposal
Together

FEATURING

Office Connections—
Pulling a Proposal Together

Understanding the features and capabilities of one Microsoft Office program is the first step to integrating your work in all of the programs.

The example in this chapter demonstrates how a proposal written by several people can be brought together using three Microsoft Office programs: Word, Excel, and PowerPoint.

Here is our scenario. Shawn is the technical assistant for a New Jersey consulting firm that specializes in installing networks for banks in the area. Her job is to understand the scope of work for any bank installation project and to create professional, eye-catching proposals and presentations to communicate her company's installation plans and costs for the network to different bank executives requesting these services.

Shawn uses Word, Excel, and PowerPoint to create each proposal. She combines Excel data and graphs and embeds network flow charts and diagrams from PowerPoint into sections of the proposal she has written in Word. For the cover pages of some of her proposals, she uses PowerPoint slides used in preliminary presentations.

Under Shawn's direction, other staff members also use Word to work on specific sections of the proposal. When these sections are ready, Shawn links them into the master proposal.

To perform these tasks, she must have a knowledge of Word, Excel, and PowerPoint and a clear understanding of how to link data from multiple Office programs.

An Overview of Inserting and Linking in Office Applications

When you have multiple files to combine or link together into one file, you can take a couple of approaches. We'll refer to the files that will be inserted as *subfiles*, and the main document into which the other files will go as the *master file* (not to be confused with Word's Master Document feature).

One approach is to insert the files at their appropriate locations in the master file using the Insert ➢ File command on the menu bar. The Insert ➢ File option inserts an entire file or a specified range (bookmark section) within a file.

The Insert ➢ File command also offers a Link to File option in the Insert File dialog box. This option allows you to *link* the multiple files into a master file. You can link an entire file or a specified range within a file.

If you are sure that no changes will be made to your inserted files, use the Insert ➢ File command without selecting the Link to File option. By doing this, you insert *copies* of the Word subfiles. If the authors of the subfiles make changes to their documents, these changes will not be reflected in your copies of their work. You will need to reinsert their files on a regular basis if you want to make sure you have the latest changes.

If you want to make changes to your subfiles, select the Link to File option in the Insert File dialog box, and the subfile will have a link to the original file. With linked subfiles, other authors can make last-minute changes to their documents which you have already incorporated in the master file. These changes will be reflected in the master file, without requiring you to reinsert their files.

To update the files and show the latest changes, you can use the Edit ➢ Links command, or you can use the Edit ➢ Select All command (Ctrl+A) and press F9 to update linked field information. You can also break a link connection through the Edit ➢ Links command.

Another approach to linking files is to select and copy data from one program file into another and choose Edit ➢ Paste Special. In the Paste Special dialog box, choose the Paste Link radio button. We'll use this method to link Excel data to a Word document.

If you simply want to copy (or move) data from one application to another, you can use the standard copy and paste through the Clipboard technique. But you can also employ a one-step method: dragging and dropping. Later in this chapter, we will use this method to design a PowerPoint slide with text created in Word.

Linking in Word

In our example, five files are involved: one master file and four subfiles created by four different authors. These are called MasterFile, SubFile1, SubFile2, SubFile3, and SubFile4.

NOTE

These are generic filenames created for use in our example and are not necessary in order to perform linking operations. You may use any normal file name (maximum of 250 characters, with spaces and periods allowed).

To link these files, do the following:

1. Open MasterFile (your main document into which subfiles will be inserted).
2. Position the insertion point at the location where you wish to insert the text from SubFile1.
3. Choose Insert ➢ File and select the file you wish to insert from the list box.
4. Click on the Link to File checkbox on the right side of the dialog box and click on OK. Figure 14.1 shows the Insert File dialog box with the Link to File option checked.

PART

II

Communicating with Word

FIGURE 14.1

While working in Word, it is easy to link multiple Word documents. Use the Insert ➢ File command and check the Link to File option.

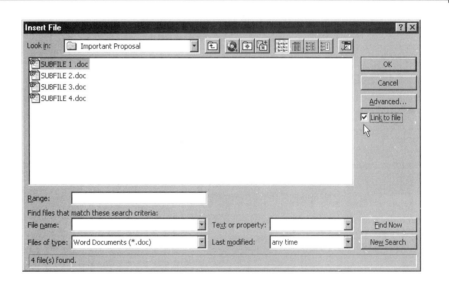

When the linked file is inserted, there is no immediate indication that you have a linked file within another file. Although it appears that you can edit the linked information, the next time you update the file link, your edits will be replaced by the original's author's changes. The linked information is really a field code that references the linked file. We will discuss field codes in the next section.

For each of the other files to be inserted and linked to the master file—SubFile2, SubFile3, and SubFile4 in our example—choose Insert ➢ File, select the file, and check the Link to File option.

If you want to distinguish the difference between a subfile's text and the original MasterFile text, change the field code options to show the field code information by doing the following:

1. Choose Tools ➢ Options ➢ View tab.
2. Click on the drop-down list next to the Field shading option.
3. Select *When selected*, if it is not already selected. Click on OK at the bottom of the dialog box.
4. When you return to the document, click in the section of information that has been inserted and linked, and you will see that section appear in gray. Figure 14.2 shows the linked file when Field shading has been turned on.

TIP

A master file with multiple links can also be a linked file within another master file.

These are the opening sentences in the <u>Master file</u>. Subfile 1 will be inserted and linked after this paragraph ends.

SUBFILE ONE:

This is the content of Subfile One. This is the content of Subfile One.
This is the content of Subfile One. This is the content of Subfile One.
This is the content of Subfile One. This is the content of Subfile One.
This is the content of Subfile One. This is the content of Subfile One.

1. This is a list in Subfile One.
2. This is a list in Subfile One.
3. This is a list in Subfile One.

This is the content of Subfile One. This is the content of Subfile One.
This is the content of Subfile One. This is the content of Subfile One.
This is the content of Subfile One. This is the content of Subfile One.

Inserting and Linking Selected Areas within a Word File

You may not want an entire subfile to be inserted into your master file. You just need to insert different sections from within the subfile. This can be done through the

Insert File dialog box, as long as a bookmark (or "range name" in an Excel file) has already been created in the linked subfile.

The first step is to have the authors of the subfiles select and give a bookmark name to the subsections that will be inserted and linked. Each author will select the paragraphs, choose Insert ➢ Bookmark, type the name for the subsection (no spaces in the name; maximum of 40 characters), and click on the Add button to add the bookmark. Repeat this procedure for each subsection you wish to insert. When checked, the Hidden bookmark option displays bookmark names that Word creates particularly for cross-references. You don't normally see these names unless the Hidden bookmark option is checked.

When the sections are marked, you can open the master file and choose Insert ➢ File. Click once on the name of the file. Click on the Link to File option on the right side of the dialog box. In the Range text box below the file list, type in the name of the bookmark section. Click on OK. Figure 14.3 shows the Insert File dialog box with a Range bookmark name specified.

You will need to insert each bookmark section separately.

PART
II

Communicating with
Word

FIGURE 14.3

You can insert and link a section of another file if the section has been given a bookmark name. Enter the bookmark name in the Range text box.

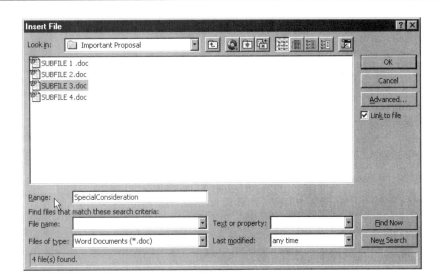

Updating Word Links

As each author of a subfile continues to make changes, you will want to update the links so that the latest changes are reflected in your master file.

To manage your Word links, choose Edit ➤ Links from the menu bar. In the Links dialog box, click on the name of the file for which you wish to update links, and then click on the Update Now button on the right side of the dialog box. Figure 14.4 shows the Links dialog box.

FIGURE 14.4

Use the Update Now button in the Edit ➤ Links dialog box to update the files so that they reflect the latest changes.

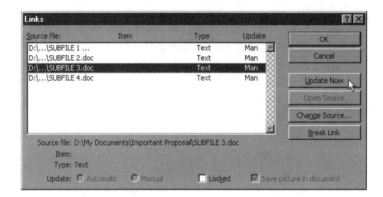

If you want to remove the link between the subfile and the master file, click on the Break Link button in the Edit ➤ Links dialog box. If you need to change the name of a linked file or the location of the file, click on the Change Source button and enter the new filename or location.

Another way to update your links is to let Word do it for you automatically when you open the master file. Choose Tools ➤ Options ➤ General tab. This page contains an Update Automatic Links at Open setting. If this option is checked, each time the file is opened, any new changes in the subfiles will automatically be reflected in the master file.

Updating Links Using Field Codes

In Word, the linked file in the master document is really just a field code—a pointer to the real file. Another method for updating the links is to click into the linked subfile text to be updated and then press the F9 key to update the field. To toggle the field codes on and off, position the insertion point in the field. You can press Shift+F9 to toggle between the display of the actual field definition, which includes the filename and path, and the text for the linked subfiles that you want to see in the finished document. If you right-click onto the field, you will see the Update Field and Toggle Field codes on the shortcut menu. These items are the same as the keystroke combinations F9 and Shift+F9, respectively. The {INCLUDETEXT} field code is what is seen when you turn on field codes. Figure 14.5 shows the subfiles with the field formats.

PART

II

Communicating with
Word

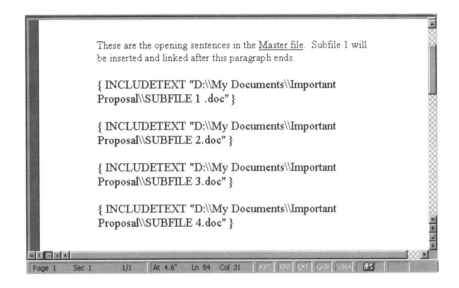

FIGURE 14.5

*Linked files can
be displayed as
fields or text by
toggling back
and forth with
the Shift+F9
keyboard
combination.*

Press Ctrl+A to Select All and then press F9 to update fields. This is an easy way to
update all of the linked subfiles at once. If you want to toggle the field codes for all of
the linked subfiles and other fields in your document at one time, press Alt+F9.

Linking Excel Data and Charts

The technical analysts in Shawn's office have created a workbook containing a number
of spreadsheets with the costs for the network installation and roll-out. These numbers
are constantly being refined to reflect changes in the costs of memory, hard drives, and
so forth in the market place. Accurate cost data is essential for the proposal, and
Shawn doesn't want to take any chances that a copy of the data in the Word proposal
might not reflect the most current numbers developed by the technical analysts. A
link to the Excel data (as opposed to a copy) will ensure that any changes to the workbook original will always be reflected in the Word proposal.

The initial steps to establish the link will be identical to those used for copying the
data. When it is time to paste the data, however, the steps will be specific to pasting
using a link to the original Excel file.

Creating the Excel Link

To create the Excel link, follow these steps:

1. Open the Excel workbook that contains the data that should be linked into the master Word file.

2. Open the Word MasterFile document created in a previous section. (If you have not been following this example, open any Word document that you wish to use.)

3. Choose Excel from the Taskbar at the bottom of the screen or hold down the Alt key and press Tab to cycle through the open applications until you find Excel.

4. Select the range of data to be inserted and linked, and then click on the Copy button on the Standard toolbar or press Ctrl+C to copy the data to the Clipboard. Figure 14.6 shows the Excel data being copied.

FIGURE 14.6

In your Excel workbook, select the range of cells to be inserted and linked into another file.

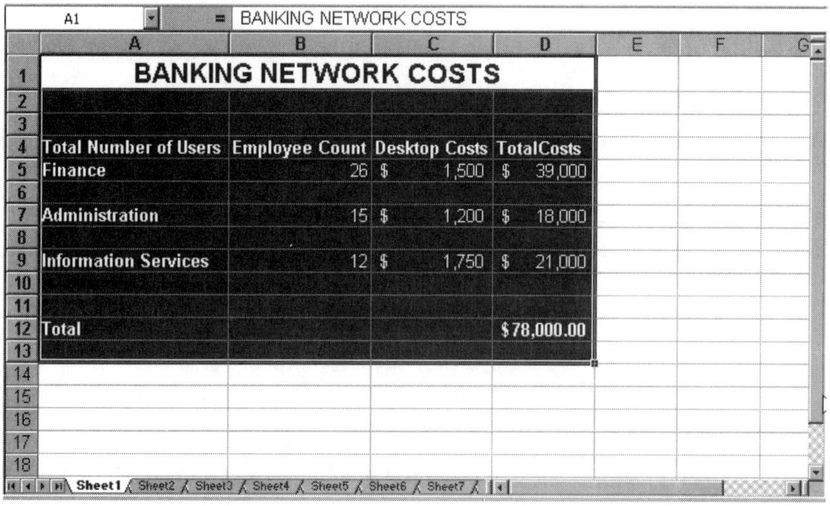

	A	B	C	D	E	F	G
1	**BANKING NETWORK COSTS**						
2							
3							
4	**Total Number of Users**	**Employee Count**	**Desktop Costs**	**TotalCosts**			
5	Finance	26	$ 1,500	$ 39,000			
6							
7	Administration	15	$ 1,200	$ 18,000			
8							
9	Information Services	12	$ 1,750	$ 21,000			
10							
11							
12	Total			$78,000.00			
13							
14							
15							
16							
17							
18							

5. After the Excel data is copied to the Clipboard, click on the Word program button on the Taskbar to make the master file active.

6. Click the insertion point at the location in MasterFile where you wish to insert the Excel data.

7. Choose Edit ➤ Paste Special from the menu bar.

8. In the Paste Special dialog box, click on the Paste Link option and choose Microsoft Excel Worksheet Object in the drop-down list, as shown in Figure 14.7. Click on OK, and the data appears in the master file.

FIGURE 14.7

*To link an Excel
Worksheet
Object, use the
Edit ➢ Paste
Special com-
mand and
select the Paste
Link option.*

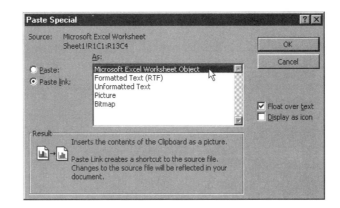

9. To put a border around the linked worksheet within Word, right-click the mouse
on the Excel worksheet object that has been inserted as a linked range. Choose
Format ➢ Object from the shortcut menu. In the Object dialog box, select the
Colors and Lines tab. In the Color box in the Line area, choose Black. In the Style
box, choose a 6-point line style—either solid line or multiple line. Click on OK.
Figure 14.8 shows pasted, linked worksheet data, with a border.

FIGURE 14.8

*You can place a
border around
the inserted
Excel object.*

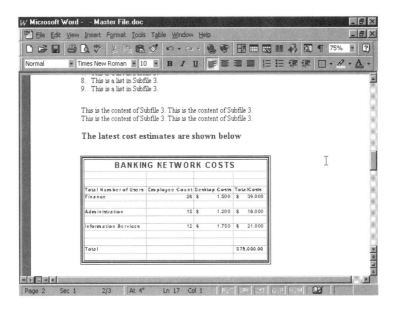

Your Excel data is now inserted into the Word main file. If you double-click on the Excel object, you will be returned to the Excel program so that you can make changes. Any changes you make are immediately reflected in the Word master file when you switch back to that file. You can also right-click on the Excel Worksheet object and select Linked Worksheet Object in the shortcut menu. Choose the Edit Link or Open Link item, and you will be returned to the Excel program that contains the data you linked into Word (if Excel is not open, the program will start and the linked file will be brought into memory). You can then make changes to the data; when you switch back to Word, the changes will be reflected automatically.

The Convert item on the Linked Worksheet Object allows you to convert data created in non-Office programs, such as Lotus 123 or Quattro Pro. There is no need to convert our Excel workbook data, because it is already an Office program.

TIP

If the Excel spreadsheet being copied, pasted, and linked using Paste Special is longer than one page, do not select to paste it as a Microsoft Excel Worksheet Object, because the object will not cross a page boundary. Instead, Paste Link it as Formatted Text (RTF). The Excel data will come in as a Word table. The table will be linked to the original Excel file, and it will reflect updates and changes like any other linked file. If you use the Unformatted Text option, the Excel data will appear as linked numbers in Word, but tabs will separate each column of data; it will not be in a table structure.

Creating and Linking an Excel Chart

You can easily create a basic chart in Excel using Excel's Chart Wizard. The Chart Wizard walks you through the process of creating a 3-D bar chart. A basic Excel chart will graph your words (labels) and your numbers (data) and allow you to display this information in a variety of graphical types: column, bar, line, pie, XY (Scatter), Area, Doughnut, Radar, Surface, Bubble, and Stock.

Here are the steps for creating a chart:

1. In Excel, select the words (labels) and then hold down the Ctrl key and select the data series associated with the words. Figure 14.9 shows the labels and data series selected for the chart.
2. Choose Insert ➢ Chart from the Excel menu bar or click on the Chart Wizard button on the Standard toolbar. The Chart Wizard dialog box appears.
3. Click on the Pie chart type on the left side of the Chart Wizard Step 1 of 4 - Chart Type dialog box. Then select the 3-D pie (in the top row, second column). Press and hold the sample button at the bottom of the box to see how the data looks with this chart type.

FIGURE 14.9

An Excel chart is easy to create. Select words (X axis) and the data series (Y axis) and choose Insert ➤ Chart.

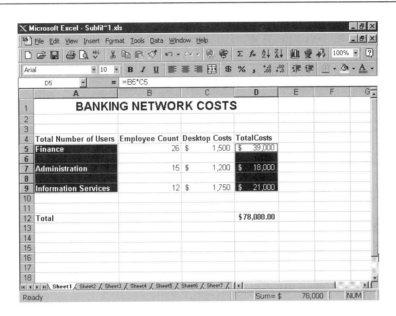

4. Click on the Next button to move to Step 2 of 4 - Chart Source Data. Then, click on the Next button to go to Step 3 of 4 - Chart Options.

5. At Step 3, type a Chart Title. For this example, we have typed **Banking Costs**.

6. Click on the Data Labels tab at the top of the dialog box and click on Show Value to make the actual costs appear next to the pie slices. Click on the Next button to move to Step 4 of 4.

7. At Step 4, Chart Location, check the As New Sheet option if it is not enabled. The default name for this sheet will be Chart1. You can change this to another name (for example, Banking Costs Pie Chart).

8. Click on the Finish button. The chart appears on its own worksheet. To return to your data, click on the Sheet 1 tab at the bottom of the chart window.

Linking the Chart in Word

You use the same procedure to link an Excel chart as you do to link an Excel spreadsheet. The contents of the linked chart reflect the labels and data series numbers in the Excel worksheet. When the numbers change in the worksheet, the chart is updated in Excel, and the linked chart in Word reflects the update.

Follow these steps to link the chart into Word:

1. Make sure you are on the Chart tab. (Look at the sheet tabs at the bottom of the window. The tab will say either Chart1 or the name you gave to the chart in Step 4. Click once on the chart to be linked; sizing handles appear around the chart object.

2. Choose Edit ➢ Copy from the menu, press Ctrl+C, or click on the Copy button on the Standard toolbar.

3. Switch to Word. Position the insertion point in the master file where the chart should be located.

4. Choose Edit ➢ Paste Special from the menu bar. The Paste Special dialog box appears.

5. Click on the Paste Link radio button. The Microsoft Excel Chart Object is the source. Figure 14.10 shows the dialog box at this point. Click on OK. The chart is inserted and linked into the Word master file.

6. If the Chart is too wide when inserted into Word, right click the mouse on the chart and choose Format Object from the shortcut menu list. In the Format Object dialog box, click on the Size tab at the top and change the Scale Height and Width to 40% and click on OK.

Remember, this chart is linked to Excel. Any changes you make in the original Excel file will be reflected in the linked Excel spreadsheet as well as the linked Excel chart.

FIGURE 14.10

The Paste Special dialog box shows the type of data that has been copied into memory.

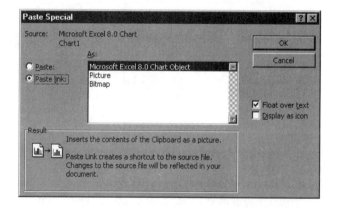

Using a PowerPoint Slide as a Cover Page

In our scenario, during an initial presentation, the bank executives were shown a PowerPoint slide show demonstrating our approach to the network installation. Shawn wants to create a new slide as the basis for the cover page of the actual proposal. The template design for the slide, however, should be the same as the one used in the original presentation.

Shawn also wants the PowerPoint slide to use a copy of text that was originally in a Word proposal designed for another client. This is a simple process of dragging and dropping. The slide will then be ready to be inserted in the master file for its cover page.

In the following section, we will create a simple PowerPoint slide, give it a template design, and then drag-and-drop text from Word to PowerPoint. Finally, we will insert and link the PowerPoint slide into the Word proposal as the cover page.

Designing a PowerPoint Slide

We first need to create the PowerPoint slide to use as a cover page. Follow these steps:

1. Launch PowerPoint using the Start button on the Taskbar.
2. When the PowerPoint dialog box appears, click on the Blank Presentation radio button, and then click on OK.
3. In the New Slide dialog box, click on the first slide format, Title Slide. Then click on OK. You will see a window with a blank PowerPoint slide, as shown in Figure 14.11. We now need apply a template design so that the slide isn't so bare.

FIGURE 14.11

A blank title slide shows the areas into which you can click and type your text.

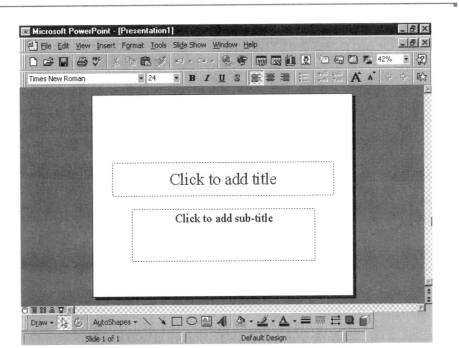

4. To use a template design, either apply one from a previously created presentation or apply a predesigned template sample supplied by Microsoft.

- To apply a template design from an existing presentation, choose Format ➤ Apply Design from the menu bar. Select the name of the existing presentation and click on the Apply button on the right side of the dialog box. PowerPoint will copy the template design of the existing presentation to your new slide.
- To choose a predefined template design, choose Format ➤ Apply Design from the menu bar. Look in the Presentation Designs folder. You can preview the different types of template designs available. When you find the template design you want to use, select it and click on the Apply button on the upper right side of the dialog box.

5. For this example, the Professional.pot (template) was selected. Once the template is loaded, click into the *Click to add title* text area and type a title for the slide. In this example the title is **Network Services**.

6. Click into the *Click to add sub-title* text area to select the text box. This is the area into which you are going to drag-and-drop text from the Word program. Leave the insertion point here at this spot.

Dragging Text from Word to PowerPoint

Our goal is to copy the text from Word into the PowerPoint slide to create the text for the new slide. As you've learned, there are various methods for copying and pasting items from one application to another, such as copying and pasting text through the Clipboard. Dragging and dropping text, data, or objects is another method of transferring items into another application. And it has the advantage of being a one-step process.

1. Start the Word program if it is not already open and open the document that contains the text that is to be dragged and dropped into PowerPoint.

2. Vertically tile the PowerPoint and Word windows. Click on the Restore button at the top of the Window of each application. Size each window into rectangles. The PowerPoint and Word windows should now be side by side, taking up equal amounts of screen space.

3. Click on the title bar of the Word document to make it the active window. (In this example the View is Normal view and the text is wrapping to the window. To make the text wrap, choose Tools ➤ Options ➤ View ➤ Wrap to Window).

4. Select the text in Word that you want to copy.

5. Hold down the Ctrl key while you drag the selected text across the window boundary onto the PowerPoint slide. Drop the text into the subtitle text box area. Holding the Ctrl key makes the drag-and-drop a copy operation, leaving the original text instead of cutting it out. Figure 14.12 shows the Word text copied to the PowerPoint slide. The subtitle contains preexisting center formatting so that when the copy is dropped, it is centered in the box on the slide.

FIGURE 14.12

You can easily restore and size the different applications so that dragging and dropping between applications is seamless.

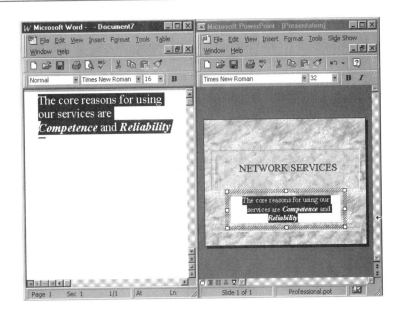

NOTE

You can also use the traditional copy-and-paste method instead of drag-and-drop. Select the text in Word, and then press Ctrl+C or click on the Copy button on Word's Standard toolbar. Switch to PowerPoint by clicking on its title bar. Click into the text area to receive the Word text. Press Ctrl+V or click on the Paste button on the PowerPoint Standard toolbar.

6. The PowerPoint window is now the active window. Choose File ➢ Save from the menu bar and type a new name for the presentation. Next, we will insert and link this file into the Word master file.

Inserting and Linking a PowerPoint Presentation into Word

You can insert and link an entire PowerPoint presentation as an object in a Word document. If you insert and link an entire presentation, the PowerPoint Viewer becomes part of the inserted presentation so you can view the entire presentation.

To link a PowerPoint presentation, follow these steps:

1. Open the MasterFile example or any other Word document.
2. Position the insertion point where you want the presentation to appear and choose Insert ➤ Object from Word's menu bar.
3. Click on the Create from File tab at the top of the Object dialog box.
4. Click on the Link to File checkbox on the right side of the Object dialog box.
5. Type in the name of the file or click on the Browse button to look for the file. Once you find the PowerPoint file, click on it, and then click on the OK button. You will be returned to the Object dialog box.
6. In the Object dialog box, the name of the PowerPoint file will appear. Click on the OK button. It will take a couple of seconds for the presentation to be inserted and linked into the Word document, with the first slide in the presentation showing. In our current example, we have only one slide.

Because the file is linked, you can make changes to the slide in PowerPoint while in the PowerPoint program, and the changes will be updated and reflected in your Word document. When you are in the Word document, you can double-click on the inserted PowerPoint slide, and the actual PowerPoint presentation will begin. Microsoft uses the PowerPoint Viewer to make it possible to view an actual slide show while you are in a different program.

NOTE

The method described here shows the first slide in a presentation in your document. If you want a slide other than the first one to appear in your Word document, switch to Slide Sorter view in PowerPoint, click on the slide that you want to link, and select Edit ➤ Copy. When you switch to Word, select Edit ➤ Paste Special and choose to Paste Link the Slide object. Double-clicking on an individual slide linked this way does not start the PowerPoint Viewer; instead, it opens the presentation file that holds the slide and allows you to edit it.

The proposal is now complete. The cover page is a PowerPoint slide, and the proposal sections are inserted and linked Word files from multiple authors. Excel worksheet data and an Excel chart are also linked as objects. Shawn can now work on the original copies of each of the inserted files, and the master proposal file will always reflect the current changes.

Adding page borders and headers with identifying information and footers with page numbers completes the proposal design. Figure 14.13 shows the proposal in Word's Print Preview screen.

FIGURE 14.13

The Print Preview's multiple-page view allows you to see the layout of the proposal.

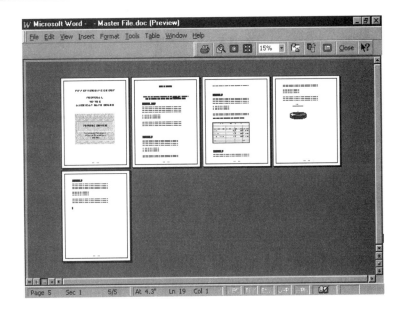

PART III

Analyzing with Excel

LEARN TO:

- *Create Financial Workbooks*

- *Create Excel Formulas*

- *Use the AutoComplete for Data Entry*

- *Graphically Chart Data*

- *Sort and Group Data*

- *Print with Headers and Footers*

- *Link Worksheets and Workbooks*

- *Customize Toolbars and Create Macros*

- *Insert Data from Office 97 Programs*

Chapter

15

The Road Map

FEATURING

The Road Map

I f you are eager to get a feel for what Excel can do for you, and you have a little understanding about electronic spreadsheet programs, review this chapter for an overview of how Excel works. For in-depth coverage of specific Excel features, check out the subsequent Excel chapters.

What's New in Excel 97

Excel 97 offers a number of new features including new Internet and intranet features, better wizards, and increased functionality.

Internet

Excel 97 provides native support for many of your Internet and intranet needs. Included in this release of Excel is the ability to insert Hyperlinks directly into your worksheets. If you have data in your workbook that can be expanded upon or validated at an Internet or intranet site, the Hyperlink can take a user directly to the location. (See Chapter 20 for more information on inserting Hyperlinks.) You can also open HTML pages directly from Excel using the File ➤ Open menu option. If that is not enough, workbooks stored on FTP Internet sites can also be opened easily from the menu bar.

Finally, if you want to take your data straight from workbook to Web, various new Wizards are available to get your information to HTML format. See Chapters 4 and 48 through 50 for Web publishing possibilities.

New Cell Formats

Previous versions of Excel provided a multitude of options when it came to formatting the data in cells. Excel 97 adds more to its list of formatting possibilities. Included in these additions are the ability to align text diagonally within cells, formatting cells with diagonal borders, and conditional formatting. Conditional formatting is the long-awaited feature that allows easy formatting of a cell based on its value without having to use long, complicated formulas. See Chapter 17 for more formatting options.

Page Break Preview

Trying to figure out where the pages break when working with spreadsheets has always been a cantankerous task. Excel now adds Page Break Preview to its printing options. This allows you to see and change the page breaks in a view similar to Print Preview.

Natural Language Formulas

Instead of having to manually name ranges, Excel now supports the use of row and column labels to reference cell values. Suppose you have a column listing the names of employees and a row listing the months of the year, with the employees' total sales for the month at the intersection. You can reference the sales figure by entering **=month name employee name**.

New and Improved Wizards

Eventually, Excel will simply ask you what you want it to do, and it will carry out your orders. Until then, you can benefit from its many Wizards, including the new ones added in this release.

The Lookup Wizard helps users create database-like lookup formulas that search for a key value and return value in another column of the same row. The File Conversion Wizard helps import other spreadsheet programs by providing batch conversion of a group of files of one type, such as Lotus 1-2-3. The HTML Wizard makes it a snap for users to create Web pages from charts or sheets in their workbooks. Finally, The Web Form Wizard takes a user through the steps necessary to create an HTML form that can be used to submit information into a database using the HTTP protocol.

Enhanced Workgroup Functionality

The last version of Excel added the capability to share workbooks simultaneously among multiple users. This feature has been greatly improved and now supports formulas and formatting.

Excel now has the ability to track changes made by multiple users of a workbook. You can highlight changes other people have made, view changes by user, time, and location, and accept or reject the changes one by one. If you have people working independently on different versions of a workbook, you can merge the different versions and consolidate the changes.

Charting Enhancements

A new user interface for creating charts makes placing charts in your workbook even easier than before. Now you have the ability to view your chart's appearance through all steps of the Wizard, choose from user-defined chart types, add series of data after the Wizard has started, show the data table with your chart, and add a chart to a sheet without having to click and drag it before the Wizard starts.

Charting has been integrated even more in Excel with single-click activation. Rather than activating your charts before formatting them, you can go directly to the various elements of the chart that you want to modify.

New chart types have also been added, including Bubble, Pie of Pie, and Bar of Pie.

Cell Data Validation

A new Data Validation feature allows you to restrict the information being placed into particular cells by applying data validation rules. These include the ability to specify the type and range of values allowed in the cell, an input message that appears like a ScreenTip when the user enters the cell, and the error message that you want to display if the data entered cannot be validated.

Briefcase Merge Support

Excel 97 now supports the merge capabilities of the Windows Briefcase. Not only can you update one workbook from another that has changed, but the Briefcase can now merge the changes from the two workbooks and update both of them.

Enhanced VBA Environment

Excel 97 brings with it the new VBA Integrated Design Environment that provides a more organized approach to handling the VBA code in your workbooks.

To help beginning VBA users, new Auto Edit features provide real-time syntax help as VBA code is typed. For example, if you typed **MsgBox** to use the MsgBox statement, Excel would provide the possible arguments directly below the line, bolding the current argument the user is typing.

Also included with the VBA enhancements are added event properties that help you program to user actions in your workbook.

Overview of Excel

Imagine you have a large workbook on your desk, stacked full of accounting spreadsheets. Excel stores this workbook in electronic form. The stack arrangement gives you the advantage of a three-dimensional work area. For example, in addition to adding numbers across or down a worksheet, you can "drill down" through a stack of worksheets to work with their numbers as well.

Not only does Excel provide easy manipulation of spreadsheets, it supplies tools you can use to store, analyze, and manipulate entire *databases* of information. If your databases grow beyond the capacity of Excel, you can convert your data into an Access database. (Access is a full-fledged database management program that is part of the Professional version of Microsoft Office. It is covered in Part Six of this book.)

No matter how much of its functionality you plan to exploit, Excel will prove to be an invaluable member of your Office team.

Jump Start into Excel

This jump start section will allow you to get started with some of Excel's basic functions. If you just want to get your feet wet, this is the way to go. If you find a feature of particular interest, turn to the related chapters for more information.

Starting Excel

1. Click on the Start button on the Windows 95 Taskbar at the bottom of the screen.

2. Highlight the Programs item. The Program menu will open.

3. Select Microsoft Excel from the list of programs.

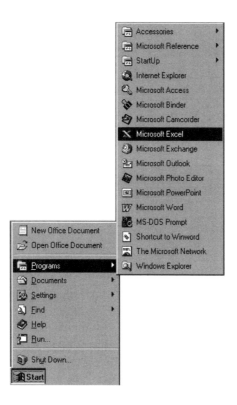

Starting a New Workbook

PART

III

Analyzing with Excel

A workbook is a collection of sheets saved together under one filename. An Excel file can have many sheets saved in one file; you are limited only by the amount of memory you have in your computer. When you launch Excel, an empty workbook titled Book1 is automatically opened (see Figure 15.1).

If you are already in Excel and do not have a file opened, you can select File ➣ New or click on the New button on the Standard toolbar to start a new workbook. The first thing you may notice is how similar the screen looks to other Office programs. The top of the Excel window shows you the program that is opened and the name of the file. Since this is a new workbook, it has been given the default name Book1. Once you have named your file, the default name will be replaced.

The workbook opens by default with a stack of three worksheets, but you can customize Excel to give you any number of sheets from one to 255 at startup. The sheet name tabs are visible at the bottom edge of the Excel window. They are labeled Sheet 1 through Sheet 3 and can be changed later. Though you can't see them all in one screen, each worksheet consists of 256 columns listed in alphabetical order and 65,536 rows listed by number.

FIGURE 15.1

The opening view of Excel

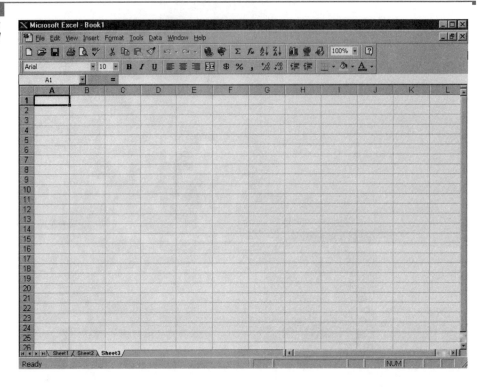

Located under the Taskbar is the formula bar, which we will explore in greater detail later in this chapter. This line will display formulas and calculations and allow for editing.

In the work area, the intersection between a row and a column is called a cell. The cell in which information is being entered is called the active cell. To be clear about where on a spreadsheet information is being entered, we refer to the cell intersection by its address. A cell address consists of the column name and the row number. A cell is activated by clicking on the intersection.

Saving Your Workbook

Even though you have a brand new workbook open, it is a good idea to go ahead and save it. Save your work regularly! This falls under the "better safe than sorry" rule. It is very frustrating to lose your most recent work due to sudden power failures or system shutdowns.

1. To save your work, select File ➢ Save from the Excel menu bar or click on the Save button on the Standard toolbar. The Save As dialog box (Figure 15.2) will open.

FIGURE 15.2
*The Save As
dialog box*

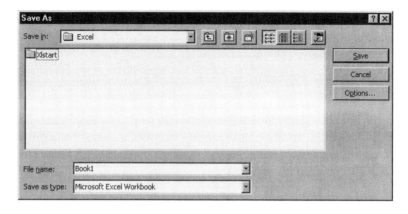

2. Type a name for your workbook. The name can be a maximum of 250 characters (including spaces). In case you forget to name your file, Excel reverts to its original default of Book1.

Don't expect to be prompted for a name every time you save a workbook. Excel only asks for the name of a workbook the first time you save it. To change the name you need to select File ➤ Save As.

Entering and Editing Data

In Excel, you have to press the Enter key on your keyboard to accept the data before you do anything with it (such as format the data or perform a calculation). You can also click on the Enter button (the checkmark) on the formula bar to accept your entry. Should you choose not to accept your entry, you can click on the Cancel button (the ×), also in the formula bar. If you wish to move to another cell immediately after entering a formula, you can use the Tab key to move to the next column or one of the arrow keys to move in their respective directions.

Listed below are some methods for editing your cell entries.

- To correct your typos as you make them, use the Backspace key. Each press of the Backspace key will erase the character to the immediate left of the cursor.
- To clear a cell already containing an entry, click on the cell you wish to clear, and then press Delete or Backspace, and the active cell will clear. The difference between the two keys in this situation is that Backspace will place you in the cell for editing and Delete will not.
- You can replace a cell entry by selecting the cell and simply typing in the new information. Accept the new information by pressing Enter or clicking on the Enter button, and the new entry replaces the original entry. To reject the new information, press Esc or click on the Cancel button, and the original entry remains.

PART

III

Analyzing with Excel

To delete entries in a range of cells, use the following steps:

1. Click on the top left cell and drag across the entire range you wish to delete.
2. Once highlighted, release the mouse and press Delete.

Formulas

To perform any type of calculation in Excel, you need to provide a formula. You can enter the formula on the formula bar or within the active cell itself. Basic editing rules still apply. You must begin with an equals sign (=) so Excel will know that an expression that needs to be *evaluated* is about to be entered. To get started let's try an example that introduces the AutoSum button. We're going to add together a series of four numbers and ask Excel to provide the answer.

1. In cells A1 through A4 (represented as A1:A4), enter numbers **1** through **4** (that is, 1 in A1, 2 in A2, 3 in A3, and 4 in A4). To do this click once on cell A1. Type **1** and press Enter. The next active cell will be cell A2. Continue to enter in the same manner until you are in cell A5.
2. Click on the AutoSum button on the Standard toolbar.
3. Notice the formula that appears. The formula that is automatically entered when you clicked on the AutoSum button uses Excel's SUM function to total the values from all the cells above the current one (cell A5).
4. Press Enter to accept the proposed action. The sum of values in the cell range A1:A4 will appear in cell A5.

Should you need assistance in choosing a function for your formula, click on the Functions button, directly to the left of the Cancel and Enter buttons on the formula bar. It will give you a list of recently used functions and an option to view all of the built-in Excel functions. By selecting one of the functions listed, you will open a dialog box with all of the arguments for that function to make entering it easier. If you select the More Functions option, you will get the Paste Functions dialog box that lists all of Excel's built-in functions broken down by category. If you do not see the Functions button, you have not yet entered an = into the cell indicating that you want to create a function.

If you have a long series of values that you would like to quickly sum, simply highlight the range and, by default, the sum appears automatically in the AutoCalculate area of the Status bar at the bottom of the Excel screen.

You can change the default operation carried out by this automatic calculating feature by right-clicking in the AutoCalculate area and choosing the function you want from the AutoCalculate shortcut menu that pops up. From that time onward, whenever you highlight a range, Excel will automatically calculate and display the result using the function you specified.

Formatting Your Work

After you have edited your data, you will want to format it, arranging it consistently or changing its looks. For example, throughout your worksheet, you can group cell entries that are of similar types by formatting them similarly. You may also want to add descriptive titles for certain rows or columns or even for individual cells. To quickly introduce you to Excel's formatting capabilities, we will first look at the formatting options on the Formatting toolbar (see Figure 15.3). If this toolbar is not on your screen, go to the menu bar and select View ➢ Toolbars. Verify that the checkbox next to Formatting is checked.

FIGURE 15.3
The Formatting toolbar

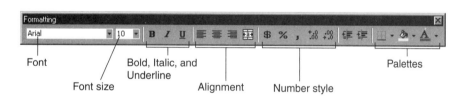

To format the contents of a cell, first activate the cell by moving your pointer to that cell and clicking on it once. Then select from the following choices:

Drop-down combo boxes - These are the first two items on the Formatting toolbar. They display the name of the current font and font size, respectively, and allow you to change them by clicking on their down-arrow buttons to display a list of choices.

PART

III

Analyzing with Excel

Bold, Italic, and Underline buttons - These buttons apply the selected style to the cell's contents.

Alignment buttons - In order, these buttons apply Left Alignment, Center Alignment, Right Alignment, and Merge and Center. The Merge and Center button is a handy tool for making a title or heading that spans multiple columns.

Number Style buttons - These include Currency, Percent, and Comma buttons. The Increase Decimal and Decrease Decimal buttons are also available for formatting the decimal precision of your numbers.

Palettes - The last three buttons, called tear-off palettes, combine a regular picture-face button with a drop-down list button. These are called the Borders, Fill Color, and Font Color buttons. When you click on the picture portion of the button, the format shown in that picture will be applied to the contents of the cell selected. You can change the picture displayed by dropping down the tear-off palette. To do this, simply click on the down arrow alongside the picture-face button, and a sample palette will drop down.

TIP

To have a tear-off palette remain displayed for ready availability, activate the palette by clicking on its down arrow. Next click on any area within the title bar of the palette and drag it away from the toolbar, letting go wherever you want it on your worksheet. Now the palette samples are handy for you to quickly redesign your efforts as you create your worksheet.

Copying Formatting from One Cell to Another

After you have formatted a cell to your liking and would like to duplicate the formatting without having to repeat all of the steps, you can use the Format Painter button on the Standard toolbar. Using it is quite simple. Select the cell that has the format you want to copy, click on the Format Painter button, and then click on the cell to which you want to copy the format. Double-click on the Format Painter button to lock it if you want to format more than one cell or range. Click on Format Painter again to unlock it.

Formatting Your Worksheet

To quickly format your worksheet to look like or serve as a table of information, you can use the AutoFormat feature. First highlight the range of data to which you want to apply a tabular format. Next select Format ➤ AutoFormat from Excel's menu bar. A dialog box will open with many tabular formats to choose from and apply (see Figure 15.4).

FIGURE 15.4

The AutoFormat
dialog box

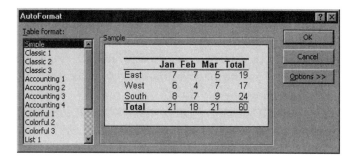

 If you enter too many digits to be displayed in a cell with a number format, Excel displays the number in scientific notation, or, if the cell is formatted with another format like Currency, uses number signs to signify a wide entry.

You can widen the column to fit your entry. The following steps show you how to adjust the column quickly.

1. Place your pointer at the top of the worksheet on the right border of the column you wish to adjust (the pointer should be in the row of column letters). Your pointer should change to a double-headed arrow.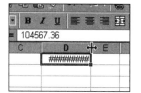

2. Double-click the mouse, and the column to the left of it will automatically adjust to fit the largest entry in the column. This procedure is called AutoFit.

TIP

If you want to adjust the column yourself, follow the first step above, but then, instead of double-clicking, click and drag the border to the width you desire.

The double-headed arrow can quickly adjust row height by following an analogous procedure. Simply place the pointer at the left side of the worksheet, on the bottom border of the row you would like to adjust, and double-click or click and drag to the desired height. (The pointer should be in the column of row numbers.)

Sorting Your Data

  On the Standard toolbar, the Sort Ascending and Sort Descending buttons sort a column of data in your worksheet in ascending or descending order. The Sort tool sorts alphabetically, numerically, and by date.

PART

III

Analyzing with Excel

Zoom Control

The Zoom control on the Standard toolbar is a drop-down box that allows you to adjust the magnification of your work area. To decrease the magnification, and therefore increase the overall view of your worksheet, you can zoom out to 75%, 50% or 25%. To increase the magnification level to make it easier to see and/or view a particular section, you can zoom in at 100% or 200% or move your pointer to the Selection option, which zooms to fit the current selection. You can also type a magnification level directly into the Zoom control box, up to 400%.

Charting Your Data

We suggest you take advantage of the tools Excel gives you to analyze your data. A graphic representation allows you to review your data more easily than viewing a lot of worksheet numbers. One of the best ways to visually represent your data is with charts. You can use the Chart Wizard button on the Standard toolbar to easily chart your data.

1. Select the range you intend to chart or place your cursor in any cell within the range; Excel will ask you to verify the range later.
2. Click on the Chart Wizard button on the Standard toolbar.
3. The Chart Wizard (see Figure 15.5) asks you to select the type of chart you wish to create. You may preview the chart to see how your data will look by clicking on the *Press and Hold to View Sample* button. Select the chart type and click on Next.
4. Verify the range of the information you wish to chart and whether you want your series to appear in columns or rows. If the range is correct, click on Next.
5. Choose from many options to customize your chart, including adding a title, setting legend options, using data labels, or even adding gridlines. Click on Next.
6. Select whether to have your chart appear on a sheet by itself or be embedded on the current sheet. Click on Finish.

NOTE

You don't need to select where your chart will appear once you have embedded it on your current sheet. Excel will create a standard-sized chart which you can move or edit later on.

If your chart is embedded, you can format different sections by double-clicking on them. (An example is shown in Figure 15.6.) For example, you can double-click on one of the axis labels to format its font or on the axis itself to format its pattern.

FIGURE 15.5

FIGURE 15.5

The Chart Wizard's four steps help you create professional-looking charts.

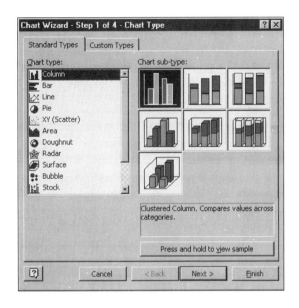

FIGURE 15.6

Formatting the axis of an embedded chart.

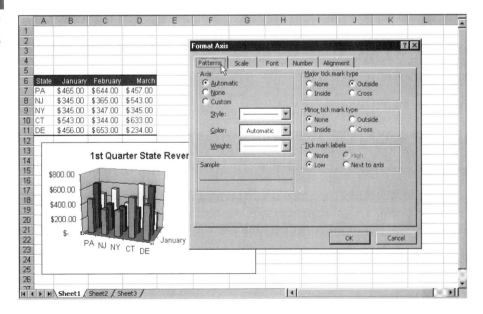

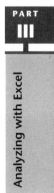

PART

III

Analyzing with Excel

Previewing and Printing Your Work

Spreadsheets can be tricky to print; therefore, previewing your work is very important. You can make the necessary changes using the Print Preview feature before you send your work to the printer. A little time put into preparing the worksheet for printing saves a lot of paper, not to mention the time it takes to wait for the printer to produce your creation.

1. Click on the Print Preview button on the Standard toolbar. Your current worksheet will appear. Excel infers that the area you want to print is the area where you have actually entered data, and by default prints the range from A1 to the last cell holding data closest to the bottom right-hand corner. Figure 15.7 shows a print preview of a worksheet with a small amount of information on it, so it only takes up one page when printed.

FIGURE 15.7

The Print Preview window shows how your worksheet will look on the printed page.

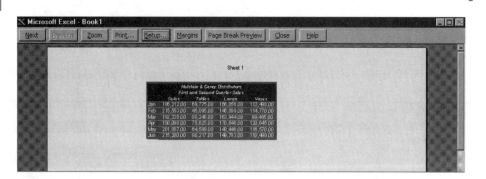

2. You can see more detail within the Print Preview window by zooming. Move your pointer to the worksheet page within the Print Preview window, and the pointer will change to a small magnifying glass. Click on any area in the sheet and the view will zoom in on that area. You can also use the Zoom button on the toolbar shown in Print Preview.

When you've zoomed into the Print Preview window and some cells display number signs, this indicates that you need to widen the columns before printing. Be sure to return to your worksheet and adjust your column widths before printing, or your printout will show the number signs instead of your numbers.

3. Select Page Break Preview to see just where and how your pages will break. Page breaks can be manually adjusted simply by clicking and dragging them to the desired area.

4. Click on the Print button to display the Print dialog box and print your worksheet. Click on the Close button to return to your worksheet and make any further modifications.

If you click on the Setup button in the Print Preview window, you can modify certain aspects of your worksheet page. Should you elect to print your work in Landscape (horizontal) orientation instead of the Portrait (vertical), select the Page tab in the Page Setup dialog box, and select the Landscape option in the Orientation group box.

NOTE

The appearance of the worksheet in Print Preview is a true representation of what will print. It's a view that may be different from what you see in the Excel application window. This is because Print Preview shows you what your printout will look like when it takes your system's printing specifications into consideration. Small adjustments may be made by Excel to make your worksheet fit proportionally on standard $8\frac{1}{2}$ by 11-inch paper. These adjustments could compromise the look you intended for your spreadsheet, so be sure to check out Print Preview before printing.

More Possibilities

There are many enhancements in Excel 97 that make it a lot easier to keep track of data and calculations. Excel allows you to perform "what if" analysis with ease. Excel can plot trends in your charts as well as in your worksheet. Exploring the following chapters will help you learn more about how Excel can work best for you.

PART

III

Analyzing with Excel

Chapter

16

Data Entry Tips and Tricks

Chapter 16

Data Entry Tips and Tricks

The more comfortable you are with the layout of the workbook and the methods available for data entry, the easier it will be for you to learn the more sophisticated features provided by Excel. This chapter focuses on shoring up your skills in the fundamental areas of data entry and navigation so that you can master the techniques in later chapters more easily.

The Worksheet

Excel's worksheet is made up of columns and rows. The intersection of a column and a row is called a *cell,* which looks like a little rectangle. There are 256 columns which are labeled alphabetically in ascending order. (A through Z, then AA through AZ, then BA through BZ, all the way to IV). Depending on your monitor's display type and resolution, you can usually see columns A through I at first view. Similarly, you can usually see rows 1 through 16, but there are far more than 16 rows in a worksheet. Each worksheet in Excel contains 65,536 rows, numbered 1 through, you guessed it, 65,536. That means that you have up to 16,777,216 cells on each worksheet available to hold information.

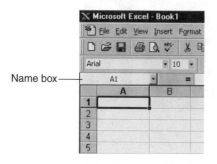

Name box

When referring to the cells in the worksheet, you must identify the letter of the column header plus the number of the row header. This combination of letter and number is called the *cell reference*, or *cell address*. You can view the cell reference for a selected cell or cells in the name box to the left of the formula bar.

Selecting Cells and Ranges

To enter data into your worksheet you must first have a cell or range selected. When you open an Excel worksheet, cell A1 is already *active*. An active cell will appear to have a darker border around it than the other cells on the spreadsheet. Only an activated cell can receive entries, so it is important to learn how to select and thus activate cells and ranges.

Selecting with a Mouse

The simplest way to select a cell is with your mouse pointer. You simply move your mouse to the desired cell and click on it.

To select multiple but adjacent cells, click and drag the mouse from the first cell in the range to the last cell in the range. Notice that the first cell in a selected range appears to not be in the selection. Even though the whole range is selected, this cell within the range is currently active and you can input information while the whole range is selected.

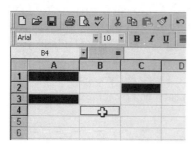

There will be times when you will want to select non-adjacent, or noncontiguous, cells on a spreadsheet. To select multiple noncontiguous cells, select the first cell or range that you want included in your selection, then hold down the Ctrl key as you select the other cells.

Navigating the Worksheet

To move around the worksheet area with your keyboard, you can use the arrow keys and the PgUp and PgDn keys, as well as various key combinations. The up, down, left, and right arrow keys will move you one cell in the selected direction. PgUp and PgDn move you one full screen, which is approximately 16 lines depending on your zoom level and formatting. Ctrl+Home will take you to cell A1 and Ctrl+End will take you to the end of the area in which you entered data on that spreadsheet.

To select data in a contiguous range using the keyboard, use your arrow keys to move to the first cell in your range, then hold down the Shift key and move the arrow keys in the direction of your range. When you have completed your selection, let go of the Shift key.

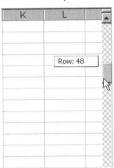

You can advance through your worksheet by rows with the vertical scroll bar or by columns with the horizontal scroll bar. When you click and drag the thumb tab on the scroll bar, a ScreenTip will appear alongside the bar identifying the row or column to which your view is advancing.

Holding down the Shift key as you scroll allows you to scroll faster through your worksheet.

PART

III

Analyzing with Excel

MASTERING THE OPPORTUNITIES

Navigating the Worksheet with the Microsoft IntelliPoint Mouse with Wheel Button

The new Microsoft IntelliPoint Mouse (and others that are sure to mimic it) provides a new twist to the standard mouse to which we have become accustomed. This new enhancement is a wheel button that is placed between the left and right mouse buttons. This new wheel makes possible a number of navigation techniques that go a long way to taming your large worksheets.

Using the scroll bars to scroll through the rows of your worksheet can become a tiresome feat, especially with 65,536 rows. With the new mouse and its wheel, you need only turn the wheel forward and backward to scroll up and down the rows of your worksheet. While it is set by default to scroll three rows per turning tick of the wheel, the mouse can be adjusted in the Control Panel to scroll in even larger increments.

Continued

Not to forget the 256 columns in your worksheet, the wheel also provides for panning (moving from side to side). Clicking the wheel initiates the panning action of the mouse. Once the wheel has been clicked, you can drag your mouse left or right and the columns will scroll by. Clicking any mouse button will turn off the panning. You can also pan up and down by clicking the wheel and dragging the mouse forward and backward.

Excel also supports zooming with the wheel. If you hold down the Ctrl key while spinning the wheel, your zoom factor will increase and decrease accordingly.

The functionality of this new wheel depends on support from applications and may be slightly different depending on the application your are currently using.

Data Entry

When you double-click on a cell, the formula bar is activated, and a cursor starts blinking in the cell. Although you may be entering characters directly into the cell, your actions are displayed in the formula bar simultaneously.

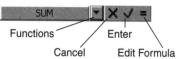

Task buttons appear on the formula bar when any activity is taking place there. The first button is the Functions button, which assists in using the built-in functions provided with Excel. The Functions button is available if there is an equals sign at the beginning of the value indicating you want to enter an expression. The next is a red ×, which is the reject or Cancel button. Clicking on it rejects whatever has been entered into the activated cell or range. The third is the accept or Enter button, a green checkmark. Clicking on this accepts, confirms, or enters whatever is in the formula bar. The last button of the group is the Edit Formula button. Pressing this button when the active cell contains an expression will open the Edit Formula dialog box, which displays the arguments for the function in the cell and their values.

Entering Numbers

Your numeric entries can be from the entire range of numeric values: whole numbers, decimals, and scientific notation. Excel displays scientific notation automatically if you enter a number that is too long to be viewed in its entirety in a cell. You may also see number signs (######) when a cell entry is too long. Widening the column that contains the cell with number signs will allow you to read the number.

Excel 97 will automatically adjust your column width to accommodate large numbers up to 11 digits. Beyond 11 digits, Excel converts your number into scientific notation and widens the column accordingly. If you have manually adjusted the columns; however, you may need to do so again when entering large numbers.

Text

You can use numbers, letters, or symbols when you enter text into a cell. Although the text that you enter into a cell may consist of both numbers and other characters, Excel will always consider as text anything it does not recognize as a pure number or date. If you have numbers that you want to be interpreted as text, such as a product ID number, simply begin the number with an apostrophe. This alerts Excel that the entry should be treated as text—or, more to the point, that it shouldn't be treated as a number, which it might automatically add, multiply, divide, or otherwise use in a calculation.

If you are unsure whether Excel accepted your entry as text or numeric, remember that numbers and dates are by default right-justified within the cell and text is left-justified. Of course, if you want to change this, you can always format the cell's alignment.

Date and Time Entries

When you enter dates and times, Excel converts these entries into serial numbers. The serial numbers are a numeric breakdown of the passage of time since the beginning of the century. Using serial numbers allows Excel to perform calculations with dates and times. The serial numbers are kept in the background, however, with Excel displaying the dates and times on the worksheet in whatever format you have selected. For instructions on the various time and date formats within Excel, consult Chapter 17.

Entering Series

When working in Excel, you will sometimes need to enter a series of data. A series may be numbers, dates, or text. You can enter a series quickly with the assistance of the AutoFill handle—that box on the bottom right side of the active cell. Below are examples of the various types of series you can quickly enter with AutoFill.

PART

III

Analyzing with Excel

Filling a Text Series with AutoFill

Follow these steps to use AutoFill to fill in the months of the year across a row:

1. Select cell A1.

2. Type **January**.

3. Move the mouse pointer to the AutoFill handle, the tiny square located at the lower-right corner of the cell's border. The pointer turns into a cross hair.

4. Using your mouse with the cross-hair pointer, click and drag the AutoFill handle across the next 11 columns, to column L.

5. Let go of the mouse button. Notice that Excel has entered all the months of the year, as shown in Figure 16.1.

FIGURE 16.1

Drag the handle over the range to input the series.

Excel also recognizes abbreviated monthly names, days of the week and their abbreviations, and quarterly names and abbreviations as well, and follows your cue when AutoFilling the rest of the range. For example, if you enter **Qtr 1** and use AutoFill, Excel will enter Qtr 2, Qtr 3, and Qtr 4. This series repeats itself in sequence throughout the range you selected. If you enter **Qtr 2** and drag the AutoFill handle for three more columns, AutoFill will know to enter Qtr 3, Qtr 4, and Qtr 1.

Filling a Number Series

Follow the steps below to enter a series of numbers that increment by a specific amount.

1. Select the first cell in your range and enter the number **5**.

2. In cell below enter the second number in the series; try **10**.

3. Select the two cells containing the numbers.

4. Click and drag the AutoFill handle at the lower right corner of your selection down the column.

5. Release the mouse button. Notice how the numbers increase by 5 down the column.

Series of Dates

You can also increment dates in a series just as you increment numbers.

1. Enter a date, **1/7/97**, in the first cell of the range.

2. In the second cell enter the second date, **1/14/97**.

3. Select the two cells.

4. Click on the AutoFill handle and drag it down three rows.

5. Release the mouse button and the incremented dates will appear.

Series: Edit ➢ Fill

For series options beyond AutoFill's capabilities, you can use the Edit ➢ Fill ➢ Series command from the menu bar. Edit ➢ Fill ➢ Series has the features of Step Value and Stop Value (Step is the increment amount, and Stop is the value at which Excel will stop), as well as a Trend option that provides best fit lines for linear growth and geometric curves for growth series. You also have Type options of Linear, Growth, and Date, as well as Auto-Fill. If you are working with date values, there is a special group of options to specify units of a desired date. With all of these options, you can select to fill either a row or column. The steps for using Edit ➢ Fill ➢ Series are as follows:

1. In the first cell of your range, enter your starting value.

2. Select Edit ➢ Fill ➢ Series from the menu bar. The Series dialog box will open (see Figure 16.2).

3. Click on or enter the options for your series.

4. Click on OK to close the dialog box.

Other options on the Fill submenu include Up, Left, Down, Right, Across Worksheets, and Justify. The first four directional choices will fill, in the direction selected, a single value across a range of selected cells. For example, if you had a formula in cell

FIGURE 16.2

The Series dialog box provides series options.

A1, highlighted the range A1:H1, and selected Edit ➤ Fill ➤ Right, the formula would be copied into all of the cells selected. Make sure that the value you wish to fill is the first cell in the selection. If the formula was in cell H1 and you selected Edit ➤ Fill ➤ Right, the result would leave all of the cells blank. If the value was in H1 and you wanted to fill the same range, you would need to select Edit ➤ Fill ➤ Left.

Filling Across Worksheets provides the capability to fill a range on one sheet to one or more other sheets. If you wanted to copy the range A1:H1 from Sheet 1 to Sheets 2 through 5, you would select the range, select the sheets including Sheet 1, and from the menu bar choose Edit ➤ Fill ➤ Across Worksheets. The range would be filled onto the other sheets.

Finally, the Justify option will take text in a selected group of cells in a column and expand it to fill as much of the column's width as possible, increasing or decreasing the number of rows when necessary.

AutoComplete

When Excel's AutoComplete feature is active, Excel automatically completes the letters of any name you type into more than one cell in the same column. All you have to do is begin typing an entry you typed earlier in the column, and AutoComplete recognizes the entry and finishes entering it for you. Look for more information about AutoComplete in Chapter 23.

Editing Data

Editing your Excel worksheet data is very easy. You can edit your entries in either the formula bar or the cell itself. First you must activate the cell you wish to edit and then use one of the following methods to enter the edit mode.

- Double-click on the cell containing the data you want to edit.
- Click once on the formula bar.
- Press F2.

The Cancel, Enter, and Edit Formula buttons, as well as the contents of the cell, will appear in the formula bar. You can position the cursor anywhere in the contents of the cell or the formula bar and begin editing the cell contents. The simplest ways to edit a cell are:

- Backspace over characters you want to change—Backspace erases the character to the left of the cursor.
- With your mouse, click and drag within a cell to highlight only the characters you want to change. Anything you type will replace the entire highlighted area.
- Simply start typing over the previous information in the cell. Note that the previous information will be lost in its entirety once you have completed your entry by pressing Enter or clicking on the green checkmark in the edit line.

TIP

Click on the Cancel button (the red ×) to keep the original entry.

Clearing the Entire Contents of a Cell

To delete the contents of a cell:

1. Click on the cell you want to clear.
2. Press Delete or Backspace
3. If you press Backspace, press Enter to confirm the empty cell.

To clear the contents without using the keyboard, try the following.

1. Right-click on the cell you want to clear. This brings up the shortcut menu for cells.
2. From this shortcut menu, click on Clear Contents. It is not necessary to press Enter or otherwise confirm this action; it's carried out immediately.

Deleting the Contents of a Range of Cells

1. Click on the first cell of what will be your range.
2. Move your pointer to the center of the cell and it will change into a solid white plus (+) sign.
3. Click again on the cell and, without releasing the mouse button, drag the mouse across the range to highlight all the cells whose contents you want to delete. Release the mouse button.
4. Press Delete to erase the contents.

Rearranging Worksheet Data

Excel gives you many tools to copy the data in your work area. The quickest way to copy within a worksheet is with drag-and-drop. For complex copying or copying between worksheets, you will probably need to use the Edit ➤ Copy commands. (You can use drag-and-drop to copy between worksheets if both worksheets are open.)

Copying Data with Drag-and-Drop

Drag-and-drop is the fastest way to copy data in your worksheet.

1. Select a cell to copy.
2. Move your mouse to the border of this cell. It changes to an arrow pointer.
3. Click your left mouse button and hold down the Ctrl key to let Excel know you are copying and not moving. A tiny plus (+) sign will appear next to your pointer. Continue holding the Ctrl key and the mouse button.
4. Drag the pointer across the worksheet to the location you would like to paste the cell contents. A small yellow box tells you the exact cell address that you are about to drop the copy. Notice also that the pointer is dragging an outline that represents the cell you are pasting.

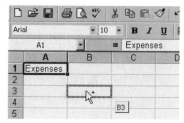

5. Let go of your mouse button and a copy of the cell's contents are pasted in the desired location.

Edit ➤ Copy

The are numerous ways to invoke the Edit ➤ Copy command in Excel. The steps below will show you how.

1. Select the cell or cells you want to copy.
2. Select Edit ➤ Copy from the menu bar or press Ctrl+C. Notice the blinking marquee surrounding your copied selection. You can also click on the Copy button on the Standard toolbar, or right-click and choose Copy from the shortcut menu.
3. Select the new cell in which to paste your copy.

4. Select Edit ➤ Paste or press Ctrl+V. You can also click on the Paste button on the Standard toolbar, or right-click and select Paste from the shortcut menu.

When you use the Edit ➤ Copy command, the information you copy is stored on the Clipboard, and you can paste it as many times as you want—that is, until you press Enter or Esc, at which point the marquee disappears from the selection being copied and it can no longer be pasted. Remember that once an item is copied to the Clipboard, you can paste it in other Windows programs. You can even arrange it so that changes made in your spreadsheet are linked to the copy in the other program and are automatically updated.

Copying Formatting from One Cell to Another

When you spend a good amount of time formatting a cell or cells and you want to apply that same formatting to another cell or range of cells, use Format Painter to accomplish the job quickly.

1. Select a cell that is in a format you would like to use elsewhere.
2. Click on the Format Painter button. Your pointer will show the Format Painter paintbrush alongside it.
3. Click on the cell (or click and drag to select a range of cells) to which you want to apply the formatting. The formatting will change accordingly.

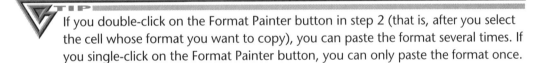

TIP
If you double-click on the Format Painter button in step 2 (that is, after you select the cell whose format you want to copy), you can paste the format several times. If you single-click on the Format Painter button, you can only paste the format once.

Moving Worksheet Data

The steps for moving your data are very similar to those for copying your data. The methods are principally drag-and-drop and the Edit menu.

Moving with Drag-and-Drop

1. Select a cell or range to move.
2. Move your mouse to the border of this cell. It changes to an arrow pointer.
3. Press and hold the mouse button. Drag the pointer across the worksheet to the location you would like to move the cell's contents. The pointer will drag an outline representing the cell you are pasting.
4. Let go of your mouse button. The cell's contents are pasted into their new location. If those cells already contain data, you will be prompted to decide whether you wish to replace that data or cancel the move.

Whether you are copying or moving with drag-and-drop, you are not limited to pasting within the same worksheet. You can also drag-and-drop into another sheet, as follows:

• If the other sheet is in the same workbook, follow the steps above, but in step 3 hold down the Alt key while you drag the pointer to the desired sheet's tab at the bottom of the worksheet (this makes that worksheet the top sheet). Release the Alt key but keep holding the mouse button, so you can continue to drag-and-drop your data anywhere within the intended sheet.

• If you have more than one workbook window open *and visible*, you can simply drag-and-drop the data from one window to the other.

Moving with the Edit menu

1. Select the cell or cells you want to move.
2. Select Edit ➤ Cut from the menu bar or press Ctrl+X. You can also click on the Cut button on the Standard toolbar or right-click and choose Cut from the shortcut menu that pops up. Notice the blinking marquee surrounding your copied selection.
3. Select the new cell to receive your data.

4. Select Edit ➤ Paste or press Ctrl+V. You can also click on the Paste button on the Standard toolbar, or right-click and select Paste from the shortcut menu that pops up.

TIP

If you selected the Edit ➤ Cut command in step 2, it is not necessary to use Edit ➤ Paste or to click on the Paste button—you can simply select the first cell of the new location and press Enter.

Transposing Your Data

You do not always have to paste cells to the same arrangement. You can quickly switch data that is in rows to data in columns by using Excel's transposing feature.

1. Select the range you want to transpose.
2. Copy the range.
3. Select the first cell of the paste area.
4. Right-click to bring up the shortcut menu.

5. Choose Paste Special from the short-cut menu to open the Paste Special dialog box.
6. Select the Transpose checkbox.
7. Click on OK. The row values will transpose to column values.

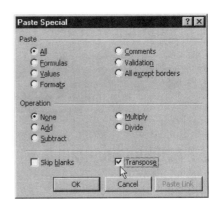

Spell-Checking

Spell-checking allows you to check for spelling errors in your worksheet. To use the spelling checker, select Tools ➤ Spelling from the menu bar, or click on the Spelling button on the Standard toolbar. Excel will check the entire worksheet. If you only want to spell-check a specific range, select that range first and run the spelling checker.

The spelling checker will prompt you before it makes a change, using a dialog box similar to the one shown in Figure 16.3. The Spelling dialog box gives you the option to change or ignore the spelling error. You may also elect to add it to the dictionary. Remember, if you have already added a word to your dictionary in any of the other Microsoft Office 97 programs, they will automatically be used in Excel since all of the programs share the dictionary.

PART III

Analyzing with Excel

FIGURE 16.3

The Spelling dialog box

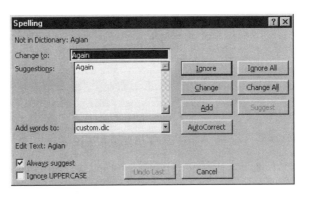

AutoCorrect

As in other Office 97 programs, AutoCorrect looks for commonly mistyped or misspelled words and automatically replaces them with the correct entry. Select Tools➤ AutoCorrect from the menu bar to see the options available. For more details about AutoCorrect and how it works, see Chapter 23.

Undo and Redo

The Undo and Redo buttons allow you to adjust your last actions. If you make a mistake on your last keystroke, you can recover by clicking on the Undo button. Excel 97 now supports multiple levels of Undo. If you continue to click on the Undo button, Excel will keep reversing the steps that you took prior to your last keystrokes. If you accidentally undo an action or actions by mistake, you can use the Redo button to "undo your undo," so to speak.

Finding Data in a Worksheet

The Edit menu allows you to search through your data to find a character or characters entered on your worksheet. Select Edit➤ Find from the menu bar and the Find dialog box (Figure 16.4) appears. You can specify what you are searching for and elect to replace it or not. You can also search within formulas rather than in values. You can find and replace all incidences of a recurring character or characters by choosing Replace All. To make your search more precise, you can also use case-sensitivity, search for whole words only, and search by rows or columns.

FIGURE 16.4

Use the Find dialog box to fine-tune your search.

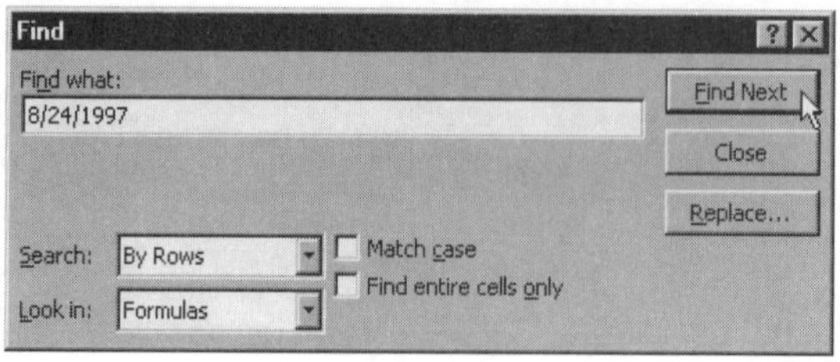

File Close

To close the current workbook, you can select File ➤ Close from the menu bar. You can also close it with the window's Close button. If you have made changes to your document before selecting close, you will be asked if you wish to save those changes. Remember, if you choose No, any changes made since your last save will be lost. If you are not sure whether you want to keep your changes, you can choose File ➤ Save As and rename the file.

TIP

Holding down the shift key while clicking File changes the Close menu item to Close All.

Chapter

17

Formatting Crowd-Pleasing Worksheets

Formatting Crowd-Pleasing Worksheets

Numbers don't need to be boring. To insure this, Excel makes available numerous formatting options to give your workbooks a polished look. You can change the size, color, and angle of fonts, add color to the borders and backgrounds of cells, and have the format of a cell change based on its value. This chapter will provide you with the tools to make your worksheets more visually appealing and easeir to interpret.

Formatting Data

In Excel, you can make many different font and format changes. Let's have a look at the capabilities of the Formatting toolbar.

Fonts

The first item on the Formatting toolbar is the Font combo box. Click on the box's drop-down arrow to see a list of available fonts. The small graphic to the left of the font name will give you an idea of how well the font will print. If the graphic shows a TT, the font is a True-Type font. This means the font will print just like it looks on the screen and can easily be scaled larger and smaller. If the graphic shows a printer, the font is a scaleable printer-resident font. This means the font on-screen might not match the printout. If there is no graphic, the font will print with the closest available match.

The Font Size box allows you to change your point size, which is a measure of the size of your font. Font sizes measure the height of your letter or number, not the width. The row height automatically adjusts to accommodate your chosen font size.

The Font Style Buttons

Excel allows you to bold, italicize, and underline your cell entries. You can apply these formats by following these steps:

1. Select the cell or cell range you want to format.
2. Click on the Bold, Italic, or Underline button on the Formatting toolbar. You can click on more than one button to impose a combination of the chosen formatting.

For even more formatting options you can use the Format Cells dialog box.

1. After selecting the cell or cells that you want formatted, select Format ➤ Cells from the menu bar (or right-click anywhere in the selected range and select Format Cells).
2. The Format Cells dialog box opens. Click on the Font tab (see Figure 17.1).

Here you can choose many font changes at once and view the result in the Preview window. Notice that there is an Effects option group box that allows you to change your data to Strikethrough, Superscript, or Subscript. If you modify selected cells and decide that you want to revert back to the Normal font, you can click on the Normal Font button. This will set the font properties on the Font tab to the Normal font style settings.

FIGURE 17.1

The Font tab of the Format Cells dialog box

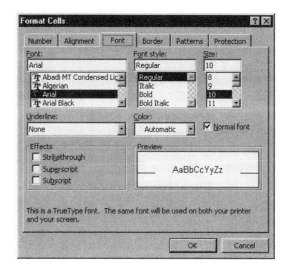

Aligning Data

The Formatting toolbar has four buttons for aligning your entries. By default, number entries are right-aligned in the cell and text entries are left-aligned. The alignment buttons will not indicate the alignment unless you modify the default. To change the alignment of a cell's entries, follow these steps:

1. Select the cell or cell range you want to realign.
2. Click on any of the first three buttons (Align Left, Center, or Align Right) to align all entries of the cell range. The entries will all align regardless of whether the they are text or numeric.
3. To reverse the action, click on the button again and it will return to the default.

The last of the alignment buttons is the Merge and Center button. Use this to place a title across a section of your spreadsheet:

1. In the leftmost cell of the range where you would like your title to appear, type the entire title.
2. Select the range across which you would like the title to appear (starting with the cell into which you placed the title).

3. Click on the Merge and Center button. You should get a result similar to the example shown in Figure 17.2.

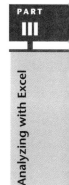

FIGURE 17.2

*A title centered
across columns*

	A	B	C	D	E	F	G	H	I	J	K	L
1					Atlantic International Publishing Journal Entries							
2												
3	January	February	March	April	May	June	July	August	Septembe	October	November	Decemb

In appearance, the columns in the row look merged together with the text in the first column centered in this space. In actuality, the entry is in the first cell only, as you can see by looking at the formula bar and the cell address box. To edit the entry, select the first cell of the range and edit either within the formula bar or the cell itself.

The Alignment dialog box offers you more options than the alignment buttons on the Formatting toolbar. For example, you can format text wrapping in this dialog box. The following steps will format the selected cell(s) so that the text inside will wrap to multiple lines, if needed:

1. Select a cell and enter text that is too long to fit in it.

2. Select Format ➢ Cells from the menu bar and click on the Alignment tab (see Figure 17.3).

FIGURE 17.3

*The Alignment
tab of the For-
mat Cells dialog
box offers more
options than
the Formatting
toolbar.*

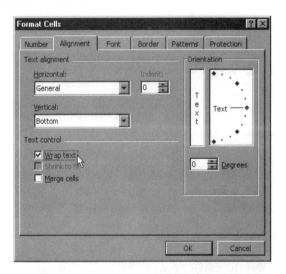

3. Check the Wrap text box and click on OK.

Your text should now wrap to multiple lines to fit within the constraints of the cell.

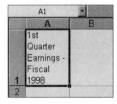

Number Style Format

The Formatting toolbar can also be used to format numbers. Select the range you would like to format and click on one of the buttons described in Table 17.1 to apply that style to your numbers.

TABLE 17.1: THE NUMBER STYLE FORMAT OPTIONS

Button		Purpose
$	Currency Style	Gives the number a dollar sign, comma, and decimal point followed by two decimal places.
%	Percent Style	Formats the number as a percentage.
,	Comma Style	Formats the number with a thousands separator and two decimal places.
+.0 .00	Increase Decimal	Increases the number of places to the right of the decimal point by one.
.00 +.0	Decrease Decimal	Decreases the number of places to the right of the decimal point by one.

If you need more number format options than are available on the toolbar, you can select Format ➤ Cells from the menu bar and click on the Number tab, which offers 11 predefined categories of formats. In addition, there is a custom category where you can define your own custom styles by combining custom codes provided by Excel.

Border and Color

You can also use the Formatting toolbar for adding borders, cell shading, and font color. These buttons are actually *tear-off palettes*. When you click on the picture portion of the button, the format of the picture displayed will be applied to the contents of the cell(s) you have selected in the worksheet. You can change the picture displayed on the button by clicking on the button's small drop-down arrow to access the palette of samples from which to choose.

PART

III

Analyzing with Excel

MASTERING TROUBLESHOOTING

Decimal Precision: What You See May Not Be What You Get

When formatting a cell for decimal precision by decreasing the number of decimal places that appear in the cell, the value of the cell does not change. For example, suppose a cell had a value of 4.35 and you decreased the number of decimal places to one. You would see 4.4 in the cell because Excel rounded the number, but if you referenced the cell in a calculation, the calculation would use the actual value of 4.35.

In order to get a true rounding effect, so that what you see and the real value are the same, you need to use the =ROUND function. The =ROUND function requires two arguments: the formula and the number of decimal places to which you want the result of the formula rounded. You would enter =ROUND(H65/B20,2) if you wanted to have the result of cell H65 divided by cell B20 rounded to two decimal places placed in a cell.

The first of the palette buttons is the Borders button. If the border you desire is on the face of the button, simply select the cell range to which you want to add a border and click on the Borders button. If you need a different border follow these steps:

1. Click on the drop-down arrow to the right of the Borders button.
2. The Border palette opens.
3. Format your selection by clicking on the style of borders you would like. The palette will close and the style you selected will be the picture on the Borders button.

If you prefer to keep the palette open and available as you work, follow these steps:

1. Click on the drop-down arrow to the right of the border picture on the Borders button.
2. The Border palette opens.
3. Instead of selecting a border, press and hold your mouse within the top area of the palette and drag it onto your worksheet (see Figure 17.4).
4. The Border palette is now open and available for repeated use.
5. To close the Border palette, click on the Close Window button.

FIGURE 17.4

Drag the palette onto your worksheet with your pointer.

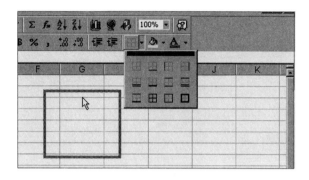

These same palette opening techniques apply to the Fill Color and Font Color buttons. For more choices when formatting borders, colors, and fonts, select Format ➤ Cells from the menu bar and choose from the Borders, Patterns, or Font tabs.

Orientation: Rotating Text

While not represented on the Formatting toolbar, another formatting option has been added to Excel 97. The contents of a cell can be aligned horizontally or vertically. This new feature is an angular orientation that makes the cell contents appear to be printed on an angle. You decide the steepness of the grade. Follow these steps to set this feature:

1. Select the cell or range of cells you wish to orient differently.
2. Select Format ➤ Cells from the menu bar and click on the Alignment tab.
3. On the right side of the dialog box, either click on the vertical box to display your text top-to-bottom or click on the right box for angular orientation.
4. Click on and hold on the word *text* in this box and drag it upward or downward to set the degree of the grade, or click on the Degrees box below this graphic and manually type a number, -90 to 90 degrees, or use the spin buttons. Use this last option for fine-tuning the degree of rotation you want.
5. Click on OK. Your text should now appear to be printed on an angle (See Figure 17.5). Notice how the cell height automatically adjusts to the height of the longest word in the series.

PART

III

Analyzing with Excel

FIGURE 17.5

Angling text can give a polished look to your spreadsheet.

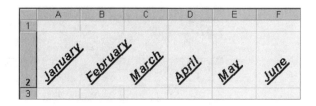

AutoFormat

Use AutoFormat to quickly format a table.

1. Select the range of data.
2. Select Format ➢ AutoFormat from the menu bar. A dialog box will open with many tabular format options.
3. Select from the many table styles. If you like one of the formats but do not want to apply every aspect of it, click on the Options button. Choose from the Formats to Apply option box and click on OK (see Figure 17.6).

FIGURE 17.6

The Options button on the AutoFormat dialog box allows you to change the format of a selected table style.

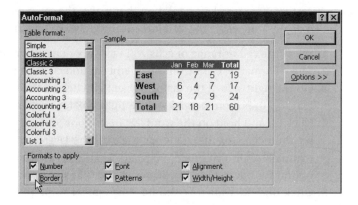

Format Style

Styles store all of a cell's formatting definitions. If you have a very complicated format and want to use it in other cells, you can apply it all in one step. To define your own format style:

1. Select a range you want to format.
2. Select Format ➢ Style from the menu bar.
3. Click on Modify.

4. Select the formats you want on any of the tabs in the dialog box and click on OK.

5. In the Style dialog box, click on the checkboxes to select or deselect styles.

6. Enter a name for the style in the Style Name box.

7. Click on OK to apply the new style format to the selected range. Clicking on Add and then on Close lets you define the new style while not applying it immediately.

If you have styles that you created in another workbook and want to use them in your current workbook, you can use the Merge button in the Style dialog box. Open the workbook from which you want to borrow styles, click on the Merge button, and select the workbook with the styles that you want.

Conditional Formatting

Excel 97 can monitor your data and alert you when the values enter a certain range or move outside of set criteria. Conditional formatting will change the formatting of a cell to draw your attention to that cell's contents. To apply conditional formatting, use the following steps:

1. Enter the following values in the cells indicated: **2000** in cell A1, **3500** in cell A2, **2750** in cell A3, **3800** in cell A4, and **1900** in cell A5.

2. In cell A6, enter the formula **=Sum(A1:A5)**. This will add the contents of cells A1 through A5. You can also click on the AutoSum button to do this automatically.

3. Activate the cell you wish to monitor—in this case cell A6. You will usually monitor a cell which contains a formula, but you could also monitor a value, particularly if you have someone else doing data entry and you want to check for the "reasonableness" of figures.

4. Select Format ➢ Conditional Formatting from the menu bar.

5. A dialog box will appear asking you to identify the conditions for which you would like your cell formatted. In our report, we want to be alerted when our total sales go below 12000. For Condition 1, select "Cell Value Is" from the drop-down box.

6. Select "Less Than" from the next box.

7. Enter the number **12000** in the third box (see Figure 17.7). If you need to enter a value from the workbook, you can use the Collapse Dialog Box button at the end of the text box. This gets the dialog box out of the way to make selection easier. Once the selection has been made, an Expand Dialog Box button is available. Now that you have defined the condition, click on the Format button in the dialog box to define the formatting you wish to apply.

8. Click on the Border tab and select Outline from the choices, then click on the Patterns tab and select the color red from the Cell Shading palette.

FIGURE 17.7

The Conditional Formatting dialog box

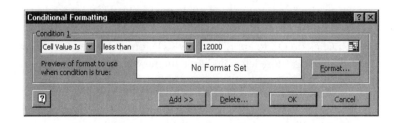

9. Click on OK and then click on OK in the Conditional Formatting dialog box (see Figure 17.7). You will not see any of your formatting in cell A6 because the value currently is greater than 12000.
10. Test for the condition by changing the contents in cell A4 to **500**. The total value has now met the condition and cell A6 should have a border and be highlighted in red.
11. Change Cell A4 back to **3800**. Cell A6 should now revert to its former formatting.

If a single condition is not sufficient to provide all of the formatting possibilities for your cell(s), you can add more conditions. The Add button on the Conditional Formatting dialog box will expand the dialog box to accommodate an additional condition—you can have a total of three conditions. If you find that you do not need an added condition, click on the Delete button. Instead of just removing the last condition, a dialog box is displayed which lets you pick the condition(s) to delete.

Formatting Workbooks

The Excel workbook contains three worksheets by default. The sheet name tabs are at the bottom of the Excel window. You can view only a few sheet tabs at a time. To adjust this view, place your pointer on the tab split bar. When it is positioned exactly on the bar, the pointer becomes a double-headed arrow, as shown in Figure 17.8. Drag it to the left or right to view fewer or more sheet tabs. To undo your adjustment, double-click on the tab split bar.

FIGURE 17.8

Drag the tab split bar to view more sheet tabs.

Arranging Multiple Workbooks or Multiple Windows

If the sheets you need to work on are in different workbooks, follow these steps to see them all.

1. Open the workbooks you need.

2. Select Window ➢ Arrange from the menu bar to open the Arrange Windows dialog box.

3. Select one of the option buttons (Tiled, Horizontal, Vertical, or Cascade) and click on OK. In Figure 17.9, the windows show the result of the Tiled arrangement.

FIGURE 17.9

The Tiled windows arrangement

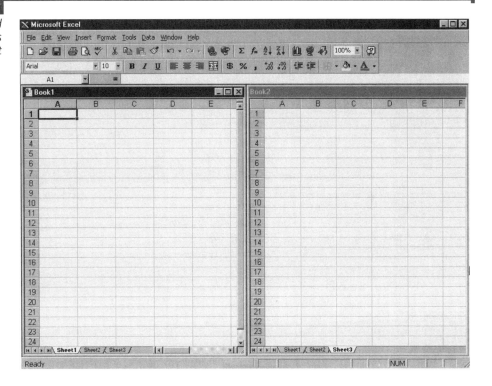

PART

III

Analyzing with Excel

To view multiple sheets within the *same* workbook:

1. Select Window ➢ New Window from the menu bar. This opens a new window with the same worksheet in it.

2. Select Window from the menu bar to switch to the new window. The new window for the workbook will have a colon followed by a 2 to indicate that it is the second view of the workbook. Select the new window.

3. Repeat steps 1 and 2 for each sheet you want to view.

4. Once you have all of the windows opened that you will need, select Window ➢ Arrange from the menu bar.

5. Click on the Windows of Active Workbook checkbox at the bottom of the dialog box and click on OK.

To restore a worksheet or workbook window to full size, click on the Maximize button at the upper right corner of the workbook window.

 MASTERING THE OPPORTUNITIES

Keeping Your Workspace As You Like It

Often your work with Excel will be in more than one workbook or one window of the same workbook. In this case, you may have a way that you like your windows arranged for easier and more logical access. The problem is that every time you open Excel and your workbook(s), you must set up this arrangement all over again. To help make working with multiple workbooks or multiple windows of the same workbook more efficient, Excel allows you to save all of your windows as a workspace.

To save your workspace, open and arrange your windows in the fashion that you normally work with them and then select File ➢ Save Workspace from the menu bar. When you save a workspace, all of the workbooks get saved independently and the workspace maintains the files included with the workspace and the number and orientation of the windows. When you open the workspace, all of the workbooks are opened and the windows are arranged just as you had them when you last saved and closed.

Hiding and Unhiding Workbooks, Worksheets, Rows, and Columns

You can hide workbooks, worksheets, rows, and columns to make your view easier to read and to help prevent unwanted changes. For example, you can hide sheets containing macros or critical data. The hidden workbook or sheet remains open, and all sheets in the workbook are available to be referenced from other documents.

To hide a column, follow these steps:

1. Select the column you want to hide by clicking on its column header, as shown in Figure 17.10.

FIGURE 17.10

A selected column

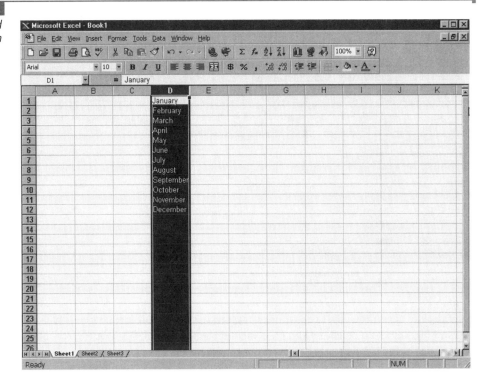

2. Select Format ➤ Column ➤ Hide from the menu bar or right-click within the selected columns and choose Hide from the shortcut menu that pops up. The column should be hidden, as shown in Figure 17.11.

To unhide the column follow these steps:

1. Select a visible range of columns that includes the hidden column.
2. Select Format ➤ Column ➤ Unhide from the menu bar or right-click within the selection and click on Unhide. The hidden column should now reappear.

You can follow the same procedures for hiding and unhiding rows.

PART

III

Analyzing with Excel

FIGURE 17.11

*After choosing
Hide, the
selected column
is hidden.*

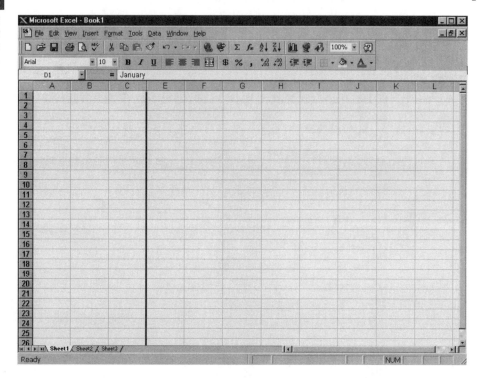

If you want to unhide all rows or columns on a worksheet, select the whole worksheet by clicking the block at the top left intersection of the row and column headings—just to the left of the heading for column A and above the header for row 1. Once everything is selected, follow the same steps for unhiding columns and rows.

To hide an active workbook, you don't need to select anything, simply select Window ➢ Hide from the menu bar. Select Window ➢ Unhide to bring it back into view using the Unhide dialog box that opens.

Inserting Columns and Rows

To insert a column or row, select the column or row header next to where the new area will appear. New columns are inserted to the right of your selection and new rows underneath. Then right-click within the selected area to bring up the shortcut menu and select Insert, or select Insert ➢ Columns or Rows from the menu bar.

Adjusting Widths

When formatting long amounts of data in a cell, you may find that your text is cut off or your numbers turn into a series of number signs. When this happens, you will need to increase the width of your column(s).

You can widen the column to show all of your entry. The following steps show you how to adjust the column quickly:

1. Place your pointer at the top right border of the column header of the column you wish to adjust. In this area your pointer changes to a double-headed arrow.
2. Double-click your pointer, and the column to the left of it will automatically adjust to fit the data entries within it. This procedure is called Best Fit.

If you want to adjust the column quickly without using AutoFit, follow the first step above, and instead of double-clicking in the second step, click and drag the border to the new width you desire.

The double-headed arrow can also adjust row height quickly, by following the same procedures listed above. The only difference is that you place the pointer on the bottom border of the row you would like to adjust.

You can also adjust columns and rows very precisely with the Format command on the menu bar. To adjust column widths:

1. Select a cell or range in the column you want to adjust.
2. Select Format ➢ Column ➢ Width from the menu bar.
3. Type a width, from 1 to 255 characters, in the Column Width box and click on OK.

Copying and Moving Sheets

The easiest and quickest way to move or copy a worksheet is to use the sheet's shortcut menu, by following these steps:

1. Activate the sheet to copy by clicking on its tab.
2. Select Edit ➢ Move or Copy Sheet. The Move or Copy dialog box appears. You can also right-click on the sheet tab and select Move or Copy Sheet from the shortcut menu.
3. Select a destination (see Figure 17.12). The To Book drop-down box lists the names of workbook destinations. You can also create a copy in a new workbook by selecting New Book from the drop-down box.

PART

III

Analyzing with Excel

4. When you select the workbook destination, the sheets of that book are displayed in the Before Sheet list box. This confusing title merely means, "The sheet has to go somewhere in the destination workbook; in front of which sheet do you want it inserted?" Select the sheet. You can also choose to move the sheet to the end of the workbook.

FIGURE 17.12

Selecting a destination in the Move or Copy dialog box

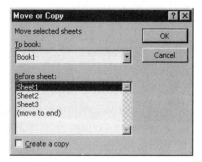

5. If you're *copying* the worksheet, select the Create a Copy checkbox, and click on OK. If you're *moving* the worksheet, just click on OK.

Another way to copy a sheet quickly is to hold down the Ctrl key while you click and drag the sheet tab to another location in your workbook. This is useful only when you can see the destination location, but don't forget that you can have multiple windows open for this very purpose.

Inserting Worksheets

Inserting is different from copying or moving an existing sheet because you are inserting a brand new sheet. When you insert a sheet, it is placed before the current active sheet. Here's how it's done:

1. Select Insert ➢ Worksheet from the menu bar, or select Insert from the sheet's shortcut menu (brought up by right-clicking on the sheet's tab).

2. If you used the shortcut menu, the Insert dialog box appears (see Figure 17.13). If the General tab isn't displayed, click on it to bring it forward. Then select the Worksheet item icon and click on OK.

FIGURE 17.13

The Insert dialog box lets you choose from a variety of objects to insert.

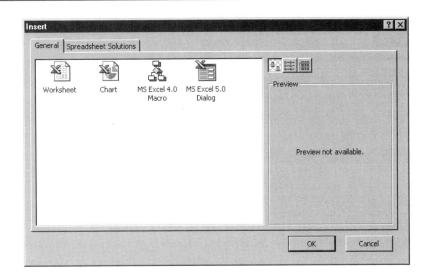

Deleting Sheets from a Workbook

To delete a worksheet, select the sheet you want to delete and select Edit ➤ Delete Sheet from the menu bar. To delete multiple sheets, first group them by clicking on the tab of the first sheet you wish to delete, holding down the Ctrl key, and then selecting other sheets by clicking on their sheet tabs. You want to be very careful about selecting multiple sheets for deletion as you will not be prompted to verify each sheet's deletion, only the deletion of the entire group.

To delete a sheet with the sheet's shortcut menu, right-click on the sheet tab and select Delete, then click on OK.

Renaming Sheets

You can immediately make your worksheets useful by naming them. (Of course, if you'd rather, you can keep the default names of Sheet1, Sheet2, and Sheet3.) To rename a sheet tab:

1. Double-click on the sheet tab or right-click on it and select Rename from the shortcut menu.
2. Type the name you want, up to 31 characters, and press Enter. Remember, you can't use the following characters in the worksheet name: slash (/), backslash (\), question mark (?), colon (:), and asterisk (*).

Your renamed sheet tab should look similar to Figure 17.14.

FIGURE 17.14

*The renamed
sheet*

Chapter

18

Formulas and Functions Built to Last

Formulas and Functions Built to Last

The real power in using a spreadsheet lies in specifying the mathematical relationship between the numbers in various cells. You do this by means of a *formula*. In Excel you literally type in these relationships, telling Excel how to formulate an answer. An example of a simple formula would be calculating base pay for hourly workers: "Hours Worked" multiplied by "Rate of Pay" equals "Dollar Compensation" or "Check" to be paid to workers. The exact values would vary depending upon the situation, but the formula would remain the same.

Creating a Simple Formula

Suppose you are making $40,000 a year in salary, and the company has announced that there will be a 10% increase for all employees. You would certainly want to know how that 10% translated into dollars. To arrive at your answer of $4,000, you would multiply the base salary by the percentage of increase. Therefore, the "formula" would be represented in words: Base Salary * Percentage of Increase. (The asterisk represents the multiplication operation on computers.)

To represent such a formula in Excel, follow these steps:

1. In cell A5, type **40000**, the amount of the base salary.
2. In cell B5, type **10%**, the percentage amount of the increase.
3. Click on cell C5. Type **=**. By using this sign you are telling Excel that you are start-ing a formula and not a simple calculation. You are now ready to represent the business formula stated above by showing (referencing) the locations (cells) that contain the numbers and typing the mathematical operators.
4. Click on cell A5.
5. Press ***** to declare that multiplication is the mathematical operator.
6. Click on B5. The formula bar at the top of the screen displays the cell references and the asterisk.
7. Click on the green checkmark next to the formula bar or press Enter. The cell displays the answer to this simple business formula and the for-mula bar displays the cell references and mathematics that were involved in producing the answer.

C5	▾	=	=A5*B5	
	A	B	C	D
1				
2				
3				
4				
5	$40,000.00	10%	$4,000.00	
6				
7				
8				
9				
10				
11				

NOTE

If you are a Lotus user and are used to beginning all formulas with a plus sign, you can continue to use the plus sign to start a formula. Excel will add an equals sign in front of your formula. But Lotus users must always remember to start even sim-ple calculations with either a plus sign or an equals sign. Excel needs the sign for all calculations, not just formulas.

Mathematical Operators

An *operator* is a special symbol that tells a program what action to take on a series of numbers. The mathematical operators to add, subtract, multiply, and divide are our most basic means of quantifying information. All computer programs use a common set of symbols to represent these four mathematical operators (see Table 18.1).

Although these mathematical operators are the most common, there are other operators represented by special symbols.

The exponentiation symbol is the ^ (caret or circumflex) character, the character above the number 6 on the standard keyboard. When Excel encounters this symbol, it is programmed to multiply the number to the left of the exponentiation symbol by the power indicated to the right of the symbol. For example, 2^3 means 2 raised to the 3rd power, which is the same as entering 2*2*2.

TABLE 18.1: MATHEMATICAL OPERATORS AND THEIR MEANINGS	
Operator Symbol	**Meaning**
+ (Plus sign)	Addition
- (Minus sign or hyphen)	Subtraction
* (Asterisk)	Multiplication
/ (Slash)	Division

TIP

To enter numbers and operators, get in the habit of using the keys on the numeric keypad to the far right side of the keyboard—it will greatly increase your data entry speed. This will also help you remember the operator symbols since they are the only ones on the numeric keypad! (Laptop and notebook computers may not have this extra keypad; however, keypads can be purchased as optional equipment for many models.)

Which Operator Takes Precedence over Another?

In Excel you can enter up to 255 characters in a single cell. This amount will allow for multiple operators and numbers to be used in a calculation or formula. The calculation capabilities of Excel are like those of a physical calculator. Begin with an equals sign and enter up to 255 numbers and operators. When you press Enter, you will get one answer.

The order in which you enter your mathematical operators, however, will produce different answers, even while using identical numbers and operators. All spreadsheet programs perform mathematical operations in a specific order. This order of operations is called *precedence*. Excel uses standard mathematical rules which give precedence to certain operations over others.

When Excel encounters more than one operator in a formula or calculation, it performs any exponentiation first and then multiplies and divides numbers before adding and subtracting them. Excel will always apply calculations in the following order:

Items in Parentheses
Exponents
Multiplication
Division
Addition
Subtraction

Analyzing with Excel

Some of us may have memorized these orders of precedence by using the sentence "Please Excuse My Dear Aunt Sally." Understanding the order of precedence is extremely important in creating Excel formulas.

Because the four core mathematical operators are the most common, let's create an example of precedence using only mathematical operators without exponentiation. Look at Figure 18.1 and try to determine the correct answer before reading further.

FIGURE 18.1

Use the order of precedence to find the answer to this formula.

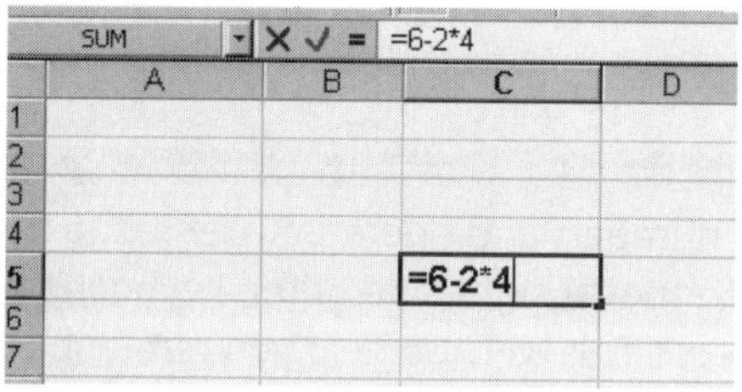

The correct answer according to the precedence rules used by Excel is -2. In our example, Excel skipped right past the subtraction and went straight for the multiplication, multiplying 2*4 to get 8. Then it went back and performed the subtraction operation: 6-8=-2. If Excel had not followed this order of precedence, it would have come up with a different answer by performing the subtraction first (6-2=4) and then multiplying that by the following number (4*4=16).

Changing the Order of Operations

To change the natural order of operations, use parentheses. In the example in the previous paragraph, to force an answer of 16 for the calculation of =6-2*4 you must change the default order of operations. Surround with parentheses the particular mathematical relationship that you want performed first. Excel will change its order of operations to perform the math within the parentheses. If you must use multiple sets of parentheses, Excel calculates the innermost pair first, then moves out through each subsequent set. Figure 18.2 shows a new answer now that parentheses have been placed around the subtraction relationship.

FIGURE 18.2

Adding parentheses alters the outcome.

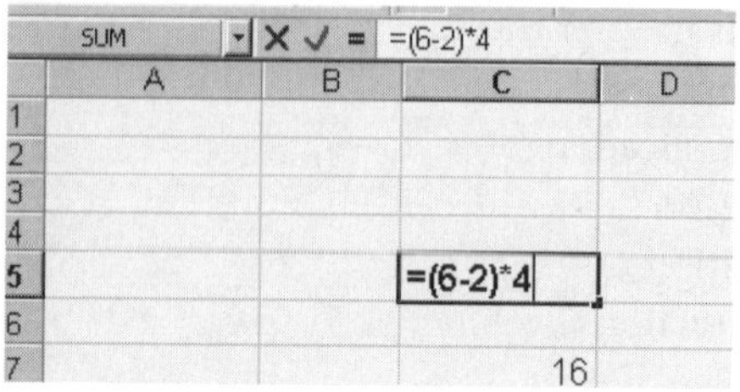

Logical or Comparison Operators

Comparison operators are used to compare one value to the other. These operators are also called *logical* operators because the resultant answer in the cell is always either True or False. Consider the calculation =4>5, where > means greater than. The comparison operator has posed a question to Excel: "Is 4 greater than 5?" The answer from Excel is False. Change the calculation to =4<5 (< means less than), and the answer from Excel is True.

Using the Comparison Operators in an IF Function

Comparison operators are used extensively within the =IF function, which we will explore in more depth later in this chapter. A *function* is a calculation engine that internally performs complex or large calculations on values placed within the function's parentheses. Functions reduce the amount of time it would take to manually calculate a complex answer. Look at the following =IF function:

```
=IF(A2>1000,"Overbudget","OK")
```

The =IF function tells Excel to evaluate a number or expression as True or False by comparing it to another number or expression. In this example, Excel must evaluate the number in cell A2 to see if it is greater than 1000. Once the evaluation has been performed, instead of printing True or False, Excel will print "Overbudget" if the answer is true or "OK" if it's false. Figure 18.3 shows the result of using an =IF function similar to the one above. Refer to Table 18.2 for the comparison/logical operators you can use in Excel.

PART

III

Analyzing with Excel

TABLE 18.2: COMPARISON OPERATORS AND THEIR MEANINGS

Operator Symbol	Comparison Meaning
=	Equal to
>	Greater than
>=	Greater than or equal to
<	Less than
<=	Less than or equal to
<>	Not equal to

FIGURE 18.3

An =IF function

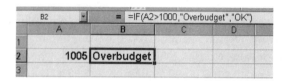

MASTERING THE OPPORTUNITIES

Not All Decisions Are Simply True or False

While a single IF function provides the first step to giving your workbook decision-making capabilities, you can accomplish far more by simply nesting IF functions within each other. Instead of providing a value for the True argument or a value for the False argument, you replace one of them with another IF function.

For example, suppose you are creating a worksheet that will determine the performance of students in a class based on a cell value representing a final grade. Using a single IF function, you could determine only whether they passed or failed. The function that you would use, assuming that the final grade was in cell F5, would be:

```
=IF(F5>65,"PASS","FAIL")
```

The value of the cell in which the function was placed would be either Pass or Fail. If you wanted to know more, such as what letter grade students should receive based on the numeric grade, nested IFs used in the following fashion would give you a result:

```
=IF(F5>=90,"A",IF(F5>=80,"B"
,IF(F5>=70,"C",IF(F5>=65,"D"
,"F"))))
```

In this formula, the value of cell F5 is evaluated to see if it is greater than or equal to 90. If it is, or rather the statement F5>=90 evaluates to True, then the True argument, "A", is used and the value of the cell becomes "A". If the statement evaluates to False, then the next IF function is evaluated in the same way. This continues until one of the conditions evaluate to True or the last nested function evaluates to either True or False.

When working with IF functions, keep in mind that no matter how complicated the nesting seems to become, it is never more complicated than the basic function of =IF(CONDITION,TRUE,FALSE). Every condition must be evaluated, starting from the left and moving into the nest of functions. Taking each IF function one at a time, insuring that all arguments are provided, you can quickly tame even the most nested IF functions. As with any use of parentheses in formulas, all open parentheses must have matching closing parentheses.

Creating and Changing Formulas

Now that you have a basic understanding of the components involved with Excel formulas, let's create a few example formulas so that you can see how easy it is to have Excel calculate the answer. The beauty of a formula is that it stays the same regardless of whether you change the specific numbers.

To calculate the gross check amount for hourly workers, you need to relate Hours and Rate. It does not matter what specific hours are entered or what specific rates are used, once you have set up the formula, Excel will automatically recalculate the gross check amount using whatever values are in the designated cells. Follow these steps to create a formula that calculates Hours multiplied by Rate. When complete, you can change the numbers and view the automatic recalculation that is performed.

1. Click on cell A1, and type the following headings in cells A1 through D1: **Name**, **Rate**, **Hours**, **Check**.
2. Click on cell A2, and type the following names in A2 through A5: **EGAN**, **COLTON**, **HINDLEY**, **WHITFIELD**.
3. Click on cell B2 and type the following rates of pay in B2 through B5: **12.5**, **13**, **14.75**, **13.5**.
4. Click on cell C2 and type the following hours worked in C2 through C5: **40**, **40**, **38.5**, **39**

5. Select B2 through C5. Click once on the Increase Decimal button on the Formatting toolbar to format both the Rate and the Hours columns for two decimal places.

	A	B	C	D
1	Name	Rate	Hours	Check
2	EGAN	12.50	40.00	
3	COLTON	13.00	40.00	
4	HINDLEY	14.75	38.50	
5	WHITFIELD	13.50	39.00	

B2 = 12.5

6. Click in cell D2 to begin typing the first formula to calculate the check amount, as presented in the following exercise.

Using the Mouse to Create Formulas

The formula to calculate the check amounts for the hourly worker model is: RATE * HOURS or HOURS * RATE. You can establish the formula by pointing out the cell locations of the values involved in the formula.

1. With the cursor in cell D2, type = to signal the start of a formula.
2. Click on Egan's rate of 12.50. The address of this cell (B2) shows up in the formula bar. Notice the moving marquee around the cell being referenced.
3. Type * (the multiplication symbol).
4. Finally, click on the cell with Egan's hours worked. The address of this cell (C2) shows up in the formula bar.

PART

III

Analyzing with Excel

5. Click on the green checkmark on the formula bar or press Enter. The formula calculates the check amount using the data in the cells specified, and the result (500) is shown in the originally selected cell (D2). Look in the formula bar at the formula itself (versus the result, 500, in the cell).

D2		= =B2*C2	
	A	B	C	D
1	Name	Rate	Hours	Check
2	EGAN	12.50	40.00	500
3	COLTON	13.00	40.00	
4	HINDLEY	14.75	38.50	
5	WHITFIELD	13.50	39.00	

6. Change Egan's hours worked to **45**. That is, click on cell C2 and type over the 40 hours with 45 and press Enter. The check amount is automatically recalculated to 562.5, because the mathematical formula has been set to multiply B2*C2 regardless of the specific values in those cells. Change Egan's hours back to **40** and press Enter.

NOTE

If you had entered the actual numbers into the formula, your answer would have still come out the same. However, if you had a change in the number of hours or the rate, you would have to make the corrections both in the source cell *and* in the formula. Using formulas that reference cells rather than specific numbers greatly reduces the chance of making data entry mistakes and increases productivity.

Changing and Deleting Formulas

There are a number of methods for changing or deleting formulas. Click on the cell whose formula you want to delete or change, and then use one of the following techniques to begin editing:

- Press Delete and start creating the formula again.
- Press F2 and perform cell editing as described below.
- Click on the formula bar and perform cell editing.
- Double-click on the cell to perform cell editing.

Once you are in the cell-editing mode, you can use the following techniques:

- Use the left or right arrows to reposition the cursor in the formula.
- Use the Backspace key to back over particular references in the formula.
- Double-click on one of the cell references within the formula and then click the mouse on the correct cell. This enters the address of that cell as the new reference in the formula. For example, suppose the formula to calculate Egan's check amount reads =A2*C2 but you want to change it to =B2*C2. After you've activated the cell editing mode, you can double-click on A2 within the formula and then click on cell B2. Excel will change A2 in the formula to the correct reference of B2.

TIP
Excel has a great shortcut to allow you to quickly toggle back and forth between the text of your formula and the value of the result. Hold down the Ctrl key and tap the backward apostrophe (`). On most keyboards the backward apostrophe is located on the same key as the tilde (~), below the Esc key. Pressing this key combination repeatedly turns on and off the ability to view the text of the formulas.

Using Colors to Read Your Formulas

New in Excel 97 is an editing feature that helps you interpret your formulas. When you first enter a cell for editing by double-clicking or pressing F2, you will notice that the cell references in your formula are different colors. The colors of the references correspond to the border colors of the cells to which they point.

This coloring of your references and their cells allows for rapid evaluation of formulas by helping you quickly find the color-coded cells in the workbook.

Copying Formulas

When the same formula is needed in multiple cells, you can usually copy the original formula to the other cells that need the formula. In our Hourly Workers example, Egan's check amount was calculated using the formula of RATE*HOURS. The other workers will need the same formula. Instead of manually entering each formula and every worker, copy the existing formula and Excel will automatically change the row numbers to reflect the appropriate rows needed for each new location. The formula change is because formulas are calculated *relative* to their position on the spreadsheet to data being calculated. For example, the original formula you created was =B2*C2. The answer which appeared in cell D2 was referencing the cell two columns to the left of the formula and multiplying that number by the contents in the cell one column to the left of the formula. The formula that will calculate Colton's check amount, on the other hand, will be =B3*C3. Notice that the same relationship exists between the column references of the values (columns B and C in both instances, two and one column to the left of the formula), but the row reference is different (row 2 in Egan's case, row 3 in Colton's).

The Copy command will change each copy of the original formula to reflect the correct row of the new formula. This property of the Copy command is called *relative referencing*: Excel takes the original formula being copied and makes each copy relate to the new row.

1. Click on cell D2, where the original formula produced the first check amount. The Copy command is not going to copy the value (500). It will copy the formula (=B2*C2).

PART

III

Analyzing with Excel

2. Click on the Copy button on the Standard toolbar, or right-click on the selected cell area and select Copy from the shortcut menu.

3. Select rows D3 through D5 (drag the mouse over these rows to select the destination for the copy).

4. Click on the Paste button on the Standard toolbar or choose Paste on the shortcut menu, or press Enter.

5. Excel copies the formula into the designated cells, but each copy uses the row number for the row on which it resides. The values calculated in each cell are different, indicating that the formula is using different values in each location.

	D3	▼		=	=B3*C3	
	A	B		C	D	
1	Name	Rate		Hours	Check	
2	EGAN	12.50		40.00	500.00	
3	COLTON	13.00		40.00	520	
4	HINDLEY	14.75		38.50	567.875	
5	WHITFIELD	13.50		39.00	526.5	

6. Make the decimal places the same for each of the check amounts by clicking and dragging to select all four check amounts (D2 through D5) and clicking twice on the Increase Decimal button on the Formatting toolbar.

Copy Tips and Tricks

Excel has a number of copy and paste methods available, including the Edit menu, the Standard toolbar, shortcut keys (Ctrl+C to copy and Ctrl+V to paste), and the shortcut menu that appears by right-clicking the mouse. In addition to these approaches, Excel allows you to press Enter instead of using the Paste command. The next sections describe alternatives to the four ways of using the two-step Copy and Paste/Enter method.

Using the Fill Command to Copy

When copying into a stack of cells, you can use Excel's Fill ➤ Down operation to copy and paste data or formulas vertically in one step. Select the original data or formula and the destination cells as one long selection. Press Ctrl+D. Excel will copy the formula down into the destination locations.

For copies across columns, select the original data or formula and the destination cells in one long horizontal selection. Press Ctrl+R to copy to the right. To copy up or to the left, select the source and destination and then choose Edit ➤ Fill Up or Left. (These operations do not have shortcut keys.)

Using AutoFill to Copy

The AutoFill command allows you to automatically fill in dates, days of the week, names of months, or series of incremental values, and is very useful as a fast copy command in Excel. AutoFill is activated when you drag the *fill handle* that resides at the lower right corner of a cell or a selected range. Follow these steps to copy the Check Amount formula for the Hourly Workers model we have been using.

1. Delete the formulas in cells D3 through D5. Leave your original check formula intact in cell D2. This will be the original source for the copy using AutoFill.
2. Click on cell D2, which contains the original formula.
3. Position the mouse at the lower right-hand corner of cell D2. Notice that a small gray button appears in this corner. The mouse pointer turns into a small black cross (See Figure 18.4).
4. Drag this cross down to cell D5 and release the mouse. Excel will copy the formula to cells D3 through D5.

This technique also works for copying and filling horizontally across columns.

FIGURE 18.4

Using AutoFill to copy a formula down a column

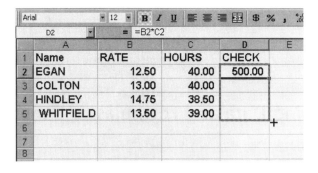

A Step-Saving Trick Using the Fill Handle

In the previous section you learned to copy by dragging the fill handle of the source cell through the destination cells. There is an added trick you can use when copying with the fill handle. This trick, however, works only with vertical destinations and requires that there be a column of data (any kind) to either the left or the right of the source cell. In addition, the column of data must already comprise the number of cells you expect the copy to occupy. In other words, if you must copy data or a formula into 20 rows, the column of data to the left or right must already extend 20 rows.

In our Hourly Workers model, the column of data containing hours worked is to the left of the formula. When we use the fill handle trick, Excel will calculate how far down to take the copy by analyzing the distance of the previous column (down to row 5). Here are the steps:

1. Click on the formula in cell D2. Make sure that there are no copies in the rest of the cells between D3 and D5.
2. Locate the small gray box of the fill handle in the lower right-hand corner of the selected cell. The mouse pointer turns into a small black cross.
3. Double-click the mouse and Excel will automatically copy the formula down to row 5 (which is the length of the column of data to the left of the formula).

PART

III

Analyzing with Excel

Copying While Entering a Formula

Our final copy trick (although not the last copy trick that Excel has up its sleeve) is to make Excel copy the formula as you create it. Use the Hourly Workers model again. This time delete the original formula in cell D2 and all of the formulas you have copied to the other workers' rows.

1. Click on cell D2 and select from D2 through D5. There should be no information in D2 through D5—just an empty selection.
2. Create the formula to calculate the check amount for Egan. Type = and click the mouse on B2, the rate of pay. Type * to specify multiplication, and then click on C2, the hours worked. Do not press Enter.
3. Hold down the Ctrl key and press Enter. This tells Excel to enter and copy into all of the selected cells the information you are entering into the first cell of the selected range.

You can also perform this operation horizontally. Simply select a horizontal range for the copy instead of a vertical range in step 1.

Copying Data and Formulas to Other Worksheets

Copying your data and formulas to other worksheets is a three-step process:

1. Select the range of data or formulas to be copied and click on the Copy button on the Standard toolbar, or choose Copy from the right-click shortcut menu.
2. Select the worksheet where the copy will be placed (click on the worksheet number or name on the bottom of the screen). Select the cell where you want to paste.

3. Press Enter or click on the Paste button. Remember you can click on the Undo button if the copy does not perform correctly.

Converting Formulas and Functions to Their Values

By default, the worksheet area of the Excel window displays the results of your formulas and functions, and the formula bar shows the actual formula and/or function. There may be times when you want to use the number from a formula or function as the basis of another set of calculations, but you need the actual *value*, not the formula or function that produced the value.

Excel has a variation on the Copy command that copies a formula but, when pasted, converts the formula or function to the actual value. Here are the general steps to convert a formula's result to an actual value:

1. Select the cells containing the formulas or function results.

2. Click on the Copy button on the Standard toolbar.

3. Click on the new location where the copy will be placed.

4. Choose Edit ➤ Paste Special, or right-click with the mouse and choose Paste Special from the shortcut menu, and click on the Values radio button. Click on OK.

5. The result of the formula appears. When you look in the formula bar, the actual value shows, not the formula references.

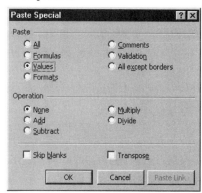

Absolute Referencing

There will be times when you want to copy a formula but you do not want Excel to perform relative referencing (as discussed earlier under "Copying Formulas"); that is, you do not want it to change the row or column coordinates of the copies. You need the capability to make a cell reference stay constant and not change to reflect the row or column to which it is being copied.

Figure 18.5 shows the result of a simple Percentage of the Total formula that calculates what percentage of the total sales each sales representative produced. When the original formula was copied, the resultant copies produced a series of errors. If you position the pointer on each cell containing the error, you will see in the formula bar that the location for the sales total (C8) is not held constant row to row.

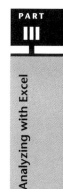

PART
III

Analyzing with Excel

FIGURE 18.5

The copies of the formula produced a Division by Zero error due to relative referencing.

	D2		= =C2/C8		
	A	B	C	D	E
1	**Sales Rep**	**Territory**	**Sales**	**% of Total**	
2	McMahon, Susan	Southern	29900	17%	
3	Lipari, Angie	Western	32800	#DIV/0!	
4	Ziemer, Karl	Eastern	41700	#DIV/0!	
5	Miserindino, Carl	Northern	38000	#DIV/0!	
6	Powers, Jessica	Mid-West	33500	#DIV/0!	
7					
8	*Total*		175900		
9					

Excel took the original formula =C2/C8 (Southern Sales divided by Total Sales = Percent of Sales) and made the copies maintain their relative positioning. This means that location C8 was copied and became C9, C10, C11, and C12 (see Figure 18.6). The problem is that Total Sales is only at location C8. Excel displays a spreadsheet error of #DIV/0!, the Division by Zero error. To avoid this error, you need to tell Excel not to change the row 8 reference.

FIGURE 18.6

When you look at the formula text, you can see that the location for the Sum of Sales is being referenced relatively, causing the error.

	A	B	C	D
1	**Sales Rep**	**Territory**	**Sales**	**% of Total**
2	McMahon, Susan	Southern	29900	=C2/C8
3	Lipari, Angie	Western	32800	=C3/C9
4	Ziemer, Karl	Eastern	41700	=C4/C10
5	Miserindino, Carl	Northern	38000	=C5/C11
6	Powers, Jessica	Mid-West	33500	=C6/C12
7				
8	Total		=SUM(C2:C7)	=SUM(D2:D7)
9				

Excel offers an *absolute reference* feature, which involves placing a dollar sign ($) in front of the column or row that should stay constant when it is copied. Thus, if you type a dollar sign in front of the row 8 reference in the original formula, =C2/C$8, then each copy knows not to change the row 8 reference. The left side of the formula is relative but the right side of the formula is absolute. Figure 18.7 shows the absolute referenced formula results, and Figure 18.8 shows the formula text where the absolute reference symbol was placed into the formula before being copied. Absolute cell references are best used in formulas that involve volatile data such as percentages or any calculable factor that changes with some frequency.

FIGURE 18.7

When the absolute reference symbol of the dollar sign is used in the formula, the results are the correct percentages.

H21		=		
	A	B	C	D
1	**Sales Rep**	**Territory**	**Sales**	**% of Total**
2	McMahon, Susan	Southern	29900	17%
3	Lipari, Angie	Western	32800	19%
4	Ziemer, Karl	Eastern	41700	24%
5	Miserindino, Carl	Northern	38000	22%
6	Powers, Jessica	Mid-West	33500	19%
7				
8	Total		175900	100%
9				

FIGURE 18.8
The dollar sign placed in a formula before the column reference dictates that that reference remain constant during a copy.

	A	B	C	D
	Sales Rep	**Territory**	**Sales**	**% of Total**
1				
2	McMahon, Susan	Southern	29900	=C2/C$8
3	Lipari, Angie	Western	32800	=C3/C$8
4	Ziemer, Karl	Eastern	41700	=C4/C$8
5	Miserindino, Carl	Northern	38000	=C5/C$8
6	Powers, Jessica	Mid-West	33500	=C6/C$8
7				
8	*Total*		=SUM(C2:C7)	=SUM(D2:D7)
9				

(Cell reference: H21 =)

TIP

If you know beforehand that you are going to need an absolute reference symbol in the formula, start the formula normally—using = and then clicking on the cell references of the formula. When you click on the cell reference that should be absolute, however, press the F4 key. Excel will automatically place dollar signs into the cell references.

Formula Error Messaging

As you saw in the previous section on absolute referencing, a problem occurred when relative-reference copying produced a #DIV/0! error. There are a number of error messages that can occur when creating formulas. Although these are Excel's attempts to be helpful in explaining the error, the messages are rather cryptic. Table 18.3 lists the error messages that occur and their meanings.

TABLE 18.3: ERROR MESSAGES FOR ERRORS IN FORMULAS

Error Message	Meaning
#DIV/0!	A division by zero has occurred in the formula.
#N/A	A value is not available to the formula.
#NAME?	An unrecognizable range name is used in the formula.
#NULL!	A reference in the formula specifies an invalid intersection of cells.
#NUM!	An incorrect number is used in the formula.
#REF!	An invalid cell is referenced in the formula.
#VALUE!	An incorrect argument or operator is used in the formula.

Formula Auditing

As you gain experience with creating spreadsheets, you may be required to explain the basis of a formula or function or to teach another person the mathematical expression being used. Excel's Auditing feature can display all of the locations involved in a formula. You can trace the precedents of a formula and the dependents of a value. Excel creates visual tracing arrows to show the various locations involved in a formula or function.

To trace the precedents in the Sales Territory model for the absolute-reference formula that calculated percentage of Total Sales:

1. Click on cell D4.
2. Choose Tools ➤ Auditing ➤ Trace Precedents from the menu bar. Blue arrows appear indicating the cells involved in the formula (see Figure 18.9).

FIGURE 18.9

Auditing arrows
displayed for a
formula

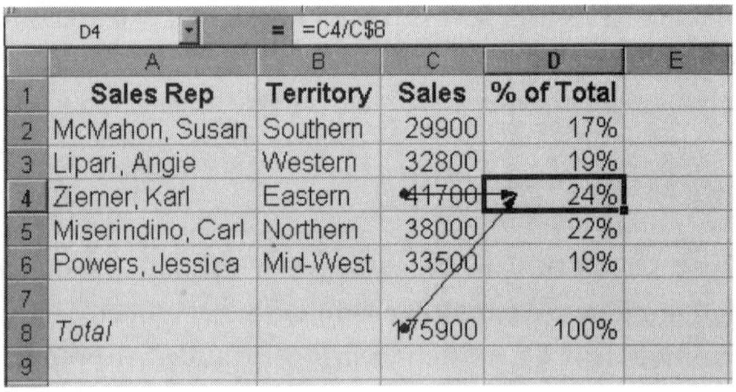

The Precedents command only works on formulas or functions. If you position the pointer on a cell containing only a value and not a formula, you can use the Tools ➤ Auditing ➤ Trace Dependents command. To remove the auditing arrows, choose Tools ➤ Auditing ➤ Remove All Arrows.

Functions

Functions are predefined formulas. They have also been called calculation engines, because functions deliver their results quickly by internally calculating multiple and sometimes complex sets of mathematical expressions.

The syntax of a function consists of the following:

- The equals sign
- The name of the function

- An opening, left parenthesis
- The arguments or ranges needed
- A closing, right parenthesis

The SUM function is the most common function used in all spreadsheet programs. This function saves you the time of adding each individual cell of data involved in the summation. To illustrate this as simply as possible, look at the difference between entering the operations on your own for a range of data and using the SUM function for the same range. If you were to add up 10 numbers starting at B1, your calculation would look like the following:

```
=B1+B2+B3+B4+B5+B6+B7+B8+B9+B10
```

The SUM function could produce the same answer using the following expression:

```
=SUM(B1:B10)
```

The SUM function requires that a range of cells be specified. The range is specified by means of its start location, then a colon to represent the word "through," and then the stop location for the range. Using the SUM function, it would be just as easy to add 500 rows as it is to add 10 rows.

Excel has over 250 functions, which perform a variety of calculations. The functions fall into ten categories:

- Financial
- Date and Time
- Math & Trig
- Statistical
- Lookup & Reference
- Database
- Text
- Logical
- Information
- User Defined

The most commonly used functions are in the categories Math & Trig, Statistical, and Financial. The SUM function falls within the Math & Trig category. If you want to find Excel Help for a function, it is useful, though not necessary, to remember the category into which a function falls. The AVERAGE function, for example, falls within the Statistical category, and the PMT (Payment function) falls within the Financial category.

 The Wizard lists all the functions, their uses and meanings, and what arguments are needed by each. Click on Insert ➤ Function to activate the Paste Function, or click on the Paste Function button on the Standard toolbar. A two-step dialog box helps you enter necessary information to the function. Figure 18.10 displays the Paste Function with the Financial category and PMT function selected.

PART

III

Analyzing with Excel

FIGURE 18.10

The Paste Function can be invaluable when searching for a particular function.

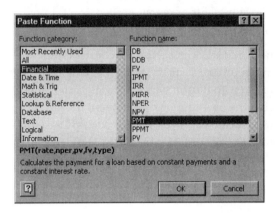

Summing Data

Because adding columns and rows of numbers is involved in all spreadsheet models, Excel provides an AutoSum button on the Standard toolbar so that you can quickly add your numbers. If your numbers are listed vertically, select a cell immediately under the last number in the column—or, if you wish, skip a cell after the last number and select the next cell down, to make the total stand out from the rest of the column. Click on the AutoSum button once. Excel will surround the column of numbers with a moving marquee, and the bottom cell will display the =SUM function

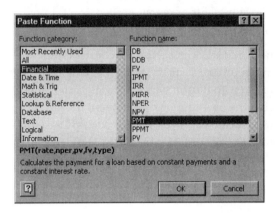

with the start and stop locations of the range of numbers. Click on the AutoSum button a second time, and Excel enters the function and displays the result.

To sum numbers at the end of a row, click on the cell to the right of the last number in the row and click on the AutoSum button twice. You can also press the AutoSum shortcut key of ALT+= (Alt plus the equals sign) instead of clicking on the AutoSum button on the Standard toolbar.

TIP

When you want to quickly view the sum of a column or row of numbers, you can simply select the series of numbers to be summed and look at the Status bar. Excel automatically displays the sum of the selected cells. (If the Status bar is not visible, select View ➢ Status Bar.)

> **WARNING**
> The location of the formula is important when using this function. AutoSum first looks up to find a number. If it does not find one in the first row directly above it, it then looks to the left and repeats this process until it finds numbers to add. If you have a space between the range of numbers you wish to add and have other totals to the left, it will add the totals to the left. Be sure to check the range *each time* you use AutoSum to be sure that you are calculating the cells you want to add.

Averaging Data

Sometimes it is easier to enter a simple function directly without using the Paste Function. The AVERAGE function's arguments are identical to the SUM function's. Unlike the SUM function, however, it has no equivalent button on the toolbar, but you can enter the name of the function and quickly select the range to be averaged.

1. Click on a blank cell below or to the right of the numbers to be averaged.

2. Type =.

3. Type the word **AVERAGE** (upper or lower case; it doesn't matter).

4. Type a left parenthesis.

5. Click and drag the mouse over the range of numbers to be averaged (see Figure 18.11).

6. You do not have to enter the right parenthesis. Click on the green checkmark on the formula bar or press Enter.

FIGURE 18.11

The AVERAGE function is easily entered without using the Paste Function.

	A	B	C	D	E	F
	SUM	▼	X ✓ =	=Average(B2:B13		
1	EXPENSES	JAN	FEB	MAR	QTR 1	
2	Item 101	104	114.4	125.84	344.24	
3	Item 102	212	233.2	256.52	701.72	
4	Item 103	784	862.4	948.64	2595.04	
5	Item 104	331	364.1	400.51	1095.61	
6	Item 105	27	29.7	32.67	89.37	
7	Item 106	508	558.8	614.68	1681.48	
8	Item 107	288	316.8	348.48	953.28	
9	Item 108	184	202.4	222.64	609.04	
10	Item 109	472	519.2	571.12	1562.32	
11	Item 110	108	118.8	130.68	357.48	
12	Item 111	487	535.7	589.27	1611.97	
13	Item 112	111	122.1	134.31	367.41	
14						
15	Total	3616	3977.6	4375.36	11968.96	
16	Average	=Average(B2:B13				
17						

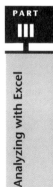

PART

III

Analyzing with Excel

TIP

You can average noncontiguous cells by clicking in the first cell, holding down the Ctrl key, and then selecting other cells to be included in the formula or you can type the cells you want included directly in the dialog box, separating the cell references with a comma.

The COUNTIF Function

The COUNTIF function is similar to the AVERAGE and SUM functions. You specify the range you wish included and Excel counts only the number of values contained in the range. The COUNTIF function allows you to use criteria to focus in on the specific values you want to be counted. The syntax of the COUNTIF function is in the following form:

```
=COUNTIF(range, criteria)
```

where *range* is the location of all the values from which the COUNTIF will choose and *criteria* are the expressions, text, or values that define which cells will be counted.

For example, you can find the number of Expense items that are over $200 for each month of the quarter with the formula:

```
=COUNTIF(B2:B9, ">200")
```

In this formula the range B2:B9 is the range of Expense costs, and the criterion is specified in quotes using the comparison operator.

Using the SUMIF Function

Like the COUNTIF function, the SUMIF function can be supplied a set of criteria by which it controls what data gets summed. A simple use of the SUMIF function would be to sum values greater than a specific value. As with COUNTIF, you must provide the function with the range of values to be summed and the criteria to be used:

```
=SUMIF(C2:C6, ">35,000")
```

In this formula the range C2:C6 is the range of sales figures and the criterion specified in quotes focuses the sum only on values over 35,000. (See Figure 18.12.)

Using the Paste Function

Some functions require that you supply information other than a range. Many of the Financial functions require multiple arguments, such as the current principal amount *and* how long an amount will be invested. It is not always easy to remember the exact

The SUMIF function is a powerful tool for focusing on specific values to include or exclude when summing the values in a range.

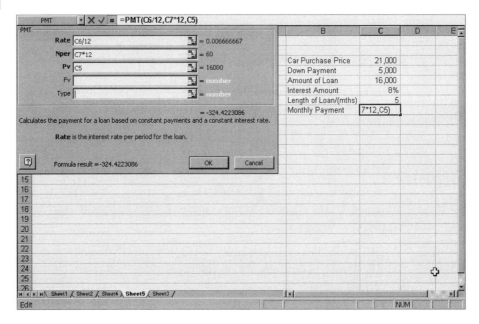

order in which the arguments should be entered. Fortunately, the Paste Function walks you through the steps of creating a function and lists the exact requirements that each function needs to work correctly.

Figure 18.13 displays a Payment model where the monthly payment for an automobile is being calculated by the PMT function. The PMT function, part of the Financial function group, requires specific arguments in a specific order. Furthermore, you can mathematically modify one of these arguments by multiplying or dividing. Let's use the Paste Function to figure out the monthly payment.

The Paste Function helps you remember the arguments required for a sophisticated function.

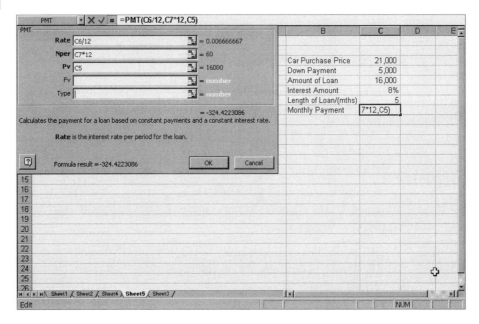

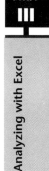

1. Create the model shown in Figure 18.13.
2. Position the pointer at C8. Widen column A until columns B and C are at the far right of your screen.
3. Click on the Paste Function button on the Standard toolbar.
4. Click on the Financial category on the left side of the dialog box. Click on the PMT function on the right side of the dialog box, then click on OK.
5. Three arguments are required for the PMT function: interest rate, the number of periods over which the loan will be paid back, and the loan amount. At the Interest Rate text box, click on the interest rate at cell C6. Divide this (yes, the location C6) by 12 to produce the following interest rate reference: **C6/12**. The interest rate will be calculated more accurately if it is divided by the 12 months of the year, since a monthly payment should be calculated by the monthly, not the annual, interest rate.
6. Click on the Nper text box to specify the number of periods. Click on C7 and multiply this reference by 12 to produce the following reference to the number of periods: **C7*12**. We're multiplying the number of periods by 12 so that the number of years is reflected as the number of monthly payments.
7. Finally, click on the PV (Present Value) text box and then click on C5, where the principal amount of the loan is located. Click on the OK button.

Excel shows the monthly payment in red to indicate a negative number. It's negative because Excel considers it to be money out of your pocket each month. To reverse the negative to a positive, if you wish, double-click on the payment located at D9 and place a minus sign in front of the function name:

```
=-PMT(C6/12,C7*12,C5)
```

Changing Your Functions

You can change your functions as you would any other formula in Excel. There are three different ways to activate the Edit mode.

- Double-click on the cell you wish to edit.
- Press F2.
- Click on the formula bar.

You can also use the Paste Function, so that you can see the descriptions of the arguments. This method offers the advantage of letting you see if you are changing the appropriate arguments.

1. Click on the cell that has the function you wish to edit. In the Payment example we have been using, click on cell C8.

2. Click on the Paste Function button on the Standard toolbar or choose Insert ➤ Function from the menu bar.

3. When the dialog box appears, click on the argument whose reference you wish to change. When you have finished, click on the OK button.

The Importance of Names in Formulas and Functions

An invaluable feature within Excel is the ability to assign a name of your choosing to a cell or range of cells. Instead of reading a function and trying to recall what the cell references mean, you could assign a real name to each of the cells referenced in the formula or function. A function that reads:

`=PMT(C6/12,C7*12,C5)`

could be easier to understand if its cell references had more descriptive terms:

`=PMT(Interest_Amt/12,Years*12,Loan_Amount)`

The ability to name a range allows for instant documentation and clarity of meaning in formulas and functions.

Defining a Cell or Range Name

You can assign a name by selecting the cell or range and then using a menu command or shortcut, both of which are described in this section. In the following steps, we'll use the Car Loan example to define a name for a single cell:

1. Select the cell or cells to be named. For this example, click on cell C6.

2. Choose Insert ➤ Name ➤ Define from the menu bar.

3. The Define Name dialog box appears. Note that Excel has already created a name for you within this dialog box—it has assumed that Interest Amount, the text label to the left of the selected cell, might already serve as a labeling function. Either keep this choice or change it. Then click on the Add button.

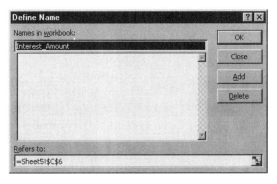

4. Click on OK. When you return to the worksheet, the pointer is still on cell C6, but now the name of the cell appears in the Name box (to the left of the formula bar).

Define the next name by using the following shortcut.

1. Click on cell C7.
2. Click on the Name box.
3. Type the name **Years** and then press Enter. You have defined another cell name.

Years		=	5	
Interest_Amount		B	C	D
1				
2				
3		Car Purchase Price	21,000	
4		Down Payment	5,000	
5		Amount of Loan	16,000	
6		Interest Amount	8%	
7		Length of Loan/(mths)	5	
8		Monthly Payment	$324.42	
9				

For practice, use either of the methods above to create a label for cell C5. Accept the suggested name Amount_of_Loan (if using the Define Name dialog box) and return to the worksheet.

You have defined three cell names. You can now use these names when creating your formulas or functions.

Inserting Cell or Range Names

The Name box is a handy and quick method for inserting names for your cells as you create a formula. To use the cell names defined above in the PMT function, delete the existing PMT function answer and start again so that you can view the process from the beginning:

1. Click on cell C8, where the PAYMENT function will be entered.
2. Type =PMT(Interest_Amount
3. Divide the Interest_Amount by 12 months and type a comma:

   ```
   =PMT(Interest_Amount/12,
   ```

4. Multiply the Years by 12 months and type a comma:

   ```
   =PMT(Interest_Amount/12,Years*12,
   ```

5. Enter the **Amount_of_Loan** range into the formula (see Figure 18.14). Press Enter. The right parenthesis will be inserted automatically. If you wish to see a positive number instead of a red, negative one, edit the formula and place a minus sign in front of the function name:

   ```
   =-PMT
   ```

FIGURE 18.14

Using names to build a formula

	A	B	C	D	E	F	G
	Arial	▾ 10 ▾	**B** *I* U ≡ ≡ ≡ ▦ $ % , ♯₀ ♯₀				
	PMT	▾ ✕ ✓ =	=PMT(Interest_Amount/12,Years*12,Amount_of_Loan				
1							
2							
3		Car Purchase Price	21,000				
4		Down Payment	5,000				
5		Amount of Loan	16,000				
6		Interest Amount	8%				
7		Length of Loan/(mths)	5				
8		Monthly Payment	=PMT(Interest_Amount/12,Years*12,Amount_of_Loan				
9							

> **TIP**
>
> You can define cell and range names on different worksheets as long as the names you use on each sheet are unique for that sheet. You can quickly position at any name regardless of its location. Select the name from the Name box. The pointer will jump to the cell or range indicated by that name. (If you have named an entire selection, the pointer goes to the top or left of the range.)

Deleting Names

To delete names, choose Insert ➤ Name ➤ Define and the Define Name dialog box appears. Click on the name you wish to delete and click on the Delete button on the right side of the dialog box. Click on OK to close the dialog box.

Natural Language Formulas and Ranges

Excel 97 makes using named ranges more intuitive than ever. This is accomplished by taking existing labels for both rows and columns and using them to reference the values that they label.

For this example, use the monthly expense account shown in Figure 18.15, suppose that you want to reference cell C5 (January's rent). The most common method for referencing this cell is to place =C5 into another cell which would return 500. Another option would be to insert a named range and reference that name. With Excel 97, you don't need to add a named range to make your formulas referencing the cells more readable. For example, you could reference cell C5 by entering =January Rent into a cell. Excel takes what is at the intersection of these two labels, C5, and uses that value. The order of column label and row label makes no difference; =Rent January would also work in a formula of a cell.

FIGURE 18.15

*A monthly
expense account*

	A	B	C	D	E	F
1						
2						
3						
4			January	February	March	
5		Rent	$ 500.00	$ 500.00	$ 500.00	
6		Utilities	$ 380.00	$ 370.00	$ 250.00	
7		Car	$ 176.00	$ 176.00	$ 176.00	
8		Insurance	$ 100.00	$ 100.00	$ 100.00	
9		Entertainmen	$ 110.00	$ 150.00	$ 80.00	
10						
11						

C14 =

Using this new natural language feature of Excel, you can also use a single label to get some interesting results. Placing =SUM(March) in a cell on the worksheet would return the sum of range E5:E9 since those are the cells directly under the label.

In some circumstances, using a single label can have different results depending on where the formula is placed. Suppose cells C11 and D11 both have the formula =Utilities. Cell C11 would show a value of 380 and cell D11 would show 370. The reason for this is that C11 is referencing the utilities for January and D11 is reflecting the utilities for February.

Providing full functionality for the true language ranges, Excel allows you to use the ranges together in calculations. Placing =January Car + January Insurance in a cell would place the value 276 (176+100) into that cell.

MASTERING TROUBLESHOOTING

When Adding a Row to a Range Is Not Reflected in Named Ranges

Sometimes when creating a worksheet you may not include all the rows or columns you need. Usually this does not cause a problem. However, when working with named ranges, the row or column additions may not get registered as part of an existing range.

The problem is that any changes outside of the range after it has been created do not

affect it. You must insert the additional row or column *before* the last row or column in the range instead of after it. Inserting a row or column in the middle of a range modifies the definition of the named ranges; inserting them after does not.

This also occurs when you have functions referencing a range to which you want to add. Inserting a row in the middle of the range will modify the function, while simply tacking on a row at the end will not.

Chapter

19

Charting and Mapping Your Data

Charting and Mapping Your Data

Data is just data until you've organized it usefully. When you can
present your data informatively,
you're providing far more than just data; you're offering *information*. One of the best
ways to convey information is with pictures. Excel offers various charting and mapping features to help you present your data most effectively.

Charting Your Data

You can use Excel's many chart options to represent your worksheet's information
visually. Charts give you a big-picture view; this makes your data easier to interpret
than when it is in spreadsheet format.

Inserting a Chart

To create a chart of your worksheet data on its own sheet, select Insert ➤ Chart from
the menu bar. To embed a chart on your current sheet, follow these steps:

1. Select the range of data you want to chart.

2. Click on the Chart Wizard button on the Standard toolbar. The Chart Wizard appears, leading you through its four steps to create your chart.

3. Select the type of chart you wish to create. To see what your chart will look like, click on and hold the *Press and hold to view sample* button located on the Chart Wizard dialog box (See Figure 19.1). When you have chosen, click on Next.

FIGURE 19.1

You can view sample charts in Step 1 of the Chart Wizard.

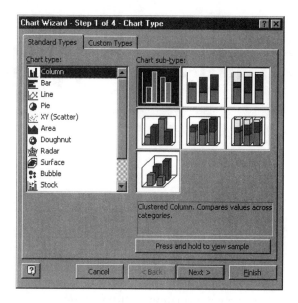

4. Accept the data range to be used by clicking on Next. If you had not already defined the range of the data, specify it in the Data Range name box. If you want to select the range using your mouse, you can click on the Collapse Dialog Box button at the end of the Data Range text box. This will collapse the dialog box, making it easier to select your range. When you are finished selecting the range, an Expand Dialog Box button is available to get you back to the other options. Once the data range is entered by either typing it or selecting it with the mouse, specify whether Excel should read the data in rows or columns when it does the charting.

5. Step 3 provides you with a multi-tabbed dialog box for detailed formatting (see Figure 19.2). Use the various tabs to add helpful details to your chart, including labels, a legend, and gridlines. Click on Next when you are satisfied with your chart's appearance.

FIGURE 19.2

FIGURE 19.2

Step 3 of the Chart Wizard lets you add detailed descriptions to your chart.

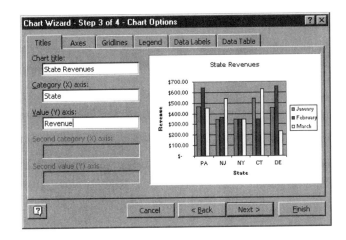

6. Step 4 asks where you would like the new chart to appear. You can insert it as a separate sheet in your workbook or as an object on an existing sheet. Once you have chosen, click on Finish. Your new chart will be created.

Editing your chart after it has been embedded on a sheet has never been easier than with Excel 97. In previous versions, you had to double-click on your chart, wait for it to activate, and then make your changes. Now, the chart is always active—you just double-click on the part of the chart that you want to format and make the changes to the formatting dialog box that opens. For example, to format a data series in your chart, double-click on it and then make changes to the Format Data Series dialog box. We'll discuss chart editing techniques later in this chapter.

TIP

You can view an embedded chart in a separate window. To do so, select the chart by clicking on it once and then select View ➢ Chart Window from the menu bar.

Chart Types

You can select from a whole palette of chart types in Step 1 of the Chart Wizard. There's also another way to choose chart types: from the Chart Types tear-off palette on the Chart toolbar. If the Chart toolbar isn't displayed, open it by selecting View ➢ Toolbars from the menu bar and click on Chart, or right-click on any toolbar and select Chart from the shortcut menu. The Chart toolbar appears. Click on the down-arrow on the Chart Type button to drop down the tear-off palette.

PART

III

Analyzing with Excel

The following paragraphs describe some of the chart types represented on this and the Chart Wizard's palette.

Area Charts—Show the relative contributions over time that each data series makes to the whole picture. The smaller the area a data series takes up, the smaller its contribution to the whole.

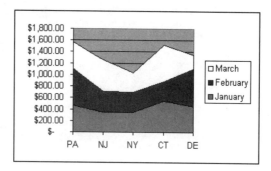

Bar Charts—Compare distinct items or show single items at distinct intervals. Use bar charts to show the results of sales contests or any competitive activity.

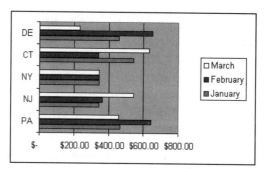

Column Charts—Similar to bar charts in that they compare distinct items. However, the two-dimensional column chart's value axis is vertical, its category axis horizontal. These charts are best suited for comparing items over time. It is important to keep the number of series in a column chart to a minimum. Too many series cause the column to become too narrow and difficult to analyze.

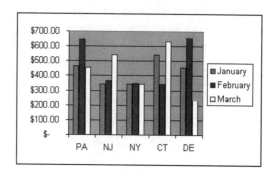

Stacked Column Charts—Selected by choosing a column chart that has a stacked style, this chart combines the power of area and column charts. Series values are stacked to show the relative contribution of each series and then reflected at discrete intervals.

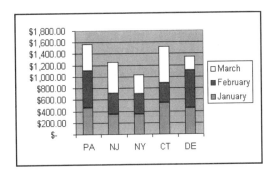

Line Charts—Reflect the changes in a series over time. Use when you are concerned more with the trend of a data series than with the actual data series' values.

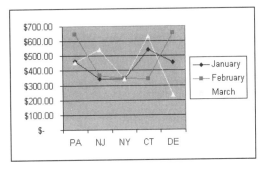

Pie Charts—Show the proportion each value represents to the whole of a single data series. Pie charts are good for showing proportional sales figures as well as population data.

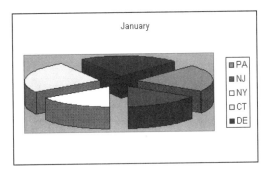

Radar Charts—Make comparisons between data series relative to a center point. They are designed much as an air traffic controller's radar screen, and are viewed the same way, as if you the viewer are the center point, and you have radar emitting a beam (the value axis) away from you in all directions. When the beam makes contact with something, a blip appears on the screen. In your chart, the blip is the data point shown with a data marker. In addition, Excel automatically draws lines from one data point to the next (that is, it connects data points that are on adjacent axes), forming polygons that make it easy to keep track of different sets of data on the same screen. In the Filled Radar chart to the left, two products are rated on a scale of 1 to 10. The polygon covering the most area represents the product ranking highest in more categories.

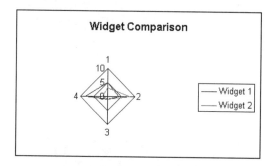

XY (Scatter) Charts—Show the relationship between numeric values in two different data series. They also plot a series of data pairs using X and Y coordinates. An XY (Scatter) chart is a variation on the line chart, in that the category axis is replaced by a second value axis. This makes it excellent for plotting survey and experiment results.

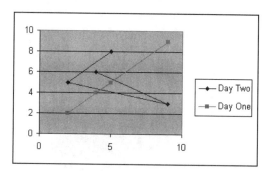

Doughnut Charts—Similar to pie charts. Like a pie chart, the doughnut chart shows the proportion of the whole that is contributed by each value in a series. Unlike a pie chart, however, you can use more than one series, because the chart can arrange a number of doughnuts concentrically. A pie chart can show the proportions of sales for each of your products within a single month; a doughnut chart can show the proportions of sales for multiple months in one chart.

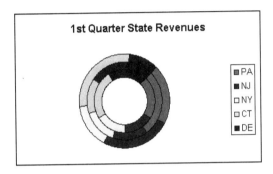

Picture Charts—By using small pictures as the units for the data series, this type of chart is great for presentations and is easy to create. We'll discuss the pictures available for these charts later in the chapter, under "Adding Clip Art to Your Charts."

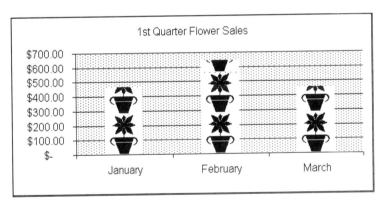

Bubble Charts—A form of XY (Scatter) charts. A bubble chart can show a third value, represented by the size of the bubbles. The chart below shows three products, revealing that while one product had more sales in quantity and dollar amount than the other two, it had the smallest amount of profit margin.

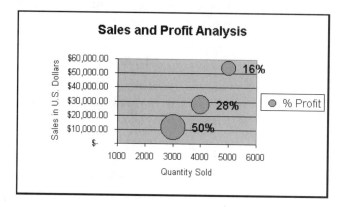

Stock Charts—Primarily used to indicate High, Low, and Close values for a stock you are tracking. When using this chart, your data must be in a specific order. Figure 19.3 shows both the data and chart for a particular stock in week intervals for one month.

FIGURE 19.3

A stock chart can show you the high, low, and closing prices of particular stocks.

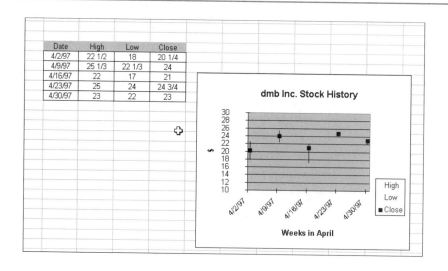

Cone, Cylinder, and Pyramid Charts —These charts are essentially the bar and column variety. There is never anything wrong with adding a bit of flare to your charts, and that is what these do best (see Figure 19.4).

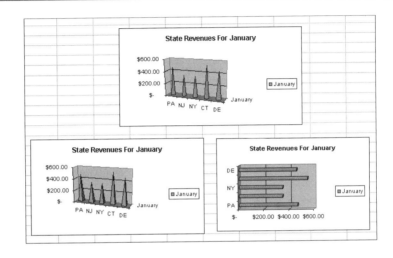

Modifying Charts

The quickest way to modify your chart is to double-click on an object within a chart to open its formatting dialog box. If you want to modify basic chart components like its titles and legend, you can select Chart ➤ Chart Options to open the Chart Options dialog box.

Advanced Charting Formats

Let's create a simple column chart and then format it using a couple of formatting tips. You will need to type in some data first and then create a basic chart.

1. In cells A1 through A6, enter **NY**, **NJ**, **PA**, **MD**, **DE**, and **VA**.
2. In cells B1 through B6, enter **76**, **77**, **66**, **55**, **88**, and **44**.
3. Select your data by clicking and dragging over cells A1 through B6.
4. Click on the Chart Wizard button on the Standard toolbar.
5. When Step 1 of the Chart Wizard opens, select Column and click on Next.
6. In Step 2, verify the data range you selected and click on Next.
7. In Step 3, click on the Titles tab and enter **Atlantic Region** in the Chart Title text box. Click on Next.
8. In Step 4, click on the radio button to place your chart as a new sheet and click on Finish.

Now that you have created a simple column chart in Excel, format it in the following ways to make it more interesting and create a better impact.

Exploding Pie Charts

First, create an exploding pie chart—a pie chart with a slice removed from the pie and set aside. This can be very useful if you want to point out a specific piece of the pie that is considered more important than the others, such as one department's budget in your organization or the profits of one fiscal quarter.

1. With the mouse pointer anywhere on the chart, right-click and choose Chart Type from the shortcut menu.
2. Select the Pie Chart type and the 3-D Pie subtype. Click on OK.
3. Click on the pie. Then click on one slice so that it alone is highlighted.
4. Press and hold down the left mouse button and drag the slice away from the center. Release the mouse button. The result should resemble Figure 19.5.

FIGURE 19.5

An exploding pie chart

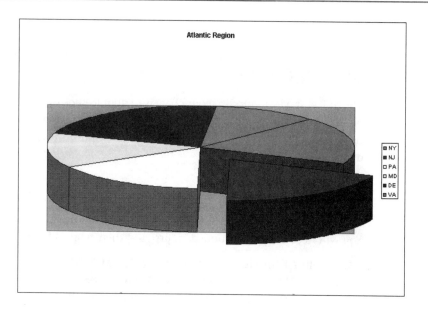

Using Clip Art in Your Chart

A little-known function of Excel is the ability to paste a clip art picture onto a chart and use that picture as units in a column. To use this feature, make sure that you have clip art installed on your computer. If you have previously done a full installation of Office, the clip art that comes with PowerPoint and Word should already be installed.

1. Click anywhere on the chart used above or on another one you may have created.
2. Change the chart type to a standard clustered column chart by right-clicking and choosing Chart Type from the shortcut menu. Click on OK.
3. Click on one of the bars in the chart. This should select the series.
4. Select Insert ➤ Picture ➤ From File from the toolbar.
5. Find the location of your clip art (the default folder should be under MSOffice/ Clipart). Select a piece of clip art and click on Insert. The clip art you chose is now used to help illustrate your chart.
6. If you want to modify the way that the picture is formatted, right-click on one of the bars in the data series and select Format Data Series.
7. Click on the Fill Effects button on the Patterns tab of the Format Data Series dialog box that opens. Select the Stack checkbox from the Fill Effects dialog box that opens. Click on OK twice to close the two dialog boxes and get back to your chart. Your final chart should look similar to Figure 19.6.

FIGURE 19.6

A two-dimensional column chart with clip art used as units of measure

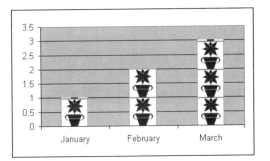

NOTE

There are several new custom chart types included with Office 97. You can choose from many professionally designed chart types or create your own. To create your own type, format a standard chart type, select Chart ➤ Chart Type, and click on the Custom Types tab. To add your own custom chart, select User-defined, then click on the Add button, enter a name and a description in the Add Custom Chart Type dialog box, and click on OK. Click on OK again to close the Chart Type dialog box.

PART

III

Analyzing with Excel

Mapping Your Data

Charts are not the only graphics you can generate from your data. Excel's mapping feature allows you to make geographic maps of your data as well. To take advantage of these mapping features, you need to create a range of data that will be appropriate to map.

1. Select the range A1:B7.

2. Enter the following information, pressing Enter after each entry:

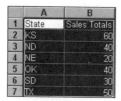

State, **KS**, **ND**, **NE**, **OK**, **SD**, **TX**, **Sales Totals**, **60**, **40**, **20**, **40**, **30**, and **50**.

Using standard abbreviations for states makes it easier for Excel's mapping tool. Each row will be represented by one region of the map. Once the map program recognizes the data, it produces a map automatically.

1. Select the range A1:B7.

2. Click on the Map button on the Standard toolbar or select Insert ➤ Map.

> **NOTE**
> If the Map button is not available on your toolbar, you may not have installed this feature with Excel. To perform mapping with Excel, rerun the Setup program, making sure that the Mapping feature is selected.

3. The pointer changes to a cross hair. Drag the pointer across the range C1:H10 to draw a rectangle in which to embed the map.

4. The Multiple Maps Available dialog box appears. From the list, select *United States (AK & HI Inset)*. Click on OK.

5. The map appears with the data entered and a Microsoft Map Control dialog box for you to make changes. (See Figure 19.7.)

In the bottom half of this dialog box, you can see the icon indicating the current map type being used. In our example, the icon for the Value Shading map appears alongside the Sales Totals column. You can change the map type by dragging a different type symbol from the bottom left of the dialog box into the editing area to the right of the symbols.

PART

III

Analyzing with Excel

FIGURE 19.7

The Microsoft Map Control dialog box appears when you select the type of map you want to display.

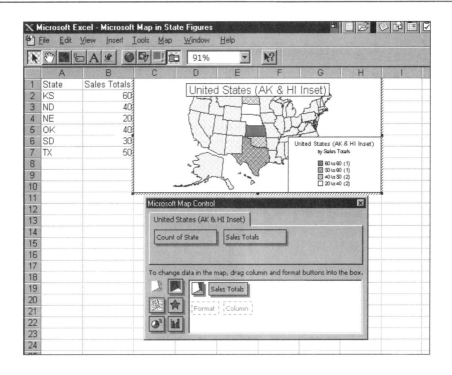

You can edit your map objects directly in the map when you are in the map window. To deactivate the map window and return to your worksheet, click anywhere outside the map but on your worksheet.

Adding Drawings to Your Charts

You can use the tools available through the Drawing toolbar to add drawings to your charts. To view the Drawing toolbar, click on the Drawing button on your Standard toolbar. The drawing tools in this toolbar (see Figure 19.8) can be used on your charts and worksheets.

NOTE

If your workspace is crowded with toolbars, you can easily move them to other places in the window. Click on the handle of a toolbar (the vertical lines at the left border of the toolbar) and drag it to the desired location.

FIGURE 19.8

The Drawing toolbar provides tools for enhancing your charts and your worksheet.

You can use the Arrow drawing tool to add an arrow to your chart for special emphasis. Click on the Arrow button on the Drawing toolbar, then click and drag from where you want the line of the arrow to begin to the item that you want the arrow to point out.

You can also format the Arrow object. To make it show up in a different color or with a different arrowhead for higher visibility, double-click on the arrow to bring up the Format AutoShape dialog box (see Figure 19.9), or right-click on it and, from the shortcut menu, click on Format AutoShape. Select from any of the options and click on OK to activate the new arrow style.

FIGURE 19.9

You have many options to format the arrow.

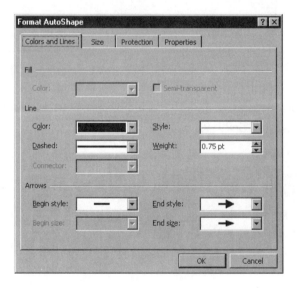

To make your arrow most useful, add a text box to its back end. Click on the Text Box button on the Drawing toolbar to add a text description to the arrow (see Figure 19.10). Move the cross-hair pointer to a place near the arrow and drag it to create a box of the size you want. Then type in the text and press Enter.

FIGURE 19.10

*A Text Box
object is added.*

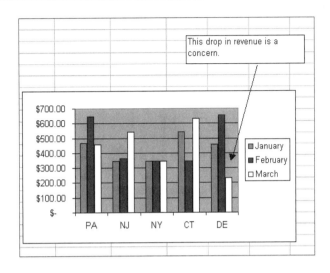

While the Arrow Text Box tools are the most useful for charts and maps, you might want to experiment with other buttons as well. You can create the shapes, group or ungroup these shapes, and specify which shapes should be in the foreground and which should be in the background. You can also apply a shadow to any selected object on your worksheet and apply a pattern to a selected drawing object. The last button on the drawing toolbar can transform your two-dimensional objects into a number of fantastic three-dimensional alternatives.

Adding WordArt to Your Charts

WordArt is a graphics tool that lets you manipulate text by adding shapes and color. You can also rotate text and customize the font size and formatting. To add WordArt to your chart, select Insert ➤ Picture ➤ WordArt from your menu. Select the style you like best and click on OK. On the next screen, enter the text to which you want to apply that styling. Once you have done that, click on OK. When your text is selected, the WordArt toolbar will appear to help you format the text to your satisfaction.

PART

III

Analyzing with Excel

Chapter

20

Linking Worksheets and Workbooks

FEATURING

Linking Worksheets and Workbooks

S preadsheet programs proved early on that they were a powerful and indispensable tool. As powerful as they were, advanced users who needed to push them to their limits quickly found that a traditional spreadsheet model, with 256 columns and 8,192 rows, simply was not enough to do the job. Not only were the number of records restricted (due to the limited number of rows), but users who wanted to keep monthly, quarterly, or yearly information would either have to divide their sheets into the appropriate number of sections or move to multiple spreadsheet files.

For instance, if someone wanted to track quarterly sales figures and then consolidate that information, they would more than likely need five separate files—one for each quarter and an additional one for the consolidation. In addition to this inconvenience, information from the quarterly sheets would have to be manually entered into the consolidation sheets every time any of the figures changed.

With Excel 97, a user has eight times as many rows per worksheet, for a total of 65,536, and a single file, called a *workbook*, that can contain hundreds of worksheets.

In addition, worksheets are no longer isolated containers of cells and numbers:

- If you have four quarterly sheets and one consolidation sheet in a workbook, you can link the totals from the quarterly sheets to the consolidation sheet so that no manual updating is necessary.
- Multiple users can link the data in their individual workbooks into one consolidated workbook, or between each other's files.

A Short Review on Selecting Cells

Becoming adept at the various methods for entering cell references and ranges will help you master linking cells from worksheet to worksheet and workbook to workbook. The techniques we'll review here for working with cell references and ranges on a single sheet can be applied in the later sections when we link between sheets and workbooks.

Entering Cell References and Ranges Directly

The most direct way to enter cell references and ranges is to type them right into the formulas of your cells. If you have gotten as far as needing to link sheets or workbooks, you are surely experienced with this skill, so we will quickly review the technique here. For more information on entering cell references using the keyboard, refer to Chapter 16.

Let's enter some data into a couple of cells on a worksheet and then use those values in the formula of another cell.

1. On a blank worksheet, enter **100** in cell A1, **200** in cell A2, and **300** in cell A3.
2. In cell A5, type the formula **=A1** and press Enter.
3. Change the value of cell A1 to **500**. Notice how cell A5 is linked to cell A1 and changes as you change A1.
4. In cell A6, type **=SUM(A1:A3)** and press Enter to reference the sum of the range of cells A1, A2, and A3.
5. Change the value of cell A2 to **600**. Note how the value of your sum formula changes when you change the value of a cell used in the formula.
6. When you want to use Excel's functions, like SUM, COUNT, AVERAGE, MAX, and MIN, to calculate the ranges of cells that are not contiguous (next to each other), you can separate the cell or ranges with commas. In cell A7, type **=SUM(A1:A3,A5:A6)** to reference the sum of the range of cells A1, A2, A3, A5, and A6.

Entering Cell References and Ranges with the Mouse

When working with worksheets, the most accurate and reliable way to refer to cell ranges is to select them with the mouse. You can click and drag over your target ranges, ensuring accuracy by reducing the risk of typos. When you start working with multiple worksheets, selecting ranges with your mouse may well prove to be the only feasible way to refer to ranges on other worksheets and workbooks.

Select a blank worksheet and try the following exercise to use the mouse to select ranges:

1. Enter **100** in cell A1, **200** in cell A2, **300** in cell A3, and **.05** in cell A4.
2. Make cell C1 your active cell.
3. Begin entering a formula by typing **=**.
4. Once you begin an expression, Excel can accept cell ranges that are selected with the mouse. Click on cell A1. The border of this cell should turn into a flashing marquee. Your formula should say =A1.
5. Click on cell A2. You may notice that your formula has changed, because Excel thinks that you are still searching for the cell or range of cells to which you want to refer. Click on cell A1 again.
6. Type **+**. Once you use a mathematical operator in your formula, Excel anchors the previous cell or range reference.
7. Click on Cell A2. Notice that because you used the plus sign, Excel now thinks that you want to add another cell reference. Your formula should read =A1+A2
8. Press Enter. The value in cell C1 becomes 300.

You can also use the mouse to enter ranges into formulas instead of just single cells.

1. Using the worksheet above, click on cell A6.
2. Type **=SUM(** into the cell.
3. Using your mouse, click and drag from cell A1 to A3.
4. Notice how Excel enters the notation A1:A3 into the formula. Type the closing parenthesis for the SUM function and press Enter.

Entering noncontiguous ranges with the mouse is as easy as selecting the first range and then holding down the Ctrl key while selecting the remaining ranges in the noncontiguous range.

PART

III

Analyzing with Excel

TIP

If you are entering a function or using only the one set of parentheses in a formula, you do not need to close the parentheses; Excel will do it for you. Simply press Enter when everything but the closing parenthesis has been entered. (Excel will *not* close any sets of parentheses if you have more than one set in the formula, even if all but one set are closed.)

1. Using the worksheet we created above, click on cell A9 and type **=SUM(**.
2. Select the cell range A1 through A4.
3. Hold down the Ctrl key and click on cell A6. Notice that Excel places a comma and then the reference to cell A6 in your formula:

   ```
   =SUM(A1-A4,A6
   ```

   Press Enter.

MASTERING THE OPPORTUNITIES

Creating Three-Dimensional Sums

Working with multiple worksheets that consolidate into one sheet creates a need for three-dimensional summing.

This means that you need to sum a range of cells in which the sheet name changes but not the cell. For example, your consolidation sheet needs to sum all of the monthly sales totals that exist in the same cell on 12 different sheets. Using the + operator, you could click from sheet to sheet, including each cell, or you could use the SUM function and create a range of sheets.

To do the latter, assume that you have 13 sheets in a workbook. Twelve of the sheets represent the months of the year, and the last sheet is used for yearly totals. The grand total of monthly sales is in cell H15 of every monthly sheet. You want to

sum all of these monthly grand totals on the yearly totals sheet. First click on any cell on the yearly totals sheet and begin a formula by typing **=SUM(**. Next, click on the first monthly sheet, presumably January, and click on cell H15. Instead of selecting a range of cells, you will want to create a range of sheets. Hold down the Shift key and click the last sheet in the range, probably December. This should select the range of monthly sheets and your formula should look like:

```
=SUM(January:December!H15)
```

Notice that the :, or the "through" symbol which represents a range, is between the sheet names this time and not between two cell references. Press Enter.

Creating a range this way provides a very clean approach to applying formulas to cells on different sheets.

Entering Cell References and Ranges with the Arrow Keys

In Excel, you can enter cells into a formula using the arrow keys on your keyboard just as easily as you can with the mouse.

1. Select a blank worksheet.
2. In cell A1 type **100**, in cell A2 type **200**, and in cell A3 type **300**.
3. In cell A4 type **=SUM(**.
4. Press the up arrow on your keyboard until the border of cell A1 becomes a flashing marquee.
5. Holding down Shift, press the down arrow key until the dotted border surrounds cells A1:A3. The formula in cell A4 should now read:

    =SUM(A1:A3

    Press Enter.

You can also use your arrow keys to enter noncontiguous cells into a cell formula. To do this, type a comma between each range that you want included. Follow these steps to total two separate ranges that are noncontiguous:

1. Using the same worksheet used in the previous exercise, select cell C1.
2. In cell C1 type **200**, in cell C2 type **400**, and in cell C3 type **800**.
3. In cell C4 type **=SUM(** and move to cell A1 using your arrow keys.
4. Hold down the Shift key while pressing the down arrow key until you arrive at cell A3. Type a comma.
5. Use the arrow keys to move to cell C1.
6. Hold down Shift while using the arrow keys to move to cell C3. The formula in cell C4 should now read:

    =SUM(A1:A3,C1:C3

    Press Enter.

SUM	▼	✗ ✓	=	=SUM(A1:A3,C1:C3	
	A	B	C	D	E
1	100		200		
2	200		400		
3	300		800		
4	600		=SUM(A1:A3,C1:C3)		
5					

Working with Worksheets

Using workbooks, you can organize your data according to separate categories, assigning each category its own sheet(s). For instance, if your workbook holds the financial data for 1995, you might want to store the data in four sheets (one for each quarter), or even 12 (one for each month). You may also want to add one more sheet to consolidate information.

PART

III

Analyzing with Excel

Excel opens a new workbook with the default of three worksheets. You can add, move, delete, or copy any of the worksheets in the workbook. You can also format multiple sheets simultaneously by selecting the sheets and then entering the data on one of the selected sheets. Sheet names can be customized with appropriate names like January or First Quarter instead of Sheet1 or Sheet2.

Naming Worksheets

You can easily edit the name of a worksheet in Excel:

1. Double-click on the worksheet tab you wish to rename.

2. Type the new name in the tab area that contains the sheet name.

3. Press Enter to apply the new name to the sheet.

Forbidden Characters

You cannot use the following characters in the name of your sheet:

:	colon
/	forward slash
\	backslash
?	question mark
*	asterisk

In addition to these forbidden characters, you cannot use the following characters as the first or last character in your sheet name.

'	accent grave or backwards apostrophe
[	opening bracket
]	closing bracket (you *can* use this as the last character, however.)

TIP

When you have many worksheets, it becomes tedious searching for the names that are further down in the tab sequence. You can see a list of all worksheet names at one time by right-clicking on the directional "Goto" arrows at the beginning of the sheet tabs.

Moving Worksheets

You may create, name, and enter data into a worksheet, and later discover you need to move it to a more logical position in your workbook. Moving worksheets is just as easy as renaming them. In many cases it is truly a matter of pointing and clicking with the mouse.

1. Click on the tab of the worksheet you wish to move and hold down the mouse button. A document icon should appear near the mouse pointer, along with a small black arrow indicating the current sheet position.
2. While holding the left mouse button, drag the sheet to its new position indicated by the black arrow (see Figure 20.1).
3. Release the mouse button to complete the move.

FIGURE 20.1

Moving a sheet

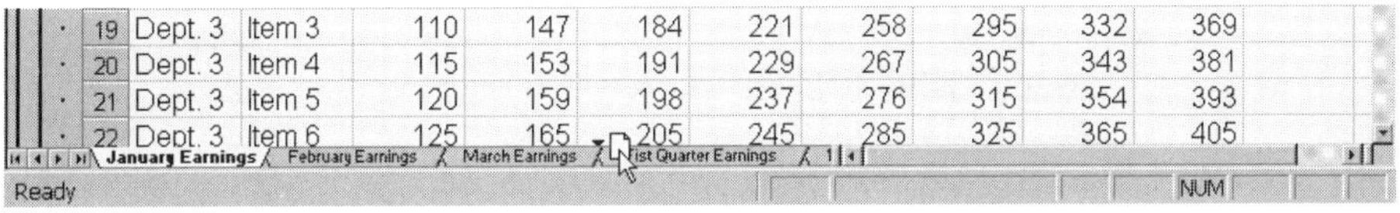

The method above works best when you can see your destination. You can even click and drag worksheets from one workbook to another if the windows of both books are visible. Before attempting this, refer to "Viewing Multiple Worksheets (Workbooks) at the Same Time" later in this chapter.

You may also use the Move or Copy dialog box to move and copy your worksheets. This method is frequently used to copy worksheets from one book to another. To run through the steps of this exercise, keep the current workbook open and open a blank workbook as the destination. Create a new workbook by selecting File ➤ New and base the workbook on a blank workbook. Click on OK.

1. If you are not in your original workbook, switch to that workbook by selecting it from the Window menu.
2. Click on the tab of the worksheet you have been using.
3. Right-click on the tab of the sheet you want to move and click on Move or Copy.
4. In the Move or Copy dialog box, select the new workbook you have created under the To Book list box.
5. Select Sheet3 from the Before Sheet list box.
6. Click on OK to move your sheet.

PART

III

Analyzing with Excel

Copying Worksheets

If you want to create a copy of a worksheet to use elsewhere in the same workbook or in another workbook, you can use the same techniques presented above, with only slight variations:

- Using the mouse, hold down the Ctrl key while you click and drag a sheet. The sheet will be copied to its new location instead of being moved.
- Using the Move or Copy dialog box, select the Create a Copy checkbox to activate the copy function.

Inserting and Deleting Worksheets

You can also insert blank worksheets into your workbook.

1. Select the tab of the worksheet where you want a new sheet to be added.
2. Select Insert ➤ Worksheet from the menu bar. Or right-click on the selected sheet to get the shortcut menu and choose Insert, making sure Worksheet is selected in the Insert dialog box, then click on OK.
3. The worksheet you selected will be shifted to the right. Excel will insert a new worksheet to the left of the selected sheet.

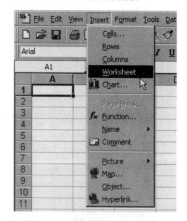

To delete a worksheet, you need only select the sheet and then either select Edit ➤ Delete Sheet or right-click on the sheet for the shortcut menu and choose Delete. You will be prompted with a dialog box to confirm your deletion.

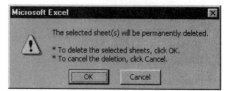

Selecting and Editing Multiple Worksheets

Sometimes you'll need to create a workbook with several worksheets that are copies of each other. For instance, if you have four fiscal quarters, and four regions in your organization, you might want five worksheets that are exact copies of each other: one for each quarter, and a fifth that totals all the quarters together. To accomplish this, you could create each worksheet separately, entering the row and column titles on each sheet. You could also create one worksheet, format it, and then copy the sheet four times. However, there is an easier way. In Excel you can select multiple sheets and edit them all at the same time.

In this situation, select the five blank sheets that you want to format alike, and then edit any one of the sheets. Any data or formatting that you apply to one of the selected sheets will show up on the other four sheets selected. Let's work through how to select and edit multiple worksheets:

1. Open a new workbook.
2. Click on the first sheet tab that you wish to edit.
3. Hold down the Shift key and click on the tab of the last sheet in the series you wish to edit.
4. Release the Shift key to finish your selection. Your series is now grouped as shown in Figure 20.2. The grouped sheet tabs all appear in white.

FIGURE 20.2

Five worksheets grouped together

NOTE

You can also select noncontiguous worksheets by pressing the Ctrl key instead of Shift when selecting the various worksheets.

You can now edit all of the selected sheets simultaneously by entering data or applying formatting on one of the sheets:

1. Select the first worksheet in the group. Choose Cell A2, type **North,** and press Enter.
2. Type **South** in cell A3.
3. Type **East** in cell A4.
4. Type **West** in cell A5.

After you finish editing the data, click on the tab of another worksheet in your group. You should see an exact copy of your data from the first worksheet in the other selected sheets.

PART

III

Analyzing with Excel

NOTE
When selecting sheets within a group, you must have another sheet in the workbook that is not included in the selection. Otherwise the selection of sheets will be undone when clicking from sheet to sheet.

It doesn't matter onto which sheet you enter data. As long as that sheet is part of the group, the data will be copied to the other sheets in that group. To see how this works, lets walk through editing some of the data on a worksheet.

1. Select the last sheet in the series by clicking on the worksheet tab.
2. Select cell A2, change North to **Northeast**, and press Enter.
3. Switch to the first sheet in the series. Northeast now appears in cell A2 of all of the sheets.

To remove the grouping of sheets, click on a sheet that is not in the group of selected sheets, or hold down Shift and click on the first grouped sheet.

TIP
Use grouped sheets when widening the same column throughout a number of sheets. The columns will widen simultaneously in all the sheets that are grouped.

Linking Sheet to Sheet

You can reference the data on one sheet to another within the same workbook. This is very useful because you don't have to enter data twice, and if data in the first sheet is changed, that change is automatically updated in the linked sheet.

Linking sheet to sheet works just like linking cell to cell. You can either enter cell references manually in formulas, or you can use the mouse.

Linking with the Mouse

Use a new, blank workbook for these examples. For this exercise, we will sum three worksheets onto one, consolidation worksheet. First we need to enter some data in our worksheet:

1. Be sure to have at least four worksheets in your new workbook. If you have only three, the Excel default, then select Insert ➤ Worksheet from the menu bar.
2. Click on the tab for Sheet2 and enter **250** in cell A1. Press Enter.
3. Click on the tab for Sheet3 and enter **500** in cell A1. Press Enter.
4. Click on the tab for Sheet4 and enter **1000** in cell A1. Press Enter.

We will now move to Sheet1 and sum the values we placed on the other sheets.

1. Click on Sheet1 and click on cell A1.

2. Type **=** and then click on Sheet2. Click on A1 and the formula bar indicates the following:

```
=Sheet2!A1
```

3. Type **+**. Notice that the cell is no longer activated.

4. Click on the tab for Sheet3 and click on cell A1. Notice that the cell is now activated and the formula bar indicates the following:

```
=Sheet2!A1+Sheet3!A1
```

5. Type **+**.

6. Click on the tab for Sheet4 and click on cell A1. Press Enter to complete the formula. The formula for cell A1 now reads:

```
=Sheet2!A1+Sheet3!A1+Sheet4!A1
```

The value in cell A1 on Sheet1 should read 1750.

Referencing Syntax

When Excel references one cell from another on the same worksheet, it simply refers to the cell by its address, such as A1 or C3. When Excel references another sheet, it also needs to reference the sheet's name.

For one-word sheet names, Excel simply places a ! (exclamation point) between the sheet name and the cell address, for example Sheet1!A1. However, if the sheet name contains a space, then Excel encloses the name in apostrophes, such as 'Fall 1995'!A1.

Linking Workbook to Workbook

Linking between workbooks is similar to linking between worksheets. As with the additional references created when linking cells between sheets, one more reference is added by Excel when you link sheets between workbooks.

TIP

Use File ➤ Open and click on the first workbook you want, then hold down Ctrl while you select multiple workbooks to open. Once multiple workbooks are open, repeatedly press Ctrl+Tab to move among the open workbooks in memory. To switch from one worksheet to another in the same workbook, hold down Ctrl and press PgUp or PgDn. Release all keys when you are at the worksheet you would like to use.

PART

III

Analyzing with Excel

Linking with the Mouse

As with linking between worksheets in the same workbook, you can use the mouse to link between sheets in separate workbooks. To use the mouse, you need to have all referenced workbooks open in Excel at the time of linking. (If you manually enter the names of the workbooks in the formula bar without using the mouse, you do not need to have the workbooks open.)

To do the following exercise, you should have two workbooks open. It will be easiest with two fresh, blank workbooks. First we need to add some data so we can see Excel at work linking workbooks:

1. Activate the first sheet of one of the workbooks and enter **200** in cell A1.
2. Activate the second sheet of the same workbook and enter **300** in cell A1.
3. Activate the third sheet of the same workbook and enter **500** in cell A1.
4. Save the workbook as **MYBOOK**.

Now we need to link the workbooks together.

1. Switch to the blank workbook by selecting Window from the menu bar and choosing the workbook from the list.
2. Activate the first worksheet and click on cell A2. Type =.
3. Select Window ➤ MYBOOK from the menu bar.
4. Click on the first worksheet tab and click on cell A1. Type +.
5. Click on the tab of the second worksheet and click on cell A1. Type +.
6. Click on the tab of the third worksheet and click on cell A1. Press Enter to complete the formula.
7. Click on cell A2 on the first worksheet. The formula should read as follows:

```
=[MYBOOK.X1S]Sheet1!$A$1+ [MYBOOK.XLS]Sheet2!$A$1+
[MYBOOK.XLS]Sheet3!$A$1
```

Referencing Syntax

Examine the formula in cell A2 and see how MYBOOK is referenced in the formula bar. To see how Excel changes the syntax when the linked workbook is closed, close the MYBOOK workbook, then look at the formula bar for cell A2 of the other workbook.

From this you can see that the complete syntax for referencing ranges in other workbooks is:

```
='PATH\[workbook name]Sheet Name'!Cell Reference
```

Because Excel can specify the path for linked workbooks, a linked workbook does not need to be open for another workbook to get information from it. If a linked workbook is not open when you open a workbook that references it, Excel will ask you if you want to update the links (see Figure 20.3).

FIGURE 20.3

Decide whether to update your workbook links.

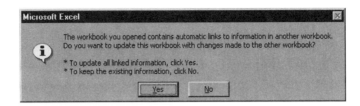

Viewing Links

To view or change the location for the links within a worksheet, choose Edit ➤ Links. The Links dialog box (Figure 20.4) appears with the name of the linked file, the type of link, and the status flag of Automatic Update. You can open the source file or change its location by selecting the options on the right side of the dialog box.

FIGURE 20.4

Use the Links dialog box to view or change the location of your work-sheet links.

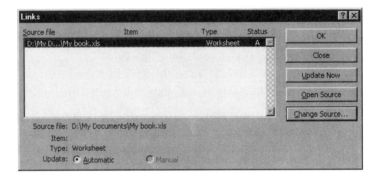

Working with Multiple Windows

Now that we've explained how to link worksheets and workbooks together, we'll learn how to view both the referencing and referenced sheets or books at the same time.

Viewing Multiple Worksheets at the Same Time

To view multiple sheets from the same workbook at the same time, you need to create a new window for your workbook by selecting Window ➤ New Window from the menu bar.

PART

III

Analyzing with Excel

Now that you have a second view of the same workbook, you need to arrange the windows so that more than one is visible:

1. Select Window ➤ Arrange from the menu bar to open the Arrange Windows dialog box.
2. Click on the Tiled radio button, select the Windows of Active Workbook option, and click on OK.

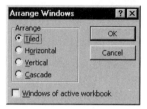

Viewing multiple windows of the same workbook allows you to select a different sheet in each window and immediately view how changing a value on one sheet affects the cells of another sheet that may be linked.

1. Open a new workbook and make sure you are on Sheet1. Type **200** in cell A1 and **200** in cell A2.
2. Switch to Sheet 2. In cell A1, type =.
3. Click on Sheet1. In cell A1 type +.
4. Select A2 and press Enter.
5. Select Window ➤ New Window from the menu bar. Select Window ➤ Arrange, click on the Tiled button, and click on OK.
6. In your first window, highlight cell A1 on the first sheet.
7. In the second window, highlight cell A1 on the second sheet.

Watch the first window while changing the value of cell A1 in the second window from 200 to **2000** and pressing Enter. The first cell in the first window should automatically update itself accordingly. Your screen should look like Figure 20.5

NOTE

When you select Window ➤ New Window from the menu bar, the window that you create is merely another view of a workbook file that you already have open. (The title bar indicates that multiple views are open by following the workbook name with a colon and the view number, as in Book1:2.) Because both windows are looking at the same workbook, when you change the value in either of the windows, Excel automatically updates both of them—they are both still views of the same workbook.

Viewing Multiple Workbooks at the Same Time - To view multiple workbooks at one time, you simply need to open each workbook and then arrange the windows by selecting Windows ➤ Arrange from the menu bar. To view separate workbooks at the same time, however, make sure that the Windows of Active Workbook checkbox is not checked.

FIGURE 20.5

Observe how changes affect related worksheets with the Tiled window arrangement.

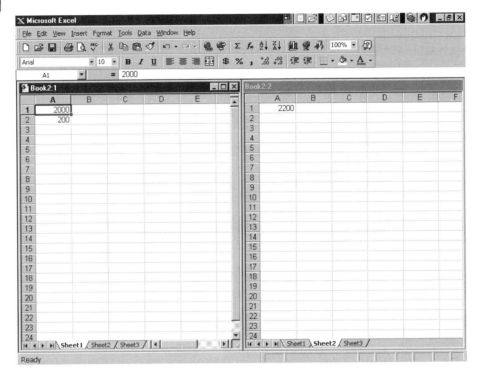

Saving Workspaces - It is possible to save your arrangement of worksheet and workbook windows so that the next time you need to work with these specific workbooks and views, you only need to open one file. Choose File ➤ Save Workspace to save the arrangement of worksheet and workbook windows. For an in-depth discussion about saving workbooks together, refer to Chapter 21.

Closing Multiple Views - You close the different views of a workbook the same way that you would close a single view, by selecting File ➤ Close from the menu bar. As you close the views of a workbook, the numerals signifying the other view numbers will decrease in number until only one view is left, at which point the colon and view number are no longer a part of the title bar.

Inserting a Hyperlink

Sharing information on a network is more important today than it has ever been. Excel has a built-in tool to help you set up links between your workbook and other files. Inserting a Hyperlink into your spreadsheet allows you to jump with a single click to another file, including Web pages.

PART

III

Analyzing with Excel

Creating a Hyperlink to Another File

Suppose your worksheet has information that comes from another file, but you want to be able to jump to the other source to view the supporting data as you might in a consolidated report. To create this Hyperlink, we will first create two files to link, following the steps below.

1. Open a new workbook.
2. In cells A1 through B6 enter the following information:

A1	**Representative**	B1	
A2	**Rose Peck**	B2	**14600**
A3	**Randy Williamson**	B3	**9860**
A4	**Penni Beaumont**	B4	**10661**
A5	**Joseph Leo**	B5	**9459**
A6	**District Total**	B6	**=SUM(B2:B5)**

3. Save the workbook as District 1.
4. Open another workbook.
5. In cells A1 through A3 enter the following:

A1	**District 1**
A2	**District 2**
A3	**District 3**
A4	**Total for Region**

6. Save the workbook as Regional Sales.
7. In the next step you will create a link to the District 1 workbook:

   - In cell B1 type = to alert Excel that a formula is being created.
   - From the menu bar, select Window and choose the worksheet District 1.
   - Click on cell B6, which is the district total, and press Enter.

8. The total for District 1 should be in cell B1. Switch to the District 1 workbook and close it.
9. Return to Regional sales and click in cell B1 to activate it. From the menu bar, select Insert ➣ Hyperlink. If you know the name and location of your file, you can type it in the Link to File or URL section of the Insert Hyperlink dialog box or click

on Browse to find the location of the file. Once you have found the District 1 file, click on OK. You can also select a sheet from that file or a single cell location by completing the named location in file section. For now, we'll just go to the linked file. Click on OK.

10. The number in cell B1 is now in color and underlined. If you hover over it, you will see a hand pointing at the cell. You can see the name of the file and the path to which the Hyperlink is linked (see Figure 20.6). Click once on the cell.

11. Excel links to the other file and automatically opens it.

FIGURE 20.6

Once the link is established, you can view the location of the linked file simply by hovering over the cell containing the link.

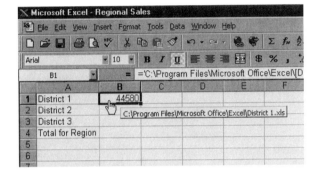

Hyperlinking to a Network Directory

You can use the previous steps for linking to a shared network directory. However, you may want to use the same address no matter where the workbook that contains the Hyperlink is saved. If so, then you will want to clear the checkmark in the Use Relative Path for Hyperlink checkbox. This will allow multiple users to access the information from wherever they are on the network.

You want to use a relative path if you may be moving or copying a file that is either referenced by or contains a Hyperlink. To update file locations and their links, open the file(s) and select File ➤ Properties from the menu. Click on the Summary tab and enter the new path in the Hyperlink base box. If you have more than one Hyperlink in a file, all of the Hyperlinks will be updated with this information.

Creating a Hyperlink to the World Wide Web

If you want to create a Hyperlink to a Web page on the Internet, you can use the same Insert ➤ Hyperlink menu option and enter the Internet or intranet Web page destination.

PART

III

Analyzing with Excel

Inserting a Hyperlink within Formulas

There may be times (in an IF function, for example) that the Hyperlink may be different depending on the current value of a cell. In this situation you will want to use the HYPERLINK function. The syntax for the HYPERLINK function in the Lookup & Reference function category is:

```
=HYPERLINK(Link_location, friendly_name)
```

The Link location is the actual link that you want executed for the current cell, and friendly name is an optional argument that you can use to make something other than the link appear in the cell.

Chapter

21

File and Print Operations

File and Print Operations

F iling and printing are the two core operations that you will perform using computer software. You must be able to store (save) and retrieve (open) the work you create and produce finished printed copies of this work. Each Office application has a File menu that holds commands for creating new files, saving and opening files, and previewing and printing. Because of the variety of financial and database layouts that are possible, Excel offers several file and print features.

Creating a New Workbook

When you launch Excel for the first time, a new worksheet appears with a generic Book# name in the title bar at the top of the screen. Excel designates a file as a book. Each book is capable of containing hundreds of multiple sheets, although only 3 of these sheet tabs are visible at one time for each new file. (Actually, depending on your system's memory, the maximum number of multiple sheets will vary. At last count we were able to insert over 1,000.) If you wish to increase the number of sheet tabs that are in a new workbook by default, select Tools ➤ Options, click on the General tab, then increase the number in the Sheets in New Workbook option.

To start another new workbook, select File ➤ New from the menu bar. Click on OK in the New dialog box and a new file will be created with the next sequential Book# (or click on the New button on the Standard toolbar). If there is an existing book (file) on the screen, the new book will "slide" in front of the existing file. You can start as many new workbook files as you wish. Excel will keep track of the workbooks in memory. Select Window from the menu bar and look at the bottom of the menu to see a list of the books that you currently have in memory. When you pull down the Window menu, you can click on one of the files in this list to make it active on the screen. An alternative is to press Ctrl+Tab to toggle back and forth between opened files or books.

Each time you create a new file, Excel will provide a new generic Book# name and increase the number. If you exit the Excel program and start again, the generic book numbering starts again at 1. This generic name will change once you formally save your work with a more descriptive name (using File ➤ Save).

Saving Your Workbook

Both during and after your work in Excel, you will want to save your work to disk to create a permanent copy of your data. When you save a workbook, you are required to provide a name. The name can be up to 250 characters and may contain spaces and periods.

1. Select File ➤ Save from the menu bar, or click on the Save button on the Standard toolbar, or press the shortcut key of Ctrl+S to save your worksheets.
2. In the File Name text box, type over the generic Book# name with your desired name. Click on the Save button on the right side of the dialog box to complete the Save operation (see Figure 21.1).
3. The name of the file appears in the title bar of the worksheet.

Once you have named and saved your file, any subsequent saves will automatically update the file on your hard drive or floppy disk. You will not see the Save As dialog box again or be prompted to rekey the filename. Make sure that you save often. Click on the Save button on the Standard toolbar for quick saves. It only takes a second and insures that your current work is safely stored on disk.

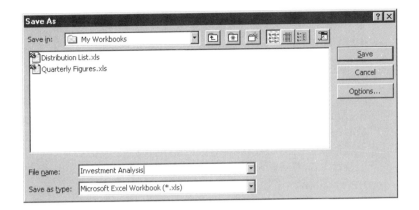

FIGURE 21.1.
*Use the Save As
dialog box to
give your work-
book a unique
name.*

NOTE

Although Windows 95 allows for filenames that can be as long as 250 characters, you can use these files under Windows 3.1. When you are running programs in DOS or under other operating systems, however, the long filenames will appear truncated and numbered with an eight-character filename: the truncated name consists of the first six characters of the long name, a tilde, and a number. For example, a long filename such as State and House Population Statistics for Electoral Votes appears as STATEA~1.XLS when viewed on the disk or from other programs.

Using the Save As Command

Once you have saved for the first time, you can use the File ➤ Save As command to make a copy of your work under another name. When you select File ➤ Save As, the Save As dialog box shows the current name of the file. Type a new name, and you will have two copies of the file. This command allows you to save the changes made to an opened file with a new name, thus preserving the original file.

Using AutoSave

Excel contains a special Add-In program that allows for automatic saves to your worksheet. You can set the time increment for the automatic save, and Excel will save the file every *x* minutes. Setting a 10-minute AutoSave can be a tremendous safeguard against unexpected power failures or machine lockups.

PART

III

Analyzing with Excel

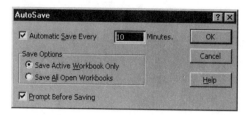

You must first "add-in" the additional program and then activate its setting. To do this, select Tools ➢ Add-Ins from the menu bar. The Add-Ins dialog box appears. Check the AutoSave option and click on OK. Now when you select Tools from the menu bar you will see an AutoSave option on the menu list. Click on it to bring up the AutoSave dialog box. You can use this box to change the time increment for saving the file. You can also specify that Excel prompt you at the AutoSave time so that you can decide whether to save or not. If you have multiple books opened, you can have AutoSave save their information in addition to the information in the active workbook.

File Management

The following sections provide some helpful hints and instructions for many common file-management operations you will be performing as you create more worksheets and workbooks in Excel.

Closing a Workbook File

To close a workbook, select File ➢ Close. If you have not performed a recent save and have made changes to your worksheet, Excel will prompt you to save your work.

TIP

Instead of closing one file at a time, you can close all the files in memory at the same time. Hold down the Shift key and, with the mouse, click on the File menu. You will see the command Close All rather than the regular Close. Select Close All and all of the files in memory will close. If any of the files need saving first, Excel will prompt you to save each one.

Opening a Workbook File

Once you have saved and closed a file, you can then open it by selecting File ➢ Open from the menu bar, pressing Ctrl+O, or clicking on the Open button on the Standard toolbar. Excel also lists the last four most recently used files at the end of the File menu. You can select a file from here. The Open dialog box will list all of the previously saved Excel files residing in the current folder as shown in Figure 21.2.

To open a particular file, double-click on the filename, or click once on the filename and then click on Open.

FIGURE 21.2

A list of Excel files is displayed when you select File ➢ Open.

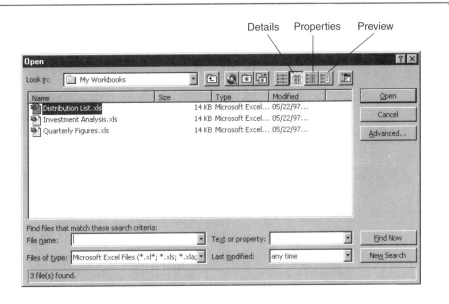

TIP

If you want, you can increase the number of recently used files that are listed on the File menu by modifying the setting in the General Options (select Tools ➢ Options from the menu bar).

Previewing and Getting Details about a File before Opening

In the Open dialog box there are a number of buttons on the right side of the Look In drop-down box (refer to Figure 21.2). These buttons control how your file list will display. The Details button allows you to see when the file was created and its size. The Preview button displays a small preview of the file. The Properties button provides details about the file's application, the date of creation, and the individual who created the file. You can also access this information by clicking on the Commands and Settings button and selecting Properties from the drop-down window.

Opening Multiple Workbook Files

Excel allows you to select and open multiple files. Click once to select the first file to be opened (do not double-click). For noncontiguous file selection, hold down the Ctrl key and click on any of the other files you wish to open.

If the files you want to open are all in sequence, click once on the first file to select it, hold down the Shift key, then click on the last file in the list to be selected. All of the files from the first to the last will be selected. Click on Open and Excel will open all of the files at once. Use the Window command on the menu bar to see the list of open files in memory. Select any file from the Window list to make it the active file.

PART

III

Analyzing with Excel

Finding Files Containing Specific Information

You can search for files containing specific words or values. Select File ➤ Open from the menu bar. On the right side of the Open dialog box, in the Text or Property area, type in the text or property you wish to find. Click on the Find Now button, and Excel will look through each file in the current folder, searching for the text or property you specified. When found, the file is displayed in the list window. Excel remembers each find that you conduct and lists the Find criteria in the drop-down Text or Property list box.

Opening Lotus and Other Spreadsheet File Types

You can open or import existing Lotus files by simply choosing File ➤ Open from the menu bar and, at the bottom of the Open dialog box, clicking on the drop-down arrow next to Files of Type. Choose Lotus 1-2-3 Files from the list and Excel will display any existing Lotus 1-2-3 files; double-click on the name of the file you wish to open.

Lotus files are opened directly into Excel with their macros preserved. You can activate one of the Lotus macros by pressing Ctrl plus the letter name of the macro. You cannot create a new Lotus macro in Excel, but you can create the macro using Lotus and once again open the file in Excel. When it is time to save your Lotus file, you can decide whether to save it as a Lotus or Excel file. Before saving it as an Excel file, consider carefully whether you or others will still need to use Lotus to open your new version of the file.

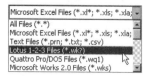

Opening or importing an ASCII-delimited text file is performed in the same manner as other file types. Select Text Files from the Files of Type list at the bottom of the Open dialog box to see the list of text files you have on the specified disk.

MASTERING THE OPPORTUNITIES

Batch Converting Multiple Files

Excel 97 comes with a File Conversion Wizard that helps convert mass amounts of one type of file into Excel format. You initiate this Wizard by selecting Tools ➤

Wizard ➤ File Conversion. The first step is to select the folder holding the files and designate their program type. Next, specify the files you want from the list box. Finally, designate where you want the converted files to be saved, and the Wizard goes about converting your files.

Renaming a Workbook File

Once you have named and saved a file, you may discover that the name is not as descriptive as you would like. You can easily rename the file. Follow these steps:

1. Select File ➤ Open to see the list of Excel filenames.
2. Click once on the filename to select it. Then click once again. (Do not perform a rapid double-click on the filename or the file will be opened into memory.) The name will be selected.
3. Type an entire replacement name or edit the existing name.

WARNING

If the filename extension was showing as part of the name, you must make sure that your new filename also includes the extension. See the next section for the importance of the extension.

4. Press Enter after you have finished renaming. The screen will flash and redisplay with the new name.
5. If you do not want to open the file at this time, you can click on the Cancel button. The file will maintain its new name.

More on Saving: Choosing a File Type

There are several different formats in which you can save your files other than Excel. You can select the file type that matches or most closely resembles the destination program type. For example, if you are sharing files with Lotus 1-2-3 users, you will need to save your work as a Lotus 1-2-3 workbook.

In the Save As dialog box, click on the drop-down arrow next to the Save As Type text box (see Figure 21.3). Excel lists the different file types available. There are a number of Lotus 1-2-3 file formats, including the .WK# extensions. If your Excel file has multiple worksheets, you will want to save it as a Lotus file type that supports multiple worksheets. (.WK4 and .WK3 files are multiple-worksheet Lotus formats.)

FIGURE 21.3

Excel allows you to save in a number of different file formats.

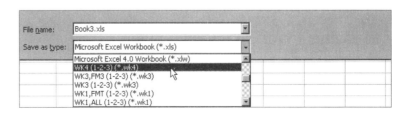

Saving in Lotus File Formats

Refer to your documentation for Lotus or ask the Lotus user who will be accessing your spreadsheet what file extension corresponds most closely to the version of Lotus to be used. Some versions of Lotus, such as Lotus Release 3.x and Lotus for Windows, permit you to use multiple-sheet workbooks. In addition, Excel macros will convert into Lotus macros; however, you should be aware that not all commands are available in both programs. If you are converting a workbook to Lotus, it is best to let the receiving program create a macro so that nothing will be lost in the conversion.

TIP

When you save in a different file format, the extension on the filename is usually different than that used by Excel. However, you will have two copies of the file: one in Excel's format and the other in the converted file type. Always keep the Excel copy of the file so that you can bring it up in Excel if the other user has questions.

WARNING

Remember that if you are saving your Excel workbook as anything other than a Microsoft Excel workbook, chances are you will lose some data in the conversion. Some spreadsheet programs do not support multiple-worksheet workbooks or workspaces. Other programs do not have very good macro languages or have extremely limited worksheet sizes. Experiment by saving in different formats and viewing the converted Excel file in the other program.

Saving as Text-Delimited

A file saved in the text-delimited ASCII format permits that file to be read by a database program, or even a computer language. Basically, there are three types of text-delimited files: space-delimited, tab-delimited, and comma-delimited.

In each case, a character is placed between fields in the file. Where that character occurs, a new field begins. For most purposes, you probably will use a tab-delimited or comma-delimited text format. Using the space format with text can cause problems. Have a systems support person work with you about how to convert your Excel worksheet properly for use in nonspreadsheet programs.

Saving a Workspace

Sometimes you will work in multiple workbooks at the same time. Excel allows you to save your work arrangement so that you don't have to manually open each file every time you work. The Workspace command allows you to save the names of all open files under one filename. Thus, you only need to remember one workspace name. When you open the workspace file, Excel will "point" to the names of the specific files contained in the workspace and open them all at once.

Follow these steps to save a workspace file:

1. Open two or three files onto the screen. (The Window menu will show the names of the multiple files.)
2. Select File ➤ Save Workspace. In the Save Workspace dialog box, Excel suggests the generic name of *Resume*. This is a reminder that the workspace file lets you resume where you left off.
3. Type a more descriptive name and click on the Save button or press Enter.
4. To close all of the files, hold down the Shift key and click on File ➤ Close All. If needed, save your work when prompted.
5. To open the workspace file, select File ➤ Open. You will see the name of your workspace file appearing in the same list as your Excel workbook files. When the workspace file is opened, Excel points to and opens the actual files involved in the workspace.

NOTE

Files have a filename extension of .xls, and workspace files have the extension .xlw.

If you have the screen split into multiple windows, Excel's workspace file will even remember the saved split screen arrangement and open the files into the same arrangement. Figure 21.4 displays three workbooks open in memory with a tiled arrangement.

Saving As an HTML File

Excel allows you to save a file in HTML format for use on the Internet. From the File menu, select Save As HTML. The HTML Wizard will give you the option of saving your existing file as a new HTML file, or to simply attach it to an existing file. See Part 7 for more information on using Office 97 and the Internet.

Shared Workbook

A new workgroup feature that was designed for Excel 95 and enhanced in Excel 97 is the ability to share workbooks for multiple-user editing. To make an Excel workbook file shareable, open the file and select Tools ➤ Share Workbook from the menu bar. When the Share Workbook dialog box appears, click on the *Allow Changes By More Than One User at the Same Time* checkbox (see Figure 21.5). You can also discover who else has this workbook open by looking at the list box on the Editing tab of the Share

FIGURE 21.4

Multiple opened files in a tiled arrangement can be saved as a workspace.

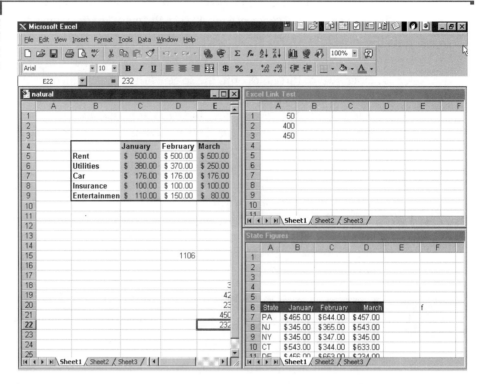

Workbook dialog box. When you click on OK, Excel will prompt you to save the file. A shared workbook can be saved just like an individual file. To track or update changes as well as resolve conflicts between users making changes to a workbook at the same time, click on the Advanced tab from the Tools ➤ Share Workbook menu.

You may wish to keep track of changes that others are making in your workbook. Select Tools ➤ Track Changes ➤ Highlight Changes from the main menu. A dialog box like the one in Figure 21.6 will appear, asking you whose and what changes you wish to track and from what point you want to track them. You can also elect to have your changes appear on screen as highlighted areas, listed on a new sheet, or both. Once you have completed your selections, click on OK.

If you want to merge copies of a workbook that has been shared, select Tools ➤ Merge Workbooks from the menu bar. Only workbooks that have been shared can be merged. Select the workbook(s) that you want to merge with the currently opened shared workbook.

FIGURE 21.5

The Share Work-book command allows multiple users to update and edit Excel Workbooks.

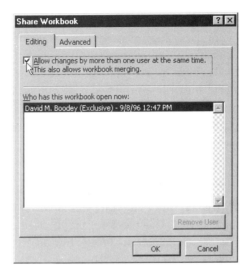

FIGURE 21.6

The Highlight Changes dialog box allows users to track changes in a shared workbook.

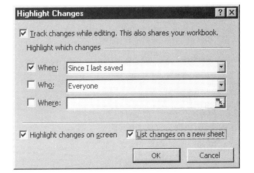

PART

III

Analyzing with Excel

File Properties

You can view important information about your file, such as creation and modification dates, file size, worksheets, and file summary information. When you have a file open in Excel select File ➢ Properties from the menu bar. Click on the General tab to see file information. If you have multiple files open, the active file will be the one whose properties are available. You can also access a file's properties before opening it. Click on File ➢ Open and select the Properties button, or click on the Commands and Settings button and select Properties from the drop-down menu.

Printing in Excel

Printing your data can sometimes be the most exhausting part of creating and producing worksheets. You may encounter columns that fall off the paper and move to the next page, page breaks that will not occur where you want them, headings that insist on printing only on the first page but not on other pages, and a host of hardware problems occurring with the printer itself. Fortunately, Excel offers solutions to 90% of printing problems—just about everything except for changing your toner or ribbon cartridge.

Print Particulars

Excel allows you to print an entire workbook, a selected sheet, selected sheets within the workbook, selected ranges with single sheets, and selected ranges across multiple sheets. When you click on the Printer button on the Standard toolbar, Excel immediately prints the active worksheet. If you select File ➤ Print, or press Ctrl+P, the Print dialog box appears, allowing you to specify your printer, number of copies, page ranges, and whether to print the Selection, Active Sheet(s), or the Entire Workbook. The default settings for printing are listed below:

Setting	Defaults
Page Orientation	Portrait
Scaling	100% (no compression ON)
Paper Size	8.5 by 11 inches
Top Margin	1 inch
Bottom Margin	1 inch
Left Margin	.75 inch
Right Margin	.75 inch
Header	(none)
Footer	(none)
Sheet	No gridlines

Printing an Entire Workbook

To print an entire workbook, select File ➤ Print from the menu bar. Click on the Entire Workbook radio button. All pages in all sheets will print. The page numbering will be sequential across all sheets in the workbook; it will not start over again for each new sheet being printed. The header containing the sheet name will change as each separate sheet is printed. If you wish to print multiple copies, type or click on the spinner buttons in the Copies option group to specify the number of copies to print.

Printing Multiple Sheets

You can always click on each individual sheet and then click on the Print button on the Standard toolbar. But to print multiple sheets at the same time, you need to group the sheets you wish to print. To group noncontiguous sheets, hold down the Ctrl key and click on the sheet names for each sheet. For contiguous groups of sheets, click on the first sheet in the group. Hold down the Shift key and click on the last sheet in the group. Grouped sheet names appear in white in the sheet tab area at the bottom of the screen.

Once you have grouped the sheets to be printed, select File ➤ Print from the menu bar or press Ctrl+P. In the Print dialog box, the Active Sheets(s) option should be on. If it isn't, activate it. Click on the Preview button to see exactly what will print.

NOTE

If you can only view a partial spreadsheet, you may have a previous print area that has been set. Ungroup the sheets by holding down Shift and clicking on one of the sheet tabs. Then select File ➤ Print Area ➤ Clear Print Area for each sheet so that your entire sheet area is available for printing.

Previewing before Printing

We recommend that you always preview before you print spreadsheets, as there are layout factors that can be unknown ahead of time (before wasting your good paper on, for example, a misaligned print job). With Print Preview you will be able to detect any print errors and fix them before sending the job to the printer.

To preview a worksheet, select the worksheet(s) with the data to be printed and select File ➤ Print Preview from the menu bar, or click on the Print Preview button on the Standard toolbar. Excel will compose a graphical representation of your worksheet in full-page view (see Figure 21.7).

The Print Preview toolbar lists the actions that are possible in Print Preview. Click on the Zoom button to adjust the Zoom setting, or click on whatever portion of the worksheet you wish to examine more closely. The Next button is enabled if there is more than one page that will print. When there are no additional pages, only the Previous button is enabled.

Analyzing with Excel

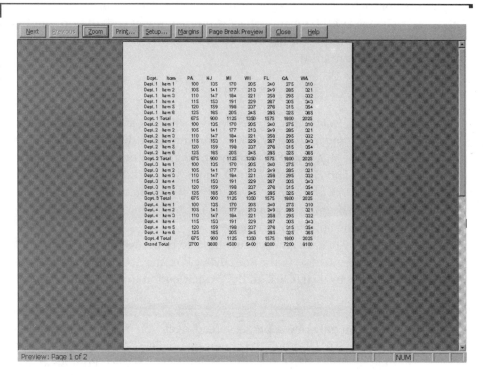

FIGURE 21.7

Print Preview helps you to correct problems before printing the worksheet.

Inserting Manual Page Breaks

If you don't like where Excel automatically breaks the page, you can insert your own page break exactly where you wish. Figure 21.8 shows a new section starting at the bottom of the page instead of on the next page, as it should. Because Excel uses a mathematical formula to figure out the page length and subtracts the margin settings from this page length, you cannot always know where the break is going to occur. Manually inserting and removing your own breaks can make a report more readable.

Both the automatic and manual page breaks can be seen in a worksheet. You can see the gray dashed lines of the page breaks as you scroll through a spreadsheet.

NOTE

If you do not see the automatic or manual page breaks in the worksheet, choose Tools ➢ Options, click on the View tab, and, in the top section of Window Options, click on the Page Breaks checkbox.

FIGURE 21.8

Excel will not always break the page where you want in a long worksheet printout.

| Next | Previous | Zoom | Print... | Setup... | Margins | Page Break Preview | Close | Help |

19	Dept. 3	Item 3	110	147	184	221	258	295	332	369
20	Dept. 3	Item 4	115	153	191	229	267	305	343	381
21	Dept. 3	Item 5	120	159	198	237	276	315	354	393
22	Dept. 3	Item 6	125	165	205	245	285	325	365	405
23	**Dept. 3 Total**		675	900	1125	1350	1575	1800	2025	2250
24	Dept. 4	Item 1	100	135	170	205	240	275	310	345
25	Dept. 4	Item 2	105	141	177	213	249	285	321	357
26	Dept. 4	Item 3	110	147	184	221	258	295	332	369
27	Dept. 4	Item 4	115	153	191	229	267	305	343	381
28	Dept. 4	Item 5	120	159	198	237	276	315	354	393
29	Dept. 4	Item 6	125	165	205	245	285	325	365	405
30	**Dept. 4 Total**		675	900	1125	1350	1575	1800	2025	2250
31	**Grand Total**		2700	3600	4500	5400	6300	7200	8100	9000
32	**Dept.**	**Item**	**PA**	**NJ**	**MI**	**WI**	**FL**	**CA**	**WA**	**MD**
33	Dept. 1	Item 1	100	135	170	205	240	275	310	345
34	Dept. 1	Item 2	105	141	177	213	249	285	321	357
35	Dept. 1	Item 3	110	147	184	221	258	295	332	369
36	Dept. 1	Item 4	115	153	191	229	267	305	343	381
37	Dept. 1	Item 5	120	159	198	237	276	315	354	393
38	Dept. 1	Item 6	125	165	205	245	285	325	365	405
39	**Dept. 1 Total**		675	900	1125	1350	1575	1800	2025	2250
40	Dept. 2	Item 1	100	135	170	205	240	275	310	345
41	Dept. 2	Item 2	105	141	177	213	249	285	321	357
42	Dept. 2	Item 3	110	147	184	221	258	295	332	369

Preview: Page 1 of 6 — NUM

PART

III

Analyzing with Excel

To insert your own page break into a worksheet, follow these steps:

1. Position the pointer on the row line that should start the new page. (Alternatively, you can think about it as positioning the pointer below the last line of text that should appear on the current page.)
2. Select Insert ➤ Page Break from the menu bar.
3. Click on the Print Preview button again to see if the page break is now in the desired location. Repeat this process as needed to manually control the page breaks for each page.

To delete a page break, position the pointer on the line where you broke the page and select Insert ➤ Remove Page Break from the menu bar. The change in the wording of the menu from Insert Page Break to Remove Page Break is how Excel shows that a manual page break has already occurred and therefore can only be removed.

WARNING

You cannot remove an automatic page break directly. The automatic break is only removed when you insert your own page break *above* the automatic break. If you insert a page break below the automatic page break, Excel will both keep its own automatic break and give you another page break. You may end up with a page that has only two or three lines on it.

TIP

If you have multiple sheets that need the page break at the same spot in all of the sheets, group the sheets before inserting the page breaks (hold down Shift and click on the last sheet in the group).

Page Break Preview

A new feature is Page Break Preview. This feature allows you to view the page breaks and click and drag them to a new location. You can only change a page break in Page Break Preview mode. Select View ➤ Page Break Preview from the menu bar, and you will see a view similar to the one in Figure 21.9. To move a page break, simply drag the page break to the new location on the spreadsheet.

FIGURE 21.9

Page Break Preview is now available in Excel 97.

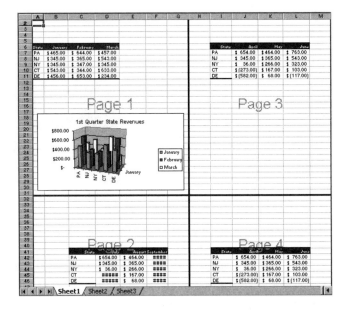

Fitting to One Page

Worksheets that break onto two pages can sometimes be adjusted so that the entire worksheet prints on one page. If you have more than two pages, Excel will attempt to adjust the sizing so that all the pages squeeze onto one page—but the font size becomes too small to read. Generally, one and a half to two screen pages can be adjusted to print onto a single page with the print remaining readable.

To adjust a worksheet to fit on one page, follow these steps:

1. Open the worksheet to be adjusted.

2. Click on the Print Preview button or select File ➤ Print Preview to see how many pages there will be for the worksheet. If there are more than two pages, do not attempt to adjust to one page.

3. While in Print Preview, select the Setup button on the toolbar. Click on the Page tab of the Page Setup dialog box.

4. In the Scaling section of the dialog box, click on the *Fit to 1 Page(s) Wide By 1 Tall* radio button. Click on the OK button to see another preview.

5. Excel has adjusted the worksheet to fit onto one page. Click on the Setup button again at the top of the Print Preview screen to return to the Page Setup dialog box. Notice the percentage of compression that was needed to squeeze the worksheet onto one page.

NOTE
You can decide on how many pages you want your spreadsheet to print by using the Page Setup dialog box to set the number of pages to your liking. Remember that the font size will compress to fit, but it will not expand to force, for example, a two-page spreadsheet onto five pages.

Printing Landscape

Another method for handling worksheets that do not fit onto a page is to change the orientation from portrait to landscape. With a landscape orientation you can fit more columns on the page but fewer rows. You may still need to use Excel's adjustment scaling of the document to force the sheet to print on a specified number of pages. The landscape orientation, however, is a tremendous help for multicolumn worksheets.

Landscape printing is very straightforward, and you will once again perform the operation from the Print Preview screen. Follow these steps:

1. Open the worksheet to be adjusted.

2. Click on the Print Preview button or select File ➤ Print Preview to view the layout of your pages.

3. Click on the Setup button on the toolbar at the top of the Print Preview screen.

4. Make sure the Page tab is selected, then click on the Landscape radio button. Click on OK to return the Print Preview screen.

5. If the landscape orientation is still not sufficient to fit all of the columns across a single page, select Setup again and repeatedly decrease the scaling until all of the columns fit on a single page. Changing the percentage of scaling compression might allow all the columns to be squeezed onto one page.

To set all sheets in a workbook to a landscape orientation, group the sheets by Ctrl-clicking on each name to group noncontiguous sheet names or Shift-clicking at the end of a contiguous range of sheet names. The grouped sheet names will be in white. Select File ➤ Page Setup, and on the Page tab click on the Landscape radio button. Click on the Print Preview button on the right side of the dialog box. All of the selected sheets will be in landscape orientation.

Changing Margins

There may be times when it is not feasible to change the scaling, as Excel simply prints in smaller font sizes to produce smaller scaling. You can change the default margins to increase the amount of data that can fit onto one page. Figure 21.10 displays the Print Preview with the Margins button selected. Notice the vertical and horizontal lines of the current margin settings. To change the margins, toggle the Margin button on and off to graphically display where the margin lines reside. Click and drag the horizontal and/or vertical margin lines to change the margins on screen. Print Preview updates instantly so that you can immediately see the implications of changing the margin. You can also select the Margin tab of the Page Setup dialog box and type in specific margin settings. These settings are saved when you save the file.

Most laser printers won't print text if the text is too close to the edge of the piece of paper. Therefore, don't decrease your margins to less than .20 inch or you may risk losing most, if not all, of your printout.

Centering the Worksheet on a Page

Excel prints all worksheets starting from the upper left corner of the page. When you have small worksheets that do not take up the full width and height of a printed page, you may want them to print centered between the margins of the page. In Excel, you can choose to print your worksheets centered horizontally and vertically on a page. Figure 21.11 shows a small worksheet printing in its default position: the upper left corner.

Select File ➤ Page Setup and click on the Margins tab in the Page Setup dialog box. If you are already in Print Preview, click on the Setup button on the toolbar and, in the Page Setup dialog box, click on the Margins tab.

FIGURE 21.10

Drag the vertical or horizontal lines to change the margin settings.

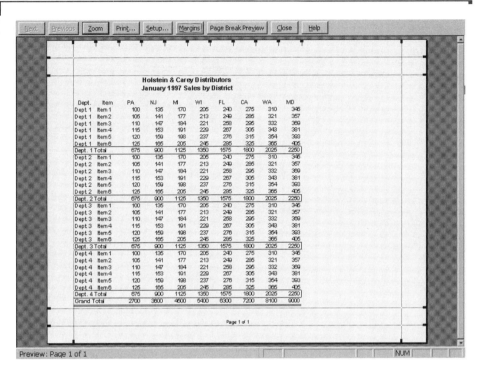

Mark both the horizontal and vertical checkboxes in the Center on Page section. (If you only want the spreadsheet to be centered between the left and right margins, then select Horizontally.) Click on OK. If you wish to see the effect, switch to Print Preview.

Printing Selected Ranges

You can have Excel print only a specified range of data using the following steps:

1. Select the range to be printed.
2. Select File ➢ Print from the menu bar or press Ctrl+P to activate the Print dialog box.
3. Click on the Selection button on the left side of the box. Then click on OK. Excel prints the selected range (see Figure 21.12).

Another method for printing only the selection you specify is to select the range to be printed, then select File ➢ Print Area ➢ Set Print Area.

FIGURE 21.11

The default position for printing: the upper left corner of the page

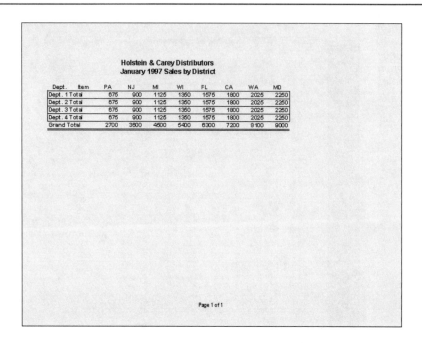

FIGURE 21.12

To print a range, select the area, select File ➤ Print, and click on the Selection button.

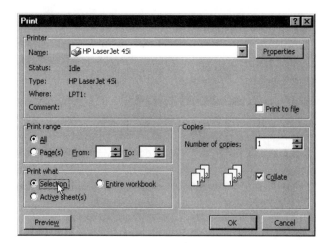

Once you have printed a selected range, you can repeatedly click on the Printer icon on the Standard toolbar and Excel will reprint the same range automatically. To clear the range from Excel's printing memory, select File ➤ Print Area ➤ Clear Print Area from the menu bar.

Printing Multiple Ranges from the Same Sheet

When you wish to print multiple ranges residing on the same sheet, select the first range and then hold down the Ctrl key and select the other ranges. Click on File ➤ Print from the menu bar. Click on Selection in the Print dialog box. Click on the Pre-view button at the lower right side of the dialog box to view your choices. The ranges will each print on a separate page.

You cannot make multiple ranges print on the same page, but you can hide columns or rows that may lie between the multiple print ranges. Select the column letters or the row numbers, then right-click and select Hide from the shortcut menu. When you print your worksheet, the hidden columns will not appear in the printout.

Printing the Same Range across Multiple Sheets

You can select the same range across multiple sheets by first grouping the multiple sheets containing the range to be printed. Hold down the Ctrl key (noncontiguous ranges) or the Shift key (contiguous ranges) and click on the names of the individual sheet tabs. The grouped sheet names will display in white. You must group the sheets first before making your across-sheet selection.

With the sheets grouped, drag the mouse over the range of data to be printed. On all the selected sheets, this same range is being selected. Select File ➤ Print or press Ctrl+P to access the Print dialog box. Click on Selection to designate that you have a range to print. Click on the Preview button at the bottom right of the Print dialog box to verify that the specific ranges across the multiple sheets will be printing. Click on the Next button on the Print Preview screen to see each page that will print.

To ungroup the sheets, click on a sheet tab not already involved with the grouping or hold down the Shift key and click on one of the grouped sheets.

PART

III

Analyzing with Excel

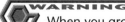

WARNING

When you group sheets and select a range, this same range will print across multiple sheets. Make sure, however, that you select File ➤ Print ➤ Selection. Do not click on Selected Sheets even though that would be the logical choice. Excel considers a selected range across multiple sheets to be a range.

Printing Different Ranges on Different Sheets

To print different ranges on different sheets within the same workbook, select the first sheet and range to be printed. Select File ➤ Print Area ➤ Set Print Area. Select the other sheets and other ranges. Note that you can select multiple, noncontiguous ranges on the same sheet by using the Ctrl key to click on the ranges. You can then select a different sheet and again specify multiple, noncontiguous ranges. Excel is extremely flexible in allowing you to specify different ranges on different sheets. Make sure that you select File ➤ Print Area ➤ Set Print Area for each of the ranges you select on each of the sheets.

Once all of the print areas for all of the ranges have been set, select File ➤ Print from the menu bar or press Ctrl+P. In the Print dialog box, select the Entire Workbook radio button. Click on the Preview button in the lower left corner so that you can see the print ranges on the different pages. When you are in Print Preview, click on the Next button to move from page to page, displaying the selected ranges.

Setting a Permanent Print Range

If there is a print range area of the worksheet that you always print, you can designate this range area in the Print Area text box on the Sheet tab of the Page Setup dialog box. All future printings can then be done by clicking on the Print button on the Standard toolbar. Excel will automatically print the data that falls in this range.

Naming Print Ranges

You can assign names to different print ranges. The name can then be referenced in the Print Area text box of the Sheet tab on the Page Setup dialog box or as the Selection option on the Print dialog box. Follow these steps to assign a name to a range:

1. Select the print range to be named.
2. Select Insert ➤ Name ➤ Define from the menu bar. Type in a name for the range and click on the Add button on the right side of the dialog box. Click on OK.

NOTE

Your name cannot include spaces. Use an underscore to represent a separation in the name, as in Year_To_Date.

3. Repeat steps 1 and 2 for each range to be assigned a name. Alternatively, note that you can also assign a name using the Name box that appears below the Font name on the Formatting toolbar (see Figure 21.13). Select range to be assigned a name. Click the mouse in the Name box, type the range name, and press Enter. To delete a name select Insert ➤ Name ➤ Define from the menu bar. Select the range name to be deleted and click on the Delete button on the right. Click on OK.

FIGURE 21.13

Range names can easily be assigned by selecting the range and using the Name box to assign a name.

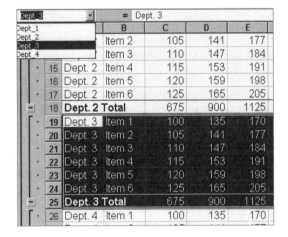

Designating Named Ranges to Print

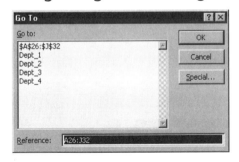

When you are ready to print the data in a named area, click on the drop-down arrow of the Name box and select the range name. The named area will be immediately selected for you to see. Select File ➤ Print and click on the Selection radio button in the Print dialog box. Alternatively, you can press the F5 Go To key, select the name listed in the dialog box, and click on OK, or double-click on the range name. The named area will be selected. Then select File ➤ Print and click on the Selection radio button from the Print dialog box.

If you want a particular range name to be the default print range, type the name into the Print Area text box on the Sheet tab of the Page Setup dialog box. You cannot select the name from a list, but you can type in the range name in the Print Area text box. This will be the default print area until you change or delete the range name.

PART

III

Analyzing with Excel

NOTE

Once you close the Page Setup dialog box and reopen it, the range name you typed in the Print Area text box will have been converted to its row/column worksheet range address.

Managing Headers and Footers

Excel allots half an inch for the header area and the same for the footer area. You may want this space shortened to fit a worksheet onto one page. You may also want the header to print but not the footer. When creating a header or footer, you can select from Excel's Header/Footer options or you can design your own. To select a predesigned header or footer, click on the drop-down arrow in the Header or Footer section of the Header/Footer tab and select the style you desire. Read the following sections to learn more about manipulating and customizing headers and footers.

Deleting a Header or Footer

Select File ➤ Page Setup from the menu bar and select the Header/Footer tab, or while in Print Preview, click on the Setup button and select the Header/Footer tab.

Click on the drop-down arrow to the right of the current header and scroll up to select the (none) option (see Figure 21.14). In the Header Preview you will no longer see a sample for the header.

FIGURE 21.14

Removing a header from a worksheet

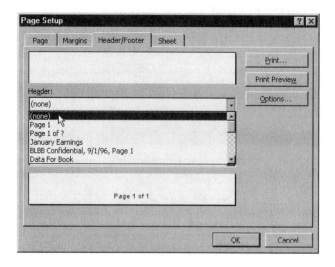

Once you have removed a header or footer, you may want to recover the half inch that Excel allots for it. Chose File ➤ Page Setup or click on the Setup button on the Print Preview toolbar. Select the Margins tab. The half-inch allotment for the header and footer appears at the top to the right of the Top Margin. Reduce to zero the amount of space Excel is holding for a header or footer to print.

Customizing a Header/Footer

Suppose you wanted the footer to print total pages, but you did not want this option centered. You preferred that the footer print in the lower left corner of each page. You can customize a header or a footer to print the words you desire or the realignment you need. Follow these steps to customize a header or footer:

1. Select File ➤ Page Setup and click on the Header/Footer tab, or, from the Print Preview screen, click on the Setup button and select the Header/Footer tab.
2. Select the Custom Header or the Custom Footer button in the middle of the dialog box. For this example we will choose Custom Footer.
3. The Footer dialog box appears. There are a number of buttons you can select to assign different options. Right-click the mouse on any of the buttons and click on What's This? to see a description of what the button will offer (see Figure 21.15).

FIGURE 21.15

When you customize a header or a footer, you can change the font typeface and size as well as other options.

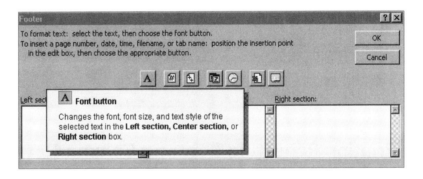

4. To change the font size and style of text that will appear at the lower left-hand corner of each printed page, click on the Left Section text box and then click on the Font button. Select a Bold Italic font, 14 pt size for the footer text that will appear on the left. Click on OK. Type the words **Draft Report** in the Left Section.

5. Click on the Right section area of the Footer dialog box and click on the Date button. Notice the ampersand symbol (&) that prefaces the Date. This symbol is used to specify *linked text*. If you wish to use the ampersand as part of your text, as in

the name Computer Resources & Training, Inc., you need to specify two ampersands next to each other so that Excel will know not to interpret the first ampersand as a special linking symbol (see Figure 21.16). If you print a single ampersand
or two ampersands with a space between them, Excel does not show any ampersands at all. When you are finished, click on OK. Figure 21.17 shows the Print Preview of a page with a customized footer.

FIGURE 21.16

*When an
ampersand
must be used in
your custom
footer, type two
adjacent amper-
sands and the
second one will
display.*

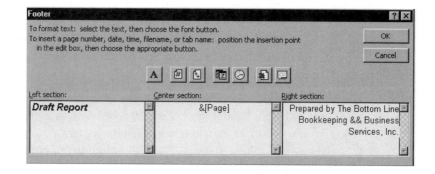

FIGURE 21.17

*Customizing
the footer or the
header can add
needed descrip-
tion to each
page of your
printout.*

115	153	191	229	267	305	343	381
120	159	198	237	276	315	354	393
125	165	205	245	285	325	365	405
675	900	1125	1350	1575	1800	2025	2250
700	3600	4500	5400	6300	7200	8100	9000

1   Prepared by The Bottom Line Bookkeeping & Business Services, Inc.

Preview: Page 1 of 1   NUM

Printing Repeating Row and Column Data on Multiple Pages

When long worksheets print across multiple pages, the headings that you typed in
the beginning rows of the spreadsheet, which print on page 1, do not print on the
subsequent pages unless you specify that they should do so. This is also the case with
multiple-column documents. When there are too many columns to fit on one page,
the trailing columns will print on the next pages. The data will now print without
any reference to what categories the data belongs. You need to specify that a specific
category column always print at the left side of the page on all subsequent pages.

Excel uses the term Print Titles to describe the option that allows you to print the same column and row headings across multiple pages of a worksheet printout. Follow these steps to set a Print Title border of rows:

1. Open a workbook with a multiple-page sheet that has a column that you would like printed across all pages.
2. Select File ➢ Page Setup from the menu bar.
3. Click on the Sheet tab from the Page Setup dialog box.
4. Click the mouse on the section called *Print Titles Rows to Repeat at Top*. Move the dialog box out of the way by dragging its title bar down or to the right so that you can see the rows you wish to be repeated at the top of each page.
5. Drag the mouse over the rows you wish to be repeated. Excel enters the row specifications into the dialog box (see Figure 21.18).

FIGURE 21.18

Rows that must repeat on each page of the printout are specified in the Rows to Repeat at Top text box.

1 2 3		A	B	C	D	E	F	G	H	I	J	K	
	1				**Holstein & Carey Distributors**								
	2				**January 1997 Sales by District**								
	3												
	4	Dept.	Item	PA	NJ	MI	WI	FL	CA	WA	MD		
	5	Dept. 1	Item								345		
	6	Dept. 1	Item								357		
	7	Dept. 1	Item				221			2	369		
	8	Dept. 1	Item 4	115	153	191	229	267	305	343	381		
	9	Dept. 1	Item 5	120	159	198	237	276	315	354	393		
	10	Dept. 1	Item 6	125	165	205	245	285	325	365	405		

Page Setup - Rows to repeat at top: ? ✕
$1:$4

NOTE

In dialog boxes that require ranges to be filled, the small button to the right of the Rows to Repeat at Top and other text boxes is the Collapse Dialog Box button. Clicking on this button will collapse the current dialog box, providing more room to select your range. When the dialog box is collapsed, use the Expand Dialog Box button to return it to full size.

---

6. Click on the Columns to Repeat at Left text box.
7. Select the columns that should be repeated at the left on every page.
8. Click on the Print Preview button on the right side of the dialog box so that you can view the repeating information before printing.

Printing Extras

With Excel you can print notes in a cell, or switch back and forth from printing formula text versus the result of formulas. You can also print column letter and row number borders. You can print gridlines, and you can direct Excel to print directly from disk. These are all features grouped into Excel's Print Extras category.

Printing Cell Comments

Excel comments are a great form of documentation for cell information (select Insert ➤ Comment, then type in the text box). When you hover your mouse over a cell that has a note, Excel displays the entire content of the note, as shown in Figure 21.19. (Note that a cell with a note in it has a little red triangle in the upper right corner.) You can also view comments by activating the Reviewing toolbar from View ➤ Toolbars and selecting Reviewing. This toolbar will allow you to add a comment, view one comment or all comments, hide comments, delete comments, create an Outlook task, or send mail.

FIGURE 21.19

The mouse pointer hovering over a comment

	Dept.	Item	PA	NJ	MI	WI	FL	CA	WA	MD

Holstein & Carey Distributors
January 1997 Sales by District

Dept.	Item	PA	NJ	MI	WI	FL	CA	WA	MD
Dept. 1	Item 1	100	135	170	205	240	275	310	345
Dept. 1	Item 2	105	141	177	213	249	285	321	357
Dept. 1	Item 3	110	147	184	221	258	295	332	369
Dept. 1	Item 4	115	153	191	229	267	305	343	381
Dept. 1	Item 5	120	159	198	237			354	393
Dept. 1	Item 6	125	165	205	245			365	405
Dept. 1 Total		675	900	1125	1350			2025	2250
Dept. 2	Item 1	100	135	170	205			310	345
Dept. 2	Item 2	105	141	177	213			321	357
Dept. 2	Item 3	110	147	184	221			332	369

David M. Boodey: Susan tells me that this item was supposed to be recalled and we're expecting a check from the manufacturer

You may want to print the content of all of the comments in a worksheet instead of viewing the comments individually on the screen. Follow these steps:

1. Select File ➤ Page Setup and click on the Sheet tab in the Page Setup dialog box. Do not use the Setup button in the Print Preview screen to access the Page Setup dialog box. The printing of comments is only available if you start through the File ➤ Page Setup command.

2. Click on the Comments drop-down box. This option will allow the comments of a worksheet to print on a separate page as displayed on the sheet or not at all. The cell references will be included if you print the comments at the end of your spreadsheet.

3. Select View ➢ Comments from the menu. You may need to move your comments around so you do not block data. To move your comments, simply click once on the comment to activate it and then hover with your mouse over any comment border until the pointer turns into a four-sided cross with a white arrow in the center. Simply click along the edge of the comment and drag it to a new location.

4. Now select As Displayed on Sheet from the Comment drop-down box on the Sheet tab of Page Setup. Use Print Preview to see your page with the comments. Note the page number at the bottom of the screen so that you can print this page only. Click on the Close button.

5. To print the one or two pages with the comments, press Ctrl+P or select File ➢ Print from the menu bar. When the Print dialog box appears, click on the Pages option in the Print Range group. Type or click on the spinner button to insert the page number in the From and To text boxes. Click on OK, and Excel will print only the pages specified.

WARNING

Your comments will not print As Displayed on Sheet unless you are currently viewing comments in the workbook. To print on the worksheet, select View ➢ Comments from the menu bar to turn them on without having to hover over the cell. You can still print at the end of a sheet even if comments are not visible on the worksheets.

Printing Formulas

You can view the formula text versus the formula result by using the shortcut key of Ctrl+' (the backwards apostrophe—located below the Esc key). This is a toggle key; use it to alternate between showing the formula text and the formula results.

To print your document with the formula text displayed, use this shortcut key to display formula text. Select File ➢ Page Setup from the menu bar and click on the Sheet tab. Check the Row and Column Headings option in the middle of the Sheet tab. Click on the Print Preview button so that you can see the printout before committing to paper. Figure 21.20 shows how a printout might look.

PART

III

Analyzing with Excel

FIGURE 21.20

Being able to print the formulas and the row and column headings can help you analyze a spreadsheet more quickly.

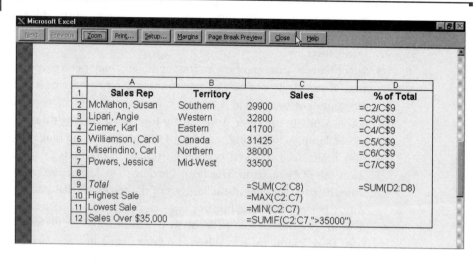

Printing Gridlines

Excel does not print gridlines unless you explicitly ask for this setting to be on. Follow these keystrokes to add and remove gridlines to and from your printed copy.

1. Select File ➤ Page Setup from the menu bar, or, if you are in Print Preview, click on the Setup button on the toolbar at the top of Print Preview.
2. Select the Sheet tab.
3. Click on the Gridlines option box to turn on gridlines. Click on the Print Preview button or on OK to see how the worksheet will look with gridlines.
4. If you like the effect, click on the Print button on the toolbar at the top of the Print Preview screen.

TIP

If you only want gridlines around a few cells but not others, don't use the gridlines options. Instead, select the range of cells that should be bordered with lines

Employee	Dept.	RATE	HOURS	GROSS	TAXES	NET
Smith, T.	1	10.00	40	400.00	110.00	290.00
Humperdink, E.	2	8.50	35	297.50	81.81	215.69
Schallow, S.	3	11.00	37.5	412.50	113.44	299.06
Johnson, A.	4	15.75	40	630.00	173.25	456.75

and select Format ➤ Cells from the menu bar. Click on the Border tab on the Format Cells dialog box. Select where you wish the line (Outline or Inside), select the specific lines you want to show, and then select a style for the line (for example, dashed, thick, or dotted). Click on OK when finished. Alternatively, you can use the selections in the Borders button's drop-down palette on the Formatting toolbar.

Printing from the Disk

To print a workbook file from disk, select File ➤ Open from the menu and select the workbook to be printed—do not double-click. Right-click to activate the shortcut menu and select Print. Excel will quickly open the file, print the sheet that was active when the file was saved, and then quickly close the file before you can change any print settings. Make sure that the file already has the correct print settings before choosing to print from the disk.

Views and Reports

To fully appreciate the View Manager and Report Manager's possibilities, you should become comfortable with the range of Excel's printing capabilities, as presented in the preceding sections of this chapter. Once you have some familiarity with what is available, you'll see the true value of these two managers. The View Manager allows you to define different print and page settings under unique view names and then, in a report, designate which views should print and in which order.

Your multiple settings might include a requirement for data to print with the formula text and the formula results. Instead of toggling to see the formula text, displaying the row and column headings, and then changing back to normal, you can name each view and Excel will automatically remember the setting that went along with the view.

Creating Views

Our example will be a printout with formula text as well as formula results. The Formula text view will be in portrait mode and have header and footer settings; the normal worksheet that displays the formula's results will have a landscape orientation and different headers and footers. Here are the general steps needed to create views and to report on them.

1. Make sure that the Report Manager program has been added to Excel. Select Tools ➤ Add-Ins from the menu bar. The Report Manager option should be checked. Click on the OK button.

2. Apply some print settings to your worksheet (for example, Landscape orientation, a specific header or footer, or shaded headings).

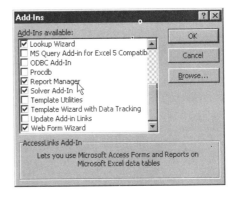

3. Select the range of cells that will be printed, and select View ≻ Custom Views from the menu bar. Click on the Add button on the right side of the Custom Views dialog box.

4. Type a unique name for your view. Click on OK.

5. Make another view by changing the formatting or the orientation and adding a different header or footer.

6. Repeat steps 3 and 4 to select and name the cells to be designated by another unique view name. In this example, there will be two unique view names listed in the Custom Views box.

Creating a Report from the Views

Your views can now be placed into a report and printed in a specific order. You will be able to name your report, and future printings will not require changing settings, since they will stored in a view. Use these steps to attach your views to a report:

1. Select View ≻ Report Manager and click on the Add button on the right side of the dialog box to add the views to print.

2. Type a name for the report in the Report Name text box.

3. In the Section to Add area, click on the drop-down arrows and select the name of the first sheet and view to print. Click on Add. The first view name appears at the bottom of the Sections in the Report part of the dialog box.

4. Select the second view in the same manner and click on the Add button. Both views are displayed in the Sections area. Click on OK to close the Add Report dialog box.

5. To print the report, click on the Print button on the Report Manager dialog box. Specify the number of copies that should print. Click on OK. Excel will save both the views and the report information, and both views will print under the single report name. Notice how each view prints with the settings you specified.

To edit the report and add or delete a view, or to print continuous page numbers, select View ≻ Report Manager and click on Edit. Make the appropriate selections.

The View Manager and Report Manager can save a tremendous amount of time and virtually eliminate the need to set up different page options like Portrait versus Landscape. Data that resides on the same sheet can be formatted differently and printed as a complete report.

Chapter

22

Ask Excel — Data Handling

Ask Excel—Data Handling

Excel's data handling capabilities are the best in the spreadsheet industry. List-management operations that previously required use of database programs such as dBASE, Access, Paradox, FoxPro, or Approach can now be handled directly in an Excel workbook. Data from any of these databases can be imported into an Excel worksheet so that you can easily use its powerful features and not struggle with the commands of the particular database program.

Excel also gives you some very sophisticated data handling capabilities. You can sort by multiple columns using the Quick Sort or Data Sort features. You can generate a data form to make data entry easier. You can filter data with AutoFilter and then subtotal your filtered lists by any column categories you designate. And finally, you can create sophisticated summary reports with the PivotTable Report command.

Creating Lists in Excel

You can easily manage your data by creating a *list*, which is information organized plainly into column headings and rows. You need only know the general methods for entering information in Excel to create useful and workable lists.

The spreadsheet list is the most recognizable data model. Figure 22.1 shows a simple spreadsheet of sales data. Each column heading is considered the field or category name for the data in that column. The row information is considered a record; each record contains related field values.

FIGURE 22.1

Column headings designate the specific categories of your list. Records are the rows of values for each heading.

	A	B	C	D	E	F	G	H	I	J
1	**Hardware Sales**									
2										
3	**Product**	**Year**	**Sales**	**Salesperson**	**Region**					
4	Computer	1997	82760	Sloan	East					
5	Computer	1997	114400	Barnhardt	South					
6	Printer	1998	15000	Sloan	East					
7	Computer	1997	68940	Leo	North					
8	Printer	1998	54820	Leo	North					
9	Printer	1998	153720	Barnhardt	South					
10	Monitor	1997	15940	Leo	North					
11	Computer	1998	110000	Sloan	East					
12	Monitor	1997	161520	Sloan	East					
13	Fax Modem	1998	98460	Sloan	East					
14	Computer	1998	163300	Barnhardt	South					
15	Printer	1997	54660	Barnhardt	South					
16	Monitor	1998	140940	Sloan	East					
17	Fax Modem	1997	138600	Sloan	East					
18	Fax Modem	1998	175020	Barnhardt	South					
19	Computer	1998	112883	Leo	North					
20										
21										

Sheet1 / Sheet2 / Sheet3 /

Entering Information into the List

As a rule of thumb, do *not* have any blank columns or rows between your data. Type your column headings in adjacent columns. Your headings can have multiple words but must be typed on a single row—do not use double-row headings. You can format the headings if you desire with bold or a different font or point size. Use only one category per column. If you are going to enter employees' names, for example, create a First Name and Last Name column, not just an Employee Name column. As your list grows, you may want to use the list for a mail merge with Word or for a formatted report in Access. You will be glad later that you made specific categories for each type of information you are tracking.

Type a value for each heading in the rows. Keep the list tight so that Excel can sense its boundaries (the white space around it). If you do not have a specific value for a column, you can leave that *cell* blank, but do not leave a whole record (row) blank. Each record must have at least one value. You can continue to add fields and records at any time. Excel will always know where the header row is and where the last record resides.

> **WARNING**
> Excel is programmed to recognize lists in a certain format, bound by blank rows and columns. Therefore, if you leave a row or column blank, Excel will not acknowledge any data beyond that space as part of your list. For example, Excel always considers the top row to be a header row. If you put a blank row between your headings and the first row of data, Excel will confuse your first row of data as the header row because of the blank row in between. So keep the blanks out!

Generating a Data Form to Add Records Easily

When entering information in a list with multiple headings, you move horizontally across the worksheet. If you have more columns than can fit on the screen, you may notice a problem: The data entry becomes tedious as you constantly scroll back and forth.

Excel has a data form feature that allows you to quickly generate a basic data-entry form from the column headings in your list. This form allows you to enter your information vertically, field by field (see Figure 22.2). Excel will then horizontally place the field values into the next blank row.

FIGURE 22.2

The data form makes data entry in long worksheets a breeze.

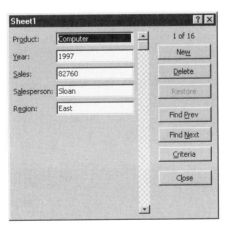

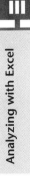

Use the following steps to create a data-entry form:

1. With a list already started (that is, with a header row and at least one record already entered), click the pointer on any cell within your list area.
2. Select Data ➢ Form from the menu bar.

3. Excel will immediately generate a form from the header row. Each field is displayed vertically, with the first record's information appearing in the form. Notice that the sheet name appears as the name on the Form dialog box. The current record of the pointer and the total number of records appear in the upper right side of the dialog box.

4. Click on the New button on the right side of the dialog box to generate a blank form. Excel will go to the bottom of the list. Fill in another record of information.

Make sure you press Tab, not Enter, to move from field to field. If you press Enter, Excel will save the current record and give you a new blank record. If this happens, click on the Find Prev button to return to the last record you were entering or editing.

Moving through Records

To look through the records one at a time, click on the Find Prev or Find Next buttons (or the up and down arrows on the keyboard), or use the vertical scroll arrows. To move to the first record in the list, press Ctrl+PgUp, or Ctrl+↑. To move to the last record in the list, press Ctrl+PgDn, or Ctrl+↓, and then press the up arrow key once or click on Find Prev.

Editing and Deleting Records

To edit your data, click on the desired field. The Home key and the End key will move you to the beginning and end of the information in that field. The left and right arrows move the pointer horizontally along the value characters in the field.

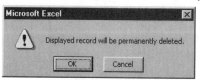

To delete a record, click on the Delete button. Excel will prompt you to confirm the deletion. Note that records deleted through the data-entry form cannot be undone with the Undo feature.

Using Criteria to Find Records

If you want to view records that match a particular set of criteria, you can use the data entry form to perform queries on your list of data.

1. Click on the Criteria button on the right side of the form's dialog box.
2. Use the blank form that appears to specify your criteria. In this example we will specify that Excel display only records from 1997 with sales equal to or greater than 100,000 (see Figure 22.3).
3. After you enter your criteria, press Enter or click on the Form button. Excel will jump to a record that matches the criteria. To find each matching record, press the Find Next button. Excel beeps when there are no more records matching the criteria. Click on Find Prev to go back through the matching records.

FIGURE 22.3

Excel will display the records that meet this criteria.

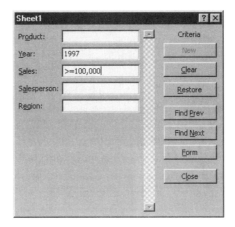

4. To clear the criteria, click on Criteria and then click on the Clear button on the right side of the dialog box. To restore your last criteria, click on the Restore button. Click on the Find Prev or Find Next buttons to continue moving through all of the records.

Sorting and Sifting through Data

Spreadsheet programs use sorting to organize data. Excel's sort feature is extremely easy to use. When you have information in an Excel list, you can use the Quick Sort buttons on the Standard toolbar to perform a sort on any particular field (column). Excel will not include your column headings as long as they are in the first row of your list. Excel also has a Sort command for more powerful sorts of multiple columns.

In addition to sorting, Excel also offers the AutoFilter, which allows you to isolate records that equal specific values. For example, to see only the sales for the Northern region, you would use the AutoFilter to exclude any sales that occurred outside this region. You can combine sorting with the AutoFilter so that, after you have isolated the records you want, you can then sort them in any fashion.

In the following sections, we will perform a quick sort and a full-blown, multiple-column sort. Then we will go on to the AutoFilter commands.

PART

III

Analyzing with Excel

Quick Sorts

To perform a sort on a column, click the pointer on the column and then click on one of the Sort buttons on the Standard toolbar. The Sort Ascending button sorts in alphabetical order (or, for numbers, low value to high value). Use the Sort Descending button to sort in backwards-alphabetical order (highest value to lowest value). Excel knows the boundaries of your list and quickly selects the range of the list. The first row is the header row and is not included with the sort.

WARNING

Do not select (highlight) a range of cells within the list before sorting. If you do, Excel will only sort the selected range and leave the other values where they were. You can undo this action with Ctrl+Z or by clicking on the Undo button. Always save your spreadsheet before sorting data.

Multiple Sort Keys

The quick sort is great for sorting one or two columns, but when you need to control the sort and assign a sort order (specifying what will sort first and then within that sort a secondary or tertiary sort), use the Data ➤ Sort option. Using the previous Sales model example, suppose you needed to sort first by Region, then by Sales, then by Salesperson. Follow these steps:

1. Click on any cell of your list area and choose Data ➤ Sort from the menu bar.
2. The Sort dialog box appears with three sort key options.
3. At the bottom of the dialog box, make sure that the Header Row radio button is selected. This option prevents the column headings from being sorted with the rest of the data in your list.
4. The name of one of the column headings may appear in the first Sort By text area. You can change this to whatever field you desire. For this example, click on the drop-down arrow of the Sort By text box and choose Region.
5. Make sure the Ascending button is checked. This will tell Excel to sort the Region column in alphabetical order (low value to high value).
6. Click on the first Then By text area's drop-down arrow and choose Sales from the list. Click on the Descending button so that the Sales will sort from the highest sale amount to the lowest sale amount.
7. Click on the last Then By text area and choose Salesperson. Click on the Ascending button so that the Salespersons' names will sort in alphabetical order. Figure 22.4 shows the Sort dialog box with the columns designated.
8. Click on the OK button to perform the sort.

FIGURE 22.4

You can use multiple criteria to complete a sort.

MASTERING THE OPPORTUNITIES

Sorting by More Than Three Rows

You can sort by one column using the Sort Ascending or Sort Descending buttons. Choosing Data ➢ Sort from the menu bar Excel provides you with up to three levels of sorting. There are many situations where three levels of sorting is just not enough.

Using either one of the basic sorting methods, you can sort by as many columns as you need; it just takes a bit of manipulation. Simply figure out in which order you want your columns sorted and then work backward.

Using the single sorting buttons, click into each desired column and click either

sorting button. The trick is to perform your main sort last. For example, suppose that you want to sort five columns with the following headings: Salesman, Region, Product, Quantity, and Amount. To sort the columns in the order listed, start in the Amount column, clicking on each column and on the appropriate sort button, and work your way backward. When finished, all of the columns will be sorted in the original order, grouping the records by Salesman, Region, Product, Quantity, and Amount.

You can achieve the same effect using Data ➢ Sort from the menu bar. Instead of sorting each column separately, you can do up to three at a time, the last three first and then the first two.

PART

III

Analyzing with Excel

Custom Sort Orders

You may need a sort order for text that is not alphabetical or numerical but adheres to other conventions. For example, the names of the months should not be sorted in alphabetical order. Excel now has a custom sort order option that uses the data of the custom list items. Excel can be told to sort in the order that the custom list displays the data. This is an invaluable feature.

Creating a Custom Sort Order List

Your first step is to create a custom sort order list. Using the Sales example, let's sort the regions in the order of North, South, East, and West instead of the default alphabetical order. If your custom list contains the items North, South, East, and West, you can assign a custom sort order by using this list.

To create the list of regional items in the order of North, South, East and West, choose Tools ➤ Options and click on the Custom Lists tab. Click on the List Entries box and type the four regional names. Press Enter after each entry. Click on the Add button when finished and then click on OK. Figure 22.5 shows the custom list items with the order of the regions specified.

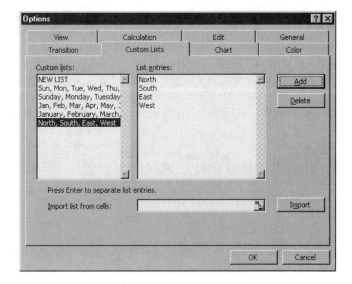

Using the Custom Sort Order List

Now that you have created a custom list, you can specify a custom sort order:

1. Click on any cell of your data list so that you are within the area of your list.
2. Choose Data ➤ Sort from the menu bar.
3. In the Sort By text area, select the Region field.
4. Click on the Options button on the left side of the Sort dialog box. The Sort Options dialog box appears.
5. Click on the drop-down arrow for the First Key Sort Order text box list. Choose the region names that were added to the Custom List (see Figure 22.6).

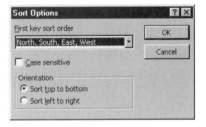

FIGURE 22.6

Use the Sort Options dialog box to specify a custom sort order.

6. Click on the OK button to return to the Sort dialog box. Click on OK to sort the data by the region name but in the order designated by the custom list items. The data is sorted in alphabetical order by region but in the custom sort order (see Figure 22.7).

NOTE

If you sort by a custom list but in descending order, Excel will use the custom list but will simply sort in the opposite order of the custom list.

Seeing What You Want to See—Using Filters

Excel's unique AutoFilter feature allows you to display only those records that match particular criteria values. Once records are filtered, you can edit or copy them to another sheet or workbook, subtotal them using the Subtotal feature (see next section), or sort them. As with the Sort command, AutoFilter is extremely easy and intuitive to use.

FIGURE 22.7

*Using a custom
sort order
enables you
to sort according
to your own
conventions.*

	A	B	C	D	E	F	G	H	I	J
1	**Hardware Sales**									
2										
3	**Product**	**Year**	**Sales**	**Salesperson**	**Region**					
4	Computer	1997	68940	Leo	North					
5	Printer	1998	54820	Leo	North					
6	Monitor	1997	15940	Leo	North					
7	Computer	1998	112883	Leo	North					
8	Computer	1997	114400	Barnhardt	South					
9	Printer	1998	153720	Barnhardt	South					
10	Computer	1998	163300	Barnhardt	South					
11	Printer	1997	54660	Barnhardt	South					
12	Fax Modem	1998	175020	Barnhardt	South					
13	Computer	1997	82760	Sloan	East					
14	Printer	1998	15000	Sloan	East					
15	Computer	1998	110000	Sloan	East					
16	Monitor	1997	161520	Sloan	East					
17	Fax Modem	1998	98460	Sloan	East					
18	Monitor	1998	140940	Sloan	East					
19	Fax Modem	1997	138600	Sloan	East					
20										

A new item in the AutoFilter list selections is a Top 10 criterion. Excel will automatically display the top ten values in a field and even let you customize this feature so that AutoFilter display up to the top or bottom 500 values in a field.

Setting Up the AutoFilter

To use the AutoFilter feature, follow these steps:

1. Click on any cell of your data list so that you are within the area of your list.

2. Choose Data ➢ Filter ➢ AutoFilter from the menu bar. Excel places drop-down arrows next to each column heading in the list.

3. Select the AutoFilter drop-down arrow next to the Region column heading. Excel displays the unique occurrences of each of the region names including the All, Top 10, Custom, and Blank options.

4. Choose North from the selection list (see Figure 22.8).

Excel immediately filters out any records that do not match the value of North in the column. Repeat step 3 for each field criteria you desire per column, then choose which region you want filtered out.

You can readily discern which column fields are involved with the AutoFilter, as both the drop-down arrow next to the columns and the row numbers are blue. This coloring indicates that AutoFilter is on. The Status bar at the bottom of the screen tells you how many records are involved in the filter and the total number of records in the

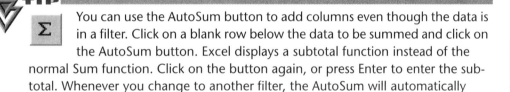

FIGURE 22.8

Excel's AutoFilter feature is available in an easy worksheet format.

whole list. Once the records are filtered, you can continue to sort these records using the Quick Sort keys on the Standard toolbar. Excel will use the displayed records as the source of the list.

To display all records again, click on the drop-down arrow next to the blue-colored fields and choose All. You may need to use the PgUp key or click on the vertical scroll box to find the All option. You can also choose Data ➤ Filter ➤ Show All from the menu bar.

Turn off the AutoFilter feature by choosing the same commands used to start it: Data ➤ Filter ➤ AutoFilter. The drop-down list arrows disappear when you turn off the feature from the menu bar.

> **TIP**
>
> Σ   You can use the AutoSum button to add columns even though the data is in a filter. Click on a blank row below the data to be summed and click on the AutoSum button. Excel displays a subtotal function instead of the normal Sum function. Click on the button again, or press Enter to enter the subtotal. Whenever you change to another filter, the AutoSum will automatically recalculate a new sum.

Defining a Custom Filter

You may want to see records that fall within a range of values and not one specific value. The Custom AutoFilter option allows you to further refine your filtering choices.

Using our example again, let's filter for records that fall between sales values of 100,000 and 150,000.

1. Make sure the AutoFilter feature is on (Data ➤ Filter ➤ AutoFilter).
2. Click on the drop-down arrow next to the Sales column heading. Excel displays each unique occurrence of each sales number, which is not very useful for selecting records.

3. Click on the Custom option in the drop-down list and the Custom AutoFilter dialog box appears.

4. Excel displays the name of the field upon which you are performing the Custom AutoFilter. Click on the drop-down arrow in the Show rows and click on *is greater than or equal to* (see Figure 22.9). Press Tab to move to the next text area.

5. Type **100000** in the text area. Make sure the And radio button is selected, as you want a compound statement.

6. Click on the drop-down arrow for the next logical expression. Choose *is less than or equal to*. Press Tab to move to the next text area.

7. Type **150000** in the text area. Click on OK to perform the filtering.

FIGURE 22.9

Defining a range in the Custom AutoFilter dialog box

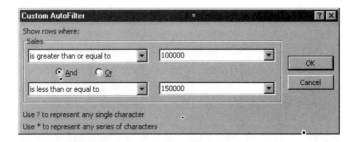

You have defined a custom filter that requests to see records whose sales are greater than or equal to 100,000 and less than or equal to 150,000. Excel displays the records that match.

You can also use wildcards in your custom filter criteria. If you need to find all values that start with the letter C and have any other characters following that letter, use the asterisk (*) to designate all characters. The asterisk is also the wildcard for a single character. For example, C* finds any word that begins with the letter C. C*t would find Cat, Cut, and Cot.

Filtering for the Top 10 Records

Top 10 is a new option in the AutoFilter drop-down list. The Top 10 option displays the 10 highest values or percentages in a particular field range. Excel even allows you to change the number of top units from 10 to as low as 1 or as high as 500. You can also find the lowest set of values. While no sorting is involved, once the records are displayed, you can perform sorts to achieve a different organization for your data.

Using the sales example, let's find the top 5 dollar sales for this list. Figure 22.10 displays the data with the AutoFilter Top 10 option selected.

FIGURE 22.10
The new Top 10 option allows you to display a specific number of high or l ow values.

Once you select this option, the Top 10 AutoFilter dialog box appears for you to specify your settings. You can choose to list any number of records in the top or bottom of your list or elect to list any percentage of the top or bottom of your list.

Creating Subtotals

The Subtotal feature allows you to mathematically summarize data by a particular field. This summary can be any of the following: Sum, Average, Count, Maximum, Minimum, Product, Standard Deviation, Count Nums, StdDevp, Varp, and Variance. If you want to see the total sales per region, for example, you request a subtotal on the Region field. At the row where the value changes from one region to the next, Excel displays a subtotal on that field that contains numeric data (for example, Sales).

When using the Subtotal feature, make sure to sort on the column field that will be used in the subtotal. Excel must have a contiguous group of the same items to give you an accurate subtotal. Follow these steps to use the Subtotal feature:

> **1.** Click on the field column by which you want to subtotal. For example, click on Product or Region or Salesperson.

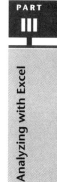

2. Click on the Sort Ascending or Sort Descending button. If you need a multiple sort as in this example, use the Data ➢ Sort menu to define multiple sort keys. In this example, the data is first sorted by region (which is the field by which we are subtotaling) and then by Salesperson so that the Salespersons' last names are sorted within the region.

WARNING

When working with multiple levels of subtotals, Excel will occasionally insert a blank column to label the subtotals. When removing subtotals, the blank columns that Excel added are the only things that it does not remove. If an added column is present after removing subtotals, simply delete the column and the worksheet will be exactly as it was before subtotaling.

Sorting is an important step needed by the Subtotal feature. Make sure that the column you are subtotaling is sorted before using the Subtotal feature. If you want to sort according to a custom sort order, see the previous section on Creating a Custom Sort Order List.

1. Choose Data ➢ Subtotals from the menu bar. The Subtotals dialog box appears for you to define the settings (see Figure 22.11).

2. In the At Each Change In text box, click on the drop-down arrow so that you can select the Region field (even though Excel suggests the first column in your list). Remember you sorted on Region because you wanted a subtotal each time that the region changed from North, South, and East.

3. At the Use Function text box, click on the drop-down arrow so that you can select the Sum function. You want Excel to add the values of the sales for each region.

4. At the Add Subtotal To checkbox options, check the Sales (numeric data) field. Uncheck any field that is not numeric—Excel cannot sum words.

5. At the bottom of the Subtotal dialog box, the additional options define what will happen each time you run the Subtotal feature and where the subtotal information should appear. Leave these settings in place for now. Once all of your settings are correct, click on OK.

Using the Subtotal Outline View

When the Subtotal feature is active, the defined subtotals are usually displayed below the field (if you kept the setting Summary Below Data in the Subtotals dialog box). Whenever the sorted column changes grouping, the subtotals appear. At the same

FIGURE 22.11

*Use the Sub-
total dialog box
to set options for
summarizing
your data.*

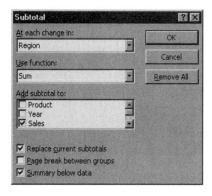

> **TIP**
>
> If you have multiple numeric fields for which you want to show subtotal summaries, add them to the field list in the Add Subtotal To text box. For example, you may have a Sales field, a Sales Commission field, and a Units Sold field. You can check all three fields so that when each Region changes, you will have subtotal information for each of these fields of information.

time, the area to the left of the subtotaled list changes automatically to provide tools for showing or hiding the level of detail shown in the columns.

The area to the left shows with outlining tools the levels of detail possible within the subtotal. At the top of the outline area, as shown in Figure 22.12, are three outline-level buttons designated by small numbers (1, 2, and 3). By default you see the total amount of detail for this particular subtotal—which is level 3 detail. Each level number expands and contracts the amount of records that are viewable. At level 3 you see all of the detail records that made up the subtotal sum.

To see different outline levels, click on the tiny number buttons at the top of the outline area. Level 2 detail shows only the subtotal records that were added to your list (see Figure 22.13). This is an extremely powerful capability, as you may need to report only the subtotals and their grouping labels of North, South, and East. Level 1 detail shows the grand total. You can immediately print any of these outline views. It is difficult to chart this data because Excel wants to display all of the values instead of the outlined values. Use the PivotTable Report feature (described later in this chapter) to achieve the same results and easily graph the data.

PART

III

Analyzing with Excel

FIGURE 22.12

Subtotals can display multiple levels of record detail.

	Product	Year	Sales	Salesperson	Region
1	Hardware Sales				
2					
3	**Product**	**Year**	**Sales**	**Salesperson**	**Region**
4	Computer	1997	68940	Leo	North
5	Printer	1998	54820	Leo	North
6	Monitor	1997	15940	Leo	North
7	Computer	1998	112883	Leo	North
8			252583		**North Total**
9	Computer	1997	114400	Barnhardt	South
10	Printer	1998	153720	Barnhardt	South
11	Computer	1998	163300	Barnhardt	South
12	Printer	1997	54660	Barnhardt	South
13	Fax Modem	1998	175020	Barnhardt	South
14			661100		**South Total**
15	Computer	1997	82760	Sloan	East
16	Printer	1998	15000	Sloan	East
17	Computer	1998	110000	Sloan	East
18	Monitor	1997	161520	Sloan	East
19	Fax Modem	1998	98460	Sloan	East
20	Monitor	1998	140940	Sloan	East
21	Fax Modem	1997	138600	Sloan	East
22			747280		**East Total**
23			1660963		**Grand Total**

FIGURE 22.13

Level 2 detail of the Subtotal Outline view

	Product	Year	Sales	Salesperson	Region
1	Hardware Sales				
2					
3	**Product**	**Year**	**Sales**	**Salesperson**	**Region**
8			252583		**North Total**
14			661100		**South Total**
22			747280		**East Total**
23			1660963		**Grand Total**
24					

Combining AutoFilter and Subtotals

You can request subtotals on a filtered list. Apply the AutoFilter first (Data ➤ Filter ➤ AutoFilter) and then define the subtotal (Data ➤ Subtotals). For example, suppose you want to see subtotals but for only one salesperson or for only those sales over a certain dollar amount. You can use AutoFilter to display the records for the specific salesperson and then define a subtotal on the filtered records. Figure 22.14 shows a filtered and subtotaled list.

FIGURE 22.14

You can apply
multiple filters
and then sub-
total the filtered
records.

	Product	Year	Sales	Salesperson	Region
1	Hardware Sales				
2					
3	**Product**	**Year**	**Sales**	**Salesperson**	**Region**
4	Computer	1997	68940	Leo	North
5	Printer	1998	54820	Leo	North
7	Computer	1998	112883	Leo	North
8			236643		**North Total**
9	Computer	1997	114400	Barnhardt	South
10	Printer	1998	153720	Barnhardt	South
11	Computer	1998	163300	Barnhardt	South
12	Printer	1997	54660	Barnhardt	South
13	Fax Modem	1998	175020	Barnhardt	South
14			661100		**South Total**
15	Computer	1997	82760	Sloan	East
17	Computer	1998	110000	Sloan	East
18	Monitor	1997	161520	Sloan	East
19	Fax Modem	1998	98460	Sloan	East
20	Monitor	1998	140940	Sloan	East
21	Fax Modem	1997	138600	Sloan	East
22			732280		**East Total**
23			1630023		**Grand Total**
24					

Removing Subtotals from the List

At any time you can remove the subtotals and return the data list to its simple column and row format. When you have finished viewing or printing the subtotaled data, click on any cell containing data; otherwise Excel will not be able to locate the data list. Then choose Data ➤ Subtotals, and click on the Remove All button on the right side of the Subtotal dialog box. Your list is returned to its original format.

Using PivotTable Report to Summarize and Organize

Even with the power of the Subtotal feature, you are still looking at a two-dimensional view of your data. Excel's list capabilities are extended with the PivotTable Report feature. While similar to the CrossTab feature in other spreadsheet programs, the PivotTable Report is a CrossTab superhero. A simple Excel list can be instantly summarized and grouped, allowing you to see your data from points of view that would not have been obvious from looking at the raw data. The PivotTable Report is interactive. You can literally "pivot" the data by quickly switching the results.

Suppose, using the sales example, you are asked to show the Years field across the worksheet in columns and the names of the salespersons along the left, going down in rows. In the intersection of each year and salesperson, you must show the sum of the sales and then a grand total for each year (column-wise) and a grand total for each salesperson (row-wise). This would be a tall order to manually rearrange and copy the list data to fit these specifications, and particularly difficult if you were told that you had only five seconds to do it. Excel's PivotTable Report feature can accomplish this easily.

Creating a Simple PivotTable Report

As with your other data list operations, make sure that you have a simple list with column headings (fields) and row values (records). There should be no blank rows between the columns or the row. Remove any subtotals or AutoFilters from the data. Our first PivotTable Report example will generate a sales summary that displays the years across the columns and the salespersons' names along the rows. The regions will be placed as page filters.

1. Click the pointer on some cell of your data list. If the pointer is outside the list, Excel cannot determine the boundaries of the list.
2. Choose Data ➢ PivotTable Report from the menu bar. Step 1 of the PivotTable Wizard appears (see Figure 22.15).

FIGURE 22.15

You can use different types of data to generate a PivotTable Report.

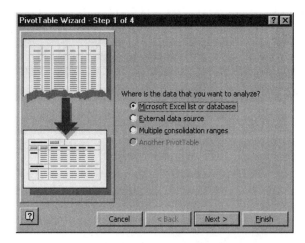

3. Make sure the *Microsoft Excel list or database* radio button is selected, and click on Next.
4. Define the range of your list. The correct range should be displayed if your pointer was already within the boundaries of your worksheet data list when you started the PivotTable Report option. If the range is not correct, enter the range in the dialog box (see Figure 22.16). Click on Next.

*Defining a
range for the
PivotTable.*

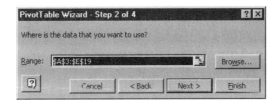

5. Now format your layout, which defines the fields to be displayed in the table. On
   the right side of the Step 3 dialog box are the different field names of your data.
   Drag the field names to the different positions on the layout to define exactly how
   the table should appear. Figure 22.17 displays the layout resulting from the following directions:

   • Drag the Region field to the Page area.
   • Drag the Year field to the Column area.
   • Drag the Salesperson field to the Row area.
   • Drag the Sales field to the Data area.

*You drag-and-
drop field names
to the different
layout areas.*

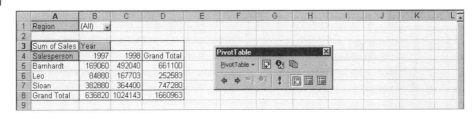

 TIP

You can have multiple fields on the columns and rows of the PivotTable layout.
Whichever field is first determines the primary grouping.

6. Do not use the Product field yet. Click on Next.
7. Specify where you want the PivotTable Report to start on the worksheet. Designate
   a cell within a range that does not contain current data. Leave this option blank
   for Excel to create a new sheet. Click on Finish.

TIP

The last step of the PivotTable Wizard provides an Options button which opens a PivotTable Options dialog box. Here you can customize some last-minute Format and Data options, such as whether you want row or column grand totals, whether you want Excel to AutoFormat the PivotTable, and whether you want to save the underlying data with your PivotTable.

The new PivotTable Report is displayed on a new sheet. Notice the generic sheet name at the bottom of the screen on the sheet tab. If you wish, you can double-click on the name and create a more descriptive name for this sheet containing the Pivot-Table. Excel also activates the PivotTable toolbar that will now be handy when working with this PivotTable. If you do not see the PivotTable toolbar floating on the screen, choose View ➢ Toolbars and verify that the PivotTable toolbar is checked.

Viewing PivotTable Report Data

Once you generate a PivotTable, the fun begins. The layout of the PivotTable Report adheres to the field arrangement you created during the PivotTable Wizard steps. You can now see the summary of the list data with the Year fields along the columns and the Salesperson fields along the rows. The sum of sales is contained in the intersection of the other fields. The Region field at the top of the table acts like a filter (see Figure 22.17). You can select a region and the summaries will reflect its sales. When South is selected, it suddenly becomes clear that Barnhardt's sales skyrocketed the second year. This information is not obvious in the flat data list. You can print and chart the PivotTable Report data (an example is shown in Figure 22.18). For more information on charting and mapping your data, see Chapter 19.

Changing the Default PivotTable Sum Function

The default calculation for a numeric field that is dragged to the Data section (center) of the PivotTable layout screen is the Sum function. If you drag a text field to the center, the default calculation is the Count function, since Excel cannot "add" words. The summary functions available for the PivotTable are Sum, Count, Average, Max, Min, Product, Count Nums, StdDev, StdDevp, Var, and Varp.

To change the type of function that Excel uses, follow these steps:

1. Click on a cell in the PivotTable that contains numeric data.

FIGURE 22.18

You can print and chart the results of a PivotTable.

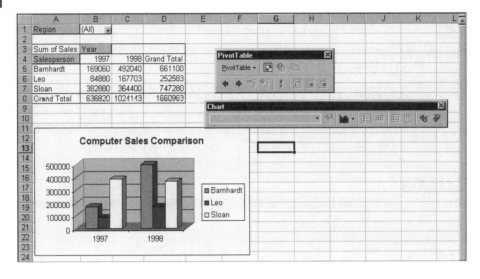

2. Choose Data ➤ PivotTable Report from the menu bar or right-click and choose Wizard from the shortcut menu. You can also click on the PivotTable button on the PivotTable toolbar and select Wizard to redisplay the PivotTable Layout screen (Step 3 of the PivotTable Wizard). Double-click on the Sum of Sales field in the middle of the layout. The PivotTable Field dialog box appears.

3. In the Summarize By list box, select another function to summarize the data. (If you choose Average and you get a Division by Zero error, you have a zero value in the PivotTable. For this exercise, choose the Max function instead.)

4. Choose OK or press Enter. If you started out with the Step 3 screen of the Pivot-Table Wizard, click on Finish.

Refreshing PivotTable Data

Don't make direct changes to the data in the PivotTable; rather, make changes to the original data and then *refresh* the PivotTable's data. For example, suppose in 1998 another salesperson was responsible for the majority of sales in that year. On the original data list, change the name of the salesperson from Barnhardt to Smythe for the 1998 sales. When you view the PivotTable, however, it still reflects the old data. You must issue the Refresh command to tell Excel to regenerate the table.

1. Click on the sheet tab that contains the original data list and correct or change the data.

PART

III

Analyzing with Excel

2. Return to the sheet where the PivotTable Report resides.

3. Click on the Refresh button on the PivotTable toolbar. (Alternatively, right-click and select Refresh Data or select Data ➤ Refresh Data.) Excel refreshes the data.

Pivoting the PivotTable

Once the PivotTable Report is generated, you can rearrange or "pivot" the fields in the table. In our example, the data has been rearranged to see the salespersons' names across the columns and the years on the rows (as shown in Figure 22.19). Use one of the following two methods for rearranging your data.

FIGURE 22.19

Rearrange the fields by selecting the first button on the PivotTable toolbar.

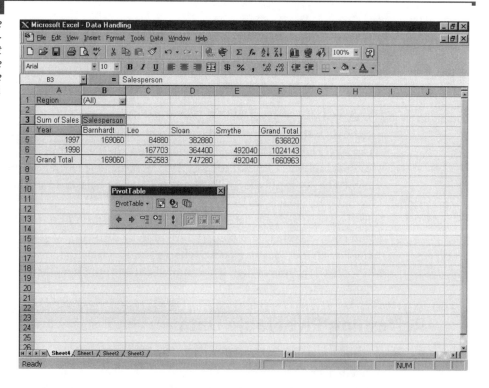

Using the PivotTable Layout Screen—Click on any cell of the current Pivot-Table and click on the PivotTable Wizard button on the PivotTable toolbar. Step 3 of the PivotTable Wizard appears on the screen. Drag the Salesperson field to the Column area and drag the Year field to the Row area. Click on the Finish button.

Rearranging Interactively—To drag the fields of your PivotTable interactively while viewing the PivotTable, click on the sheet tab that contains your PivotTable. Drag the field(s) that lie on the column to the row position. Notice that the small icon which represents the field name switches its direction. Figure 22.20 shows a PivotTable that has no column field, only two row fields. You can cluster fields on one axis; the first field in the cluster determines the primary grouping.

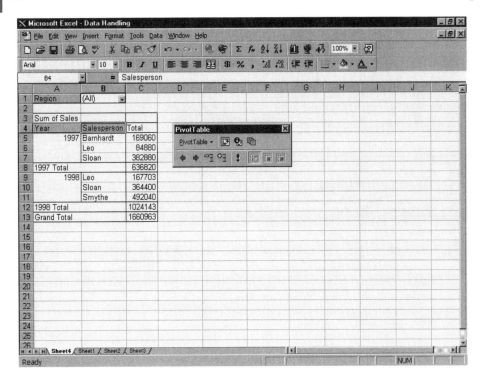

FIGURE 22.20

A PivotTable with two row fields

Adding, Removing, and Renaming Fields from the PivotTable

Once you see the capabilities of the PivotTable, you will want to add fields to the layout so that you can perform more in-depth analysis. To add fields, activate the PivotTable layout form by clicking within the range and then clicking on the PivotTable Wizard button on the PivotTable toolbar. The PivotTable Wizard's Step 3 dialog box appears. From here you can drag additional fields to the columns or the rows, or reposition existing fields.

To quickly remove a field from the layout, drag the field outside the white layout area onto the gray background of the PivotTable Wizard Step 3 dialog box. You can also drag fields back to the list of fields displayed on the right side of the dialog box.

To rename a field, double-click on the field name on the PivotTable's Layout (Step 3) screen. The PivotTable Field dialog box appears. Type over the existing name to change it to something more descriptive. You can also change the numeric format of a numeric field by clicking on the Number option on the PivotTable Field dialog box. Choose from among the various numeric formats.

To change the appearance of the PivotTable, click on a cell of the PivotTable and choose Format ➢ AutoFormat from the menu bar, then choose from among the suggested table layouts.

Chapter

23

Excel's Reusability Features

Excel's Reusability Features

Advanced and beginning users alike will be able to take advantage of the reusability features in Excel. These features range from customized lists to workbook templates.

Some reusability features are the same ones available in other Office applications. For example, any AutoCorrect entries that you make in Excel are available in Word and PowerPoint, and vice versa. The spelling dictionary used by Word can be shared with Excel and PowerPoint to eliminate the tedious reentry of specialized words.

Other features are unique to Excel. AutoComplete provides a way for you to reuse entries typed in a column. You will save time and avoid typos when you do not need to rekey the same data that already occurs in the column. The Custom Lists feature forms the basis of the AutoFill (pretyped months, days, and dates) and the Custom Sort Order features. You can add entries to the Custom Lists tab of the Tools ➤ Options dialog box and use them to automatically fill in cells.

The final feature we will discuss in this chapter is Excel's templates. Excel allows you to format spreadsheets and then reuse their layouts and formulas. You no longer need to open, copy, and clean out an old spreadsheet. You can use Excel's predefined templates (a cadre of built-in templates for home and business use now accompany Excel), modify the AutoTemplate (the one used every time you select to create a new workbook), and create and save your own custom templates.

Working with AutoCorrect

Some of the most common English words are also the ones most people have difficulty spelling. Words like *accommodate*, *balance*, and *occasion* give even the most confident spellers just a slight pause of uncertainty. And the simplest words are the ones that we mistype again and again. How many times have you accidentally transposed the letters in the words *the, and,* and *but*?

The Excel AutoCorrect feature looks for common, incorrect letter patterns and replaces them with the correct spelling of the word. To access the AutoCorrect feature, select Tools ➤ AutoCorrect from the menu bar. A dialog box like the one in Figure 23.1 will appear.

FIGURE 23.1

All five options are checked in the AutoCorrect dialog box.

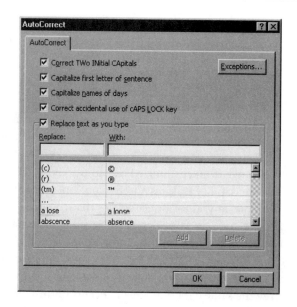

The AutoCorrect options work as follows:

Correct Two Initial Capitals—Tells AutoCorrect to look for two initial capitals (a common typographical error) and change the second capital letter to lowercase.

Capitalize First Letter of Sentence—Automatically capitalizes the first letter of sentences.

Capitalize Names of Days—Automatically capitalizes the first letter of day names.

Correct Accidental use of Caps Lock Key—Watches for inadvertent use of the Caps Lock key, fixes the case of words incorrectly entered, and toggles off the Caps Lock key.

Replace Text As You Type—Allows you to add your own replacement text as you type. Under this checkbox are boxes labeled Replace and With. The Replace list shows common symbol shorthand and spelling and typing mistakes, and the With list shows the correct symbols and spellings. Excel will automatically replace the listed errors with the correct versions as you type.

> **NOTE**
>
> AutoCorrect's initial capitals feature only works with words containing three or more letters (two capital letters together will not be changed). AutoCorrect is unable to distinguish intended usage of capitalization, so it will merely follow the rule. For example, if you are typing *USA* and accidentally capitalize the first two letters (the *U* and *S*) but not the third (*a*), AutoCorrect will change the second letter to lowercase, resulting in *Usa*.

If you prefer that Excel not automatically correct the types of mistakes represented by an AutoCorrect checkbox, click once to remove its checkmark.

Using the scroll bar to the right of these entries, scroll through to see the large number of entries that come with Excel. There are 350 predefined AutoCorrect entries. You may also add your own—as many as you wish. You can add words to the Replace and With lists to replace any characters you type with any new characters.

Adding AutoCorrect Entries

Adding your own AutoCorrect entries can save you lots of typing. For example, suppose your company name is extremely long; you can use an abbreviation instead of typing in the long company name. Add the abbreviated name to the Replace list and the full name to the With list (you can use capitalization and spaces); Excel will then make the change automatically.

To see how this works, step through this example using your own name:

1. Select Tools ➤ AutoCorrect.
2. Click on the empty text box area under the word Replace.
3. Type your initials. If the three letters of your initials spell a real word, use only two or add another character. You don't want Excel to replace a real word that has the same letters as your initials.

4. Click on the empty text box under With or press the Tab key.

5. Type your full name. As soon as you begin typing in the With box, the Add button becomes enabled.

6. When you have finished typing your entry, click on the Add button. The entry will now appear alphabetically in the list. Figure 23.2 shows an example of an entry added to the AutoCorrect list.

FIGURE 23.2

Adding an entry in the Auto Correct dialog box

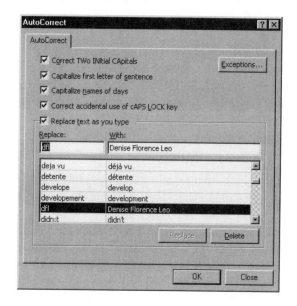

7. Click on OK to close the dialog box and return to your spreadsheet.

8. Place your cursor in cell A1 and type your initials. When you have finished, press the spacebar, Enter, Tab, or any of the arrow keys. Your full name should now appear.

 TIP

Remember that the Office 97 suite shares several features, including AutoCorrect, so if you have already entered several custom AutoCorrect entries in another Office application, you don't need to repeat them in Excel.

Deleting AutoCorrect Entries

You may find it necessary to delete certain word patterns in the AutoCorrect list because they conflict with what you want to do. For example, if your name is Carl Nathaniel Adams and you want Excel to replace your initials (cna) with your name, you would need to delete the AutoCorrect entry that already exists for that word pattern or select another abbreviation. Otherwise, each time you type your initials, the word *can* will appear, not your name, because Excel "corrects" this typo.

To delete an AutoCorrect entry, select Tools ➤ AutoCorrect and click once on that letter pattern. Once you have highlighted the entry, it will appear in the Replace and With text boxes. Click on the Delete button on the right side of the dialog box. The selection will be deleted from your list. Keep in mind that if you delete an AutoCorrect entry in Excel, it will be deleted from the other Office applications as well.

TIP

Instead of scrolling through the long list of AutoCorrect entries, you can jump to an entry. Click once on any entry name in the list. Press the first letter of the entry you are seeking, and Excel will jump to the first entry that begins with that letter (only the first letter works, however).

Filling in Cells with AutoComplete

The AutoComplete feature performs two functions: it keeps track of list entries you type in columns, and it attempts to fill in following cells with repetitive list items as it begins to recognize the word pattern. The feature can be disabled and enabled.

There are three basic things to remember about AutoComplete:

- The function works in columns, not rows.
- Skipping an entirely blank row will cause AutoComplete to reset.
- AutoComplete completes only entries that contain words or words combined with numbers. Entries that contain only numbers, dates, or times are not captured for completion.

Using AutoComplete

To see how AutoComplete works, start a new worksheet and follow these steps:

1. In cell A1, type the name **David**. Press Enter.
2. In cell A2, type the letter **D**. Do *not* press Enter. AutoComplete attempts to fill in the remainder of the cell with the name *David*. Complete the name **Denise** and press Enter.
3. In cell A3, type the letter **D**. AutoComplete has not completed the word since it has more than one entry that begins with *D*.
4. Type the letter **a**. AutoComplete attempts to fill in the name *David* since it now recognizes a unique word pattern. Complete the name **Daniel** and press Enter.

5. In cell A4, type the letter **D**. Now hold down Alt while pressing the down arrow key. A drop-down list of all the entries found in the prior cells will appear.

6. Select *David* from the list and press Enter. (You can also right-click and select Pick from List to display the list of AutoComplete entries.)

7. Activate cell A6. Type the letters **De**. AutoComplete cannot fill in the name because there is a blank row between the current active cell and the original list. When there is a break in the line, AutoComplete resets its list of values.

Disabling and Enabling AutoComplete

In some cases, you may not want Excel's help in filling in your list. You can disable or enable AutoComplete through Excel's Options dialog box. Select Tools ➤ Options from the menu bar. Click on the Edit tab. The last checkbox on this tab is for Auto-Complete. A checkmark here enables the option.

Filling In Cells with Custom Lists

Excel's Custom Lists feature can help you avoid the repetitive typing of items commonly listed in worksheets, such as month names. When you type any word in a defined list of words, Excel recognizes the name as being part of a custom list. Then you can use Excel's AutoFill feature to automatically complete the rest of the list.

If the number of cells you select is more than the number of items in the custom list, Excel will repeat the list until all the selected cells are filled. You do not need to use the first name in the list for Excel to recognize it as belonging to the group; you can start anywhere.

Using Custom Lists

Excel has predefined custom lists of common repetitive items, such as the 12 months of the year and the seven days of the week. To see how this works, start a new sheet and follow these steps:

1. Click on cell A1. Type the word **Sunday** and press Enter.

2. Click again on cell A1.

3. Drag the AutoFill's fill handle across the cells in row 1 to column I. To drag this handle, place your mouse pointer over the bottom-right corner of cell A1, where a small gray box appears. The pointer turns from the white cross shape to a small black cross, which you drag to the right across the row. Release the mouse at column I. Excel will fill in the cells with the day names, as shown in Figure 23.3.

PART

III

Analyzing with Excel

FIGURE 23.3

Excel automatically fills in the days of the week.

Notice that after AutoFill completed the cycle, it began again. You can leave your list selected and format it (bold, centered, and so on).

Creating Your Own Custom Lists

You can create your own custom lists for use with the AutoFill feature. For example, you might define lists with the names of people, departments, or complex labeling systems. Then you will only need to type them once for use in all your workbooks, old and new. Through the Custom Lists tab of the Options dialog box, you can either type in your own lists or import existing text for your custom lists.

Typing In a Custom List

To add your own custom list, follow these steps:

1. Select Tools ➤ Options and select the Custom Lists tab.
2. In the Custom Lists list box, highlight New List. A cursor will appear in the List Entries list box.
3. Type your list in this box, pressing Enter after each entry.
4. When you have finished typing your list, click on the Add button. Your list will now appear in the Custom Lists box on the left. To add another list, simply repeat these steps.
5. Click on OK to save your custom list(s) and close the dialog box.

Importing Text into a Custom List

If a workbook already contains a list of entries that you would like to make into a custom list, follow these steps:

1. Highlight the cells that contain the list you wish to import.
2. Select Tools ➤ Options and select the Custom Lists tab.
3. Check that the Import List from Cells text box at the bottom of the dialog box shows the correct cell range (the cells you selected). If it does not, type in the cell range where the list resides on the worksheet.
4. Click on the Import button in the lower-right corner. Your list should now appear in the Custom Lists box. Click on Add if you would like to import another list.
5. Click on OK to save your custom list(s) and close the dialog box.

Setting Up with Custom Lists

Now try this example to create and use two custom lists:

1. In cell A1 of a new sheet, type **Marketing**.

2. In cell A2, type **Sales**.

3. In cell A3, type **Client Services**.

4. Select Tools ➤ Options and select the Custom Lists tab.

5. Click once on New List in the Custom Lists box.

6. In the List Entries box, enter the following names, pressing Enter after each one: **Stephen Nicholas, Alexandra Florence,** and **Deborah Shockley**. Click on the Add button so that the names will be listed in the Custom Lists text area.

7. In the Import List from Cells box, type **A1:A3**.

8. Click on the Import button. Both of your new lists should now appear in the Custom Lists box, as shown in Figure 23.4.

FIGURE 23.4

You can either type a custom list into the List Entries area or import a list of typed items from a worksheet.

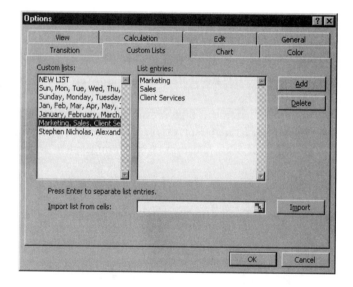

9. Click on OK to return to your worksheet.

10. In cell A5, type the word **Sales**.

11. Grab the fill handle and drag across to cell C5. Widen the columns if necessary.

12. In cell A6, type the name **Stephen Nicholas**.

13. Grab the fill handle and drag across to cell C6. The names flow from the list.

As the example demonstrates, custom lists can save you hours of typing and reduce your typographical error rate dramatically. Now you only need to worry about the numbers, not the text. What a relief for spreadsheet users!

You can also tell Excel to use a custom list as the basis of a sort. For example, you might want to sort in calendar month order instead of alphabetical order. See Chapter 22 for more information about using the Custom Sort Order List feature.

About Templates

You've done all the work. The report looks exactly as you want it. The formatting is attractive and easy to read, the columns perfectly spaced, the cell references finally where you want them, and the macros are debugged. Your workbook should look just like this every time you create this report. It can, if you save the workbook as a template and use the template as the basis of your next report.

Templates serve as patterns for creating new workbooks, sheets, charts, modules, and dialog boxes. They can save you a lot of time and hard work and add consistency to your workbooks. Templates can also give you a jump start on worksheets that use complex calculations by storing them for repeated use. Just as you can create Word templates for form letters, you can create Excel templates for "form worksheets."

In addition to creating custom templates, you can also alter Excel's default template, the AutoTemplate. For example, you can change the font size, column widths, page orientation, and headers that will be the defaults for every new workbook. You may also find that Excel has anticipated your needs. Excel comes with a number of predefined templates for you to use.

In the following sections, you will learn to create a new AutoTemplate and set up your own custom templates. Then you will take a tour of Excel's predefined custom templates.

Creating a Workbook AutoTemplate

Excel uses a default workbook AutoTemplate every time you click on the New button on the Standard toolbar or select the Workbook icon on the General tab of the File ➤ New dialog box. The default workbook AutoTemplate contains the column widths, styles, formatting, page setup, and other settings for the new workbook.

You can change these default settings by customizing any blank workbook and saving it as the new default AutoTemplate. The name of the template must be Book. It must be saved as a template in a specific folder under the Excel folder called XLSTART.

As an example, suppose you want every new workbook to have a 14-point font, column widths of 15, a currency format (with two decimal places), and the current date in cell A1. You can create a workbook that has these formats, column widths, and a date formula and save it as the new AutoTemplate. Follow these steps:

1. Select the entire workbook by clicking on the empty button to the left of the column A letter and above row 1. The mouse pointer will change to a white cross.

- Select a 14-point font using the Formatting toolbar.

- Click on the Currency format button.
- Select Format ➤ Column ➤ Width. Type in **15** and click on OK.
- Click in cell A1, type the function **=NOW()**, and press Enter.
- With cell A1 selected, select Format ➤ Cells, select the Date format on the Number tab, select a date style, and click on OK.
- If you want to modify the page setup, select File ➤ Page Setup and make changes (such as landscape versus portrait or removing the header).

2. Once the workbook has been formatted, select File ➤ Save or Save As.

3. In the File Name text box, type the name **Book**. You must use this name if you want the new template to be the AutoTemplate.

4. In the Save As Type text box, click the drop-down arrow and change the type from Microsoft Excel Workbook to Template. Immediately, Excel switches to the Templates folder.

5. In the Save In text box at the top of the dialog box, find and click the XLSTART folder within the Microsoft Excel folder, as shown in Figure 23.5

FIGURE 23.5

Select the XLSTART folder to save your file as an Auto-Template.

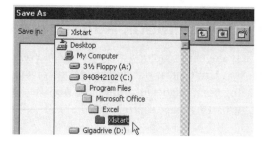

6. Click on the Save button on the right side of the dialog box. Your file is saved with an .XLT (template) extension instead of the usual .XLS (sheet) extension.

7. Close the file (File ➤ Close) so that there are no open workbooks.

8. Click on the New button on the Standard toolbar or select File ➤ New, select the General tab, and click on OK. The new workbook now contains all of the defaults you defined and saved. The NOW function produces the current date in the first cell.

If you want to change or enhance your new default AutoTemplate, make the changes on any new workbook and then repeat steps 2 through 6 to save it as the new default worksheet template.

When you want to use the AutoTemplate for the workbook, click on the New button on the Standard toolbar or select the Workbook icon from the General tab of the File ➤ New dialog box. To revert back to the default workbook template, simply delete BOOK1.XLT from the XLSTART folder.

Creating Other AutoTemplates

Excel uses a number of AutoTemplates to manage the defaults for new sheets, charts, dialog boxes, and programming modules. All the AutoTemplates must be stored in the XLSTART folder, and they must have specific names, as follows:

Sheet Type	Default AutoTemplate Name
Workbook	BOOK.XLT
Worksheet	SHEET.XLT
Chart	CHART.XLT

Set up the AutoTemplate by creating a workbook with the sheet names and text, chart settings, or programming code that you wish to insert automatically. Save the workbook under the identifying AutoTemplate name, choosing to save it as a template in the XLSTART folder. Make sure that the active sheet is the one you want to use as the template when you save the workbook.

When you want to use your new sheet, chart, or workbook, select the item from the Insert menu on the menu bar.

Creating Custom Templates

When you have set up a worksheet with formatting and other items that you will use again in certain worksheets, you can create a custom template. Begin by setting up the existing workbook just as you want it to look for the template. For example, if you are setting up a periodic report, you may want to erase the numbers that change from report period to report period—but not formulas.

To create a template from an existing workbook on the screen, select File ➤ Save As from the menu bar. Type any name for the workbook. Change the Save As Type setting from Microsoft Excel Workbook to Template. Templates are saved in a default folder called Templates. You can have as many custom templates as you desire.

Once your template is saved, you can select it from the list of templates in the File ➤ New dialog box. The workbook that appears on the screen will be a copy of the template, not the original. Your custom template name followed by the number *1* appears in the title bar (like the AutoTemplate Book1 name).

As an example, here are the steps to create a simple custom template:

1. Select a new workbook.
2. In cell A1, type **Bank of Cordell Monthly Analysis Report**.
3. In cell H1, type **=NOW()** so that the default system date will appear each time you use the template.
4. Press Ctrl+1 to activate the Format ➤ Cells dialog box. Select the Date category and select a date format type.
5. Select File ➤ Save As.
6. Type the filename **Bank of Cordell**.
7. For Save As Type, select Template from the drop-down list.
8. Click on the Save button
9. Close the workbook.
10. Select File ➤ New. You will see an icon for your template on the General tab of the dialog box.
11. Select the Bank of Cordell icon to open the template.

Bank of
Cordell

Your new sheet will already have the name Bank of Cordell Monthly Analysis Report in cell A1 and the current date in cell H1. Any other information you saved as part of your workbook template will also be included.

Editing or Deleting a Custom Template

To edit an existing template, select File ➤ Open from the main menu or click on the Open button on the Standard toolbar. Enter the name of the template as the filename. For Files of Type, select Template. Browse to the Templates folder, which should be in your main Office folder. Once you have located the file, select Open.

Make your changes directly to the open template file. When you have completed your edits, simply save the file with the changes, and then close it.

You can delete templates in the same way that you delete other files. Select the file directly from the Excel file list screen (File ➤ Open or File ➤ Save) and right-click to access the shortcut menu. Select Delete from the shortcut menu (See Figure 23.6).

FIGURE 23.6

Use the short-cut menu to delete a template.

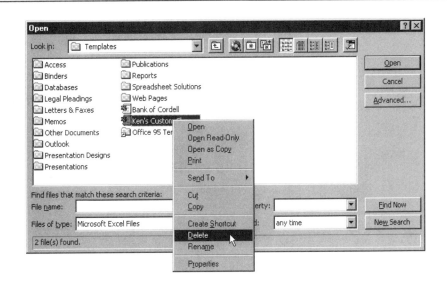

As when you delete other files, Excel will ask for confirmation. Remember, the deleted file will be sent to the Recycle Bin. If you delete the wrong file, return to the Desktop (right-click on the Taskbar and minimize your applications). Then double-click on the Recycle Bin icon, select the file to be restored, and select File ➣ Restore to restore the deleted file. The file will be returned to the proper folder.

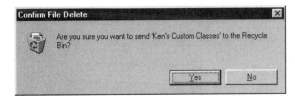

Creating a Custom Template Folder

If you have created a number of custom templates, you may want to group them in their own categories in the File ➣ New dialog box. To create your own pages with tabs within the New dialog box, create a folder within the Templates folder under Office 97. You can use the Explorer to find the Templates directory and create the folder there, or you can create a new folder using Excel.

PART

III

Analyzing with Excel

The following steps guide you through creating a new folder using Excel and placing your custom template within this new folder.

1. Select File ➢ Open and open the custom template used in the previous example or one of your own custom templates. Remember, change the Files of Type option at the bottom of the dialog box to Templates and locate the Templates folder under Office 97 using the Look In text box at the top of the dialog box.
2. Open the custom template and select File ➢ Save As.
3. In the Save As dialog box, click on the Create New Folder button (the third yellow folder button at the top of the dialog box). The New Folder dialog box appears.
4. Type the folder name that you want to appear on the tab, and click on OK.

The new template folder is listed with the other template folders. Figure 23.7 shows an example of a new folder in with the other templates. Our next steps are to save the custom template into this new folder.

FIGURE 23.7

You can create new folders within the Templates folder by using the File ➢ Save As command and selecting the new folder button.

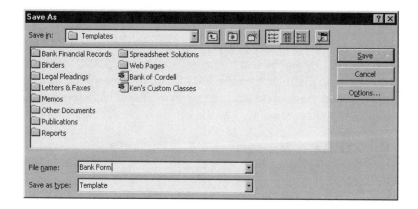

5. With the Save As dialog box still on the screen, double-click on the name of the new template folder you just created. The folder will be empty.
6. Because your custom template is still on the screen behind the dialog box, you can save the template into this new folder. You will delete the extra copy of the template that is the General folder in a later step.
7. Click on the Save button on the right side of the Save As dialog box. You will be returned to your custom template workbook.
8. Close the workbook and select File ➢ New from the menu bar to see your new tab in the dialog box. Click on the new tab to see the saved contents of your custom folder, as shown in Figure 23.8.

FIGURE 23.8

You can add your custom template to a new folder within the Templates folder.

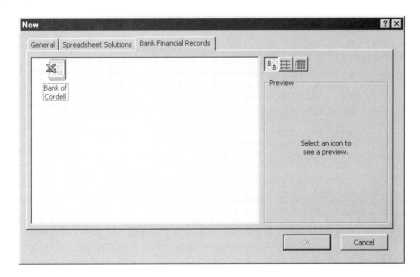

9. To remove the extra copy of the custom template from the General tab, select the General tab and select the template.

10. Right-click to access the shortcut menu, but hold down Shift before you click on the Delete option. The Shift key combined with the Delete option tells Excel not to send the deleted object the Recycle Bin. Since you already have a copy of the template in the correct folder, there is no need to have an emergency copy in the Recycle Bin. Excel asks you to confirm your choice.

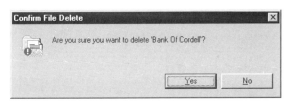

11. Click on Yes to remove the extra copy of the template.

Using Excel's Predefined Templates

You can select from among Excel's predefined templates when you select File ➤ New. Excel has placed four business and personal templates in the Spreadsheet Solutions folder, as shown in Figure 23.9. Double-click on any of these templates and examine their formats and formulas to see if any of them can be of use to you. For example, the

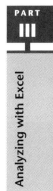

MASTERING TROUBLESHOOTING

Missing Template Folders

After creating template folders to organize your custom templates, you may notice that a folder does not show up as a sheet tab when you select File ➢ New from the menu bar.

This will happen if there are no templates for the current application inside the folder. So, if you have a new folder in which you have not yet placed a template, it will not show up when starting a new document.

This behavior is the same across all of the Office applications. The template folders are subfolders of the Office Templates folder. If you click on the New Office Document button from either the Start Menu or the Office Shortcut Bar, all of the folders, as long as they have at least one template in them, will be represented as sheet tabs in the New Office Document dialog box. If you attempt to create a new document from within one of the Office applications, only those folders with templates for the specific application will appear in the New dialog box.

Invoice template, shown in Figure 23.10, includes multiple sheets for tracking different budget categories, such as entertainment, credit card expenses, and so on. You can customize these forms to fit your business needs.

FIGURE 23.9

Excel has a number of templates for your business or personal use.

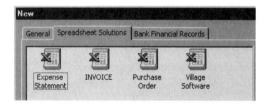

When you select File ➢ New and select an Excel predefined template, you are given a copy of the template to serve as the basis for a new workbook. You can make whatever changes you wish, and then save the file either as a workbook or as a new template with a different name.

FIGURE 23.10

FIGURE 23.10

Excel's pre-defined Invoice template is a tremendous time saver and has an attractive design.

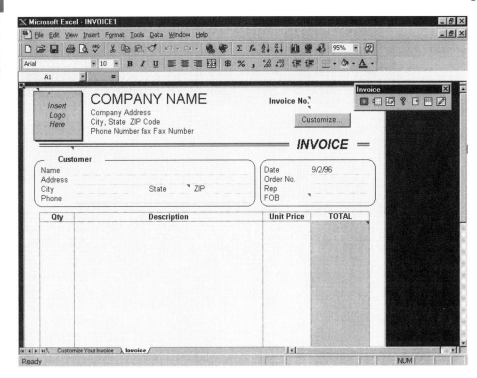

As you learned in this chapter, Excel provides many reusability features that save you time and make your work more accurate. The next chapter describes how you can customize Excel toolbars and use macros to maximize your efficiency.

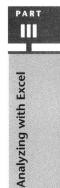

Chapter

24

Customizing Excel with Toolbars and Macros

Customizing Excel with Toolbars and Macros

The toolbars and menu bars within all of the Office 97 programs can be customized with different buttons to suit your needs and preferences. The default toolbars and menu bars reflect only some of the commands that are available to you. Excel provides buttons for almost every command. For example, you may want to add buttons for inserting and deleting rows or columns, or for the equals sign and the four basic mathematical operations (add, subtract, multiply, and divide).

Of course, not every command you want to automate is currently a part of the Excel program. Excel does, however, provide you with the ability to create macros that automate any number of your spreadsheet tasks and to assign them to custom toolbar buttons or menu items.

In this chapter, we'll begin with the ways that you can customize Excel's toolbars and menu bars. Then we'll discuss the basics of macro design and creation.

Customizing Toolbars and Menu Bars

Excel places the Standard and Formatting toolbars on the screen when you launch the program. Some of the toolbars, such as Chart and PivotTable, are automatically shown during certain operations. If you do not see a toolbar that you need, select View ➢ Toolbars from the menu bar to select the desired toolbars (see Figure 24.1). You can also right-click on any part of a toolbar and use the shortcut menu to view toolbar choices.

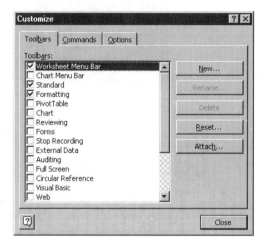

Adding and Removing Commands

To add a command to any toolbar or menu bar, select Customize from View➤ Toolbars or the Toolbars shortcut menu and select the Commands tab (shown in Figure 24.2).

The list box on the left side of the Commands tab shows the categories of commands. The items to the right are the available commands. In Figure 24.2, you can see that some of the buttons in the File category are already on the Standard toolbar or on the file menu. You can view the purpose of each command by selecting it and clicking on the Description button at the bottom of the Customize dialog box.

As an example, let's add the Columns command to the Standard toolbar. This command lets you quickly insert a column where you place the pointer. Follow these steps:

1. Select View ➤ Toolbars ➤ Customize or right-click on any toolbar. Select the Commands tab.
2. Click on the Insert category (the fourth category in the list).
3. When the Insert commands appear, find the Columns command (it is the third command).
4. Click on the command and drag it onto a toolbar or the menu bar. A copy of the command is dragged onto the toolbar or menu bar and a button is created.
5. Drop the button where you want it to appear on the toolbar. You can move it by dragging directionally across the toolbar.
6. Close the Customize dialog box.

To test your button's capabilities, click on a column of text and then click on the new button to insert a new column.

You can also remove commands from toolbars and menu bars. To get rid of a command you do not need, select View ➤ Toolbars ➤ Customize, or point to any button on a toolbar, right-click, and select Customize from the shortcut menu.

When the Customize dialog box is visible, point to the command to be removed, press and hold down the mouse button, and drag the command off the toolbar or menu bar into the workbook area.

TIP

If you want to quickly remove a command without having to open the Customize dialog box, hold down the Alt key and drag the command off the toolbar. This shortcut will only work with command buttons on toolbars and menus on the menu bar; to remove menu items, you must open the Customize dialog box.

Floating and Docking Toolbars and Menu Bars

When you add commands, the toolbar or menu bar may not be able to display every item. Each additional command pushes down the other commands. Eventually, you will not be able to see the buttons on the far right side of the toolbar or menu bar.

Excel lets you *float* and *dock* the toolbars and menu bars. When you float a toolbar, you can place it in any position on the screen. You can then shape the toolbar to see all of its buttons.

Floating a toolbar does not require the Customize dialog box to be active. On the left side of each toolbar and menu bar is a handle that looks like a grip with two vertical bars. Use this handle to click and drag the toolbar down into the middle of the

PART

III

Analyzing with Excel

screen. Then drag the sides to narrow or widen the toolbar to put the buttons in multiple rows so that you can see all of them. Figure 24.3 shows an example of a floating Standard toolbar with its commands on two columns.

FIGURE 24.3

When you float a toolbar or menu bar, you can position it anywhere on the screen and arrange the buttons in rows.

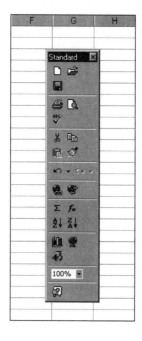

To dock the toolbar to another position or back to its original position, drag the title bar that contains the toolbar's name to either the top, bottom, left, or right sides of the screen. If you double-click the title bar, the toolbar will dock to its last position. Figure 24.4 shows an example of a toolbar docked at the bottom of the screen.

FIGURE 24.4

A toolbar docked at the bottom of the screen.

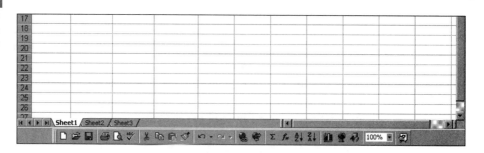

Creating New Toolbars and Menu Bars

You may want to create your own toolbar or menu bar that contains only the commands you need to efficiently perform your worksheet operations. The Insert category in the Customize dialog box is a favorite because it holds the buttons relating to creating worksheet formulas: equals sign, mathematical operators, and so on. In the following example, we will first create a new menu bar and then populate that menu bar with commands from the Insert category.

1. Select Tools ➢ Customize from the menu bar.
2. Click on the New button on the Toolbars tab and type **My Menu** in the New Toolbar dialog box. Click on OK.
3. Click on the Commands tab of the Customize dialog box and select New Menu in the Categories area. In the Commands area, drag the New Menu command to the My Menu bar.
4. Right-click on New Menu on My Menu and change the Name property that appears on the shortcut menu to **Operations**. Press Enter to accept your change. If your toolbar disappears behind the Customize dialog box, move the dialog box out of the way by dragging its title bar.
5. Select the Insert category on the left-hand side of the Commands tab in the Customize dialog box.
6. Scroll down the Commands list and drag the Plus, Minus, Multiplication, and Division Sign commands on top of the Operations menu on My Menu so that they become menu items. When you drag a command to be a menu item, you must drag to the menu option, let the menu drop down, and drop the command on the menu as a menu item.
7. Drag the Equals Sign command to the menu bar to the right of the Operations menu so that it is at the same level.
8. Close the Customize dialog box. Your new menu should look similar to the one in Figure 24.5.

PART

III

Analyzing with Excel

FIGURE 24.5

A new menu containing commands of your choice.

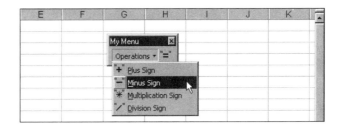

Your new menu bar can now be docked. Double-click the blue title bar with the name My Menu, and the menu bar will dock itself at the top of the screen. You can also click on the toolbar's title bar and drag it where you want it to appear on the screen. When you right-click on any toolbar or menu bar, you will see the name of your new menu bar listed with the others.

To delete one of your own toolbars or menu bars, select Tools ➤ Customize from the menu or right-click on any toolbar and select Customize. Select the name of your toolbar from the Toolbars tab on the Customize dialog box. When you click on the name of your toolbar, the Delete button becomes available. Click on Delete and Excel will ask you to confirm the deletion. Click on OK.

Understanding Macros

If you are often repeating particular workbook tasks, you may have candidates for macros. Repetitive keystrokes and mouse movements can be directly recorded as instructions for these tasks. A single name is given to each set of instructions. Thus the origins of the name macro—one overall name that represents multiple, micro steps.

When you are recording your keystrokes and mouse movements, Excel writes down these movements as a list in a special language called Visual Basic for Applications (VBA). You can then run this list of instructions by activating the macro.

While Excel provides several built-in macros in the form of shortcut commands and toolbar buttons, you may find Excel lacking some specific commands that you use often. Some functions that may be candidates for your own macros include printing specific sections of a report, exporting or importing data, applying particular formats to different ranges, and changing printer settings and print ranges.

Recording Macros

When you record a macro, do not type any characters or perform any actions that are not part of the macro recording. Although you can edit your macros (as described later in the chapter), it is best to plan your steps before you begin recording.

We will record a simple macro that types a company name and address. Follow these steps:

1. Click on cell A1 of a blank worksheet.

2. Select Tools ➤ Macro ➤ Record New Macro. The Record Macro dialog box opens (see Figure 24.6).

FIGURE 24.6

*Use the Record
Macro dialog
box to name
and describe
your macro.*

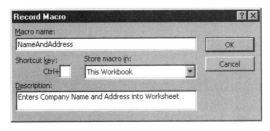

3. Type **NameAndAddress** in the Macro name text box. Macro names can be up to 255 characters and must begin with a letter. You can have numbers and underscores in the name, but not spaces or other punctuation marks.

4. Type a description for the macro, **Enters Company Name and Address into Worksheet**, in the Description area of the dialog box. Although this is an optional feature, we recommend that you always enter a short description of what your macro does.

5. If you want to designate a shortcut key for your macro, enter it into the Shortcut Key text box. If you choose an existing Excel key combination, your macro will be invoked instead of the built-in action.

6. Click on OK. An error message will appear (or the Office Assistant will inform you) if you included spaces or other punctuation in the macro name. Click on OK (or press Esc) to make corrections to the name.

When the recording starts, Excel displays the Stop Recording toolbar and the word *Recording* appears on the Status bar at the bottom of the screen. There are two buttons on the Stop Recording toolbar: Stop Recording and Relative Reference. Stop Recording is pressed when you are finished performing the steps. Relative Reference should be pressed when you want Excel to record your movements in a workbook relative to your current location as opposed to absolute, cell-specific jumps. For example, if the Relative Reference button was pressed, and you clicked on cell A10 after having the active cell marker on A1, Excel would record that you moved nine rows down. If Relative Reference was not pressed, Excel would record that you moved specifically to cell A10. If you later ran the macro with the active cell marker on cell D1, cell D10 would be activated if Relative Reference was on while recording. Cell A10 would be activated if Relative Reference was not on. For this example, the Relative Reference button should be pressed.

7. With the Macro Recorder on, type your company address information. Use a separate row for each part of the address.

PART

III

Analyzing with Excel

8. Drag the mouse over the rows of information and click the Bold button. Click on the next blank cell below the company name. Your screen should look similar to the example in Figure 24.7.

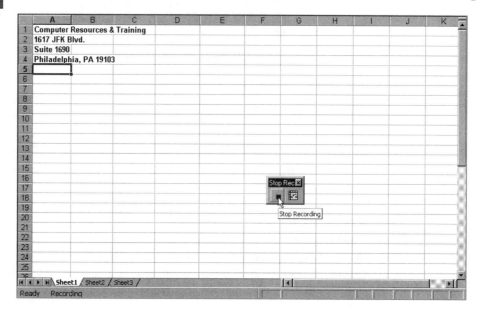

9. Click on the Stop Recording button, or select Tools ➤ Macro ➤ Stop Recording.

Running Macros

After recording a macro, you will want to test your keystrokes immediately to see if they perform correctly. If you recorded the macro on a worksheet that you want to keep, save your file before running the macro, in case something goes wrong.

1. Position the pointer in a blank area of the worksheet and select Tools ➤ Macro ➤ Macros.

2. In the Macro dialog box, select the name of your macro and click on Run. Excel plays back the keystrokes that enter the company name and address information and apply the bold format.

3. Click into another empty cell and run your macro again. Your screen might look something like Figure 24.8.

FIGURE 24.8

*Run your macro
a couple of times
to test it.*

	A	B	C
1	Computer Resources & Training		
2	1617 JFK Boulevard		
3	Suite 1690		
4	Philadelphia, PA 19103		
5			
6			
7			
8	Computer Resources & Training		
9	1617 JFK Boulevard		
10	Suite 1690		
11	Philadelphia, PA 19103		
12			
13			
14	Computer Resources & Training		
15	1617 JFK Boulevard		
16	Suite 1690		
17	Philadelphia, PA 19103		
18			
19			
20			

TIP

An easy way to repeat a macro that has just been run is to select Edit ➢ Repeat Macros or simply press Ctrl+Y.

Notice that no matter what cell the pointer is in, when you run the macro, the company information appears. This is why you chose Relative Reference. If you had not, the macro would only run in the cells in which you performed the recording, regardless of where you positioned the pointer.

The sample macro that you recorded only works in the current workbook. If you close the file containing this macro, no other workbook will be able to access it. Later in this chapter, you'll learn how to make a macro global to all workbooks.

When you want to run a macro, you can always use the formal method of selecting the macro name from the Macro dialog box and clicking on Run. But you probably want a quicker way. Excel lets you assign your macros to keyboard combinations, menus items, toolbar buttons, or custom worksheet buttons. These alternatives are discussed in the following sections.

Creating a Macro Shortcut Key

To assign your macro to a keyboard combination, follow these steps:

1. Open the workbook that contains your macro and select Tools ➢ Macro ➢ Macros.
2. Select the name of your macro. The buttons on the right side of the Macro dialog box become available.
3. Click on the Options button. Another dialog box, Macro Options, appears. Here is where you can assign a keyboard shortcut.

PART

III

Analyzing with Excel

4. Ensure that the insertion point is in the Shortcut Key text box area.

5. Press the keys that you want to use in combination with the Ctrl key as the short-cut for your macro. For example, to assign the keyboard combination Ctrl+Shift+N (N=Name) to the sample macro we created, hold down the Shift key and tap the letter N. (The Ctrl key is already set.) The keys you pressed will appear as the shortcut key, as shown in Figure 24.9.

FIGURE 24.9

The Macro Options dialog box allows you to assign a shortcut key after the macro has been created.

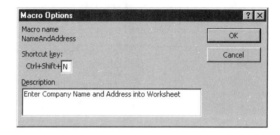

6. Click on OK in the Macro Options dialog box.

7. Click on the Cancel button in the Macro dialog box.

8. Once you return to the worksheet, click on a blank cell and press your shortcut key combination (such as Ctrl+Shift+N) to activate your macro.

Assigning a Macro to a Toolbar or Menu Bar

Follow these steps to assign your macro to its own button on a toolbar or menu item on a menu. You may want to assign all of your macros to a new, custom toolbar instead of placing them on existing toolbars or create a separate menu to hold them.

1. Select Tools ➢ Customize or right-click on a toolbar and select Customize from the shortcut menu.

2. Select the Commands tab and scroll down through the categories until you get to Macros. When you select Macros, you will see Custom Menu Item and Custom Button appear in the Commands list.

3. Drag-and-drop the Custom Button to a toolbar. Close the Customize dialog box. (If you wish to add a custom menu item instead, simply drag Custom Menu Item to a menu and then place it as a menu item when the menu drops down. The remaining steps in this procedure are the same.)

4. Click on your new button. The Assign Macro dialog box opens.

5. Select the name of your macro and click on OK. Your macro can now be activated by clicking its new button on the toolbar.

As mentioned earlier, this sample macro only works for the current workbook. When you close this workbook and try to access the macro in a new workbook, it is not available through the Tools ➢ Macro dialog box. If you assigned the macro to a shortcut key, it would not be available in other workbooks—only the original one in which it was created.

The one exception is when you have assigned the macro to a button on a toolbar or menu bar, and then click on the button or menu item while in a new workbook. Excel loads the workbook that contained the macro and then activates the macro on the new workbook. In other words, you now have two workbooks in memory: the workbook on the screen and the workbook that contains the macro. Select Window from the menu bar to see the name of your other workbook that contains the macro.

Creating Worksheet Buttons for Macros

You can also create your own custom command button objects that appear directly on the worksheet instead of on a toolbar. Follow these steps to assign a macro to a worksheet button:

1. Display the Forms toolbar by selecting View ➢ Toolbars ➢ Forms from the menu bar or point to any toolbar, right-click, and select Forms.
2. On the Forms toolbar, click on the Button icon.
3. Position the mouse pointer where you want the button to appear on your worksheet. Click and drag a box across one column and down three rows. When you release the mouse button, Excel displays the Assign Macro dialog box. Your screen should look similar to the one shown in Figure 24.10.
4. When the Assign Macro dialog box appears, select the name of your macro from the list or begin recording a new macro by clicking on the Record button on the right side of the dialog box. If you are assigning an existing macro, click on OK after selecting the macro name. The button is on the worksheet, and it is selected, as you can tell by the sizing handles around the button. The generic name *Control 1* appears.
5. Drag across the generic name and type a more appropriate name for the button. (Don't press Enter while you're typing the name, unless you want two lines of text on the button.)
6. Click on another part of the worksheet to move away from the button.
7. Test the button by clicking on an empty cell and clicking on the button. Notice that the mouse pointer changes to a hand pointing a finger. When you click on the button, the macro runs.

You can assign a macro to a worksheet button by using the Forms toolbar's Button choice.

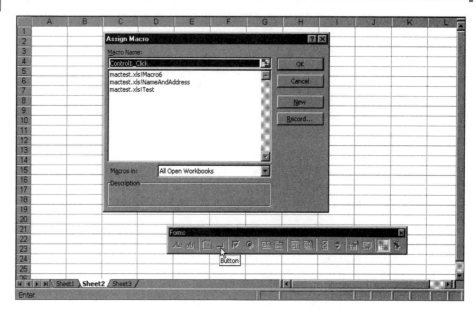

After you've created a worksheet button, you can change it, but you need to select it first. You cannot just click on the button, because that activates the macro. Hold down the Ctrl key while you click on the button, and you will be in edit mode for that button. You can change it in the following ways:

- To change its name, click on the name, delete it, and then type a new name.
- To resize the button, pull on the small, gray boxes called sizing handles that surround the button.
- To move the button, point to any edge of the button (in between the sizing handles). The pointer changes to a white arrow with four smaller arrows pointing in different directions. Drag the button to another location.
- To reassign another macro to the button, hold down Ctrl and right-click it, then select Assign Macro from the shortcut menu.

When you're finished making changes to the worksheet button, click on a blank cell or press Esc.

Editing Macros

If you discover a mistake in one of your macros (such as a typo in our sample company name macro), you can rerecord the entire series of keystrokes again, or you can edit the macro code directly. The macro is written in VBA programming language and resides in a module that can be viewed using the Visual Basic Editor (VBE).

To see and edit your macro, select Tools ➤ Macro ➤ Visual Basic Editor from the menu bar. You could also press Alt+F11, which is the shortcut key combination that switches to the VBE (see Figure 24.11). If you are not in the workbook that contains the macro, select Tools ➤ Macro ➤ Macros, select your macro, and click on Edit.

FIGURE 24.11

To edit your macros, use the Visual Basic Editor.

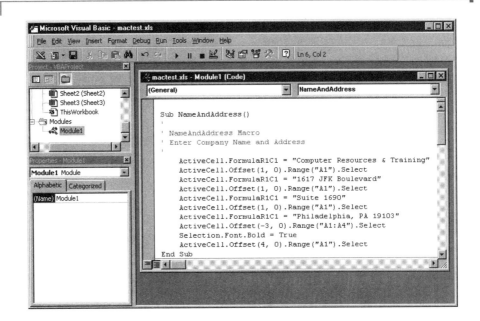

The VBE comprises three different windows. The Project window lists all of the current projects that are open. Your workbook is a VBA project. Other projects you will see include add-ins that are installed with Excel to enhance its capabilities.

You may also see a Properties window. The Properties window allows you to view and edit the properties of whatever object is currently selected, whether it be a project, a worksheet, or the module in which your macro is stored.

The largest window will contain the module that holds your macro; it should be to the right and take up most of the space. There are three main sections to Module window. The largest section stores the code and two combo boxes that control what you see in the main section. The first combo box will have General selected. For our purposes, don't change that text box. The second text box is the Procedure text box. If you click on the drop-down arrow for this combo box you should see your macro in the list. Select it to see its code in the main section of this window.

Once your macro is selected you should see Sub NameAndAddress( ), followed by some lines of code and then End Sub. The total of your macro resides within the Sub and End Sub lines. Quickly glancing over the code, and knowing what you do about how it was created, you can get an idea of what it will do. You will notice that there are

PART

III

Analyzing with Excel

words enclosed in quotation marks following equals signs. As you can guess, the words in quotes are the words you typed for your NameAndAddress macro when you were recording it.

Click into the module window, modify the text in between the quotes (for example, to fix typos), and switch back to Excel by selecting File ➤ Return to Microsoft Excel from the menu bar. When you run the macro again, the changes you made in the VBE will be used.

WARNING
Unless you know the VBA programming language, do not make any changes to the macro code. Just edit the text that you typed for the macro, such as your own company information. For more information about working with VBA, see the Sybex book, *Excel 97 Macro & VBA Handbook* by Lonnie Moseley and David Boodey.

Storing Global Macros

Excel gives you the ability to record and store global macros. You can create your own macro library full of commonly used macros to use on all workbooks. Global macros are stored in a Personal Macro workbook. The first time you create a global, personal macro, Excel creates this hidden workbook, which is stored in the Xlstart folder. The workbook actually stays in memory but is hidden.

Creating a Global Macro

Our sample company name macro cannot become a global, personal macro after the fact. You must select the option to make the macro global before you begin recording it. In the following steps, we will rerecord another version of our company name macro as a global, personal macro.

1. Start a new workbook or select a blank cell range on the workbook that is currently on the screen.
2. Select Tools ➤ Macro ➤ Record New Macro.
3. In the Record Macro dialog box, type a name for the new macro (don't use the same exact name that you used for the earlier sample macro, because we want to keep the original macro for now). As always, enter a description for your macro.
4. Select Personal Macro Workbook in the Store Macro In combo box (see Figure 24.12) and click on OK. In the worksheet, you will see that the Macro Recorder is on. The Stop Recording toolbar should be visible and the word *Recording* should appear on the Status bar. Be sure that the Relative Reference button on the Stop Recording toolbar is pressed.
5. Type your company name and address. Select the cells and make them bold. Then click on the blank row below the company name and address cells.

FIGURE 24.12

To create a global macro, select the Personal Macro Workbook as the location to store it.

6. Click on the Stop Recording button or select Tools ➢ Macro ➢ Stop Recording.
7. To run this macro, select Tools ➢ Macro ➢ Macros from the menu bar. The name of the global, personal macro is listed (see Figure 24.13).
8. Select the macro and click on Run.

FIGURE 24.13

Select your global macro from the Macro dialog box.

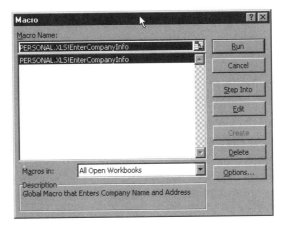

Assigning and Editing Global Macros

You can assign a global, personal macro to a menu item, shortcut key, toolbar button, or worksheet button in the same way that you assign shortcuts for local workbook macros (described earlier in this chapter).

To edit the global macro, however, you must first unhide its workbook. Select Window ➢ Unhide from the menu bar. When the Unhide dialog box appears, select Personal. Click on OK to unhide the workbook with your global macro.

Once the Personal Macro workbook is unhidden, Excel displays the workbook which contains one worksheet called Sheet 1. To view the macros for the Personal Workbook, press Alt+F11 or select Tools ➤ Macro ➤ Visual Basic Editor from the menu bar. In the Projects window you will see the VBAProject(PERSONAL.XLS). Below the project is a Modules folder—you may need to use the scroll bar to see it—containing Module1, where the macro you recorded is stored. If the Module window is not already open, double-click on Module1 to open the module to view your macro. You can make your changes to the global macro in the Module window, select File ➤ Save PERSONAL.XLS to make your changes permanent, and close the Visual Basic Editor to return to Excel.

Rehide the Personal Macro workbook by selecting Window ➤ Hide from the menu bar. The workbook is immediately hidden back into memory.

NOTE You can hide any workbook that is active on the screen by selecting Window ➤ Hide from the menu bar. Be careful, because you might forget that you hid your workbook, and you may waste time looking around your desk for it. Use Window ➤ Unhide to make any of your hidden workbooks visible.

Creating Print Macros Using VBA

One of the most common requests for macros in a spreadsheet program is to print various ranges of data. The actual values may change weekly or monthly, but the area of the spreadsheet where the data resides does not change. In other spreadsheet programs, you can create names for these print ranges and design a quick macro that prints a specific range. It is just as easy to do similar tasks in Excel, but the use of the VBA programming language is necessary.

So far in this chapter, you have learned how to record macros and view the code on the Module sheets. In this next example, you will write the code from the beginning, without recording the macro first, and then assign the macros to worksheet buttons.

Writing the Macros

The following VBA print macro requires you to have four print ranges defined with range names.

1. In the workbook that contains the various print ranges, select (highlight) the first print range and click on the Name box above the A column. Type a name (no spaces are allowed) and press Enter. You can also select Insert ➤ Name ➤ Define, type a name for the range (we'll use Qtr1 in this example), and click on OK.

2. Repeat the process described in step 1 to define three more print range names. (The range names Qtr2, Qtr3, and Qtr4 are used in this example.)

To delete a range name, select Insert ➢ Name ➢ Define. Select the name, click on Delete, and click on OK.

3. Select Tools ➢ Macro ➢ Macros to open the Macro dialog box. Type PrintQuarter-One in the Macro Name text box and click on Create.

4. The Visual Basic Editor opens with the first and last lines of your new macro. The following lines of code should be entered between the Sub **PrintQuarterOne** line and the End Sub line.

You are now ready to write your lines of code. A subroutine reference must precede the name of each macro. Each macro must have a unique name. The name must be followed by parentheses.

5. Insert a line after Sub PrintQuarterOne() and type the following:

```
Range("Qtr1").PrintOut Preview:=True
```

This line says "On the Range defined as 'Qtr1,' perform the PrintOut method or action." The range name is in quotation marks because quotation marks represent literal text that is typed. The macro name is not in quotation marks. The optional parameter of Preview is set to TRUE so that the printout will appear on the screen before it is printed to the printer. You will remove this optional parameter after you test the macros.

6. Switch back to Excel and repeat steps 3 through 5 for each of the three remaining ranges, substituting "Qtr1" with the appropriate name. Figure 24.14 shows the four macros in the Module window of the Visual Basic Editor.

7. Save the workbook.

8. Select Tools ➢ Macro ➢ Macros. You will see your new macros listed in the Macro dialog box, as shown in Figure 24.15.

9. Select the name of the print macro you wish to preview and click on Run. Repeat to test each of the macros.

10. After you have tested the macros and are sure they work as you intended, remove the Preview:=True statement from each macro so that the macro prints directly to a printer. To edit the macro to remove the statement, select Tools ➢ Macro ➢ Macros, select the name of the macro, and click on Edit.

PART

III

Analyzing with Excel

FIGURE 24.14

The print macros print four different print ranges. These macros can be assigned to buttons on a worksheet, toolbar, or menu bar.

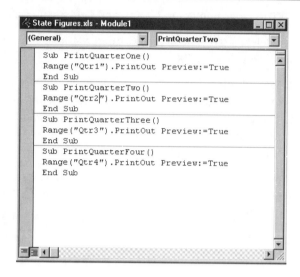

FIGURE 24.15

The Macro dialog box displays the names of each of your subroutines, just as if you had recorded the macros.

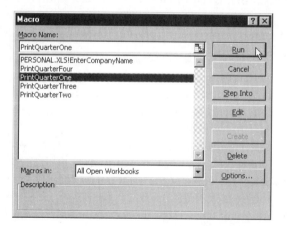

Now that you have created and debugged your macros, you can assign each one to a worksheet button for easy access. Follow the steps outlined earlier in the chapter for assigning macros to the toolbars and menu bars.

This chapter has described how to customize toolbars and automate your work with macros. The next chapter is about integrating your work in Excel with other Office 97 applications.

Chapter

25

Office Connections—Handling a Table That Keeps on Growing

FEATURING

Office Connections—Handling a Table That Keeps on Growing

Microsoft Office is known for its enhanced ability to integrate data from multiple applications. In Chapter 14, we focused on linking files between Word and Excel and Word and PowerPoint.

The example in this chapter demonstrates how you can integrate a "simple" project that starts in Word, expands to Excel, and finally finds a true home in Access. You'll learn more about Access and its query and reporting features in Part Six.

The Project's Route through the Office

Renee is a marketing specialist for Washington-based Entertainment Television. One of her projects involves developing a table that lists focus group participants and their preferences about the show. She needs to track the focus group dates, the questions asked, and the names and demographics (for example, age, sex, income, and marital status) of participants.

Renee initially creates the table in Word. She uses Word's Database toolbar and buttons to create a database form. Then she uses the sort buttons on the toolbar to quickly organize her data.

As the table grows, individuals in her department begin to depend more and more on the information it contains. The table continues to expand as columns of new data are added. It becomes obvious that Renee needs to move the table to another program that allows her to add new categories of information more easily. She decides to move the table to Excel.

As more focus groups are conducted, the table continues to grow. Renee learns to use the Access data-entry form. Eventually, the table becomes too unwieldy to manipulate in Excel. Renee's colleagues are asking more questions about the data than Excel can answer with its current tools. It's obvious that the query and reporting features of Access are needed by the department members, so Renee exports the table to Access. Her coworkers praise her efficient data management skills.

Many times a project "evolves." At the start of a project, it is hard to predict how the project will grow over time. Renee's information eventually had to be organized differently, and her single table divided into multiple related tables. Mass mailings are now conducted on the data using Word form letters. The process comes full circle. Let's get started and follow Renee's route around the Office.

Creating a Database in Word

Word's Table feature is ideal for managing columnar and row information. A Word table is used as the data source for the mail merge feature because it can organize information in database-type fields and records.

Follow these steps to create a Word database:

1. Create a new file in Word.

2. To change the page orientation to landscape (to allow for ten columns of information), select File ➤ Page Setup and click on the Paper Size tab. Select the Landscape option.

3. To change the margins, select the Margins tab and set all four margins to **.5**, as shown in Figure 25.1. Click on OK in the Page Setup dialog box.

4. To create the table, select Table ➤ Insert Table. In the dialog box, click the up spinner buttons and change the settings to **10** columns and **10** rows. Click on OK.

5. Enter the following column headings into the first row, using the Tab key to move from column to column (use Shift+Tab to move backward from right to left):

   Focus Group Name, **Date of Group**, **Last Name**, **First Name**, **Gender**, **Date of Birth**, **Marital Status**, **Income**, **Race**, and **Address**

6. Click on the row of column headings, and then select Table ➤ Select Row. Click on the Bold and the Center buttons on the Formatting toolbar.

FIGURE 25.1

Setting the margins for a table with landscape orientation

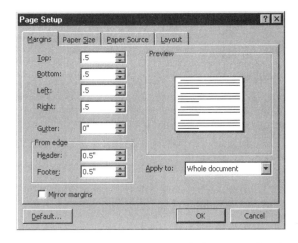

7. Click on the second row of the first column below your first heading, and select View ➤ Toolbars ➤ Database.

8. Click on the Data Form button, the first button on the Database toolbar. A data form appears, as shown in Figure 25.2. Click the on Add New button.

FIGURE 25.2

Use this data entry form to transform a Word table into a simple database.

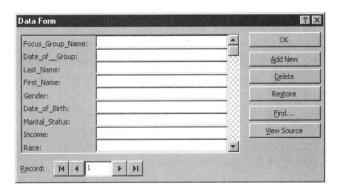

9. Enter some sample records to represent Renee's data.

Focus Group Name	**Diana Ross, comeback tour**
Date of Group	**8/1/96**
Last Name	**Frierson**

PART

III

Analyzing with Excel

First Name	**Mary**
Gender	**F**
Date of Birth	**8/23/35**
Marital Status	**S**
Income	**37,000**
Race	**B**
Address	**Stover Ave., DC**

10. Click on the Add New button or press Enter when you have typed the information into the last field of the data form.

> **NOTE**
>
> If you use the table and not the form to type the information, press the Tab key on the last column and last row to add a new, blank row. To move from the data form to the table, click on the View Source button in the Data Form dialog box. To return to the form, click on the first button on the Database toolbar.

Sorting a Word Database

Once the data is in a Word table, separated in columns and rows, you can organize it with the Database toolbar's sort buttons. If this toolbar is not on your screen, select View ➤ Toolbars and check the Database option.

If you are in the Data Form, click on View Source to return to the table. Click on the Last Name column of the table, making sure that you do not select the entire table. Click on the Sort Ascending button (A to Z). Select the Date of Group column and click on the Sort Descending button (Z to A).

You can also use the Sort dialog box, shown in Figure 25.3, to sort by different columns at once. Use the Table ➤ Sort command to get to this dialog box.

Copying Word Tables to Excel

When a table outgrows Word, you can transfer it to Excel. This is a simple copy-and-paste operation. The table does not need to be linked, because it will no longer be managed in Word. Here are the steps to copy and paste the Word table:

1. To select the Word table, click on any cell of the table and select Table ➤ Select Table, or hold down Alt and press 5 on the number pad at the right side of the keyboard (Num Lock must be on).

FIGURE 25.3

You can use Word's Sort dialog box to sort by multiple fields.

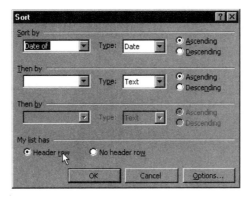

2. Copy the table information into the Clipboard (click on the Copy button on the Standard toolbar or press Ctrl+C).

3. If Excel has not been launched, click on the Start button on the Taskbar and select Programs. Click on the Excel program menu item to launch the program.

4. Make sure the pointer is in cell A1 on a blank worksheet in Excel. Click on the Paste button on the Standard toolbar or select Edit ➤ Paste from the menu. The Word table flows into the columns and rows (see Figure 25.4). Widen the columns as needed.

FIGURE 25.4

The Word table copied to Excel

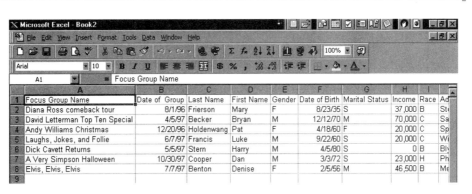

PART

III

Analyzing with Excel

5. Before continuing, save the Excel file under the name Focus Group Data (select File ➤ Save or press Ctrl+S).

Using Access Wizards in Excel

As new columns are added to a table, it becomes more difficult to fill in the data horizontally across the wide rows. An Access data-entry form makes it easier to enter more records. From Excel, you can initiate the Access Form Wizard and set up your form in a few steps. You can also use the Access Report Wizard to design sophisticated reports for your Excel data.

Using the Access Form Wizard

The Access Wizards are options on Excel's Data menu. If you do not see them, select Tools ➤ Add-Ins from the Excel menu bar, check AccessLinks Add-In, and click on OK. Once you have the Access Wizards available, follow these steps to create the Access data entry form:

1. With the cursor in any cell of the Focus Group Data, select Data (MS Access Form) from the menu. If you did not save your Excel file before choosing to create an Access form, Excel will prompt you to do so.

2. In the Create Microsoft Access Form dialog box, make sure that the New Database option button is selected. Make sure the Header row button at the bottom of the dialog box is selected. The first row of column headings is considered the header row, and these headings will be the field names used on the Access form. Figure 25.5 shows the dialog box with these settings. Click on OK to begin designing the form.

FIGURE 25.5

Create the form in a new database and specify that your list has a header row.

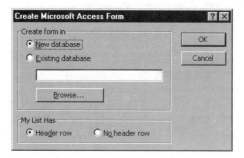

You may need to wait a minute or more for your Access connections from Excel.

3. Access welcomes you to the Access Form Wizard and allows you to select particular fields to be used for data entry. Because you need all of the fields on the form, click on the >> button to copy all of the fields to the Selected Fields box on the right. Click on Next.

4. The Access Form Wizard asks you to select a layout for your form. Select Columnar (you can click on the other layout choices and see a preview of each before you make your final selection). Click on Next to continue.

5. Select the International style for your data form. The fields of your Excel sheet will appear against a background of a world map. Click on Next.

6. Type a name for your data-entry form and select the *Open the form to view or enter information* option. Then click on Finish.

The finished form is attractive and easy to use. Use the Access toolbar buttons to sort and filter your data. See Part Six for information about using the Access program.

NOTE

When you are finished viewing or entering data in your Access form, close Access. After the last column of data in the Excel file, you will see an Access form button. Whenever you want to use your data-entry form, click on the View MS Access Form button to launch the form you just designed.

Using the Access Report Wizard

In addition to creating an Access data-entry form, you can use the Access Report Wizard to design a sophisticated report from your Excel data. Here are the general steps for using the Report Wizard:

1. Save your Excel data and make sure your pointer is within the data area.

2. Select Data ➤ MS Access Report from the menu bar.

3. In the Access Report Wizard dialog box, select the fields you want on the report. Click on Next to move to the next screen.

4. The Access Report Wizard asks if you would like to have the data on the report grouped by a particular field. For this example, select Gender as the field for grouping.

5. The Access Report Wizard asks you to select a sort order. Click on the drop-down arrow next to item 1 and select the Focus Group Name field. The report will be grouped by the Gender field, and within that field, the names will be sorted by the group names. You can have up to four sort fields in the report. Click on Next to continue.

6. The Access Report Wizard asks you to select a layout for your report. Select the Outline1 layout. Click on Next.

7. Your next step is to specify a typeface and font style for the report. For this example, select the Compact style. (You can select each of the style types and see a preview before making your final selection.) Click on Next after you make your selection.

8. When you are at the "Finish" line, the Access Wizard asks for a name for the report. Type in a descriptive name and click on Finish.

Excel to Access—The Final Transition

The connections to Access from an Excel file are certainly helpful, but they are also slow. After Renee, our marketing specialist, became comfortable with the Access data entry form and the Access report, it made sense to move the entire table to Access. The powerful tools provided by Access are appreciated by everyone in the department who uses the focus group table. Renee saves Access queries and reports so that users can run them simply by clicking on the objects she creates. Access' powerful relational database capabilities allow Renee to divide her data into smaller, more manageable tables as she begins to reinterview the same people during different focus groups.

Converting Excel data to an Access database is a quick and straightforward process. Here are the steps:

1. Save your worksheet data. Then select Data ➤ Convert to MS Access from the menu bar.

2. In the Convert to Microsoft Access dialog box, select the New database option. Click on OK.

3. Select the First Row Contains Column Headings option to let Access know that the column headings are to be used as the field names for the database. Click on Next to continue.

4. Access then asks if you want to store the data in a new table or an existing table. Select In a New Table and click on Next.

5. The next dialog box will allow you to provide details about each field. For each field you will be able to assign a new name, choose to have Access create an index on the table using the field, choose a data type if applicable, or completely skip the particular field when importing and not include it in the Access table. For this exercise leave all of the fields at their default settings and click on Next.

6. A primary key is an index that specifies a field or combination of fields that are unique for each record in a table. You can elect to have Access create the primary key, you can choose a field to be the primary key, or you can choose not to have one created at this time. Let Access create the primary key and click on Next.

7. This is all the information that Access needs to convert your data. When you are prompted for the table name, accept the default name or type a more descriptive one. Then click on Finish. You will be alerted when the Wizard completes the conversion of your worksheet into an Access table.

NOTE

If you want Access to analyze your table once it is imported, you can check *I would like a Wizard to analyze my table after importing the data.* Once the data is imported, an Access Wizard will review your table and make suggestions as to what you could do to better organize your data. '

8. Click on OK to continue.

9. Double-click on the name you gave to the table, and your Access table will appear.

After the data has been converted, you can begin using Access commands to query and report on the data. See Part Six for more information.

Mail Merging with Access Data

It is the start of a new year, and Renee wants to invite the participants from last year's focus groups to participate in a new round of discussions. Letters must be sent to all of the participants. Once again, the focus group data is being managed through Word, but at another level of operation. Renee now uses Word to design form letters to send to the focus group members. The data resides in Access, however, not in Word or Excel.

Word allows Renee to design and format the letter to be printed on snappy, special marketing letterhead. Word's Mail Merge Helper guides her through the process of merging the names of the focus group participants with the letter.

In Step 1 of the Mail Merge Helper (Tools ➤ Mail Merge), Renee designs the letter. In Step 2, she selects to open the Access Focus Group database as her data source and add any of the fields to the letter. In Step 3, she merges the letter with her Access table. For a more detailed discussion of using Mail Merge Helper in Word, see Chapter 47, the Office Connections chapter of Access.

As you have seen in this example, Office 97's flexibility and power allow for productivity gains. Small applications can grow and move into more sophisticated tools as your knowledge of the Office suite grows.

PART

III

Analyzing with Excel

PART — IV

Presenting with PowerPoint

- *Create impressive presentations easily*

- *Add multimedia to your presentations*

- *Give your presentation in person or online*

- *Use templates to create presentations easily*

- *Take your presentation on the road*

- *Turn your presentation into a Web page*

Chapter

26

Road Map—Jump Start
into PowerPoint

Road Map—Jump Start into PowerPoint

Before presentation software became available, speakers and meeting leaders relied heavily on professional printers and graphics designers to outline, edit, and create graphical representations for visual aids. Often it took several weeks between original concept and final design to take all the necessary steps, which cost hundreds or even thousands of dollars. Most large organizations established their own graphics design departments for in-house manufacturing of presentations. Not only did this offer employees a great convenience, it helped keep confidential information from having to leave the premises.

Today with PowerPoint, anyone can create a complete slide show presentation. Instead of taking weeks to complete a presentation, you can organize an entire conference within a few hours. No longer is security an issue, since one person can design and implement the entire presentation from one computer, without any need for outside organizations. And if your work is part of a team effort, PowerPoint can help you merge everybody's best ideas into one effective presentation.

Main Features of PowerPoint

To maximize your presentation potential with PowerPoint, you must first be familiar with the parts that make up the PowerPoint whole. The next few sections provide the information you need.

Slides

Anyone who has taken a class or attended a meeting where an overhead projector was used is familiar with slides. The term *slides,* in the context of PowerPoint, refers to the individual pages of your presentation. You can use the pages, or slides, for on-screen presentations that take advantage of animation features or to print as transparencies or slides. Figure 26.1 shows a basic PowerPoint slide.

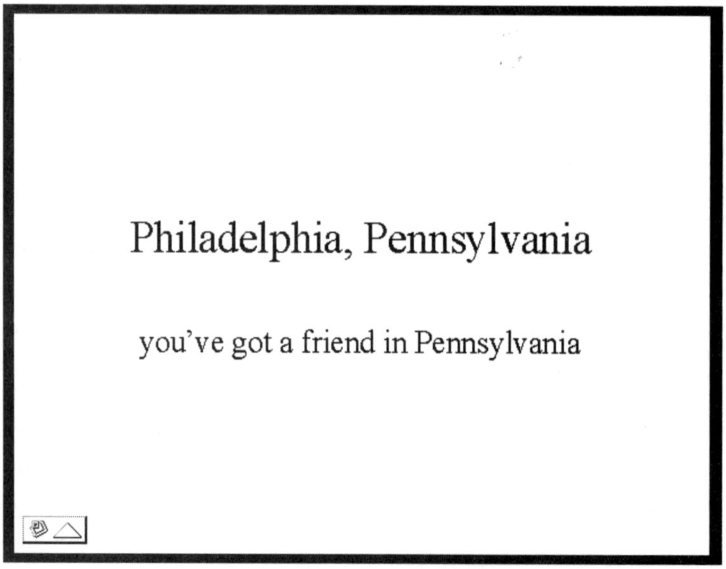

FIGURE 26.1

A sample slide as it appears in PowerPoint

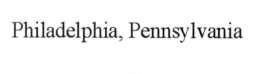

Philadelphia, Pennsylvania

you've got a friend in Pennsylvania

With PowerPoint 97, you can turn those slides into Web pages, enabling your clients, coworkers, friends, and family to visit your presentation online.

Speaker Notes

Speaker Notes are designed to assist the speaker in a presentation. If you have spent time sifting through note cards during a speech, you know the anxiety that can occur without organization. PowerPoint handles the organizing for you. With each slide, you can create a complete set of notes, as detailed or basic as you like, from a complete script to just a general outline. The audience does not see the notes, but they are printed for the speaker's use. Accessing Speaker Notes is as easy as this:

1. Select View ➤ Notes Page from the menu bar.
2. Use the bottom block to type any notes you will need for your presentation.

Figure 26.2 shows the Speaker Notes for the slide in Figure 26.1.

FIGURE 26.2

*Speaker Notes
for the slide in
Figure 26.1*

PowerPoint 97 makes Speaker Notes easier to use than ever; you simply type the notes you want to add and PowerPoint does the rest. You can type the notes directly onto the bottom of the Notes Page, as the preceding steps illustrated, or you can use the Speaker Notes option in the View menu to display a 3 x 5 card on which you can enter your notes. It's really as simple as making a few note cards. The great thing is that the notes never get separated from your presentation; they are saved in the file, attached to their corresponding slide. And once you've created the notes, you can reuse them by using the text in Lotus Notes or saving the notes in a Word document.

Return to the Slide view of your presentation by selecting View ➤ Slide from the menu bar.

What's the Difference between Notes Page and Speaker Notes?

PowerPoint gives you two different methods for annotating your presentation. In Notes Page view, one of the standard views in which you can display your slides, the slide is at the top and room for note-taking is at the bottom. You can add notes simply by clicking on the bottom portion of the page and typing.

When you enter Speaker Notes for a specific page, you do so by choosing View ➤ Speaker Notes. A small dialog box appears so you can enter the notes you need. When you close the dialog box by clicking on Close, PowerPoint automatically attaches the note to the slide. When you view the slide in Notes Page view, the note you entered using Speaker Notes will be visible there.

TIP

The view items on the menu bar correspond with the view buttons at the bottom left of the PowerPoint window. If you want to switch quickly to one of the views, you can click on the buttons instead of going through the menu bar.

Organization Charts

You can use organization charts in a presentation to visually display the hierarchical structure of a company, organization, or even a conceptual design. In the past, special programs were needed to create organizational charts, but with PowerPoint, you can easily create these charts and incorporate them into slides or export them to other applications in Office 97. Figure 26.3 shows an example of an organizational chart created in PowerPoint.

Media Clips

The term *media clips* includes the sound, animation, and video clips you may want to insert into your presentation. Once you have inserted a media clip into a slide, you can activate it with a simple click while viewing your presentation. Whether you want to play a message from the chairman in a company meeting or take a tour of your state-of-the-art facility in a sales demonstration, media clips can really pump up your presentation. New picture editing capabilities and features that help you create your

FIGURE 26.3

*Organizational
chart in a slide*

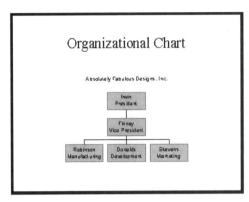

own animation bring even more sparkle to your work. Figure 26.4 shows a media clip
waiting to be activated.

FIGURE 26.4

*A media clip
waiting to be
activated: Click-
ing on the
image will acti-
vate a live-
action video.*

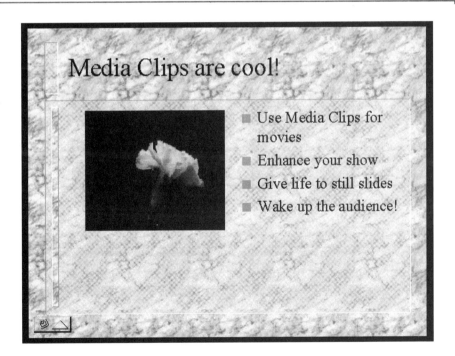

Graphs

Nothing shows sales trends better than a graph. You can insert graphs into your slides to add visual punch to the numbers you want to get across to your audience. Power-Point uses Microsoft Graph and all its available formats, including three-dimensional formatting (see Figure 26.5). And Microsoft Graph 97 now offers additional chart types and graph animation capabilities. Another new feature enables you to literally "grow" your chart right in front of your audience. By animating chart elements, you can lengthen or shorten bars, lines, and areas on the chart, showing sales trends and capturing your audience's attention at the same time.

FIGURE 26.5

A three-dimensional graph showing the increase in sales over five years

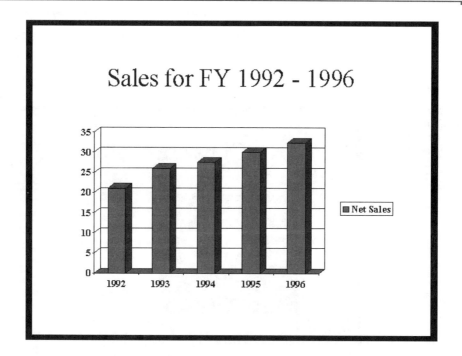

Clip Art

Whether you use the collection of clip art that comes with PowerPoint or decide to supplement your library with one or more of the innumerable libraries available through other sources, clip art is a nice way to add descriptive visuals to your presentations. If you don't overuse it, clip art helps you emphasize the points you are trying to make. When appropriate, many of the clip art selections can also add a bit of levity to your presentation. The new Microsoft ClipArt Gallery 3.0 enables you to share clip art with other Office applications more easily than ever. Figure 26.6 shows a slide that uses clip art from PowerPoint.

FIGURE 26.6

A slide filled with a number of samples from PowerPoint's clip art collection

Web Pages

Presentation slides are perfect for generating Web pages. Once you add the text, graphics, and charts in the format you like, you can save your slide as an HTML (HyperText Markup Language) document, ready for use on the World Wide Web.

Views in PowerPoint

PowerPoint consists of multiple views to help you in the creation, presentation, and maintenance of your presentations. The various views, which you access through View on the menu bar or the View buttons at the bottom left of the PowerPoint window, are described in the following sections.

Slide

Slide view is the default view when you open PowerPoint. Think of Slide view as a picture of your slide as it will appear when printed or shown in the slide show. Only one slide is visible at a time in Slide view.

Choose Your View

One of the great things about PowerPoint is the flexibility it offers you in the way you create your presentation. You are sure to find a view that fits you best. Some people think best in outlines; others think best in visuals.

If you find yourself relying on to-do lists, feeling more comfortable when you've got the basic game-plan of a meeting, or getting more done when you outline your plan of action first, chances are you'll like structure your presentation using Outline view. With Outline view, you can write the basic presentation in a matter of minutes and then go back and consider, slide by slide, what visual elements you want to add.

If you think visually, accessing what's needed and what's missing by considering images, balance, color, and format, working in Slide view will give you the creative space in which to work. With Slide view, you can "slop on" text, charts, and images like a painter puts paint on a canvas, removing what doesn't work and building on what does.

Outline

Outline view provides an organized way to view your slides in the order in which they will appear in your presentation. Using Outline view, you can step back and look at the big picture of the message you will be trying to get across. Figure 26.7 shows a slide presentation in Outline view.

Notice the numbers that appear to the left of each slide. These numbers represent the order of the slides in the presentation. The small Slide icon next to each number represents a slide. The new addition of the Slide Miniature window shows you what the current slide will look like in Slide view.

FIGURE 26.7

Sample outline for a slide presentation

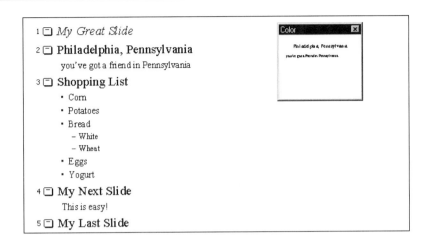

TIP

Double-clicking on a slide listed in Outline view allows you to jump back quickly to Slide view.

Slide Sorter

Slide Sorter provides a more detailed view than Outline view, which shows only the text and titles of slides. Slide Sorter view shows the completed slides as they will appear in the presentation. The number at the lower right of each slide indicates the order in which it will appear.

In addition to showing slides in their completed form, Slide Sorter view lets you change the presentation order. For instance, moving Slide 1 after Slide 2 in Slide Sorter view reverses the order in which they will appear.

Slide Sorter view not only allows for changes in slide order, it permits you to create effects for the slide show. For instance, suppose you want to include a repeating element on each slide, like a special design box, but throughout the presentation, you want to move the box from left to right across the screen, a little at a time. By viewing the presentation in Slide Sorter view, you can see where your design box is positioned in each slide and make adjustments as necessary. Figure 26.8 shows the example presentation in Slide Sorter view. You can also add sound to a slide, enhancing your presentation.

FIGURE 26.8

The slide presentation in Slide Sorter view

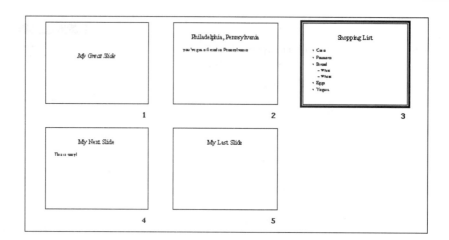

Notes Page

Notes Page view allows you to see both your notes and the slide that will be viewed during a presentation at the same time. You might use Notes Page, for example, to help you remember key points you want to stress. You could also print handouts that include your notes and circulate them among team members to get your group's input before the big meeting. Figure 26.9 shows a slide with its notes in Notes Page view.

FIGURE 26.9

A slide with its notes in Notes Page view

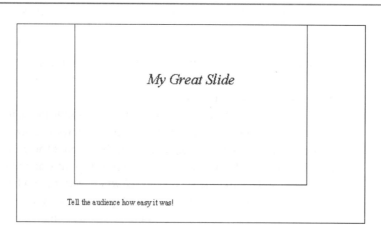

Slide Show

Slide Show view for your presentations is equivalent to Print Preview in Word for documents. When in Slide Show view, you are completely out of design mode; you see the slide as your audience will. In fact, if you want to take advantage of the animation effects of PowerPoint, you will need to use Slide Show view instead of the PowerPoint Viewer to give your on-screen presentations.

Design Tips for PowerPoint

Although PowerPoint provides you with some very powerful tools to give top-notch presentations, making the wrong design choices can defeat all your efforts. Making the right decisions is not difficult. By following the guidelines below and taking time to step back and look at your slides with a critical eye, you will be on your way to bringing your audiences to their feet.

- Pick fonts your audience can read easily. Fancy fonts are fine if they are readable, but use them mainly for emphasis.
- Use clear, easy-to-understand language in your slides. Remember to keep it simple and to the point.
- Choose font and screen colors that will contrast enough to be viewed at a distance and in low light.
- If you use symbols, graphics, or sound effects, make sure they are appropriate and easy to identify.
- Remember, less is more. Don't overburden your audience with many slides when just a few are needed.

Launching PowerPoint

Launch PowerPoint by choosing Start ➤ Programs ➤ Microsoft PowerPoint. Remember, you can always create a shortcut icon on your desktop to launch PowerPoint directly. Refer to Chapter 2 for the specifics of how to do this.

Starting with a Blank Presentation

When you begin PowerPoint, you see a dialog box that asks whether you want to open an existing presentation or use the AutoContent Wizard, a template, or a blank presentation, as shown in Figure 26.10. To start a new presentation from scratch, choose Blank Presentation.

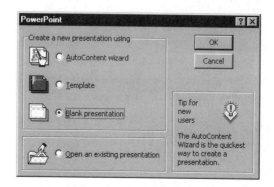

When you first start PowerPoint, the default is Template. If you've used PowerPoint previously, the default is the option you used last. All the options are listed here:

AutoContent Wizard—Select this option to take advantage of the Wizards in PowerPoint; you'll get help at every step along the way in creating a new presentation.

Template—If you want to create a new presentation using one of the several presentation templates included with PowerPoint or, perhaps, using a template of your own, choose Template on startup. This choice is ideal for those who get writer's block when looking at a blank piece of paper.

Blank Presentation—Just as the name implies, there are no templates, master slides, notes, or slides included in a blank presentation. You might want to use this option if you have a new approach or if none of the templates suit your needs.

Open an Existing Presentation—Make this choice if you want to work with an existing presentation—for instance, if someone gives you a presentation file to edit or if you have already set up a presentation and want to continue working with it.

> **TIP**
>
> If you are a new PowerPoint user, the AutoContent Wizard is a helpful starting point. Many people like to work for a while with a Wizard, until they have gained experience, and then work from templates or blank presentations.

To choose a blank presentation, click once on the radio button next to Blank Presentation and click on the OK button. When you select Blank Presentation, you will have a new presentation without slides, notes, templates, or outlines. The first thing you need to do is choose the format for your first slide in the New Slide dialog box. From that point on, you add the text, colors, graphics, and multimedia objects that you want on the slide.

If you wish to skip the Startup dialog box every time you open PowerPoint, you can change your startup option by following these steps:

1. After you've started PowerPoint, select Tools ➤ Options from the menu bar.
2. Click once on the Startup dialog checkbox under the Show options in the View tab (shown in Figure 26.11). The check should disappear from the checkbox.
3. Click on OK.

Presenting with
Powerpoint

The View tab of
the Options
dialog box

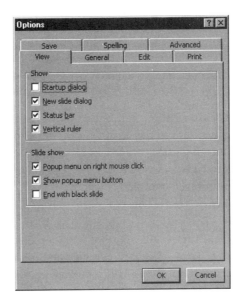

Your changes have now been saved into PowerPoint. From this point forward, each time you start PowerPoint, you will not be asked to open an existing presentation or select one of the other forms for a new presentation. Instead, PowerPoint will automatically default to a blank presentation.

Adding a New Slide

Once you have chosen a blank form for your new presentation, the New Slide dialog box appears on the screen. Again, PowerPoint helps you each step of the way. In this dialog box, shown in Figure 26.12, you are asked to choose how you want the first slide of your presentation to appear.

FIGURE 26.12

PowerPoint prompts you for a format for your first slide.

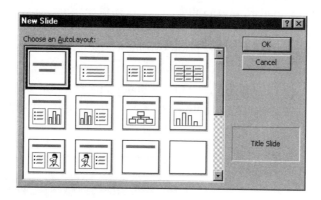

There are 24 different slide layouts from which to choose. You simply make your selection and click on OK. Each choice, described below, dictates how your completed slides will appear.

Title Slide—This option is useful for beginning a presentation or a major section of a presentation; use this slide if you want to include subtitles or smaller text underneath a title.

Bulleted List—Anytime you need to make a list of things that fall underneath a general subject, choose this layout.

2 Column Text—This is a useful option for doing pro/con lists.

Table—This option is perfect for organizing and classifying things.

Text & Chart—This option is good for showing a chart with explanatory text.

Chart & Text—This is a reversed variation of the Text & Chart layout.

Organization Chart—This is a great option for corporate hierarchical structures or flows of command.

Chart—Use this layout if you want to include a graph or chart.

Text & Clip Art—Use this layout to show a graphic with text.

Clip Art & Text—This is a reversed variation of the Text & Clip Art layout.

Title Only—This option is great for the beginning of a presentation; no subtitles are included in this layout.

Blank—Use this layout if you want a blank slide formatted according to the Master Slide.

Text & Object—If you want to include text with a linked object, such as a spreadsheet, graph, or database, choose this layout; it's the perfect choice to take advantage of OLE.

Object & Text—This is a reversed variation of Text & Object layout.

Large Object—This layout allows a large object to be linked to the slide without any text; this format is ideal for workbooks or spreadsheets from Excel.

Object—Use this option to place a title over one linked object.

Text & Media Clip—This layout uses media clips embedded in a slide; media clips can be animation, sound, or video files that you want to embed in a presentation.

Media Clip & Text—This is a reversed variation of the Text & Media Clip layout.

Object over Text—Use this option to place one linked object over text.

2 Objects over Text—This option is a combination of Object over Text and Text & 2 Object layouts.

Text over Object—This is a reversed variation of Object over Text layout.

Text & 2 Objects—This is a variation of Text & Object layout, but with two embedded objects.

2 Objects & Text—This is a reversed variation of Text & 2 Objects layout.

4 Objects—This is a very useful layout if you need to include multiple objects from one or more applications.

If a slide *almost* meets your needs, you can always use it as the foundation for your new slide and then modify it as you see fit.

Possibilities

PowerPoint can bring your presentations alive. Use PowerPoint to graphically present data from a spreadsheet or database. You can create graphs to show sales reports in a more colorful form.

With the multimedia tools, not only can you create a slide show with quotations, you can now embed an actual video movie and sound, as well. Just imagine a presentation in which the CEO of a company not only outlines sales plans for the coming year in text but *talks* to the audience from the company headquarters.

The Pack and Go Wizard lets you save all the files you'll need for your presentation on a disk to take on the road. You can even include a Viewer so you can give your presentation on a computer without PowerPoint.

This is only the beginning. You'll see how powerful PowerPoint is in the following chapters. Don't be afraid to experiment. If you wonder what will happen when you click on a button or choose a layout or template, go ahead and try it. PowerPoint has a multiple-level Undo feature, which you access by clicking the Undo button on the Standard toolbar, that will keep you from making permanent errors. And most importantly, have fun!

Chapter

27

Text Tips and Formats

Text Tips and Formats

Now that you understand the process of creating a presentation, you'll need to know how to work with the text in the presentation. Being able to give a presentation doesn't mean much if there are spelling errors, problems with the text format, incorrect slides, or misplaced text. With PowerPoint, you can be sure that whatever text you create for a presentation, you can always change or enhance it later. No one wants to hear snickering from the audience or be embarrassed because of a spelling error or out-of-date information. Now there's no reason your presentation can't be perfect.

Text and Text Objects

Before we jump into the subject of working with text, you need to understand a few concepts. PowerPoint holds text in text *objects*. All the text contained in a text object is affected by the formatting of the object. Because of this, you can change the way all the text will appear by selecting and formatting the object, or you can select just a few words to change.

If you click on the text in a text object, an *insertion point* (blinking vertical line) appears. However, you can select a text object without getting an insertion point. As shown in Figure 27.1, if you hold down the Shift key as you click on the text, you select the entire object.

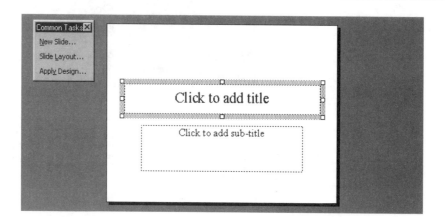

You can always toggle between the text contained in an object and the object itself. To do this, just press F2 after you have selected the text or object.

Editing Text

Editing text in PowerPoint is just a matter of pointing and clicking. As long as you have an insertion point, you can work with the text you have typed or add new text to your slide.

When opening a new slide with text in the layout, you don't have to select the text object to add text. Just begin typing when the slide appears on the screen, and PowerPoint automatically adds the text to the title text object.

Selecting Text

To select any text in an object, click on the desired text. A single-click creates an insertion point for inserting text. A double-click selects an entire word. A triple-click selects an entire paragraph. To select all the text in an object *without* selecting the object itself, press Ctrl+A after clicking on the text object to get an insertion point.

Deleting Text

Once you have selected the text you wish to delete from your slide, you can delete it by pressing the Delete key on your keyboard. If you choose, you can use the Cut button on the Standard toolbar or even select Edit ➢ Cut from the menu bar. Use Ctrl+X as a shortcut to delete text.

If you select Edit ➢ Clear or press the Delete key, you will not be able to paste your deleted text. But remember, if you make a mistake, just click on the Undo button to bring back your text.

Inserting Text

To insert text, click on the position where you need to add text. You will see an insertion point at that location. If you need to move the insertion point, you can use the arrow keys on your keyboard to move the point left, right, up, or down. Once you have placed your insertion point where you want it, type the text you want to insert. If you just need a space between two words, press the spacebar. To add a blank line, press Enter. Any text you insert into a text object will have the same formatting as the text directly to the left of the insertion point.

Although PowerPoint will automatically size a text object for you to fit your text, it cannot become any larger than the slide. If you type too much or if your text is too large, PowerPoint will not enlarge your text object to a size greater than the slide to fit the added text. Unlike Word, PowerPoint cannot create a new slide for you; the text that doesn't fit on your slide will be cropped from the slide, and your audience will not see it. Be careful!

If you have too much text for the object but it will fit on the slide, you can enlarge the text object to fit the text.

Copying Text

Not only can you delete text, you can copy it. To copy, first select the text and then press Ctrl+C. This procedure saves a copy of the text to the Clipboard. Then move your mouse to the location where you want to copy the text. You can copy text to another place in a text object, to a different text object on the same slide, or to another slide in an open presentation. You can also use the Copy button on the Standard toolbar or select Edit ➢ Copy from the menu bar.

Moving Text

You can move text in PowerPoint from one place to another on a single slide or between slides and presentations. If you have a lot of text to move or feel "lost" between your slides, you can use Outline view to move your text between slides. If you have more than one presentation open and need to copy between them, you can select Window from the menu bar to switch between open presentations.

To move text, follow these steps:

1. Select the text you want to move.
2. Cut the text by selecting Edit ➤ Cut from the menu bar or pressing Ctrl + X.
3. If you are moving the text to another slide, move to that slide using the scroll bar at the right of the screen.
4. Click on the text object at the point where you want to insert the text.
5. Select Edit ➤ Paste from the menu bar or pressing Ctrl + V.

If you are moving text to a new location on the same slide, you can highlight the text, hold down the left mouse button, and drag-and-drop it at the new location. If you make a move you aren't happy with, remember that you can easily reverse the action by selecting Edit ➤ Undo or pressing Ctrl+Z.

TIP

If you are planning on moving several lines around, or you want to move text from one page to another, you can move text easily in Outline view. Display the presentation in Outline view and then highlight the text you want to move. Drag the text to the new location and drop it where you want it. The text is moved to the new place

Formatting Text

At times you may want to make a word or sentence stand out from other text. For instance, if you want to indicate a new term used in a presentation, you can choose to make it italic or bold. You can underline words to indicate stress or change the font or color to make the word stand out even more.

When you are creating a presentation, remember to be careful about the size and color of your text. If you want to create 35mm slides, you should use a font that is at least 18 points in size.

> **NOTE**
>
> Because color choice is critical when creating a presentation, PowerPoint has virtually eliminated the guesswork. PowerPoint has chosen colors that work well together, but be careful. If your text and background are too close in color, the text could be invisible during the presentation. It's best to use the actual projection equipment or test print slides before your presentation to make sure the colors will look right.

Italics, Bold, Underline, and Shadow

To format text with italics, bold, underline, or shadow, select the text you want and click on the appropriate toolbar button. You can also use the shortcut keys: Ctrl+I for italic, Ctrl+B for bold, and Ctrl+U for underline. There is no shortcut for shadow.

> **TIP**
>
> If you are unsure how your text is formatted, you can select the text and check the toolbar. If the text is bold, italic, or underlined, the associated button appears depressed or "gray" on the toolbar.

Text Color

You might want to change the color of the text on your slide so it stands out against the background. Be sure the new color doesn't conflict with the background.

To change the color of your text:

1. Select the text you want to color.

2. Click on the arrow beside the Font Color button on the Drawing toolbar.

3. Select the color you want from the palette that pops up.

When choosing a different color for your text, you are not limited to the colors listed in the drop-down palette. If you want to pick another color, follow these steps:

1. Select your text.

2. Click on the Font Color button on the Drawing toolbar.

3. Click on More Font Colors to see the Colors dialog box shown in Figure 27.2.

4. Select the color you want from the hexagon of colors on the Standard tab. As soon as you select the color, your choice is shown in the preview area of the Colors dialog box.

FIGURE 27.2

The Standard tab in the Colors dialog box offers an array of color choices for text.

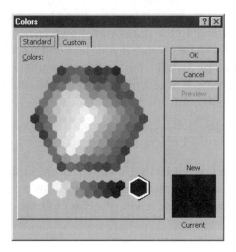

If you don't see a color you like on the hexagon of colors, you can select a specific color from the Custom tab of the Colors dialog box, as shown in Figure 27.3. This option is useful if you have a specific color in mind or if your company uses a particular color scheme. When using custom colors, you can create almost any color in the rainbow. To create a custom color, select the Custom tab from the Colors dialog box. Move the cross hairs until you find your desired color and click on OK.

FIGURE 27.3

You can create almost any color from the Custom tab.

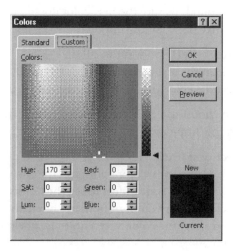

New to PowerPoint 97, you can return text to its original color by clicking on the Font Color button and choosing Automatic from the pop-up palette.

Embossing

You can emboss your text, although you should use this option with caution. It may look impressive on the screen, but it may not print or present as you think it will. Again, test any changes you make to your text before giving your presentation. To emboss your text, select the text you want to emboss, select Format ➤ Font from the menu bar, and click on the Emboss checkbox in the Font dialog box (shown in Figure 27.4).

PART

IV

Presenting with
PowerPoint

FIGURE 27.4

From the Font dialog box, you can change font attributes such as embossing.

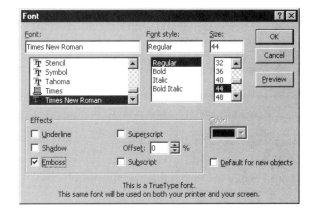

> **TIP**
>
> You can change your default font style by clicking on the Default for New Objects checkbox in the Font dialog box. Simply choose a font, size, and style, and then click on the checkbox to set this as the default font for new text. If you do this, all the text on your new slides will be formatted accordingly.

Changing Case

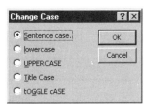

If type your text in a hurry, you might make capitalization mistakes. In PowerPoint you can easily change the case of any selected text. However, you should use this option only for small selections of text. PowerPoint has a more powerful tool called Style Checker, discussed later in this chapter, that can scan your entire presentation to make sure your text is formatted properly. To change case for a small selection of text, select the text you wish to change, select Format ➤ Change Case from the menu bar, and click on the appropriate radio button in the Change Case dialog box.

Aligning Text

You can align your text any way you want in PowerPoint. You can left-align, right-align, center the text, or use full justification, which expands the text to fill an entire line. If you are creating a presentation with a large font, avoid using this option; your text will look awkward and the lines and paragraphs will appear "empty."

Click on the text you wish to align. You can place your insertion point anywhere within the paragraph you want to align; you don't need to highlight it. Select Format ➢ Alignment from the menu bar and select the appropriate alignment from the submenu.

 **TIP**

Notice that the first three alignment options—Left, Center, and Right—have corresponding buttons on the Formatting toolbar. Just highlight the text you want to change and click the button of your choice.

Line and Paragraph Spacing

You can change the line and paragraph spacing in PowerPoint. Line spacing is the space between lines in the same paragraph, and paragraph spacing is the space between separate paragraphs. Remember, PowerPoint starts a new paragraph each time you press Enter while entering text. Since it works just like Word, you will recognize the look and feel immediately.

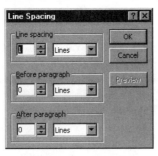

To change line and paragraph spacing, select the text you want to format for spacing and select Format ➢ Line Spacing from the menu bar. The Line Spacing dialog box appears. Choose the line and paragraph spacing appropriate for your text.

Text Objects

PowerPoint holds all of your text in text objects for easy editing. You can format text objects to add colors, lines, and even shadows. You can add a text object easily by opening the Insert menu and choosing Text Box. You then drag the mouse on the slide to where you want the new text box to appear. A new text box is added to the current page, ready for you to enter text.

FIGURE 27.6

*Tables are ideal
for definitions
or terminology.*

Although you can create a table by clicking on the Insert Microsoft Word Table button on the Standard toolbar, it is easier to create a new slide and select the slide layout for a table. The reason is that the table will overlay anything you have on your slide, and if you have not chosen a blank layout, you could accidentally end up with a table lying on top of a text object. Let's examine both ways to create a table, and you can decide the best way for you.

Tables from the Toolbar

To create a table from the toolbar, you can use the Insert Microsoft Word Table button. When you click on this button, PowerPoint opens up a Table tool that uses the same commands as the Table tool in Word. You may find it works a little slowly, but it is well worth the wait. This versatile tool provides the ability to create borders and shading just as in Word and to change column widths and numbers. You will soon wonder how you ever lived without it.

Let's walk through the steps for creating a table from the toolbar:

1. Choose the slide into which you want to insert your table.
2. Using the Insert Microsoft Word Table button on the toolbar, choose the number of columns and rows you want in your table. A Table menu appears in the menu bar, and a table is created on the page. The table has horizontal and vertical rulers so you can create it to match your specifications.
3. Type your text and press Tab between entries.
4. Press Esc when you are in the last cell.
5. Press Esc to deselect the table.

Creating a Table from a New Slide

Let's take a look at the steps for creating a table with a new slide. You will probably find that creating a new slide based on the Table layout is easier than inserting a table into an existing slide.

1. Click on the Insert New Slide button on the Standard toolbar.
2. Choose the Table layout and click on OK.
3. Once you see your new slide, double-click on the Table icon.
4. Choose the number of columns and rows and click on OK. The Table menu appears in the menu bar.
5. Enter your text just as you would in any table.
6. Press Esc to return to Slide view.
7. Press Esc to deselect the table.

TIP

If you press Tab in the last cell of your table, a new row is created. If you don't want a new row, you can click on the Undo button on the toolbar or choose Edit ➢ Undo from the menu bar.

NOTE

For more information about inserting objects onto a slide in PowerPoint, see Chapter 32, which discusses linking and embedding objects.

Using Tools in PowerPoint

PowerPoint provides some very useful tools to help you work with your text. You can find and change text throughout your presentation. You can check your style and spelling. You can even replace one font with another in your presentation. Some of the tools work just like those in Word, but two are unique to PowerPoint. Let"s take a look at those that Word and PowerPoint have in common and then look more closely at those only found in PowerPoint.

Finding Text

You can use the same tool that Word provides to find any text you want in your presentation. Select Edit ➢ Find from the menu bar and type the text you want to find in the Find What text box. Click on Find Next. When you are finished finding your text, click on Close.

TIP

Find and Replace are two of those procedures you will like to do quickly. You can find something fast by pressing Ctrl+F or start the Replace procedure by pressing Ctrl+H.

Replacing Text

You can replace text just as easily as in Word, using the same dialog boxes. Select Edit ➢ Replace from the menu bar and type the text you want to find and what you want to replace it with. Click on Replace or Replace All and click on OK. When you are finished replacing text, click on Close. If you mistakenly replace any text, you can use Undo to restore your text to its original form.

Spelling

The Spell Checker in PowerPoint works exactly like the one in Word. To check the spelling of your presentation, just press F7 or select Tools ➢ Spelling from the menu bar. You will see a dialog box similar to the one Word provides to help you with suggestions for your spelling errors.

When you type something PowerPoint 97 doesn't understand, the program underlines the unrecognized word to call it to your attention. You can then right-click on the word to see a list of possible suggested spellings. PowerPoint underlines unknown, misspelled, and repeated words.

AutoCorrect

PowerPoint now has the same AutoCorrect option that Word does. To access AutoCorrect, just follow the same steps as in Word. You can always add text to AutoCorrect to change any errors you frequently make when typing. You can also choose to turn it off or delete any changes you don't want PowerPoint to make. To use the AutoCorrect option, follow these steps:

1. Select Tools ➢ AutoCorrect from the menu bar.
2. In the AutoCorrect dialog box (see Figure 27.7), add and delete any items you wish, or change any options.
3. Click on OK to accept the changes or Cancel to keep your old settings.

TIP

PowerPoint 97 also enables you to set up exceptions to the rule. If there are certain letters, words, or abbreviations you don't want corrected automatically, you can click on the Exceptions button in the AutoCorrect dialog box to enter the items you want to remain the way they are entered.

*You can change
your AutoCorrect
options in the
AutoCorrect
dialog box.*

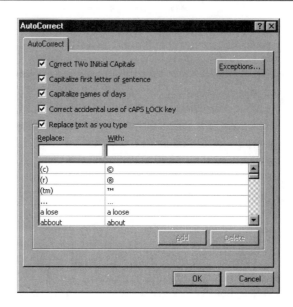

Replacing Fonts

This tool is unique to PowerPoint. If you find that you have used a font in your presentation that does not work well on your slides, you can always change that font to another one more suited to your presentation's formatting and colors. To do so, follow these steps:

1. Select Format ➤ Replace Fonts from the menu bar.

2. In the Replace Font dialog box, select from the Replace list the font that needs to be replaced.

3. From the With list, select the font that will replace the current font.

4. Click on Replace.

5. Repeat steps 2 through 4 to replace other fonts.

6. Click on Close when you are done.

Style Checker

Finally, after you have created your presentation, are happy with the fonts, and are pleased with the layout, you can let PowerPoint perform a final check for you, to make sure there are no inconsistencies. Although this tool may take some time to run, it is so valuable, it is worth the wait. You can always help yourself to another cup of coffee or take a break if it's taking too long. This tool is only found in PowerPoint.

You can set the options for Style Checker. For instance, if you have already performed a spell check, you can open the Style Checker dialog box by choosing Tools ➢ Style Checker and uncheck the appropriate box.

Take a look at the steps for changing the options in Style Checker to see whether they are appropriate for your presentation:

1. Select Tools ➢ Style Checker from the menu bar.
2. In the Style Checker dialog box (shown in Figure 27.8), click on the Options button to see what Style Checker uses as benchmarks.
3. Make any necessary changes on the Case and End Punctuation tab in the Style Checker Options dialog box, as shown in Figure 27.9.
4. Click on the Visual Clarity tab, and make changes to the way Style Checker will check your slides for clarity and visibility. If you want to return the settings to their default values, click on the Defaults button.
5. Click on OK when you are satisfied with the options.
6. Click on Start to begin Style Checker.
7. After PowerPoint is finished checking your presentation, the Style Checker Summary dialog box appears. When you are finished reviewing the errors, click on OK to return to your slide.

FIGURE 27.8

*Style Checker
dialog box*

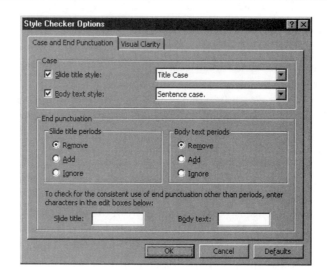

What's Next?

In this chapter you have seen how to edit and format the text in your presentation. In the next chapter we will look at adding clip art and media clips to give your presentation a life of its own.

Chapter

28

Animation, Art, and Sound

FEATURING

Animation, Art, and Sound

Because of the explosion in multimedia applications, more and more computers are being sold as "multimedia" or "family" machines. The word *family* once implied "general use" or "suitable for children;" but now, in the world of computers, family means entertainment. No longer limited to using personal computers to balance budgets and write letters, today's individuals and families are buying full-blown entertainment boxes with sound, video, and CD-ROM capabilities. Where once only a handful in Hollywood could edit movies digitally, now, with only a small investment, anyone can buy such a machine.

In this chapter, you'll learn how to add exciting multimedia objects to your PowerPoint presentations, including animation and sound. You'll also use the ClipArt Gallery to add artwork and create your own professional-looking organization charts.

PowerPoint and Multimedia

You can think of multimedia as taking any picture from your photo album, any song from your favorite singer, or any scene from a great action flick and digitizing it. When you digitize something, all you are doing is reducing its form to something a computer can read and reproduce.

PowerPoint takes such advantage of multimedia that it's almost like having a producer, director, and a small cast working with you to create your slide show. You can play sounds, show video clips, use clip art, animate text and slides, and have PowerPoint run other programs from a slide show. Just imagine the possibilities. You could communicate a record sales quarter by inserting a slide into your presentation that shows a graph of regional sales, alongside a media clip that plays a rocket launching, all introduced by the sound of an audience clapping.

Adding Art to Your Presentation

First, let's take a look at creating a new slide with art. You don't have to be a Picasso or Rembrandt, because PowerPoint has included both the tools you'll need and sample clips for creating a very impressive slide with art. You can also use other vendors as a source for art.

WordArt

WordArt gives you the ability to morph your text into various shapes and designs. The important thing to remember for our purposes in PowerPoint is that WordArt is *not* plain text. It is an object and therefore behaves like an object. This means that if you make a spelling error using WordArt, the Spell Checker will not alert you to your mistake. You must edit the WordArt object by double-clicking on it.

Creating WordArt

Let's walk through the steps of creating WordArt in PowerPoint. If you have used WordArt before in Word, this procedure will seem familiar. However, you must perform some extra steps to ensure that the object embeds properly. First, you need to have a presentation open. If you don't have a presentation open, go ahead and open either one of your own presentations or a blank one. Then follow these steps:

1. Click on the Insert New Slide button on the Standard toolbar or use the New Slide button in the Common Tasks window (see Figure 28.1).

TIP

The Common Tasks window is a small window with three buttons that appears to the left of a slide in Slide view. If you close it, you can reopen it later by opening the View menu, choosing Toolbars, and selecting Common Tasks from the popup menu.

2. Select a layout that is based on an object—for example, the Large Object layout. Figure 28.1 shows a slide with WordArt based on this layout.

FIGURE 28.1

*A slide with
WordArt based
on the Large
Object layout*

3. Click on the OK button.

4. Double-click on the Object icon to add an object.

5. Make sure that Create New is selected in the Insert Object dialog box. Select Microsoft WordArt 2.0 from the Object Type list box and click on OK.

6. Type your text in the *Enter your text here* text box, and select a shape from the drop-down combo box on the toolbar. The box will display Plain Text. You can add any other properties you like from the toolbar.

7. When you are finished creating the WordArt, press Esc twice to return to your slide.

Instead of creating a new object, you can always select an object you created earlier by clicking on the Create from File radio button. You can browse your drive(s) or floppy for the proper file.

As mentioned earlier, if you don't see a layout you want in the New Slide dialog box, you can embed an object on a blank slide. You can also choose a slide layout that is close to the one you want and delete, copy, or edit object sizes to suit your needs.

Clip Art versus Drawing

Working with clip art is basically the same as working with WordArt. Although you can create your own art, you may want to find clip art that fits your needs instead. If you are not familiar with the Paint program or another drawing program or you have minimal artistic abilities, sticking to clip art may be your safest bet in making a nice-looking presentation. You can spend a lot of time creating a picture, but in the end it may not be as effective as a similar picture already available in clip art.

Creating Images from Scratch

To create images from scratch, follow these steps:

1. Click on the New Slide button in the Common Tasks window.

2. Choose a layout that contains an object and click on OK.

3. Double-click on the Object icon to create the picture.

4. From the Object Type list box, choose either Bitmap Image or Paintbrush Picture. The Paintbrush window appears. Draw a picture using the Paint tools.

5. Press Esc twice to return to PowerPoint and your slide.

Figure 28.2 shows the result of a time-consuming effort in Paintbrush.

FIGURE 28.2

A plane created in Paintbrush

Clip Art

Now that you have created your own picture, let's try to insert an image already created by PowerPoint. This should be simpler and will probably be more attractive than anything most of us could create with Paintbrush.

The next slide, shown in Figure 28.3, is based on the Text & Clip Art layout from the New Slide dialog box. After inserting the art, you select the text object and delete it by pressing the Delete key. You then reposition the clip art object on the slide.

TIP

If you're uncertain about what type of art will best fit your presentation, you can use the AutoClipArt feature to let PowerPoint make suggestions for you. Choose Tools ➢ AutoClipArt and PowerPoint will evaluate the words in your presentation and display clip art that might illustrate your key concepts.

FIGURE 28.3

*An example of
clip art*

A Clip Art Example

Here are the steps:

1. Create a new slide by clicking on the Insert New Slide button on the Standard toolbar or choosing New Slide in the Common Tasks window.
2. Select either the Text & Clip Art (or Clip Art & Text) layout and click on OK.
3. Double-click on the clip art object. When the Microsoft Clip Gallery 3.0 dialog box opens, select one of the categories listed on the left and then, on the right, select a piece of clip art under that category.
4. Click on Insert and move or resize the object as desired. Notice that when the clip art is placed on the slide, the Picture toolbar appears. Using these tools, you can change the brightness, contrast, line style, or color of the art. You can even reset the clip art to its original state or replace it with a different piece of clip art.
5. Press Esc twice to return to PowerPoint or the slide.

TIP

If you don't like the way your clip art appears on your slide, you can always replace it with another piece of clip art by double-clicking on the object and inserting a different piece of art. You can also right-click and select Replace Clip Object from the shortcut menu.

MASTERING TROUBLESHOOTING

Art and Web Pages: Do They Mix?

One of the great things about Power-Point 97 is the ease with which you can create Web pages. The Save As HTML option in the File menu lets you create a Web-ready document complete with all the necessary coding embedded for you. But will the visitors to your Web site be able to see your page the way you do?

Even though the massively popular Web browsers Netscape and Internet Explorer (along with many others) have the ability to view graphics, there are many users who cannot view graphics—that is, clip art, photos, etc.—with their Web browsers. As you create your Web page, consider this portion of your audience and make sure you include enough text to get your point across.

AutoShapes

AutoShapes are probably the easiest objects to add to a slide in PowerPoint. You simply click on the AutoShapes button on the Drawing toolbar and choose the shape type you want from the palette; then choose from the submenu that appears (see Figure 28.4) There are many shapes from which to choose, so feel free to select whichever one you like.

AutoShapes give you several palette of shape choices.

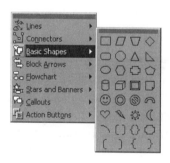

To add an AutoShape, follow these steps:

1. Click on the AutoShapes button on the Drawing toolbar at the bottom of your screen.

AutoShapes ▾

2. Point to the shape or symbol you want. A submenu showing more choices appears. Click on the shape you like.

3. Place and size the shape on your slide by holding down the left mouse button and dragging.

4. Type the text you want in the AutoShape.

5. Press Esc twice when you are done.

Graphs

You can easily add a graph to your slide. You can also insert an Excel spreadsheet or graph, but this section focuses on creating a graph from scratch. (For more information about embedding a graph and linking it to a spreadsheet, see Chapter 32, which discusses integrating PowerPoint with other Office programs.)

Let's run through the process of creating a graph from scratch and then placing it onto a slide:

1. Create a new slide by clicking on the Insert New Slide button.

2. Select the Chart layout and click on OK.

3. Double-click on the Chart icon to create the graph.

4. There is already data in the datasheet, so you need to delete it by clicking and dragging to select the cells and pressing Delete. Type your own data in the datasheet.

5. Choose a form for the graph using the Chart Type button at the top of the screen that shows a picture of a chart and a drop-down arrow. Figure 28.5 shows a datasheet being edited.

6. Close the datasheet by clicking on the Close button (×) in the upper right-hand corner.

7. To leave graph mode, press Esc three times.

Organization Charts

If you have ever tried to create an organization chart from a table in Word or from lines in an Excel spreadsheet, you probably have spent hours creating your perfect chart, only to later discover that you left out a level or you weren't basing your chart on your company's new organization structure.

Microsoft has included an Organization Chart utility to use with the Office programs. Let's take a brief look at using this tool:

1. Create a new slide by clicking on the Insert New Slide button.

2. Choose Organization Chart from the New Slide dialog box and click on OK.

3. Double-click on the Organization Chart icon to add the chart. Your screen should look similar to the one in Figure 28.6.

FIGURE 28.5

Editing the datasheet

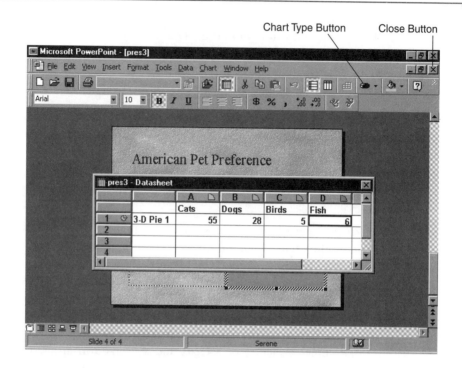

To edit a position in the organization chart, click on it and fill in the name, title, and any other information associated with the position. When you are finished with a position, just choose another, and the box will automatically resize itself to fit the text.

You can add positions by clicking on one of the position buttons on the organization chart's toolbar and, with the position now attached to your mouse pointer, click on the box where you want the new position to be attached, as shown in Figure 28.7.

WARNING

If you delete positions, your organization chart will automatically shift all the subordinate positions to fit the chart style. Be careful—you can completely change your organization chart by deleting one position.

When you are finished creating your chart, select File ➤ Close and Return to Presentation from the menu bar. You are asked whether you want to update your slide. Click on Yes if you want to include the chart. If you click on No, your work is discarded.

FIGURE 28.6

*Creating an
organization
chart*

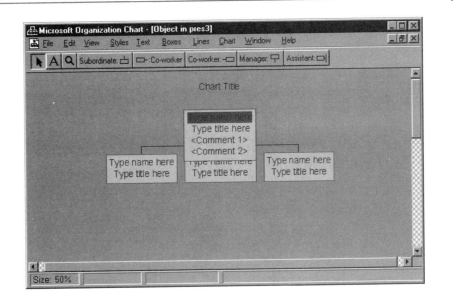

FIGURE 28.7

*Attaching a
new position to
an organization
chart*

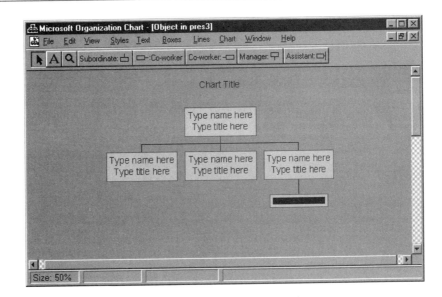

Slide Transition, Animation, and Sound Effects

You can manipulate how your slides and objects appear and disappear in your slide show. One slide might fade in, while the following slide might open like a Venetian blind. You can have text appear to fly into position, word by word or letter by letter. You can have bulleted lists materialize one level at a time. You can even give sound to your slides, either by using a sound effect already in PowerPoint or by choosing another sound file you have available.

Slide Transition

Transition controls the way each slide will appear as it opens on the slide show screen. You have a long list of effects from which to choose, and since a picture is worth a thousand words, this would be a good time to see how using this option will affect the slide's appearance in the show.

To open the Slide Transition dialog box shown in Figure 28.8, choose Slide Show ➤ Slide Transition from the menu bar. You can change the picture on the sample slide in the dialog box by clicking on it.

FIGURE 28.8

Slide Transition dialog box

If you want to see how each transition will affect the way your slide appears in the slide show, click on the down arrow next to the effect listed and use your arrow keys to scroll through the list. As you scroll, each transition effect is demonstrated for you. You can also determine at what speed (slow, medium, or fast) you want the transition to play.

Presenting with PowerPoint

The Random Transition effect at the end of the list randomly chooses an effect for use in the presentation. If you are preparing a slide show you plan to use a lot, picking this transition effect will add variety to your show.

In the Slide Transition dialog box, you can also set slide advancement to occur after a certain number of seconds. This is a useful feature for either self-running demos or presentations you have timed well enough that you can let the computer handle the slide advancement, freeing you to move around.

If you want a sound to play at the transition of a slide, you can choose from the sounds listed in the Sound combo box in the bottom right-hand corner of the Slide Transition dialog box. You can also select another sound by choosing Other Sound at the bottom of the combo box list and selecting a new sound. Clicking on the Loop until Next Sound checkbox determines whether the sound you choose will continue until another sound is activated or just play once. If you choose to loop your sound, you should view the slide show to see whether the sound is effective or distracting. A typewriter sound may be a good effect, recreating the teletype sounds that television news shows once used. On the other hand, a cash register sound played in a loop may become distracting.

Once you have made your selections, just click on the Apply button to save your settings for that slide. If you want to set these changes for all the slides in your presentation, click on the Apply to All button.

Animation

You can change the order in which objects enter the slide and the manner in which each object appears on the slide. You can also attribute sound to individual objects on a slide.

To change the settings for an object, choose Slide Show ➤ Custom Animation. Remember, you can choose multiple objects on the same slide by clicking on each object while holding down the Shift key. If you select more than one object type, you will be able to modify only the properties the objects have in common.

The Custom Animation dialog box provides you with four different tabs to control the various aspects of the animation. You can set the timing, control when sounds and text items are introduced, determine how you want charts animated, and set play settings to control when and if an object is animated on the slide.

You can display the Custom Animation dialog box quickly by right-clicking on the object you want to animate and choosing Custom Animation.

Start in the Timing tab of the Custom Animation dialog box to determine whether an object is animated. Choose the slide objects you want to animate from the list on the left and click on Animate or Don't Animate, depending on how you want the objects on the slide to appear.

The Effects tab, shown in Figure 28.9, is where you choose the special effects you want to use—for example, Fly from Left or Dissolve—and assign any sounds. Click on the down arrows in the Entry Animation and Sound Area of the Effects tab and make your choice for each setting. The options available depend on the type of object you have selected to animate.

FIGURE 28.9

Choices for animating objects

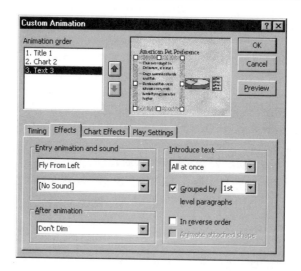

If you have chosen a text object to be animated, the Introduce Text options are available. You can have text appear all at once, word by word, or letter by letter. You can also determine how you want the text grouped, in what order you want the text to appear, and whether you want to animate a shape that is attached to the text. Finally, you tell PowerPoint whether you want the object dimmed, hidden, or displayed in a different color after the animation plays.

When you choose a chart object, the Chart Effects tab gives you the options you need for animating. You can introduce the chart elements one by one or all at once, and you can decide on the special effect and sound you want for the chart animation.

If, on the active slide, you have several objects that use animation, you can choose the order in which they appear. Simply select the object you want to change and click on either the up or down arrow to the right of the Animation Order box to rearrange the items. If you change the order of one object, the others will change order automatically.

If you have a chart or other object (other than text), you can choose the Play Settings tab and choose from the play options, as you can see in Figure 28.10. In the Object Action box, if you choose Open, you actually open, during the slide show, the program that produced the object, such as the graph program. If you choose Edit, you can edit the data in the graph. This might be useful if you want to interactively change a graph or spreadsheet on a slide during a presentation.

FIGURE 28.10

Animation settings for a non-text object

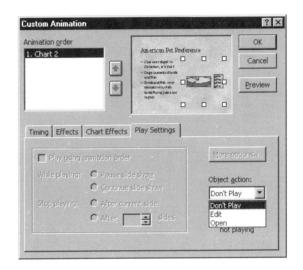

Action Settings

You can add another setting to an object on a slide by using the Action Settings dialog box shown in Figure 28.11 (select Slide Show ➤ Action Settings). Action settings affect how an object will react when you click on it or pass the mouse over it during a slide show. You have five options from which to choose: None, Hyperlink To, Run Program, Run Macro, and Object Action.

If you want to move to another slide when you click on an object in a slide show, you can pick any slide in your show as the destination. Simply right-click on the object and choose Action Settings to display the Action Settings dialog box. Then click on the Hyperlink To radio button and use the down arrow to display the list of pages you can select. Select the page to which you want to move. When you click on the object during the presentation, PowerPoint moves you to the slide you have selected. For example, you may want to reference numbers previously mentioned in another slide if audience members have questions; being able to jump back to your justification without fumbling around is very impressive. You can even jump to a different presentation or to a Web page using the Hyperlink To option.

FIGURE 28.11

*Action Settings
dialog box*

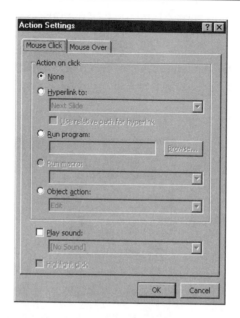

NOTE

If you move to another slide, PowerPoint continues the presentation from that slide and does not return you to the calling slide. If you know you will be jumping from one slide to another, be sure you have an interactive way to jump back to the original slide.

Finally, you can choose to run a program from the Action Settings dialog box. If you select the Run Program radio button, simply type the name of the program you want to run when you click on the object, or click on the Browse button and select a program in the Select a Program to Run dialog box. PowerPoint opens the application on top of your slide during the slide show.

TIP

A very good use of the Run Program option is to run Calculator when showing numbers in a presentation. If you are presenting a graph during a slide show, you can run Calculator and quickly do calculations to show the audience confirmation of what you are stating.

MASTERING THE OPPORTUNITIES

Launching into Action

The Action Settings dialog box is a launching pad for all kinds of possibilities. Suppose that you are presenting a new budget proposal to the board of directors of your company. You anticipate that they will have questions about your projections, but you don't want to use up valuable presentation time to go into the details unless you're asked. You can link an object on your presentation slide that discusses the projections to the Excel spreadsheet that shows the total calculations. When the questions start rolling in, you can click on the button and display the spreadsheet.

Think about what extra"side trips"might add depth or impact to your presentation. Perhaps a voice-over clip from the CEO. Maybe a video clip showing a recent trip through your company's warehouse. You might keep a short library of interviews to show prospective hires to the recruitment committee. Whatever the need, you've got the resources and the ability to access them at a moment's notice.

Action Buttons

Action buttons are another element you can easily add to your presentation slides. Use them to add a preprogrammed button so you can move easily from one slide to another, a home page button for the slide you're preparing for your Web site, or a sound button to play a greeting or musical introduction when you click on it.

To add an action button, choose Slide Show ➤ Action Buttons to display the palette of 12 buttons (shown in Figure 28.12). Then just click on the button you want and place it on the slide.

FIGURE 28.12

*Action buttons
are easy to add
and use.*

Media Clips

Finally, you can insert multimedia clips into a slide in PowerPoint. Now you can run a video clip, play music, animate charts, and more. Here is where PowerPoint really shines. If you plan on using sound, just make sure you have a sound card installed in your machine.

To insert a media clip, open a new slide based on the Media Clip & Text or Text & Media Clip layout. Although you can insert an object using Insert ➤ Object from the menu bar, we'll walk through the process of creating a new slide to put a media clip onto the slide. (In Chapter 32 we will discuss linking objects and the advantages and disadvantages of inserting objects into a slide.)

1. Create a new slide by clicking on the Insert New Slide button.
2. Choose either the Media Clip & Text or Text & Media Clip layout and click on OK.
3. Double-click on the Media Clip icon. The Insert Movie dialog box appears.
4. Choose the particular clip you want and click on OK. The object is added to the slide, as shown in Figure 28.13.
5. If you want to change the clip, right-click on the object. When the popup menu appears, choose Edit Movie Object.
6. Click elsewhere on the slide to insert the media clip and return to Slide view. To play the media clip, double-click on it.

FIGURE 28.13

Adding a media clip to a slide

You can also add a moving or sound object by choosing Insert ➤ Movies and Sounds. When you position the pointer on that option, the submenu shown in Figure 28.14 appears. You can load a movie or sound file from the Microsoft Clip Gallery 3.0 or from a separate file. Additionally, you can play an audio CD track as an object in your presentation.

FIGURE 28.14

*You can add
movies and
sounds from the
Clip Gallery or
from a file.*

If you choose to use media clips, be aware that these files can be extremely large, making your presentation much bigger each time you include one. Also, media clips behave poorly on slower computers. Experiment with different types and lengths of media clips to see how each will work on your system. Some video boards are designed specifically to work with multimedia. You can greatly enhance your media clip performance by working on a system that has such a board, although it is not necessary.

What's Next?

In Chapter 32 we will look at how you can insert these objects from existing files, how you can link your presentation to those individual files, how that will affect your slide show, and how to resolve any errors you might encounter.

In the next chapter, however, you will see how all the objects and their settings will work in the completed presentation. You'll see the different tools at your disposal, and you'll learn about creating handouts and printing your notes to get the most out of your slide show.

Chapter

29

Making the Presentation

Making the Presentation

Now that you have learned how to create your own presentation, you're ready for the moment when all the hard work pays off. You can give your presentation in person or in cyberspace, thanks to PowerPoint's presentation conferencing feature. And you can use several Power-Point tools to help you deliver your message clearly, effectively, and impressively. When you're ready to present, you can use the Meeting Minder, Write-Up, Slide Meter, and Pointer Options to help you make the best total impact with your work.

Setting Up the Show

Different types of slide shows are needed for different types of audiences. If you are creating a presentation that a single user will navigate through herself, for example, you need to build in controls so she can easily move from slide to slide. For a presentation projected on a big screen monitor in the board room, however, you may want to use automatic timing so the slides advance "by themselves," and each slide takes up the maximum space available on-screen.

PowerPoint gives you the means to decide what type of slide show you want with the Set Up Show option. Choose Slide Show ➤ Set Up Show. The dialog box shown in Figure 29.1 appears.

FIGURE 29.1

Setting up the type of show you want

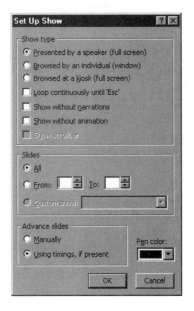

For a typical presentation, leave the first option selected. If you want the presentation to appear in a window on the screen, choose *Browsed by an individual.* If you want the presentation to run full-screen, choose *Browsed at a kiosk.* Choosing *Loop continuously until 'Esc'* will keep the presentation running until someone presses the Esc key. Finally, you can present the show without narration and without animation, if the situation, hardware, or time constraints require that you do without those added effects.

In addition to choosing the basic type of show you want, you can determine which slides you want to show and elect whether to manually advance the slides yourself (by clicking the mouse or pressing PgDn or Enter) or use timings you set up using Rehearse Timings. After you make your selections, click on OK.

NOTE

Choosing and hiding slides, determining manual or automatic slide advance, and selecting pen colors are all discussed later in this chapter.

Meeting Minder: Keeping Track

Where will you give your presentation? Most likely, in a meeting of some kind. For that reason, PowerPoint includes the Meeting Minder, a feature that includes a scheduler, room for meeting notes, and a record page for "action items" to be completed after the meeting's close.

You can access Meeting Minder during the creation or editing of a presentation and while viewing it in Slide Show view. To access Meeting Minder while editing your presentation, select Tools ➤ Meeting Minder from the menu bar. To access Meeting Minder during the slide show, right-click and choose Meeting Minder from the shortcut menu. In either case, you will see the screen shown in Figure 29.2.

FIGURE 29.2

*Meeting Minder
dialog box*

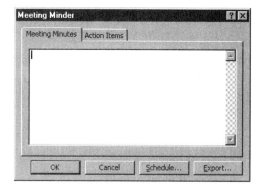

Meeting Minutes

As the name implies, the Meeting Minutes tool allows you to take minutes during a meeting pertaining to your presentation or even during your slide show. If you choose to use this tool during your slide show, you can keep track of discussions from the audience or speakers. Later, you can export your Meeting Minutes to Word for printing.

Scheduling Meetings

One feature within Meeting Minder enables you to schedule appointments and meetings you have coming up. By clicking on the Schedule button in the Meeting Minder dialog box, you can display the Appointment window in which you enter pertinent information about the meeting: the subject, the location, the start and end times. You can even have your computer remind you of the meeting by setting a Reminder value (perhaps 15 or 30 minutes prior to the meeting) and assigning a Reminder Sound that will ring when the reminder is due. You may never miss a meeting again!

The Meeting Planner tab of the Appointment dialog box enables you to list the people attending your meeting, plan out the times they can attend, and invite others to your meeting group. The Appointment dialog box is actually part of Microsoft Outlook, the personal information manager included with Office 97.

Action Items

Action Items is a handy tool that allows you to track specific items needing attention as a result of the presentation. You can write specific tasks that need to be completed now or jot down subjects that may need attention in the future. When you add an item to the Action Items tab in Meeting Minder, PowerPoint creates a final slide in your presentation entitled "Action Items," which outlines in bulleted form those specific tasks you placed in the Meeting Minder. You can see an example of an Action Items slide in Figure 29.3. As with Meeting Minutes, you can export Action Items to Word for editing and printing. Further, you can assign the tasks to a specific person or group, so you know who to contact to make sure the task is complete.

NOTE

PowerPoint creates only one Action Items slide at the end of your presentation. If you enter too many items, they will not fit on the slide. Try to limit yourself to placing five or six items under Action Items.

FIGURE 29.3

Action Items slide created by PowerPoint

Using Meeting Minder

To use Meeting Minder in Slide view, select Tools ➤ Meeting Minder. If you want to add any minutes for this slide, just click on the Meeting Minutes tab and type. To add specific items that will become bulleted in a final slide, click on the Action Items tab, and add the item, the person or group to whom it is assigned, and the due date, if necessary; then click on Add. PowerPoint adds the item to the list in the bottom left corner of the dialog box.

If you want to change one of the action items you have added, simply select it in the action list by clicking on it; then click on Edit. You can then change the information as needed. If you want to remove an item from the list, select it and click on the Delete button.

To use Meeting Minder, follow these steps:

1. Select Tools ➢ Meeting Minder.
2. Click on the Meeting Minutes tab and enter your minutes.
3. Click on the Action Items tab and enter each item you want to follow up.
4. Click on OK to save your changes to Meeting Minder.
5. Select another slide and repeat steps 1 through 4.

After you have entered all the Meeting Minutes and Action Items for your presentation, you can create a Word document based on the items entered into Meeting Minder:

1. Select Tools ➢ Meeting Minder.
2. Click on the Export button to see the Meeting Minder Export dialog box shown in Figure 29.4.

FIGURE 29.4

Meeting Minder Export dialog box

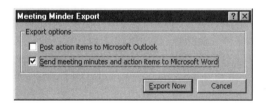

3. Make sure the *Send meeting minutes and action items to Microsoft Word* checkbox is selected.
4. Click on Export Now. Microsoft Word opens and a document based on your Meeting Minder items is created. You can now print this document or save it.
5. Exit Word and return to PowerPoint.

Turning "To-Do" Items into "Done-That!" Items

Microsoft Office 97 is big on integration: You create something in Word, you can use it in Excel, PowerPoint, Access, and more. Data moves smoothly back and forth among the applications, making it easier than ever for you to create something once and use it many times, cutting down both on your effort and your error margin.

Microsoft Outlook is a program included with the Office 97 suite that helps you organize all the important things you do during the day, week, and month. You can schedule appointments, track phone calls, receive and send e-mail, remind yourself of important events, and prioritize your commitments.

The Action Items offered in PowerPoint's Meeting Minder are a perfect fit for this kind of efficiency—now you can move your action items right into Microsoft Outlook, making sure that the action items you've listed are, in fact, acted upon. No more falling through the cracks or "Gosh, I meant to do that..."—you can remember, or remind yourself, using Microsoft Outlook.

To make sure the action items get to Microsoft Outlook, click on the Export button on the Meeting Minder dialog box. When the popup window appears, select the *Post action items to Microsoft Outlook* checkbox. See Part Five for a full discussion of Outlook.

Write-Up: Exporting to a Word Table

The Write-Up tool is quite useful. You can choose to have all the notes and slides for your presentation exported to a Word table. Each slide will appear as a picture next to any notes for that slide. Write-Up lets you easily fit several slides onto a page in Word. Handouts (hard copies of the slide presentation) in PowerPoint can print only two, three, or six slides on each page, without notes. You can also elect to print only the outline or the notes pages of your presentation. To access Write-Up, follow these steps:

1. Select File ➤ Send To ➤ Microsoft Word to display the Write-Up dialog box shown in Figure 29.5.
2. Select the layout you want.
3. Choose whether you want to Paste or Paste Link and click on OK.
4. Word opens, and a table with your slides and notes is created. You can edit this document, save it if you want, and then print it.
5. Exit Word to return to PowerPoint.

The Write-Up
dialog box
helps you
export your
PowerPoint
presentation to
Word.

> You can easily send your presentation to others using your mail utility. Choose File
> ➢ Send To and then choose either Mail Recipient, Routing Recipient, or Exchange
> Folder. Additionally, if you want to send your slides to a professional slide produc-
> tion company, you can select Genigraphics for instructions on how to do that.

Slide Meter: Rehearsing Your Presentation

Before you give your presentation in front of an audience, it's a good idea to rehearse
your slide show and make note of slide timings. PowerPoint allows you to time your
presentation and then rehearse subsequent shows using your previous times. You can
choose to use the Slide Meter, a timing device that shows you whether your presentation is running too slowly or quickly according to the times you recorded previously.
You can also let PowerPoint automatically advance each slide according to the times
you record for a dry run.

Rehearsing Slide Timing

Let's run through the procedure for creating a base time for your slide show and then
see how you can use the tools in PowerPoint Slide Show view to enhance and speed up
your presentation. You'll need to have a presentation open. If you don't have any presentations, use one of the complete template presentations from PowerPoint.

1. Select Slide Show ➤ Rehearse Timings. The first slide appears, along with a Slide Timer in the lower right-hand corner of your screen. Also note the dim pointer in the lower left-hand corner of the screen.

2. Advance through each slide by clicking on the next arrow in the Rehearsal dialog box or clicking on the slide. If you make an error, you can repeat the slide, and the timer will start from 0:00 again. You can  also click on the Pause button in the Rehearsal dialog box to pause the timer.

3. When you have finished your show, a dialog box appears asking whether you want to record the new times for your slide show. Click on Yes.

MASTERING TROUBLESHOOTING

Avoiding Timing Troubles

Figuring out just how long is long enough—and not too long—for each individual slide takes some practice. Use the Slide Meter and the Rehearsal dialog box to help you find a comfortable length of time for each slide.

Generally, consider how long you'll need to spend with each slide. Text with the following items needs a longer span of time than title slides or slides used primarily for visual effect:

- A slide with several bullet points

- A slide with a chart you need to explain

- A slide with an organizational chart

- A slide showing a table of information

If you're using a slide as a "filler" or to set up or close a section of the presentation—for example, a title slide, an introductory slide, a review slide, or an art slide positioned between segments in your presentation—

you should be able to get by with between 15 and 30 seconds for display.

For longer slides with more information, leave one to two minutes or longer, if you think more discussion is needed.

What problems can bad timing cause?

- If your timing is too long, your audience could get bored—their minds will wander.

- If your timing is too quick, your audience could miss your point.

- If your timing is uncomfortable, you and your audience will be, too.

As a general rule, use PowerPoint's tools to help you time the presentation correctly. Then practice it a few times and present it to someone whose judgment you value. Ask whether the slides were too slow, too fast, or just right. Use the feedback to further revise the timings of your presentation. Your experience will make you more effective later.

When you have completed your dry run through the presentation slide show, PowerPoint asks you whether you want to review the timings in Slide Sorter view. Click on Yes and the presentation appears in Page Sorter view, where you can see each of the slides in your show, along with the times recorded for each slide.

Viewing and Hiding Slides

After rehearsing your presentation, you might choose to delete or edit some slides. However, you may first want to see how the slide show will be affected before you make the changes permanent. You can hide any of the slides in your presentation from the Slide Sorter view. To hide a slide, select Slide Show ➢ Hide Slide. Or, if you prefer, you can right-click on the slide you want to hide and select Hide Slide from the shortcut menu.

You can also hide a slide from Slide view by using the same menu selection when the slide is displayed on the screen. To redisplay a hidden slide, select the slide in either Slide view or Slide Sorter view and click on Slide Show ➢ Hide Slide to disable the feature.

NOTE
You may be surprised to see that when you choose the Hide Slide option, the slide doesn't disappear from view. The slide remains intact in both Slide view and Slide Sorter view but is hidden during the slide show presentation.

Letting Slide Meter Run the Show

Once you have recorded your time for the slide show and hidden any slides you no longer need, you can rerun your slide show, timing yourself against your original time to see whether you can repeat your performance. If you find you have to talk too quickly or there are too many pauses between slides, you can always rerun your slide show and record new times.

Once you are satisfied with your times, you can let the computer rerun your slide show using the times you recorded. PowerPoint automatically advances your slides. All you have to do is give your speech for each slide. To let the computer run the slide show, follow these steps:

1. Select Slide Show ➢ View Show.
2. Deliver the script for each slide as you normally would.

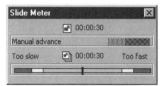

PowerPoint automatically uses the timings you rehearsed with the Rehearse Timings option. When the slide show finishes, PowerPoint returns you to your original view. Use the Slide Meter tool to see whether your original times are too slow or too fast.

To access the Slide Meter during a slide show, right-click and select Slide Meter from the shortcut menu. Within a few seconds, PowerPoint places the Slide Meter in the lower right-hand corner of your screen. To advance through the slides, either press N (for Next) or click on the slide.

As you give your slide show, you will notice that the black arrow in the Slide Meter moves either to the left, indicating that you are taking too long with your presentation, or to the right, meaning that you are moving too quickly. The meter updates itself as soon as you advance to the next slide. You can use the running clock in the Slide Meter to see how long you have taken with each slide.

The Pointer: Your Toolbox during Presentations

You have seen the pointer in the lower-left hand corner of the screen in Slide Show view. Think of this pointer as your toolbox to use during a presentation. You can access several items that may come in handy during your presentation. Available from the pointer are:

- A pen for writing in a variety of colors on slides.
- Access to the Slide Meter, Speaker Notes, and Meeting Minder tools.
- A Slide Navigator that permits you access to hidden slides during a presentation.
- The option of blacking out the screen to take the audience's attention off the present slide and onto something else in your presentation.

Displaying the Pointer

If your pointer is not visible in Slide Show view, right-click, select Pointer Options, and uncheck the Hide Now option. If your pointer is still not visible, right-click again, select Pointer Options, and make sure the Hide Always option is not checked. If it is, uncheck it. If you are not already in a slide show, switch to Slide Show view and activate your pointer.

Navigation

The first three selections on the Pointer popup menu deal with slide navigation. The first and second selections on the menu permit you to go to either the next or the previous slide. Of course, if you are at the first slide in your presentation, you cannot go to a previous slide. If you are at the last slide in your presentation, choosing Next exits you from the slide show.

The third option on the menu is Go, which allows you either to go to a specific slide in your slide show or to reveal hidden slides. If you choose Hidden Slide from Go, you will go to the next hidden slide. This option is available only if the next slide is hidden. If you need to go to an indiscriminate hidden slide, use the Slide Navigator.

If you choose Slide Navigator from Go, you will see a dialog box like the one in Figure 29.6, displaying the names of all your slides in the order in which they appear in your presentation. If the number is enclosed in parentheses, that means the slide is hidden. From this dialog box you can go to any particular slide in your presentation. For instance, if you are on slide 1 and you choose to go to slide 4, you will skip slides 2 and 3. Likewise, if you are on slide 6 and you choose to go to slide 3, you will move directly to slide 3.

FIGURE 29.6

The Slide Navigator dialog box shows you the presentation order of your slides.

If you choose to move through your slide show using Slide Navigator, you will not return to the slide from where you activated the Navigator. If you go back through your slide show, you will have to use Slide Navigator to return to your previous position. Likewise, if you move ahead in your presentation, you will have to navigate back to your starting point by displaying the Slide Navigator, clicking on the slide you want, and clicking on Go To.

PART
IV

Presenting with
PowerPoint

NOTE

If you want access to either the Meeting Minder, Speaker Notes, or the Slide Meter during a slide show, you can do so from the Pointer popup menu. Just remember, your Meeting Minder, the Speaker Notes, and the Slide Meter will appear to your audience if you use these tools during a live presentation.

Pens and Arrows

The third set of tools available from the Pointer popup menu consists of the Arrow, Pen, and Pointer Options choices. You can choose to use an arrow as a pointing device during your slide show, or you can switch to a pen. If you choose a pen, you will still be able to access different tools from the Pointer popup menu by right-clicking to access the shortcut menu, but you will not be able to advance to a slide by clicking on the present slide, and you will not be able to activate any of the text-building options of interactive programs you may have associated with objects on your slide.

You can use the pen to write on the surface of your slide without making any changes to the slide itself. For example, you can circle important items or draw the audience's attention to another item by underlining it. You can use several different color "inks" on the same slide. And when you have finished marking your slide, you can erase everything you did with the pen and return your slide to its original form.

NOTE

If you have access to a Pen Pad, experiment to see whether you can use it effectively during your presentation. The mouse does not offer a great amount of agility; consequently, when you use the pen, your handwriting appears uneven, not unlike the contestant sign-ins on Jeopardy.

To use the pen, click on the pointer and choose Pen. You can write anywhere on the slide; it will not affect the slide's transition in the show.

If you want to change the color of the pen, select Pointer Options ➤ Pen Color from the Pointer menu and select a new color for your pen.

When you need to erase any marks you have made on your slide, click on the pointer, select Screen, and select Erase Pen.

Go to Black

You can black out the screen at any time during your presentation by selecting Screen ➤ Black Screen from the Pointer popup menu. You can still use the pen to write on the black screen if you wish. To return your slide to its normal view, select Screen ➤ Unblack Screen from the Pointer popup menu.

View on Two Computers

Even though you have been working on a presentation on your own computer, creating, editing, enhancing, and modifying what you do, it's always a good idea to get another opinion of your work before you give the presentation. PowerPoint includes the View on Two Computers option that enables you to run the presentation on two computers at the same time. You might use this feature when you're in your "rough draft" stage and are inviting feedback from a coworker or superior or when you are doing a kind of training that would benefit from having two computer users at the same time.

To give the presentation on two computers, choose Slide Show ➢ View on Two Screens. The dialog box shown in Figure 29.7 appears. The instructions on the screen tell you how to choose the connection and set up the other computer. Click on OK when you're finished. When you give the presentation, it is displayed both on your computer and on the computer to which you are connected.

FIGURE 29.7

*Viewing the
presentation
on two screens*

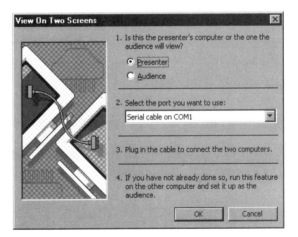

Presentation Conference: Adding Other Computers

A Presentation Conference enables you to give your presentation while others view it online. This is a great forum if you're preparing your presentation as a team effort; each person on the team can attend the Presentation Conference and make suggestions for further revisions.

To use Presentation Conference you first have to take note of a few items. If you are unsure about the information, contact your network administrator or Help Desk staff. They should be able to help you in creating your Presentation Conference.

First, you need to make sure your computer is on a network or has access to the Internet. You will know whether you are networked with other computers if you double-click on the Network Neighborhood icon on the desktop and can browse your entire network. If your computer is not networked, contact your systems staff to either correct the problem or find a computer that is on your network.

Second, you need to know the addresses or "names" of the computers you wish to join to your presentation. For some offices, this is usually the same as a person's logon. For others, it is a special inventory code. And for still others, it is a personalized name for the computer. It's traditional with network administrators to pick a theme for a network. If you have any trouble locating the names of the computers, again, talk with your systems staff.

Starting a New Conference

Follow these steps to begin a new conference. The Wizard walks you through the process, enabling you to set everything up, get everyone online, and give the presentation.

1. Select Tools ➤ Presentation Conference to see the Presentation Conference Wizard dialog box shown in Figure 29.8.

Use the Presentation Conference Wizard to set up a new conference.

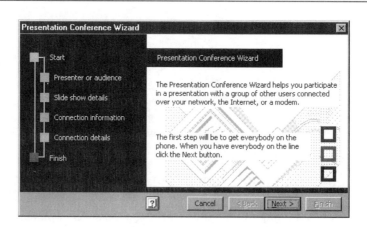

2. Click on Next to continue to the next page of the Wizard. If you need help, click on the Help button at the bottom of the dialog box. The second page of the Wizard enables you to choose whether you'll be the presenter or the audience (see Figure 29.9).

FIGURE 29.9

The Wizard's second dialog box lets you decide whether you are presenting or observing.

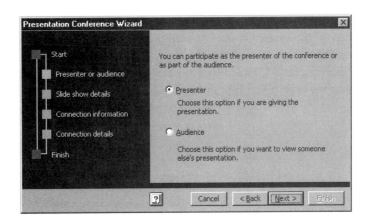

3. Next PowerPoint shows you which slides are to be included in the presentation. Unless you've previously hidden slides, all slides will be shown by default. If you want to omit some slides, cancel the Presentation Conference Wizard, choose Slide Show ➢ Set Up Show to make your changes, and then restart the Presentation Conference Wizard. When you return to this page of the Wizard, click on Next.

4. Connect to your Internet service provider or get everyone connected via modem. Once everyone is connected, click on Next.

5. Now enter the computer address for each participant in the presentation conference. Choose the computers you wish to invite to your Presentation Conference. Type in the name of the computer (not the user's logon, but the computer name) and click on Add. PowerPoint searches your network to find the computers. You can add just one or several computers to your conference. If PowerPoint cannot find the computer on your network, contact your systems staff for assistance. (Note: In future conferences, after you have added computers to your conference list, you can click on the Open List button to display the Open Conference Address List dialog box and choose the participants from the entries there.) Click on Next once you have added all the computers you want in your conference.

6. Finally, click on Finish so PowerPoint can find the computers on your network.

Joining a Conference

Once they have been invited, your viewers must link their computers to your conference. To join, open the Presentation Conference Wizard by selecting Tools ➢ Presentation Conference. On the second page of the Presentation Conference Wizard, click on Audience. Click on Next and choose the connection option that applies: either a LAN or an Internet connection. Click on Next and make sure the computer name is displayed accurately. (If it is not, contact your system administrator for help.) Finally, click on Finish to prepare to view the presentation.

What's Next

Making a success of one presentation is an accomplishment; providing consistent quality in your presentations, even at a moment's notice, should be the quest of anyone relying on PowerPoint as a key ingredient to getting their job done. Chapter 30 delves into the PowerPoint features that allow you to provide this desired consistency.

Chapter

30

Master Templates and Reusability

30

Master Templates and Reusability

Now you've spent hours perfecting your presentation, placing graphics and tables in their proper positions, and customizing text and colors. You've invested a considerable amount of thought, planning, and effort to get your presentation just the way you want it. How easy it would be to save the things you like most about this presentation and use them again in other presentations you create. Through the use of templates and presentation designs, PowerPoint makes this possible.

With PowerPoint, you can create your own templates or complete presentations for your own use or for PowerPoint users in your organization. Although the process can take time to perfect, it is well worth the effort: future presentations will be easier to create and edit.

Reusability Terminology

To take full advantage of the reusability features in PowerPoint, you need to be familiar with the following terminology.

Templates

A template is a slide that has predefined properties, such as background color, text color, text font and size, and interactive settings. A template can either contain no slides, such as the templates in the Designs tab of the New Presentation dialog box, or have numerous completely formatted slides, with text and bullets. PowerPoint includes several templates that already contain slides in the Presentations tab of the New Presentation dialog box.

Templates, Templates Everywhere

Your first glance at the New Presentation dialog box will reveal several different templates from which to choose. How do you know which template you need? Are some better than others? How do you decide? Here's a quick look at what each of the tabs contains and how they differ:

General—Includes only the presentations and templates you create. When you create your own presentation files and templates, they are added to the General tab.

Presentations—Contains 33 complete presentations, each based on a particular theme. The actual content of the presentation—or suggestions for how you can supply your own—are included on the slides. Additionally, all the design elements are there, so all you need to do is plug in your own text and data.

Presentation Designs—Offers 17 more presentation designs. These files are strictly designs, meaning you create your own slides, text, and charts and use the design built into the template.

Web Pages—Includes only two items, both of which are files that include slides with objects you may want to use in a presentation you're designing for the World Wide Web. You can easily create links to these objects, which can include your company name, URL, or other important information.

Presentation Templates to Help with Content

PowerPoint goes beyond helping you manage the look of your presentation and actually helps you create the content. Are you preparing to give a technical report? Introduce a new product? Sell your idea? No matter what your purpose, PowerPoint offers you pre-designed presentations you can simply use with your own data. To choose one of PowerPoint's content templates, choose File ➤ New and click on the Presentations tab.

You can click on different presentation icons to see how they look in the preview window. When you've found the one you want, click on OK. The presentation is opened in Slide view and you can enter your own information. Figure 30.1 shows a presentation based on a financial template displayed in Slide Sorter view. PowerPoint has created the title, bullet items, tables, even charts—now all you have to do is enter your own data.

FIGURE 30.1

The Presenta-tions selections are complete presentations that include a number of slides, text, graphics, and charts.

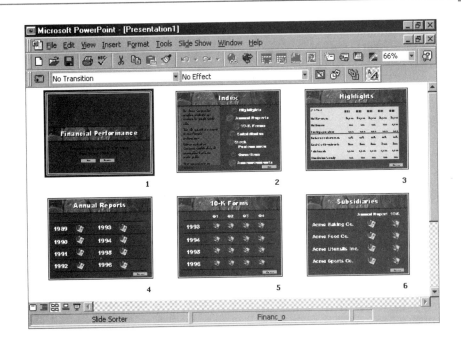

Presenting with PowerPoint

Web Page Templates

PowerPoint also includes templates for Web pages you may want to create from your presentation. Display the New Presentation dialog box by choosing File ➤ New and select the Web Pages tab. Choose the file you want and click on OK. The files available include banners you may want to use on your Web pages.

Layouts

Slide layouts contain the number and placement of objects on the slides themselves. When you create a slide, AutoLayout prompts you for a layout for your slide. You can choose from 24 different layouts. If you need to create a custom layout, you can use the blank layout and place those objects you need on the slide or modify a formatted layout to fit your slide's needs.

Even though you want to select just the right slide layout for each slide in your presentation, you can still rely on PowerPoint's expertise to do the design work. When you choose File ➤ New and select the Presentation Designs tab, you see a number of different designs on which you can base your presentation. Click on an icon to see a preview of the design it represents. When you find the one you want, click on OK, and PowerPoint displays the New Slide dialog box so you can choose the layout you want to use with the new design template you have chosen.

Title Slide

The term *Title Slide* is somewhat misleading. It does not refer to the first slide in a presentation or to the slide that contains the name of your presentation. It refers only to a particular layout, the Title Slide layout. You can have as many Title Slides as you want in your presentation. Although this may at first seem redundant, having one layout to control the Title Slide is important if you want to break down your presentation into several sections and introduce each section with a Title Slide.

The Title Only layout is *not* considered a Title Slide. If you want to create a Title Slide without any subtext, do not place any text in that object. Remember, the dotted lines surrounding objects do not appear in the presentation; they are used only for reference in editing slides.

Masters

Masters control the appearance of slides, handouts, and notes in a presentation. With a presentation open on the screen, select View ➤ Master to select the Master you want from the Master menu. You can choose any one of the following Masters: Slide Master, Title Master, Handout Master, and Notes Master.

Masters control the appearance and placement of the footer, date, page number, and any graphics or lines you want to add to all your slides, handouts, and notes. Masters also control the color of your text and background and the interactive settings for objects.

Although you can change the Interactive settings for a Master, you cannot change the Slide Transition, Build Slide Text, or Animation Settings options here. You must activate these settings from the individual slides and objects.

Slide Master

The Slide Master, shown in Figure 30.2, contains the formatting that controls how layouts will appear for existing or new slides in a presentation. The Slide Master can control the appearance of all the slides in a presentation or template, but if you want the Title Slide to be treated differently, use the Title Master to control the layout for that slide.

FIGURE 30.2

The Slide Master controls the formatting for all slides in a presentation.

Title Master

The Title Master, shown in Figure 30.3, changes the formatting for only the Title Slide layout. You can have numerous Title Slides in a presentation, and they can appear at any position in a presentation. However, PowerPoint considers only the Title Slide layout as a Title Slide, so if you change the Title Master, it will not affect any other slide layouts in the presentation.

FIGURE 30.3

The Title Master only changes the formatting for the Title Slide.

Handout Master

The Handout Master, shown in Figure 30.4, controls the appearance of the handouts you choose to print and then distribute to your audience or presentation staff. You can include a header, footer, date, and number in your Handout Master.

You also can choose from four different Handout Master designs by choosing the look you want from the Handout Master toolbar. The first handout design is for 2-Per-Page handouts, in which two slides are printed on each page. The second design, 3-Per-Page, gives you room for three slides. The third design, 6-Per-Page, arranges six slides on a single page; and outline displays the Outline only used for the handouts.

*Handout
Master and
its toolbar*

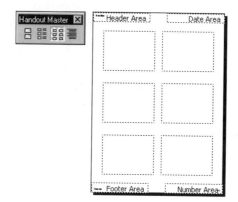

Notes Master

By choosing View ➤ Master ➤ Notes Master, you will get the display shown in Figure 30.5. The Notes Master controls the placement of the header, footer, date, number, notes body area, and slide image.

Master Layouts

Each Master also has a layout. The layout elements are visible only when viewing a Master, and then only the layout for that Master is accessible. To view the layout of any Master, just display the Master view you want to see and click on the Master Layout button on the Standard toolbar. Figure 30.6 shows the Notes Master layout dialog box that appears.

FIGURE 30.5

*Use the Notes
Master for
placement of
note text and
header and
footer areas.*

FIGURE 30.6

*The Notes
Master Layout
dialog box lets
you alter what
appears on the
Notes Master.*

The dialog box shows the objects that are currently available on the Master. In this case, all of the items are selected because the Notes Master is currently in its original form. If you want to add an item that you had previously removed, click on the Master Layout button and check the appropriate checkbox to add the checkmark. That would return the item to the Master.

Although you can delete any object from a Master by selecting it and pressing Delete, you cannot delete it from the Layout dialog box. Likewise, you cannot add an object directly to the Master. You must access the Master Layout dialog box, select what you wish to add, and click on OK.

TIP

Editing Masters is almost as easy as editing a layout or individual slide. But because Masters affect all slides in a presentation or a template, take care when making changes to any Master. You can always undo them, but make sure your template and Master look as you wish before putting them to wide use.

MASTERING THE OPPORTUNITIES

Let the Master Do It!

If your eyes start to glaze when you think about working with the Masters in your presentation, you're not alone. Many people have trouble deciding what, if anything, they need to include on a Master.

Masters can save you an enormous amount of time you might otherwise spend redesigning the same basic effects over and over again. Here are a few ideas for deciding which items to include on your Master pages:

- Look at a presentation you particularly like. Make a list of the things that appeal to you. Include items like color, background, text style, and chart types.

- Notice the placement of text, especially in headers and footers.

- Does the presentation include a logo? You can add your company logo at an out-of-the-way place on every slide of your presentation.

- Do you want to add a button, like a Home button for a Web page, to each page of the presentation? That's a good candidate for a Master.

Using Existing Templates

Before you jump in with both feet and try to create a template from scratch, work through the following steps required to edit an existing template that PowerPoint has included for you.

If you have any presentations open in PowerPoint, it is a good idea to close them all at this time. Although making changes to a template or Master affects only the current presentation, you could mistakenly switch between open presentations and alter a presentation you don't want to change.

 TIP

When you edit a template, PowerPoint prevents you from accidentally overwriting an existing template by prompting you for a name. Because of this, you can feel free to experiment.

Deciding on a View

First, you need to decide on the view for your template. You don't want any of the slides already in your presentation, so choose from the list of blank templates:

1. Select File ➢ New.
2. Click on the Presentation Designs tab.
3. Select the FIREBALL template. Click on OK.
4. When the New Slide dialog box appears, click on the Blank slide. Click on OK.

Now you should have a blank presentation slide on your screen. This particular template is useful to work with because it reveals some of the mystery about templates. The background image that you see is actually just one large piece of clip art, which you can replace with a different graphics image.

Replacing Graphics

At this point you need to switch your view so you are viewing the Slide Master. Remember, this is a blank slide, so if you want to make changes to the images on the Title Slide after you add one, you have to view the Title Master. Also remember that even though you can change the background color and color scheme from Slide view, those changes will affect only this individual slide. To create a new template and make changes that will affect all the slides you create in any future presentations based on this template, follow these steps:

1. Select View ➢ Master ➢ Slide Master from the menu bar.
2. Click on the multicolored bar stretching across the slide background. The graphics image should be selected.
3. Press Delete. The image should disappear.

4. Click on the Insert ClipArt button on the Standard toolbar.
5. Choose a piece of clip art you like and click on Insert.
6. Repeat steps 4 and 5 if you want other pieces of art.

You should now have the Slide Master on your screen with clip art. You can copy, move, or resize the clip art to suit your needs. You can even resize the clip art to fill the entire slide. However, if you choose to do this, be careful to pick clip art that doesn't interfere with the text on the screen. The text will appear on top of the background image, but if the colors conflict or there is too much clutter, the text will be difficult to see.

Changing the Font

Let's also change the font for the title on the Slide Master:

1. Select the title for the slide by pressing Shift and clicking on the title.
2. Select Format ➤ Font from the menu bar.
3. Select a font you like from the dialog box and also change the color.
4. Click on OK to close the Font dialog box and return to the Slide Master.

Adding a Name and Logo

Finally, let's put a company name and logo on the Title Master. Change to the Title Slide, if necessary, and display the Title Master. If you have your own company logo that you have used before in another application, you might want to see how it will look on this slide. If not, just choose any piece of clip art. To add a logo, follow these steps:

1. Click on the Insert ClipArt button on the Standard toolbar.
2. Locate your logo or choose a piece of clip art you like and click on Insert.
3. Resize the image if needed.
4. Place the image in the lower right-hand corner of the slide.

Now that you have added the logo for this slide, you need to add your company name to the footer on the Title Master. Do not add any text to the text objects on the slide. Since this is the Master, the text would appear on every Title Slide in your presentation, and you would not be able to use titles. To add your company name, follow these steps:

1. Display the Title Master, if it is not already displayed.
2. Click on the Footer Area.
3. Type the name of your company.

The footer area resizes automatically to accommodate the text you enter. You may want to resize it so the text is distributed differently, however. For example, if your company name wraps around to a second line, you might want to lengthen the footer area so the entire name fits on one line.

To resize the footer area:

1. Select the footer.
2. Drag one of the handles in the direction you want to resize the object.
3. Click on an area outside the object.

NOTE

The term *footer* is somewhat misleading. You don't have to keep the footer at the bottom of the slide. You can move it anywhere on the slide and even make a copy of it so you can have it appear in two places on your Title Master. This may be a good idea if you want to distinguish a division of your company from the entire company.

The identifying names of the objects will not appear on the slide when you return to Slide view. They are there only to help you refer to the objects as you work on the Title Master.

Now that you have created a Title Master, you need to create a Slide Master so that all the slides in your presentation will have the same format. When you create a Slide Master, you can change the attributes for all the slides in a presentation without affecting the Title Slides.

Creating a Slide Master

To create a Slide Master, follow these steps:

1. Select View ➢ Master ➢ Slide Master. Notice that you are back to your original format.
2. Choose Format ➢ Background.
3. Click on the drop-down arrow next to the color box and choose Fill Effects. The Fill Effects dialog box appears. Select the Pattern tab (see Figure 30.7).
4. Select a pattern. Be sure to select one that will not interfere with the text on the screen.
5. Click on OK; then click on Apply to change the background of the Slide Master without changing that of the Title Master.

At this point you should save your template:

1. Select File ➢ Save from the menu bar.
2. In the Save As Type dialog box, change the file type to Presentation Templates.
3. Type the name of the template and click on Save.

Now, close this template so you can create a new presentation based on it. You should be able to find it alongside the other templates in the General tab in the New Presentation dialog box. If it's not listed there, open the template again by selecting it

FIGURE 30.7

*Choosing a
pattern for the
Slide Master
background*

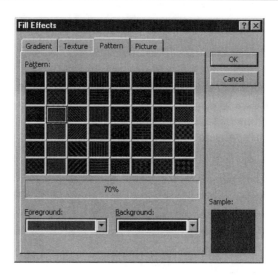

from the most recently used file list under the File menu, and then repeat the steps
above for saving a template.

Creating a New Presentation

To create a new presentation based on the template:

1. Select File ➣ New from the menu bar and click on the General tab.
2. Select the template you just created. Click on OK. The New Slide dialog box
   appears.
3. Select the Title Slide layout and click on OK.
4. If you want to select a layout different from the Title Slide, click on the Slide Layout tool and then choose a different layout.
5. Click on Reapply.

If you are not in Slide View, switch to it. Then switch between your two slides to
confirm that they are formatted the way you want. The Title Slide should be as you
formatted it. It should be different from the second slide you created. If you are
unhappy with the formatting or need to change something, you can always repeat the
steps above to reformat the Masters.

You can use Masters to change the settings not only for templates, but also for existing presentations. Now that you have learned how to edit the Slide and Title Masters,
you might want to reopen a presentation you created previously and redesign the
slides. Don't be afraid to tinker; you can always close your presentation without saving, preserving you original presentation.

Design Presentations

PowerPoint has created numerous templates for you. Open each and see how the Masters are designed. Feel free to copy any graphics images you like onto another Master for a different presentation. Browse freely; you might find that certain effects you cannot create yourself have been created for you.

You will find all kinds of personalities represented in the templates that are available, from whimsical to professional, from stodgy to stylish. Experiment with the various templates to get just the right look for your presentation.

Although we created a template based on an existing design presentation, don't feel limited to using a predesigned template. You can always create a template from scratch, but you might want to wait until you are thoroughly familiar with PowerPoint before attempting this.

Experiment with different patterns and textures to see how they will work with different text colors. Create your own colors. Use your imagination and be creative. Remember, it will take some time to become comfortable with everything you can do with slide layouts, Masters, and templates.

What's Next

With the reusability techniques covered in this chapter, you are now versed not only in creating powerful presentations, but in how to recycle the pieces of your presentations that will aid you in making future presentations easier to create with the same level of quality.

The next chapter explores the considerations you need to take into account when making presentations out of the office, possibly without the comfort of the computer that was used to create the presentation. The chapter also reviews basic file-management techniques that will focus on where and how you keep your presentations on your computer.

Chapter

31

File Management and Taking It on the Road

FEATURING

File Management and Taking It on the Road

I n this chapter we focus on three major aspects of file maintenance: locating files, preparing files for the World Wide Web, and taking presentations on the road. One of the great features of PowerPoint is that you can take it wherever you need to make powerful presentations. At a client's office, in a booth at a trade show, or even as a Web page on the World Wide Web, you can use PowerPoint to deliver your message with impact.

Changing the Default File Location

Windows 95 provides a folder named My Documents. Many people, especially new users, will want to save their files here so they know where they are. When you save a presentation in PowerPoint, your presentation files are saved in the My Documents folder. When you prepare to open a presentation, using File ➤ Open, PowerPoint displays the contents of the My Documents folder (see Figure 31.1). You may want to change this default folder location so you can keep all your PowerPoint files together.

You can change this PowerPoint option of defaulting to the most recently saved folder by defining a path, or a place for PowerPoint to save all your files. This simple process takes just a few seconds. Follow these steps to change this option so you will know exactly where your files have gone:

1. Select Tools ➤ Options from the menu bar.

FIGURE 31.1

*The Open
dialog box in
PowerPoint*

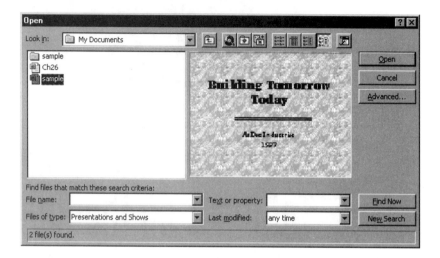

2. When the Options dialog box appears, click on the Advanced tab (see Figure 31.2).
3. With your mouse, click on the Default File Location field and type the name of the folder where you want your presentations to be saved. For example, if you wanted the default to be a folder you created and named My Work, you would type **C:\My Work** into the field.

FIGURE 31.2

*Changing the
default folder*

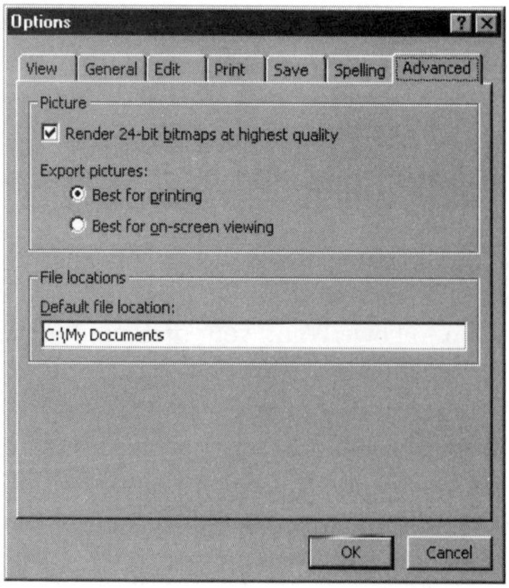

Saving Your Presentation as an HTML File

Maybe you didn't know it—but your presentations may be ideal Web pages, created to interest, enlighten, and inform readers who visit your Web site in cyberspace.

You can easily turn your presentation into a document ready to be used on the World Wide Web by using PowerPoint's Save As HTML option. HTML is an acronym for HyperText Markup Language, and it is a type of tagging system that controls the placement, style, and color of text and graphics on your page.

Deciphering Cyber Lingo

If you are new to the Internet and just getting your beginner's stripes on the World Wide Web, some of the terms and acronyms may be new to you. Here are some terms you'll see as you investigate Internet possibilities:

GIF—An acronym for Graphics Interchange Format, the format for graphics files available on the Internet and popular online services.

JPEG—A compressed format for high-quality graphics often used in multimedia.

HTML—An acronym for HyperText Markup Language, a tagging system that formats documents for the World Wide Web.

Web Page—A page of information on the World Wide Web with links that enable visitors to move from page to page.

World Wide Web—An interactive method of navigating the Internet through a series of linked pages.

URL—An acronym for Universal Resource Locator, commonly referred to as a Web page address (example: http://www.microsoft.com).

Link—A "hotspot" on a page that takes you to another location or activates an object to accomplish a predefined task, such as run an animation, play a sound, or download a file.

1. Choose File ➤ Save As HTML, and the Save As HTML dialog box appears (see Figure 31.3). A Wizard will lead you through the process of turning your presentation into an HTML document. To continue, click on Next.

2. First you are asked whether you want to choose a layout or create a new one. New layout is selected automatically. Make your choice and click on Next. If you choose to create a new layout, the HTML Wizard gives you a choice of two different page styles, Standard or Browser Frames (see Figure 31.4). Choose the style you want and click on Next.

FIGURE 31.3

The HTML Wizard helps you prepare an HTML document

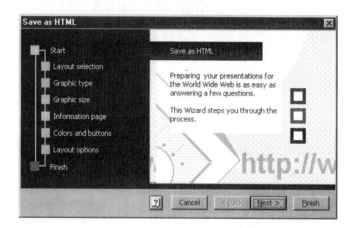

FIGURE 31.4

Choosing a page style

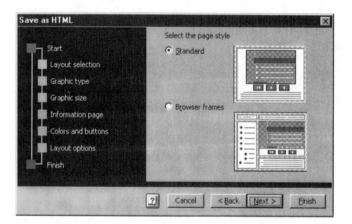

3. The next page asks you what type of graphics you plan to use. Choose GIF or JPEG. If you include animation in the presentation, click on the PowerPoint Animation button. Visitors to your Web page will be prompted to get the PowerPoint Animation Player in order to view the animated objects on their own systems. Click on Next.

4. You are asked to choose how you want the graphics on your page displayed. Different monitors will have different capabilities, and on the Web you can be sure that your site will be accessed by all kinds of users with many different system setups. The lowest standard, 640 by 480, is selected by default, and you can leave this setting selected to be sure the largest number of users can view the graphics you include. You can also select the width of the graphics by clicking on the Width of Graphics down-arrow and choosing from the drop-down list. Click on Next.

5. Enter your e-mail address, your home page address, and any other information you want to include. To allow visitors to download your original presentation file in addition to viewing it online, click on the Download Original Presentation checkbox. Click on Next.

6. To let visitors' browsers determine the colors they see, click on Use Browser Colors (see Figure 31.5). If you want to specify your own colors, click on Custom Colors and choose from background, text, link, and visited link colors. Also, if you want the buttons to appear transparent, click on the Transparent Buttons checkbox. Click on Next.

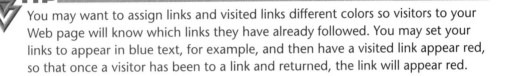

TIP

You may want to assign links and visited links different colors so visitors to your Web page will know which links they have already followed. You may set your links to appear in blue text, for example, and then have a visited link appear red, so that once a visitor has been to a link and returned, the link will appear red.

FIGURE 31.5

*Selecting page
and button
colors*

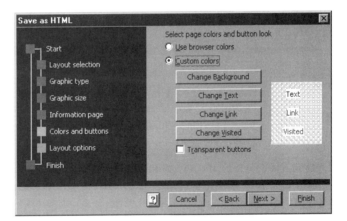

7. You will see a page on which you determine where the buttons are placed: above, below, to the right, or to the left of the page. If you want to add the slide notes to pages, you can click on the checkbox to do so. Click on Next.

8. The final page of the HTML Wizard asks you where you want to create the HTML directory that will store the files you create for your presentation. Type the folder name or click on Browse and select the folder from the list. Click on Next. Finally, click on Finish.

9. You are then asked to enter a name for these same HTML conversion settings in case you'd like to use them again. This is a kind of template approach to creating HTML documents, so if you think you may make these same choices the next time you create a Web page, enter a name for the settings and click on Save. If you want to discard the settings, click on Don't Save.

10. PowerPoint displays an HTML Export in Progress message window, telling you how the operation is going. When the process is complete, click on OK on the displayed message; you are returned to the presentation in Slide view.

Using the Pack and Go Wizard

One of the most useful tools now available in PowerPoint is the ability to "pack up" all your work. Not surprisingly, the tool responsible for this is called the Pack and Go Wizard. Pack and Go compresses your presentation and any files you have linked to it to a floppy disk so you can make your presentation on another computer. This Wizard also gives you the option of installing the PowerPoint Viewer on the floppy so you can view your presentation on a computer that does not have PowerPoint installed.

 NOTE

The PowerPoint Viewer *will* work on a computer running Windows 3.1 or Windows 3.11. However, the Viewer does not support all the functionality of the full PowerPoint product.

Packing Up

To use the Pack and Go Wizard, first be certain your presentation is in its final form. If you use the Wizard and later make changes to your presentation, you will have to rerun the Wizard to repack your presentation in its new form.

1. To start saving your presentation on a floppy disk, select File ➢ Pack and Go from the menu bar. You will see the screen shown in Figure 31.6. The Wizard prompts you to click on Next or Cancel. Choose Next.

2. The Pack and Go Wizard now prompts you to either pack your current presentation or choose Other Presentation(s) (see Figure 31.7). If you choose Other, click on the Browse button to find the presentation you wish to pack. Once you have selected the presentation, click on Next.

3. Now the Wizard asks for a destination for your compressed presentation file. Choose Drive A (or B) if you want a floppy to be the destination, or select Choose Destination if you want to save the file to another drive. Click on Next.

FIGURE 31.6

*The first screen
in the Pack and
Go Wizard*

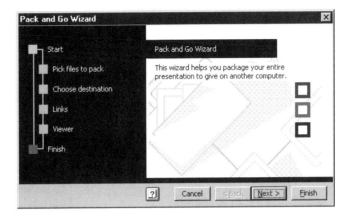
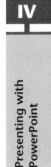

FIGURE 31.7

*Selecting which
presentation to
pack and take
on the road*

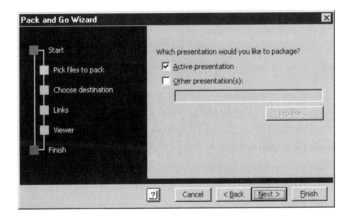

4. The Wizard now asks whether you want to include linked files and embed True-
Type fonts. If you have linked any files, make sure this box is checked. If you have
any special fonts on your machine that may not be available on the machine
where you will be doing the presentation, you should also check the Embed True-
Type Fonts box. Once you have made your selections, click on Next.

5. Check the *Viewer for Windows 95 or NT* checkbox if you will be taking your presentation to another computer that does not have PowerPoint. Click on Next.

6. The final screen asks to go back, cancel, or finish. If you are satisfied and wish to
continue creating your compressed presentation file, click on Finish.

PowerPoint now creates a compressed file on your floppy drive, or another drive if you chose one, that you can run, or execute, when you arrive at your presentation location. Look for the file PSNGSETUP.EXE to begin the unpacking process.

Unpacking the Presentation

Once you have reached your destination, run the file PowerPoint created while packing up your presentation.

1. From the Start button on the Microsoft window, select Run. Then type **A:\PNGSETUP.EXE** and press Enter.
2. The dialog box in Figure 31.8 asks you for a destination for your presentation. Select the folder or type its name directly into the destination field.

After designating the folder, your presentation will be uncompressed for viewing (see Figure 31.9), and a dialog box will open asking whether you want to view the presentation now.

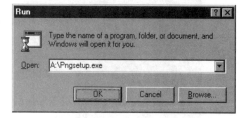

MASTERING TROUBLESHOOTING

Opportunities to Use the Pack and Go Wizard

How could you use the Pack and Go Wizard?

- To show a proposal to a client.

- To run in your booth at a trade show.

- To take a presentation to display as part of your off-site training program.

- To present your annual report at the corporate meeting in Bali.

- To have sales people at a remote site become familiar with your product.

Presenting with
PowerPoint

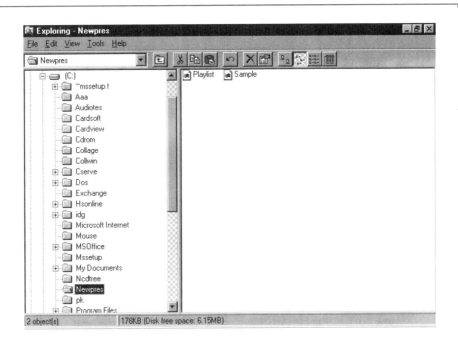

What's Next

The presentations you will be making, whether they are on the road or in-house, will at one time or another benefit from the other Office applications you use. The next chapter illustrates how you can greatly increase the functionality of PowerPoint and significantly reduce the duplication of effort by incorporating the other Office applications into the creation of your presentations.

Chapter

32

Office Connections—
Presenting with the
Help of Other Office
Programs

Office Connections—Presenting with the Help of Other Office Programs

O ne of the most powerful features of PowerPoint is its ability to share information between the other programs in Office. You can copy and paste between any of the other Office programs with the same ease with which you would copy and paste from within PowerPoint. You can either create a working copy of an object from another program or create a link to the original file so all changes will be updated in your PowerPoint presentation.

To Link or Not to Link

One of the biggest questions you will face as a writer of a presentation is whether you should link or embed the objects you place on your slides. Up to this point, we have addressed only embedding an object in a presentation—that is, placing a complete copy of the file within your presentation. This technique, however, has some drawbacks.

One problem is that your presentation file can become rather large if you embed enough objects in it. Another problem is that you have no access to updated information. If you embed an Excel spreadsheet in your presentation, and someone updates the data in that spreadsheet, your presentation will still reflect the old data. The same is true if you plan to embed a chart based on a spreadsheet or an Access table.

However, when you link the original file instead of embedding it, the original file is always referenced and updated in the link. When someone updates the original spreadsheet, your presentation will reflect the new data.

Of course, there is an advantage to embedding a file. If someone moves or deletes the original file, your copy is still securely embedded in your presentation. Also, you don't have to worry about accidental changes in your presentation, because you have "locked" the copy of the file by embedding it.

Another problem with linking is that it does not work over networks. You must still embed any objects you want in your presentation, even if you have permissions on a network to access and edit information in that file.

Also be aware that if you plan to use the Pack and Go Wizard, your embedded or linked objects will work only if your presentation computer has the resident Office program installed. For instance, if you attempt to show a presentation with an embedded Access table on a computer that does not have Access installed, you will not be able to use that table. If you do not plan to take a computer with you for your off-site presentation, be sure to request a computer that has all the necessary programs already installed. If you are able, carry a laptop that has a complete version of Office 97, just in case.

WARNING

If you move a linked file, PowerPoint will not be able to locate it. You must delete the object and reinsert it with the new link.

Up to this point, when you created a new slide, you embedded objects rather than linking them. It is a good idea to continue to create your slides in this fashion until you feel secure enough with PowerPoint to break with tradition and explore the options associated with objects in presentations.

A Review of Embedding an Object

Let's quickly review creating a slide with a simple object, such as a chart:

1. Create a new slide from the New Slide option in the Common Tasks window.
2. Select an AutoLayout that includes a chart and click on OK.
3. Double-click on the chart icon, highlight the existing data, and press Delete.
4. Enter your new data, choose a format for the chart, and edit it if you like.
5. Close the datasheet to view your finished slide with the embedded chart.

Now that you know how to create a slide with a chart embedded in it, take a closer look at what has just happened. You created a chart from scratch with new data that you entered onto a datasheet. You then chose a form for the chart and, optionally, edited it.

When you closed the datasheet, PowerPoint automatically updated your slide by inserting your chart into an object. You really didn't have to worry about files, their locations, or linking and embedding.

This is the simplest way to create an object on a slide. Every time you created a new slide with an object, what you were really doing was either creating a new object from scratch, such as your chart or organizational chart, or embedding an existing object, such as clip art. But now you need to look at creating a slide with existing objects by linking and embedding them.

You can embed or link an object in PowerPoint in two ways. One way is to copy just the portion of the file you want and then paste it on a slide. The other way is to insert an entire file into the slide.

Copy and Paste When Embedding and Linking

Perhaps the easiest way to insert an object into a slide in PowerPoint is to switch to the application in which the object was created, select the object, copy it, and then paste it onto the slide. You have two choices of insertion when you create objects on slides in this manner:

- Pasting
- Pasting with a link

If you paste without a link, you are creating a copy of that file on the slide. If you paste with a link, you are directing PowerPoint to the file so it can create the slide. Since you have not made any copy, your data can update as needed. In Office Connections for Word, you copied and linked a chart to a Word document. You use the same process to insert a chart into a PowerPoint document (slide), first without the link and then by linking the Excel chart.

Copying a Chart

Here are the steps for copying a chart:

1. Enter Excel and open a spreadsheet. If you do not already have a chart made for this sheet, create one now using the Chart Wizard.
2. After you have placed the chart on a sheet, select the chart and press Ctrl+C, choose Edit ➤ Copy, or right-click on the selected chart and select Copy (see Figure 32.1).
3. Switch to PowerPoint, and if you have not already done so, create a new slide based on the Blank layout and choose OK.
4. Press Ctrl+V or choose Edit ➤ Paste.

FIGURE 32.1

*Copying a chart
from Excel to
PowerPoint*

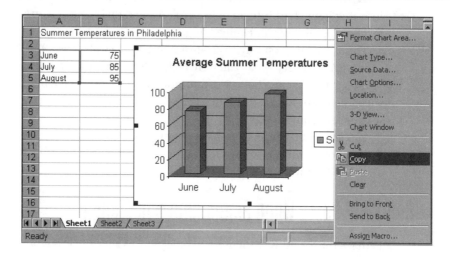

When you copy and paste a chart in this fashion, you are creating a copy of it on the slide. If you edit the original chart, your slide will remain unchanged. This would, of course, be advantageous if you were making a chart of a spreadsheet that changed daily, but you only wanted to graphically reflect the data as of one date. In this instance, you would want to embed the chart with no link.

Linking a Chart

But what if you wanted to have your presentation updated every time the original spreadsheet changed? Then you would create a link between your slides and the original files.

Once again, we'll work with an Excel chart. Try to work with the same chart you used in the preceding example so you can see the difference between the two slides you have created.

Here are the steps for linking a chart:

1. Enter Excel and open a spreadsheet. If you do not already have a chart made for this sheet, create one now using the Chart Wizard.

2. After you have placed the chart on a sheet, select the chart and press Ctrl+C or choose Edit ➤ Copy.

3. Switch to PowerPoint, and if you have not already done so, create a new slide based on the Blank layout and choose OK.

4. Choose Edit ➤ Paste Special. You will see the Paste Special dialog box shown in Figure 32.2.

5. Select the Microsoft Excel Chart Object choice.

6. Select Paste Link and click on OK.

FIGURE 32.2

*Pasting an Excel
chart with a
link into
PowerPoint*

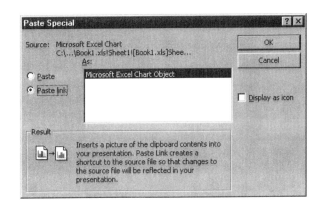

Now go back to your original Excel spreadsheet and change some of the data used
to create the chart. Notice that in Excel, the chart will automatically update to reflect
the changes in the data. If you now switch back to PowerPoint, you'll see that your
original slide, with the embedded (pasted without a link) chart, is unchanged. However, the chart you pasted with a link back to the original Excel spreadsheet has
changed to reflect the new data.

Inserting an Entire File

You can also insert an object into a slide in PowerPoint by using the Insert ➤ Object
menu. When you place an object on a slide in this manner, you are not selecting one
section, such as a chart, sheet, or page, to be inserted into the slide. You are placing the
entire document on the slide. This technique is advantageous if you want a user to
have access to a copy of a file. For instance, you may want to actually show the spreadsheet that produced a particular chart, or you may want to enter the spreadsheet to
view other data that you did not use to create your chart.

As with cutting and pasting, you have the option of creating a link when you insert
an object into your slide. Just click on the Link checkbox in the Insert Object dialog
box (see Figure 32.3).

Here are the steps for creating a link:

1. Choose the Insert ➤ Object menu.
2. Click on the Create from File radio button.
3. Click on Browse, select the file you want to insert, and click on OK.
4. Click on the Link checkbox and click on OK to insert the file.

FIGURE 32.3

Check the Link box to create a link.

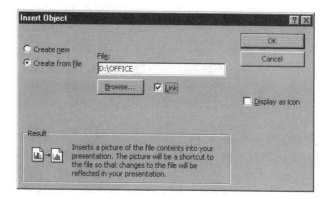

 TIP

You can display the file as an icon, which will allow you to enter the file and edit information, but the file will appear only as an icon on your slide. You can choose this option to speed up the painting of a slide with linked information on it. If an object is large, it can take several minutes to appear.

You can also insert a new object that you create from scratch using this method. In this case, instead of clicking on the Create from File radio button, you would click on the Create New radio button and choose the object type you wish to insert.

The advantage of using this method to insert objects is that you have greater control over the creation process. Instead of relying on PowerPoint to choose a layout for you based on clip art, a chart, an organization chart, a media clip, or an object, you can automatically request a Microsoft Equation or WordArt object. Some users like to use this method of object insertion. Others prefer using AutoLayout. The method you choose will not affect your object's appearance or behavior.

Real-Life Situations

Now let's take a look at a Visitor's Service Center in Philadelphia, where one of the managers, Susan, must create a presentation bringing together elements already created by other employees in the company.

Susan needs to create a simple presentation to welcome employees moving into Philadelphia. This product will be provided free of charge to any company that needs to orient new employees. But Susan has just moved to Philadelphia herself, and she doesn't know much about the city or its attractions. She decides to put her thoughts down in outline form first, before jumping into PowerPoint.

Susan uses Word's Outline view to create an entire document representing the order in which she thinks the information should be presented (see Figure 32.4).

FIGURE 32.4

The Outline view of a document

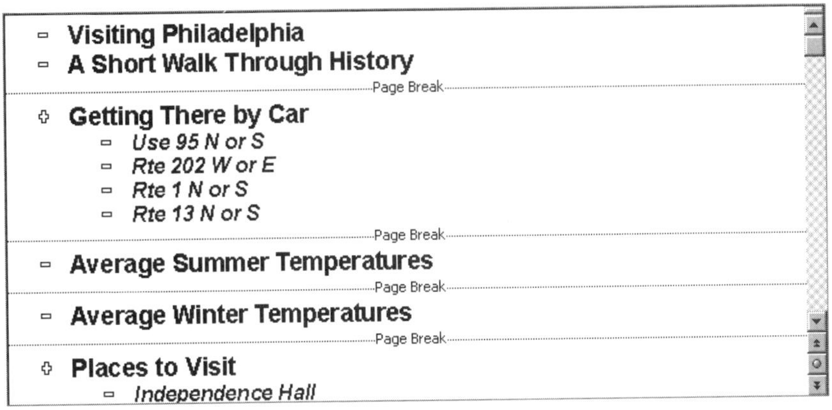

Using a Word Outline as a PowerPoint Presentation

Susan knows she can use Word outlines as the basis of PowerPoint slides, and she decides to create the slide show presentation directly from the outline. She uses Word's Outline view (View ➤ Outline) to create a few headings. Heading 1 items will become new slides. Heading 2 items will become bullet points under Heading 1. Heading 3 items will become subitems under Heading 2. She then saves the Word file and closes it.

Here are the steps for creating the PowerPoint presentation from the Word outline:

1. Create a blank presentation in PowerPoint and choose the Blank layout.
2. Select Insert ➤ Slides from Outline from the menu bar.
3. Choose the Word file containing your outline and click on Insert.
4. Save your presentation.

Copying Excel Data to a PowerPoint Slide

After Susan has created the slides from the outline, she notices that each slide is a little empty. She thinks the slide show needs something more. She has included summer and winter temperatures but not the supporting data. Susan decides to create a workbook in Excel with two charts that graphically display the winter and summer temperatures in Philadelphia. Integrating the data from Excel into the PowerPoint slide will require Susan to open her new presentation in PowerPoint so she can edit the slides.

Next, she will need to start Excel and open the workbook containing the charts. Then she can start to insert her charts.

Here are the steps:

1. After opening both Excel and PowerPoint, move to the slide where you want the chart and delete any empty text boxes.
2. Switch to Excel using the Taskbar.
3. Click on the chart in Excel that you want to insert. Sizing handles will appear around the chart to indicate that it is selected.
4. Press Ctrl+C to copy the chart.
5. Switch back to the PowerPoint slide using the Taskbar, and press Ctrl+V to paste the chart.
6. Place and resize the chart as needed on the slide.

The slide should resemble the one shown in Figure 32.5.

FIGURE 32.5

Excel chart data in a PowerPoint slide

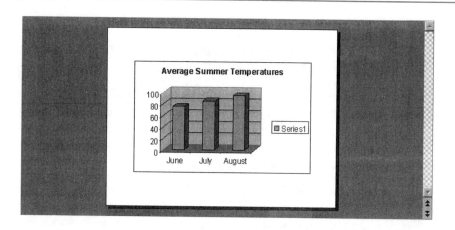

Susan has placed her charts on the appropriate slides, but she decides that the slide showing how to get to Philadelphia should have a map to give the employees a good idea of where Philadelphia is in relation to other cities. She creates a map using Microsoft Map in Excel. After including major cities on the map and some geographic features and highways, she saves the workbook. Susan launches both PowerPoint and Excel. She opens the workbook she created. She then starts to work through the steps for copying the map onto her slide:

1. If there is an empty text box on the slide, delete it.
2. Switch to Excel using the Taskbar.

3. Select the map and press Ctrl+C to copy it.

4. Switch to PowerPoint using the Taskbar.

5. Press Ctrl+V to insert the map.

6. Place and size the map as needed.

7. Save your presentation.

Susan now has a completed slide show ready for the employee orientation. She decides to make some minor changes before her presentation by applying a design template to change the look of her slides. She does this by using the following steps:

1. Choose Format ➤ Apply Design from the menu bar.

2. Select a style you want and click on Apply.

3. Save your presentation.

Susan shows the slide presentation to members of the Visitor's Service Bureau board, and they decide to include the disk with other marketing materials provided to companies and individuals seeking information about Philadelphia. She also discusses the possibility of turning the presentation into a Web page as soon as her company gets their Web site up and running.

The entire slide show, shown in Slide Sorter view in Figure 32.6, was created in Power-Point using elements from other Office 97 applications.

FIGURE 32.6

*Previewing the
slide show in
Slide Sorter View*

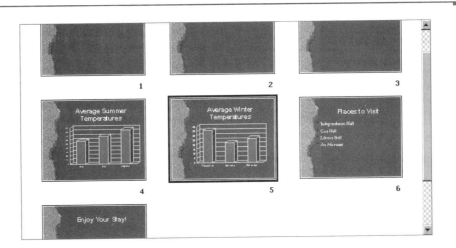

Power Moderation

In this part of the book, you have learned how to create a new presentation, create and edit slides, use the powerful tools included in PowerPoint, such as organization charts and clip art, create templates, make presentations, use the Pack and Go Wizard, and share information between other applications in Office 97. Of course, no text can be exhaustive in its exploration of a program as powerful and flexible as PowerPoint. From here, you should practice your art.

The best way to learn more about PowerPoint is to jump in and start creating new presentations. Try using all the concepts introduced in this part, even if you don't think you will be using them immediately. You will learn more from trial and error than you could ever gain from one textbook. If you aren't sure whether something will work, try it. You can always undo your work later. Keep a backup copy of your presentation on hand, just in case you cannot undo any changes to your file. Soon you will find that you have become a PowerPoint expert, and people will be coming to you for advice and help in creating their own presentations.

PART V

Organizing with Outlook

LEARN TO:

- *Navigate the numerous Outlook folders*

- *Manage your contacts*

- *Track tasks and appointments*

- *Send meeting requests and replies*

- *Track Office application activity with the Journal folder*

- *Create and organize notes*

- *Browse your disk folders*

- *Send and receive e-mail using the Inbox folder*

- *Use Outlook with the other Office applications*

Chapter

33

The Basics of Outlook

FEATURING

The Basics of Outlook

Outlook—the newest member of the Office suite—is a powerful information manager that combines the best features of its predecessors Schedule+ and Microsoft Exchange Client. Outlook brings personal information management capabilities to the Office, helping users track contacts, maintain schedules, and manage tasks. In addition, Outlook performs as a universal e-mail client and file management utility. Fully integrated with the other Office applications, Outlook makes it easier for you to communicate and coordinate effectively in personal and business environments.

What Outlook Can Do for You

Outlook wears many hats as a personal information manager. The following sections will give you a brief overview of Outlook's capabilities as a mail manager, time scheduler, contact manager, and disk navigator. While each of these features by themselves are not ground-breaking technologies, used together they provide tremendous help toward making your work more efficient and effective.

Outlook as a Mail Manager

Outlook acts a universal inbox—a depository for all of your sources of electronic mail, including Internet messages, e-mail from online services like Compuserve and MSN, faxes, and your local network e-mail. To compose messages, you can use the basic Outlook mail editor or WordMail editor, which provides Word editing features. In either editor, you can compose messages that are Rich Text Formatted to allow multiple font colors, sizes, and styles. If your organization uses Microsoft Exchange as its mail server, Outlook lets you take advantage of the powerful workgroup features of Exchange's public folders.

Scheduling Your Time

Outlook manages your time commitments by tracking your appointments, monitoring your progress on specified tasks, and reminding you about important events such as a monthly management meeting or your mother's birthday. Advanced scheduling features include Wizards that help you organize and coordinate meetings among people in your address book. And finally, keeping in mind that your computer is not always at hand, Outlook supports many printing formats for both basic calendars and popular paper organizers.

Contact Management

Keeping track of your contacts is essential whether you are a small business owner trying to provide personal service to customers, an employee of a large company who needs to have instant access to contacts both inside and outside the organization, or simply someone who takes advantage of the Office for personal use to keep family ties intact. Outlook lets you store essential information about a contact in predesignated information fields; if you desire, you can create custom fields specific to your needs. To track any activities you have with your contacts, you can use Outlook's Journal feature to automatically track e-mail, appointments, phone calls, and even usage of other Office documents.

Disk Drive Navigation

Because you frequently use your computer's resources—hard drive, CD-ROM, network, and floppy drives—Outlook makes them easy to access without leaving the Outlook interface. Outlook also lets you start new Office documents, adding more incentive to use it as the centerpiece for your computer activity.

A Quick Tour of Outlook

When you install Office 97, the Inbox icon that was previously on your desktop is replaced with a shortcut to Outlook. Double-click on the Microsoft Outlook desktop shortcut or select Start ➤ Programs ➤ Microsoft Outlook from the Taskbar. If you get a Choose Profile dialog box, select your profile or accept the default profile if no other profiles exist (profiles are discussed in Chapter 37). When Outlook starts, the Office Assistant appears offering a number of introductory help topics; click on OK to close the Assistant for now.

Outlook lets you manage your major tasks using a single window from which other windows can be opened when necessary. This window, known as the Information Viewer, can contain several sections, including the Inbox folder (see Figure 33.1). To the left of the window is the Outlook Bar, showing command icons that help you navigate your way through the program. Above the Information Viewer is the Folder List button, which, when pressed, displays the list of Outlook folders.

PART

V

Organizing with
Outlook

FIGURE 33.1

*Viewing the
Inbox folder in
the Outlook
window*

Folder List Button

Outlook Bar

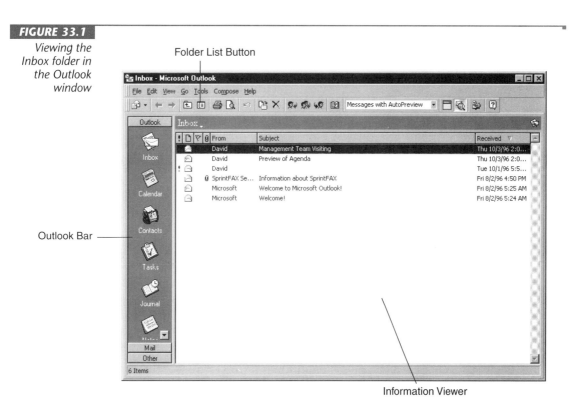

Information Viewer

The Outlook Bar

The Outlook Bar is your tool for navigating tasks, schedules, contacts, and e-mail. The bar is divided into three groups: Outlook, Mail, and Other. If necessary, you can add icons and groups to the bar.

The Outlook Group

The Outlook group contains icons, described in Table 33.1, that switch you between the major functions of the program.

TABLE 33.1: OUTLOOK ICONS AND THEIR FUNCTIONS

Outlook Group Icon	Function
Inbox	Allows you to view the contents of your Inbox folder.
Calendar	Accesses your Calendar, from which you can choose a number of different views such as Day, Week, or Month.
Contacts	Allows you to view your contacts in various address book views such as Address Cards or Phone List.
Tasks	Lets you view tasks by category, including person to whom task was assigned, different levels of details, active or overdue, and more.
Journal	Opens the Journal Information Viewer, which allows you to view entries grouped in different ways. You can automatically track contact activities like e-mail, faxes, meeting requests, phone calls, and usage of Office documents, or you can manually add journal entries one at a time.
Notes	Lets you post small, miscellaneous notes in the Notes folder, much like jotting down quick thoughts or reminders on sticky notes.
Deleted Items	Stores any items deleted from within Outlook.

The Mail Group

The Mail Group contains icons to access to your mail folders. From this group you can get to your Inbox, Sent Items, Outbox, and Deleted Items folders. These folders are described in Table 33.2.

TABLE 33.2: MAIL GROUP FOLDERS AND THEIR FUNCTIONS

Mail Group Folder		Function
Inbox	Inbox	Receives your incoming mail.
Sent Items	Sent Items	Contains copies of outgoing e-mail messages.
Outbox	Outbox	Serves as a temporary storage area for mail that you plan to send but have not yet delivered to its appropriate service.
Deleted Items	Deleted Items	Stores any items deleted from within Outlook.

The Other Group

The Other Group comes with direct links to views of three important folders on your machine's hard drive. Table 33.3 provides a description of each folder.

TABLE 33.3: OTHER GROUP FOLDERS AND THEIR FUNCTIONS

Other Group Folder		Function
My Computer	My Computer	Shows the contents of My Computer in the Information Viewer. From here you can navigate any of the local or mapped folders.
My Documents	My Documents	This is the default location to which the Office applications save. If one folder is not enough to organize your documents, you might consider adding subfolders under My Documents to make accessing your files a bit easier.l

Continued ▶

PART

V

Organizing with Outlook

TABLE 33.3: OTHER GROUP FOLDERS AND THEIR FUNCTIONS (CONTINUED)

Other Group Folder		Function
Favorites		When you add documents to this folder using the Windows interface, shortcuts are placed there so that you can keep the documents in their original location while still being able to access them among other commonly accessed documents.

Custom Groups and Buttons

If you want, you can add groups of your own to the Outlook Bar. Right-clicking an empty area of the bar will display a shortcut menu with an Add New Group option. Select this option and a new grouping bar will appear in the Outlook Bar, ready for you to type a name for it. If you give it the name "My Stuff," your Outlook Bar may look like Figure 33.2. Once the new group is added to the bar, you can add folders or Outlook items specific to your work habits in Outlook.

FIGURE 33.2

We've added the "My Stuff" group to the Outlook Bar.

To add buttons to a custom or existing group, right-click on the Outlook Bar and select Add to Outlook Bar from the shortcut menu. From the dialog box that appears (see Figure 33.3), select from File System or Outlook entries to add to the bar. Click on OK and that item will be added to your chosen group and be available until you decide to remove it

The Information Viewer

Clicking on any button on the Outlook Bar switches the contents of the Information Viewer to show the contents of the associated folder. Depending on which folder you select, the Information Viewer may appear differently to accommodate the type of information stored in that folder. You can change the views in each folder or customize them to suit your needs. To change the current view of a folder, select a view from the Current View combo box on the Standard toolbar.

If the views available do not give you exactly what you want, select View ➤ Define Views from the menu bar. The Define Views dialog box for the current folder will open (see Figure 33.4), and you can manipulate the view to your own standards.

FIGURE 33.4

Use this dialog box to customize your view of the Inbox folder.

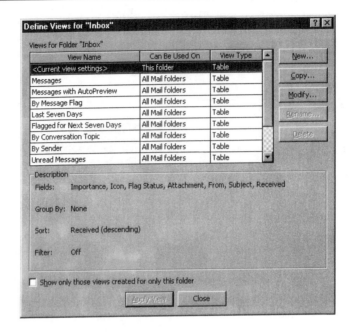

Folder List

To switch to another folder while you are in an Outlook view, click on the Folder List button above the Information Viewer. A folder list of either Outlook or File System items will drop down, allowing you to switch to a folder not directly available on the Outlook Bar. To display the folder list permanently next to the Information Viewer, select View ➤ Folder List from the menu bar or click on the Folder List icon on the Outlook toolbar.

The Outlook Standard Toolbar

The Standard toolbar in Outlook changes slightly depending on the current folder, but some buttons remain consistent (see Figure 33.5).

FIGURE 33.5

The Outlook Standard toolbar

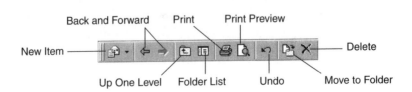

The first button is the New Item button. The default item will change based on the current folder. You can either click on the button to create a new default item or click on the drop-down arrow to the right of the button to choose from another item type. The Back and Forward buttons act like Web-browser buttons as they cycle you through all the places that you have been within Outlook. The Forward button becomes active once you have used the Back button. The Up One Level button helps you navigate through hierarchies of folders. The Folder List button will toggle the Folder List on and off. The Print and Print Preview buttons are followed by an Undo button, a Move to Folder button for moving items from one folder to another, and a Delete button to delete selected items.

WARNING

Be aware that the Delete button on Outlook's Standard toolbar will *not* prompt you with a warning before it deletes selected folders.

The Find Items button is also available while viewing all of the folders. This button accesses the Find dialog box (see Figure 33.6), which performs detailed searches of items within Outlook. The same dialog box can be accessed from other Office applications by selecting Start ➣ Find ➣ Using Microsoft Outlook.

PART
V

Organizing with
Outlook

FIGURE 33.6

The Find dialog box lets you search for items within Outlook.

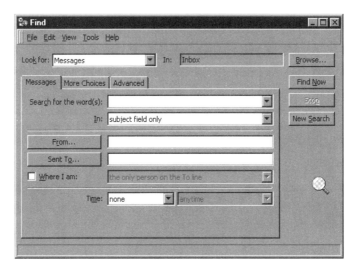

This chapter presented a brief overview of the information management functions of Office's newest application. The following chapters will explain in much greater detail the various functions of Outlook.

Chapter

34

Keeping Track of Your Contacts with Outlook

Chapter

34

Keeping Track of Your Contacts with Outlook

Outlook takes the contact management features previously found in Schedule+ and enhances them to provide tighter integration with other Office applications, including the ability to merge your contact information into your Word documents. Basic features like names, addresses, and phone numbers can now be classified by categories. You can also track e-mail and home page addresses and much more. This chapter will show you how to establish a contact list, classify contacts by a variety of categories, and view your lists in several different ways.

Getting Your Contacts into Outlook

New users of Outlook will fit into two basic categories: those who have never kept track of their contacts with a computer and those who have invested a great deal of time entering their information into another program's format. Users who are taking the electronic tracking plunge for the first time will benefit from many of the features designed to make data entry easier than ever. Users migrating from other applications will find that Outlook's emphasis on seamless conversion via Import Wizards makes moving to Outlook a breeze.

Entering a New Contact

The first step to entering a new contact into Outlook is to bring up a fresh Contact window. There are a number of ways to do this:

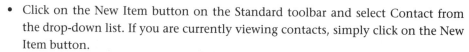

- Select File ➤ New ➤ Contact from the menu bar.
- Press Ctrl+Shift+C.
- Click on the New Item button on the Standard toolbar and select Contact from the drop-down list. If you are currently viewing contacts, simply click on the New Item button.

The Contact dialog box will appear (see Figure 34.1). Your insertion point will be in the Full Name text box on the General tab.

FIGURE 34.1

Entering a new contact begins with the Contact dialog box.

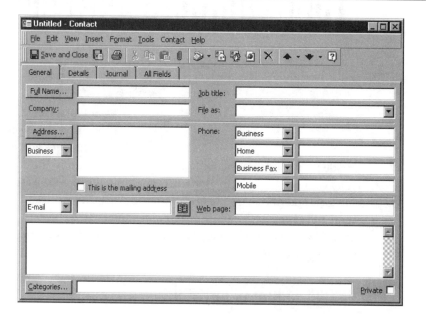

Entering the Name

Type in your contact's first name and then their last name. Press Tab to move to the Job Title field. The File As combo box will fill with the last name first. If you want, you can click on the combo box and choose another option. The options for filing the name in the combo box will grow once you enter a company name.

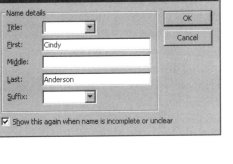

To ensure that Outlook recognizes the name or if you want to add a title, middle name, or suffix, click on the Full Name button to the left of the text box. This will open the Check Full Name dialog box. Here you can make changes or additions to the name. When you are finished click on OK, and the changes will be reflected. Continue by entering Job Title and Company information if appropriate.

Entering Address Information

There are three address choices for a contact: Business, Home, and Other. All of these addresses use the same text box area. Be careful to choose the address type that you are entering in the combo box *before* entering an address. Next type the address into the Address text box and press Tab.

If Outlook cannot interpret the address, it will display the Check Address dialog box for you to provide verification. If you want to have the assistance of the Check Address dialog box from the beginning, simply click on the Address button and enter your address directly into the dialog box.

If a contact has more than one address, change the text box on the left to indicate the address' category and enter it into the text box. Use the checkbox beneath the address to designate which of the three addresses to use when corresponding. It can be checked for only one address at a time.

Entering Phone Numbers

Outlook allows four phone numbers per contact. Each of the number fields has a combo box to identify its type. Choose a type for the number and click on the corresponding number text box. Enter the number without any extra symbols like dashes or parentheses and press Tab. When you leave the number text box, Outlook will format it based on how many individual digits you entered. If there are only seven digits, Outlook adds your local area code and the formatting characters. If there are ten digits in the number, Outlook pulls out the first three as the area code and the last seven for the number. If it is unable to identify the number based on the quantity of digits, it displays a message box asking you to be more specific, such as using parentheses for the area code or a plus sign for an international number.

PART

V

Organizing with
Outlook

Entering Electronic Addresses

Outlook provides space for three e-mail addresses and one home page address per contact. Enter e-mail addresses the same way you would enter a normal address. Select which type of e-mail address in the combo box and type the address in the text box. If you have addresses stored in another area, such as your Personal Address Book or a global address book in Exchange, you can click on the Address Book button next to the text box and choose from there.

When entering a home page address, you can leave off the HTTP:// accompanied by most location addresses and enter the main portion of the address. Once you leave the text box, Outlook will add the prefix for you.

General Contact Notes

Beneath the e-mail area in the Contact dialog box is a free-form text box. You can use this area to keep notes on a contact. Text can be formatted using the Formatting toolbar, which becomes active when you enter the text box.

Taking Full Advantage of the Contact Notes Area

In addition to supporting text formatting, the notes area also supports embedding OLE objects that you may want to store with your contact. Suppose, for example, that one of your contacts has given you an electronic version of her resume to distribute to anyone who might benefit from her services. Instead of storing it on a floppy disk or in a folder on your hard drive, you can insert the file into the notes section of her contact listing.

1. Click on the notes area.
2. Select Insert ➤ File from the menu bar or click on the Insert File button on the toolbar.

3. Find the file that you want to insert using the Insert File dialog box that opens.
4. Make sure that Attachment is selected in the Insert As option group and click on OK. Selecting Attachment stores the file with the contact and makes it available even if you delete the original file. You can select to insert a shortcut, and a pointer will indicate where the file is stored. If you choose to insert it as text, the contents will be inserted into the notes area.

The document will now be stored indefinitely with the contact.

Assigning a Contact to Categories

Outlook facilitates a list of categories to which you can assign various items to track, including contacts. Click on the Categories button to open the Categories dialog box, which presents a list of categories you can assign to your contacts (see Figure 34.2).

FIGURE 34.2

Assigning categories to a contact using the Categories dialog box

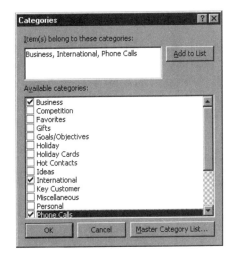

Check the categories to which you want your contact to belong. Later, you can use these designations to group your contact with other members of the same categories. If you need a category not on the list, enter the name into the Item(s) Belong to These Categories text box and click on Add to List. This will add your contact to the new category and place it in the Master Category List so that it will be available to other items in Outlook.

If you want to delete a category, click on the Master Category List button, select the category, and press Delete.

If you want to designate categories without the Categories dialog box, you can simply type them into the Categories text box at the bottom of the Contact dialog box. Any categories that Outlook does not recognize will be treated as new categories, but they will not be added to the Master List. This will prevent them from being assigned to other items, thereby voiding the main purpose you are using categories: to group items together.

PART

V

Organizing with Outlook

Making Your Contacts Private

If you are using Outlook in a workgroup environment where other people will be able to view your Outlook file, you may want to keep some of your contacts private. Click on the Private checkbox for all contacts that you do not wish others to view.

Fields, Fields, and More Fields

There are two more tabs in the Contact dialog box: Journal and All Fields. We will discuss the Journal tab in Chapter 36.

On the All Fields tab, you can select from 11 groups of fields, including All Contacts fields which list in table format just about any field possible. Here you can enter other field information that you want to track. Simply find the field in which you want to store a value and enter it into the table next to the field name. Figure 34.3 shows the Spouse field being selected so that the spouse name can be entered.

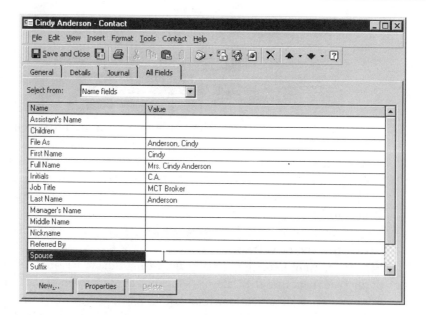

Saving Your Contacts

After you have entered all of the information for the contact, select File ➢ Save from the menu bar. If you want to continue adding contacts, you can use File ➢ Save and New to save the current contact and start a new one. If you are entering multiple contacts from the same company at one time, then select File ➢ Save and New in Company.

Can't Find It?...Create It!

If a field is not available in Outlook but you need it for your contacts, you can create a custom field.

To create a new field, open a Contact dialog box and click on the All Fields tab. Click on the New button at the bottom of the tab and fill in the Name, Type, and Format text boxes in the New Field dialog box. Click on OK.

Your new field will now be available for all of your contacts on the All Fields tab when User Defined Fields in Folder is chosen in the Select From combo box. If you ever want to modify a custom field's properties or view the properties of built-in fields, click on the Properties button.

Once all of your contacts are saved, select File ➤ Close from the menu bar or click on the Close (×) button on the Contact dialog box to return to the main window of Outlook.

Importing Contacts

Outlook's Import Wizard will help you import contacts already entered into another program.

1. To begin importing a file, select File ➤ Import and Export from the menu bar. The Import and Export dialog box will appear (see Figure 34.4).

FIGURE 34.4

The Import and Export Wizard's opening dialog box

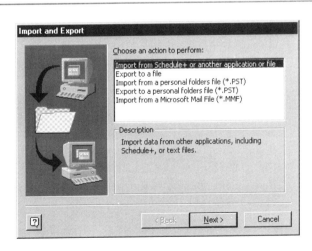

2. You need to tell Outlook where to find your data. You can import from the Personal Folders files, a Microsoft Mail File (*.MMF), Schedule +, and some other applications. Select the appropriate format and click on Next.

3. In the Wizard's second dialog box, scroll through the list box to select the specific application that holds your contacts. Click on Next.

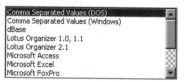

NOTE

If your specific program is not listed, do not despair. It is very likely that your application can export to one of the formats listed. Return to the application that currently has the contacts, export them into one of the formats, and return to the Outlook Import and Export Wizard. You can now specify the exported file that you will now want to import into Outlook.

4. Now you need to specify the actual filename and location. You also need to choose your duplicate import option. You can choose to allow duplicates to be created, update old existing duplicate records with new data being imported, or simply not import duplicate records at all. Click on Next.

5. Select which Outlook folder will receive the imported data. A basic Folder List will appear in the Wizard dialog box. Select Contacts and click on Next.

The Wizard now provides two new buttons: a Change Destination button and a Map Custom Fields button. With the first you can modify your selection of which Outlook folder you want to import. The second button opens the Map Custom Fields dialog box (see Figure 34.5). Default mappings might already have been done by the Wizard. The fields available from the file you are importing are listed on the left and the Outlook fields are listed on the right.

6. You have several options in the next step of the Wizard:

- If you want to add mappings or modify an incorrect mapping done by the Wizard, click on and drag a field from the file being imported on top of an Outlook Field.
- If you want to completely clear the mappings that Outlook made, click on the Clear Map button.
- If you make changes to the mapping and want to revert back to its original format, click on the Default Map button.

- If you want to scroll through the current values of the fields from the application from which you are importing, use the Next and Previous buttons under the application's field listing.
- If there is no Outlook field to match one coming from your application, you can drag the application's field to one of the User Defined fields at the bottom of the Outlook field list named User1 through User4.

Once the mappings are correct, click on OK.

FIGURE 34.5

Mapping fields from the file being imported to Outlook

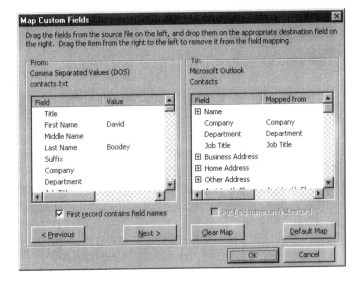

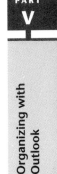

PART

V

Organizing with Outlook

7. After finishing the mapping, return to the main Wizard dialog box and click on Finish.

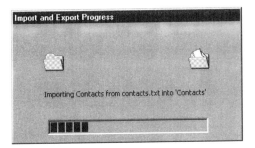

Using your mappings, Outlook will proceed to import your records, displaying the Translation Monitor dialog box until finished. Once all importing is completed, your contacts should be accessible from within Outlook.

Viewing Contacts

Because people have different preferences for working with data, Outlook offers table, card, and icon views of contacts. Each of these views can be formatted a number of different ways to accommodate user needs.

 Outlook is shipped with a few predefined views based on the three basic types. When viewing Contacts, you can choose from the ones that come with Outlook by selecting them from the Current View combo box on the Standard toolbar.

NOTE

While you may see views available other than the three mentioned, they are not discussed in this chapter because they apply more to time-centric events and not contacts. See Chapter 35 for a discussion of the time views.

Card View

Card views provide index-card-like listings of Outlook items. The index cards are stacked on top of each other, fitting as many as possible per column and then wrapping to fit the screen.

There are two predefined views for contacts using Card view: Address Cards and Detailed Address Cards. Figure 34.6 shows the Address Cards view, accessed by selecting Address Cards from the Current View combo box. The Detailed Address Cards view is identical, but with more fields included on each card. On the right hand side of both of these views is a column of lettered buttons that, when pressed, cause the view of cards to jump to the contact names that begin with the letter(s) on the button.

Table View

For the most part, Table views are of the columnar and row variety, much like an Excel worksheet or an Access datasheet. The Phone List view option of the Current View combo box shows a basic Table view with field names at the top of each column and rows representing individual contacts (see Figure 34.7). The first column in Table view includes the icon to identify the Outlook item type, and the second column will have a paper clip in it if there are any attachments in the contact's notes area.

The other views based on a Table view—By Category, By Company, and By Location—demonstrate Outlook's ability to group information in Table view. When you select one of the table grouping views, a Group By section displays above the table list,

FIGURE 34.6

The Address Cards view is one way to view your contact lists.

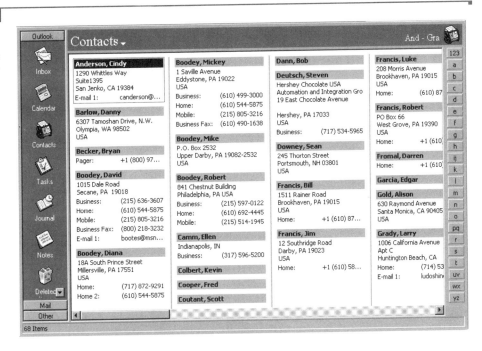

showing the fields by which the list is grouped. If you don't want to use one of Outlook's groupings, you can switch to Phone List view and click on the Group By button on the Standard toolbar. Once the Group By box is atop of the table view, you can click and drag any of the column headings by which you want to group. Whenever you switch views, Outlook displays a dialog box asking if you want to save any changes to the view as a custom view.

Custom Views

You can define your own custom views by selecting View ➢ Define Views from the menu bar. The Define Views for *"Contacts"* dialog box opens. The grid in the dialog box will contain all of the views that are available in the Current View combo box on the Standard toolbar.

If you want to modify one of the views, you can select its row and click on the Modify button. A View Summary dialog box opens with five buttons that access various dialog boxes with options to modify the selected view.

To create a new view:

1. Click on the New button. The Create a New View dialog box opens (see Figure 34.8).

FIGURE 34.7

The Phone List
view shows
contacts in
a columnar
format.

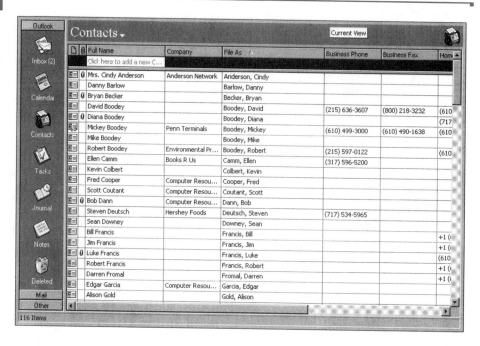

2. In the Name of New View text box, enter a name for the view.
3. Select the type of view. In this example, choose the Icon view. This is the only remaining contact view type that we haven't yet seen.
4. Choose the *This folder, visible to everyone* option in the Can Be Used On group. Click on OK.

FIGURE 34.8

Use the Create a
New View dialog
box to custom-
ize a format
for viewing
contacts.

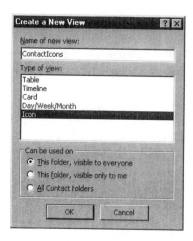

The View Settings for *"Name"* dialog box opens. Three buttons are enabled on the dialog box to modify the view. The Sort button, when pressed, opens the Sort dialog box, which allows you to sort the contact icons up to four levels. The Filter button opens a dialog box for applying criteria requirements to contacts you want to be visible in the view. The Format button opens the Format dialog box, which allows you to format the view; in Icon view it allows you to set icon size and placement. Once you are finished customizing the view, click on OK in the View Settings for *"Name"* dialog box.

Once you are back in the Define Views for *"Contacts"* dialog box, select your new view and click on Apply View. Your new view will appear in the Outlook Information Viewer.

> **NOTE**
>
> If you have made any changes to the previous view before applying the new view, you may get a Save View Settings dialog box. You must decide whether to discard the changes, save the current view settings as a new view, or update the current view with the new settings. Select the appropriate option and click on OK to continue.

The icon view will display your contacts as icons. If you want to see the details for a contact, double-click on the corresponding icon.

Creating and tracking contact information is a critical part of Outlook's information management tasks. Outlook can track your contacts to associate them with appointments in your calendar. The next chapter discusses creating appointments associated with your contacts as well as Outlook's ability to track events and tasks.

PART

V

Organizing with Outlook

Chapter

35

Managing Your Time with Outlook

Managing Your Time with Outlook

Outlook's major function is to schedule your time and help you manage it. Outlook divides your time into four categories—appointments, events, tasks, and meetings—and provides efficient organizational tools to keep track of increasingly complicated schedules.

Time Folders

Outlook uses two folders to help you manage your time: the Calendar folder and the Tasks folder. The Calendar folder lets you view your schedule with simultaneous access to other tasks and calendars. You can also view your appointments in table format, with data grouped by similar attributes. The Tasks folder allows you to manage your appointments and duties in a more task-oriented manner. You can organize calendar entries by whether they are current, overdue, or completed or by who is responsible for them. Both folders let you customize the views to suit your needs most effectively.

Calendar Folder

To access the Calendar folder, click on Calendar on the Outlook Bar. The default view shows the current day's appointments and events (see Figure 35.1). Also shown is the Date Navigator, which allows a quick glance at the current and following month, and the TaskPad, which lists your current tasks.

FIGURE 35.1

The Day/Week/ Month view is the default view of the Calendar folder.

Date Navigator

TaskPad

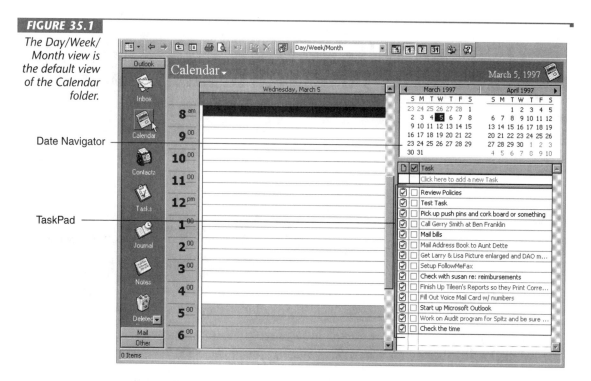

To customize the Date Navigator, place your mouse pointer over its left or bottom border; the mouse pointer will change into a double-headed arrow symbol. Click and drag the mouse to increase or decrease the space in the Date Navigator. The number of months displayed will change accordingly.

You can also change the daily schedule to weekly or monthly. Select View ➤ Day, Week, or Month from the menu bar to switch your view of events and appointments accordingly. Selecting a range of days in the Date Navigator will change the view specifically to those days. Note that the selected days in the Date Navigator in Figure 35.2 are displayed in the appointment calendar.

FIGURE 35.2

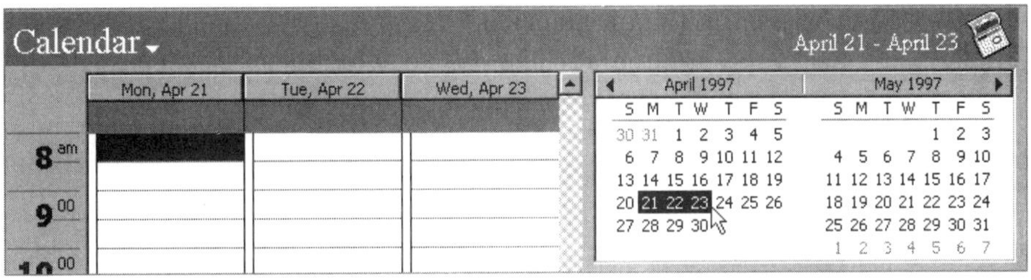

*The days
selected in Date
Navigator are
reflected in the
appointment
and event
viewer.*

TIP

If you select View ≻ Month from the menu bar or the equivalent button on the Standard toolbar, the Date Navigator and the TaskPad seem to disappear. They actually have just decreased in size. To show the Date Navigator and TaskPad, position the mouse over the right hand side until you see the resizing pointer and click and drag it to the left. The size of each day will decrease, but you will have access to the TaskPad and Date Navigator.

Tasks Folder

Clicking on the Current View combo box on the Standard toolbar will show the various views in which Outlook can display your tasks. Click on Tasks on the Outlook Bar to select one. Figure 35.3 shows a Simple List table view, which details whether your task is complete, the subject of your task, and its due date. Other views offer more columns for detail, filters to show tasks with similar traits, and groupings to make organization easier. While most of these views are in a table format, the Task Timeline view will display a timeline with your tasks along it (see Figure 35.4).

Appointments

Most of the time that you schedule in Outlook will be in the form of an appointment. You can specify a subject, location, start and end dates and times, whether the appointment is an all-day event, reminders, and any descriptions or comments you might have. Appointments can also be grouped to enhance your organization.

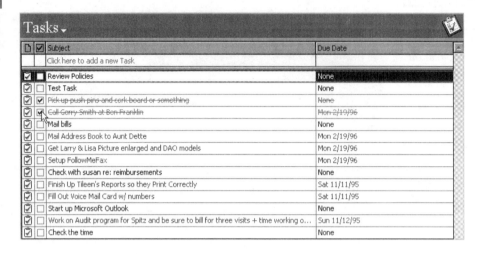

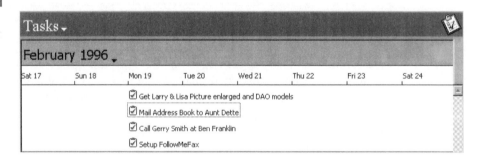

Creating New Appointments

You can create new appointments in Calendar view by any of the following methods:

- Selecting Calendar ➤ New Appointment from the menu bar.
- Clicking on the New Appointment button on the Standard toolbar.
- Pressing Ctrl+Shift+A or Ctrl+N.
- Right-clicking on the Appointment and Event view and selecting New Appointment from the shortcut menu.

Figure 35.5 shows the Appointment dialog box that opens to accept your new appointment information.

FIGURE 35.5

Adding a new appointment

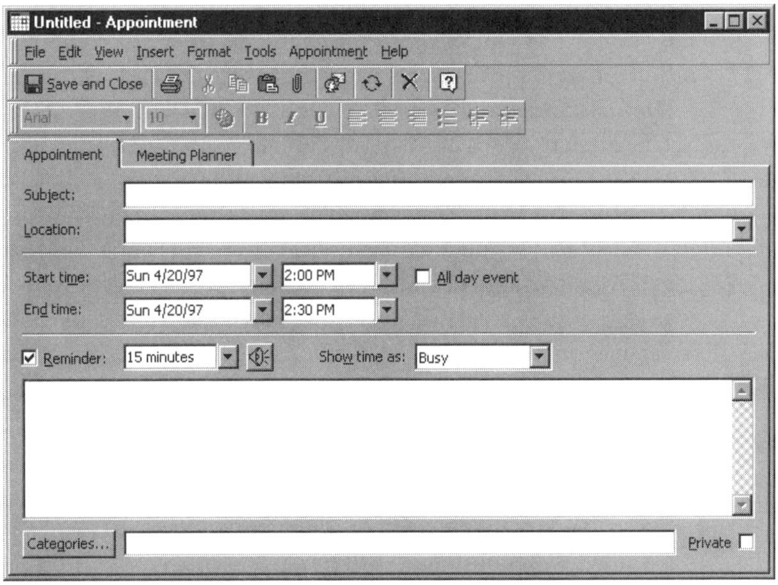

PART

V

Oarganizing with Outlook

Enter the Subject—The Subject box is where you place a primary description of the appointment. The information entered here will be used to identify the task in the various views.

Enter the Location—Specify a location for the activity in the Location combo box. The location will be available for other appointments by clicking on the drop-down arrow.

When Will It Take Place—Use the Start and End Time fields to specify the date and time for the appointment. If you check the All Day Event checkbox, the hour portion in the fields is removed and you need only provide the start and end dates. If you click on the drop-down boxes for the dates, a calendar is displayed to help you pick a date. Clicking on the drop-down boxes for the times provides a list of times in half-hour increments.

Just in Case You Forget—Click on the Reminder checkbox to be reminded ahead of time of an appointment. The combo box to the right of the checkbox will become enabled, and you can indicate how far in advance you want to be reminded. If you want to specify a time other than the predefined list of time options, you can type it into the combo box directly. If, for example, you want to be reminded four days before an appointment, you simply type **4 Days** in the combo box. Clicking on the Sound button next to the reminder allows you to specify the sound to be used when it is time to remind you of the appointment.

Show Time As—You can choose to identify an appointment in four different ways, which are indicated by colors on your schedule: Free (white), Tentative (cyan), Busy (blue), and Out of Office (purple). This color association is helpful when you or others are trying to schedule a meeting using Outlook's Meeting Planner.

Detailed Description—The large text area with the vertical scroll bar is used for detailed description information. This area can also be used to embed OLE objects, such as a Word document that contains the agenda for a conference you are attending.

Categorize It—You can organize your appointments by assigning them to Outlook categories. If you have a number of accounts and want to group your appointments for reporting purposes, you could create a category for each account and assign your appointments accordingly. Later you could view your categorized appointments in a table format to see which accounts are taking the most time.

Make It Private—You may have personal appointments, and you want others in your workgroup to know only that your are "unavailable." Click on the Private checkbox in the bottom right-hand corner of the Appointment dialog box to insure that only you see the detailed information.

Save It—When you are finished entering information in the Appointment dialog box, click on Save and Close on the Standard toolbar or select File ➢ Save and File ➢ Close from the menu bar. Your appointment will be saved, and you will be returned to the main Outlook window.

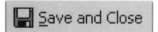

Recurring Appointments

Certain appointments may occur at regular intervals instead of just once. Perhaps you have a weekly department meeting every Thursday at 3 P.M. or a monthly breakfast meeting of a charity board to which you belong; both of these are examples of recurring appointments.

You can create a recurring appointment in the Calendar folder by selecting Calendar ➢ New Recurring Appointment from the menu bar. Or you can create a regular appointment and select Appointment ➢ Recurrence or press Ctrl+G or click on the Recurrence button on the Standard toolbar. A new appointment is created and the Appointment Recurrence dialog box shown in Figure 35.6 opens.

Setting the Time—Specify the time that the appointment will take place. Enter a Start time and then specify either a Duration or an End time; the latter two fields are linked so that one adjusts when the other is changed.

What Is the Recurrence Pattern—Specify how often your appointment will occur by checking Daily, Weekly, Monthly, or Yearly.

FIGURE 35.6

*Creating a
recurring
appointment*

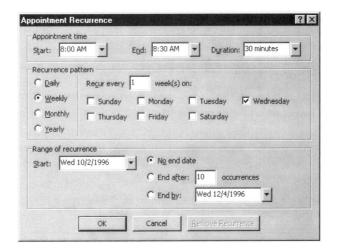

- If you want daily recurrence, you need to specify whether it should happen every weekday or enter the number of days between the appointments. Selecting Daily and entering Recur Every **1** Day(s) will place it in your calendar every day.
- For weekly recurrence you must specify which days of the week and the week frequency. Checking Tuesday and Thursday and specifying a frequency of **2** weeks will enter the appointment every other week on Tuesday and Thursday.
- With a monthly recurrence you can pick on which day of every month you want the appointment to occur, or you can specify a pattern such as the first and third weekends, or a specific day of the week and the monthly recurrence interval.
- For a yearly recurrence you must designate a specific day of the year, or you can specify a pattern such as the third Friday of every April.

How Long Should the Appointment Recur—Once you have designated the pattern of occurrence, you must tell Outlook how long it should apply the pattern. The Start date is usually the day that you are creating the appointment, but you can change it if necessary. Select from the radio buttons when to stop the recurrence and fill in the appropriate dates, as necessary. Click on OK when you are finished scheduling the recurring appointment.

The Basics—When you are finished with the Appointment Recurrence dialog box, you need to specify the basic appointment information like sub-

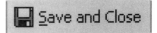

ject, location, and whether you want to be reminded before each occurrence. Instead of date and time information, a sentence describing your chosen recurrence options is displayed on the appointment. After putting the final touches on your appointment, save it by selecting File ➤ Save from the menu bar or click on the Save and Close button on the Standard toolbar.

Viewing Appointments

Most viewing of appointments is done using the Day, Week, and Month views of the Calendar folder (See Figures 35.7 and 35.8). Appointments are indicated by white space spanning the time set aside for the appointment. If you choose to be reminded of the appointment, a small bell will display in the white space. If you create a recurring appointment, two arrows forming a circle will display. To the left of the appointment will be the color representing how you wanted the time to be shown: Free (white), Tentative (cyan), Busy (blue), or Out of Office (purple).

FIGURE 35.7

The Day and Week views of scheduled appointments

When viewing your appointments, you can click and drag them to change the times that they occur in daily view or the day that they occur in weekly or monthly view.

You can also view your appointments in various table formats. Figure 35.9 shows a table view that lists only recurring appointments, and groups them by their type of recurrence. The first two columns in Table view identify what type of Outlook item you are viewing and whether there is an attachment.

PART

V

Oarganizing with
Outlook

FIGURE 35.8

A Monthly view
of appointments

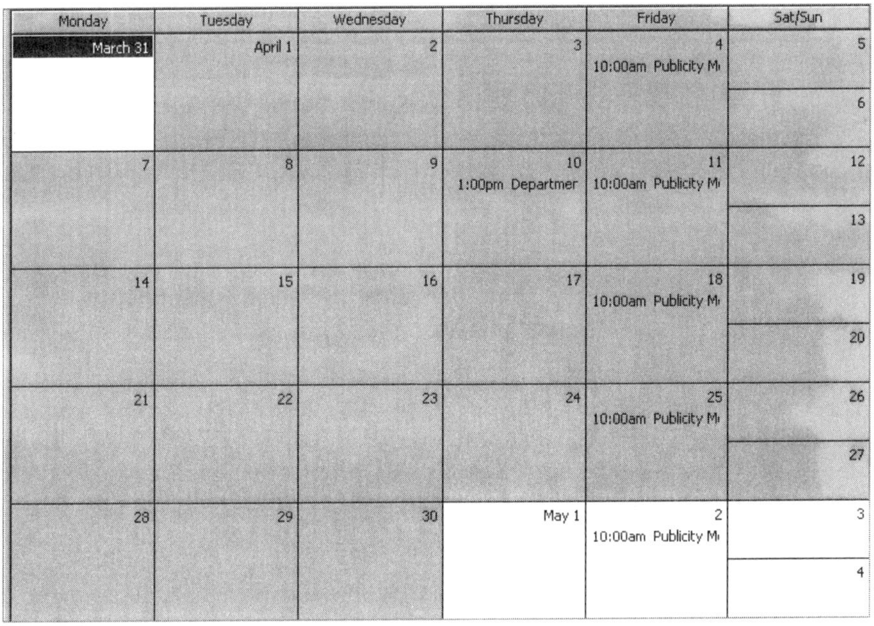

Monday	Tuesday	Wednesday	Thursday	Friday	Sat/Sun
March 31	April 1	2	3	4 10:00am Publicity M	5
					6
7	8	9	10 1:00pm Departmer	11 10:00am Publicity M	12
					13
14	15	16	17	18 10:00am Publicity M	19
					20
21	22	23	24	25 10:00am Publicity M	26
					27
28	29	30	May 1	2 10:00am Publicity M	3
					4

FIGURE 35.9

A Table view
of recurring
appointments,
grouped by
categories

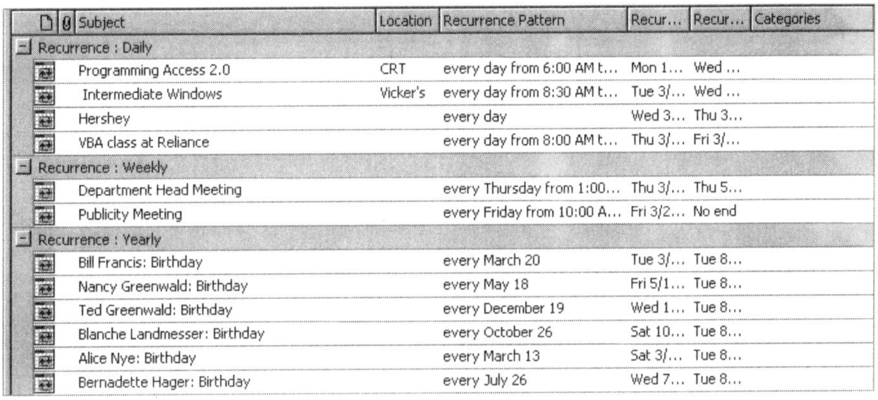

	Subject	Location	Recurrence Pattern	Recur...	Recur...	Categories
Recurrence : Daily						
	Programming Access 2.0	CRT	every day from 6:00 AM t...	Mon 1...	Wed ...	
	Intermediate Windows	Vicker's	every day from 8:30 AM t...	Tue 3/...	Wed ...	
	Hershey		every day	Wed 3...	Thu 3...	
	VBA class at Reliance		every day from 8:00 AM t...	Thu 3/...	Fri 3/...	
Recurrence : Weekly						
	Department Head Meeting		every Thursday from 1:00...	Thu 3/...	Thu 5...	
	Publicity Meeting		every Friday from 10:00 A...	Fri 3/2...	No end	
Recurrence : Yearly						
	Bill Francis: Birthday		every March 20	Tue 3/...	Tue 8...	
	Nancy Greenwald: Birthday		every May 18	Fri 5/1...	Tue 8...	
	Ted Greenwald: Birthday		every December 19	Wed 1...	Tue 8...	
	Blanche Landmesser: Birthday		every October 26	Sat 10...	Tue 8...	
	Alice Nye: Birthday		every March 13	Sat 3/...	Tue 8...	
	Bernadette Hager: Birthday		every July 26	Wed 7...	Tue 8...	

No matter what view you use for your appointments, you can always see the detail or edit it by double-clicking on the appointment or right-clicking on it and selecting open from the shortcut menu.

Events

Creating a new event is identical to creating a new appointment, except that the appointment is specified as an All Day Event. Rather than specify start and end times, you choose start and end dates. Or you can select Calendar ➤ New Event and enter the appropriate data.

To establish a recurring event, select Calendar ➤ New Recurring Event or press Ctrl+G after creating a new appointment. Select All Day Event to access the Appointment Recurrence dialog box.

Events are distinguished from normal appointments with a border and shaded background. In the Day, Week, and Month views, the events are listed at the top of each day (see Figure 35.10).

FIGURE 35.10

The different Calendar views show events at the top of each day.

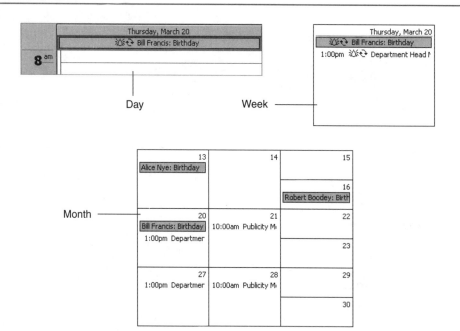

Tasks

In Outlook, tasks are items to be completed but not within a specific time frame. You can specify a task's target completion date, its priority, and, as you keep track of it, what percentage of the task is complete.

Entering New Tasks

Create a new task by selecting File ➤ New ➤ Task, Task ➤ New Task, pressing Ctrl+Shift+K, or clicking on the first line of the TaskPad that reads *Click here to add a new task*. If you want to send a task to someone else's task list, choose New Task Request from the menu options. Clicking on the first line of the TaskPad makes the Subject field and the Due Date text box available. Using the other two options or double-clicking on the new task on the TaskPad opens the New Task dialog box (see Figure 35.11). Here you can enter or modify the Subject field, which is the primary listing for the task.

FIGURE 35.11

The Task dialog box

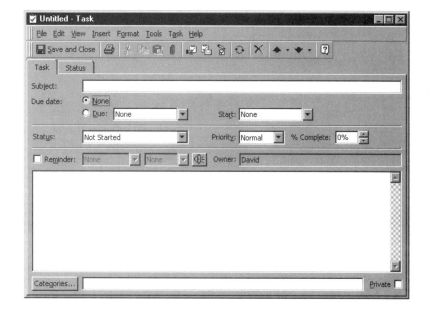

Indicating a Due Date—Specify a due date by clicking on the Due option button and entering a date. To indicate a start date, specify it in the Start combo box. When a due date is specified, Outlook adds a line to the task indicating the length of time until the due date. If there is no start date, the combo box will accept None and the Due line is removed from the task.

Status, Priority, and % Options—You can assign the initial status and priority of the task by filling in the corresponding combo boxes. As work is done on the task, these options can be modified as well as the % value, which is used to monitor the task's progress.

Reminder—To prevent a task from getting lost in the shuffle, you can set a reminder to go off at a predetermined time before the task is due.

Description—Enter detailed information regarding the task in the large text box, or you can embed OLE documents that may be related to the task.

Categories—Like the other items in Outlook, you can assign the task to categories for use in grouping.

Private—Finally, you can also mark a task as private so that other users cannot view it.

The Status Tab of the task is available for you to provide information on how long you have worked on the task, what resources you have used to complete it, and what companies and contacts were involved in its completion.

When you are finished editing the new task, select File ➤ Save and File ➤ Close or click on the Save and Close button on the Standard toolbar.

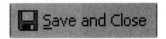

Recurring Tasks

To set a recurring task, press Ctrl+G, select Task ➤ Recurrence from the menu bar of the Task dialog box, or click on the Recurrence button on the Standard toolbar. Follow the guidelines under "Recurring Appointments" earlier in this chapter for establishing a recurring task.

Assigning Tasks

If you are in a position where you delegate tasks to individuals, then the Assign Task option will be useful. When you assign a task, you essentially bundle the task up like an e-mail message and send it to the assignee.

To assign a task, select Task ➤ Assign Task from the menu bar of the Task dialog box, or click on the Assign Task button on the Standard toolbar. The dialog box gains a To field in which you enter the person responsible for the task. Figure 35.12 shows a task being assigned to another user.

You can be updated on the task's progress and its completion by checking the corresponding checkboxes before sending the task to its new owner. Once all of the assignment information is entered, click on the Send button on the toolbar to deliver it to the assignee.

PART

V

Oarganizing with
Outlook

FIGURE 35.12

*Assigning a task
to another user*

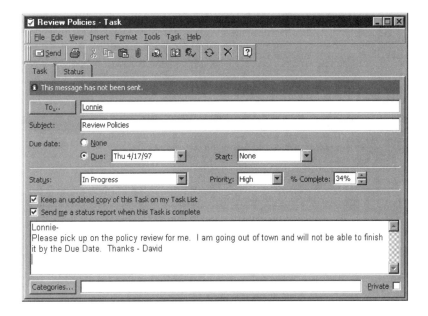

Viewing Tasks

There are a number of options for viewing tasks. Use the Task folder to view your tasks
in a variety of formats. If you want the tasks integrated into the views of your Calendar, you can take advantage of the TaskPad.

Calendar Folder

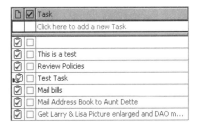

To view your tasks alongside of your appointments and events, use the TaskPad in the Calendar folder. To modify the TaskPad, select View ➣
TaskPad View to choose a view for the pad or
select View ➣ TaskPad Settings to modify which
fields are displayed, grouping categories, and the
format of the font.

Tasks Folder

The Tasks folder is the place to go when you want to focus on your tasks. Like the other
folders, you have a number of viewing options, most of which are table-type formats for

ease of viewing. You can use variations of the views to limit the listed tasks to overdue or active tasks, tasks due in the next seven days, Task Timeline, or various grouping options. You can select an existing view from the Current View combo box on the toolbar, or select View ➤ Define Views from the menu bar to customize the existing views or create your own. Figure 35.13 shows the predefined Task view Detailed List.

FIGURE 35.13

The Detailed List view in the Task folder

	!	0	Subject	Status	Due Date	% Complete	Categories
			Click here to add a new Task				
✓				Not Started		%	
☑			This is a test	Not Started	None	0%	
☑			Review Policies	Not Started	None	0%	
☑			Test Task	Not Started	None	0%	
☑			Pick up push pins and cork board or something	Completed	None	100%	
☑			Call Gerry Smith at Ben Franklin	Completed	Mon 2/19/96	100%	
☑			Mail bills	Not Started	None	0%	
☑			Mail Address Book to Aunt Dette	Not Started	Mon 2/19/96	0%	
☑			Get Larry & Lisa Picture enlarged and DAO models	In Progress	Mon 2/19/96	43%	
☑			Setup FollowMeFax	Not Started	Mon 2/19/96	0%	
☑			Check with susan re: reimbursements	In Progress	None	75%	
☑			Finish Up Tileen's Reports so they Print Correctly	In Progress	Sat 11/11/95	35%	
☑			Fill Out Voice Mail Card w/ numbers	Not Started	Sat 11/11/95	0%	
☑			Work on Audit program for Spitz and be sure to…	In Progress	Sun 11/12/95	90%	
☑			Check the time	Not Started	None	0%	

Meetings

Another form of appointment is a Meeting Request, in which you set up an appointment that you want other people to attend. If other users publish their schedules, you can determine beforehand the availability of the people you want to attend.

Requesting a Meeting

There are two ways to initiate a meeting. You can use the Plan a Meeting dialog box or you can create a Meeting Request directly, which is an appointment with a To field for the attendees, and fill in the Meeting Planner tab.

Using the Plan a Meeting Dialog Box

To use the Plan a Meeting dialog box, select Calendar ➤ Plan a Meeting from the menu bar or click the Plan a Meeting button on the Standard toolbar. When the Plan a Meeting dialog box opens (see Figure 35.14), you should fill the All Attendees column with the people whom you want to attend the proposed meeting.

FIGURE 35.14

Use the Plan a Meeting dialog box to invite participants to a meeting.

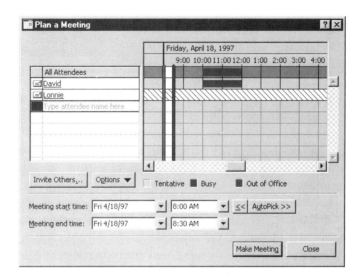

After filling in the Attendees list, be sure to establish the Meeting Start and End Times. The grid to the right of the attendees' names indicates whether they are busy, have tentative appointments, or are out of the office. If there are diagonal hash marks in their row, it means that Outlook was unable to determine their availability. If you are trying to get a group of very busy people together, you can use the AutoPick button. This option will find the next available opening of time when everyone is free. Once you have selected a meeting time, you can click on the Make Meeting button.

A Meeting dialog box will open with the names of the attendees listed in the To field. When you are satisfied with the meeting settings, click on the Send button so that all of the attendees are notified of your meeting request.

Creating a Meeting Request

You can create a Meeting Request directly by selecting File ➢ New ➢ Meeting Request from the menu bar or by pressing Ctrl+Shift+Q. You will access the Meeting dialog box. You will not have the information culled from the Plan a Meeting dialog box, but you can still review free and busy times of attendees by using the Meeting Planner tab of the Meeting dialog box. When all of the meeting options have been entered, click on Send to route your request to the attendees.

PART

V

Oarganizing with
Outlook

Accepting or Declining a Meeting Request

If you receive a meeting request, it will appear in your Inbox like a regular e-mail message. When you open the

message, however, you will find three special buttons. You use these buttons to accept, tentatively accept, or decline the meeting request. When you choose one of the first two options, the appointment will be entered into your calendar. If you choose the third option, your calendar will not be affected.

When choosing any of the options, you will be prompted with a dialog box informing you that a response will be sent to the person requesting the meeting. You have the option to send the default response, edit the response so that you can provide an explanation for your decision, or cancel sending a response altogether. The meeting initiator will receive your decision by mail, indicated both in the subject of the e-mail and in the header of the e-mail when it is opened. Outlook will also supply a current listing of those who accepted, tentatively accepted, and declined the meeting to date.

Chapter

36

Journal, Notes, and Other Folders

Journal, Notes, and Other Folders

Outlook offers a couple of additional folders that you will find useful in managing your day-to-day scheduling. The Journal folder helps you record and track specific items, and the Notes folder lets you create instant reminders to post onto your work.

Journal Folder

The Journal folder is used to track selected portions of your daily work flow. Items that can be tracked include communications with your contacts and, if desired, documents created in Word, Excel, Access, PowerPoint, and the Office Binder. The journal entries can be created manually or be tracked automatically.

Manually Entering Journal Entries

You can enter a new journal entry by selecting Journal ➤ New Journal Entry from the Journal folder menu bar, selecting File ➤ New ➤ Journal Entry from any Outlook menu bar, or pressing Ctrl+Shift+J. Figure 36.1 shows the Journal Entry dialog box that appears.

FIGURE 36.1

*Creating a new
journal entry*

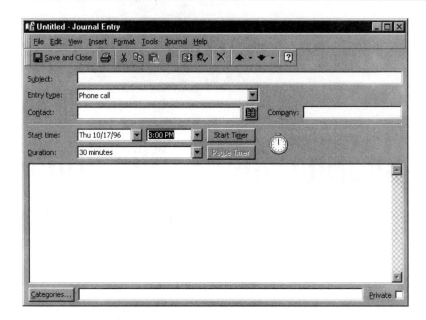

Subject—Like all Outlook items, the Subject field for the journal entry is the primary field of identification. You will want to be as descriptive and concise as you can.

Entry Type—This journal-specific field is used to qualify the type of action that is being recorded. A drop-down combo box provides a finite list of options from which to choose. If one of the items provided does not exactly match what you want to record, you may want to consider selecting Note from the list and using it whenever you need a generic value for this field. You can always elaborate in the description text box about the specific journal entry.

Contact—Most of your journal entries will have a connection to a contact. Clicking on the Address Book button will open the Select Names dialog box for you to pick your contact. If you are using multiple address books you can select the specific address book from the Show Names combo box. When you select the contact and click on OK, the Company field will be filled in automatically if a corresponding value is stored with the contact.

Start Time—A start time can be specified for the item, and if you want, you can specify a duration for the journal from the Duration combo box. If the item should be timed for billing or similar purposes, use the Start Timer and Pause Timer buttons to record the actual time duration of the entry.

PART

V

Organizing with
Outlook

TIP

If you do not want to pick your contact from a list box, you can type a portion of the contact's name into the Contact text box and press Alt+K. Outlook will attempt to resolve the portion of the name you entered. If there is only one possible match, the name will be completed and underlined to signify that it is recognized by Outlook. If the portion of the contact name that you entered could be matched with multiple contacts, a dialog box will open with the possible contacts listed; select one of the contacts and click on OK.

Description—Any elaboration you need to make about the entry can be done in the description text box at the bottom of the dialog box. Any OLE objects, like Office documents, can be embedded into this area to keep related items closely tied to the entry.

Private—If you need a journal entry to be designated as private so that others cannot view it, you can do so using the Private checkbox at the bottom right-hand corner of the dialog box.

Categories—The Categories button will open the Categories dialog box from which you can assign the entry to any applicable categories to use for future sorting and grouping. When you return to the Journal Entry dialog box, the selected categories will be listed, separated by commas.

Save It—When all of the information for the entry is filled in, select File ➤ Save from the menu bar or click on the Save and Close button on the toolbar. Your entry is now stored in Outlook.

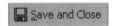

Automatically Recording Journal Entries

You can designate that certain actions associated with specific contacts be automatically recorded in your journal. To pick contacts and their associated items to automatically track, select Tools ➤ Options from the Outlook menu bar and choose the Journal tab (see Figure 36.2).

There are three list boxes on the Journal tab. In one you can choose which item types to automatically record in the journal. The next list box lets you select which contact associations you want to track for each selected item type. Any of the applications checked in the last list box will be tracked with automatic journal entries in Outlook. If you double-click on a journal entry group, you can specify whether the journal entry itself or the Office document opens when you double-click on a journal entry icon. After selecting all of the options items to be automatically tracked in the journal, click on OK. See Chapter 38 for more information on tracking Office documents.

FIGURE 36.2

The Journal tab of the Options dialog box

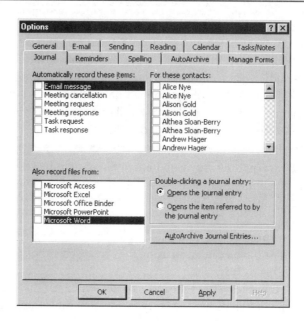

Viewing Journal Entries

Timeline views and Table views are best suited for use with the Journal folder. Timeline views can show you in which order your journal entries took place. Some views may be grouped by a particular characteristic of the journal entry. If there is grouping, the entries will be separated by gray bars that can be collapsed to see only one type of entry. Figure 36.3 shows a Timeline view grouped by type.

FIGURE 36:3

A Timeline view of journal entries grouped by type

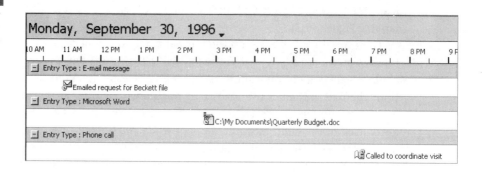

Table views of your journal entries make sorting by various columns a snap. Figure 36.4 shows a table view of journal entries sorted by Entry List. Like the other items in Outlook, all of the view types are available to build new views, but the Timeline and Table views are most appropriate.

FIGURE 36.4

A Table view of journal entries sorted by Entry List

		Entry Type	Subject	Start	Duration	Contact	Categories
		E-mail message	Request for Training Dates	Fri 9/27/...	0 hours	Denise Leo	
		E-mail message	Emailed request for Beckett file	Mon 9/3...	0 hours		
		Microsoft Word	C:\My Documents\Quarterly Budge...	Mon 9/3...	2 minutes		
		Phone call	Wright, Christine	Tue 9/24...	0 hours	Christine Wright	
		Phone call	Called to coordinate visit	Mon 9/3...	0 hours	Alice Nye	

Notes Folder

The simplest of inventions, the Post-it® note, has become a key tool for many in remembering those small tidbits of information that need to be temporarily kept but are not substantial enough to file. Outlook has taken the basic Post-it® note functionality and implemented it in the Notes folder.

Creating a New Note

Creating a note could not be easier. You can select Note➤ New Note from the menu bar of the Notes folder or press Ctrl+Shift+N from anywhere within Outlook. Either one of these options will create a note.

The note will display over whatever part of Outlook you have open. Type your thought on the new note and press the Esc key. The note will be saved and you will return to where you were before creating the new note.

9/30/96 7:01 PM

TIP

If you are in the Notes folder you can right-click on the Information Viewer and select New Note from the shortcut menu.

Changing the Colors of Notes

To color-code your note, right-click on the note that you want change, select Color from the shortcut menu, and choose the new color. To modify the default color of the

PART

V

Organizing with Outlook

notes, select Tools ➣ Options from the menu bar and change the Color option in the Notes Defaults section of the Tasks/Notes tab. You can also change the size, the font, and whether to show the time and date.

Viewing Notes

The view most commonly used for the Notes folder will be the Icon view (see Figure 36.5). If the text of the note is too long to display normally, you can move your mouse over the note and, after about a second, the note will display in full.

As always, the number of views is limited only by what your imagination can do with the basic view types. One example of a different view is a table view using Auto-Preview. When AutoPreview is on, you can see the first portion of the note, which for most of your notes will be the complete thought (see Figure 36.6).

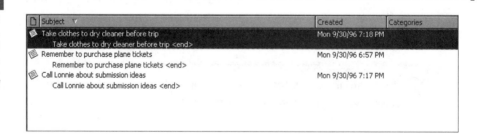

To activate AutoPreview for any view, select View ➣ AutoPreview or click on the AutoPreview button on the toolbar.

Other Folders

The Other section of the Outlook toolbar has shortcut buttons to My Computer, My Documents, and the Favorites folder. Clicking on these buttons will switch the Information Viewer to the specified folder. You can navigate the subfolders and files in the Information Viewer as you would with Windows Explorer. Double-clicking on any folder or container object will open the folder and display its contents in the Information Viewer window. If you find a file that you want to access, you can double-click on the file to open it.

Adding Folders to the Outlook Bar

If you want to create a shortcut to a particular folder that you frequently access, click and drag the folder onto the Outlook Bar. If you right-click on the Outlook Bar and select Add to Outlook Bar, you can pick a folder to add from the Add to Outlook Bar dialog box.

Viewing Folders

You can select from a number of predefined views for your disk drive. These default views are based on the same view types on which other Outlook folders can be based. Figure 36.7 shows the Details view of a C-drive.

PART

V

Organizing with Outlook

FIGURE 36.7

The Details view of a C-drive is one of several options for viewing your disk drive.

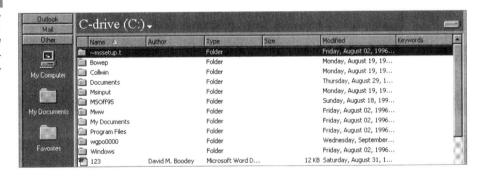

Chapter

37

Outlook As Your Mail Client

Outlook As Your Mail Client

One of the primary folders within Outlook is the Inbox folder, which can accept any variety of communications from outside your program. The Inbox folder is the default delivery location for all e-mail services that you choose to install with Outlook. By taking advantage of its special features, you can use Outlook as a universal client for all your communication needs.

A Universal Client

When it comes to working with e-mail, Outlook acts as a universal inbox, which means that you can go to one place for all of your sources of electronic mail. Before, if you subscribed to multiple online services, used the e-mail system at work, and sent faxes electronically, you would need to access several programs, having to manage each source separately. By taking advantage of Outlook's *services* and *profiles*, you can use Outlook as a central depository from which you can send, receive, and manage all of your electronic mail, no matter what type it is.

Services

When you want to use a printer with Windows, you must install a printer driver so that your programs can communicate with the printer. Outlook's *services* are like printer drivers for your information services. There is a separate service for each on-line source of electronic mail. By combining multiple services, Outlook can manage multiple types of e-mail using the same inbox.

Figure 37.1 shows the Services dialog box, which you access by selecting Tools ➤ Services from the menu bar. From here you can add and remove sources of e-mail that you want to use through Outlook. Each service stores the information Outlook needs to connect, send, and retrieve each source of e-mail.

FIGURE 37.1

The Services dialog box

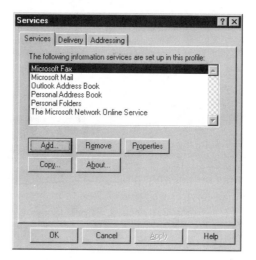

Profiles

A collection of services and their settings are stored in *profiles*. Profiles allow you to create multiple configurations of Outlook and to configure Outlook so that more than one user can access it. Each profile contains user and password information for the services used and makes available specified personal folder files and address books. When you start Outlook, the dialog box shown in Figure 37.2 appears. You can select an existing profile or create a new profile from here.

NOTE   If you do not get the Choose Profile dialog box, select Tools ➤ Options and select the General tab. Specify *Prompt for a profile to be used* in the Startup Settings group. Click on OK and restart Outlook. You should now get the dialog box shown in Figure 37.2.

FIGURE 37.2

*The Choose Pro-
file dialog box*

You can choose an existing profile from the Profile Name combo box or click on the New button, which initiates the Inbox Setup Wizard shown in Figure 37.3. The primary services that an Outlook profile uses are listed; check any ones you want to include for the new profile. You will also need to enter a name for the new profile and specify the details for each of the services.

PART

V

Organizing with
Outlook

FIGURE 37.3

*The Inbox
Setup Wizard*

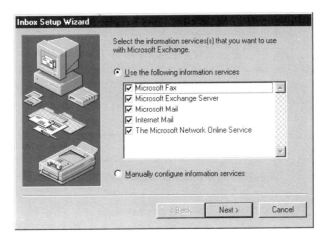

One use of profiles is to allow multiple people to access the same Outlook program while maintaining separate inboxes to hold their mail. You can have your own personal folder, so there is no worry that others will see your Outlook information when they are using the same application.

After starting Outlook and specifying the profile that contains the services you want to use, you can send and receive e-mail via your universal inbox.

Using E-Mail

Sending e-mail messages to contacts through various services is becoming more of a common, day-to-day activity. Even though Outlook has provided many other time management functions, it has not forgotten the basic e-mail message and makes working with it as easy as ever.

Sending Mail

You can send an e-mail message by pressing Ctrl+Shift+M from anywhere in Outlook or Ctrl+N while in the Inbox folder. You can also select File ➤ New ➤ Mail Message from the menu bar, or click on the New button on the Standard toolbar. Figure 37.4 shows the Message dialog box in which you can create your new message.

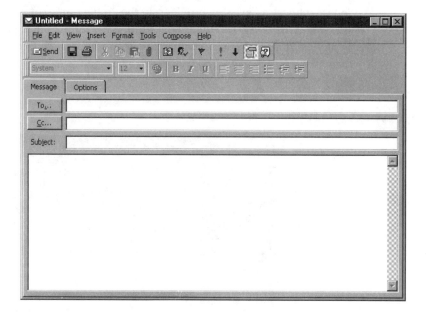

Destinations—First you need to indicate to whom it is going. You can either click on the names in the To text box directly or click on the To button to open the Select Names dialog box, from which you can choose the recipients (see Figure 37.5). If you use this dialog box, you can also add recipients to the Cc field, which sends a copy of your message to its addressees, and the Bcc field, which is a blind carbon copy of the e-mail, meaning that the other recipients do not know that the Bcc recipients also received the e-mail. By default the Bcc field does not show in your Message dialog box. To view the Bcc field, select View ➤ Bcc Field from the menu bar of the Message dialog box. If the mail service to which a recipient belongs supports special send options, they can be accessed using the Send Options button in the Select Names dialog box.

Subject—All e-mail messages have a subject, which should give an indication of the contents of the message. The Subject field is what the recipients will see when browsing their inbox.

FIGURE 37.5

*Selecting
Names for the
To text box*

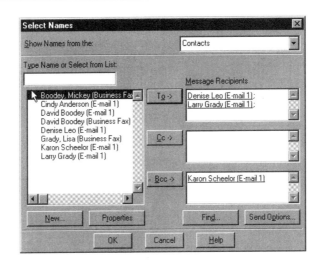

Message—The text area below the Subject field is where you want to type the main text of your e-mail message. This is a Rich Text Format area in which you can put formatted text and any attachments that you may want to send to the recipients.

Options

The Options tab in the Message dialog box can help add functionality to your e-mail messages (see Figure 37.6).

In the General Options group, you set the importance and sensitivity levels of your e-mail message. You can also choose to have voting buttons added to your message so that your recipients can quickly answer or vote on the contents. Their replies will be returned with their answers in the Subject field and in a line above the From area which reads "The sender responded: Yes (qr No)." You can route replies to specific people and save a copy of a sent message to a folder other than the Sent folder.

In the Delivery Options group, you can delay mailing your e-mail until a certain date. You can also specify an expiration date after which the message is not available. Both of these options provide a drop-down calendar from which you can choose a specific date.

Finally, the Tracking Options group notifies you when the message has been delivered and/or when the message is read by the recipient. You can also assign categories to your e-mail by clicking on the Categories button.

When all e-mail options have been selected, you can press Alt+S, Ctrl+Enter, or select File ➢ Send from the menu bar.

PART

V

*Organizing with
Outlook*

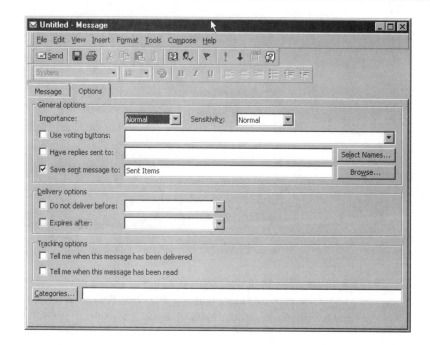

Reading Mail

When receiving and reading your e-mail, you will depend on the views of the inbox. Default views for the inbox include a basic Messages view, which simply lists your messages in a table view, allowing you to sort by any of the columns.

If you select a view that uses AutoPreview, you can see the first part of the message before opening it to help you determine whether you want to bother reading it or simply delete it.

When you want to read an e-mail message, double-click on it to open the message to read its full contents. If the message that you receive is attempting to poll its recipients for answers, you can click on the answer buttons available on a special toolbar to send your response without missing a beat.

Chapter

38

Office Connections

FEATURING

Chapter

38

Office Connections

O utlook was designed to fully integrate with the entire suite of Office
applications. From importing con-
tact data previously stored in Excel or Access to tracking Office application usage, Outlook is a full-fledged team member ready to cooperate to get the job done.

Outlook and the Office

Outlook can track your usage of any Office application.
Select Tools ➤ Options from the menu bar and choose the
Journal tab to access the Also Record Files From options. By
checking any of the Office applications in the list box you
can record your usage of that application's documents.

When you check one of the Office applications, any of the
files that you use in that application will be recorded in the Outlook Journal. Figure
38.1 show an example of a journal entry automatically created to track Excel usage.
The same type of entry can be created for any Office document if the application is
selected in Outlook.

FIGURE 38.1

A journal entry automatically created for an Excel workbook

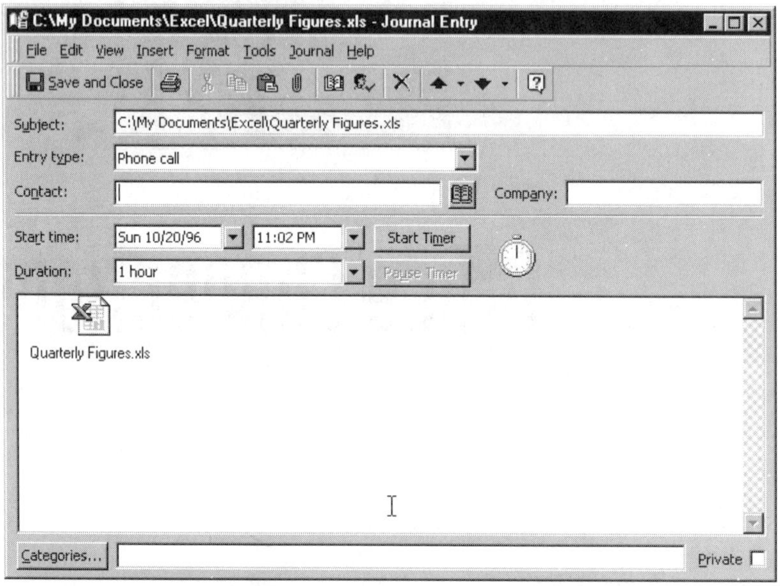

Importing Access and Excel Data

You may have previously kept your contact information in either Excel or Access. Now, with Office 97 and Outlook, you may nearly be convinced to commit to Outlook to track all your contacts. All of your contact data, however, has already been entered once into another application, and you do not want to repeat all that tedious work.

Outlook supports importing both Access and Excel data into its folders. To import data from another application into Outlook, select File ➤ Import and Export from the Outlook menu bar. Figure 38.2 shows the Import and Export dialog box from which you can choose to import data from an Office application.

Selecting *Import from Schedule+ or another application or file* from the dialog box will, when you click on Next, provide a number of application file formats from which Outlook can import. As you progress through the Wizard, Outlook will assist you in matching up your old fields with the ones in Outlook. Once the data is in Outlook, it no longer has a connection to the original data.

PART

V

Organizing with
Outlook

FIGURE 38.2

*The Import and
Export Wizard*

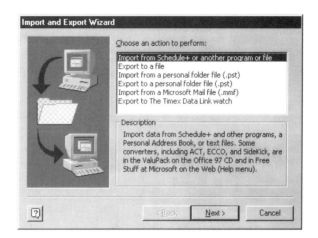

Mail Merging with Word

The tightest integration that exists with Outlook is its integration with Word. Using
the Mail Merge Helper in Word, you can select the Outlook Address Book as the source
for any merge documents that you want to create. There is no need for you to import
the data into Word before you can use it. The mail merge capabilities of Word can help
you send out form letters to specific contacts, create mailing labels for mass mailings,
and accomplish any other task that requires you to print multiple documents, changing only the information pertaining to specific people.

To work with Word and Outlook, you need to start in Word. Then select Tools➤ Mail
Merge from the menu bar. The Mail Merge Helper dialog box opens (see Figure 38.3).

The Mail Merge Helper is divided into three steps. Step 1 is to create the main document. Clicking on the Create button drops down a list of Merge letter types from
which to choose. While you can select any of the options, the Form Letters option is
the most common because it allows you to create a number of variations of form letters based on a blank sheet of paper on which you can insert fields.

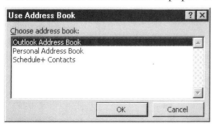

Once the Main document type has been
selected, you need to tell Word where to get
its data to merge; this is where Outlook
comes in. Clicking on Get Data will provide
choices for the data source of your merge letter. Select Use Address Book to open the Use
Address Book dialog box.

FIGURE 38.3

Access the Mail Merge Helper dialog box from Word.

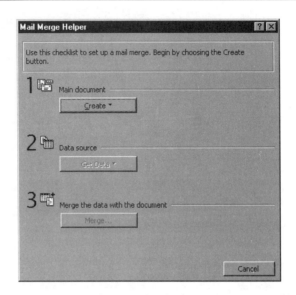

The Outlook Address Book is available in the list of address books; select it and click on OK. The hard drive of your computer will churn for a bit as Word accesses this data. From the dialog box, choose to edit the main document. Figure 38.4 shows the Mail Merge toolbar that will be available in your merge document. The first two buttons on the toolbar are Insert Field buttons for the merge fields of your data source (Outlook in this scenario) and Word.

FIGURE 38.4

The Mail Merge toolbar

Clicking on Insert Merge Field on the Mail Merge toolbar will list the field options from the Outlook Address Book. Selecting a field from the list will insert it at the location of the insertion point. After inserting a number of fields, your document may look like Figure 38.5.

After inserting all of the fields that you want in your main document, select Tools➢ Mail Merge from the Word menu bar. The third step of the Mail Merge Helper is active and the Merge button enabled. Click on the Merge button.

FIGURE 38.5

*Name and
Address fields
inserted from
Outlook into a
Word document*

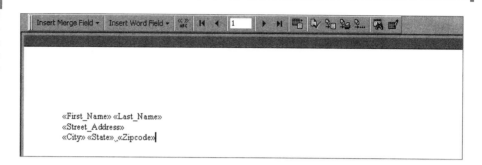

«First_Name» «Last_Name»
«Street_Address»
«City» «State» «Zipcode»

The Merge dialog box will open with some last-minute mail merge options, including the option to Merge to a New Document, Printer, Electronic Mail, or Electronic Fax. Once all options have been selected, you can click on the Merge button, and the source that you designated will receive the merged document. You can save the main document once you are finished and reuse it to perform subsequent merges using the document as is or modified.

PART
V

Organizing with
Outlook

PART VI

Data Management with Access

LEARN TO:

- *Create a database quickly with Access Wizards*

- *Design tables*

- *Create a form either manually or with the Form Wizard*

- *Design, update, and navigate query databases and reports*

- *Create and run macros*

- *Import and export data*

- *Integrate Access with other Office products*

Chapter

39

The Road Map—Jump-
Start into Access

The Road Map—
Jump-Start into Access

Access is a Relational Database Management System (RDMS) that you can use to store and manipulate large amounts of information. Because its tools are user-friendly and because it is a powerful development environment, Access is equally appropriate for novices and MIS professionals. Bernadette User, who works primarily with Microsoft Word to produce documents, can use Access to quickly and easily create a database of mailing list information that she can merge with Word documents. Nadine Professional can use Access to develop a database application that tracks customer and order information, which data entry people can operate without ever knowing they are in Access.

Beginners can use Access to:

- Store and manage various types of inventories such as recipes, stamps, baseball cards, or other hobby collections.
- Log information such as auto repairs for one or more cars, doctor visits for multiple family members, or daily exercise lists for training programs.
- Create contact management databases that can track not only contacts, but phone calls, meetings, and any other interactions with contacts.

Developers and MIS professionals can use Access to:

- Develop order-entry systems.
- Create applications that manage survey results.
- Manage front ends for enterprise-wide databases such as SQL server.
- Establish help-desk applications.
- Produce any other database application that the departments in their organizations might need.

The above are, of course, only suggestions; the possibilities for end-user and developer use of Access are limited only by the needs of an organization and the imagination of the user or developer.

The Main Elements of Access

Access is an object-oriented program; that is, everything in Access is an object, including the application itself. Each object has properties that define how it looks and performs.

In this chapter we will define the main object types and then use the Wizards to build a basic database that uses most of these objects. This information may seem overwhelming, but don't let it deter you from continuing further. This chapter provides a breadth of information regarding Access and all of its parts; the following chapters will explain each part in greater detail.

The Database Window

In Access, all objects of a database are stored in a single file, and the filename has an .MDB extension. You manage objects through the Database window (see Figure 39.1).

FIGURE 39.1

The Database window of the Northwind sample database

At the top of the Database window are tabs representing each of the six main object types: Tables, Queries, Forms, Reports, Macros, and Modules. Selecting a tab switches the view of the window to reveal a listing of the current objects under that type.

On the right side of the window are three buttons.

- The top button is labeled Open, Run, or Preview, depending on which tab is selected. Clicking on this button activates the selected object.
- Clicking on the Design button opens the selected object in Design view so that you can modify its structure and properties.
- Clicking on the New button starts the process of creating a new object of the selected type.

TIP

To quickly bring the Database window to the front of your screen from behind other open windows, press F11.

Tables

Tables are the primary building blocks of any Access database. All data is stored in tables. Every table in your database should focus on one subject, such as Customers, Orders, or Products. Every row, or record, in your table is a single unique instance of that subject (for example, each record in a Customers table would provide information about one customer). The characteristics of each customer are separated into the fields. For example, First Name, Last Name, Address, City, State, Zip, Phone, and Birthday would all be fields that could make up a record in a Customers table.

Figure 39.2 shows a table in Design view. The top pane of the window lists the individual fields of a table, the type of data those fields can store, and, optionally, a description of the fields. The bottom pane shows the properties of the current field selected in the top pane. Field properties determine how data is formatted in the field and whether that data must meet any specific criteria. You build the structure of your tables in Design view, telling Access which fields and which types of fields you want to store in the table. If the possible values for a field will be coming from another table or query, the properties on the Lookup tab make it easier for you to place controls on forms by predefining the type of control to use and designating from what table or query to pull the value list.

You enter or view data in Datasheet view (see Figure 39.3). Here every row is a record in the table, and the columns are the fields of the records. Using this view, you can add, modify, delete, view, sort, find, filter, and format the data in the table. Once you have the table datasheet looking the way that you want it, you can print the datasheet. Because formatting is limited in Datasheet view, however, you'll generally want to print from Report view.

PART

VI

Data Management
with Access

FIGURE 39.2

The Design
view of a table

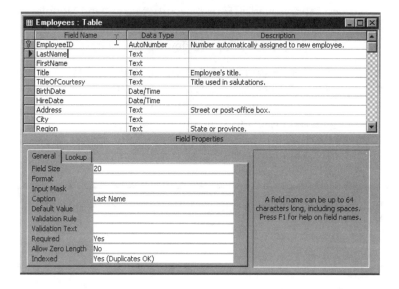

FIGURE 39.3

The same table
in Datasheet
view

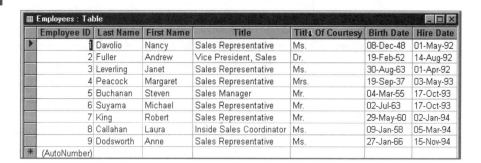

NOTE

Although accessing table data through the Datasheet view is the most direct
method, you can also access table data through forms that you create—a more
visually appealing experience.

Queries

A query is a question that you ask of the data stored in the tables of your database. For
example, you can create a query that asks for only those customers in the state of California or that finds all employees who have birthdays in the current month. You can
also use queries to determine which fields of a table will be included in a new datasheet.

Most Access databases contain more than one table, and you can use queries to pull specific fields from multiple tables into one datasheet. The datasheet that a query returns is called a recordset.

Some queries do not provide recordsets. These special queries, called Action queries, perform bulk updates on your data. For example, Action queries can find and delete the records of customers with no sales activity in the past year. You use these queries to update, append, or delete records in tables or to construct new tables from the results of the query.

Figure 39.4 shows the Design view of a query. The top pane lists the tables that are supplying the data for the query. The bottom pane shows the Query by Example (QBE) grid in which you place fields from the table(s) in the top pane that will be included in the results of the query. The QBE grid is also the place where you can specify any criteria or sorting that will be applied to any fields.

FIGURE 39.4

You can construct a query in Design view, using the list of tables and the QBE grid.

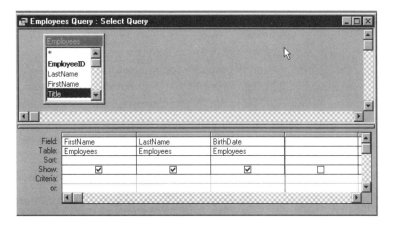

PART

VI

Data Management
with Access

To view the answer of a query, you open the query in Datasheet view. The Datasheet view of a query looks just like the Datasheet view of a table. You manipulate the data in a query datasheet just as you do in a table datasheet. One primary difference between the two, however, is that the fields in a query datasheet may not always be updatable. This situation may occur when you are using more than one table in a query and do not include enough fields in the query to make a valid record in the table(s) on which it was built, or if you include calculated fields that are based on expressions that use values from multiple fields. A nonupdatable query can also occur if that datasheet is the result of a totals query, which groups data instead of providing the details.

NOTE

An important concept to remember about queries is that you are storing the question and not the datasheet. If you run a query that asks for all companies in the state of Oregon, you will get a datasheet of those records that match your criterion. If you close the query, add new records of Oregon companies to the table(s) on which the query is based, and then run the query again, the datasheet will reflect your changes. Your query runs every time it is opened, and it asks the question of the current data.

Forms

Access forms serve two functions. The first is to present the table or query's data in a format that is easy to view or update. These fields of data are available to use on a form when it is bound to a table or query. You can then edit the form just as you would edit the datasheet of the bound table or query, or you can set parameters that restrict the form's use to only viewing data, only adding data, or only editing data without the ability to add records.

The second function of forms is to create the interface portion of an Access application. This function is primarily for applications developers. You can, for instance, create forms called Switchboards that help navigate to other forms and functions of the application (see Figure 39.5). You can also create forms to use as dialog or message boxes or forms on which a user can enter information and then click on a button that dynamically creates a report or a query based on the information.

FIGURE 39.5

A form called a Switchboard can be used as the control center of a database.

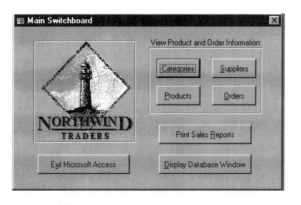

The easiest way to design forms bound to a table or a query is to use the Form Wizards. Whether you are a novice or an advanced user, you can use the Form Wizards to design the bulk of a form and then make any necessary changes in Design view. Figures 39.6 and 39.7 show the same form in Form view and Design view. To learn more about the Design view of a form, see Chapter 41.

FIGURE 39.6

FIGURE 39.6

A data-entry form in Form view

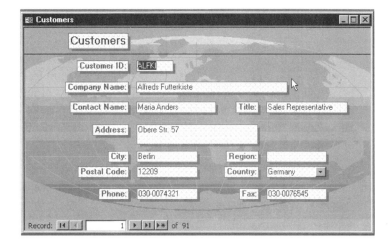

FIGURE 39.7

You can make changes to the form in Design view.

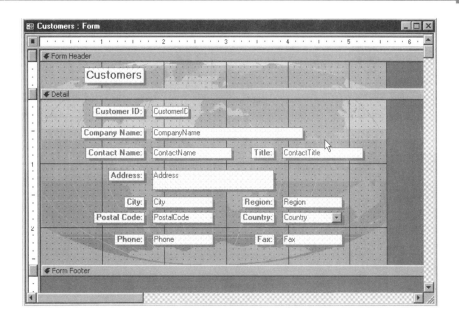

PART

VI

Data Management with Access

Reports

Whether we like it or not, we are still a paper-based society; printing the results of the data we store—reports—is still necessary. With Access, you can quickly and easily design such reports based on your data.

Like forms, reports can incorporate fields from one or more tables. Report Wizards can help make report writing a cinch. Like the Form Wizards, Report Wizards may not provide exactly what you want, but you can always make adjustments in Design view. See Chapter 43 for more detailed information about designing reports.

An Access report is not restricted to your basic row and column format. A report can be a catalog of products, mailing labels, a graph, or any other form that can take advantage of the WYSIWYG (what you see is what you get) capabilities of the Design view. Figure 39.8 shows the preview of a basic report, and Figure 39.9 shows a preview of a mailing label report.

FIGURE 39.8

A basic colum-nar report created through Design view

FIGURE 39.9

*A mailing label
report*

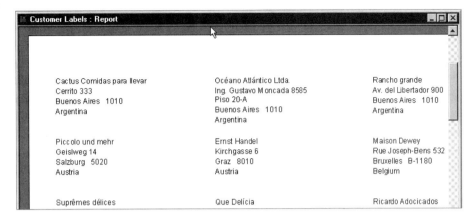

Macros

Macros provide an easy, effective method for automating many database tasks. You can use macros for tasks as simple as displaying message boxes to validating data entered into a record before it is saved.

Macros are composed of actions. In Access, you can choose from 49 actions. You create a macro by listing the actions in the order that you want them to be performed. Each action appears in an individual row in the top pane of the macro Design view, as shown in Figure 39.10. The bottom pane shows the arguments or the specifics for the current macro action in the top pane.

The top pane is divided into four columns, only two of which are visible at first. The main column is the Action column, in which you specify the action for the row. The other visible column is the Comment column, in which you can place comments about the actions that the macro will perform. The two other columns are labeled Condition and Macro Name. To open either column, you can click on its toolbar button, choose it from the View menu, or right-click on the Design view title bar. You can use the Condition column to test an expression. If the condition returns true, the action on that row is run; if the condition returns false, the action is skipped. The Macro Name column provides a way to group a number of small macros into one macro design window, thus reducing the number of macros listed in the Database window.

When you design forms and reports, they and the objects that you place on them all have event properties. An event is something that can happen to an object. For example, a form has a Before Update property that gets triggered right before a record on the form is saved. If you have placed the name of your macro in the Before Update property of the form, your macro will run right before the current record of the form is saved. If you place a button on a form, the button has an On Click event that is triggered whenever the button is pressed. If the name of a macro that opens the Employees form is set to the On Click event of a button on another form, the Employees form opens when the button is clicked on. More discussion of events and examples of using macros to automate your database are found in Chapter 44.

Macros can be as simple as the one in Figure 39.10, which displays "Hello World!" in a message box. Or they can be as complicated as the one in Figure 39.11, which validates the postal codes entered into a form and displays the results in a message box.

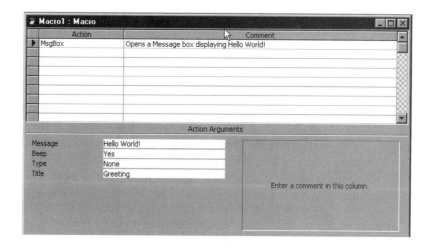

FIGURE 39.10

Design view of a simple macro that opens a message box

FIGURE 39.11

A more complicated macro that validates data entered into a form

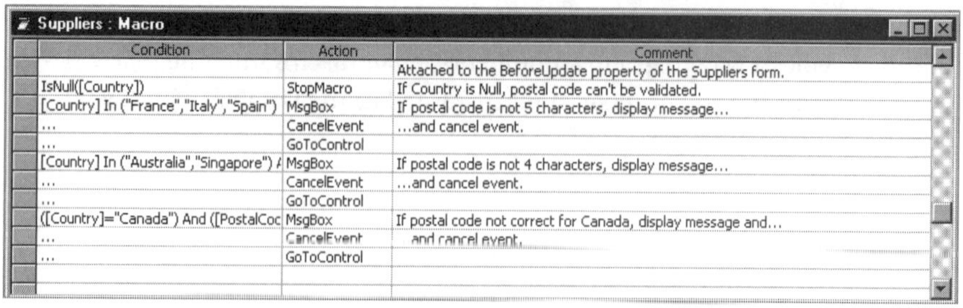

Modules

Modules are the containers for any programming code written in an Access database. The two types of modules are global and form or report.

Global modules are listed in your Database window. The code that you store in these modules is available everywhere in your application, hence, the name global.

Every form or report that you design has its own module that can store code. If you import or export the form or report to another database, the code travels with it. This code is available only when the form or report is open and, even then, can only be called from the form or report in which it is stored.

The language that Access uses for code is Visual Basic for Applications (VBA). If you have written code for previous versions of Access using Access Basic, the transition should be relatively smooth. Syntax changes are minor, and with only a slight bit of tweaking, your code should run smoothly with VBA.

NOTE

Programming with VBA is generally the preserve of more skilled users and developers. Although the scope of this book does not cover VBA completely, Chapter 44, which discusses automating Access, will provide you with a foundation.

Relationships

When working with Access, you can create and use multiple tables to help reduce redundancy in a database. For example, to track customer orders in a spreadsheet program, you would have to repeat the customer information, such as name, address, and phone number, for every order. In Access, you can create a table to store customer names and another table to store order information, and then establish a relationship to connect the two tables. In the Customers table, you would create a field, called a primary key, that uniquely identifies each customer. In the Orders table, you need store only the primary key of the customer from the Customers table to access that data. You use primary keys all the time in your day-to-day life. Your driver's license number, your frequent flyer account, and your credit card numbers are all examples of primary keys. Chapter 46 provides more explanation on creating and working with relationships.

Creating a Database Quickly with the Help of Access Wizards

Now that we've explained the basic components of Access, we'll run through a couple of exercises that, when finished, will produce a complete Access database. With the help of the Access Wizards, these exercises will demonstrate that a fully functioning database can be created with almost no knowledge of Access.

Starting Access

The first step is to start Access and begin a new database.

1. From the Start button menu, select Programs ➤ Microsoft Access.
2. In the Microsoft Access dialog box, select the Blank Database option button and click on OK.
3. In the File New Database dialog box (shown in Figure 39.12), type **My Application** in the File Name text box and then click on Create.

TIP

If you are really new to creating databases and have no idea where to start, you might want to create a database by selecting the Database Wizard from the opening Microsoft Access dialog box instead of clicking on the Blank Database button. You can also access the Database Wizard by selecting File ➤ New Database from the menu bar. The Database Wizard handles everything from selecting the tables and fields to building the forms and reports you will need.

FIGURE 39.12

Naming your file in the File New Database dialog box

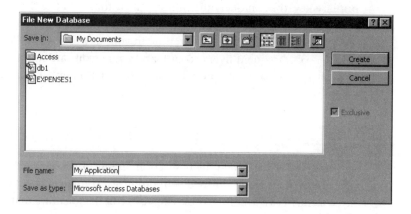

After you have specified the database name, you are presented with an empty Database window. Your job now is to create all the objects you want in your database. Our example database will track basic phone book entries.

Building a Table to Store Phone Book Entries

The first step in creating a database is to design the table(s) that will hold your data. Using the Table Wizard, this is a snap.

1. Select the Tables tab of the Database window.

2. Click on New in the Database window. The New Table dialog box will open.

3. Select Table Wizard from the list and click on OK. The Table Wizard dialog box will open.

4. You can choose which type of table you want to use as a sample: Business or Personal. Select Personal.

5. Select Addresses from the Sample Tables list.

6. In the Sample Fields list box, select the following fields and click the > button after each one to send them to the Fields in My New Table list box: AddressID, FirstName, LastName, SpouseName, Address, City, StateOrProvince, PostalCode, HomePhone, WorkPhone, Birthdate, and Notes. Your Table Wizard dialog box should look like the one in Figure 39.13.

FIGURE 39.13

Building an Address table with the Table Wizard

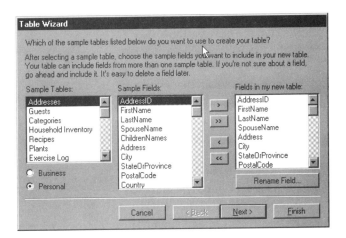

7. Click on Next, and the second Table Wizard dialog box opens.

8. Accept Addresses as the name of your table and allow Access to create a primary key for you. (Primary keys are discussed in Chapter 46.) Now, click on Next.

9. In the last dialog box for the Table Wizard, select Modify the Table Design radio button and then click on Finish. The Wizard will generate the table and then display the Design view of the Addresses table as shown in Figure 39.14.

FIGURE 39.14

The Addresses table in Design view

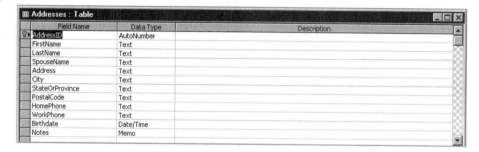

10. After investigating the design, select File ➤ Close from the menu bar or click on the Close button in the title bar.

Making Data Entry Easy with a Form

The next object that we want to create is a form so that entering data in the table will be easy.

1. In the Database window, select the Forms tab.

2. Click on the New button.

3. In the New Form dialog box, select Form Wizard from the list box at the top and select the Addresses table in the combo box in the middle as the source for the data. Click on OK to continue.

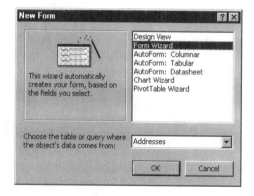

4. In the first Form Wizard dialog box, select the fields to include on the form. Send over all fields except for AddressID by clicking on the >> button and then double-clicking on the AddressID field to send it back. The dialog box should now look like the one shown in Figure 39.15. Click on Next.

5. Choose a Columnar form layout and click on Next.

FIGURE 39.15

All fields except
for AddressID
will be placed on
the new form.

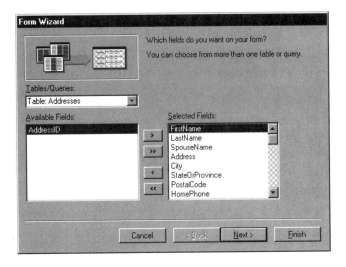

NOTE

We left AddressID off the form because it is an automatic number field that Access increments on its own. There really is no reason for it to be on this form since the user does not need to enter the number. The number is being used to uniquely identify each Address.

6. The Form Wizard prompts you for a style for your form. Select Standard and click on Next.

7. The last dialog box will ask you to name the form and what you want the Wizard to do when it finishes designing it. Leave the default of Addresses for the name and the *Open the form to view or enter information* radio button. Click on Finish.

Your form will open in Form view so that you can enter some records. If the cursor is not already in the First Name text box, click in the box and type the name of your first address entry. Now press Tab to move from field to field and press Shift+Tab to move back field by field. When you reach the last field on the form, in this case the Notes field, press Tab; Access moves you to the next record. Some basic data entry techniques are listed below. Refer to Chapter 41 for more detail on creating and using forms.

TIP

You can also use the Enter key to move from field to field. To modify the behavior of the Enter Key, select Tools ➢ Options ➢ Keyboard from the menu bar and modify the Move After Enter value. It can be set to Don't Move, Next Field, or Next Record.

PART

VI

Data Management
with Access

- To add a new record, choose Insert ➤ New Record from the menu bar.
- To delete the current record, choose Edit ➤ Delete Record.
- To move from one record to the next, press PgUp and PgDn.
- To undo changes to the current field or record, press the Esc key once.

After entering the information about some of your addresses into your database, close the form by choosing File ➤ Close from the menu bar or by pressing Ctrl+W.

Creating a Query to Question Your Data

You might want to generate a list of only the names and phone numbers at each address. You can do this by using a query to select only those fields that you want to view.

1. From the Database window, select the Queries tab.

2. Click on the New button.

3. In the New Query dialog box, select Simple Query Wizard and click on OK.

4. In the Simple Query Wizard dialog box, send the FirstName, LastName, and HomePhone fields to the Selected Fields list box using the > button or by double-clicking on them. Click on the Next button when you are ready to continue.

5. In the last Simple Query Wizard dialog box, change the name of the query to Phone Numbers, but leave the radio button selected to *Open the query to view information.* Click on Finish.

6. You query will run, showing you only the three fields that you chose from the Addresses table. You will see information based on the records that you entered. Our query datasheet/recordset reflects that there are eight records in the Addresses table.

First Name	Last Name	Home Phone
Lisa	Grady	(714) 555-4322
Bill	Francis	(215) 623-9853
Pat	Holdenwang	(812) 342-4521
Bernadette	Hager	(404) 353-1356
Robert	Francis	(908) 642-2153
Blanche	Landmesser	(516) 423-5214
Luke	Francis	(310) 432-4543
Ray	Montalvo	(818) 908-3413

7. When you are finished viewing the datasheet, choose File ➤ Close.

Generating a Report to Print Your Data

You could print the datasheet that results from the query; however, its formatting is limited. Creating a report from which to print the data is a more attractive option.

1. From the Database window, select the Reports tab.

2. Click on the New button.

3. In the New Report dialog box, select Report Wizard and the Phone Numbers query as the data source. Click on OK.

4. Using the >> button, send all the Available Fields of the query to the Selected Fields list box so that the Report Wizard dialog box looks like the one in Figure 39.16. Click on Next.

5. The Report Wizard will ask if you want to group anything in your report. For this example you don't, so click on Next.

6. The Report Wizard will prompt you for the fields that you want to use to sort your report. Select Last Name in the first combo box. Click on Next.

7. The Report Wizard then prompts you for report layout information with some defaults already chosen. Accept the defaults of Tabular Layout and Portrait Orientation by clicking on Next.

8. Figure 39.17 shows the Report Wizard requesting that you choose a style for your report. Select Bold and then click on Next.

FIGURE 39.16

Selecting all fields from the Phone Numbers query

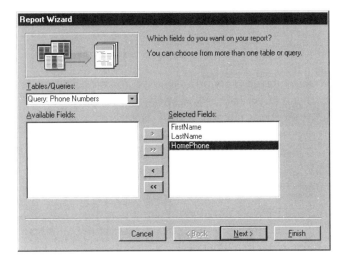

PART

VI

9. The last stage of the Report Wizard requests a name for the report. Leave Phone Numbers as the name and leave the radio button selected to *Preview the report.* Click on Finish. Your report will open in Print Preview.

10. When you are finished looking at the report, select File ➤ Close from the menu bar.

Data Management
with Access

FIGURE 39.17

Selecting the Bold style for the report

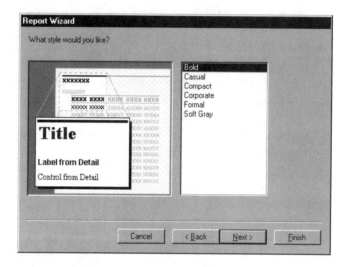

Setting Database Startup Options

You now have a functional database. You have a table to store the data, a form to make data entry easier, a query to select only certain fields from your table, and a report to print the data from your query—in this case a phone list. One last exercise will set an option that polishes your Access database.

Generally, you have one main form when you first open your database. For that form to open automatically when you open the database, you need to set a database option.

1. Select Tools ➤ Startup to open the Startup dialog box.

2. In the Display Form combo box, select the Addresses form and click on OK.

3. From the menu bar, select File ➤ Close.

4. Select File ➤ 1 My Application from the most recently used file list off of the menu bar.

5. Now, when your database opens, the form you specified opens automatically.

There are, of course, more advanced uses for all the objects we have reviewed here, and you can choose from among many other options to determine how your database will perform.

MASTERING THE OPPORTUNITIES

From Database to Application in a Few Easy Options

The dialog box that opens when you select Tools ➢ Startup from the menu bar of Access provides you with a number of options that assist in making your database more polished, more like a professional form. Without having to write a line of code you can:

Change the name that appears in the Access title bar by providing the new name in the Application Title text box. This new name will appear both in the title bar of the Access window and in the task bar.

Customize the icon that is displayed in the title bar and task bar by either typing in directly or browsing for the path of the Application Icon file.

Specify a new default menu bar if you have created a custom menu for your database. This menu bar will appear for every form or report that does not have a menu bar already specified in its properties.

Restrict easy access to Design views and other menu bar options that may alter parts of your database. Making sure that the Allow Full Menus checkbox is not checked will restrict menu choices to those who work with the data and not the design of your database.

Disable the right mouse button and the default shortcut menus by not checking the Allow Default Shortcut Menus.

Keep the Database window from appearing by clearing the Display Database Window checkbox. This will help keep innocent users from straying into areas not intended for their use.

Remove the Status bar while your database is open by unchecking the Display Status Bar item.

Create a custom shortcut menu bar to appear when users press their right mouse button while using your database. This is done by specifying the name of the shortcut menu bar you create in the combo box.

Disable Access design keyboard shortcuts like F11 (show database window), CTRL+G (show the coding debug window), and Ctrl+Break (pause running code) by clicking the Advanced button and deselecting the Use Access Special Keys checkbox.

If you are using any of these features and get locked out of one feature or another while designing your database, you can hold down the Shift key while opening the database and none of the options in the Startup dialog will be implemented.

PART

VI

Data Management with Access

Chapter

40

Working with Data in Tables

Chapter 40

Working with Data in Tables

A s mentioned in Chapter 39, all Access data is stored in tables. Tables are made up of records, and records are made up of fields. You can do quite a bit with tables using the Wizards while not really understanding the structure beneath the datasheet. If you plan to work with Access and not use the Wizards, however, a small primer on the types of fields you can use and the properties available for the field types is necessary.

The goal of this chapter is to help you understand Access table design and to introduce you to the navigation tools with which you maneuver the resulting datasheet.

Designing a Table Manually

To create a new table, you first select the Tables tab from the Database window and then click on New. The New Table dialog box appears. The options are Datasheet View, which allows you to enter sample data and have Access define the field type; Design View, from which you build a table from scratch, defining all your fields and their properties; Table Wizard, which steps you through the process; Import Table, which brings in existing tables in other file formats; and Link Table, which aids you in attaching to tables outside your current database (we'll talk about that in Chapter 45). Because you want to build a table from scratch, select Design View and click on OK.

The window in Design view consists of a top pane and a bottom pane. Enter or name each field needed and decide on its data type in the top pane; specify properties for each field in the bottom pane.

Field Names

In the Field Name column in the top pane, you type the name of the field you are adding to your table. The field name can have as many as 64 characters and can contain any characters, numbers, and spaces except for the period (.), an accent grave (`), square brackets ([ ]), and exclamation marks (!) (these characters have reserved meanings in conjunction with filenames in Access). Leading spaces are also not allowed, so you will need to begin each field name with a valid character or number.

Although you can have 64 characters in the field name, keeping your field names as small as possible is advisable. Smaller names are easier to remember and type when you need to refer to the field in a form, macro, or expression or in code. Even though spaces are allowed in a field name, try to avoid using them; they only make working with the field more cumbersome.

Data Types

The data type of a field determines the kind of data the field can store. You can choose from nine data types, ranging from Text, which stores characters, to OLE Object, which stores OLE objects such as Word documents, Excel workbooks, bitmaps, sounds, and even video files.

Field Properties

Field properties are characteristics of a field such as size, format, and data restrictions. Depending on the data type, a field may or may not have certain properties. The list of properties below includes the data types to which they apply and any special considerations.

Text	The Text data type can store as many as 255 alphabetic or numeric characters. You use this data type to store data such as names, addresses, descriptions, and numbers that will not be used in calculations, such as phone numbers.
Memo	The Memo data type can contain the same type of data as the Text data type, but it can hold as many as 65,535 characters. You do not, however, have as much flexibility with this data type as you do with the Text data type. You cannot sort or index a table using a Memo data type field.
Number	The Number data type stores numbers that will be used in mathematical calculations. The size of the number that you can store in a field is determined by the Field Size property (discussed later in this chapter).
Date/Time	The Date/Time data type is a special number data type that allows you to store dates and times in a field. The Format property of this data type allows you to specify how the date will appear in a field (for example, 4/10/70; 4/10/70 8:00:34 AM, or Sunday, April 10, 1970).
Currency	The Currency data type stores numbers representing currency that will be used in calculations. This data type has special built-in logic that corrects rounding errors.
AutoNumber	If you select this data type for a field, Access handles the entry for that field in every record. You can set AutoNumber to increment 1 number at a time or to generate random numbers. You can have only one AutoNumber data type per table. If an AutoNumber data type field is used, it is usually the primary key of the table (discussed later in this chapter).
Yes/No	The Yes/No data type is a logical field that can store either True or False. The field accepts True/False, On/Off, Yes/No, -1/0 for its values although you can use its Format property to customize what it shows for True and False.
OLE Object	The OLE Object data type stores large binary OLE objects such as Word documents, Excel workbooks, bitmap files, sound files, and video files.

PART

VI

Data Management
with Access

Hyperlink The Hyperlink data type stores any combination of text and numbers that make up a Hyperlink address. Each Hyperlink address can contain three parts: the display text, address, and subaddress. Each part can contain 2,048 characters a piece.

Lookup Wizard The Lookup Wizard, although not a data type, assists you in defining the data type and properties of a field whose values can be chosen from a static list or from values in an existing table or query. Selecting the Lookup Wizard from the Data Type combo box of a field in Table Design view initiates the Lookup Wizard. It steps you through filling out the properties on the Lookup page in the properties pane in Table Design view. The Lookup properties define the default display control to be used for the field and the properties associated with control.

 MASTERING THE OPPORTUNITIES

Providing Access Information To Make Building Forms Easier

As you design the tables of your database, take time to fill in the Lookup properties page for as many text and number fields as you can. This time spent will provide a great return when you are designing your forms and reports. Instead of having to create combo or list boxes for those fields that will have finite choices, you can simply click and drag the desired field from the field list in the Design view of a report or form. Access will use the properties on the Lookup page to build the appropriate control.

Whether you are using the Lookup Wizard or filling in the properties manually, you can specify whether you want the choices for the field to come from a table or query or a static list that you provide.

If you decide to use a static list, be sure the list will be modified rarely, if at all, after you are done designing the database. An example of this type of list would be the options for shipping a package: generally there is Federal Express, US Postal Service, UPS, and possibly another overnight courier. If you have a field that fits this category, you can list the options, separated by semicolons, in the Row Source property of the Lookup page. You also need to specify Value List as the Row Source Type. The major drawback to this choice is that if you want to modify the list of choices, you must do so in Design view, and other users will usually find it too difficult to modify.

Continued

The more common option for providing a list of choices for a field is to use a table or query. This option allows others using your database to easily make modifications outside of Design view by using a form or datasheet. You can use the Lookup Wizard to fill in the properties for you, and it will create a special query for the list that pulls in only the fields you need from the designated query or table. If you are doing this manually, then you need to set the Row Source Type property to Table/Query and specify a table or query from which you want to pull the list in the Row Source property. You will also want to make use of the Bound Column, Column Count, and Column Widths properties.

The Bound Column property specifies which column from the table or query

you want to store in the field; this is usually the primary key when you are creating relationships. The Column Count property specifies how many columns you are using from the table or query. If the column you want to use is the third column, then you need to specify three columns. If you specify one, Access will use the first column. The Column Widths property allows you to keep unwanted columns from showing. You specify a number, in inches, for each column with the numbers separated by semicolons. For example, if you have a Column Count of three and you want to hide the first two columns, you would type **0;0;1** in Column Widths. Only the third column would show since it is set at 1 inch.

Field Size

Text, Number, and AutoNumber data types have Field Size properties. For the Text data type, you can specify a length from 1 to 255, which is the number of characters the field will hold. The Field Size property of a Number data type is actually a subtype that determines the range of numbers allowed. The table below lists the Field Size options for the Number data type.

Field Size	Range
Byte	0 to 255
Integer	-32,768 to 32,767
Long Integer	-2,147,483,648 to 2,147,483,647
Single	-3.402823E38 to -1.401298E-45 for negative values; 1.401298E-45 to 3.402823E38 for positive values

Field Size	Range
Double	-1.79769313486232308 to -4.94065645841247E-324 for negative values; 4.94065645841247E-324 to 1.79769313486232E308 for positive values
ReplicationID	Globally Unique Identifier (GUID) used with AutoNumber for replication

When choosing a Field Size property for a number, be careful. You want to avoid a number that is too small, but you also don't want to choose a number that is needlessly large. The larger the number a field can hold, the more space the field takes up in your database.

NOTE If you need to work with decimals, you must choose either a Single or Double Field Size property because the other Field Size properties do not have decimal precision.

Although the AutoNumber data type has a Field Size property, it is almost always set to Long Integer. If it is not set to Long Integer, it is being used for a process called replication, which is beyond the scope of this book.

Format

All data types except for OLE object have a Format property. The Number, Date/Time, AutoNumber, Currency, and Yes/No data types all have predefined formats. If none of the predefined formats is suitable for your situation or if you are formatting a Text or a Memo field, you can create custom formats. To find a list of formatting codes available for different data types, click on the Format Property of a field in Table Design view and press F1.

A format is applied after the user enters information into a table or form. For example, if you have an ID field that formats all characters in uppercase letters and all user types in lowercase, the table stores the entry in lowercase. But whenever that entry is viewed in a table, form, report, or query, it appears in all uppercase.

Input Mask

Some data types have an Input Mask property. This property is similar to the Format property except that it formats the text as the user enters it and can even provide a template guiding how the data should be entered. A phone number Input Mask, for instance, could look like:

(X X X) X X X - X X X X

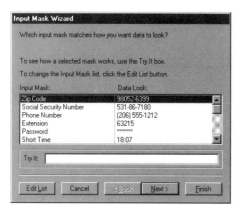

The easiest way to apply an Input Mask to a field is to click on the Input Mask property of the field. Then click on the Build button or the button with the ellipsis (...) that appears directly to the right of the property. When you click on the Build button for either a Text or Date/Time data type, the Input Mask Wizard opens. Simply follow the steps.

Caption

All data types have a Caption property. The Caption property provides an alternative name for Access to use for your fields when creating labels or references that the user will see. For example, a field called FNAME on a form could be labeled as First Name if this was the caption for the field. Captions help keep field-name size small while providing users with meaningful names.

Decimal Places

The Number and Currency data types have a Decimal Places property, which determines how many decimal places are shown. Remember, only Number data types with a size of Single or Double have decimal precision.

Default Value

All data types except AutoNumber and OLE Objects have a Default Value property, which specifies the value of a field when a new record is started. Default Values are not permanent; they can be changed. You use Default Values when the value of a field is almost always the same, with few exceptions. Declaring a Default Value reduces the amount of data entry.

Validation Rule and Validation Text

The Validation Rule and Validation Text properties are available for all fields except AutoNumber and OLE Objects. A Validation Rule qualifies the data entered into a cell. If, for example, you had a Quantity field that must never accept quantities less than 100, you could place >=100 in the Validation Rule. Access would then not allow any numbers less than 100 to be entered into the field. Validation Text is the text that you want a message box to show when a user violates the Validation Rule. If you have a Validation Rule, be sure to have Validation Text; otherwise, Access will present its own cryptic message.

PART

VI

Data Management
with Access

Required

The Required property specifies whether a field must contain a value before the record is saved. This property does not apply to fields with the AutoNumber data type because Access always provides a value for such data types.

Allow Zero Length

Applied to the Text, Memo, and Hyperlink fields, the Allow Zero Length property determines whether a zero length string qualifies as a valid value.

Indexed

Access stores the indexed property in a special table, much like the index listing in the back of a book. This property makes searching the records easier. Running a query that searches for all customers in a specific zip code goes much faster, for example, if the zip code field has the Indexed property. The three possible values for the Indexed property are No, Yes (No Duplicates), and Yes (Duplicates OK). The No value obviously tells Access not to store an index on that field. The Yes (No Duplicates) value tells Access to index the table on the field and not to allow duplicate values in the field. For example; if one record has ABC as an ID number, no other record can have ABC. The Yes (Duplicates OK) value tells Access to index the table based on the field and to allow multiple records to have the same value in the field.

Primary Key

The primary key of a table is the table's main index. In addition, the field or fields that make up the primary key are used to uniquely identify each record; no two records can have the same value stored in the primary key field(s).

Although Access does not require a primary key, we strongly suggest that you have one. Every time you try to modify the structure of a table without a primary key, Access prompts you to create one or to allow Access to create one. If you are new to working with databases, let Access set the primary key for you.

When Access sets the primary key of a table, it uses a field with the AutoNumber data type. If you already have a field in your table of this type, and you can have only one, Access uses that field as the primary key. If the table does not have an AutoNumber field, Access inserts one, names it ID, and sets it as the primary key.

The Index property of the field(s) set to be used as the primary key is automatically set to Yes (No Duplicates) to ensure that the value in the primary key field(s) is not duplicated.

To set the primary key manually, follow these steps:

1. Open a table in Design view.

2. Click on the gray field selector to the left of the field name that you want to be the primary key. The field row will be selected as shown in Figure 40.1.

3. From the menu bar, choose Edit ➣ Primary Key or click on the Primary Key toolbar button or right-click on the field selector and choose Primary Key from the shortcut menu. A key appears in the field selector to signify that the primary key has been selected.

FIGURE 40.1

Selecting a field to be the primary key

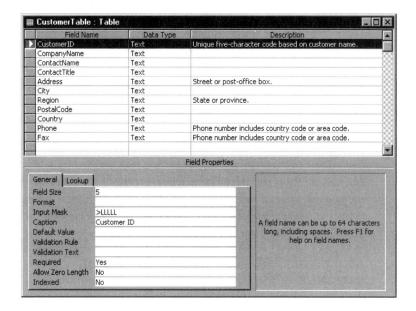

 NOTE

Fields with Memo, OLE Object, or Hyperlink data types cannot be indexed and therefore cannot be primary keys.

A primary key can be made up of more than one field if you do not have any one field that can uniquely identify a record. To have more than one field make up a primary key, select all the fields to be included before setting the key.

1. From Design view, open a table.

2. To select the first field for your primary key, click on the field selector.

3. While holding down the Ctrl key, select the other fields to be included.

4. Choose Edit ➤ Primary Key from the menu bar or click on the Primary Key toolbar button. All the selected fields should have the key symbol in their field selectors, as shown in Figure 40.2.

Field Name	Data Type	Description
CustomerID	Text	Unique five-character code based on customer name.
CompanyName	Text	
ContactName	Text	
ContactTitle	Text	
Address	Text	Street or post-office box.
City	Text	
Region	Text	State or province.
PostalCode	Text	
Country	Text	
Phone	Text	Phone number includes country code or area code.
Fax	Text	Phone number includes country code or area code.
test	Hyperlink	

Designing a Table in Datasheet View

If selecting data types and field properties seems a little daunting for your first time out, you might want to try creating a table in Datasheet view. Using Datasheet view is slightly different from using the normal datasheet. When designing a table with the datasheet, Access gives you a blank datasheet with generic fields and default field names such as FIELD1, FIELD2, and so on. Your job is to fill the first row of the table with sample data so that Access can determine the data types.

1. Open a database and select the Tables tab.

2. Click on the New button.

3. In the New Table dialog box, select Datasheet View and click on OK. A blank datasheet opens.

4. In the first row of the datasheet, type the following:

Field 1	**Mickey**
Field2	**Francis**
Field3	**208 Morris Avenue**
Field4	**Lockhart**
Field5	**PA**

Field6	**19000-2822**
Field7	**10/20/46**
Field8	**HTTP://www.brookhome.com**

Your datasheet should resemble Figure 40.3.

5. From the menu bar, choose File ➤ Save. Accept the default name of Table# (where # is the next number in the succession of tables that you have created during your current session of Access), and answer Yes when asked if you want Access to define a primary key.

6. From the menu bar, choose View ➤ Design View or click on the View button on the Table Datasheet toolbar.

FIGURE 40.3

Entering data to design a table in Datasheet view

Field1	Field2	Field3	Field4	Field5	Field6	Field7	Field8	Field◄
Mickey	Francis	208 Morris Avenue	Lockhart	PA	19000-2822	10/20/46	http://www.brookhome.com	

Table2 : Table

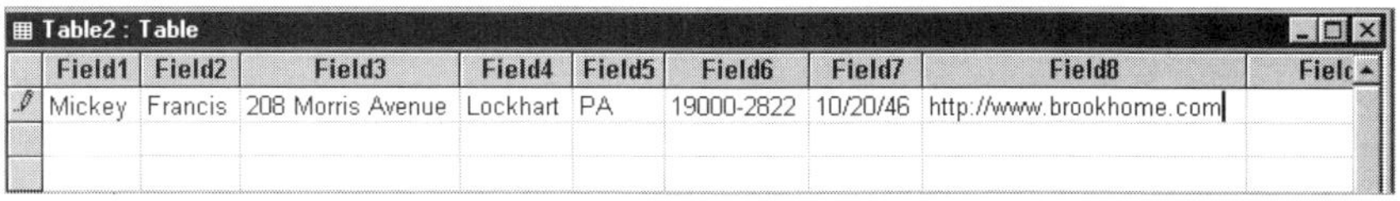

Notice that Access has defined the data types and properties for you. You can now make any changes you feel are necessary; for example, you might want to alter the field names.

Working with the Table Datasheet

Once you have designed your tables, you will need to know how to navigate your datasheet so that you can add, edit, and delete records, sort records on specific fields, search for records containing specific information, and apply formatting.

Navigating the Datasheet

Figure 40.4 shows the datasheet of the Customers table that is in the Northwind sample database located in the Samples folder under your main Access folder. To view a table in Datasheet view, follow these steps:

1. From the Database window, select the Tables tab.

2. Select the table you want to see in Datasheet view and click on the Open button. The datasheet opens and is similar to the one in Figure 40.4.

PART

VI

Data Management with Access

FIGURE 40.4

The Table datasheet of the Customers table

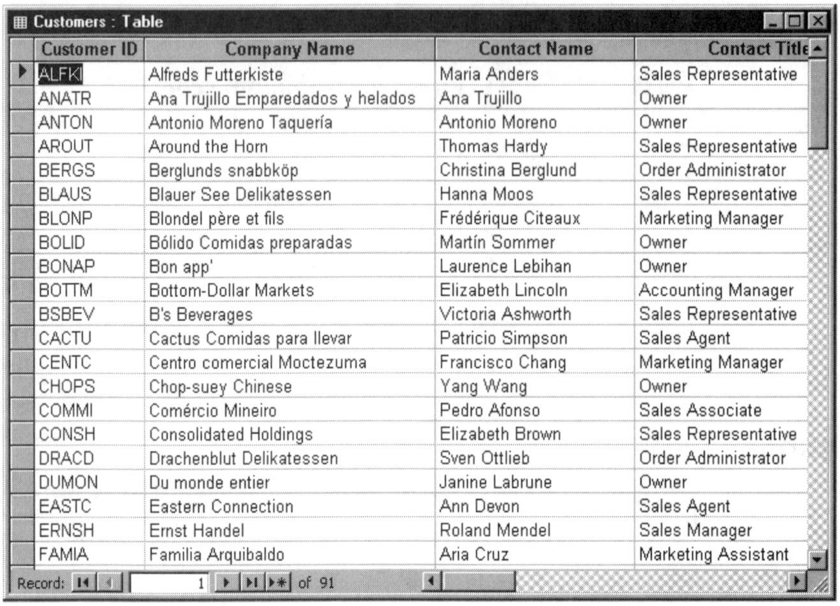

Customers : Table

Customer ID	Company Name	Contact Name	Contact Title
ALFKI	Alfreds Futterkiste	Maria Anders	Sales Representative
ANATR	Ana Trujillo Emparedados y helados	Ana Trujillo	Owner
ANTON	Antonio Moreno Taquería	Antonio Moreno	Owner
AROUT	Around the Horn	Thomas Hardy	Sales Representative
BERGS	Berglunds snabbköp	Christina Berglund	Order Administrator
BLAUS	Blauer See Delikatessen	Hanna Moos	Sales Representative
BLONP	Blondel père et fils	Frédérique Citeaux	Marketing Manager
BOLID	Bólido Comidas preparadas	Martín Sommer	Owner
BONAP	Bon app'	Laurence Lebihan	Owner
BOTTM	Bottom-Dollar Markets	Elizabeth Lincoln	Accounting Manager
BSBEV	B's Beverages	Victoria Ashworth	Sales Representative
CACTU	Cactus Comidas para llevar	Patricio Simpson	Sales Agent
CENTC	Centro comercial Moctezuma	Francisco Chang	Marketing Manager
CHOPS	Chop-suey Chinese	Yang Wang	Owner
COMMI	Comércio Mineiro	Pedro Afonso	Sales Associate
CONSH	Consolidated Holdings	Elizabeth Brown	Sales Representative
DRACD	Drachenblut Delikatessen	Sven Ottlieb	Order Administrator
DUMON	Du monde entier	Janine Labrune	Owner
EASTC	Eastern Connection	Ann Devon	Sales Agent
ERNSH	Ernst Handel	Roland Mendel	Sales Manager
FAMIA	Familia Arquibaldo	Aria Cruz	Marketing Assistant

Record: 1 of 91

Moving from Field to Field and Record to Record

In the datasheet, you can move from field to field and from record to record using the arrow keys or Tab and Shift+Tab. Pressing Tab is the same as using the right arrow key, and pressing Shift+Tab is the same as using the left arrow key. Notice that when you move up and down, a triangle marker moves in the record selector, indicating the current record.

Editing

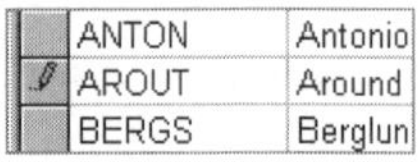

ANTON	Antonio
AROUT	Around
BERGS	Berglun

To edit the contents of a field, press the arrow keys until the field that you want is highlighted and then press F2. Pressing F2 removes the highlight and allows you to edit the field. If you are using the mouse, simply click on the field you want to edit. If you are replacing the entire contents of a field, you need not press F2. Instead, highlight the desired field and start typing. Your new entry replaces the entire contents of that field. When you are editing a field, a picture of a pencil appears in the gray record selector for that row.

Undoing Changes

If you begin changing a field and make a mistake, press the Esc key to undo the change. If you continue to make changes in other fields of the same record without moving to another row, pressing the Esc key undoes the changes to the entire record.

This works only if you have not moved off the current record, because Access saves the changes to your record whenever you move off the field.

TIP

If you move to another row or record and find that you made an error, press Ctrl+Z or Click the Undo button or select Edit ➣ Undo to restore the last record you edited. Be careful, however, not to rely on this, because it only works for the last record saved. If you make even a minor change in another record before noticing your error in a previous record, you will not be able to undo the change.

Adding New Records

When you want to add a new record to a table, you first need to get to the very last row of the datasheet. You can do this in a several ways (see Figure 40.5).

- Use the down arrow key on your keyboard to move to the last row.
- From the menu bar, choose Insert ➣ New Record.
- Click the New Record button on the Table Datasheet toolbar.
- Use the Goto New Record navigation button at the bottom of the datasheet.

If you look at the blank row at the bottom of the datasheet before you move to it, you will notice an asterisk in the record selector. This signifies that the row is really not a record yet, but a place to add new records to the table. Once you enter the row, the asterisk turns into the normal triangle record marker.

Deleting a Record

To delete a record in a table, select it by clicking somewhere on the row of the record and follow one of the steps below.

- From the menu bar, choose Edit ➣ Delete Record.
- Click on the Delete Record button on the Table Datasheet toolbar.
- Select the current record by clicking on the record selector and pressing the Delete key or right-click on the record selector and choose Cut from the shortcut menu.

PART

VI

Data Management
with Access

FIGURE 40.5

Options for inserting a new record

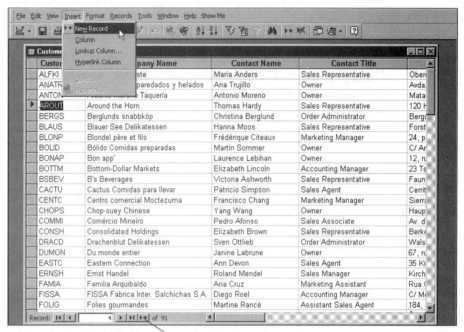

Goto New Record

Sorting and Filtering Your Data

You don't necessarily enter information into a table in the order that you need to view it. You may also need to view only certain records at a time. Using the sorting and filtering functions in Datasheet view gives you this flexibility.

Sorting

Sorting data in Datasheet view is a snap. First, click on the field column by which you want to sort, and then do one of the following: (1) Click on one of the sort buttons in the toolbar (see Figure 40.6); (2) choose Records ➤ Sort ➤ Ascending or Descending from the menu bar; or (3) right-click on a field and choose either Sort Ascending or Sort Descending.

You can also sort by multiple columns, but the columns must be adjacent, or side by side (see "Changing the Column Layout" later in this chapter). If the field columns are adjacent, select the first column by clicking on the column header, then hold down Shift and click on the last column header of the columns by which you want to sort. Your datasheet should now resemble that shown in Figure 40.7, and you can use any of the previously mentioned methods for sorting.

FIGURE 40.6

Sorting by Contact Title, using either the toolbar or the menu bar

FIGURE 40.7

Sorting by multiple columns: Contact Title and Contact Name

Filtering by Selection

Filter by Selection is the quickest and easiest method to filter information in your datasheet, albeit the most limited. First, place the insertion point in the field that has the data value you want to extract, and then do one of the following: (1) Choose Records ➤ Filter ➤ Filter by Selection from the menu bar; (2) click on the Filter by Selection toolbar button; (3) or right-click on the desired value and choose Filter by Selection from the shortcut menu.

PART

VI

Data Management with Access

To practice filtering, display the entire, unfiltered Customers table in the sample Northwind database. Suppose you want to see the records for only those customers in Oregon. The first step is to find a record that has Oregon in the Region field and then click on that field. Figure 40.8 shows such a record.

Mario Pontes	Rua do Paço, 67		Rio de Janeiro	RJ
Carlos Hernández	Carrera 22 con Ave. Carlos Soublette #8-35		San Cristóbal	Táchira
▶ Yoshi Latimer	City Center Plaza		Elgin	OR
Patricia McKenna	8 Johnstown Road		Cork	Co. Cork
Helen Bennett	Garden House		Cowes	Isle of Wight

Next, choose Records ➤ Filter ➤ Filter by Selection from the menu bar. Figure 40.9 shows the results.

To clear a Filter by Selection or to clear any filter applied to a datasheet, do one of the following: (1) Choose Records ➤ Remove Filter/Sort from the menu bar; (2) click on the Apply Filter toolbar button; or (3) right-click on any field and choose Remove Filter/Sort from the shortcut menu.

Customers : Table

Contact Name	Address	City	Region
▶ Howard Snyder	2732 Baker Blvd.	Eugene	OR
Yoshi Latimer	City Center Plaza	Elgin	OR
Fran Wilson	89 Chiaroscuro Rd.	Portland	OR
Liz Nixon	89 Jefferson Way	Portland	OR
*			

Filtering by Form

Filtering by form in a datasheet allows you to filter the records that you want by selecting field filters from a combo box. To filter by form:

1. In Datasheet view, open a table.
2. From the menu bar, choose Records ➤ Filter ➤ Filter by Form, or click on the Filter by Form button on the toolbar.
3. Your datasheet will reduce to one row (see Figure 40.10). When you click on any field, a combo box arrow appears.

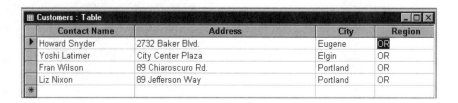

Customers: Filter by Form

Customer ID	Company Name	Contact Name	Contact Title	
▶				

4. To select a filter value for the current field, click on any of the drop-down arrows. You can select criteria from other fields, if desired.

5. After the criteria for the filter are chosen, choose Filter ➢ Apply Filter/Sort from the menu bar or right-click on the title bar of the Filter by Form window and choose Apply Filter/Sort from the shortcut menu. Or click on the Apply Filter button on the toolbar.

To modify the above filter, choose Records ➢ Filter ➢ Filter By Form from the menu bar and make the changes in the filter row. To clear the filter and see all records, choose Records ➢ Remove Filter/Sort from the menu bar or right-click on a field or the window title bar and select Remove Filter/Sort.

Advanced Filtering

Using Advanced Filter/Sort is similar to creating a query except that you do not specify the fields to show or hide; instead, you specify criteria. To learn how to use the Advanced Filter/Sort option, review Chapter 42 on designing a query with the QBE grid.

Formatting the Datasheet

Although you will probably want to use the formatting capabilities of forms and reports instead of formatting the datasheet, some formatting techniques can make working with datasheets a little more effective.

Changing the Font

If the font in your datasheet is too small, too big, or just not right, you can modify it.

1. From the menu bar, choose Format ➢ Font.

2. In the Font dialog box, select the options you want and click on OK.

 NOTE

You cannot change the font for only one field, column, or row. The whole table must use the same font.

Changing Column Widths and Row Heights

At times you will want to change the height of rows or the width of columns to facilitate viewing your data.

To change the column width:

1. From the menu bar, choose Format ➢ Column Width.

2. In the Column Width dialog box, specify the number of characters you want to see in the column.

3. Click on OK.

PART

VI

Data Management
with Access

You can also change the width of columns by placing your mouse pointer over the top right border of the column you want to change and clicking and dragging the border until it is the desired width. Double-clicking on the column header's right border will "best fit" the column to the largest entry, which occasionally will be the field name/caption in the header itself.

Changing row height changes all rows; you cannot specify different row heights for only some rows. To change the height of rows:

1. Choose Format ➤ Row Height from the menu bar.
2. Type a number, measured in points, in the Row Height dialog box. Click on OK.

You can change the row height by clicking and dragging the top border of one of the gray record selectors on the left side of the datasheet.

Changing the Column Layout

To change column order while viewing the datasheet, you need only click and drag the columns that you want to move.

1. In Datasheet view, open a table.
2. Position your mouse pointer over the gray column header of the column that you want to move and press once.
3. Position your mouse pointer back over the column header and click and hold the left mouse button. A box is now attached to the bottom of your mouse pointer.
4. Drag your mouse pointer until the black column separator that moves with it is in the desired location.
5. Let go of the left mouse button. Your column will move into its new position.

Freezing Columns

If you have a large number of fields in a table and you need to keep one or more columns in view as you scroll through the other fields, you can freeze those columns.

1. In Datasheet view, open a table.
2. Click anywhere in the column that you want to freeze, and choose Format ➤ Freeze Columns from the menu bar, or select the column, right-click on the column header, and choose Freeze Columns on the shortcut menu. The column you selected will move to the far left and freeze.

More Mouse for Your Money with the Secondary Mouse Button

The secondary mouse button (for most mice the right mouse button) provides great efficiency when working in Access. Datasheets specifically offer a number of options for the secondary mouse button to increase your productivity.

Clicking this button inside of your datasheet provides quick access to a number of menu bar and toolbar options via a shortcut menu.

Clicking this button within a field that does not have anything selected gives you sorting and filtering options. If you have something selected when you click, the Cut, Copy, and Paste options are enabled. If the field you click is a Hyperlink, then a submenu appears showing Hyperlink options, including Open the Destination of the Hyperlink, Edit the

Link, Copy the Link, Add the Link to Your Favorites, and Select the Link. If the field you select is an OLE field, then an Insert Object option is enabled to allow you to put an object in the field. If there is already an object there, then options appear that allow you to edit and open the object.

If you select one or more columns of your datasheet first, and then click your secondary mouse button, a whole new list of options becomes available. By selecting columns first, you can sort (if you have multiple columns selected you need to hold down the Ctrl key to sort them together from left to right), copy, change column width, run the Lookup Wizard, and hide, freeze, insert, delete, and rename columns.

By taking advantage of the secondary mouse button, you can cut mouse clicks and key strokes off your daily tasks and reduce a great amount of wasted time.

PART

VI

Data Management with Access

3. If you scroll to the right to view other fields, the frozen column will always stay in view.

4. To freeze more than one column, repeat the steps above for each new column.

5. To unfreeze columns, choose Format ➤ Unfreeze All Columns from the menu bar.

NOTE

When you unfreeze columns that were not originally on the left side of the datasheet, Access keeps the columns on the left side and does not move them back to their original position. When you close the table, you will be asked if you want to save changes to the layout of the table. Click on No and the columns will revert to their original position.

Hiding Columns

To hide a column in Datasheet view, click on the desired column and choose Format ➤ Hide Columns from the menu bar or select the column and right-click on the column header to choose the Hide Columns option on the shortcut menu. To unhide a column, choose Format ➤ Unhide Columns from the menu bar, check the column you want to unhide in the Unhide Columns dialog box, and click on Close.

TIP

The easiest way to hide multiple columns is to choose Format ➤ Unhide Columns from the menu bar, uncheck all the columns you want hidden in the Unhide Columns dialog box, and click on Close.

Inserting Columns

Access allows you to add fields or columns to a datasheet.

1. In Datasheet view, open a table.
2. Click on any column to the left of which you want a new column inserted and choose Insert ➤ Column from the menu bar, or select a column and right-click on the column header to choose the Insert Column option on the shortcut menu.
3. Type a sample of the data for the field in a record.
4. Switch to Design view by choosing View ➤ Table Design from the menu bar. Your field is added to the structure and a data type is chosen.

Renaming Columns

You can change a column name in Datasheet view.

1. Click on the column whose name you want to change.
2. From the menu bar, choose Format ➤ Rename Column.
3. Type the new name of the column in the header and press Enter. Or double-click on the column header and edit the name. Or select the column, right-click on the column header, and choose Rename Column from the shortcut menu.

Chapter

41

Using Forms with Your Data

Using Forms with Your Data

Access provides a number of methods for generating forms. If you're a beginning user, you will likely use the Form Wizards and AutoForms, which offer help and guidance. If you're more adventurous or if you're an advanced user, you'll probably want to use the Design view to create forms or to modify a form that was created with the Wizards. This chapter will review all of these methods.

Designing a Form

You have several options for creating new forms. To see them for yourself, click on the New button on the Forms page in the Database window (see Figure 41.1).

When specifying one of the following methods in the New Form dialog box, you must also specify the record source. The record source is the table or query from which the form will get its data. A form can have only one record source.

FIGURE 41.1

*Options for cre-
ating forms in
the New Form
dialog box*

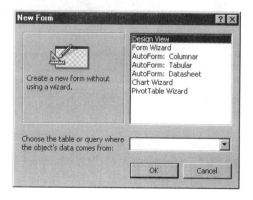

Design View	For the experienced user who wants to create a form from scratch.
Form Wizard	Takes a user step by step through the creation of Columnar, Tabular, Datasheet, and Justified forms.
AutoForm	Automatically creates a Columnar, Tabular, or Datasheet form without any user interaction, except for selecting a particular AutoForm.
Chart Wizard	Helps a user easily create a form that displays a graph of the chosen data.
Pivot Table Wizard	Steps a user through placing an Excel pivot table, based on Access data, on a form. (For more information on pivot tables, see Chapter 22 on Excel database capabilities.)

The Form Wizard and AutoForms

With Form Wizard or one of the AutoForms, you can create four kinds of forms:
Columnar, Tabular, Datasheet, and Justified. This section will walk you through the
steps for using the Form Wizard.

For this example we will use the Northwind database in the SAMPLES folder under
\Program files\Microsoft Office\Office.

1. Open the Northwind database.

2. From the Database window, select the Forms tab and click on the New button.

3. Select the Form Wizard option and select the Customers table for the record source. Click on OK.

4. Select the fields you want on your form from the Form Wizards dialog box.

5. Click the >> button to send all the fields from the Customers table to the selected fields list, as shown in Figure 41.2. Click on the Next button.

FIGURE 41.2

Selecting all fields from the Customers table for the form

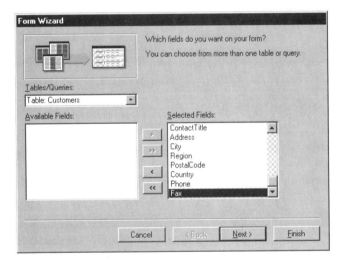

6. Next, the Form Wizard asks you to select a layout. The choices are Columnar, Tabular, Datasheet, and Justified. Select Columnar. (We will see samples of all four later.) Click on the Next button to continue.

7. Select a style for the form. Select International for this example and click on Next.

8. Now title your form **My Customers**, without changing any of the other options, and click on Finish. Your form opens for use and is similar to the one shown in Figure 41.3.

PART

VI

Data Management
with Access

FIGURE 41.3

*The completed
My Customers
form in the
International
style*

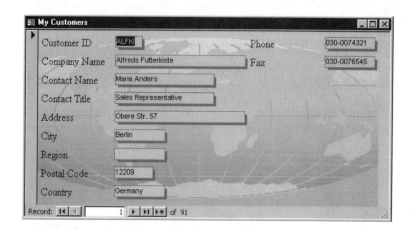

Selecting Fields from Multiple Tables

You can select fields from multiple tables or queries; however, this does not mean you can have more than one record source per form. If you select fields from more than one table or query, Access creates a main form with either a subform or a linked form. You might do this when you want to show the relationships between tables or queries. For example, you might want the Customers fields on a main form and the fields from the Orders table on a subform or linked form. The subform and linked form will be created to show only the orders for the current customer record.

Using a subform allows you to have all of your data easily accessible on one form. You can establish one by placing a second form within a subform control on the main form. A linked form is a separate form usually opened by clicking on a command button on the main form. Linking forms keeps your forms simple and uncluttered while still giving you access to detail information.

Choosing other layout options would render different results, as shown in Figures 41.4 through 41.6.

FIGURE 41.4

The form using the Tabular layout

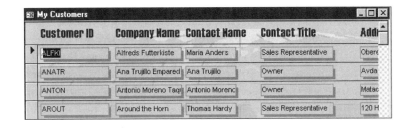

FIGURE 41.5

Now, in Datasheet layout

FIGURE 41.6

Finally, with the Justified style

If you select one of the AutoForms in the New Form dialog box, Access automatically (without asking you any questions) creates the form by using all the fields in the table or query that you select.

The Form Design Screen and Its Components

The Form Design Screen is used to create a form from scratch or to modify a form that was created with a Wizard. Although the Access Form Design Screen is easier to use than many form design utilities in other databases, it takes practice and time to become adept and effective at using it. The best way to learn is to practice modifying existing forms. Once you are comfortable with modifying forms, you can take the plunge and create a new form using only the Form Design Screen and no Wizards.

NOTE

Even if you become extremely adept at creating forms, you will probably find that using the Form Wizard will save time—even if the only things that the Wizard-created form and your final form have in common are the controls that are bound to fields.

In our example, we use an existing form in the Northwind database.

1. Open the Northwind database and select the Forms tab.
2. Select the Employees form and click on Open. Or right-click on the form name and select Open from the shortcut menu. Or simply double-click on the name. The form opens.
3. Click on the Personal Info tab to switch to the next page and on the Company Info tab to return to the top of the form.

To see how this form was constructed, we need to look at it in Design view. Using one of the methods described below, switch to Design view.

- From the menu bar, select View ➤ Design View.
- Click on the View button on the Form View toolbar, or click on the down arrow button next to it and select Design View from the list.

The Sections in a Form

Forms are divided into sections, and a form can have as many as five sections. Each one begins with a gray section header that contains its name. The five sections in the blank form shown in Figure 41.7 are:

Form Header and Form Footer The items you place in the Form Header or Footer appear once and only once at the beginning or end of the form. When you create a new form in Design view, the Form Header and Footer are not visible by default. To make them visible, select View ➤ Form Header and Footer from the menu bar while in Design view or right-click on the window title bar and select Form Header and Footer from the shortcut menu.

Page Header and Page Footer	The information you place in the Page Header does not appear onscreen. It only appears in the printed form. When creating a new form, the Page Header and Footer are not shown by default. To show them, select View ➢ Page Header and Footer from the menu bar while in Design view or right-click on the window title bar and select Form Header and Footer from the shortcut menu.
Detail	A form always has a Detail section in which you place the fields of records that you want to view or anything else that will be the focus of the form.

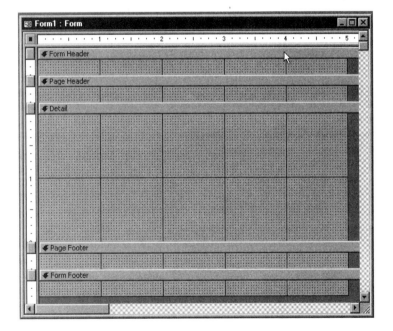

FIGURE 41.7

The five sections of a form

Field List

When working with a form that has a record source, you can open a field list window to show a list of fields. You can click and drag any of these fields onto the form. To view the field list of the Employees form, select View ➢ Field List from the menu bar or click on the Field List toolbar button.

PART

VI

Data Management
with Access

The Toolbox and Controls

The Toolbox is a special toolbar that contains every type of object that you can place on a form. These objects are called *controls*. If you want to place a control on a form, click once on the control in the Toolbox and then click on the section of the form in which you want the control. You can view the Toolbox by choosing View ➤ Toolbox from the menu bar or by clicking on the Toolbox toolbar button. The various control options are described in Table 41.1 below.

If you cannot see a button that you are certain is on a toolbar, check to make sure that you do not have two toolbars docked at the same level. If this happens, you may need to click and drag one toolbar so that it is either floating or docked at a different level.

TABLE 41.1: TOOLBOX CONTROLS

Control	Description
Label	Used to place descriptive text on a form that does not need to be bound to any data.
Text Box	The most common control used to display data from underlying tables and queries. It can also show results of calculations.
Toggle Button, Option Button, and Checkbox	When used alone, these controls can be bound to fields that are of the Yes/No data type. Multiple controls of these types can be used within an Option Group to provide mutually exclusive options. The Option button is the control usually used in an Option group, although all three will work if you want to use them.
Option Group	Control used on a form to group Option buttons, Toggle buttons, or checkboxes to facilitate mutually exclusive options. When using the Option group, the controls within it provide a value and the Option group is bound to a data field.

Continued ▶

TABLE 41.1: TOOLBOX CONTROLS (CONTINUED)

Control	Description
Combo Box	Provides both the features of a text box and a list box because you can either type right into it or select from a list of choices. Generally chosen over a list box when you need the ability to pick from a list without taking up as much space on a form or report as a list box.
List Box	Provides a pick list of options from which a user can select. Uses more space than a combo box but allows for easier identification of choices since a user does not need to click anything to see at least some of the items.
Command Button	Primary control used when automating a database with macros or code. The name of the procedure or macro is placed in the On Click event of the command button so that it will run when the button is pressed.
Image	Used to place pictures that do not need to change or be edited onto forms and reports. This cannot be a bound control.
Unbound Object Frame	Used to place OLE objects *not* stored in your database on a form or report.
Bound Object Frame	Used to place OLE objects that are stored in your database on a form or report.
Page Break Control	Placed on a report to cause a page break at a specific point in the report. On a form it can be strategically placed to create a two-page effect using the PgDn and PgUp keys or buttons on the form.
Tab Control	When placed on a form, provides tabbed pages to logically organize controls.
Subform/Subreport	Commonly used to visually show one-to-many relationships between a table or query of the main form and the table or query of the subform or report.
Line	Allows the creation of indiscriminate lines on a report or form.
Rectangle	Used to easily create rectangles on a form or report.

PART

VI

Data Management
with Access

Continued ▌▶

TABLE 41.1: TOOLBOX CONTROLS (CONTINUED)

Control	Description
More Controls	Provides a list of all installed ActiveX controls that can add to the functionality of Access.
Select Objects	This button, the first on the toolbox, is not a control. When this button is pressed, your mouse can be used to manipulate the controls that are already on the form. After you place a control on the form, the Select Objects button is automatically selected.
Control Wizards	When pressed, the second button on the toolbox activates the Wizards for form controls that could benefit from assistance in filling out their properties.

When placing controls on a form, you are not always thinking about the order in which the fields will need to be accessed. Selecting View ➢ Tab Order from the menu bar will allow you to easily change the Tab Index property of the controls, which lists the order in which the controls will receive the focus when tabbing through the form.

Extending Access with ActiveX

ActiveX is the new name for OLE controls. Microsoft, third-party developers, and even your in-house developers can use ActiveX controls with Visual Basic or C++ programming languages to extend the capabilities of Access. ActiveX controls provide functionality such as user-friendly controls with no interface, complex programming tasks, marquee-like scrolling text, and special interfaces like calendars, gauges, outline views, and much more.

When using an ActiveX control, you will usually find a special properties sheet in addition to the standard one. It can be accessed by clicking on the Builder button on the Custom property or right-clicking on the control, selecting the name of the object on the context menu, and clicking Properties.

Take special precautions to test the ActiveX controls used in your database as they take advantage of some advanced technology in Access. Unless written correctly by the provider, they can cause undesired results.

Properties

As mentioned earlier, everything in Access is an object, and objects have properties. Properties determine how an object looks and performs. To view the Properties window, select View ➤ Properties from the menu bar or click on the Properties button on the Form Design toolbar (see Figure 41.8). There is only one Properties window. To view properties for different controls, select the control; the Properties window changes to show you the properties for the selected object. You can see the change in the title bar of the Properties window. Remember that the form itself is an object, and you can select it by clicking the intersection of the two rulers in the top left corner of the Form window. The various functions of the most common properties are described in Table 41.2.

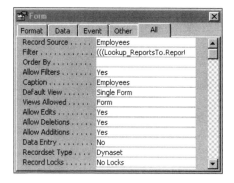

TABLE 41.2: COMMON PROPERTIES

Property	Description
Caption	The displayed text that is associated with a control like a label control or a command button.
Control Source	This is usually the name of the field to which the control is bound. It can also contain a calculation.
Default Value	When inserting a new record, this is the value that will be placed in the control.

Continued

PART

VI

Data Management with Access

TABLE 41.2: COMMON PROPERTIES (CONTINUED)

Property	Description
Format	Specifies how the data should be displayed in the particular control. This will override the Format property at the table level for the field if it contains a different format. This does not affect how the data is stored.
Hyperlink Address	Causes any control to act as a Hyperlink to the specified address.
Hyperlink Subaddress	Used to jump to a name tag, bookmark, or range of the location specified in the Hyperlink Address. If the Address is left blank, can be used to create a Hyperlink to an object in the current database.
Input Mask	Provides the user with a template for filling in the data for the control. This can modify the data as it is being entered and does affect the way it is stored.
Name	Identifies the object.
Tab Stop	Yes or No value specifying whether it will ever gain focus if the user tabs through the form.
Validation Rule	A rule that the data being entered into the control must meet or Access will not let the focus leave the control. Do not have a Validation Rule without Validation Text because the default messages Access gives are a bit cryptic.
Validation Text	The text displayed in a message box when the Validation Rule is violated.

TIP

If you want to know what a particular property does, click on the property's value in the Properties window and press F1 for context-sensitive help.

The Form View of a Form

Once you create a form, whether with Wizards, from scratch in Design view, or by a combination of the two, you can use the form to add, edit, and view the data in the table or query that is the form's record source. The way you work with data in a form is similar to the way you work with data in Datasheet view.

Navigating Your Data in a Form

To open a form in Form view, select the form in the Database window and click on Open or select View ➤ Form View from the menu bar while in Design view.

Editing - To edit fields on a form, use Tab, the arrow keys, or the mouse to get to the field that you want to edit. Once the contents of the field are highlighted, press F2 to begin editing.

Undoing Changes - If you change a field and then want to restore it to its original state, press the Esc key. If you want to undo changes to an entire record, press the Esc key as well.

Moving from Record to Record - To move from record to record, you can use PgUp and PgDn or the record navigation buttons in the bottom left corner of the Form window.

NOTE

If you use PgUp or PgDn to move from record to record and a form has multiple pages in the detail section, PgUp and PgDn switch pages before changing records. If you are on the last page of a form for the current record and you press PgDn, you will go to the next record, on the last page of the form.

Adding a New Record - To create a new record using the form, select Insert ➤ New Record from the menu bar or click on the New Record toolbar button. You can also use the Go To New Record navigation button on the bottom left corner of the Form window, if it is available.

Deleting a Record - To delete a record in a form, select Edit ➤ Delete Record from the menu bar or click on the Delete Record toolbar button. Or, if it is visible, right-click on the record selector, the gray bar on the left side of the detail section of the form or at the beginning of a record in a datasheet subform, and select Cut from the shortcut menu. Not all forms will have the record selector visible.

PART

VI

Data Management
with Access

Filtering Records

You can filter the information in a form using Filter by Selection or Filter by Form.

Filter by Selection

When you select Filter by Selection, you filter the records displayed in a form based on the value or part of the value in the field of the current record.

1. Open the Employees form of the Northwind database. Notice the number of records available to the right of the navigation buttons at the bottom left corner of the form.
2. Tab to the Title field of Nancy Davolio so that it is selected, as shown in Figure 41.9, and then do one of the following:

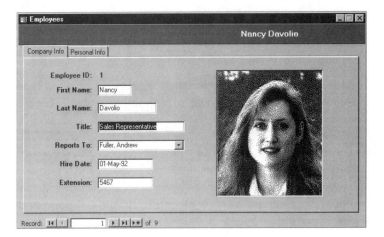

- Click on the Filter by Selection button on the toolbar, *or*
- Select Records ➤ Filter ➤ Filter by Selection, *or*
- Right-click on the field containing the value on which you want to build a filter, and then select Filter by Selection from the shortcut menu.

3. The number of records available is reduced to include only those in which the employee is a sales representative. To the right of the navigation buttons is the term *(Filtered)*, as shown in Figure 41.10.

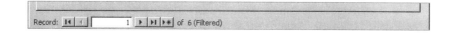

FIGURE 41.10

Filtering records based on Sales Representative

4. To restore all records, do one of the following:

- Click on the Remove Filter button on the toolbar, *or*
- Right-click anywhere on the form and select Remove Filter/Sort in the shortcut menu, *or*
- Select Records ➤ Remove Filter/Sort from the menu bar.

> **TIP**
>
> If you select only part of the value in a field, Access filters only that selected part. For example, choosing Sales instead of the entire Sales Representative would filter Sales Manager as well as Sales Representative.

Filtering by Form

When you use Filter by Form, you specify the fields that you want to include in your filter by setting the values right in your form and then applying the filter based on your criteria.

1. Open the Employees form of the Northwind database.

2. Select Records ➤ Filter ➤ Filter by Form from the menu bar or click on the Filter by Form toolbar button. Or right-click on an open area of the form and select Filter by Form from the shortcut menu.

3. The controls on your form will all go blank, as shown in Figure 41.11, so that you can specify criteria.

4. If you click on the field for which you want to specify criteria, a drop-down arrow appears to allow you to select from a list of values.

5. After you specify the criteria, select Filter ➤ Apply Filter/Sort from the menu bar or click on the Apply Filter toolbar button. Or right-click on an open area of the form and select Apply Filter/Sort from the shortcut menu. The recordset is extracted/sorted based on the criteria you specified.

PART

VI

Data Management with Access

> **TIP**
>
> If you need to specify OR criteria—for example, you want to see everyone bearing the title of President or Chairman—you can use the OR tabs at the bottom left of the Filter by Form window and specify separate pages of criteria for OR conditions.

FIGURE 41.11

The form is ready for you to specify criteria.

Employees: Filter by Form

| Company Info | Personal Info |

Employee ID:

First Name:

Last Name:

Title:

Reports To:

Hire Date:

Extension:

Look for / Or /

Forms without Data

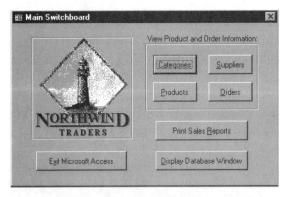

You may want to create some forms that will not have a record source. For example, you might want to use a form to access all the other forms in your database, or you might want to use forms as message boxes or dialog boxes. The Northwind database form Main Switchboard is a good example of a form that is used for interface purposes rather than for direct data access. These types of forms must be created from scratch using the Design view without the help of any Wizards.

Chapter

42

Asking Questions of Your Data with Queries

Asking Questions of Your Data with Queries

Designing a query has never been easier than with Access 97. The five Query Wizards step you through the query creation process, asking which fields you would like in the final datasheet/recordset and how you want to sort the resulting datasheet/recordset.

Designing a Query

At the root of all query-building interfaces is Structured Query Language (SQL). SQL is command-line-like language that requires a user to select fields from a specific table where certain conditions are true. Microsoft has gone to great lengths to provide interfaces to shield the user from SQL for a reason: It is hard to learn! Unless you are an adventurer at heart or an experienced SQL database person, put this aspect of Access on the back burner until you fully understand the other parts. Instead, build your queries with the Wizards and modify them easily using the Query Design Screen and its Query by Example (QBE) grid.

Using the Wizards

Previous versions of Access relied on the Query Design Screen for the creation of all queries except for the four more difficult queries that were and still are supported with Wizards of their own. The Simple Query Wizard has been added to help with creating basic queries. You can now use any of the following to design a query:

Design View
Opens a new Query Design Screen and allows you to create queries from scratch.

Simple Query Wizard
Asks which fields you want in the resulting datasheet, whether you want the information grouped, and whether you want to perform a function such as sum, count, or average on any field.

Crosstab Query Wizard
Creates a spreadsheet-like result from three fields: a field to use as a row heading, a field to use as a column heading, and a field on which to perform a function at the intersection of the row and column headings. If, for example, you want to know how many orders each employee has in each country where you have customers, you would take the following steps: (1) Specify the EmployeeID field as the row heading so that all employee IDs are listed down the left column; (2) specify the ShipCountry field as the column heading so that the countries are listed across the top in the column headings; and (3) specify the count of the OrderIDs as the value that you want at the intersection of EmployeeID and Country.

Find Duplicates Query Wizard
Helps you generate a query that looks to see if records in a table have duplicate values in specific fields.

Find Unmatched Query Wizard
Looks at two related tables to see if there are any records with values in a specific field that do not appear at least once in the related field of the other table.

You will use the Simple Query Wizard to create, or at least start, most of your queries. The following example is indicative of how to use most Query Wizards.

1. Open the Northwind database in the Samples folder under \Program Files\Microsoft Office\Office folder.
2. Select the Queries tab and click on the New button.
3. In the New Query dialog box, select Simple Query Wizard and then click on OK.
4. The Simple Query Wizard (Figure 42.1) asks you to select the fields for the query.

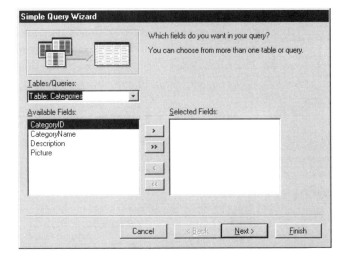

The first window of the Simple Query Wizard has three parts: the Tables/Queries combo box, the Available Fields list box, and the Selected Fields list box. In the Tables/Queries combo box, you select the table or query from whose fields you want to choose. The Available Fields list box shows you the available fields for the table or query you selected in the combo box. The Selected Fields list box holds the fields you want to include in your query.

A nice feature of this window is that you can select all the fields from all the tables that you want to include. Once you have selected fields from one table or query, you can select another table or query from the combo box and choose from its fields. You can continue to select tables, queries, and fields until you have chosen all the fields you want in your query.

PART
VI

Data Management
with Access

WARNING

Be aware that if there are no direct or indirect relationships between the tables that hold the fields you choose for your query, Access will prompt you to either change your relationships and restart the Wizard or remove the fields from the tables that are not related.

When all the fields you want to include are listed in the Selected Fields list box, you can continue.

5. From the Tables/Queries combo box, select the Customers table.

6. Send the CompanyName field from the Available Fields list box to the Selected Fields list box by clicking on the > button. Or simply double-click on CompanyName.

7. From the Tables/Queries combo box, select the Orders table.

8. Send the OrderID, OrderDate, and ShippedDate fields to the Selected Fields list box. When your screen looks like the one in Figure 42.2, click on Next.

FIGURE 42.2

Selecting fields from multiple tables

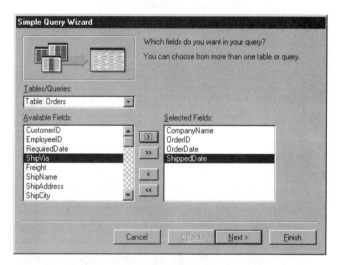

In the next step, the Wizard asks whether you want detail (*Show me all of the records in their entirety*) or a summary (*Summarize my information for me*).

9. Leave the default of *Detail (shows every field of every record)* and click on Next.

10. Next, the Wizard asks for a title for your query. Type **My Query** and click on Finish, leaving the other settings in the window with their defaults.

Figure 42.3 shows the datasheet that results from the query you just created. Note that it lists the name of the company every time there is an order. If you wanted a cleaner presentation, you could create a report from this query and sort, group, and format the information.

FIGURE 42.3

A maximized datasheet for My Query

Company Name	Order ID	Order Date	Shipped Date
Alfreds Futterkiste	10643	25-Sep-95	03-Oct-95
Alfreds Futterkiste	10692	03-Nov-95	13-Nov-95
Alfreds Futterkiste	10702	13-Nov-95	21-Nov-95
Alfreds Futterkiste	10835	15-Feb-96	21-Feb-96
Alfreds Futterkiste	10952	15-Apr-96	23-Apr-96
Alfreds Futterkiste	11011	09-May-96	13-May-96
Ana Trujillo Emparedados y helados	10308	19-Oct-94	25-Oct-94
Ana Trujillo Emparedados y helados	10625	08-Sep-95	14-Sep-95
Ana Trujillo Emparedados y helados	10759	29-Dec-95	12-Jan-96
Ana Trujillo Emparedados y helados	10926	03-Apr-96	10-Apr-96
Antonio Moreno Taquería	10365	28-Dec-94	02-Jan-95
Antonio Moreno Taquería	10507	16-May-95	23-May-95
Antonio Moreno Taquería	10535	13-Jun-95	21-Jun-95

Although the Simple Query Wizard makes query creation a breeze, a few restrictions will generally require that you modify the query using the Query Design Screen. The Simple Query Wizard does not allow you to sort, specify criteria, create calculated columns, or limit to top values. When these situations arise, the Query Design Screen becomes useful.

The Query Design Screen and the QBE Grid

The Query Design Screen, as shown in Figure 42.4, consists of a top pane that holds the field lists of the queries or tables being used as the data source and the QBE grid. The QBE grid is where you specify the fields to be included in the query and select any sorting or criteria that you want to apply to those fields.

Field Lists

To add tables and queries to the field lists, select Design View from the New Query dialog box. This creates a new query in Design view and opens the Show Table dialog box. From here you can add the tables or queries to be used. If you need to add tables after you close the Show Table dialog box, you can always open it by choosing Query ➤ Show Table from the menu bar or by clicking on the Show Table toolbar button. Or right-click on the top pane and choose Show Table from the shortcut menu.

FIGURE 42.4

The My Query design screen

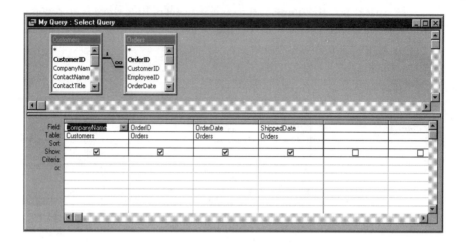

If you are using more than one table in the query, any relationships that have been created are reflected in the top pane. If a table is not related to any other table in the query, it can be linked by clicking and dragging from a field in the unrelated table to a field in another table. For more information on relationships and joins, see Chapter 46.

WARNING

Never run a query if there is a field list in the top pane of the Query Design Screen that is not related to another field list with a join line identifying which fields should be used in each of the lists to match up their records. If the query is run and there are field lists that are not joined to other field lists, the datasheet will reflect what is called a Cartesian Result. For example, assume you have two unconnected tables in a query and you run it. If one table has 100 records and the other table has 10 records, the resulting datasheet will consist of 1000 records. Because the query does not know how to relate the two tables, it matches every record in one table with every record in the other table—a meaningless result that can be costly in terms of time and memory.

The QBE Grid

Once you have the field lists in the top pane of the Query Design Screen, you need to specify which fields to use with the query. You do so by moving fields from the top pane into the QBE grid. Use any of the following techniques.

- Click and drag the desired field from a field list in the top to a column in the QBE grid.

- Double-click on a field in a field list to place it in the next available column.
- Click on the field row of a column and then click on the drop-down arrow to choose from the list of available fields.
- Click on the field row of a column and then type the expression of a calculated field that you want to use in the query.

TIP

If you want to use all the fields from a field list, the quickest way to add them is to place the asterisk (*) located at the top of a field list into one of the columns of the QBE grid. The asterisk represents the entire record, and when the query runs, all fields in that field list are included in the datasheet. The only downside to using the asterisk is that you cannot specify criteria for individual fields. To quickly get all fields from a field list in their own individual columns, double-click on the title bar of the field list to select them. Click and drag the selection to the QBE grid, and the fields are placed into their own columns.

Once the fields are in the QBE grid, you can specify sort order, set criteria, and determine whether a field will be shown or used only to set criteria or sort.

Building the Query

To demonstrate the capabilities of the Query Design Screen, we will rebuild the query we constructed with the Simple Query Wizard and expand on it in ways not possible with the Wizard.

1. Select the Queries tab of the Northwind Database window and click on the New button.
2. From the New Query dialog box, select Design View and then click on OK.
3. In the Show Table dialog box, select the Customers table and click on Add.
4. Select the Orders table and click on Add.
5. With the two tables added to your query, click on Close in the Show Table dialog box. Your Query Design Screen should look like the one in Figure 42.5.
6. Point to the CompanyName field in the Customers field list and drag the field to the first column of the QBE grid.
7. Double-click on the OrderID field in the Orders field list. The field appears in the second column of the QBE grid.

FIGURE 42.5

*The Customers
and Orders
tables are added
to the new
query.*

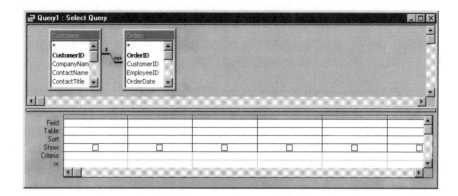

8. Click on the field row of the third column and click on the drop-down arrow that appears. Select the Orders.OrderDate field from the list

9. Add the ShippedDate field from the Orders field list using one of the above methods.

10. Using the Query Design Screen, you can add calculated fields to your query. Click on the Field row of the fourth column.

11. In the fifth column, type the following exactly as it appears:

```
DAYS ELAPSED:[SHIPPEDDATE]-[ORDERDATE]
```

The text to the left of the colon is the caption, or the name of the calculated column, and the expression to the right of the colon generates a value for the column. When referring to fields, field names are enclosed in square brackets. Your Query Design Screen should look like the one in Figure 42.6. You may not see the entire calculation if it is too wide for the column. To widen the column, double-click the top of the column divider on the right side of the column that is too narrow.

FIGURE 42.6

*New query
with a calcu-
lated column
to figure the
days elapsed
between
OrderDate and
ShippedDate*

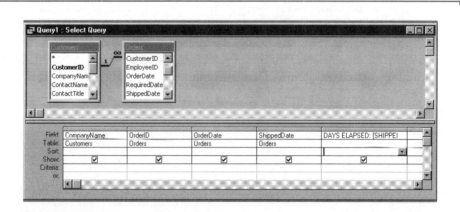

PART

VI

Data Management with Access

> **TIP**
>
> If you find it hard to type in the limited space of the column cell when creating calculated columns or specifying criteria, you can press Shift+F2 to zoom in on the cell, or you can right-click on the field row cell and choose Zoom from the shortcut menu. This will open a dialog box in which you can type the formula without the size restraints of a column.

12. We want to sort by OrderDate and then by CompanyName, but we want CompanyName to appear first in the Datasheet view of the query, and Access sorts from left to right. All is not lost though. We can bring OrderDate down to the grid a second time, this time placing it before CompanyName. To do so, click and drag the OrderDate field from the Orders field list on top of the CompanyName field in the QBE grid. All columns shift right.

13. Click on the Sort row under the OrderDate field in column one, and choose Ascending from the drop-down list displayed by clicking the down arrow button. We also want to sort by CompanyName after OrderDate, so choose Ascending in the Sort row under CompanyName as well.

14. Even though we needed OrderDate in the first column for sorting, we do not want it to show in the query datasheet; so uncheck the checkbox in the Show row under OrderDate in the first column.

15. In the Criteria column under the DAYS ELAPSED column, type **>10**. This criterion restricts the records to only those whose orders took more than 10 days from the order date to ship. Figure 42.7 shows the finished QBE grid.

FIGURE 42.7

The finished query, sorted by date and company name

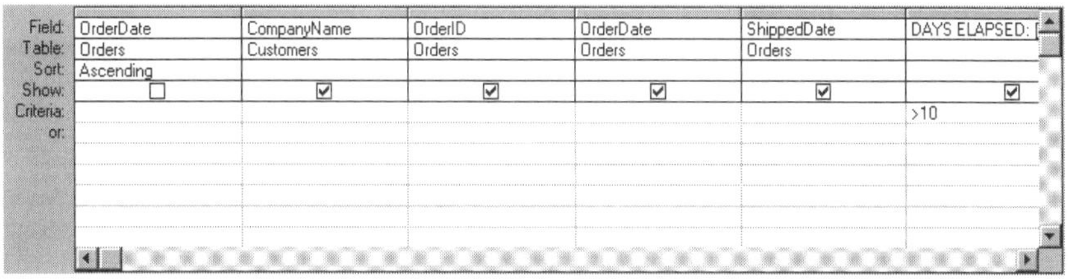

Field:	OrderDate	CompanyName	OrderID	OrderDate	ShippedDate	DAYS ELAPSED:
Table:	Orders	Customers	Orders	Orders	Orders	
Sort:	Ascending					
Show:	☐	☑	☑	☑	☑	☑
Criteria:						>10
or:						

When you are ready to view the results of your query (see Figure 42.8), choose View ➤ Datasheet View from the menu bar or click on the View button on the Query Design toolbar. You can also click on the Run button on the same toolbar.

Remember that although this query was created from scratch with the Query Design Screen, you can redesign any query created with the Simple Query Wizard and add sorting, specify criteria, or create calculated columns.

FIGURE 42.8

The resulting datasheet with five columns

Company Name	Order ID	Order Date	Shipped Date	DAYS ELAPSE
Vins et alcools Chevalier	10248	04-Aug-94	16-Aug-94	12
Chop-suey Chinese	10254	11-Aug-94	23-Aug-94	12
Que Delícia	10261	19-Aug-94	30-Aug-94	11
Folk och fä HB	10264	24-Aug-94	23-Sep-94	30
Blondel père et fils	10265	25-Aug-94	12-Sep-94	18
Split Rail Beer & Ale	10271	01-Sep-94	30-Sep-94	29
Berglunds snabbköp	10280	14-Sep-94	13-Oct-94	29
Reggiani Caseifici	10288	23-Sep-94	04-Oct-94	11
Tortuga Restaurante	10293	29-Sep-94	12-Oct-94	13
Suprêmes délices	10302	11-Oct-94	09-Nov-94	29

MASTERING TROUBLESHOOTING

When You Misspell a Field Name

When manually entering field names into the field row or the QBE grid or when entering complicated calculations, you may occasionally misspell a field or table name. When this occurs, instead of an error occurring like you might expect, the query attempts to execute by prompting you with a dialog box. The title bar of the dialog box will contain *Enter Parameter Value*, and the message will be the misspelled table or field.

This happens because queries are dynamic, and Access allows you to enter values when the query is run. For example, if you had a query that returned sales between certain dates, you could prompt for the dates using parameters. Parameters are placed in the criteria section just as you would place a table or field name, in effect creating a new field for which the user can provide a different value every time the query is executed. When you misspell a table or field name, Access interprets it as a parameter since the name does not match a table or field.

To resolve the problem, go to Design view and correct the misspelled field or table name that appeared in the dialog box.

Top Values

You can easily set the properties of a query so that it returns only the top percentage or some top number of records. If you click in an open area of the Query Design Screen and choose View ➤ Properties from the menu bar or double-click in the open area of the screen, the Properties window for the query will open. The Top Values property has a combo box list of suggested top values, such as 5, 25%, and All. By selecting the value directly in the Top Values property or by using the Top Values list box on the Query Design toolbar, you can restrict the records returned to a certain number.

In the example, you might want only the top 10 orders with the worst elapsed shipped times. To get the 10 worst, remove the previously entered sort parameters and then sort by the Elapsed Days column in descending order. Specify a Top Values property of **10**, which you will need to type into the Top Values combo box because it is not available in the drop-down list. Figure 42.9 shows the results in Datasheet view.

FIGURE 42.9

The results of the modified Top Values query

Company Name	Order ID	Order Date	Shipped Date	DAYS ELAPSE
Vins et alcools Chevalier	10248	04-Aug-94	16-Aug-94	12
Chop-suey Chinese	10254	11-Aug-94	23-Aug-94	12
Que Delícia	10261	19-Aug-94	30-Aug-94	11
Folk och få HB	10264	24-Aug-94	23-Sep-94	30
Blondel père et fils	10265	25-Aug-94	12-Sep-94	18
Split Rail Beer & Ale	10271	01-Sep-94	30-Sep-94	29
Berglunds snabbköp	10280	14-Sep-94	13-Oct-94	29
Reggiani Caseifici	10288	23-Sep-94	04-Oct-94	11
Tortuga Restaurante	10293	29-Sep-94	12-Oct-94	13
Suprêmes délices	10302	11-Oct-94	09-Nov-94	29
*	(AutoNumber)			

NOTE

Figure 42.9 shows 10 records since it is a Top Values query set to 10. If there is a tie for the lowest value, Access does not cut off any records because it has no way of determining which records take precedence over others. You may, therefore, receive more records back than the query specified.

Behind the Scenes with SQL View

Once you have finished designing a query, you might want to see what you were really creating: a SQL statement. You can view the SQL of a query by choosing View ➤ SQL View from the menu bar or by clicking on the drop-down arrow of the View button on the toolbar and choosing SQL View. Figure 42.10 shows the SQL view for the query we just created.

FIGURE 42.10

The query in SQL view

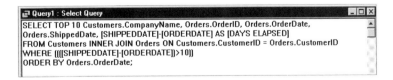

```
Query1 : Select Query
SELECT TOP 10 Customers.CompanyName, Orders.OrderID, Orders.OrderDate,
Orders.ShippedDate, [SHIPPEDDATE]-[ORDERDATE] AS [DAYS ELAPSED]
FROM Customers INNER JOIN Orders ON Customers.CustomerID = Orders.CustomerID
WHERE ((([SHIPPEDDATE]-[ORDERDATE])>10))
ORDER BY Orders.OrderDate;
```

TIP

You can switch from Design view to SQL view and back again, which is useful when you are learning SQL. Write the SQL statement first in SQL view and then switch to Design view to see if your statement gives the expected results

Updating and Navigating Query Datasheets

Query datasheets can be both updateable, allowing you to edit or add records, or restricted, preventing you from making any modifications. This is because some queries pull in enough information from individual tables to pinpoint the exact field or record that needs to be updated. Generally, if the datasheet of your query comes from only one table, it can be updated without a problem. Records can be added to the single table query as long as all required fields are included in the datasheet.

If you are working with multiple table queries, as will be the case most of the time, query datasheets can also be updated. If you want to add records using multiple table queries, you need to make sure that all of the required fields from each of the tables from which you pulled fields are included; otherwise, a complete record cannot be formed, and you will be unable to add to the datasheet.

Your query, whether it is based on a single or multiple tables, cannot be updated if it does any sort of totaling or grouping. For example, if you turn on the Totals row of the QBE grid, Access will group information instead of listing the detail. Hence there is no way for Access to know which field you want to update. The Crosstab query also cannot be updated. By definition it is a Totals query because it totals a field based on row and column values and therefore returns a *snapshot*, or a non-updateable query.

Chapter

43

Publishing Your Data with Reports

FEATURING

Chapter 43

Publishing Your Data with Reports

Since its beginning, Access has been superior to other database programs in its publishing capabilities. Using the Report Design Screen and its graphical controls, you can quickly become proficient at generating professional-looking reports.

When working with the Report Design Screen, don't limit your concept of reports to the bland, columnar reports of old. Not only can you spice up a columnar report with different fonts, but you can also create reports in the form of catalogs, invoices, labels, and much more.

Designing a Report

Clicking on the New button on the Reports tab of a Database window opens the New Reports dialog box, which gives you six options:

Design View   Allows you to build a report from scratch.

Report Wizard	Steps you through the creation of a report, asking which tables and fields you want to use. It also allows you to specify levels of grouping, such as grouping all orders by customers. This Wizard provides you with a number of layout options based on your grouping choices, asks whether you want to sort within groups, which type of style you want, and so on. The Report Wizard is now so user-friendly that the beginner need not create a query to include fields from multiple tables. If you do not specify a table or a query to use, the Report Wizard asks which tables and fields you want. It then creates a SQL statement for you to use as the record source for the report.
AutoReport Columnar	Generates a columnar report based on the table or query you choose in the New Report dialog box and a set of report defaults.
AutoReport Tabular	Generates a tabular report based on the table or query you choose in the New Report dialog box and a set of report defaults. To use either AutoReport, you must first specify a table or a query; however, after you do so, the rest of the report is generated using default settings. You don't have to answer a single question.
Chart Wizard	Assists in creating a report that requires a chart.
Label Wizard	Makes creating labels of any size based on a table or query a complete snap. Most of the time, you can select a size from the Avery Label collection. Because Avery is the most popular brand of computer-generated labels, most of its competitors put a reference to the corresponding Avery label number on their packages. If your label format is not available, you can easily specify a custom format.

Using the Wizards

The Wizards provide a fast and easy path to report creation. The two Wizards that you will probably use most often are the Report Wizard and the Label Wizard. All the Wizards are by nature easy to use and generally self-explanatory.

The Report Wizard

You can use the Report Wizard to create most of the reports you will ever need. In our example, we will create a report without using a single table or preexisting query. Creating a report from a preexisting table or query would eliminate several of these steps.

1. Open the Northwind database found in the Samples folder under \Program Files\Microsoft Office\Office.

2. Select the Reports tab and click on the New button to open the New Reports dialog box.

3. You do not need to specify an available query or table to use the Report Wizard as you do with other Wizards, so select the Report Wizard, leave the combo box empty, and click on OK.

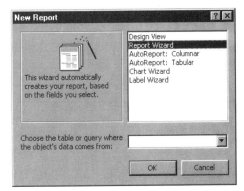

The first window of the Report Wizard (see Figure 43.1) has three main areas: the Tables/Queries combo box, the Available Fields list box, and the Selected Fields list box. In the Tables/Queries combo box, you select the table or query that contains the fields you want. The Available Fields list box changes to show the available fields for the table selected in the combo box. The Selected Fields list box will hold the fields that you want to include in your report.

One of the nice functions of this step is that from this one window you can select all the fields from all the tables you want to include. Once you have selected fields from one table or query, you can make another selection from the combo box and choose the fields from that table or query. You continue to select tables, queries, and fields until you have chosen all the fields to be included in your report.

> **NOTE**
> The Report Wizard uses the relationships created in the Relationships window to determine which tables to include in the query that it creates as the source for your report. To view the relationships for the Northwind database, select Tools ➢ Relationships from the menu bar. See Chapter 46 for more details on relationships.

PART
VI

Data Management
with Access

FIGURE 43.1

The first window of the Report Wizard lets you select fields from various tables and queries to include in your report.

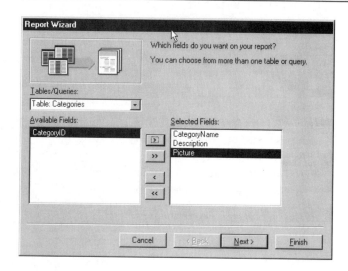

Once all the fields to be included are listed in the Selected Fields list box, you can continue.

4. From the Tables/Queries combo box, select the Categories table.

5. Send the CategoryName, Description, and Picture fields from the Available Fields list box to the Selected Fields list box by clicking on the > button or by double-clicking on the field names in the Available Fields list box.

6. From the Tables/Queries combo box, select the Products table.

7. Send the ProductName, UnitsInStock, and UnitsOnOrder fields from the Available Fields list box to the Selected Fields list box. Click on next.

8. Next, the Report Wizard asks how you want to view the information on your report. In our example, each product listed in the Products table is related to a category in the Category table by CategoryID; if we choose to view our report by categories, all the products for specific categories will be grouped together. Select By Categories as the viewing method and click on Next.

9. Next, the Report Wizard asks if you want to create any additional grouping. We have no need for another grouping in this example, so click on Next.

10. The Report Wizard now asks how you want to sort the detail section of your report. You can have as many as four levels of sorting, as shown in Figure 43.2. Select ProductName in the first sorting combo box. Notice the sort buttons on the right of these combo boxes. They are toggle buttons that switch between Sort Ascending and Sort Descending for the chosen field. Click on Next.

FIGURE 43.2

Sorting by ProductName

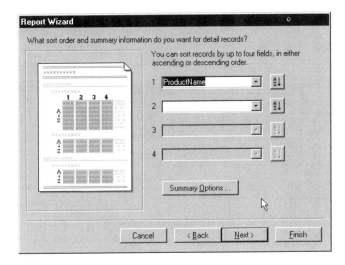

11. Next, the Report Wizard asks about the layout of your report (see Figure 43.3). Select Outline 1 in the Layout box and click on Next, leaving all other options at their defaults.

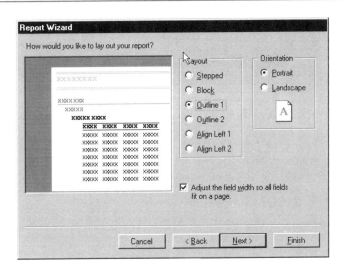

PART

VI

Data Management
with Access

12. To choose a style, click on each of the views to see how the different styles appear. We'll use Corporate in our example, so select it and click on the Next button.

13. The final step is to enter a title for the report. Replace the default title Categories with **Products by Category Report** and click on Finish, leaving all other options at their defaults. Your report should look similar to that in Figure 43.4.

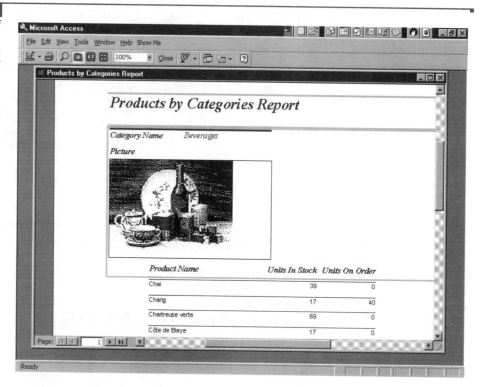

The Label Wizard

The Label Wizard takes you by the hand to help you create professional-looking labels. Like the other Wizards except for the Report Wizard, the Label Wizard requires you to have a table or a query ready to use.

1. Open the Northwind database.
2. Select the Reports tab and click on the New button.
3. In the New Report dialog box, select Label Wizard and choose the Customers table in the combo box. Click on OK.
4. The label size list box provides descriptions of labels for which it already has dimensions: the Avery number (found on almost every box of laser or inkjet

labels), the dimensions, and the number of labels across a page (see Figure 43.5). This list contains most of the labels that you should ever need. You can modify the list's Unit of Measure or Label Type by changing the appropriate option button below the list box. You can also click on the Customize button to define your own label if it is not listed. Select Avery number 5160, which is a sheet-fed label, and click on Next.

FIGURE 43.5

Selecting a label size

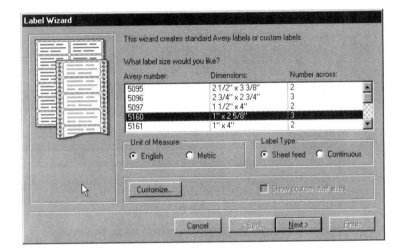

5. Next choose a text format for your labels. The options you choose will be applied to all text, fields, and data. The preview on the left of the dialog box will reflect any changes that you make. Remember, you are generally working with small labels, so don't make your font size too large. For this example, you can simply accept the defaults and click on Next.

   In the next stage, you design a template for your label using the fields from the table or the query that you selected earlier. If any extraneous punctuation marks or text need to appear on your labels, you can type them directly into the Prototype label.

6. From the Available Fields list, select CompanyName and then click on the > button or simply double-click on the field name. Press Enter to move to the next line in your Prototype label.

7. Select Address in the same way, and press Enter to move to the third line.

8. Select the City field as above, type a comma (,), and then press the spacebar once.

9. Select the Region field, press the spacebar twice, and select PostalCode.

10. When you're done, your screen should like that in Figure 43.6. Click on Next.

PART

VI

Data Management
with Access

FIGURE 43.6

*Designing a
prototype label*

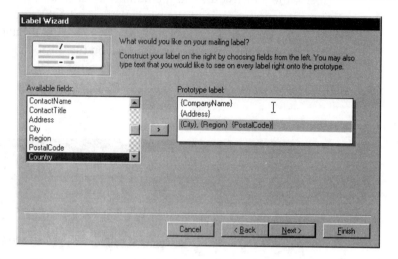

In the next step, the Label Wizard asks if you want to sort the information in any particular order. If you choose to sort by more than one field, the report is sorted in the order in which you selected the fields. Since we will use these labels for a mailing, let's sort by PostalCode and within each PostalCode by CompanyName.

11. Select PostalCode from the Available Fields list box and click on the > button to move it to the Sort By list box or double-click on the field name.

12. Select CompanyName in the same manner and click on Next.

13. Change the title/name of the report to **Customer Mailing Labels**. Click on Finish, leaving the other options at their defaults.

Figure 43.7 shows the resulting mailing label report in Print Preview mode. Notice that the information is in three columns, matching the Avery label sheet on which it will print.

Report Design Screen

As helpful as the Wizards are for creating reports, they could not possibly accommodate everyone's specific needs. These special needs can be met by modifying reports created with the Wizards or by creating reports from scratch. Both options are done in Design view. The Design view of a report is in five sections, similar to the Design view for forms. With reports, however, you can create new sections in which to group data to allow for subtotals or special formatting. The main tools for building the report in Design view are the same as those used in building forms: the field list, the Toolbox, and, as always, properties.

FIGURE 43.7

Figure 43.11: Print Preview of the Customer Mailing Labels report

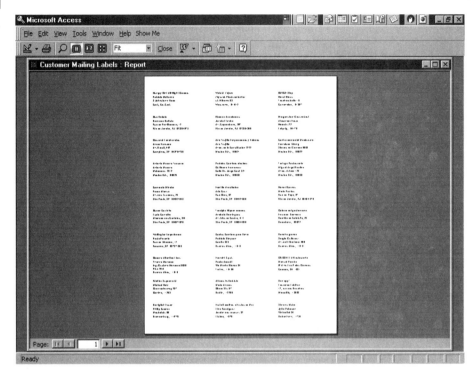

Sections

Each section begins with a gray section header that contains its name. The five primary sections in a report are:

Detail	A report always has a detail section in which you place the fields that repeat for every record.
Report Header and Report Footer	The items you place in the Report Header and Report Footer appear once and only once—the Report Header at the beginning of the report, and the Report Footer at the end of the report. You place controls that calculate grand totals in the Report Footer. When you create a new report in Design view, the Report Header and Footer are not visible by default. To make the Report Header and Footer visible, choose View ➤ Report Header/Footer from the menu bar while in Design view or right-click on the Report window's title bar and choose Report Header/Footer from the shortcut menu.

PART

VI

Data Management with Access

Page Header and Page Footer
The Page Header holds information that you want to appear at the top of every page in your report, and the Page Footer holds information that you want to appear at the bottom of every page. You can set the Page Header and Page Footer properties not to print on the first and last pages of the report.

Sorting and Grouping

If you elect to group the report by specific fields, you can add new sections to a report. You can also set the group to have a header and/or footer section of its own to hold section totals.

1. Open the Northwind database.
2. Select the Reports tab and click on New.
3. In the New Report dialog box, select AutoReport: Tabular and the Customers table. Click on OK. A new report based on the Customers table opens in Print Preview.
4. Click on the Close button on the Print Preview toolbar. The report is now in Design view, as illustrated in Figure 43.8.
5. From the menu bar, select View ➤ Sorting and Grouping to open the Sorting and Grouping dialog box.

FIGURE 43.8

Design view of our tabular report

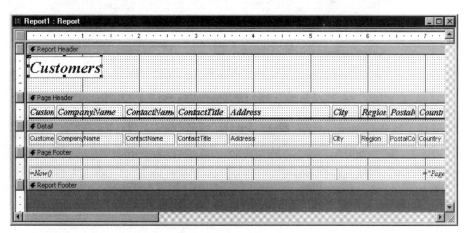

6. In the top pane of the Sorting and Grouping dialog box, click on the first row of the Field/Expression column.
7. Click on the drop-down arrow and select the Country field from the list. When you select a field, a bottom pane appears that lists the Grouping Properties for that field.

8. In the Group Header and Group Footer properties, change the setting to Yes by typing over what is there or by clicking on the down arrow button and selecting from the drop-down list.

9. Select the CompanyName field in the second row of the Field/Expression column in the top pane. Since we want to sort by CompanyName after Country, leave the Group Properties with their default settings. Your dialog box should look like that in Figure 43.9.

FIGURE 43.9

The Group Properties are shown for CompanyName.

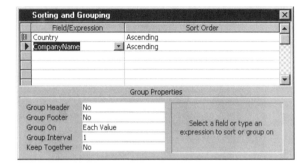

10. Close the Sorting and Grouping dialog box by clicking on the Close button or simply typing Alt+F4. Notice the new sections created in your report design.

11. From the menu bar, select View ➤ Field List.

12. Click and drag the Country field from the field list to the left of center area in the Country Header, as shown in Figure 43.10.

FIGURE 43.10

Dragging the Country field from the field list to the Country Header

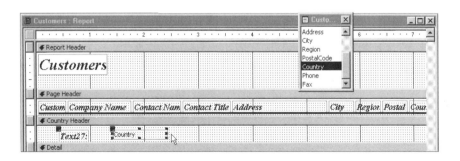

PART

VI

Data Management with Access

13. Dragging the field from the field list will also bring a label for the Country field. The name in the label is meaningless for our report, so point to the label, click on it, and press Delete.

14. From the menu bar, select View ➤ Print Preview or File ➤ Print Preview or click on the Print Preview toolbar button, or right-click on the title bar of the report and select Print Preview. Figure 43.11 shows the result of grouping by country.

The report is now grouped by country.

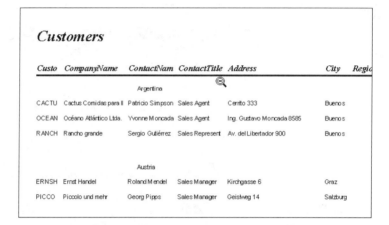

Field List

When working with a report that has a record source, you can open a Field List window to show a list of fields. Click and drag any of these fields onto the report. To view the field list, select View ➤ Field List from the menu bar or click on the Field List toolbar button.

If you cannot see a button that you know should be on a toolbar, check to make sure that you do not have two toolbars docked at the same level. If this happens, you may need to click and drag the toolbar so that it is either floating or docked at a different level.

Toolbox and Controls

The Toolbox is a special toolbar containing the main objects that you can place on a report. These objects are called *controls*. To place a control on a report, click once on the control in the Toolbox and then click on the section of the report in which you want the control. You can view the Toolbox (see Figure 43.12) by selecting View ➤ Toolbox from the menu bar or by clicking the Toolbox toolbar button. The Toolbox controls are described in Table 43.1.

> **NOTE**
> The last button on the Toolbox gives you access to ActiveX controls (previously know as OLE Controls), which are provided by Microsoft and third-party software vendors to extend the form and report capabilities of Access. These controls require more resources than the basic controls but can provide you with very rich functionality for your forms and reports. The provider of the controls should offer additional documentation and help to use them.

FIGURE 43.12

The Toolbox holds the primary control types that can be used on a report.

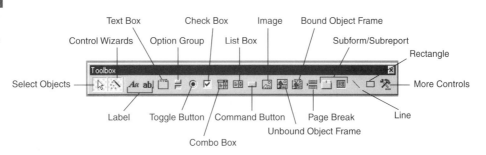

TABLE 43.1: TOOLBOX CONTROLS

Control	Description
Select Objects	This button, the first on the toolbox, is not a control. When it is pressed, your mouse can be used to manipulate the controls that are already on the report. After you place a control on the form, the Select Objects button is automatically selected.
Control Wizards	When pressed, the second button on the toolbox activates the Wizards for controls placed on a report that could benefit from assistance in filling out their properties.

Continued ▶

PART

VI

Data Management
with Access

TABLE 43.1: TOOLBOX CONTROLS (CONTINUED)	
Control	Description
Label	Used to place descriptive text on a report that does not need to be bound to any data.
Text Box	The most common control used to display data from underlying tables and queries. It can also show results of calculations.
Toggle, Option, Checkbox	While not as functional when used on a form, these controls can add a nice touch to reports that show Yes/No field values.
Option Group	Can be used to group Checkboxes, Option Buttons, or Toggle Buttons visually and functionally on a report.
Image	Used to place pictures that do not need to change or be edited onto forms and reports. This cannot be a bound control.
Unbound Object Frame	Used to place OLE objects *not* stored in your database on a form or report.
Bound Object Frame	Used to place OLE objects that are stored in your database on a form or report.
Page Break	Placed on a report to cause a page break at a specific point in the report. Commonly placed in a group footer to force a page break when a group value changes.
Subform/ Subreport	Commonly used to visually show one-to-many relationships between a table or query of the main report or form and the table or query of the subform or subreport.
Line	Allows the creation of indiscriminate lines on a report or form.
Rectangle	Used to easily create rectangles on a form or report.
More Controls	Provides a list of all installed ActiveX controls that can add to the functionality of Access.

Properties

Properties determine how an object looks and performs. To view the Properties window, select View ➤ Properties from the menu bar or click on the Properties button on the Report Design toolbar. There is only one Properties window. To view properties for different controls, select the control; the Properties window changes to show you the properties for the selected object or section. You can see the change in the title bar of the

Properties window. Remember that the report itself is an object, and you can select it by clicking on the intersection of the two rulers in the top left corner of the Report window.

NOTE

Chapter 40 provides more information about the Field list, the Toolbox, and the Properties window. Remember the design screens for forms and reports work the same except for some minor differences that depend on whether you are printing to paper or formatting for the screen.

Previewing Your Report

Instead of opening reports, you preview them. The sole function of reports is to generate output suitable for printing, so there is no "screen view" other than Print Preview, which shows you exactly how the report will print.

WARNING

When exiting from Print Preview, be sure to click on the Close button on the Print Preview toolbar or press Esc. Selecting File ➤ Close from the menu bar or the Close button on the report's title bar closes the report object completely, not just the preview.

MASTERING TROUBLESHOOTING

PART

VI

Data Management with Access

When Blank Pages Plague Your Printouts

When printing a report to a preview or to the printer, you may find that you are getting blank pages for no apparent reason. This occurs because of a conflict in your report width, your report margins, and the paper size of the report.

The first issue is your margins. When you create a new report, the default margin size is 1 inch on all sides, the default paper size is portrait $8\frac{1}{2}$ inches by 11 inches, and the

default report width is 5 inches. Most people soon find that they are losing $1\frac{1}{2}$ inches of space since a report 5 inches wide with 1 inch margins consumes only 7 inches, $1\frac{1}{2}$ inches less than the default paper size. The next logical step to maximize the available space is to increase the width of the report. When doing this, it is not uncommon to click and drag the width just a bit too far.

Continued

MASTERING TROUBLESHOOTING CONTINUED

When the addition of margins and report width are greater than the available paper width, blank pages are created. When Access attempts to convert your design into print, it cannot logically place more information than is available on the page, so it creates a second page to complete the printing of the information, even if it is only blank space because a report is too wide.

To quickly correct this problem, check your margins and paper size and be sure that your report width, when added to the margins, does not exceed the paper width. If it does, simply click and drag the width back to the appropriate setting.

One last note: You may remember placing your report at the right width, but the width increased anyway. If you attempted to place a control towards the right hand side and there was not enough space, Access automatically increased the width to accommodate the control.

Chapter

44

Making the Access
Parts a Whole

Making the Access Parts a Whole

Bringing all parts of your database into an efficient whole is the job of Access macros and the programming language of Access, Visual Basic for Applications (VBA). Unlike the other applications in Office, Access differentiates between macros and VBA. In Access you create macros using Macro Design view, choosing from 49 actions for each step of the macro. Macros provide most of the automation that users will ever need. Developers and more advanced users, however, can use VBA, which provides faster execution of automation procedures. You can use VBA to manipulate other applications, including Word and Excel, and to tap into the core functions of Windows.

Both macros and VBA code center around the event properties of objects. An event, as we've mentioned, is something that can happen to an object. For example, a Command button on a form has an Onclick event that is triggered when you click on it. The event properties hold the name of the macro or code that you want to execute when a particular event occurs. By using events to trigger when macros or code run, you can create a database that fits seamlessly into an application.

Macros

Access macros allow you to automate tasks step by step. In Macro Design view, you list actions in the order that you want them to be performed.

Designing Macros

The Macro Design view screen, like many of the design screens, is divided into a top and bottom pane. In the top pane, you list the actions to be performed. The bottom pane reveals the arguments for the current action, which is marked by the cursor in the top pane.

The top pane has four columns: Macro Name, Condition, Action, and Comment. The Macro Name and Condition columns are not visible by default, because they are not necessary for basic macros. To view all the columns (see Figure 44.1), do one of the following: (1) Select View ➤ Macro Names and View ➤ Conditions from the menu bar; (2) Click on their corresponding buttons on the Macro Design toolbar; or (3) Right-click on the title bar in Macro Design view and choose Macro Names and/or Conditions from the shortcut menu.

FIGURE 44.1

Macro Design view with all columns in the top pane in view

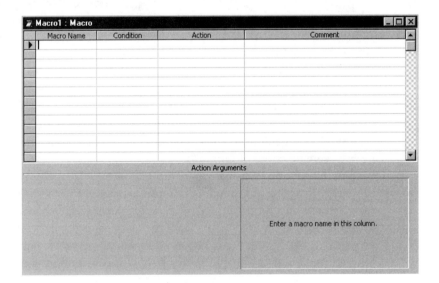

Actions

An action is a command that has a specific function. Forty-nine actions are available to use in each line of a macro. Some of the actions are:

OpenForm, OpenReport, OpenQuery, OpenTable	Each opens its respective object.
MsgBox	Displays a message dialog box.
ApplyFilter	Applies a filter to a form, report, or table.
OutputTo, TransferDatabase, TransferSpreadsheet	Exports, imports, or links Access objects to certain file formats.
RunCode, RunMacro	Run other automation routines from within a macro.
RunCommand	Executes built-in Access commands that can appear on menu bars, toolbars, and shortcut menus.
Quit	Exits Access from a database.

By listing the actions one after the other in successive rows, you can easily automate your database.

Arguments

Form Name	
View	Form
Filter Name	
Where Condition	
Data Mode	Edit
Window Mode	Normal

For every action you specify in the top pane of the Macro Design view screen, corresponding action arguments appear in the bottom pane. The arguments in the bottom pane change as you move from action to action in the top pane.

PART

VI

Data Management with Access

 TIP

After you select an action in the top pane, a short description of the action is displayed in the area to the right of the action arguments. If you need more information about the action, press F1. Help opens directly to the section on the selected action. You can get the same kind of help for the individual arguments for each action.

Conditions

The Condition column is not visible when you start a new macro because you don't need it for building macros. If all the actions in your macro execute every time the macro runs, the Condition column can remain hidden. This column provides a way to test the result of an expression that returns either True or False. If the expression returns True, the action executes; if it returns False, the action does not execute. Here are two ways to use Conditions:

- Check to see if a form is open before referring to a control on the form. An error would result if the form was closed.
- Check the current value of a control on a form before saving the record, to ensure data integrity.

Macro Names

You use the Macro Name column to group small macros into a logical whole. For example, you have a group of small macros that are used to respond to the On Click event of four buttons on a form. If you create an individual macro for each button, four macro icons are displayed in the Database window. In the Macro Name column, you specify the name of each macro within the current Macro Design view screen, the name of which will be the only one listed in the Database window. When the first action of a macro is listed in Macro Design view, a name is specified in the Macro Name column. This column remains empty until the next macro begins. Figure 44.2 shows the Macro Design view of four small macros, each having two actions. Each macro opens a different form and closes the form from which the macro was called—more than likely a Switchboard form of some sort that has multiple buttons to open other forms and run reports.

FIGURE 44.2

Four small macros are shown in the Macro Name column.

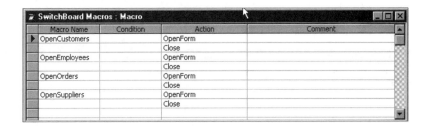

Creating a Macro

When creating a macro, you need to think in very linear terms. Access will process each of your actions in the order that you list them, stopping only to check if there is an expression in the condition column to the left.

The following steps will walk you through creating a small macro that will export a table from the Northwind database.

1. Open the Northwind database.
2. Click on the Macros tab and click on New.
3. In the first row of the Action column, click on the drop-down arrow and choose TransferSpreadsheet. The Argument list at the bottom of the design screen will activate with the arguments for the current action.
4. Change the Transfer Type argument to **Export**, Spreadsheet type to **Microsoft Excel 8**, Table Name to **Customers**, and File Name to **c:\customer.xls**. Leave the other arguments blank.
5. In the top pane, move to the second row and choose the MsgBox action.
6. In the bottom pane, type **Export Complete** in the Message argument box.
7. To test the macro, Select Run ➤ Run from the menu bar. Save the macro as **Export Customers**. After you save the macro, it will run, exporting the Customers table to an Excel spreadsheet and displaying a message box when it is complete.

Running Macros

Running a macro from the design screen is not very useful in the real world. You will find it more helpful if you run macros in the following places in your database:

The Macro Design View - You may want to test a macro as you build it to verify that it works. To run your macro from Macro Design view, you need to save it first or be prompted to do so by selecting Run ➤ Run from the menu bar or by clicking on the Run button on the Macro Design toolbar.

The Database Window - Although most macros are not meant to run from the Database window, they can if the need arises. Select the macro on the Macros page and click on the Run button.

In Response to Events - The purpose of most macros is to respond to the events of various objects: the click of a Command button, the opening of a form or a report, and before the update of a record in a form.

From Another Macro or from a Code Module - If one macro or module triggers the execution of another macro, you can use the appropriate macro action or VBA statement. To execute a macro from within another macro, put RunMacro in the macro action of a line in your macro and specify the macro in the arguments for the action. To execute a macro from within VBA code, use the RunMacro method of the DoCmd object, followed by the necessary arguments.

MASTERING THE OPPORTUNITIES

Maximizing the Potential of Macros

Many new users feel that anything to do with automating must be out of their league of abilities, and many seasoned programmers new to Access feel that since they can write code, Macros are a waste of their time. Both of these assumptions are false.

For new users, Macros provide an easy and painless path toward creating useful applications. The beginner can start small with easy macros that open one form and close another. The same new user, once more comfortable with macros, can continue to exploit their power without ever having to place code in the database.

The advanced programmer will find that even though code is needed for applications built for mass distribution, those same applications will need to contain at least two macros. The AutoExec macro will initiate any procedures at startup (without specifying a form in Tools ➤ Startup), and AutoKeys will provide universal shortcut keys throughout the application.

Visual Basic for Applications

Visual Basic for Applications is the programming language of the Microsoft Office programs. You move from VBA when macros no longer provide the functionality your database needs.

Functions and Procedures

When you write VBA code, you create either a sub procedure or a function procedure. The main difference between a function and a procedure is that the function returns a value and the procedure does not.

For example, if you simply want to write code that has Access perform a list of commands and finish, with no need for information to be returned, then you would want to write a sub procedure. A sub procedure is similar in function to a macro.

A function procedure should be created when you not only need Access to perform a list of steps, but you also want it to return a value. What you do with that value depends on the situation. You may need a function to perform a complicated mathematical routine and return an answer for use in other computations. Some functions are written to use the return value as a method of the code. The function calls it to determine if it successfully finished processing without an error. Functions of this type are generally set up to return True, if completed, or False, if an error occurred and all of the steps were not executed.

Procedures are stored in large code modules that can hold multiple procedures. Because of this, it is necessary to contain the code of each procedure and set it off from the other procedures. The container consists of beginning and ending lines that signify the start and end of each procedure. For a sub procedure the syntax is:

```
Sub NameofProcedure()
...
...
End Sub
```

The syntax for a function procedure is:

```
Function NameofProcedure()
...
...
End Function
```

The fact that a sub procedure does not return a value and a function does makes the way that you execute them different as well. When you want to call, or execute, a sub procedure, you simply list its name followed by any arguments that it may require; if there are multiple arguments, they should be separated by commas. An example of calling a sub procedure declared as:

```
Sub DisplayMessage(MSG as String, Title as String)
```

would be:

```
DisplayMessage "Hello There", "Greeting"
```

Give special attention to the fact that there are no parentheses around the argument and you do not need to assign the procedure to a variable since it is not returning a value.

There are two basic ways to call a function procedure. The first method is similar to calling a procedure. The second way is by including it in an expression or calculation and treating it like a built-in Access function. To call a function declared as:

```
Function SquareIt (X as integer)
```

you could assign the value being returned by typing something like:

```
Answer=SquareIt(6)
```

or you could use the function in an equation by typing:

```
Result = (5+SquareIt(6))/2
```

PART

VI

Data Management
with Access

The important thing to remember is that a sub procedure does not return a value and a function procedure does. You can simply call a sub procedure, but you must do something with the value that a function procedure returns, like assign it to a variable.

MASTERING TROUBLESHOOTING

Expected: = and Expected: End of Statement Errors

If you receive compile errors when you attempt to execute procedures, you may get an Expected: = error or an Expected: End of Statement error. These errors are not very clear in explaining the real problem. Generally when you receive one of these errors it means that you attempted to execute a sub or function procedure incorrectly.

If you get the Expected: = error, which is the most common among the two, you may have used parentheses around the arguments of a sub procedure. When calling a sub procedure, the arguments are simply listed after the procedure name without parentheses.

If you get the Expected: End of Statement error, you probably forgot to place parentheses around the arguments of a function while trying to assign its return value to a variable or using it in an expression.

Modules

A module is a generic term for a container object that holds the VBA code written for your Access database. *Global modules* are the modules listed in your Database window. The procedures and functions in these modules are available from anywhere in your application. Code written for use with specific forms or reports is stored in special *form* and *report modules* that are saved with the form or report. This code is available only within the form or report in which it is stored and while the form or report is open.

To create this CBF (Code Behind Form), you program to existing event procedures of various objects on a form or report. To get to the existing procedures, you find the event to which you want to program on the object's Properties sheet, click in the Event text box, and then click on the Builder button that appears. Selecting Code Builder in the Choose Builder dialog box opens the form or report module and places you in the event procedure, where you can enter the code that you want to execute when the event is triggered.

Code Sampling

The following example procedure lets you work in a Code window. The code that we create will be stored in a global module that is available anywhere in your application.

1. Open the Northwind database.
2. Click on the Modules tab and click on New.
3. In the new module, type **(Sub SayHello)** and press Enter. Figure 44.3 shows the procedure header and footer in which you type the code.

The procedure header and footer for SayHello

4. Type **Dim A as String** and press Enter.
5. Type **A=InputBox("What is your name?")** and press Enter.
6. Type **MsgBox "Hello " & A & "! Here is the Employees Form."** (be sure to put a space between Hello and the closing quotation mark) and press Enter.
7. Type **DoCmd.OpenForm "Employees"** and press Enter. Your Code window should look like that in Figure 44.4.

PART

VI

The completed SayHello procedure

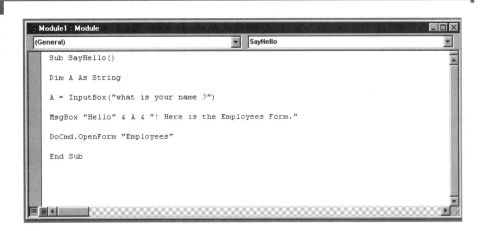

Data Management with Access

8. To test the procedure, we can use the Debug window. Select View ➤ Debug Window or press Ctrl+G.

9. In the Debug window, type **SayHello** and press Enter. Your procedure should run, ask your name, say hello to you, and open the Employees form.

10. When you are finished, select File ➤ Close from the menu bar.

Since we are running this procedure from the Debug window, it will cover up the Employees form when it is opened. The Debug window is used primarily for debugging programs and not for real-life execution of code.

To run this procedure from a Command button on a form, you use the Code Builder to write code for the event, using the Builder button to create an event procedure in which you could specify SayHello as the only line of code.

This sampling of VBA code is not meant to be anything more than a demonstration. To learn more about VBA and how you can use it in Access, see *The Access Macro and VBA Handbook* by Susann Novalis, Sybex, 1996.

Help with Writing Code

The new VBA Auto Edit features make it easy for beginners to write VBA code. These features provide real-time prompting of arguments for statements, properties and methods for objects, and current values for variables that you select.

The easiest way to learn these features is to write a short procedure that adds numbers and execute it using the Debug window.

1. Open the Northwind database.

2. Click on the Modules tab and click on New.

3. Type **sub addem(x as Integer, y as Integer)** in the new module and press Enter. The Addem procedure will be created. Notice how the Auto Edit feature provides the possible data types a variable can be (see Figure 44.5).

FIGURE 44.5

Auto Edit Features can provide possible data types for variables.

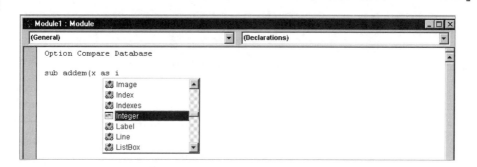

4. Next, type **Msgbox "The answer is " & x+y.** Access provides the syntax of the Msgbox statement (shown in Figure 44.6).

FIGURE 44.6

*The syntax for
VBA statements
is provided as
you type.*

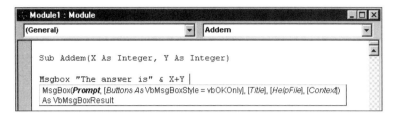

5. Press Ctrl+G to bring up the Debug window. In the bottom pane, try to run the procedure you just created by typing **addem 5,5**. Notice how Access now uses Auto Edit to provide the arguments needed to execute your procedure (see Figure 44.7).

FIGURE 44.7

*Auto Edit will
also provide
assistance with
the procedures
that you write.*

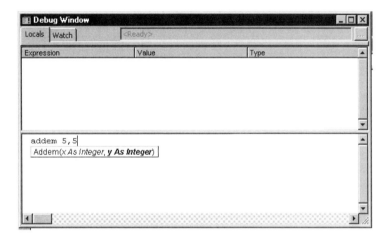

As you can see, Auto Edit will not write the code for you, but it definitely reduces the number of times you will need to jump back and forth to online help for assistance.

NOTE

If you would like to turn the Auto Edit features off, Select Tools ➤ Options from the menu bar and deselect the Auto features on the Options tab.

PART

VI

Data Management
with Access

Chapter

45

Connecting Access to
the Outside World

Connecting Access to the Outside World

I t would be wonderful if all data was in the same format; the truth is, it isn't. Data stored in older programs, data we receive from other users' database programs, and data to which we connect on larger mainframe and SQL platforms are all in different formats. Access can accept and communicate with external data from many different sources in two ways: by importing it and by linking to it.

Importing Data

When importing data, Access reads a file in another format and saves a copy of it as a table in your database. When you import a table, there is no connection between the original data and the new table in Access.

Many people import data when they know that they'll never again need the data in its original format. A mailing list is an example. Mainframe data is often imported because it is not accessible from the machine that has the Access database. When data is being imported from a mainframe or a large database system, the importation is generally automated with macros because the tables containing the mainframe data, such as addresses on a macro list, may need to be updated frequently.

To import data, follow these steps:

1. While you have a database open (whether empty or containing tables), select File ➤ Get External Data ➤ Import from the menu bar.

2. In the Import dialog box, select the type of file that you want to import from the Files of Type combo box in the bottom left corner (see Figure 45.1).

FIGURE 45.1

Select the file type and folder of the data to be imported in the Import dialog box.

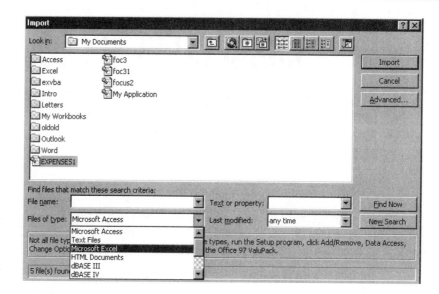

3. Select the folder that contains the file you want to import.

4. Click on the Import button.

5. If successful, you will receive an appropriate message (see Figure 45.2), Click on OK. The imported data is listed as a table.

FIGURE 45.2

Data has been successfully imported to a new table in your Access database.

Depending on the file type that you are importing, other steps may be involved. When importing a spreadsheet program, for example, Access will ask if you want an entire worksheet or only a specified range (see Figure 45.3). If you are importing delimited or fixed-width files, Access may require additional information (see Figure 45.4).

The Import Spreadsheet Wizard dialog box for spreadsheet files containing multiple worksheets

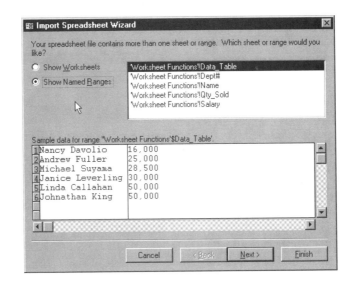

The Import Text Wizard dialog box for delimited and fixed-width files

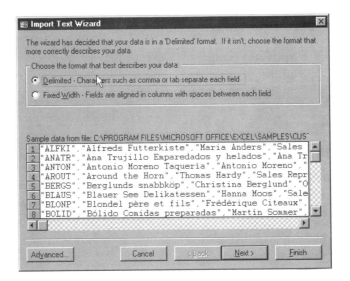

PART

VI

Data Management
with Access

You can also import objects other than tables from one Access database into your current database. When importing from Access, the Import Objects window shown in Figure 45.5 opens to allow you to select the object.

FIGURE 45.5

Use the Import Objects window to import objects from one Access database to another.

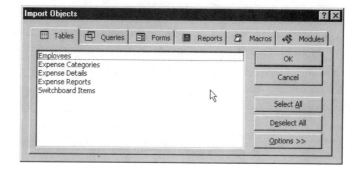

Import Errors

If Access encounters errors while importing tables, especially when appending data to an existing table, it will display an error message and create an Import Errors table that tracks the records not imported and the error that caused their exclusion. The table includes the field names and row numbers of the data that caused the errors.

If Access reports errors, open the Import Errors table and try to determine the reason for the errors. The following are some possible reasons:

Field Truncation	An imported field value is too large for the specified field width.
Type Conversion Failure	An attempt was made to import the wrong data type for a field.
Key Violation	A record's primary key value duplicates a record that already exists.
Validation Rule Failure	The value of a field in a record would break rules set using the Validation Rule property for this field or for the table.
Null in Required Field	A null value appears in a field where null values aren't permitted because the Required property for the field is set to Yes.
Unparsable Record	Access cannot understand the value of a field.

Linking Tables

When you are working with external data that needs to remain in its original format (perhaps the original application still needs to use the data), linking to the external data is the way that you want to go.

Linking to a table, previously known as attaching, allows Access to perform as a front end to the data, writing and reading it in the original format and application. When linked to the external data, Access works with the original data. If Access alters that data, the original application sees the changes; if the original application changes the data, then Access can see the changes.

To link to a table outside your Access application:

1. From the menu bar, select File ➤ Get External Data ➤ Link Tables.
2. In the Link dialog box (shown in Figure 45.6), specify the file type that you want to link in the Files of Type combo box and find the file using the dialog box options. To select the file, click on the filename once and then click on the Link button.

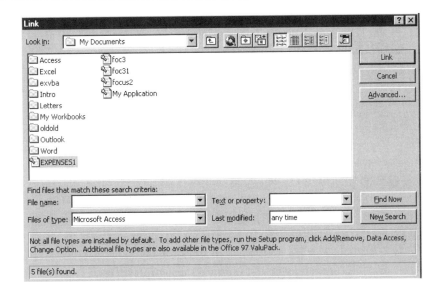

FIGURE 45.6

The Link dialog box

3. If you are linking to a spreadsheet or to text files, Access presents you with a Linking Wizard. If you are linking to a dBase or a Paradox file, Access may ask if there are index files that it will need to keep updated.

4. When you are finished, Access confirms a successful link with a message box.

5. Linked files appear on the Tables page of your Database window. The little black arrows to the left of the filename signify that the file is linked, and the little icon indicates the file type. Figure 45.7 shows a Database window with three linked tables.

FIGURE 45.7

The Database window with three linked tables

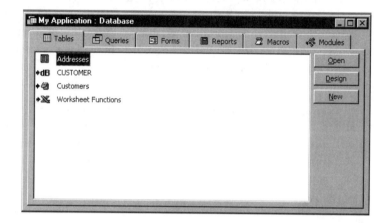

ODBC

To link to foreign data sources, Access takes advantage of Open Database Connectivity (ODBC). ODBC is a data access standard that acts as an interpreter from the foreign data source to Access or to any other database that supports ODBC. Every database format needs its own ODBC driver—the program that you install so that programs supporting ODBC can read and write in the driver's format. To install an ODBC driver, select Start ➤ Settings ➤ Control Panel. The Control Panel window contains a 32bit ODBC icon on which you double-click to access the install procedure. When linking to a database format supported by ODBC, select ODBC Databases as the file type.

Exporting Data

On occasion you will want to transfer information to someone who does not have Access. To export a table or query to another file type, select File ➤ Save As/Export from the menu bar. Select the To an External File or Database button and click on OK. In the Save In dialog box, you specify the folder in which you want to store the exported file, the filename, and the file type. After you specify these options, click on the Export button to create the file.

Finding the Right File Format

Sometimes when exporting information from Access, you may need to export to a file format that doesn't have a corresponding file type in the Save In dialog box.

All is not lost. First find out which file types the receiving application can import. Even most of the older programs still hanging around can import at least one or two file types other than their own.

Next decide which of these types you will use to save your data. There are three standard file formats that work best when trying to transfer data between applications that don't talk directly to each other. While none of these maintain complicated property information like Validation Rules, the data is assured to come across whole and unharmed because these formats are so popular and easy to create.

The first and most basic type is text-delimited format. The fields in this format are usually separated by commas, the records by carriage returns and linefeeds, and strings are wrapped in quotes. Even a common text editor can open and modify this format.

The second type is DBF, or dBASE III, format. dBASE was among the first and certainly the most popular databases available when personal computers were first being used. Because of its popularity and the need for vendors to support the format, exporting and importing to and from dBASE has long been a perfected art.

Finally, the last tried-and-true format for exporting is the Lotus .WK3 file format. If you plan on exporting to a spreadsheet other than Excel, this format is the way to go. People have used this format for many years to get information into new spreadsheets (later versions of Lotus 1-2-3, for example) because the file format information for the newer file versions were too complicated and not well supported. Every spreadsheet, however, can import Lotus 1-2-3 .WK3 files, essentially for the same reasons they can import dBASE III.

So don't let the lack of supported export formats thwart your conversion duties. Discover what format both Access and the destination application can support and use that as the middle man for your conversion.

PART

VI

Data Management
with Access

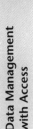

Chapter

46

Access As a Relational Database

Access As a Relational Database

Access is a *relational* database. A relational database consists of multiple tables or subjects of data that are joined by common fields or characteristics. Using multiple tables instead of a single table (a flat file database) improves speed and makes storage more efficient.

As an example, let's compare how a flat file database (Excel) and a relational database would track customers and orders. Excel can track customer information without difficulty. But you will run into problems if you try to use Excel to also track customer orders. Every time that you enter an order for a customer, you must enter not only the order information but also the customer information. You end up with a table or a flat file that stores customer information every time it stores order information. On the other hand, a relational database creates a table for every subject. For example, the database creates a Customers table, and each customer has one record of information in that table. Another table holds information pertaining to the order subject, and every order has one row in that table storing information about it. A relational database uses relationships to associate the orders in one table with the customers in the other table.

Relationships provide a logical link from one table to another. In the above example, a relationship exists between the Customers table and the Orders table. The relationship connects the primary key, which is a field that uniquely identifies one customer in the Customers table, to a field in the Orders table that stores the primary key of the customer who placed the order. Once this relationship is defined, Access can determine the address of a customer who places an order even though that information is not stored in the Orders table. Access simply follows the relationship from the value of the customer identifier in the Orders table back to the record with that value in the primary key field of the Customers table, which holds the basic information for each customer.

Types of Relationships

Three types of relationships can exist in database programs: one-to-many, one-to-one, and many-to-many. To take full advantage of the relational nature of Access, you must clearly understand these basic relationship types.

One-to-Many

Perhaps the most commonly used relationship, one-to-many allows a main subject in one table (Customers) and multiple instances of related records in another table (Orders). Because one customer can have many orders, one record in Table A can correspond to many records in Table B. Table A has a primary key field that is indexed and that allows no duplicate values; the primary key is the unique identifier for the records in that table. Table B can have multiple records that relate to a single record in Table A and an index on a field that references the primary key in Table A. Table B is indexed to allow for duplicates.

One-to-One

In a one-to-one relationship, one record in Table A corresponds to one record in Table B. You use a one-to-one relationship when some fields in your records are not used by a sizable percentage of the records. For example, an Employees table tracks employee information, including benefits. If 40 percent of the employees work part time and are not eligible for benefits, 40 percent of the records in the table have blank fields.

To relieve this inefficiency, you can create a second table and call it Benefits. The primary key field for the Benefits table is exactly like the one in the Employees table. The only difference occurs when the primary key data type in the main table (Employees) is AutoNumber; in that case, the data type of the related table (Benefits) is a Long Integer. The data type cannot be AutoNumber because you will need to enter values that match the primary key of the other table, and AutoNumber is self-numbering.

In a one-to-one relationship, both sides of the relationship must have a unique field that identifies the records in the respective tables, and the second table can be considered an extension of the first table. Each record in the first table can have no more than one record in the related table. The related table, however, is not required to have any records that relate to the main table. For example, the 40 percent of employees who work part time do not have records in the Benefits table.

Many-to-Many

In a many-to-many relationship, several records in Table A would correspond to several in Table B. This type of relationship cannot directly exist in Access, but you can form individual one-to-many relationships that give the effect of a many-to-many relationship.

For example, the Orders table and the Products table have a many-to-many relationship. Many orders can include many products. The solution is to create an intermediary table that has one-to-many relationships with each of the two tables. The relationship of the Orders table to a new table, Order Details, would be one-to-many (one order has many products); the relationship of the Products table to the Order Details table would be one-to-many, (one product is ordered many times). The two direct one-to-many relationships have created an indirect many-to-many relationship.

Creating Relationships in Access

You create relationships using the Relationship window. In this window, you can add or delete tables and click and drag from one table to another to set relationships.

To open the Relationship window, select Tools ➤ Relationships from the menu bar or click on the Relationships toolbar button. Figure 46.1 shows the Relationships window of the Northwind database.

All relationships in the Northwind database are one-to-many. The symbols on either side of the relationship indicate its type. The *1* represents the "one" part of a relationship, and the infinity symbol (∞) represents the "many" part. If a relationship has a *1* on both sides, it is a one-to-one relationship. If you do not see these symbols, then the line between the tables is a simple join which is used to match up records in queries but not enforce any data entry rules.

To delete a relationship, click on the middle of the line joining the two tables and press Delete. Deleting a table (by clicking on the title bar and pressing Delete) simply removes the table from the layout screen and does not remove the relationship.

PART

VI

Data Management
with Access

FIGURE 46.1
The Relationships window of the Northwind database shows several one-to-many relationships.

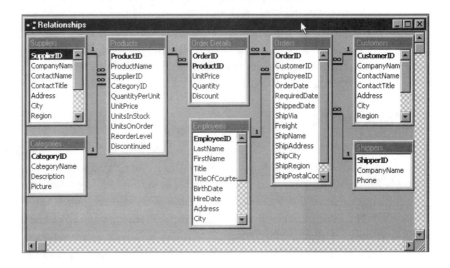

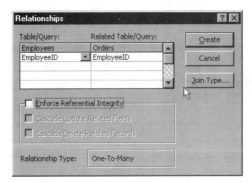

When you click and drag from one table to another in the Relationships window, the Relationships dialog box opens. In the Relationships dialog box, indicate whether you want to enforce referential integrity, turn on cascading updates and deletes, specify the type of join you want for your relationship, and click on the Create button to create your relationship type, which Access automatically determines.

How Access Determines Relationship Types

Access determines the type of relationship you will be creating by following some rules of thumb:

- If only one of the related fields is a primary key or has a unique index, Access creates a one-to-many relationship.
- If both of the related fields are primary keys or have unique indexes, Access creates a one-to-one relationship.
- If neither field is a primary key or has a unique index, Access creates an undefined relationship.

Referential Integrity

When you select Enforce Referential Integrity, you are instructing Access to watch over your tower of data. When referential integrity is enforced, the relationships created will insure the integrity of your data.

You cannot enter data, using any method, into a table on the many side of a one-to-many relationship if the value in the foreign key relating to the table does not have a corresponding value in the table on the one side. You cannot, for example, add orders for a customer that does not exist.

You cannot delete records in a table on the one side of a one-to-many relationship if records on the many side refer to that record. Doing so would create the orphan record syndrome—child records without a parent; orders without a customer. Unless the Cascade Delete option is set, you would have to delete the many records before you would be allowed to delete a record on the one side.

Cascade Update

Cascade Update is an option of referential integrity. If Cascade Update is engaged for a relationship, changing the primary key value of a record on the one side of a one-to-many relationship causes Access to cascade the change in number to the child, or to the many records. For example, if a Customer with the primary key of ABC123 must be changed to 789XYZ, all orders for that customer must reflect the change. In most situations, this is a not an option but a necessity.

Cascade Delete

Don't be as quick to use the Cascade Delete option as you would be to use Cascade Update. Cascade Delete will eliminate all records on the many side of a relationship if you delete the record in the table on the one side. Although this takes care of having to delete many children records before deleting the one parent record, there are consequences. Be sure that the information stored in the tables that would be erased with Cascade Delete is not needed elsewhere in the database, even if it is not necessary for the section that you are deleting. For example, an accounting application uses the data in the Orders table for its calculations; past data may be needed even if a customer ceases to buy in the present.

Joins

To open the Join Properties dialog box, click on the Join Type button in the Relationships dialog box. You can choose from three types of joins: the inner join, the left outer join, and the right outer join. The join type of a relationship determines which

PART

VI

Data Management
with Access

records from the tables involved in the relationship will be included in the recordsets of the queries that use the tables.

Inner Join—This is the default. When two tables are connected with an inner join, only those records that have equal values in the joined fields appear in the results of a query. For example, if you create a query based on a Customers table and an Orders table that are related on the Customer ID field, the only customers that will be included are those that have orders in the Orders table.

Left Outer Join—In this join, all records in a table on the one side of a relationship are listed at least once, and only those records that have a value in their foreign key that equals the joined primary key of a record in the table on the one side are included in a query. For example, if you have a one-to-many relationship between the Customers table and the Orders tables, every customer is listed each time they have an order in the Orders table. Those who do not have an order record in the Orders table are listed once. Only those orders in the Orders table that match an existing customer are included in a query. If a customer does not have a corresponding record in the Orders table, any fields included in a query from the Orders table will be blank.

Right Outer Join—All records in a table on the many side of a relationship are listed, and only those records that have a value in their primary key that equals the joined foreign key of a record in the table on the many side will be included in a query. For example, if you have a one-to-many relationship between the Customers table and the Orders table, every order is listed once, including those that do not have a customer record in the Customers table. Only those customers in the Customers table that have an order record(s) in the Orders table will be included in a query. This join type is popular for finding orphan records—those records in tables on the many side of relationships that do not have a corresponding record in the table to which they are related.

The toughest part of creating a database application is the design process—deciding which tables are needed and determining the relationships. Some people devote their lives to studying how to make databases more efficient and how to better the design standards. If you are serious about developing applications with Access, be sure to refer to books devoted solely to Access that have a substantial section on table design.

Chapter

47

Office Connections—
Integrating Access with
Other Office Products

Office Connections— Integrating Access with Other Office Products

A ccess is the real powerhouse member of Office. If you use all the programs, it's likely that Access is the center of your Office world. Access makes an excellent hub to the spokes of the other applications.

You can merge letters created in Word with current mailing lists stored in Access. You can include and interpret Access data in an Excel workbook or on a form in your database. PowerPoint, an unlikely compatriot, can use objects like the Data Map to query the Access data and represent it graphically for presentations. Not only can Access provide data to the other applications, but you can use Access forms in Excel.

This chapter will guide you through Access' Office connections by looking at what the folks at Northwind Traders Company do with the data stored in the Northwind database, located in the Samples folder under \Microsoft Office\Office.

Access and Word

Northwind Traders is planning a monthly mailing to customers who placed orders that month, thanking them for their continued business. First, they will create a totals query that groups sales of the past 30 days by customer, and then they will create a merge letter in Word that they can print every month.

Creating the Query

The first step is to create a query that asks the data, "Which customers have ordered in the past 30 days, and how much did they spend on all orders?" To create the query, take the following steps:

1. Open the Northwind database. Click on OK in the Welcome window that appears.
2. Select the Queries tab and click on New.
3. Select the Design View option and click on OK.
4. In the Show Table dialog box, select Customers and click on Add.
5. Select Orders and click on Add, and then select Order Details and click on Add.
6. Click on the Close button. Your Query Design Screen should look like Figure 47.1.

TIP

You can select all the tables that you want to add at one time. To do so, select the first table with your mouse. Hold down Ctrl and continue clicking on the other tables you want to add. When all the tables are selected, click on Add.

FIGURE 47.1

The Query Design Screen with the Customers, Orders, and Order Details tables

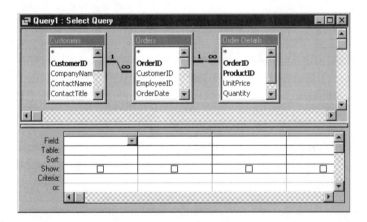

7. Point to the title bar of the Customers table field list and double-click to select all the fields except the asterisk.

8. Click and drag the selection from the field list to the QBE grid in the lower pane. Your QBE grid should now have in it all the fields from the Customers table.

9. From the Orders table field list, click and drag the OrderDate field on top of the Customer ID field in the QBE grid. The Customer ID and other fields will shift to the right.

10. Click anywhere on the OrderDate column of the QBE grid and select Insert ➤ Columns from the menu bar. Your grid should look like Figure 47.2.

FIGURE 47.2

The QBE grid after adding the OrderDate field and inserting a blank column

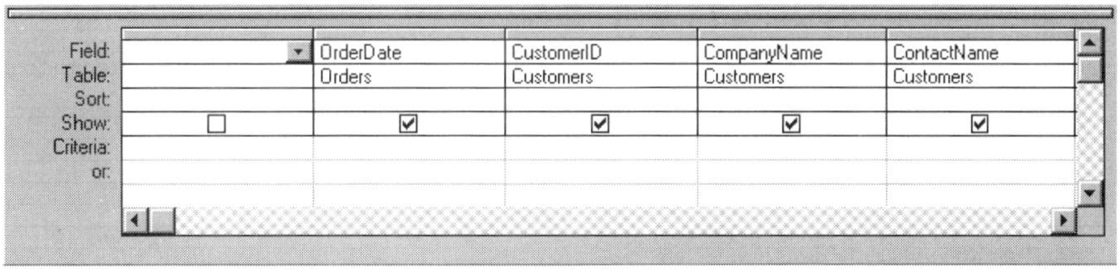

We need a column in our query for the total amount spent on orders for the month. To do this, create a calculated field:

11. Your insertion point should still be in the Field row of the blank column. If not, click on there now.

12. In the cell, type **Total:[unitprice]*[quantity]**. The result will be the value of the current quantity from the Order Details table multiplied by the value of the current records' unit price, also from the Order Details table.

13. Because we want one line per customer with a grand total in the Total row, select View ➤ Totals from the menu bar or click on the Totals button on the Query Design toolbar to create a totals or grouping query. A Total row appears in the QBE grid with Group By in each column.

14. Change the value of the Total row under the first Total column to Sum and the value under the OrderDate column to Where. Your grid should now look like Figure 47.3.

FIGURE 47.3

The Totals query with Sum in the Total column and Where in the OrderDate column

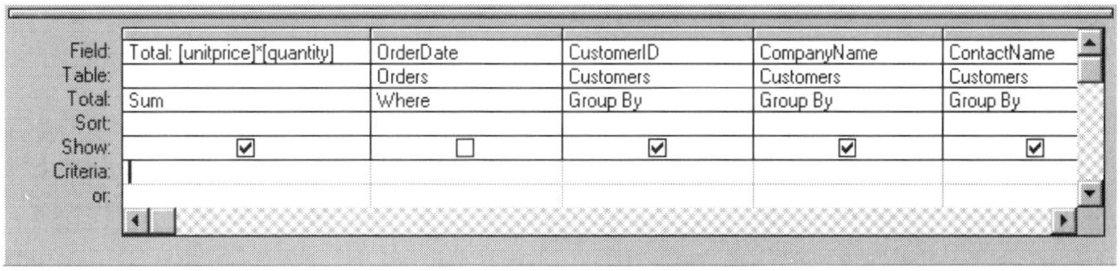

PART

VI

Data Management with Access

15. We want to total records only for those orders placed during the past 30 days. Normally, you would place >Date()-30 in the Criteria row under OrderDate. This specifies orders with order dates that are greater than 30 days prior to the current date on which the query is run. Because we are using data with order dates that may not fall within the past 30 days, place **>11/30/94-30** in the Criteria row under OrderDate.

16. From the menu bar, select File ➢ Close or press Ctrl+W and name the query **Monthly Customer Sales Merge**.

We now need to link Word and Access so that Word can merge letters using the Access data. Thankfully, Access and Word Wizards make this a breeze.

Creating the Merge Document

To perform a merge with Word, you need not exit Access and open Word. Access and the Word Mail Merge Wizard will walk you through all the steps.

1. Be sure the cursor is on the Queries tab of the Database window.

2. Select the query that you want to use for a merge to a Word document, in this case Monthly Customer Sales Merge, and select Tools ➢ OfficeLinks ➢ Merge It with MS Word from the menu bar or click on the OfficeLinks button on the toolbar. The Microsoft Word Mail Merge Wizard opens, as shown in Figure 47.4.

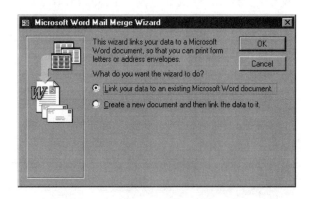

3. You can merge the query with an existing document or with a new document. Select *Create a new document and then link the data to it* and then click on OK.

4. After a bit of hard drive churning, Word opens a new document that has a data source of your query (see Figure 47.5).

The Word win-
dow as it
appears when
you link a merge
document with
an Access query

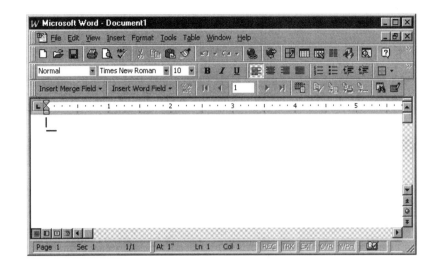

5. Your insertion point should be at the top of the new document. Press Enter five times.

6. From the Word menu bar, select Insert ➢ Date and Time. From the Available Formats list, select the date format you want in your letter. Be sure that the Update Automatically checkbox is checked and then click on OK.

7. Press Enter three times.

8. Click on the Insert Merge Field button on the Mail Merge toolbar and choose CompanyName from the list. Press Enter. In the same way, add ContactName and Address, pressing Enter after each.

9. Now, add the City field, type a comma and a space, add the Region field, type two spaces, and add the PostalCode field. When finished, press Enter twice. Your Word document should look similar to Figure 47.6.

10. Because there is no field for the first or last name of the contact or even an honorific to address the person properly (for example, Mr., Ms., or Mrs.), type **Dear Customer:**. Press Enter twice.

11. Type the following:

> **Greetings from Northwind Traders! Everyone here would like to express their thanks for your business.**
>
> **This is just your monthly reminder of our appreciation for your business. This month you have spent**

FIGURE 47.6

Merge fields inserted for the opening of our letter

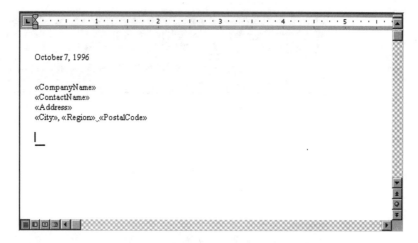

12. After the word *spent*, press the spacebar and insert the Total field using the Insert Merge Field button.

13. Now press the spacebar again and finish the sentence with:

worth of our products.

14. Start a new paragraph and type:

As always, if there is ever anything that we can do to make your experience with our company any better, please do not hesitate to call and speak with anyone here.

Thank You,

Northwind Traders

The final merge document should look like Figure 47.7.

The final stage is to test the merge document by performing a merge to a new document.

1. From the menu bar, select Tools ➤ Mail Merge.

2. In the Mail Merge Helper dialog box click on the Merge button.

3. The Merge dialog box, shown in Figure 47.8, is set to merge with a new document. If you are certain that the merge is correct, you can merge with a printer instead of a new document. Click on Merge.

FIGURE 47.7

*The merge doc-
ument ready to
be merged*

October 7, 1996

«CompanyName»
«ContactName»
«Address»
«City», «Region» «PostalCode»

Dear Customer:

Greetings from Northwind Traders! Everyone here would like to express their thanks for
your business.

This is just your monthly reminder of our appreciation for your business. This month you
have spent «Total» worth of our products.

As always, if there is ever anything that we can do to make your experience with our
company any better, please do not hesitate to call and speak with anyone here.

Thank You,

Northwind Traders

FIGURE 47.8

*The Merge
dialog box can
be set to merge
with a docu-
ment or a
printer.*

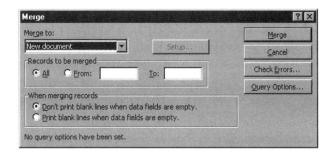

4. All customers in the Access query merge with your form letter into a single document called Form Letters1, separated by section breaks so that every merged letter
starts on a new page.

5. You can now print the form letters from the document or close the merged document and rerun the merge, directing the output to the printer (once you are certain that everything is printing correctly). Figure 47.9 shows a letter from Form
Letters1 with customer information from the Access query.

PART

VI

Data Management
with Access

October 8, 1996

Comércio Mineiro
Pedro Afonso
Av. dos Lusíadas, 23
São Paulo, SP 05432-043

Dear Customer:

Greetings from Northwind Traders! Everyone here would like to express their thanks for your business.

This is just your monthly reminder of our appreciation for your business. This month you have spent $1,641.75 worth of our products.

As always, if there is ever anything that we can do to make your experience with our

No need to store customer information in a Word table *and* in Access, no need to manually insert monthly numbers into merge fields—the Office is truly coming together. Once you have written the letter, you can save it and merge it every month. Because the document is linked to your query, the data will be as up to date as your Access database every time you merge the letter.

NOTE

When saving documents in Word that you want to merge, never save the resulting Form Letters# document. Save the original document that contains the field codes. Saving Form Letters# is the same as saving the result of the merge and will do you no good when you want letters with new data.

Access and Excel

As efficient and powerful as Access is, if you want to summarize your data in a variety of ways, you will need to rely on the PivotTable, which is available through Excel. In Access, the Form Wizard helps you generate a form on which you can view a PivotTable.

Creating the Query

The first step is to create a query whose results you want to analyze with the PivotTable:

1. In the Northwind database, select the Queries tab and click on New.

2. In the New Query dialog box, select Design View and click on OK.

3. In the Show Table dialog box, add the Categories, Products, Order Details, and Orders tables to the query and click on Close.

4. Add the CategoryName Field from the Category table to the first column of the QBE grid.

5. Next add the OrderDate field from the Orders table to the second column of the QBE grid.

6. In the Field row of the third column, create a calculated column by entering:

Total:[order details].[unitprice]*[order details].[quantity]

 NOTE

Table names should be included in calculations like the above when your query contains tables with identical field names. In our query, the Products and Order Details tables both have a UnitPrice field, so we must specify the table. While the Quantity field does not exist in two tables, making full table and field declarations can help make your expressions easier to read later.

7. Save the query as **Category Sales**.

Creating the Form with the PivotTable Wizard

Once we have the query on which we want to base the PivotTable, we can create a form using the PivotTable Wizard.

1. In the Database window, click on the Forms tab and then click on New.

2. In the New Form dialog box, select PivotTable Wizard and click on OK.

3. The first dialog box of the PivotTable Wizard tells you about PivotTables. Click on Next.

4. Select the Category Sales query and all its fields as the Field source for the PivotTable. Click on Next.

5. You will be presented with a PivotTable Wizard dialog box in which you place the fields on the PivotTable layout. Drag CategoryName to Row, OrderDate to Column, and Total to Data. Click on Next.

6. The PivotTable Wizard provides a button for some final options, leave the defaults and click on Finish.

7. When you are prompted that the entire table will not fit, click on OK.

8. You are returned to your Access form with the PivotTable on it. Click on the Edit PivotTable button at the bottom of the form. This returns you to Excel so you can make modifications.

PART

VI

Data Management
with Access

9. Once in Excel, right-click on the gray OrderDate cell. Choose Group and Out-line ➤ Group from the shortcut menu. You may get a message box requesting that you refresh the underlying data of your PivotTable. If so, click on the Refresh Data command.

10. Change the Starting At date to 1/1/1994 and select years from the By list in the Grouping dialog box, as shown in Figure 47.10. Click on OK.

FIGURE 47.10

The Grouping dialog box

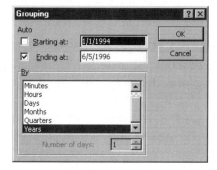

11. Select *Close & Return to Pivot Form.*

12. Save the form as **Category Sales**.

Access and PowerPoint

Let's suppose you are the sales manager for Northwind Traders, and it is your job to make the yearly presentation to the board, briefing the board members on sales progress. If you already have the sales data in Access, you will not have to spend time collecting the data for your presentation.

To create a visual representation of European sales figures, for example, you can create a query that groups sales by country and then use the Data Map feature to place a map on a PowerPoint slide.

Creating the Query

The first thing we need to do is build the query to gather sales by country.

1. From the Northwind database, select the Queries tab and click on New.

2. Select Design View and click on OK.

3. In the Show Tables dialog box, add the Orders and Order Details tables to your query and then click on Close.

4. From the Orders table, bring down the OrderDate and ShipCountry fields to the first and second columns of the QBE grid.

5. In the third column, click on the Field row and type:

Total:[unitprice]*[quantity]

6. Change the query to a totals query by selecting View ➤ Totals from the menu bar or by clicking on the Totals button on the Query Design toolbar.

7. In the Total row of column three, change Group By to Sum.

8. Change the Total row of the OrderDate column to Where.

9. In the Criteria row of the OrderDate column, type:

year([orderdate])=year(date())

and be certain that the checkbox in the Show row is unchecked so that only orders from the current year are included in the query result and this column does not show.

10. Save the query as **Yearly Sales by Country** once it looks like the one in Figure 47.11, and then close the Query Design screen.

FIGURE 47.11

The query to group sales by country for the current year to date

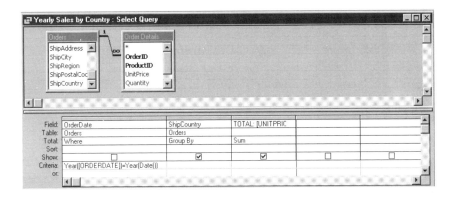

PART

VI

Data Management with Access

Creating the Slide with a Data Map

We now need to create a slide in PowerPoint and place a Large Object on it to use for a data map.

1. Open PowerPoint and start a blank presentation.

2. In the New Slide dialog box, find the Large Object slide (see Figure 47.12) and click on OK.

Selecting the Large Object slide layout

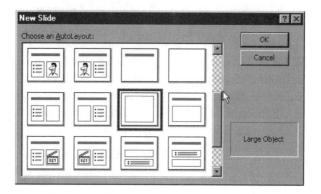

3. Double-click on the Large Object in the middle of the slide.

4. In the Insert Object dialog box, select Microsoft Map and click on OK.

5. From the menu bar, select Insert ➢ External Data.

6. Select Microsoft Access as the data source and click on OK.

7. In the Open Database dialog box, find and open the Northwind database and click on Open.

8. In the Select External Data dialog box (shown in Figure 47.13), select the Yearly Sales by Country query and send all the fields to the *Fields to display in map* list box. Click on OK.

Selecting the Yearly Sales by Country query

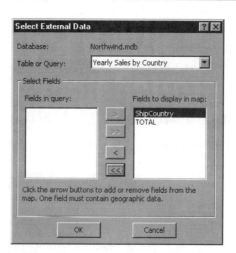

9. The data map will begin generating; however, it will not recognize the abbreviation *USA* which is used for the United States. Select US and then click on Change.

10. The recordset is read-only so that the USA change will not be permanent. Click on Continue to ignore the error. The Data Map with the results of our query appears. A Microsoft Map Control also appears. We will not use it to make changes in this example but you can review Chapter 19 for more information about this dialog box. Figure 47.14 shows the global map with shadings that represent our numbers.

FIGURE 47.14

*The Data Map
that results
from our query*

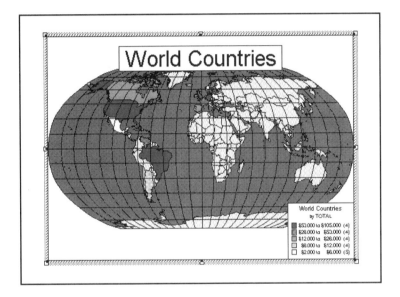

We will zoom in on the European countries so that we can distinguish the shading that is being applied to the countries with sales.

11. Click once on the Center Map button on the Data Map toolbar.

12. Position your mouse with the Center Map pointer over the center of the European countries and click once. Now change the zoom percentage of the map using the Zoom combo box on the toolbar. If the European countries are off center, use the Center Map pointer to refine the position of the map.

13. Double-click on the World Countries label, type **Europe,** and delete the remaining text.

14. Resize the legend, using the frame handles, and adjust the level of zoom to make the map look similar to the one in Figure 47.15.

FIGURE 47.15

The European Countries Sales map with detailed legend

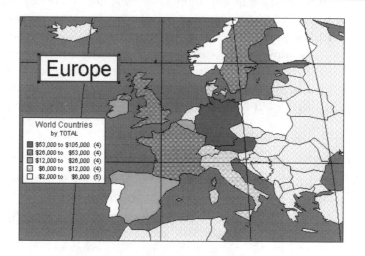

15. Click on the Map Labels button on the Data Map toolbar to get the Map Labels dialog box. The labels will be chosen from World Countries. Choose OK. Click on the European countries that you want to label.

16. When you are finished, click outside the map area on the border of the slide to end the editing of the Map object and see the final slide, as shown in Figure 47.16.

FIGURE 47.16

The final Power-Point slide

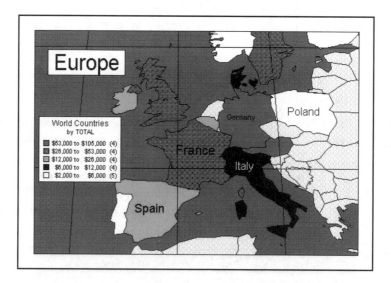

You can now use the map in your presentation. If you ever need to update or modify the information, you can simply double-click on the map on the slide and make the changes.

As you can see, you need only enter data once into Access to have it available for all of your Office applications. Microsoft Office, with Access as its central data source to link to and from the other Office applications, helps reduce redundant data entry and makes the way you work much more efficient.

PART

VI

Data Management
with Access

PART VII

Office 97 Internet Tools

LEARN TO:

- **Connect Office Documents Using Hyperlinks**

- **Create Your Own Web Pages**

- **Create Links to Internet or Intranet Sites in Your Office Documents**

- **Put Access Data on the Web**

- **Save Excel Workbooks as Web Pages**

- **Save Word Documents as Web Pages**

- **Save PowerPoint Presentations as Web Pages**

Chapter

48

Creating Hyperlink Documents

Creating Hyperlink Documents

n Chapter 4, you were introduced to the Internet, the World Wide Web, and hyperlinks. As you learned, the World Wide Web is a document linking system. Documents on the World Wide Web are also referred to as *pages*. These pages can reside on the same computer or on different computers in different locations around the world, and they are linked to other pages by hyperlink addresses inserted within them.

With the advent of Office 97, you can also insert links to different documents that were created using the Microsoft Office products. A Word report or proposal, for example, could contain a link to an Excel spreadsheet or to an Access database. How the link looks to your readers is your decision. The reader could see the actual computer file address as the clickable link to the Excel spreadsheet, or you may choose to use words or even a graphic to create a clickable link to the spreadsheet (or any Office document).

When inserting hyperlinks, you are not limited to just World Wide Web documents or Office 97 documents. Hyperlinks can be inserted that reference any program on your computer or network. However, the reader who clicks on this type of hyperlink must also have the program residing on their own computer or network for the hyperlink to work.

This chapter will explain how to use the Office applications to insert hyperlinks that connect you to documents around the world.

Understanding Hyperlinks

Stated simply, *hyperlinks* are references in a document to the location (*address*) of other information. Also known as *hot spots*, you click on a hyperlink to jump to a location within the same document, another Office document (*file*) on your local computer or network, an HTML page on a local intranet, or an HTML page on a remote computer on the World Wide Web.

A hyperlink object, also known as an anchor, can be the file address of another location, or any word or graphic that has been assigned an address. If an address or text is used as a hyperlink, it is usually represented by colored and underlined text. If a graphic is the hyperlink object, there may be no obvious indication of this until you pause your mouse over the graphic.

To create a hyperlink address, place the insertion point at the spot in a file (document, spreadsheet, database, slide) where you want the hyperlink. Then, click on the Insert Hyperlink button on the Standard toolbar or press Ctrl+K. The Insert Hyperlink dialog box will appear; in it you select the file you want the hyperlink to jump to. The file's address will be inserted into the document as a hyperlink.

To create a hyperlink from text, type the text and select it; then click on the Insert Hyperlink button on the Standard toolbar and find the file to be linked to the text. If you are using a graphic as the hyperlink, click on the graphic to select it; then click on the Insert Hyperlink button and assign the file to be linked to the graphic.

All hyperlink objects (addresses, text, graphics) in Office 97 applications show the mouse pointer as a pointing finger and a ScreenTip showing the location of the link's destination. Figure 48.1 shows a Word document with three examples of the same file being referenced by the three different types of hyperlink objects—address, text, and graphic (created using WordArt). When you click on any of the hyperlink objects, the destination document will be brought into memory and shown on the screen.

After you jump to a hyperlink destination and then return to the file containing the original link, the color of the link will have changed. The new color reminds you that you have "hit" this link at least once—in other words, you have already been to this destination. Graphics that have been used as hyperlink objects do not change colors once they have been clicked on and returned to; only text and file address hyperlink objects do this.

To move through linked Office files on your own computer or network, click on the Web Toolbar button, located on the Standard toolbar of each application, to call up the Web toolbar. Then, use the Back and Forward buttons on the Web toolbar to move backward and forward between hyperlinked documents that were opened during a computer session.

FIGURE 48.1

A hyperlink object can be the address of the destination file. Words and graphics can also be used as the hyperlink objects.

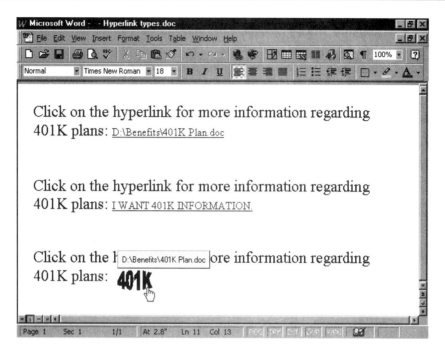

The buttons on the Web toolbar also move you between any files that were opened using the Address box, located at the right side of this toolbar. The Address box lists the last 25 hyperlinked files opened using the Address feature.

The Internet Explorer browser can also be used to move through linked Office documents, but its power is better tapped when you use it to open and navigate through World Wide Web documents (Web pages).

Hyperlink History

The documents in which hyperlinks are inserted are called *hypertext documents*, a concept invented in the late 1960s by computer scientist Ted Nelson in his attempt to create new ways for exploring information. While reading a document, he wanted the reader to be able to click on a highlighted word or phrase that was linked to another document. When the other document opened, additional information would be available about the meaning or purpose of the hyperlink word. Once the additional information had been opened, the reader could then click on a button and return to the original document.

Using a business example, imagine that you are reading your benefits plan in the electronic employee handbook of your company, and the word 401K is underlined and in another color. When you click on this hot spot, another document is then opened that contains the history of 401K plans in America and additional information about the benefits of joining the plan. You then click on a button to return to the original employee handbook document you were reading.

The creators of the World Wide Web saw the benefits of this concept and used it as the basis for their Web document system—documents that link to other documents that link to other documents from computer to computer across the Internet.

In Office 97, however, you need not create a Web page in order to use hyperlinks. You can create a hypertext document by placing hyperlinks in regular reports, proposals, spreadsheets, databases, and business presentations. A simple memo created in Microsoft Word, for example, could contain a hyperlink to a section within an employee handbook that is located on the local network, to a file located in Japan, and to a video clip of the company president's last speech to the stockholders.

What You Need to Link

Creating hyperlinks to other files or sections within the same file is a straightforward process. However, your ability to link to these files will depend on your current computer configuration. If you are referencing files that reside on your own computer or network, you can have instant access as long as you know where the file is located.

If you are referencing files that reside on a remote computer, you must also have a computer configuration that supports dialing out to other computers. You must know the Fully Qualified Domain Name (FQDN), also known as the URL (Uniform Resource Locator), address for the file. And your computer must have a personal modem or a network modem connection to the Internet. (See Chapter 4 for background information on FQDNs, URLs, and the Internet.)

If you are not on a network connected to the Internet, you must obtain an Internet connection through an Internet service provider (ISP) or one of the online services such as Microsoft Network (MSN), America Online (AOL), CompuServe, or AT&T. The ISP will guide you through installing special transmission software needed to make your computer talk to other computers on the Internet.

Corporate network servers connected to the Internet use a special protocol called TCP/IP, to allow each user's workstation on the network to dial up other computers. TCP/IP (Transmission Control Protocol/Internet Protocol) software is a set of rules and agreements on how to send information across the Internet.

If you are going to view documents on the World Wide Web, you will need another special software program—a *browser* (such as, Internet Explorer, Netscape, Mosaic). Browser software allows you to view documents that are created using the Hypertext Markup Language (HTML). Browsers also allow you to navigate among different Web sites and assist you in using special file types such as virtual reality, sound, and video files. Internet Explorer is supplied free of charge with Office 97. Chapter 4 contains background information about browsers, and Chapter 50 discusses the Internet Explorer browser.

Creating a Hyperlink

The steps to create hyperlinks are the same for each of the Office 97 applications. Remember, a hyperlink is an object onto which is inserted the location (address) of the file you want to link to. The address of the file you want to link to itself can be the reference, or you can use text or a graphic as the reference to the file.

To insert a hyperlink into any Office 97 application:

1. Create the document, spreadsheet, database, or slide that will contain the hyperlinks.

2. If you are going to insert the link address itself, position the insertion point at the location where you want the link to be. If you are going to use text or a graphic as the reference, type the text or create a graphic, and then select the text or the graphic.

3. Click on the Insert Hyperlink button on the Standard toolbar or press Ctrl+K. Word will recommend that you first save the file if there is current unsaved work you have done on the file. Choose Yes to save your work first before inserting the link.

4. When the Insert Hyperlink dialog box appears, type the location of the destination file (see Figure 48.2). The file can be another Office 97 file located on your computer or network or a Web document located on a remote computer.

5. If the destination is a location that you have previously used, don't type the information. Click on the drop-down arrow next to the Link to File or URL text box and find the local document's filename or remote document's URL.

6. If you are unsure of the local filename or remote file's URL, click on the Browse button to search the hard disk. Remote URLs can be found in the Favorites Folder where your favorite Internet locations are stored. The Link to File dialog box displays the folders on the hard disk. Find the filename.

7. At the bottom of the dialog box is the Use Relative Path for Hyperlink checkbox. If this option is checked, when you insert the hyperlink reference, the Path section on the dialog box will only show the name of the file and not the drive letters. This is so you can move the file later to another directory without having to reinsert a new hyperlink for the new location.

The Insert Hyperlink dialog box allows you to enter or find the destination file for the link.

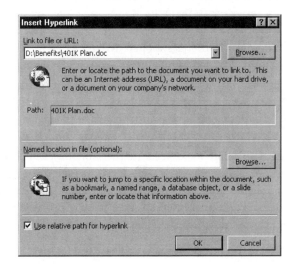

> **TIP**
>
> If you are referencing a document that resides on your network, use the UNC (Universal Naming Convention) path to designate the network drive that is shared by multiple users on the network—for example, \\Training\Documents\Hyperlink Rules (note the double backslash in front of the network reference). Talk to your network administrator about the UNC.

Removing a Hyperlink

To remove a hyperlink address, drag the mouse across the hyperlink address and press the Delete key; this is the same method for deleting any text in a Windows file. To remove the hyperlink reference from text or a graphic, however, you must follow these steps:

1. Place the mouse over the hyperlink reference and right-click.

2. Choose the Hyperlink option from the shortcut menu.

3. In the hyperlink submenu, choose Edit Hyperlink.

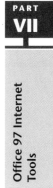

4. The Edit Hyperlink dialog box will appear. Click on the Remove Link button in the lower left corner of the box. The text or graphic remains, but the hyperlink reference is removed.

Reassigning a Hyperlink

To assign another destination to an existing hyperlink reference, place the mouse over the reference and right-click. Choose the Hyperlink option from the shortcut menu. In the hyperlink submenu, choose Edit Hyperlink. When the Edit Hyperlink dialog box appears, click on the drop-down arrow next to the Link to File or URL text box and choose another file or URL. Use the Browse button if the file is not in the most recently used list. Click on OK when finished.

Types of Hyperlinks

When you click on a hyperlink in Office 97, you may be referencing any of the following types of files:

- Office 97 documents created in Word, Excel, PowerPoint, or Access
- A section further down in the same document as the link
- HTML documents residing at remote locations or on the local intranet
- Sound files
- Video files
- Virtual reality animation files
- Other organizations' computer files

When you are creating a hypertext link, you should know where the file is located (that is, on your computer, the network, or a remote computer); you must also decide the *type* of link that should be used to reference that file. A hypertext document can contain links to other files using one of three types of hyperlinks:

- Target links
- Relative links
- Absolute links

If you link text or a graphic to information in another section of the same document or a section of a different document, this type of link is known as a local target or *target* link. For example, you could create a hyperlinked table of contents at the top of a document, so that when the reader clicks on a topic in the table of contents, the link jumps to corresponding information further down in the document—not necessarily in another file. In Office 97 applications, a target link is created using the Named Location section on the Insert Hyperlink dialog box.

Relative links are the default types of inserted hyperlinks in Office 97. These links are based on the location of the current file rather than the full path to the file. A link that is relative is easily moved to another computer or to another subfolder on the same computer. For example, suppose you keep all sound files in a folder called Sounds. If you move these files to another computer, the link still works even though the files no longer reside at the original destination, as long as you create a folder with the same name that the files had before. If these files are going to be the link destinations on an actual Web page, the same folder name must be created on the Web server as was created on the original computer. (In this example that would be a Sounds folder.) If you check Use Relative Path for Hyperlink on the Insert Hyperlink dialog box, the link address never has to be changed just because the files are moved to a Web server.

Absolute links are references to documents located at different sites (different folders or different computers). This is commonly used for documents stored on a host computer elsewhere on the World Wide Web. The addresses of these links will not change and the full file location or URL must be used in the link. You would uncheck the *Use relative path for hyperlink* option on the Insert Hyperlink dialog box (see Figure 48.2, above) to create an absolute link in an Office 97 application.

Named Locations in Hyperlinked Files

In the Hyperlink dialog box, you can select a Named Location in File (see Figure 48.3) as the destination for a hyperlink. You select a named location in this box to create target links, which reference different sections within the same document or different sections in another file.

FIGURE 48.3

You can have a hyperlink jump to a particular section within a document.

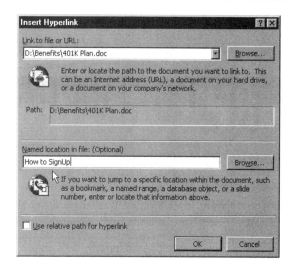

For example, suppose you insert a hyperlink into a document#1 that references document#2, but the specific information you want to reference in document#2 is far down in the document. You need to establish a link not only to document#2, but to the exact spot where the information resides, by specifying a named location. (If you don't specify a named location in document#2, the link drops the reader off at the top of the document.) This same idea can apply for one document where the different sections linked to are further down within the same document.

For example, say that the electronic employee handbook from our earlier example is 100 pages long, and each page contains sections of information grouped under the page heading. A hypertext table of contents can be created at the top of the 100-page document, so that when the reader clicks on a table of contents link, they are taken to the exact spot of the information on the page (the named location).

In order to reference a named location, the location within the file must be specially named. In Word, you use the bookmark feature to name a section of text as a named location. In Excel, you use the range name feature to name a section of the spreadsheet as a named location. In PowerPoint, you use the specific slide number as the named location.

To specify a named location, choose the Insert Hyperlink command and enter the filename for the link in the Link to File or URL area. Then, go down to the Named Location in File area and click on the Browse button to see any bookmarks, named ranges, or slides located in the destination file. Select the specific item that will appear when the link is clicked. If you are linking to a named location within the same file, you don't need to fill in the Link to File section at the top of the Insert Hyperlink dialog box. The program defaults to using the name of the current document on the screen.

If you are referencing a remote file or a another organization's page on the World Wide Web, you will not be able to insert a named location into your hyperlink reference, since you will not have access to the file to create a named location within it. The best you can do is insert a hyperlink reference to the file itself. Since your reader will be dropped off at the top of the file, you can include instructions before the hyperlink that tells them to scroll to a specific location.

Hyperlinks to Sound and Video

You can insert hyperlinks to sound and video files, which can be heard and viewed using Windows 95 by users who have installed the Multimedia capability. The recipients of sound files must have a sound card and speakers (or headphones) to hear the content of such files.

When inserting a hyperlink to sound or video files, the convention is to use a graphic that represents sound or pictures so that your reader knows to expect a sound file or video file. To do this, create or find a graphic that represents the sound or video file and insert it into your hypertext document. Click on the graphic to select it, then click on the Insert Hyperlink button or press Ctrl+K. When the Insert Hyperlink dialog box appears, find the sound or video file that is to be the destination link and click on OK. When your reader clicks on the graphic, the sound or video file will play and the reader must listen or view until the file is finished playing.

Click me to hear the opening to Chopin's Sonata in B flat minor

ChopinSoundfile.wav

> **WARNING**
>
> Care should also be taken when hyperlinking to sound and video files. These files tend to be very large. Readers may wait a number of minutes for a file to be loaded into their computer's memory only to see that the file was not what they were looking for. Keep your video and sound files small and they will be more effective.

You can obtain sound files (WAV files or MIDI files) by downloading them from the Internet, buying them, or recording your own. To record your own voice sound file:

1. Place a microphone jack into the sound card at the back of your computer.
2. Choose Start ➤ Programs ➤ Accessories ➤ Multimedia ➤ Sound Recorder to view the Sound Recorder dialog box.
3. Click on New on the File menu (nothing will seem to happen), and then click on the red Record button to record your message.
4. Start speaking into the microphone.
5. When you've finished, click on the black square Stop button to stop recording, then select Save from the File menu to type a name for the sound clip. Note the directory so that you can reference this location in your hyperlink.

To record from a CD, you follow the same steps for recording your own voice, but you won't need the microphone:

1. Choose Start ➤ Programs ➤ Accessories ➤ Multimedia, and open the Sound Recorder. Then, choose Start ➤ Programs ➤ Accessories ➤ Multimedia again, and open the CD Player. You will see both dialog boxes on the screen at the same time.
2. Place the CD into the CD-ROM disk holder.
3. Click on New on the File menu in the Sound Recorder dialog box, and then click on the red Record button.
4. Start the CD track you want to play. The Sound Recorder will tell you how much recording time you have.
5. Click on the Stop button when you are finished recording, then select Save from the File menu to type a name for the sound clip. Note the directory so that you can reference this location in your hyperlink.

Likewise, you can obtain video (AVI) files by downloading them from the Internet or buying them. Although Windows 95 offers no built-in features for capturing (recording) or editing video clips, you can use third-party software to transfer your own video files. Video transfer programs such as Snappy create "still" shots from video camcorders or VCR tapes. Intel's VideoRecorder is a video capture program that captures moving video and plays it back as a file. Adobe's Premiere is a video editing software program that allows for the editing, enhancement, and rearrangement of your video captures. All of these programs have good reputations for capturing and editing video. Note the directory into which you have stored the video file, so that you can reference this location in your hyperlink.

To play a multimedia file before inserting it into your document as a hyperlink, select Start ➤ Programs ➤ Accessories ➤ Multimedia ➤ Media Player. Select the type of file you want to play from the Device menu. When you find the file in the Open dialog box, click on Open. The first button is the Play button. Select it to hear or see your multimedia file to test for problems. (To listen to a sound file, make sure your speakers or your headphones are inserted into the sound card at the back of the computer.)

NOTE

If you do not see the Media Player option in the Multimedia folder in the Accessories menu, you will need to install it. Have your Windows 95 CD or disks ready and choose Start ➢ Settings ➢ Control Panel, then double-click on the Add/Remove Programs icon. Select the Windows Setup tab in the Properties dialog box and scroll through the list of options until you find Multimedia. Double-click on Multimedia, then check as many programs as you wish to install. Click on OK until you back out of the menus, and follow the instructions on the screen for inserting the correct Windows 95 disk(s) or CD.

The Web Toolbar

The second Internet button on the Standard toolbar is the Web Toolbar button. Clicking on this button displays the Web toolbar, which contains commands you will need as you work with online documents.

The Web toolbar (shown in Figure 48.4) allows you to easily open and navigate around documents that contain hyperlinks. When you click on a hyperlink, the destination file opens into memory; to move back to the original file, click on the Back button on the Web toolbar. If you open a Web page, the Internet Explorer browser will load into memory to take over the management of the Web pages (coded in HTML). Although you can also use Internet Explorer to navigate through non-HTML documents, it is better to use the Web toolbar for this purpose.

FIGURE 48.4

The Web Toolbar helps you navigate among hypertext documents containing hyperlinks.

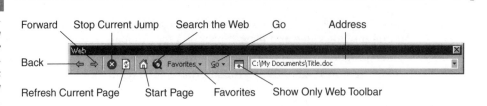

The Web Toolbar offers the following buttons:

- Back—displays the previous hyperlink document.
- Forward—displays the next hyperlink document.
- Stop Current Jump—terminates a jump.
- Refresh Current Page—updates the information on a page.
- Start Page—displays the home page of the current site.
- Search the Web—uses the Internet Explorer to explore Web pages.
- Favorites—adds sites to a Favorites directory for future return jumps.
- Go—displays a list of all the commands on the toolbar.
- Show Only Web Toolbar—hides other toolbars.
- Address—shows a history of documents and sites visited.

Using the Address Box

The Web toolbar's Address box is an additional method for opening Word documents and Internet documents. The Address box displays the last 25 documents or Web pages viewed in memory.

To use the Address box, make sure that the Web toolbar is displayed by selecting the Web Toolbar button on the Standard toolbar. Click on the drop-down arrow next to the Address box on the right side of the toolbar to see the list of previously opened Office documents or Web page URLs. Select a file, and it will immediately load into memory, if the current application created the file. If you select a file created in another application than the one on the screen, the application will load and then the file will display. This Address list will appear in all applications with the same files showing.

Both local files and Web pages show up in the Address History list. Local files have addresses that show the drive letter of the computer on which the file resides. Web pages are recognized by the letters http:// as part of the Fully Qualified Domain Name.

For example, say you are in Word, and a previously visited page was an Excel hyperlinked document. When you choose the file from the Address list on the Web toolbar, the Excel program will load, followed by the document referenced in the hyperlink.

If you choose a Web page address from the History list, the Internet Explorer browser will load. The Address list is a handy option when you know you have visited a site but forgot to add the name to your Favorites shortcuts (or write it down anywhere else) and then want to visit the site again.

Hyperlinks throughout the Office

In the next sections, you will learn how to create hyperlinks for specific files and named locations in each of the Office 97 applications. Links can reference Office 97 documents on your local computer or network, or they can reference remote documents residing on host computers on the World Wide Web.

Inserting Hyperlinks into Word

In the section above on "Creating Hyperlinks," you learned the simple steps to create a hyperlink to a local or remote file. The procedure is the same for inserting hyperlinks into Word documents: Create a Word document (or use an existing one), then place your insertion point anywhere in the document and click on the Insert Hyperlink button or press Ctrl+K to insert hyperlink references to other file locations. These locations can be destinations further down in the same document (named locations), another document on your computer or the local network, or a remote site on the World Wide Web.

In a Word document, you can create hyperlinks to files created in any of the other Office 97 applications (for any of the Office suite versions—4.2, 4.3, and 95). This means that there can be references to Excel, Access, PowerPoint, and Outlook files within your Word document.

NOTE
You can also create hyperlinks to any program that resides on your computer or network. When this external program launches, however, it will not have a Web toolbar or buttons you can use to return to the source file. Instead, you will have to close the file to return to the source file.

You can reference any address or file located on another server, provided that you know the URL (Uniform Resource Locator) address.

Decide the destination file and what text or graphic will be used as the hyperlink object in the Word document and then:

1. Select the text or graphic or, if inserting the hyperlink address itself, position the insertion point at a blank spot.

2. Click on the Insert Hyperlink button on the Standard toolbar or press Ctrl+K.

3. When the Insert Hyperlink dialog box appears, find the file reference or the URL and click on the OK button.

4. The hyperlink will be colored and underlined unless you chose a graphic.

Creating the Destination and Source Files

For you to get a good feel for hyperlinks in Word, let's create a hyperlink reference to two other Word files. (The destination files could also be Excel, Access, or PowerPoint files, sound or video files, or an external program's files.) Follow these steps:

1. Start a new Word document that represents the destination file that the hyperlink will jump to. In this document, type the following sentence, which will represent a full document of text:

   ```
   I am the file containing the information about 401K plan.
   ```

2. Save the file under the name 401K Plan. Note the directory into which you are saving the file.
3. Close the File.
4. Create another Word document and type this sentence:

   ```
   I am the file containing the information about the Credit Union.
   ```

5. Save this file under the name Credit Union. Note the directory into which you are saving the file.
6. Close the File.
7. Create a new document as the source file that contains the hyperlink to the destination files. Type this sentence:

   ```
   If you would like more information on our employee benefits,
   click the appropriate icon:
   ```

8. Press the Enter key three times. You will now create 401K and Credit Union icons using the WordArt program.

Creating a WordArt Graphic Hyperlink

You are now going to create two icons: one that says "401K" and one that says "Credit Union." The icons will be created using the WordArt program.

1. Click on the Drawing button on the Standard toolbar to display the Drawing toolbar.
2. Click on the Insert WordArt button.
3. When the WordArt gallery appears, move down four rows and over three columns to the sample that is in a gradient yellow and has a shadow effect to it and click on it. Click on OK.
4. The Edit WordArt Text dialog box appears with the words "Your Text Here." Type the letters **401K** over the other text. Don't click on OK yet.

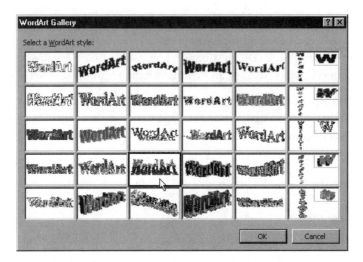

5. Change the font point size from 36 to 16 by clicking on the Size drop-down arrow at the top of the dialog box and choosing 16, then click on OK.

6. The WordArt graphic appears in your text (it's not positioned correctly, but we will take care of that in a few seconds). If you find that you have a typo in the graphic or didn't change the point size, click on the Edit Text button on the WordArt toolbar that appears at the bottom of the screen. If you don't see the WordArt toolbar, make sure that you click once on the graphic, the toolbar shows when the graphic is selected. If the toolbar still doesn't appear, choose View ➤ Toolbars and select the WordArt toolbar and then click on the Edit Text button.

7. To move the graphic, make sure it is selected and point to the middle of it. The mouse pointer becomes a four-headed arrow. Drag the WordArt icon to the left side of the sentence and then click below the graphic so that it is no longer selected. You are ready to create the second WordArt graphic.

8. Repeat steps 2–7 to create a Credit Union graphic. If the Drawing toolbar disappears, go back to step 1.

9. Save the file under the name Employee Benefits. Figure 48.5 shows the results after creating the two graphics.

Inserting Hyperlinks Using WordArt Graphics

The WordArt graphics you created in the previous section are now ready to become hyperlinks. To make the 401K WordArt graphic a hyperlink:

1. Select the 401K graphic by clicking on it once. Ignore the WordArt toolbar that appears when you select the graphic—you won't need it right now.

FIGURE 48.5

The WordArt feature can create a graphical word that can be used as a hyperlink anchor.

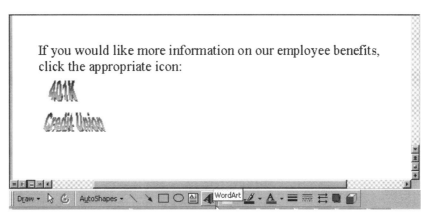

2. Click on the Insert Hyperlink button on the Standard toolbar or press Ctrl+K to activate the Insert Hyperlink dialog box.

3. In the Link to File or URL area, click on the Browse button and find the file called 401K Plan that you saved previously. When you locate the file, double-click on it; you will be returned to the Insert Hyperlink dialog box.

4. Click on OK at the bottom of the dialog box to return to your document.

5. Repeat steps 1–4 for the Credit Union graphic.

6. When both graphics have become hyperlink objects, click outside the currently selected graphic to deselect it. Pause the mouse over the graphic and notice that the mouse pointer changes to a pointing hand and the hyperlink address to the destination file appears as a ScreenTip above the graphic. Save the Employee Benefits file.

7. Click on the Web Toolbar button on the Standard toolbar, next to the Insert Hyperlink button. You will need this toolbar when you are testing your hyperlinks.

8. Test your hyperlinks. Click on the 401K graphic, and the 401K Plan document will load. On the Web toolbar, the Back button is lit up with a blue left arrow. Click on the Back button to return to the Employee Benefits file. Now click on the Credit Union graphic to test that link. You can return back to the original file using the Back button on the Web toolbar.

You can begin to see how hyperlinks could also be inserted into each of the destination files (401K Plan and Credit Union) for different words or graphics that were placed into these files. The group of documents with links is your hypertext collection of documents.

Named Locations in Word

When you insert a hyperlink into any document, you must indicate the document's address location in the Link to File area of the Insert Hyperlink dialog box. You might also need to designate a subsection further down into the document as part of the hyperlink. To do this, you use the Named Location in File area of the Hyperlink dialog box, in which you can indicate a particular section (*named location*) of a document for a hyperlink to jump to. As you learned earlier in this chapter, a link that you indicate in the Named Location in File area is called a target link (see "Types of Hyperlinks," earlier in the chapter).

In Word, bookmark names must be given to the subsections within a document that you wish to reference in the Named Location in File area. When the reader clicks on the hyperlink, the entire file will load *and* the reader will be placed at the particular named subsection within the document.

Assigning Bookmarks to Subsections

Open the destination file that contains different sections of text that you want to be referenced by hyperlinks. Then, follow these steps:

1. Select the first text section that will be referenced as a named location (or just select the heading of that section).
2. Choose Insert ➢ Bookmark from Word's main menu.
3. Type in a name for this bookmark. Since the name cannot have spaces in it, use underscores instead. The bookmark name can be a maximum of 40 characters.
4. Click on the Add button at the bottom of the dialog box.
5. Repeat these steps for each subsection in the document you want to create a bookmark for.

Inserting Bookmark Names into a Hyperlink

Now, you can insert hyperlinks that will take your readers to bookmarked sections of the destination file. To do so, indicate the names of the bookmarks in the Named Location in File area of the Insert Hyperlink dialog box. Here are the steps:

1. Create or open the source file that has the text or graphic to which hyperlink references and named locations need to be assigned.
2. Select the text or graphic that will be the hyperlink object.
3. Click on the Insert Hyperlink button on the Standard toolbar or press Ctrl+K.
4. In the Link to File or URL text box, type (or browse and insert) the location of the destination file.

PART

VII

Office 97 Internet Tools

5. Click in the Named Location in File box and click on the Browse button. The Bookmark dialog box (Figure 48.6) will appear; in it, you can click on one of the bookmark names you previously created.

You can include a hyperlink reference to a bookmarked subsection of a Word document by using the Named Location in File option in the Insert Hyperlink dialog box.

Inserting Hyperlinks into Excel

Use the steps you learned about hyperlinks in the previous sections to insert hyperlink references into cells of an Excel spreadsheet. Create an Excel document (or use an existing one), then place your insertion point anywhere in the spreadsheet, and click on the Insert Hyperlink button or press Ctrl+K to insert hyperlink references to other file locations. These locations can be destinations further down in the same spreadsheet (named locations), another file on your computer or the local network, or a remote site on the World Wide Web.

Excel users find the hyperlink feature a great boon when working with multiple spreadsheets. Hyperlinks are inserted for other spreadsheet files that must be quickly viewed. You can use the Web toolbar to move back and forward between the multiple hyperlinked spreadsheets.

Named Locations in Excel

When you insert a hyperlink into any workbook, you must indicate the workbook's address location in the Link to File or URL section of the Insert Hyperlink dialog box.

You might also need to designate a subsection range within that workbook as part of the hyperlink. To do this, use the Named Location in File section of the Insert Hyperlink dialog box.

Assigning a Range Name

A range name must be used to mark a range of a workbook that you want to be referenced by a hyperlink, and this name must be used in the Insert Hyperlink dialog box.

Open the destination file that contains the ranges to be named, then follow these steps:

1. Highlight the range of data you want to reference as a named location.
2. Choose Insert ➤ Name ➤ Define from Excel's main menu.
3. Type in a name for the range. Since the name cannot have spaces in it, use underscores instead, as shown in the graphic below. The range name can be a maximum of 255 characters.
4. Click on the Add button and click on OK.
5. Repeat these steps for each range in the workbook.

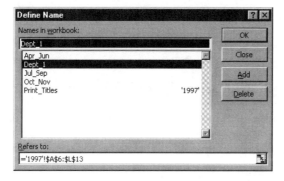

Inserting Range Names into a Hyperlink

When you have assigned range names to the different data ranges of the workbook(s), you are ready to reference these names in the Named Location in File part of the Insert Hyperlink dialog box. Here are the steps:

1. Select the graphic or text, or position the pointer in a blank cell.
2. Click on the Insert Hyperlink button on the Standard toolbar or press Ctrl+K.
3. In the Link to File or URL text box, type the full path to the destination workbook file.
4. Click into the Named Location in File box and click on the Browse button. The Browse Excel Workbook dialog box will appear, in which you can select a range name.
5. Click on the Defined Name option button to see a list a list of range names. Select the named location that should be part of this hyperlink.

Inserting Hyperlinks into PowerPoint

Create a PowerPoint presentation and insert hyperlink references onto an object on any slide of the presentation. The hyperlink reference should generally be to other PowerPoint slides either in the same file or in another file; but theoretically you can create a hyperlink reference to any other file from any other application.

1. Use text or create an object or use a piece of clip art on a slide.
2. Select the text or object.
3. Click on the Insert Hyperlink button on the Standard Toolbar.
4. In the Insert Hyperlink dialog box assign a file location to the object. If the reference is in the same PowerPoint presentation, you only have to use the Named Location in File.
5. Click on the Browse button in the Named Location in File area, and you will see a listing of the other slides in the presentation. Choose the slide that will be the destination for the link and click on OK.
6. Click on OK at the bottom of the Insert Hyperlink dialog box.
7. The link is not active until the PowerPoint presentation is run. Click on the Slide Show button in the bottom left side of the PowerPoint window to start the show. When the slide appears with the hyperlink, click on the link to launch the destination file.

Inserting Hyperlinks into Outlook

Although Outlook does not contain the Insert Hyperlink button, the Web toolbar is displayed when you use Word as your e-mail editor. When you use Word as your e-mail editor and compose a new message, the Standard, Formatting, and Web toolbars are shown with all the features and commands available for use in your e-mail message. If you do not see the Web toolbar when you are creating a new message in Outlook, choose Tools ➣ Options and select the E-mail tab. At the bottom of the E-mail dialog box, check the box *Use Microsoft Word as the e-mail editor.* Click on Apply and then click on OK to close the dialog box.

When Word is your e-mail editor, you can give the recipient of an e-mail the URL to a particular Web page: Choose Insert ➣ Hyperlink or press Ctrl+K to display the Insert Hyperlink dialog box. Then, enter the URL or select it from the Link to File or URL text box and click on OK. The hyperlink address is displayed in your e-mail. When the recipient gets the e-mail, the hyperlink will be shown. If the recipient has an Internet connection and clicks on the link, the Internet Explorer (or whatever browser they are using) will launch, and the Web page will be located.

MASTERING THE OPPORTUNITIES

Creating Named Locations the Easy Way

Although Microsoft is fairly explicit in its documentation that you must use the Named Location section of the Insert Hyperlink dialog box to reference data that is in a section further down in a file, there is a simpler method for creating a named location in Word, Excel, or Power-Point (this method is not available for Access). This technique does not require that you first create bookmarks in Word, range names in Excel, or slide numbers in PowerPoint. Follow these steps:

1. Select the text in Word (usually a heading), the range in Excel, or the slide content in PowerPoint that will be the named location section that the hyperlink will jump to.
2. Click on the Copy button on the Standard toolbar.
3. Switch to or start the file (within the same application) that will display the hyperlink. Position the insertion point where you want the hyperlink to appear, or select text or a graphic that will be the hyperlink anchor.
4. Choose Edit ➢ Paste as Hyperlink from the menu bar.
5. The hyperlink address will appear in the document, or the anchor text or graphic will have the hyperlink address.

When the reader pauses the mouse over the hyperlink, they will only see the name of the entire file. However, when the reader clicks on the hyperlink, the destination file will be loaded into memory, and the insertion point will jump to the specific location that was selected and copied.

In addition, you can insert a hyperlink to a file located on your hard disk in an e-mail message, but you must also attach the file (select Insert ➢ File or click on the Insert File icon on the new Message toolbar). Instruct the recipient to first save the file to their disk before clicking on the hyperlink. Otherwise, their computer will alert them that the hyperlink file does not reside on their computer, only on yours. Although it is possible to insert a hyperlink to a regular file in the e-mail, it is easier for the recipient if you just insert the file as an attachment.

Creating hyperlinks to files located on a network is a very effective method for displaying the addresses of multiple documents related to a particular e-mail subject. When working in a corporate network environment and inserting hyperlinks to files on the network, it is unnecessary to also attach the file, as the recipient's computer will be able to find the file on the network when they click on the hyperlink to the file.

When you attach a document that contains hyperlinks, the same considerations as mentioned above are to be used: If sending Internet URLs, make sure you are sending hyperlinks to individuals who have an Internet connection. If an attached document contains links to file locations, make sure the recipients have access to the files being referenced by the link, or else attach these files.

Inserting Hyperlinks into Access

Hyperlinks in Access can be placed in datasheets, forms, and even reports. The links can jump to other Microsoft Access objects in the same or another database, Word, Excel, and PowerPoint documents, or Web documents on the Internet.

Hyperlinks to be placed in a datasheet must be in a special hyperlink field. Click on the Design button for your table or create a new table and create a field for the hyperlink reference. Type a name for the field and designate the field data type as Hyperlink, as illustrated in Figure 48.7.

There is a special Hyperlink field available for Access records to store hyperlink references.

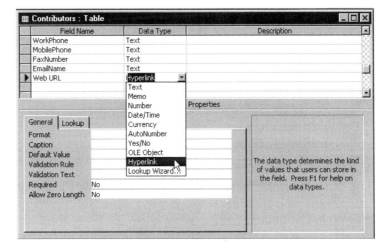

You can type or insert hyperlink references for each record using any file location as well as the locations of Internet URLs. For example, in a database of suppliers in which, in addition to physical address information, you store home page Internet URLs, a hyperlink to each supplier's Web page can be inserted into the field that was created using the hyperlink data type instead of the text data type. As you are entering record information, choose Insert ➤ Hyperlink from the Access menu to type in a supplier's URL, or browse your Favorites folder for the supplier's URL if you have previously saved it.

TIP If you need a new column in your table that will hold your hyperlink addresses, you can insert a Hyperlink column directly into the table without going into Design view. Select Insert ➤ Hyperlink Column. The new column will be inserted to the left of the column where the insertion point is placed. A new field will show in your table as Field1. Double-click on the column heading to change the field name to something more appropriate for the table. To delete the column, select the column by clicking on the column heading, then choose Edit ➤ Delete column.

If you import data into an Access table (File ➤ Get External Data ➤ Import) that contains URL information in its column(s), the Import Spreadsheet Wizard will convert the column that contains URLs or UNC paths to a hyperlink field—as long as all of the data in the column includes recognizable protocols. For example, if every value in the imported column starts with http: or \\, Access converts the column to a hyperlink field. If just one value in the column doesn't start with a recognized protocol, Access cannot convert the column to a hyperlink field.

Inserting Graphics on Access Forms and Reports

You can use hyperlinks in forms and tables to jump to objects in the same or another Access database. Hyperlinks in Access can also jump to documents created with Word, Excel, and PowerPoint, and to documents on the global Internet or on a local intranet. You can also add hyperlinks to reports. Although hyperlinks in a report won't work when previewed in Access, the hyperlinks will work if you output the report to Word or Excel, or convert it to HTML.

To add a hyperlink graphic in Access:

1. Open a form or report in Design view.
2. Click on the Image Control tool in the toolbox, and then click on the form where you want to create the picture.
3. In the Insert Picture dialog box, locate the picture you want to use. Microsoft Access then adds the image control to the form or report.
4. Make sure the image control is selected, and then right-click the mouse and choose Properties from the shortcut menu.
5. In the HyperlinkAddress property on the Format tab, specify a UNC path or a URL. For example, enter **d:\training\registrations\cost_center.xls** or **http://www.microsoft.com**. If you need to browse for the address, click on the Build button to open the Insert Hyperlink dialog box.
6. If you want to jump to a sublocation within a file, enter the sublocation in the HyperlinkSubAddress property.
7. To test the link, return to the Form view and click on the hyperlink picture. The destination file will load. Click on the Back button on the Web toolbar to return to the Access form or report.

Chapter

49

Creating Web Pages with Microsoft Word

FEATURING

Creating Web Pages with Microsoft Word

n Chapter 4, you learned about the World Wide Web, a document delivery system that rides on top of the Internet. This document system was invented by Tim Berners-Lee and his colleagues, physicists at the CERN research center in Switzerland, who wanted to be able to present information in documents that could be linked to other documents. The documents would be stored on computers (host servers) throughout the Internet.

The CERN scientists developed a special series of communications protocols called Hypertext Transport Protocol (HTTP), which enabled the scientists to locate one document on the Web and from that first document easily access documents on other computers elsewhere. All of this was possible without the use of complicated commands. This network of documents connected across the network of computers called the Internet became known as the World Wide Web.

Web Page Concepts

The fundamental component of information on the Web is a document (known as a *page*). A Web page can contain varied types of information: text, graphics, sound, animation, video, and 3-D images. The purpose of a Web page varies: It may contain information about a person or a corporation; it may display information about products you can purchase over the Internet, such as books and music; or it may show government census information about a particular area. There are Web pages that display the news from the various news bureaus, such as the Reuters News service. Some Web pages allow you to search for other Web pages on a specific topic—these are known as *search engines.*

In addition, many corporations today are creating and storing Web pages on their own internal networks. Known as *intranets*, these internal webs let users move from corporate documents linked to other corporate documents.

Web pages may contain links to graphics, sound, animation, or video files. One page can contain hyperlinks to many other pages or files which then contain hyperlinks to many other pages or files.

Web pages are written in Hypertext Markup Language (HTML). This language uses codes before and after different sections of text to designate the content type (for example, headings, body text, bulleted or numbered lists) and the type of formatting you desire for the text (bold, italic, underline, and so on). Codes are also used to indicate links—called *hyperlinks*—to other files and other documents. No special program is needed to code a document in the HTML language. Any ASCII text editor, such as Notepad, will do fine—and, of course, a knowledge of what the codes are and how to use them.

To translate HTML-coded documents into text, images, or sounds that your personal computer (client) can display or play, a special program called a *browser* (such as Microsoft Internet Explorer, Netscape Navigator, and NCSA Mosaic) is needed.

In this chapter, you will learn the concepts and steps needed to create Web pages using Microsoft Word's Web Page Wizard, which walks you through the entire process and has a number of predesigned Web pages. You will also learn about Web design elements, such as colorful backgrounds, animated and scrolling text, graphics, video, and sound.

Why Web Pages?

In Chapter 48, you learned how to insert hyperlinks into Office 97 documents. However, people connected to the Internet can only view Office documents if they also have a copy of Windows 95 and Office 97 on their local machines. Then, if they click hyperlinks that lead to a Word document, an Access database, or an Excel spreadsheet, Windows 95 will load the appropriate Office 97 program and display the document.

The creators of the World Wide Web system of documents wanted a platform-independent method of linking documents that did not require multiple programs be loaded in order to view documents created within those programs. To do this, they developed a set of rules, known as Hypertext Transfer Protocol (HTTP), and the

Hypertext Markup Language (HTML). Together, HTTP and HTML allow you to specially code any document so that only one program is required to translate the codes and display the document. This translator program is known as a *browser*.

Office Documents in HTML Format

In order for your Word report, Excel budget, PowerPoint presentation, or Access database to be viewed using a browser, these documents must contain the special HTML codes used in Web documents. Each Office 97 application offers a feature that allows you to create your documents in their native formats and then save them in the HTML format. Each document becomes specially coded and Web-ready. Chapter 50 goes in depth into the steps required to take an existing Office document and convert it to an HTML page for viewing on the World Wide Web.

Web Page Templates

The other HTML feature that Office 97 offers is an HTML editor that is part of Word 97. Using your word processor instead of an ASCII text editor or third-party software, you can create beautiful Web pages with links to graphics, sound, video, and animation. Special Web page templates and commands that are a part of these Word templates allow you to create pages with colorful backgrounds, fancy fonts, and scrolled text (File ➤ New ➤ Web Pages tab).

There are three templates that are available from the Web Pages tab of the New dialog box: Blank Web Page, More Cool Stuff, and Web Page Wizard, as shown in Figure 49.1. The More Cool Stuff template takes you online with Microsoft to obtain additional Web utilities or page design elements. Only Blank Web Page and Web Page Wizard create HTML documents.

Using either the Blank Web Page or Web Page Wizard templates, you create a document, and Word inserts the correct HTML codes behind-the-scenes; these codes are not visible until you specifically request to view them (View ➤ HTML Source). The wonder of Office 97 is that it is possible to create these Web-ready documents without ever learning or using one single HTML code. Instead, you can concentrate on page layout, design, and links. As you gain experience with Web page design, you may want to see the coded document so that you can make changes more quickly by working directly with the underlying source HTML codes.

Even though you can use the Word HTML templates to create pages and view them, you truly will not know how these pages will look until you preview them using your browser. The Web Page Preview button on the Standard toolbar launches the Internet Explorer, and displays your page as others will see it on the Internet's World Wide Web.

You can use the Web Page templates to either create a Web page on your own or to be walked through the design of a page.

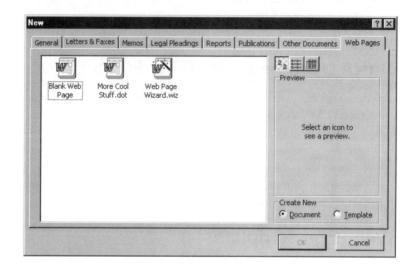

A Web *home page* is the first HTML page that a person or organization presents to you when you visit their site. The home page is a "Welcome to my site" page that describes the purpose of the company and generally allows you to click onto links to other parts of the site. The home page can be the only page that makes up the Web site or can be the first page of a collection of interconnected pages.

Using the Web Page Wizard

The Web Page Wizard, a Word 97 template, walks you through the design steps of creating your first Web page. Before using the Web Page Wizard, there are design elements with which you should be familiar, as you will be asked a few questions by the Wizard. Table 49.1 displays the most common design elements used in Web page design.

TABLE 49.1: WEB PAGE DESIGN ELEMENTS

Design Element	Meaning
Anchors	Graphics and text that represent hyperlink addresses. For example, a microphone graphic may be used as an anchor to represent a sound file that will play when the user clicks on the microphone.

Continued ▶

TABLE 49.1: WEB PAGE DESIGN ELEMENTS (CONTINUED)

Design Element	Meaning
Backgrounds	Colored backdrops to the text. Add texture and visual interest to the page (Format ➤ Background).
Bullets	Small, attractive graphics to set off lists of information (Insert ➤ Picture ➤ From File). Located in the Microsoft Office\Clipart folder, the Bullets folder contains a variety of bullet types you can use in your Web page design.
Font size	The size of text.
Graphics	Clip art or scanned photos that can be placed on a Web page to give visual interest to the page.
Headings	Text categories that label different sections of information (Style box on the Formatting toolbar).
Horizontal lines (rules)	Horizontal separation lines between different sections of text (Insert ➤ Horizontal Lines).
Hyperlinks	Addresses (URLs) or text or graphics that can be clicked on to bring other files into memory (Insert Hyperlink button on the Standard toolbar).
Numbered lists	Chronological lists of information that use Arabic or Roman numbers to set off items (Numbering button on the Formatting toolbar).
Scrolling text	Moving, marquee text that focuses the eye on short messages (Insert ➤ Scrolling text).
Sound	.wav files that contain recorded music or voice that can be played through the computer's sound card (Insert ➤ Background Sound).
Tables	Used to control page layout when multiple columns of information are needed (click on the Tables and Borders button, then use the Draw Table tool).
Text	Used to communicate the purpose and information of the Web page.
Text colors	The color of the text or hyperlinks (Format ➤ Text Colors).
Video	.avi files that contain video or animation (Insert ➤ Video).

Let's use the Web Page Wizard to create a sample Web page, so that these design elements can be seen. Start the Word 97 program and follow these steps:

1. Select File ➤ New from the menu bar (don't click on the New icon on the Standard toolbar).

2. When the New dialog box appears, click on the Web Pages tab. The Web templates are contained on this page.

3. Double-click on the Web Page Wizard icon to start the Web Page Wizard. The Web Page Wizard dialog box appears with a Simple Layout template in the background. The text prompts in brackets are not HTML codes; they simply let you know where to type your information.

4. Click on another page type in the dialog box to view some of the other templates available. Figure 49.2 displays the Web Page Wizard dialog box with the Simple Layout template selected.

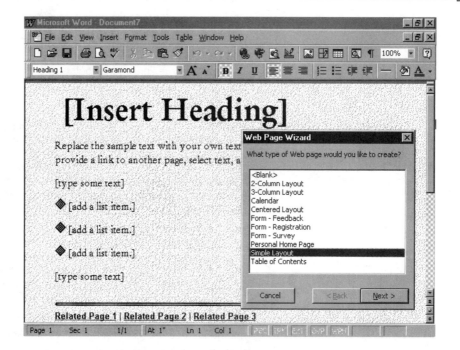

5. For this example, click once on the Simple Layout template in the Web Page Wizard dialog box and click the Next button at the bottom of the box.

6. When asked *What visual style would you like?* select each different style to see if the presentation is what you want for your page. Word refreshes the background screen to display each style's presentation.

7. For this example, select the Jazzy style and click on the Finish button. Choose File ➤ Save and save the Web page. If you don't like the looks of this Web page, close the file without saving (File ➤ Close) and start again with step 1.

Filling in the Web Wizard Template

Once you have a Web page template you like, you will fill in the sample areas with your own text. Look where it says "Replace the sample text with your own text, graphics and multimedia files"—this information is the instruction that tells you how to proceed on the page. All of the locations that have square brackets are sample text areas that will be removed when you type your own information.

Web Template Buttons and Commands

There are additional Web page design buttons located on the Standard and Formatting toolbars that only appear when you're using the Web Page Wizard or the Blank Web Page template: Web Page Preview, Form Design Mode, and Insert Picture. The Web Page Preview button is identical to the File menu option called Web Page Preview. This feature allows you to see what your page will look like when viewed through the Internet Explorer browser. You will be asked to save the Web page first before the Preview can be shown. Form Design Mode (also available on the View menu) allows you to create forms to capture user input; and Insert Picture (also available on the Insert menu) displays the clip art gallery for you to insert graphical files onto your Web pages.

The Formatting toolbar shows two new buttons when a document is saved as an HTML document: Horizontal Line and Background.

The Insert menu also contains six Web page design options: Horizontal Line, Picture, Video, Background Sound, Forms, and Scrolling Text. These options will be discussed later in this chapter.

Headings

"Insert Heading" is the first sample text that you should fill in with your own information. Click the mouse anywhere into the prompt area; the entire prompt is selected so that you can type over the generic information. Type your own heading.

In the prompt "type some text," type the text for the heading, purpose, or subject of your page. You can type as much as you want, but you should frequently break up the text into small paragraphs to make your text easier to read on the screen.

If you wish to add additional headings, use the Style box on the Formatting toolbar (the first button on that toolbar). Click on the drop-down arrow and select either the Heading 1.6 styles or scroll down until you find the H1 through H6 styles. The H1 through H6 styles are the styles used in the HTML coding and contain larger font sizes than the traditional Headings.

You can either select the text first and then apply the heading or select the heading style and then type your text. If you don't like the heading after seeing its effect, click on the Undo button on the Standard toolbar.

Font Size Changes

When you create a Web page, you will need to know how to change the size of words or parts of your text. When an HTML template is used as the basis of a new document, the Formatting toolbar's Font Size box will be replaced with the Increase Font Size and Decrease Font Size buttons. These buttons appear as a large A and a small A. When you select text and click on either of these buttons, the font size will increase or decrease.

Bulleted Lists

In the bulleted list section, click once on the prompt that says "add a list item" to select the sample text. Then, type your list. To copy a bulleted item, select the entire line and click on the Copy button on the Standard toolbar. Click the insertion point where you will want the copy, then click on the Paste button on the Standard toolbar to retrieve your selection. You can also select a line and delete it.

Even though the Web page Wizard supplies a particular bullet, Microsoft has a number of other graphical bullet styles you can insert on your Web page:

1. Click directly on the existing bullet to select it. The Picture toolbar appears.
2. Click on the Insert Picture button or choose Insert ➤ Picture ➤ From File from the menu bar. If asked if you want to save the document, click on Yes. The Insert Picture dialog box appears with the Clipart folder open.
3. The Clipart folder contains a number of subfolders with graphics that can be used in Web page design. Double-click on the Bullets folder and select one of the bullet files. Each bullet file name ends with a .gif extension.

When you return to the document, the selected bullet has been replaced with the bullet chosen in the Bullets folder. Figure 49.3 shows the initial development for a Chopin Web page. Hyperlinks have not been inserted yet onto this page.

Hyperlinks

Below the horizontal rule (the graphical line displayed across the width of the page), there are hyperlink placeholders where you can insert hyperlink addresses. These placeholders are formatted with a blue color and bold.

To insert a hyperlink, drag across the first placeholder, Related Page 1. Click on the Insert Hyperlink button on the Standard toolbar, press Ctrl+K, or right-click and select hyperlink from the shortcut menu. When the Insert Hyperlink dialog box appears,

FIGURE 49.3

The Web Page Wizard gives you a template design that you customize with your own text.

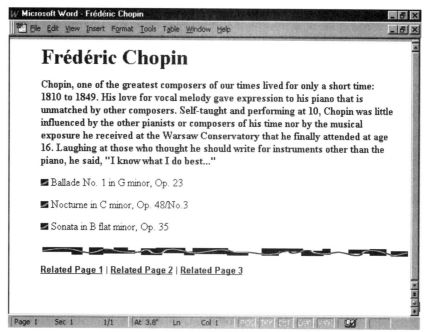

type in the name of the destination URL, or select it from the list of recently viewed documents. You can also Browse your hard disk for the name, if the destination is a file stored on your local machine.

If you do not wish to link other pages to this page, drag over all three hyperlink placeholders and press the Delete key. And of course, you do not have to use the hyperlink placeholders—you can select any word or phrase and turn it into a hyperlink. In our Chopin Web page, the names of each favorite piano piece will be selected and a hyperlink inserted that references the file location (URL) of the .wav file for that piano piece.

Once a hyperlink is inserted, you can assign another file or URL to the hyperlink by right-clicking on the link and choosing Hyperlink from the shortcut menu. Within the hyperlink submenu, choose Edit Hyperlink. The Edit Hyperlink dialog box appears; you can change the hyperlink URL or file at the top.

Clip Art and Graphics

Clip art and graphics enhance the visual appeal of your pages. To insert a clip art file or other graphic into the Web page, select Insert ➢ Picture ➢ From File or click on the Insert Picture button or right-click and select Picture. The graphic files can be used as design elements or as hyperlink anchors that, when clicked, link the reader to another file.

When you insert a graphic into a Web page that contains text, you may not like the way the text wraps around the graphic. To change the way that the text wraps around a graphic, select the graphic and right-click. Choose Format Picture from the shortcut menu, then click on the Position tab at the top of the Format Picture dialog box. Next, click on the None or Right option to set the Text wrapping style, and then click on OK.

If you are using a Web page template, a Settings tab will appear in the Format Picture dialog box. Select the Settings tab to change the Path and Use Absolute Path options in the Link area, which are available when GIF or JPEG graphic files are selected. (GIF and JPEG are the two graphic file types that can display on Web pages.)

The Settings tab also contains a Text option in the Picture Placeholder area. This option allows you to put a text reference for the graphic for those Web browsers that cannot display GIF and JPEG graphics. The text you type will be shown instead of the graphic.

Moving Graphics - To move a graphic, point to the middle of the graphic and drag it to the position where you want it on the page.

Figure 49.4 shows the next step in the Chopin Web page. The bulleted items have been turned into hyperlinks to Chopin sound files, and a picture of a conductor has been inserted so that the text flows to the right of the picture.

Creating a Graphic Hyperlink - To make a graphic a hyperlink anchor, click on the graphic to select it and then press Ctrl+K or click on the Insert Hyperlink button on the Standard toolbar. Fill in the Link to File or URL text box with the name of the destination file. You can test your graphic hyperlinks by previewing the page: Select File ➤ Web Page Preview from the menu bar; Internet Explorer will launch. You can then click on your graphic links to see if you are taken to the correct Web page or file. If you have not saved the document after the last changes, you will be required to do so.

After you have inserted a hyperlink onto a graphic, it is difficult to select it to delete, copy, move, or format the graphic, because you will activate the hyperlink. In order to select the graphic, right-click on the graphic and choose Hyperlink ➤ Select Hyperlink from the shortcut menu. Once you see the sizing handles, you can press the delete key or right-click to move or copy the graphic.

Saving the HTML File

When you save a file created with the Web Page Wizard or with the Blank Web page template, the default file format is as an HTML document with an extension of .htm or .html; this is the format needed to display this document on the World Wide Web.

To save a file as an HTML file, select File ➤ Save from the menu bar, or click on the Save icon on the Standard toolbar, or press Ctrl+S. When you save a file created with the Web Page Wizard, the Save As HTML dialog box appears with a suggested name in

FIGURE 49.4

Inserting graphics and hyperlinks are core Web Page techniques.

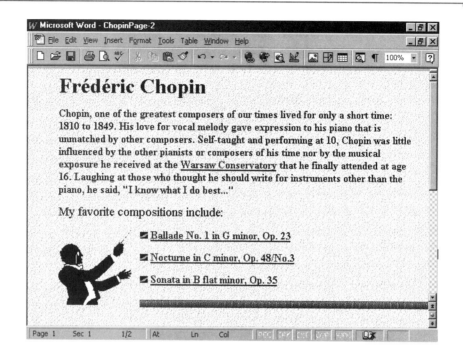

the File Name text box. (The suggested filename will be the first line under the Web page heading plus the .html extension.) Type over this suggested name with a more appropriate name for the file, if desired.

If you do not wish to save the file in HTML format at this time, choose File ➤ Save as Word Document; a .doc extension will be given to the file. You can then send the file to others who are using previous versions of Word or who don't have a Web browser program. Others can still view your page with its formatting.

Saving as a Web Template

If you have heavily customized a Web page, you can create a template from your own Web page. When you save the file, choose File ➤ Save As, and the Save As dialog box will appear. In the Save As Type text box area, click on the drop-down arrow and scroll to the top of the list of file types until you find Document Template (*.dot). When you select this file type, the various template folders are shown. Choose the folder in which to save your new template. Remember, you can save this template with a name that is different from the name you gave it when you saved it as an HTML or Word document. When ready, click on the Save button on the right side of the dialog box to complete the save action.

Your new template should now appear in the New dialog box when you start a new document by choosing File ➤ New. Your template will appear on the tab page that corresponds to the folder you saved the template in, as shown in Figure 49.5.

FIGURE 49.5

Use the Web Page Wizard to get you started and then save your page as its own template. It will appear in the New dialog box when you select File ➤ New.

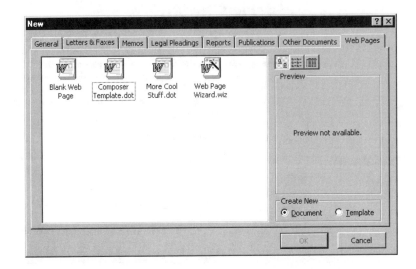

Web Page Preview

It is important as you are building your page to continuously view it through the browser, because this is the medium through which the world will be viewing your page. Various browsers may not display the same page in the same way; text may wrap differently when viewed in the browser than in the Word HTML template. And because of the room that the browser takes up on the screen, you may not be able to see as much of the page in one screen of the browser as you could when you created the page using a Web page template in Word.

In order to see how the Web page currently on the screen will look when displayed in Internet Explorer, you must first save the file as an HTML document. Once you save, select File ➤ Web Page Preview. The Internet Explorer browser will launch and bring up your page at the same time.

When the Save As HTML dialog box appears, the suggested name in the File Name text box is the first line that was typed under the Web Page heading plus the .html extension. Type over this suggested name if you want a different name and click on the Save button on the right side of the dialog box.

When you are in Web Page Preview mode, make sure you click on the links that you inserted into your page, so that you will get the same experience as your audience. Pause the mouse over each link and look at the filename at the bottom of the browser to make sure that your references appear correctly. Evaluate whether the page looks too busy or there is not enough writing on the page. Should there be more graphical elements? Try your pages out on colleagues to get their reactions.

When you have finished previewing, select File ➤ Close from Internet Explorer's menu. You will be returned to your HTML document.

WARNING

You do not always have to close Internet Explorer after previewing. Switch back to Word using the Taskbar and continue to make and save your changes to your Web page. When you switch back to Explorer, however, these changes will not be reflected until you refresh the file by pressing F5 or choosing View ➤ Refresh from the menu bar.

Web Page Design Elements

Your Web page is well on its way to being a superior product, but you still may want to change some of the design elements supplied by the Web Page Wizard or add other elements to your page. The items listed below are Web page design elements you may want to use, from the most frequently used elements to the least frequently used elements. Video is at the bottom of the list because the display of video files tends to be slow on most computers.

- Headings
- Font sizes
- Bulleted or numbered lists
- Graphics
- Background colors or textures
- Text colors
- Horizontal lines
- Hyperlinks
- Scrolling text

- Tables
- Sound
- Video

In our first Web page example, you found that you could change the heading styles supplied by the Web Page Wizard. There are six levels of headings that you can use on your Web pages. Click on the Style box on the Formatting toolbar and find the H1 through H6 heading styles--these are the styles that are supported by all of the browsers.

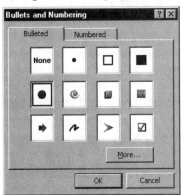

Bullets and numbering can be easily turned on and off using the Bullets and Numbering buttons on the Formatting toolbar. If you wish to have fancier bullets than the solid dots format supplied with Word, select your previously bulleted text and then choose Format ➤ Bullets and Numbering. Word displays a number of graphical bullets. These bullets are only available if your document is saved in HTML format.

You also have learned that you can insert graphics and clip art into a Web page by selecting Insert ➤ Picture from the menu bar or clicking on the Insert Picture icon on the Standard toolbar. When you save the file, the graphics are stored in separate files named image1, image2, and so on.

NOTE
When you save the Web page, the bullet is saved in the GIF format (Graphical Interchange Format), the file format needed to display a graphic in a hypertext Web document. Different bullet styles are named sequentially--Bullet1.gif, Bullet2.gif, and so on.

Adding Background Colors or Textures

The Web Page Wizard offers a number of background styles to you when you are going through the steps of creating your page. You may, however, want to use another background than the one supplied. It is very easy to change the background color or texture. Be careful, though, to pick a color that contrasts well with the text color you choose.

TIP
Different browsers may display the colors of your page differently. Continuously preview your page using the Internet Explorer (File ➤ Web Page Preview).

To change the background color of a Web page:

1. Select Format ➤ Background from the menu bar or click on the Background button at the right side of the Formatting toolbar.
2. Select a color and see if you like the effect. Also, evaluate how the color looks with your other Web page design elements. If you want to try another color, click on the Undo button or press Ctrl+Z to reverse the action and start again.
3. You also have available to you Fill Effects from the Background submenu. Select Fill Effects and scroll through the samples of background textures until you see one you like. Choose Other Texture from the bottom of the Fill Effects dialog box to search for graphic files that you downloaded from the Internet or purchased and installed on your computer.
4. Again, use the Undo button or press Ctrl+Z to reverse the action if you don't like the effect of your selections.
5. Select File ➤ Web Page Preview to see how this color looks in the Internet Explorer browser.

Adding Text Colors

The default color of the text on your page is black. If you change the text colors, you will also want to change the colors of your hyperlinks (the color before a hyperlink has been visited and the color after the hyperlink has been visited). To change the text color:

1. Choose Format ➤ Text Color.
2. Click on the drop-down arrow next to Body Text Color, and select a color that will complement your background color or texture.
3. In the Hyperlink list box, select a color for hyperlinks that have not been followed.
4. In the Followed Hyperlink list box, select a color for hyperlinks that have been followed.
5. Click on OK when finished.

Experiment with this dramatic combination: choose a Black background, Red body text color, Blue hyperlink color, and Yellow for followed hyperlinks. The red letters with the blue hyperlinks on a black background cause the blue hyperlinks to appear to stand-out—almost raised from the page. The yellow followed hyperlinks let the reader see quickly what their favorite path of links were.

NOTE

As you are experimenting and clicking links to see the hyperlink colors change, turn on the Web Toolbar so that you can use the Back and Forward buttons to return to your home page from files you jump to.

Horizontal Lines

Horizontal lines, also known as *rules,* are graphical elements used to separate sections of text so that the reader can understand the organization of the information on the page more easily. Not as popular as they once were, horizontal lines should be used sparingly, as they can be distracting. To insert a horizontal line into your page:

1. Click on the line where you want the horizontal line.
2. Select Insert ➤ Horizontal Line.
3. The Horizontal Line dialog box displays various horizontal line styles. Select the line you like and click on OK.
4. To size the horizontal line so that you can center it across the page, click on the horizontal line graphic and shorten the line by dragging the sizing handles toward the center of the screen.

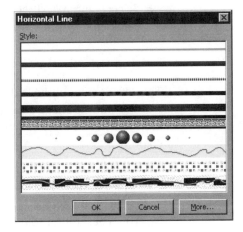

To delete, move, or copy horizontal lines, select the line and either press Delete or right-click the mouse and choose Cut or Copy.

Again, this design element is an actual file that accompanies your Web page. The filenames used for horizontal lines are Line1.gif, Line2.gif, and so on.

Hyperlinks

In Chapter 48, you learned how to insert hyperlinks of every type into your documents. These same hyperlink procedures are used for inserting hyperlinks into Web pages.

In a multipage Web site, you must link your pages together using hyperlinks so that readers can move through your site. It is a good idea to place a hyperlink graphic on each page at the bottom that links back to the home page of your site.

Hyperlink anchors are the graphics or text onto which a hyperlink has been inserted. When the viewer clicks the underlined and colored text or a graphic, the Web page or file is loaded into their browser.

Here's a quick run-through of the steps to create a hyperlink:

1. Position the insertion point where the URL or filename will appear, or select some words or a graphic to be the hyperlink anchor.
2. Press Ctrl+K or click on the Insert Hyperlink button on the Standard toolbar.
3. In the Insert Hyperlink dialog box, type the URL or filename of the destination file, which can be a Web page, a document, a graphic, or a sound or video file.
4. If the link is to information further down in the same page or in the destination file, use the Named Location section of the Insert Hyperlink dialog box to designate the location within the file (this must be a bookmark location in Word, a range name in Excel, or a slide number in a PowerPoint presentation).
5. Click on OK when done. The hyperlink color and underline will appear unless the anchor is a graphic.
6. To change the color of your hyperlinks, choose Format ➤ Text Colors.

Microsoft WordArt graphics don't translate to HTML coding; they are generally used in creating online documents that are not HTML documents. So for documents that will become Internet Web pages, use a third-party program such as Photoshop to create 3-D or rotated text as graphics. Save the graphic in GIF (Graphic Interchange Format) or JPEG file format (Joint Photographic Engineering Group), the file formats that browsers support to display graphics on a Web page.

There are also thousands of clip art graphic files already on the Internet. For example, Microsoft regularly adds new graphics to their site that you can download for use on your Web pages. Save these files on your computer and insert a hyperlink reference to them on your Web pages or insert them as a picture directly into the Web page.

Web Page Courtesy

It is considered good Web page form to have a couple of links to URLs outside of your site, because you don't want to force the viewer of your page to have to type the address of another URL themselves in order to get out. Links that you provide to other sites enhance the interest of your own site and let fellow surfers know you thought carefully about the content of your Web site. You can include links to search engines like Yahoo, Excite, or CNET, or to sites that you think reinforce or complement the purpose of your page(s). The previous section explains how to insert hyperlinks.

NOTE

For excellent examples of the current innovative thinking about Web site layouts and human interaction, see *Mastering Web Design* by John McCoy (Sybex, 1996).

Scrolling Text

The Internet Explorer 3.0 browser supports marquee-style scrolling text. If you have a short message you need your readers to pay attention to, use this feature—you're guaranteed your readers will read your message at least once. After the first reading, scrolling text becomes annoying, so don't set your text on an infinite loop. Have the message come into the page from the left or the right and then lock on the screen.

You can create a scrolling text message with more than a thousand words, but it is to your advantage to keep the message short. You can select different background colors to allow the text to stand out. Figure 49.6 shows the various options you can set for scrolling text.

FIGURE 49.6

Scrolling text is a great tool to use to grab a Web surfer's attention for a couple of seconds.

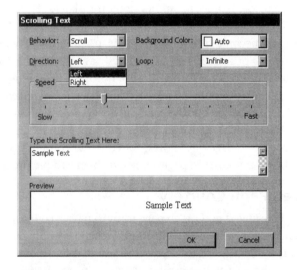

To insert scrolling text:

1. Click where you want to the text to appear.

2. Select Insert ➤ Scrolling Text.

3. In the Type the Scrolling Text Here text box, type a text message.

4. Slide the Speed dial to increase or decrease the speed at which the message scrolls across the screen.

5. In the Loop box, set the number of times the message scrolls across the screen. Use Infinite looping sparingly.

6. You can change the direction from which the message scrolls; the background color of the message area; and the behavior of the scroll. Click on OK when you have finished customizing your settings.

You can start and stop the play of the scrolling on your Web page by right-clicking on the scrolling text and choosing Stop from the shortcut menu. To delete the scrolling text select the scrolling text on the screen and the text box will appear with sizing handles. Choose Edit ➤ Clear to delete the box from the Web page design screen.

Your readers cannot delete your scrolling text from the Web page once it is loaded into their browser. You should set up scrolling text so that they don't want to delete it.

Using Tables to Control Page Layout

One of the most important elements in Web page design is the table, which is used to control the flow of text and graphics. Fourth-generation Web pages—pages with multiple columns of text, colored tables of contents on the left, and WordArt graphics—are the latest rage on the Web. Sites such as `http://www.cnet.com` offer examples of excellent Web design using the table features.

Because it is not possible to accurately line up text with graphics using HTML codes (there just are not enough design layout elements in the language), Web designers use HTML table codes to maintain multiple columns of text and graphics. The HTML coding for simple tables is overwhelming to the new Web designer and tedious at best for the experienced designer. If you were to code tables yourself, you would have to use table codes to define the beginning and end of the table, each column's beginning and end boundaries, and each row's beginning and end boundaries.

Fortunately, you can easily insert tables into your Web pages in Word. Start with the Blank Web Page template or let the Web Page Wizard get you started. To create evenly spaced columns, choose Table ➤ Insert Table. To draw your own split-cell table designs, click on the Draw Table button on the Tables and Borders toolbar. Whichever method you use, Word has taken a tremendous amount of tedium out of the process of using tables in HTML pages.

Using the Web Page Wizard for Table Design

The Web Page Wizard also offers you two columnar layouts that allow you to set up Web pages in table format. To set up a three-column Web page using the Web Page Wizard:

1. Select File ➤ New.

2. When the New dialog box appears, click on the Web Pages tab at the end of the template tabs.

3. Double-click on the Web Page Wizard. The Web Page Wizard dialog box appears.

4. Select 3-Column Layout from the Wizard list of layouts and click on the Next button at the bottom of the dialog box.

5. Decide the visual style you like. This example will use Elegant.

6. Click on the Finish button.

7. Click the mouse in the sample text area and type a heading.

8. Type text into the first column. Because this is a table, you can let the text wrap around to multiple lines. Continue typing information in the different cells of the table.

Figure 49.7 shows a table used to lay out a list of professional services that contains clip art in the bottom row. The border lines around the table were created by choosing Table ➢ Borders and clicking on the Grid option.

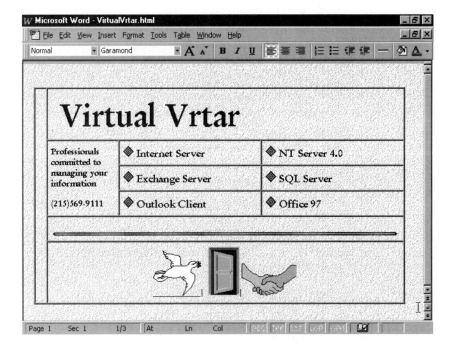

You can insert rows into a Web Page table by placing the insertion point on a table row and repeatedly clicking on the Insert Rows button on the Standard toolbar.

Adding Sound and Video to Web Pages

You can insert a hyperlink reference to a sound file (.wav) or video file (.avi), just as you would reference another Web page file. When a person clicks on a sound file, however, they must have the necessary sound equipment (sound card) to hear the .wav file.

Some browsers do not support the playing of video files. When you insert a video file into a Web page, its a good idea to have a static alternate image in case a browser does not support the video.

Word's Web Page Wizard and Blank Web Page templates have two commands in the Insert menu to handle sound and video: Background Sound and Video.

If you wish for a background sound to be played when a reader first clicks on your page, choose Insert ➤ Background Sound ➤ Properties. Click on the Browse button to find the .wav file that you want to start playing when the page loads into the viewer's browser. Decide how many times you want the sound file played—you have a range from 1 to 5 times or an infinite amount of times that the sound plays. Other sound files that the reader has the option to listen to should be inserted as hyperlinks into the Web page.

To insert a video file into a Web page:

1. Select Insert ➤ Video.
2. Click on the Browse button to find the name of an .avi video file.
3. Since some browsers don't support the viewing of videos, designate a "still" picture to represent the video in the Alternate Image box and type some text in the Alternate Text box that describes what the video displays. This will help visitors to your site get the point of the video if their browser does not support viewing video.
4. You can designate video options, such as how many times the video file plays and when the video should start playing. You can also show Video Controls that the reader can use to control the replay of the video. Check the Video Controls option to allow the reader more control of the video play.

5. When you've finished, click on the OK button. If you have not designated an alternate image, you are prompted by the program to do so.

6. The video graphic button appears in your page.

Preview your page through the Internet Explorer browser by selecting File ➤ Web Page Preview. Click on the video button to see how the video behaves in the browser.

Viewing HTML Source Code

As you learned in Chapter 4, all Web pages must be created using the Hypertext Markup Language (HTML), which is a coded system to represent structural layout, formatting styles, and hyperlinks. The coding is not hard to learn, but it can be tedious and error-prone to code a Web page in HTML. Word 97 has taken almost all the pain out of creating Web pages with the Web Page Wizard and the Blank Web Page templates. These templates allow you to focus on your creativity and formatting without worrying which codes to use.

Although it is not necessary to see the actual HTML codes in order to create beautiful Web pages in Word, veteran HTML Web page designers will want access to these codes so that they can quickly make changes to items such as graphic size or inspect the URLs at one glance.

To see the real HTML coding, select View ➤ HTML Source. A Web page template must be active on the screen for this command to be available. When you select this command, you are prompted to save the document before viewing the codes if you have made recent changes. To close the HTML Source code view, click on the Exit HTML Source button that appears as the first button on the Standard toolbar.

HTML codes are used to give the text of your document structure. Every blank line, heading, list, indentation, graphic, hyperlink, or font change is represented by a special code. For example, the browser will not know what to do with blank lines in your Web page if you merely press the Enter key between paragraphs. A code, <P>, is used to represent blank paragraph lines.

The six levels of headings are shown with beginning and ending codes of <H1>*Heading Text*</H1>. The slash in front of the ending H1 code represents the ending code. The text between these two codes will be in a large font because the H1 through H6 styles have been designed to represent decreasing heading font sizes and are a natural part of the HTML language.

NOTE

If you want more information about using HTML codes, use some of the search engines on the Internet to search for HTML primer information. Yahoo's site contains information that all Web page designers should know plus plenty of downloadable graphics and backgrounds. Point your browser to `http://www.yahoo.com` and type **HTML** in the search text box.

Looking at the Code

If you are not an experienced Web page designer, do not make changes to the HTML source code; the smallest error may cause the page to be display improperly. Do your designing using the Web page templates (Blank or Web Wizard).

Below is an example of HTML coding for a simply designed Web page created using the Blank Web Page template. The page, shown in Figure 49.8, uses the H1 and H2 styles. Three plain bullets are used; the last is a hyperlink to the Microsoft Web page.

FIGURE 49.8

A short and simple Web Page designed using a Web template.

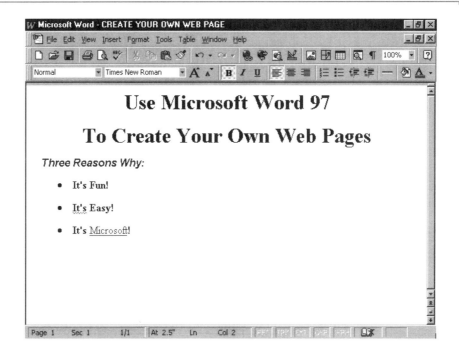

Once the page was typed and various heading styles applied, the page's HTML code could then be viewed (View ➤ HTML Source). Here's what it looks like:

```
<HTML>
<HEAD>
<META HTTP-EQUIV="Content-Type" CONTENT="text/html; charset=windows-
   1252">
<META NAME="Generator" CONTENT="Microsoft Word 97">
<TITLE>CREATE YOUR OWN WEB PAGE</TITLE>
<META NAME="Version" CONTENT="8.0.3311">
<META NAME="Date" CONTENT="7/11/96">
<META NAME="Template" CONTENT="D:\Office97\Office\HTML.DOT">
</HEAD>
<BODY TEXT="#000000" LINK="#0000ff" VLINK="#800080"
   BGCOLOR="#ffffff">

<H1 ALIGN="CENTER">Use Microsoft Word 97</H1>
<H1 ALIGN="CENTER">To Create Your Own Web Pages</H1>
<P><B><I><FONT FACE="Arial">Three Reasons Why:</P>

<UL>
<LI></I></FONT>It's Fun!</LI>
<LI>It's Easy!</LI>
<LI>It's </B><A HREF="http://www.microsoft.com/">Microsoft</A><B>!</
   LI></UL>

<P> </P></B></BODY>
</HTML>
```

Note the different beginning and ending codes. Also notice the beginning code at the very top, <HTML>, and its accompanying ending code at the very bottom, </HTML>; every Web page must begin and end with these codes. The body text code , <Body Text>, shows the hexadecimal notation for the color of the text, the hyperlinks, and the Web page background.

Getting Your Page to the Web

Now that you have created your page(s), in order to make them accessible to others on the World Wide Web, it is necessary to store the page and the accompanying graphic, sound, and video files on a host computer (server) that is configured with special Internet and World Wide Web software. Remember from the discussion in Chapter 4, computers that connect onto the Internet must be running TCP/IP software, and have a unique IP (Internet Protocol) address and a domain name registered with the InterNIC committee. Your Web pages must be stored on such a computer.

Storing Pages on the Corporate Network Server

If you are on a corporate network with a host computer connected to the Internet, all of the registration and Internet software issues have been handled by your network administrator and Webmaster. Talk to the administrator about the necessary procedures to copy the Web page files to the Web server. There will be specific directories on the server that the administrator will want to use to store Web pages and the accompanying files. The administrator also has security issues to manage and will have special *firewall* software that prevents hackers from depositing virus programs onto the network server. These security issues may limit whether the administrator will let you use interactive forms on your Web pages. Also find out how often you can update the pages and whether the administrator will allow you personally to upload the new changed Web pages to the Web server or whether the administrator wants to do it.

Planning Your Own Web Server

If you are the person who is going to become the Web server administrator, you must have access to a powerful host computer (the processor, hard disk, and memory specifications will vary depending on what you want the host server to do), your own direct (and costly) connection to the Internet, and a registered IP address and domain name. Also contact Microsoft's home page (http://www.microsoft.com) for information on obtaining Microsoft's Internet Information Server (IIS) software, or Netscape's home page (http://www.netscape.com) for information on obtaining Netscape's Web Server.

Web server software is necessary for configuring a computer to be connected to the Internet and display Web pages. Particularly look at the information for Microsoft's FrontPage software. This is a powerful Web page editor (like Word 97's Web page templates) and HTML page management tool. FrontPage also is the software that allows you to upload your Web pages directly to the server and handles a lot of server management security issues. Microsoft provides a lot of support to individuals working with the Internet and World Wide Web documents.

Storing Pages with an ISP

If you are an individual with a single modem dial-up connection to the Internet through an independent service provider (ISP), contact the ISP to find out what services they have for placing your Web pages on their host computer. There may be a small charge for the hosting in addition to the monthly Internet connection fees; but remember you won't have the expense of buying a Web server or the special Web server software and paying for and maintaining the connection to the Internet. The

ISP will manage all of this for you. The browser software may even be free, as in the case of Microsoft Internet Explorer.

A new category of businesses have emerged on the Internet that host Web sites for a small fee, but these companies are not your independent service providers. They buy host servers and connect to the Internet, and take care of maintaining, advertising, and updating Web sites on a regular basis. Search for the words *Web Site Hosting* on any of the Internet search engines to obtain the listing of companies that provide these services.

Storing Pages with an Online Service

If you are a member or are thinking of becoming a member of an online service, you should know that many online services offer Web page hosting for free (included in your normal monthly online fees)—America Online, CompuServe, and Prodigy allow you to store your own Web pages on their Internet servers as part of their monthly fees. You are allotted a certain amount of server disk space (sometimes between one and five Web pages are allowed); temporary IP addresses and domain names are then provided to you.

Listing and Marketing Your Web Site

Once your network administrator, online company, ISP, or hosting service gives you the URL address to your page, you are ready to give the location of your site to friends, business clients, or industry colleagues, so that they can find and view your Web page through the Internet. Your Web page should be listed on some of the major search engines within thirty days of obtaining your URL, as search engines generally update their indexes once a month. To make sure that different search engines list your page, contact them directly through the e-mail address listed on their home pages. Find out their procedures for listing your page in their indexes and find out how often they update their indexes.

If your Web page advertises services or products, you may need to do more than list your page with a search engine for indexing. The Internet public must learn about your services or products. You may want to investigate bulk e-mail list companies (use a search engine to find the words "bulk e-mail"). For a fee of approximately $50–$100, these companies will sell you e-mail addresses and software for sending mass messages to individuals.

Another method for gaining interest in your page is to join newsgroups. Use a search engine to search on the word "newsgroups" to find the lists of existing groups and steps for signing up. Newsgroups are groups of individuals who share common interests, such as Faulkner novels, wine, mud wrestling, Denzel Washington, and so on. Becoming part of a group of people who you know have a direct interest in your product will increase your sales opportunities. You must be careful, however, because direct solicitation of sales to these newsgroup members usually ends up with you being censored or disregarded as a correspondent. Spend some time as a corresponding member of a couple of newsgroups that could have an interest in your product or service category. After you have gained acceptance by this community, you can begin to talk more directly about your products or services.

There are also Internet marketing books and articles both online and printed that have flooded the Internet consciousness. Use a search engine to search for the words "Marketing on the Internet"; there are many, many pages of current information on how to successfully market the products that your Web site may be advertising.

Chapter

50

Displaying Office Documents on the Web

Displaying Office Documents on the Web

I n the preceding chapters, you learned a number of document management techniques—including techniques for creating hypertext documents (Chapter 48) and Web pages (Chapter 49), and for accessing files created in any of the Office 97 suite of products from the Web toolbar.

But what about data you have created in Office products that you want to display at a Web site? To re-create all of your Office information in HTML format would be frustrating, and the necessary and constant updating of the data would be overwhelming. To the rescue comes one of the best Web features of the Office programs: the Save as HTML command found on the File menus of Word, Excel, PowerPoint, and Access.

Office Documents as Web Pages

With Office 97's ability to create Web pages from existing documents, you can concentrate on creating spreadsheets, documents, and databases—not on being a Web designer. One click of the Save as HTML command on the File menu and your information can become available to hundreds of thousands of viewers.

The process for converting data to HTML format is different for each of the programs, even though the results are the same: Web-ready data. With Word 97, information is instantly converted when you select Save as HTML from the File menu, although the appearance may have to be adjusted once the Word data is viewed through a Web browser. For example, information that was tabbed in Word will not display correctly when viewed through a browser. (It is better to use the table feature instead of tabs to separate columns of data when saving data as HTML.) Headers and footers cannot be saved in HTML format in Word.

In Excel, choosing File ➤ Save as HTML launches an Internet Assistant Wizard that asks questions regarding the ranges of data to be saved as HTML. Large workbooks may be too wide for the Internet browser programs that display the HTML documents, so the Wizard helps you manage the look of this data. You can create an independent Web page with your Excel data or have the data inserted into an existing Web page. Header and footer information can be saved with an Excel HTML document.

PowerPoint uses a Save as HTML Wizard to convert a slide show to the needed Internet format. By far, PowerPoint has the best looking, Web-ready documents. A PowerPoint presentation saved in HTML format saves the entire slide show presentation into a folder on the hard disk. A table of contents page is automatically generated as the first page of the Web page presentation. Navigation buttons are created on each page that the user can use to move back and forward through the presentation. Each slide is shown in the graphical template style in which you created the presentation; in case the viewer's browser does not support graphics or graphics are too slow when loading, they can change to a text-only style.

Access uses a Publish to the Web Wizard, which lets you create a Web publication from a table, query, form, or datasheet and from reports. Businesses will want to utilize this extremely powerfulfeature to display any type of database information—for example, the amount of inventory of a product. This is database information that customers could view themselves instead of calling the distributor.

The Access Publish to the Web Wizard gives you your choice of saving an Access database to a Web server so that Web viewers can interact with the data themselves; you can also publish the data in static form so that it is only viewed at a Web site. There is tremendous potential for product selling using Access's Publish to the Web feature.

Word Documents on the Web

Because Word 97 is the official HTML editor, you can use a Web template to create your own Web pages easily (see Chapter 49). But if there are existing documents that would require a lot of data entry to put them into HTML format, use the Save as HTML command to instantaneously convert the information to the Web format. There may be some clean-up required on your part once you view the data through the browser.

To save a Word document in HTML format:

1. Open the existing Word document.
2. Make any heading and formatting changes.
3. Select File ➢ Save as HTML.
4. The Save as HTML dialog box appears and the existing name of the file appears in the File Name box with an .html extension.
5. Click on the Save button on the right side of the dialog box.
6. The file may appear somewhat different once the HTML formatting has been applied. You will not see the formatting codes unless you choose View ➢ HTML Source from the menu bar. Figure 50.1 shows how the file looks in Word as an HTML document.

FIGURE 50.1

When you convert a Word document to an HTML file, there may appear to be very little formatting changes until you see the data through the browser.

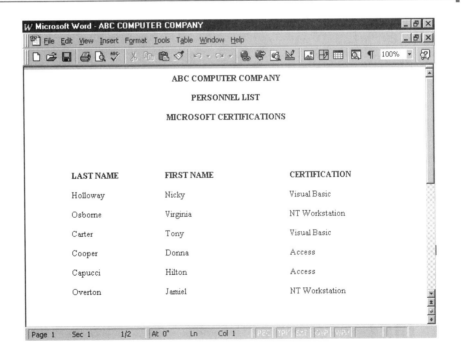

7. You will still need to see how the document looks through your Web browser. Note where you saved the file and start Internet Explorer: Click on the Start button, choose Programs, and select Internet Explorer. If your actual Internet connection starts, cancel it. You only want the browser to load without an accompanying Internet home page.

8. Choose File ➢ Open from the menu bar of the Internet Explorer browser and browse to find the document you saved in HTML format. Click the Open button on the dialog box. Figure 50.2 shows how the document shown in Figure 50.1 now looks through the browser—as you can see, there are problems.

FIGURE 50.2

This data is the same data as in Figure 50.1. Tabbed columns don't translate well into HTML codes.

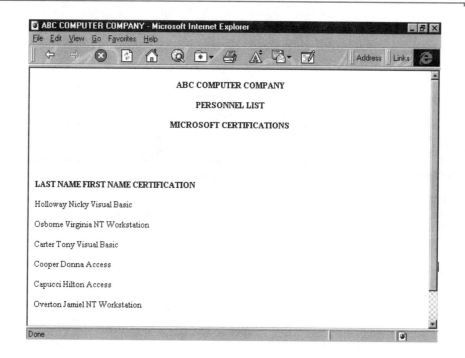

The problem is that the columns of information were tabbed in the Word document, and HTML codes don't do a good job of keeping the alignment. This information will have to be converted to a table so that the columnar alignment is preserved. Tables convert easily to HTML coding.

If this happens to you, find the original Word document and open it. To convert the tabbed text to a table, you will want to use the Convert Text to Table command on the Table menu. You can only have one tab stop between columns of data, so you *must* delete any additional tab stops between columns before you perform the conversion.

Figure 50.3 shows the data as a Web page after it was correctly tabbed, converted to a table, and again saved in HTML format.

PART

VII

Office 97 Internet
Tools

FIGURE 50.3

The table feature is the only reliable tool to use to preserve columnar layout for data that will be converted to HTML.

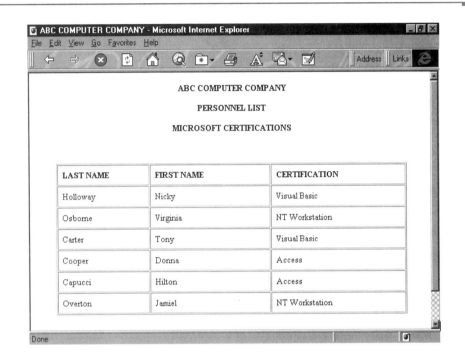

Excel Workbooks on the Web

Excel workbook data is also easily converted to HTML formatting, but Excel uses a Wizard to walk you through the process of converting your data. Because of the large workbooks that Excel can maintain, the data must be able to fit into the browser screen for proper viewing on the Web. The Internet Assistant lets you set the range parameters of the worksheet that define the areas you want saved as an HTML page.

To save Excel data in HTML format:

1. Open the Excel workbook with the data.

2. Select the range to be saved in HTML format.

3. Select File ➢ Save as HTML.

4. Step 1 of 4 of the Internet Assistant appears. Your data range is shown in the Ranges and Charts to Convert section. To add another range or a chart, select the Add button. The dialog box will collapse so that you can select an additional range or chart. Click on OK and the dialog box will expand again. Use the Remove button to eliminate ranges or charts from the list. The up and down Move buttons allow you to move a selected range up and down in the list. When you've finished, click on the Next button at the bottom of the dialog box.

5. In Step 2, you must decide if the data should become a Web page itself, complete with headers and footers, or be inserted into an existing Web page. The default is for an independent Web page. Click on the Next button.

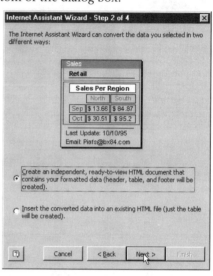

6. In Step 3, specify the title you want displayed on the title bar at the top of the Internet Explorer browser; it can be different than the filename for the workbook. This title is used by some search engines as a way of indexing your Web page.

7. In the Header section, type the words you want to actually appear on the Web Page above the data (this is more like the real title of the spreadsheet). It may be the same name you used for the title bar. You can also enter text in the Description Below the Header box. These lines of text will appear two lines below the header.

8. Step 3 also allows you to insert horizontal lines, the date the file was updated, and your Internet e-mail address—giving a professional look to your Web page. When you have finished with Step 3, click on the Next button.

9. Step 4 uses the default code page related to the U.S. and Western keyboard conventions. There is no need to change this if you reside in these areas of the world. If you use FrontPage and want to integrate this Web page with a FrontPage Web site, check that option.

10. You must save the spreadsheet file. Don't use the generic name supplied. Browse the folder in which you want to store the file and type a name for the file including the extension of **.htm**, or the file will be saved without an extension and the browser will be unable to locate it. Click on Finish.

11. To view this Web page as it will look through the browser, start the Internet Explorer and choose File ➢ Open from the browser's menu. Locate the file you just converted and saved and see how it will appear to other Internet Explorer users (see Figure 50.4).

FIGURE 50.4

*You can select
ranges of your
workbook and
save them as
HTML pages.*

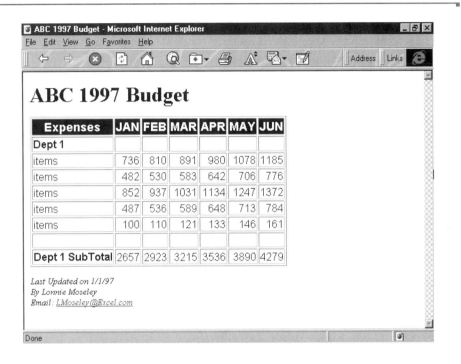

If the default country code appears at the top of your Web page and you don't wish
for it to appear, choose View ➢ Source from the Internet Explorer menu. The HTML
code for your Excel Web page appears in a Notepad window. You will be able to see the
country code at the top of all the other codes. Select it and press Delete. Your Web page
should then start with the <HTML> code and nothing else above it. Remember to save
the Notepad file (File ➢ Save) and then exit Notepad. Back at the browser, press F5 to
refresh the Web page so that Explorer will reread the page into memory.

If you don't want the Header centered on the Web page, select View ➢ Source and
find the Center codes around the header text (<CENTER> </CENTER>). Select and
delete each code. Save and exit the Notepad. To see the changes in Internet Explorer,
press F5 to refresh the page.

If the Save as HTML command did not appear in step 3, select Tools ➢ Add-Ins and
make sure that the Internet Assistant Wizard is checked. (An Add-In program is an
optional program provided with Excel. The information for the Internet Assistant is
stored in an Add-In program called Html.xla.)

If you check the Add-In option, but the Save as HTML command still does not
appear on the File menu, the Internet Assistant for Excel may not have been installed
when Office 97 was installed. To install it, choose Start ➢ Settings ➢ Control Panel ➢
Add/Remove programs and choose Microsoft Office 97.You will be asked to insert the

Office 97 disk. Click on the Add/Remove button on the Office 97 dialog box, then select Microsoft Excel from the list of options and click on the Change Option button. When you see the Excel options, select the Add-ins option and click on OK. Follow the Install procedures on the screen.

In case the Html.xla file was moved to the wrong directory, try this: Click on the Start button and choose Find ➢ Files or Folders, then search for the Html.xla file. If you find that it is on your hard disk, copy it to the Office\Library directory so that it appears in the Add-Ins list.

You can also download the Add-In Html.xla file directly from Microsoft's Web site.

PowerPoint Presentations on the Web

PowerPoint presentations brought to the Web are well produced. A Save as HTML Wizard walks you through the many steps needed to customize your presentation for the World Wide Web. You can insert Excel, Word, or Access data into a PowerPoint slide, and place the entire slide show at a Web site.

To convert a PowerPoint presentation to HTML, you must first create the presentation. To follow this example, open an existing presentation that you created or use PowerPoint's AutoContent feature to create a presentation. Then, follow these steps to save the presentation as an HTML file:

1. Save the presentation normally by choosing File ➢ Save and giving it a name.Then, select File ➢ Save as HTML from the PowerPoint menu bar.
2. When the Save as HTML Wizard dialog box appears, click on the Next button.
3. The New Layout option button is selected. (You can save the answers to all of the questions that will be asked on the subsequent series of dialog boxes in a layout file. This first question asks if you want to use a previously saved layout file. Since this is the first time you are using the Wizard, there is no existing layout file.) Click on the Next button.
4. The Select the Page Style option is already set to Standard. Click on the Next button.
5. The Graphic Type defaults to GIF (Graphics Interchange Format), one of the most frequently used graphic formats on the Web. JPEG (Joint Photographic Engineering Group) formats are better for displaying photograph images. For this example, use the default GIF selection. Click on Next.
6. When asked for the Graphic Size, use the default of640 by 480 as this is the display resolution of most computers. Below this option is the Width of Graphics list box. Change this option to allow the presentation to take up a larger or smaller

part of the screen. The default is $\frac{1}{2}$ Width of Screen, which is the best size. If you change to a larger width than $\frac{1}{2}$ width, the reader will have to scroll up and down to see all of the slide. Click on the Next button.

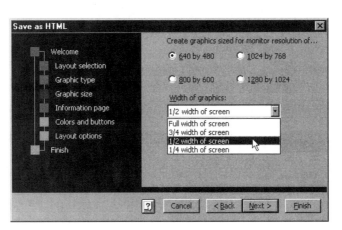

7. At the Information Page, indicate your e-mail address and your home page URL (if any). Click on the Next button.

8. When the Colors and Buttons page appears, you can select the page colors and button look.Change the background colors to whatever would complement your slide colors. You can also define the text and links colors. Click the on Next button.

9. When asked to Select a Button Style, choose the style you like and click on the Next button.

10. At the Layout options Page, decide where you want the navigation buttons that move the reader back and forward through the presentation. The default position is at the top of each slide. You can also include the slide notes on each of the Web pages.

11. When the Create HTML Directory In option appears, click on the Browse button to find the folder in which you want the presentation to be stored. The entire presentation will be stored as a subfolder within the folder you specify here. (You do not have to create the folder the presentation is stored in—the saved filename of your presentation will be used as the folder name.) Click on the Next button and then click on the Finish button.

12. When asked if you want to keep the responses you made during this Wizard walk-through, type a name for the Layout file and click on the Save button. Otherwise, click on the Don't Save button, in which case the answers to the questions will not be saved, but the presentation will still be saved as an HTML file. PowerPoint makes a folder and gives it either the name of the presentation or the generic

name *Presentation* if there is no saved filename. PowerPoint then begins to convert each slide to HTML. You will be notified when the presentation has been successfully saved.

13. Start or switch to Internet Explorer (Start ➢ Programs ➢ Internet Explorer) to see how the presentation will look through the browser. Choose File ➢ Open from the Explorer's menu and find the folder in which the presentation resides. Then, click on the Index.html file, as this is the first page of the presentation. Click on Open and OK. Figure 50.5 shows the first page of the PowerPoint presentation.

FIGURE 50.5

The PowerPoint Save as HTML Wizard produces a clickable presentation complete with a table of contents.

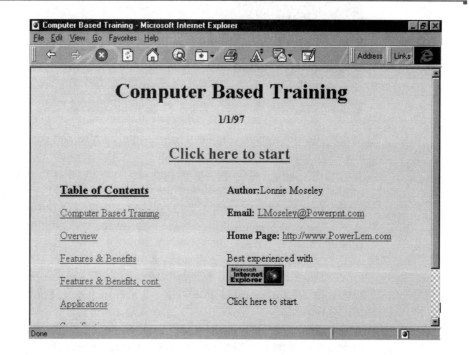

Start the presentation by clicking on the Click Here to Start button below the presentation title. The first slide appears with navigation buttons at the top (see Figure 50.6):

- The Next button (single right arrow) moves you forward slide by slide.
- The Back button (single left arrow) moves you back slide by slide.
- The First button (double left arrow) moves to the first slide in the presentation.
- The Last button (double right arrow) moves to the last slide.
- The Index button (with the letter I) returns to the page that contains the table of contents.

- The Home button only appears on presentations where the URL of a home page was designated in the Wizard.
- The Text button turns the presentation into a text-only show, if the reader is not able to view graphics or the graphic movement is too slow.

FIGURE 50.6

The slide show on the Web comes with its own navigational buttons.

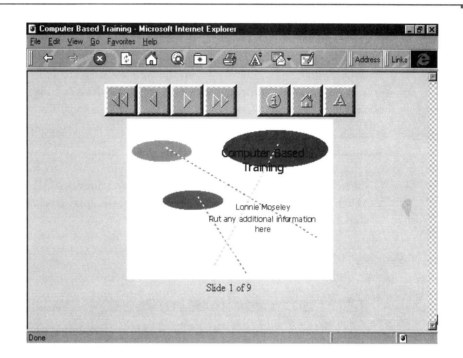

If you see changes that should be made to your presentation, switch back to or start PowerPoint and make changes to the slides, then save your changes. You will have to process the presentation through the Save as HTML Wizard again. If you saved the style information in a layout file (in step 12, above), you will be able to reuse it without again going through each step of the Wizard.

Access Databases on the Web

Information that resides in your Access database can be organized in many ways (tables, forms, queries, and reports) to provide answers to every audience—employees, clients, customers, colleagues, suppliers, shippers, creditors, managers, and so on. The ability to organize the information in large databases and display it easily on the Web will be a tremendous boon to businesses, corporations, and individuals. Given the proper security measures, you can even allow World Wide Web viewers to interact with your Access database by storing your databases on a Web server and publishing a form or table that viewers can type information into.

Before you can display a database on the Web, you must create, organize, and report the data correctly in Access (see Part 6 on Access for how to create and manage your Access database). Once you have the information in the format you want, you can use the Save as HTML Wizard to publish this data on the Web.

To show you how to publish data on the Web, we are going to use the sample North-wind database that accompanies the Access program, which contains made-up company and customer names. First, we will preview the report to be published on the Web:

1. Start Access 97, and in the opening Microsoft Access dialog box, make sure that the option Open an Existing Database is checked. The Northwind database is among the list of existing databases in the Program Files\Microsoft Office\Office\Samples folder. Select this file and click on OK.

2. When the opening Northwind description screen appears, click on the OK button to remove it.

3. The Northwind database window appears with the different object tabs: Tables, Queries, Forms, Reports, Macros, and Modules. Select the Reports tab to see the currently available reports.

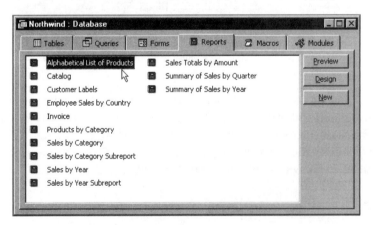

4. Double-click on the first report, Alphabetical List of Products (a five-page report). You will publish this report to the Web so that Northwind customers that have connections to the Internet can view the product offerings.

5. When you select the report, Access gives you a preview of the report; look at the layout and content. To zoom in and out of the report, click on and off of the report preview. To see the layout of the data from the report, click on the TwoPages or Multiple Pages button on the toolbar.

6. When you have finished viewing the report, click on the Close button on the toolbar to return to the database window. You are now ready to publish this report to the Web (make it an HTML file).

Converting Access Data to HTML

In the previous section, you identified the particular report that will be published to the Web. You can now use the Publish to the Web Wizard to make that report—the Alphabetical List of Products report—an HTML document that can be viewed on the World Wide Web:

1. Make sure the Northwind database is open. You do not need to have any particular object selected.

2. Select File ➢ Save As HTML from the menu bar.

3. The Publish to the Web Wizard dialog box appears with important information about the publishing capabilities inherent in the Wizard (see Figure 50.7).

FIGURE 50.7

The Publish to the Web Wizard describes the range of Web publishing possibilities in the opening dialog box.

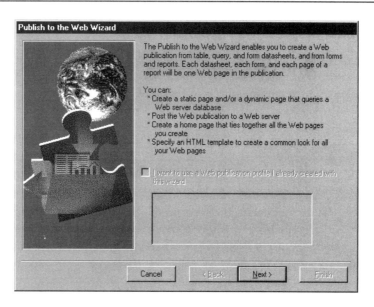

4. Take a minute to read the information in the dialog box and then click on the Next button.

5. When asked *What do you want to publish?*, click on the Reports tab in the sample database window and check the box next to Alphabetical List of Products. Then, click on the Next button at the bottom.

6. You will now be asked *What HTML document, if any, do you want to use as a default template?*. If you have an existing Web page template that has your company or personal HTML codes for address, e-mail, and navigation buttons, for example, specify it here as the default template. Then, click on the Next button.

7. Make sure that the option next to Static HTML is checked. You are going to create a *static* HTML page that readers can view but not interact with, as opposed to a *dynamic* page that readers can fill in themselves.

NOTE

If you want your pages to be dynamic, you must specify the name of a Web server. To find out the name of the server, check with your network administrator or Webmaster. You should also discuss security issues with the Webmaster, if you are going to allow readers on the Internet to store information on the Web server at your company.

8. Click on the Next button.

9. When asked *Where do you want to publish to?*, you must specify the folder in which you want the Access Web pages to reside. If you do not specify a particular folder, the My Documents folder will be used. Also, make sure that the option button next to *No, I only want to publish objects locally* is checked. This way, the pages will be stored on your local computer. (You can always copy these pages to your Web server administrator later, and the administrator can copy them to the Web server.) Click on the Next button.

10. Do not check the *Yes, I want to create a home page* box at this time. Click on the Next button to go to the last page of the Publish to the Web Wizard dialog box.

NOTE

The home page that Access creates is a table listing the names of the multiple objects (tables, reports, or forms) from which the Web pages were generated. The home page that Access creates is not very glamorous, and you could do a better job yourself using the Web Page Wizard in Word 97 to create links to multiple Access Web pages.

11. When asked if you want to save the Wizard's answers to a publication profile, check on the box next to Yes. This way, if you need to resave the Alphabetical List of Products as HTML again, the Publish to the Web Wizard will not have to ask for answers that you gave already. Thus, you will be able to easily update the report on the Web as you add information to your Access database.

12. Type **Product Spec** for the Profile Name and click on the Finish button. The Wizard will begin processing the Web pages for the report. You can see the processing of each of the five pages of this report in the Printing dialog box.

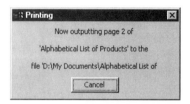

Now that you have saved the report pages as HTML pages, you can do anything with them—including opening them in Word and working exclusively with them as online documents without publishing them to the Internet at all.

Viewing Access Data in Internet Explorer

Now that you have created Web pages from an Access report, you will want to view them through the eyes of your Internet Explorer browser to make sure that they are acceptable for viewing by your corporate customers on the World Wide Web. You published these pages locally (on your own computer) in a folder you specified to the Publish to the Web Wizard.

To view the pages through the Internet Explorer browser, follow these steps:

1. Start or switch to the Internet Explorer (Start ➢ Programs ➢ Internet Explorer).
2. Select File ➢ Open from the Explorer's menu.
3. On the small Open dialog box, type the name or click on the Browse button and find the name of the folder you specified during the Publish to the Web process.
4. The browser will show you a complete list of all the HTML files you have stored in that folder.
5. Double-click on the Alphabetical List of Products.htm file to open it in the browser, then click on the OK button. Figure 50.8 shows the Access report in the window; at the bottom of (each page) of the report, there are Navigation hyperlinks to the other pages of the report. Click on the Next link at the bottom of the report to move through it, page by page. The Previous link moves you back page by page, and the First and Last links jump you to the first and last pages of the report.

FIGURE 50.8

When the Access Publish to the Web Wizard creates HTML pages from your data, it places navigational links at the bottom of each page of the data.

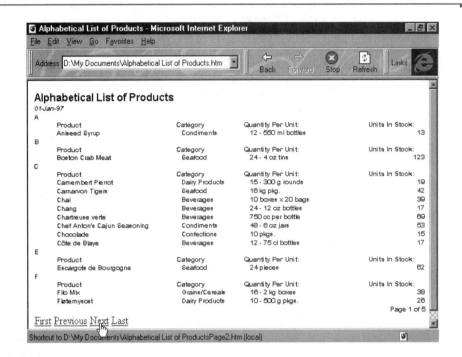

> **TIP**
>
> You can open any HTML file in Word 97 and make changes to it using regular word processing tools. You can also view and modify the source HTML code from within Word by choosing View ➤ HTML Source. Remember to save the file after you update the HTML codes.

6. When you have finished viewing the report, exit the browser.

If you need to make formatting changes to the report that are not Access-related changes, open the Access HTML document in Word 97. The data will appear in a table format, ready for you to make your formatting changes. The pages are ready to be integrated with the rest of your Web site and given to your Web administrator for storing on the Web server.

Appendix

A

Installing Microsoft Office

INSTALLING MICROSOFT OFFICE

There are two editions of Microsoft Office 97 for Windows 95/NT— Standard and Professional. The Standard Edition includes Word, Excel, PowerPoint, Outlook, Microsoft Binder, and Microsoft Photo Editor. The Professional Edition adds Access to the group.

There are a few things you should know before you begin your installation. For one, if you are upgrading from a previous version of Office, you don't need to remove the existing version of Office. Office 97 will install itself to a new location on your hard disk, and you can choose later whether to remove the older version. Documents, templates, and other files you created using the older version of Office will be preserved.

If you know that you wish to overwrite the old version of Office 97, select the same directory folder as the old version when prompted to designate where Office should be installed. Make sure that you have backed up important templates (especially Normal.dot). Even though there are assurances that old templates will be preserved, you should take no chances.

Before you begin the installation, you should take a moment to do a little inventory to make sure the installation will be easy and hassle-free.

- Make sure you have all the installation diskettes or CD-ROM.

NOTE
Important: On the back of the CD there is a CD key number that you will be required to provide at some point in the installation. Write it down so you have it handy before you begin installation.

- Be sure your computer is already running Windows 95 or Windows NT. Office 97 will not run under earlier versions of Windows.
- If you are installing from a CD, make sure your CD-ROM player is working properly in Windows 95.
- Make sure you have enough space on your computer to install Office 97. For a Typical install without Access, you need approximately 80MB of space on your

hard drive. Access requires an additional 39MB. Regardless of the type of installation you choose, you will also need about 20MB to 40MB of free space *after* installing Office 97, to allow space for Windows 95 to work properly and space for you to save your files.

If you do not have enough disk space, you can install parts of Office now, then install more later—after you make room on your hard disk by using the Windows Explorer to find files that can be deleted or sent to another drive.

TIP

If you really tight on free space, Office 97 can be run from the CD, so that you are actually using the files on the CD instead of having the programs installed on your hard disk. With this approach, Office will still need to copy approximately 24 MB of files to your Windows 95 folder, but not the entire Office suite of program files.

A few last things to do before you start installing:

- Close any open programs.
- Set aside enough time to complete the installation. A typical Office 97 installation can take anywhere from 30 minutes to an hour, depending on your machine.

Running Setup the First Time

To start the installation of Office for Windows for 95:

1. The first step depends on the installation medium:

Installing from the CD—Insert the Microsoft Office 97 CD in the CD-ROM drive.
Installing from floppy disks—Insert Disk 1 into your floppy disk drive (A or B).
Installing from a network location—Connect to the proper network location, using Network Neighborhood from the Windows Desktop to search for shared drives. Your network administrator can assist you with this.

NOTE

You can find additional information about installing across the network by reading the Office 97 resource kit, available for downloading from Microsoft's Web site at http://www.microsoft.com.

2. Click on the Start button on the Taskbar and choose the Run command. Designate the drive letter from which you will be installing the Office, by typing the drive letter, a colon, and then **Setup**. Figure A.1 shows the Run dialog box for a CD-ROM installation.

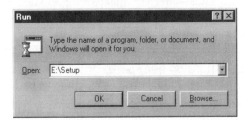

3. When the Setup Welcome screen appears, Microsoft reminds you to close any open files before continuing with Setup. Once you are ready to continue, click on the Continue button at the bottom of the dialog box, as shown in Figure A.2.

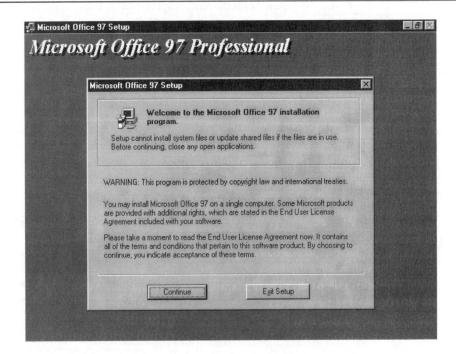

4. Enter your name and organization in the Name and Organization Information dialog box. Microsoft uses this information for future installs.

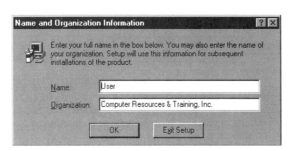

You will be asked to confirm the name and organization information. If there are any typos, or you just wish to change the information, click on the Change button and Setup will redisplay the dialog box. Click on OK.

5. A key or ID number is needed to authorize the installation. This step depends on if you are installing from a CD, floppy disks, or a network:

Installing from the CD-ROM—A dialog box will appear asking you for your CD Key number. Enter your 10-digit CD Key number in the slots provided if you are installing from a CD-ROM and click on the OK button. You will be presented with a Product ID verification dialog box. Click on the OK button.

Installing from floppy or from a network drive—A dialog box will appear with your Product ID number. This information will be important if you need to contact Microsoft about any problems you are having with Office 97. Although you may want to write down your Product ID number, note that this number will always appear on the About dialog box (Help ➢ About) for each Office 97 application. Click on OK on the Product ID dialog box.

Designating the Installation Folder

When prompted to verify the folder into which Office for Windows 95 will be installed, check to see if the default folder path is agreeable to you. You can choose to Change Folder, Exit Setup, or choose OK to continue. If you click on the Change Folder button, you can install Office to another folder on the same drive or on another drive, even a network drive.

Figure A.3 shows the Microsoft Office 97 Setup dialog box.

Office allows you to change the folder where you want the installation to occur.

If the settings are correct, click on the OK button.

Choosing a Type of Install

Office now asks you what kind of installation you want to perform. There are three choices: Typical, Custom, or Run from CD-ROM. The Typical installation is generally the wisest choice, if you have the required amount of free disk space (80MB to install the Standard Edition and an additional 39MB for Access). If you don't have enough space for a typical install, a Custom install will allow you to narrow down the installation to the components that you absolutely need installed. Figure A.4 shows the installation options and the disk space required for each.

TIP

If you want to install *everything*, you must choose the Custom installation, which allows you to install more components than the Typical installation.

If you do not want the Office for Windows 95 programs on your hard disk at all, you can run the entire suite from the CD. Only a few important files will be copied to the hard disk. Of course, to run any of the Office programs using this installation method, you must keep the CD in the drive whenever you wish to use Office 97.

FIGURE A.4

*Office for
Windows 95
Installation
options*

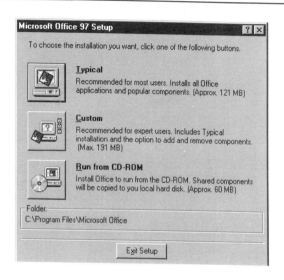

Typical

In a Typical installation, the programs and tools most commonly used in Office will automatically be installed on your computer. Your main programs will be installed, along with some frequently used tools. Choose this installation option if you are a first-time user of Office, or if plan to use only the most common features of Office.

Custom

Choose Custom installation if you plan to install either more or less options than are provided by the other installations. For instance, you can choose Custom installation to install everything that comes in the box. You can also use Custom installation if you want to install certain tools but leave out others. (Use this latter option only if you are experienced with Office, and know what a particular tool or item does.)

One particularly good use of Custom is to spread out your programs to several drives. For instance, if your C drive is nearly full, but you have a D drive that is almost empty, you can install some files on C, and the rest on D.

Figure A.5 displays the Custom dialog box. Note that there is not enough disk space on Drive C for all of the options to be installed, so some options will need to be deselected or installed to another drive.

If you want to install all of the Office 97 components, just click on Select All. Alternatively, to install only certain tools, select the option that would include the tools you want, and then click on Change Option. In the Change Option dialog box, you can turn on and off the installation of additional components for the selected option.

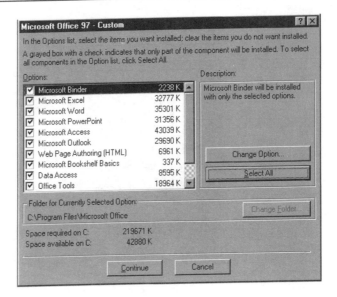

Run from CD-ROM

If you do not have the space to install Office, do not select the Typical or Custom installations. Instead, use the Run from CD-ROM option on the Microsoft Office 97 Setup dialog box, so that the Office suite will run primarily from the CD and not your hard disk. There is still a minimum requirement of 60MB of disk space for files that Office needs to keep on your hard disk.

TIP

It is usually faster to run the suite from your hard disk instead of the CD-ROM drive (depending how fast your CD-ROM drive is).

Reinstalling Office 97

If you leave anything out of Office 97 in this initial setup, and you find later that you need it, you can always run Setup again from the original disks or from the network folder where Office was installed:

1. Click on the Start button and choose Run from the Start menu. The Run dialog box will appear.

2. In the Open box, type the drive letter (the letter and a colon) to tell Windows where to find the CD-ROM, the floppy, or the network folder. Type the word **Setup** and click on OK. The Installation Maintenance dialog box will appear.

3. Choose Reinstall to install another entire version of the Office suite, or choose Add/Remove to add or take out options.

Figure A.6 displays the Installation Maintenance Program screen.

FIGURE A.6

*Add or remove
components or
reinstall the
Office suite in
the Installation
Maintenance
dialog box.*

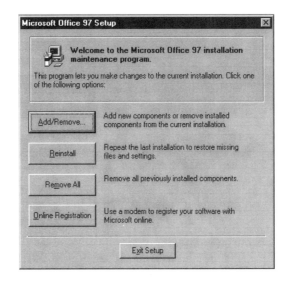

Installation Announcements

After you have started the installation, a meter shows the progress as Setup continues to copy files from your source drive onto your hard drive or network. In addition, various prompts will appear during the installation asking you for further information about what you want installed or requiring you to do something.

If you chose a Typical Setup, Office will ask you if you want to install a number of options, including Microsoft Map and Web Page Authoring. If you have sufficient space on your hard drive, choose Yes; if you don't have sufficient space, or are unsure about the amount of space you have, click on No. You can always install it later, if you need it.

If you are running the installation from floppies, Setup will install all of the files from the first diskette and then prompt you to load another diskette into your floppy drive. If you did not choose to install the entire Office 97 program, Setup may skip a diskette in the series. Don't be alarmed—Setup knows where to find the proper programs, and will prompt you for the needed diskette to insert in your floppy drive. If you place the incorrect diskette in the drive, Setup will let you know.

During the installation process, you will also be presented with colorful dialog boxes describing Office 97 features that you will enjoy using, as shown in Figure A.7.

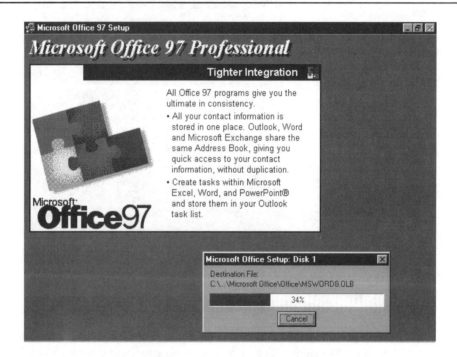

After Office has completed its installation, a dialog box reminds you to fill out and send (or transmit via modem) your registration of the software (see Figure A.8).

After this, you can start using Office as you like. Click on the Start button on the Taskbar and then choose Programs to find the Microsoft Office folder that contains your Office 97 programs. Within the Office folder you will see the different icons for each of the Office programs; select the program you wish to start.

FIGURE A.8

*Finish Installa-
tion dialog box*

Installing Access Separately

Access is only included in the Professional Edition of Office, not the Standard Edition. If you bought the Standard Edition, you may purchase Access and install it separately. The instructions below will help you to do just that.

Access requires approximately 39MB of disk space. The procedures for installing Access are identical to those for installing the Standard Edition of Office:

1. Insert the CD-ROM version or Disk 1 of Access into the appropriate drive. Click on the Start button on the Taskbar and type the drive letter, a colon, and **Setup** in the Run dialog box. The Access installation will begin.
2. The Name and Organization dialog box will appear with the information you entered when you installed the Standard Edition. If this information is still the same, click on the OK button. Access verifies that the information is correct and shows you the Product ID dialog box.
3. After searching for installed components, the Setup menu returns for one final verification of the drive on which you want to Access to be installed. Click on OK and begin the installation.

Installing Office 97 from the Network

If you have a license from Microsoft to install Office 97 on more than one client computer, there are two ways you can approach the installation: you can distribute the Office CD-ROM or disks to each end user, or you can install Office on a network and have each end user install from there.

To have users install from the network, you should first tell each user which network drive contains the software files or the shared CD-ROM drive. Then, each user should:

1. Choose Start from the Taskbar and click on the Run command.
2. At the Open text area, type the letter of the shared Network drive where the Office files reside.
3. Type the word **Setup,** then press Enter or click on the OK button.

Alert the user as to the folder they should name when prompted to designate where Office should be installed. When prompted, the user must also know which drive letter to use for their hard disk, in case there are multiple hard disk drive letters. The installation will proceed normally.

If you want additional information on performing network installations, read the online Office 97 Resource kit information that can be downloaded from Microsoft's Web site at http://www.microsoft.com.

Master's

Reference

MASTER'S REFERENCE

Alignment

Alignment refers to the position of the text within a cell, text box, or the margins or paragraph indents on the page. Data can be aligned within your document both horizontally and vertically.

Aligning Data Horizontally

Use the buttons described below, found on the Formatting toolbar in Excel, PowerPoint, and Word, to horizontally align your data.

- Click on the Align Left button to align the data in selected cells in an Excel worksheet along the left edges of the cells, selected text within a text box along the left edge of the text box in PowerPoint, or the selected paragraph along the left margin in a Word document.

- Click on the Center button to center the selection within selected cells, within a text box, or between the left and right margins.

- Click on the Align Right button to align the selection along the right edges of cells, within a text box, or along the right margin.

- Click on the Justify button to align selected data evenly between the cell edges, the sides of a text box, or the left and right margins.

Alternatively, use the following commands to align a selection:

- In Excel, choose Format ➣ Cells (Ctrl+1) and select the Alignment tab. In the Horizontal drop-down list, choose Left (Indent), Center, Right, or Justify. Choose OK.

- In PowerPoint, choose Format ➣ Alignment, and then choose Left (Ctrl+L), Center (Ctrl+E), Right (Ctrl+R), or Justify (Ctrl+J).

- In Word, choose Format ➣ Paragraph and select the Indents and Spacing tab. In the Alignment drop-down list, choose Left (Ctrl+L), Centered (Ctrl+E), Right (Ctrl+R), or Justified (Ctrl+J). Choose OK.

Aligning Data Vertically

To align data vertically in the active cell or text box:

- In Excel, choose Format ➣ Cells (Ctrl+1) and select the Alignment tab. In the Vertical drop-down list, choose Top, Center, Bottom, or Justify.

- In Word, choose File ➣ Page Setup, click on the Tables and Borders button on the Standard toolbar, and then click on the Align Top, Center Vertically, or Align Bottom button.

To align text vertcally on a page in a Word document, you must first create a separate section for it, because all the text in a section has the same vertical alignment. You can insert a section break anywhere in your document.

To align a paragraph vertically on a page, follow these steps:

1. If necessary, choose Insert ➣ Break ➣ Next Page to create a section break both before and after the text that is to be vertically aligned.

2. Position the cursor in the section, and then select File ➣ Page Setup to display the Page Setup dialog box.

3. Select the Layout tab.

4. In the Vertical Alignment drop-down list, choose one of the following options:

   - Select Top to align the top line of text along the top margin.

   - Select Center to center the text between the top and bottom margins.

   - Select Justified to align the text along both the top and bottom margins.

5. Choose OK in the Page Setup dialog box.

Auditing

Use buttons on Excel's Auditing toolbar to trace cell dependents, cell precedents, and errors in a worksheet. The Auditing tools display *tracer arrows* from the active cell to any cells containing related data.

Tracer arrows point in the direction of the data flow (always toward the formula). The dot at the end of a tracer arrow indicates a value that is a direct dependent or precedent. Tracer arrows appear in blue on a color monitor, and with a worksheet icon attached if a dependent or precedent is in a different worksheet.

To display the Auditing toolbar, choose Tools ➢ Auditing ➢ Show Auditing Toolbar.

Tracing Dependents

Cells that contain formulas referring to other cells are called *dependents*. A cell that contains a formula that refers to the active cell is called a *direct dependent*. An *indirect dependent* is a cell that refers to a direct dependent or another indirect dependent.

1. Click on the Trace Dependents button on the Auditing toolbar or choose Tools ➢ Auditing ➢ Trace Dependents to display tracer arrows to all direct dependents.

2. Click on the Trace Dependents button or choose Tools ➢ Auditing ➢ Trace Dependents again to display the first level of indirect dependents.

3. Repeat step 2 for each subsequent level of indirect dependents you want to trace.

Click on the Remove Dependent Arrows button to remove the arrows that are farthest away from the active cell. Click again to remove each subsequent level of arrows.

Click on the Remove All Arrows button on the Auditing toolbar or choose Tools ➢ Auditing ➢ Remove All Arrows to remove all the arrows from the worksheet.

Tracing Errors

When the formula in a cell displays an error message, trace the error to discover the source of the values that produced the error.

1. Select a cell that contains an error value.

2. Click on the Trace Error button on the Auditing toolbar, or choose Tools ➢ Auditing ➢ Trace Error.

Tracing Precedents

Cells from which a formula obtains values are called *precedents*. A cell that is referred to by the formula in the active cell is called a *direct precedent*. An *indirect precedent* is a cell that is referred to by a direct precedent or another indirect precedent.

1. Click on the Trace Precedents button on the Auditing toolbar or choose Tools ➢ Auditing ➢ Trace Precedents to display tracer arrows to all direct precedents.

2. Click on the Trace Precedents button or choose Tools ➢ Auditing ➢ Trace Precedents again to display the first level of indirect precedents.

3. Repeat step 2 for each subsequent level of indirect precedents you want to trace.

To remove the farthest set of precedent arrows from the active cell, click on the Remove Precedent Arrow button. Each additional click removes the subsequent level of tracer arrows.

AutoCorrect

With Microsoft Office's AutoCorrect feature, you can save an abbreviation for often-used text or a graphic, such as a company name or logo. You can then type the abbreviation followed by a space to insert the text or graphic in a document.

Microsoft Office comes with many AutoCorrect entries already defined.

Changing an AutoCorrect Entry

Access, Excel, PowerPoint, and Word allow you to edit AutoCorrect entries. An entry you insert in any application is shared by all of them.

To edit an AutoCorrect entry, choose Tools ➢ Auto-Correct to display the AutoCorrect dialog box, and then use any of the following methods:

- To add the same entry with a different name, select the entry in the Replace Text As You Type list box, type the new name for the entry in the Replace text box, and then choose Add.

- To change a plain text entry's contents, select the entry in the Replace Text As You Type list box, type the new contents for the entry in the With text box, and then choose Replace.

- To edit a formatted text entry, make the necessary changes in the document, and then select the entire entry and display the Auto-Correct dialog box. Type the name of the entry in the Replace text box, and then choose Replace. Choose Yes to confirm that you want to redefine the entry, and then choose OK.

- To delete an AutoCorrect entry, select the entry in the AutoCorrect dialog box's list box and choose Delete.

Creating an AutoCorrect Entry

Each AutoCorrect entry must be defined with a name you create. The name can contain as many as 31 characters, but it cannot contain any spaces. Do not use a real word as the name of an Auto-Correct entry, because when you type the word followed by a space, the AutoCorrect entry will be inserted rather than the word.

In Word, you can specify whether text selected as replacement text is entered as plain text or formatted text. Plain text has no formatting, and the entry can contain up to 255 characters. Formatted text is saved with the formatting applied in the document and can be as long as you wish, depending on the memory available in your computer.

1. If necessary, select the text (for a paragraph or long entry) or the graphic for which you want to create a name.

2. Choose Tools ➤ AutoCorrect to display the AutoCorrect dialog box.

3. If necessary, select the Replace Text As You Type checkbox.

4. Type the name (an abbreviation) of the entry in the Replace text box.

5. If you did not select text in step 1, type the text you want to enter each time the AutoCorrect entry name is typed in the With text box.

6. If you selected text in step 1, choose either Plain Text or Formatted Text.

7. Choose Add to insert the entry in the list box.

8. If necessary, repeat steps 4 through 7 to create additional AutoCorrect entries.

9. Choose OK in the AutoCorrect dialog box.

To turn off the AutoCorrect feature, clear the Replace Text As You Type checkbox, and then choose OK in the AutoCorrect dialog box.

AutoFormat

Both Excel and Word have an AutoFormat feature. Excel's AutoFormat and Word's Table AutoFormat allow you to select one of the built-in formats for the data in a worksheet or table. Word's AutoFormat can analyze your document and select one of the built-in document formats for you.

Using AutoFormat in Excel and Table AutoFormat in Word

Excel's AutoFormat and Word's Table Auto-Format automatically apply number formats, data alignments, fonts, and borders and patterns, and change the row height and column width as necessary in a selected table.

When you use AutoFormat, Excel automatically selects an active area of the table and displays the AutoFormat dialog box. If the Excel data contains any blank rows or columns, you must select all the cells in the range before you choose Format ➤ AutoFormat.

To use AutoFormat or Table AutoFormat:

1. Select one cell in a column or row of data, and then choose Format ➤ AutoFormat in Excel or Table ➤ Table AutoFormat in Word.

2. Select the name of a format in the Table Format or Formats list box.

3. In Excel, choose Options to display the formatting options.

4. Clear the checkboxes of any of the types of formatting you do not want to change in the Formats to Apply area.

5. In Word, select the row or column to which special formats are to be applied in the Apply Special Formats To area.

6. Choose OK in the AutoFormat or Table Auto-Format dialog box.

Using AutoFormat in Word

Use Word's AutoFormat feature to apply consistent formatting to a document. With AutoFormat, you type the text, then Word analyzes the document and suggests styles to apply to each part of the document. Word uses any formatting you have already applied to help in the analysis. If you accept Word's formatting suggestions, the corresponding styles are applied to the document text.

AutoFormat applies only Word's built-in styles. To have AutoFormat apply your own styles, redefine Word's built-in styles with your own formats.

To have Word quickly analyze and format the current document or selected text, click on the Auto-Format button on the Standard toolbar. Alternatively, choose Format ➤ AutoFormat, select AutoFormat Now, select General Document, Letter, or Email in the *Please select a document type to help improve the formatting process* drop-down list, and then choose OK.

To have Word analyze and suggest appropriate formatting for a document or selected text:

1. Place the insertion point anywhere in the document or select the text you want to format.

2. Choose Format ➤ AutoFormat, and then choose AutoFormat and Review Each Change in the AutoFormat dialog box.

3. Select General Document, Letter, or Email in the *Please select a document type to help improve the formatting process* drop-down list, and then choose OK.

4. Choose one of the following actions:

- Choose Accept All to agree to all the changes Word has proposed.

- Choose Reject All to discard all the formatting changes.

- Choose Review Changes to display the marked changes and the Review AutoFormat Changes dialog box.

- Choose Style Gallery to display its dialog box.

Using AutoFormat to Review Changes

If you choose Review Changes in the AutoFormat dialog box, Word inserts the following marks in the document:

- A blue ¶ at the end of the paragraph indicates that Word applied a style.

- A red ¶ indicates a deleted paragraph mark.

- Deleted characters appear with a red - (strikethrough character).

- Inserted characters appear with a blue _ (underline character).

The following options are available in the Review AutoFormat Changes dialog box:

- Choose ← Find to return to the previous AutoFormat change.

- Choose → Find to proceed to the next Auto-Format change.

- Choose Reject to reject the highlighted change.

- Choose Hide Marks to display the document as it will appear if all the changes are accepted, or Show Marks to display the hidden change marks in the document.

- Choose Undo to reverse the last rejected change.

When you are finished reviewing the changes, choose Cancel to return to the previous AutoFormat dialog box, and then choose Accept All or Reject All to specify what to do with all the changes you did not reject during the review.

AutoSummarize

Use Word's AutoSummarize feature to automatically create a summary using the important points in a document. AutoSummarize identifies the key points in a document by analyzing the sentences that contain the words used most frequently. Auto-Summarize is useful for structured documents such as reports, articles, and scientific papers.

AutoSummarize works best when the Find All Word Forms tool (installed by default) is installed. In addition, text that is formatted with the No Proofing option in the Language dialog box and text in a language other than English cannot be automatically summarized.

1. Choose Tools ➤ AutoSummarize to display the AutoSummarize dialog box.

2. In the Type of Summary area, select one of the following options to specify the appearance of the summary:

   • Choose Highlight Key Points to have AutoSummarize highlight the key points in the document without hiding any existing text.

   • Choose *Create a new document and put the summary there* to have AutoSummarize open a new document and insert a copy of the key points in it.

   • Choose *Insert an executive summary or abstract at the top of the document* to have AutoSummarize place a copy of the key points at the beginning of the document.

   • Choose *Hide everything but the summary without leaving the original document* to have AutoCorrect apply hidden text format to all the document text except for the key points.

3. Specify the length of the summary in the Percent of Original drop-down list. A larger percentage covers more key points in the document; a smaller percentage covers fewer key points.

4. Select the Update Document Statistics checkbox (selected by default) to have AutoSummarize copy the keywords and the sentences that contain the most frequently discussed points to the Keywords and Comments text boxes on the Summary tab in the document's Properties dialog box.

5. Choose OK. The AutoSummarize toolbar appears.

6. If necessary, adjust the length of the summary using the options available on the AutoSummarize toolbar.

AutoText

Use AutoText to quickly insert entries you have saved in a Word document. You can create named entries for text or graphics that you use often, such as the return address or closing of a letter.

Word comes with many built in AutoText entries, including salutations and closings for letters.

Creating an AutoText Entry

AutoText entry names can contain as many as 32 characters and can include spaces. You can also specify that AutoComplete inserts the AutoText entry when the first four letters of the entry's name are typed in a document. When an AutoText entry appears in a comment box in your document as you are typing, you can press Enter to insert it or continue typing to refuse it.

1. Select the text or item you want to save as an AutoText entry, including any spaces or punctuation you want to insert when you insert the entry in your document. If you want to save the format of selected text, make sure you also select its paragraph mark (¶).

2. Choose Insert ➤ AutoText ➤ AutoText to display the AutoText tab in the AutoCorrect dialog box.

3. Select the *Show AutoComplete tip for AutoText and dates* checkbox (selected by default) to have AutoComplete suggest the AutoText entry when the first four letters of the entry's name are typed.

4. If necessary, type a new name for the entry in the Enter AutoText Entries Here text box.

5. If necessary, select the name of the document template where the entry will be saved in the Look In drop-down list. By default, entries are saved to the NORMAL.DOT template.

6. Choose Add to add the entry to the Enter AutoText Entries Here list box.

You can quickly add a selection to the list of AutoText entries by either clicking on the New button on the AutoText toolbar or choosing Insert ➤ AutoText ➤ New (Alt+F3) to display the Create AutoText dialog box. If necessary, type a different name in the Please Name Your AutoText Entry text box, and then choose OK.

To delete an AutoText entry, choose Insert ➤ AutoText ➤ AutoText, highlight the name of the entry in the Enter AutoText Entries Here list box, and then choose Delete. Choose OK to return to your document.

Displaying the AutoText Toolbar

You can easily display the AutoText tab in the AutoCorrect dialog box, insert an AutoText entry, or create a new AutoText entry using the buttons on the AutoText toolbar. Use either of the following methods to display the AutoText toolbar:

- Choose Insert ➢ AutoText ➢ AutoText to display the AutoText tab in the AutoCorrect dialog box, and then choose Show Toolbar.

- Right-click on any displayed toolbar, and then choose AutoText.

Inserting an AutoText Entry

To insert an AutoText entry in a document, select it in the list of AutoText entries that appears on the Insert ➢ AutoText submenu or when you click on the Entries button on the AutoText toolbar. The AutoText entry list contains only the entries that were created in the same paragraph style as the paragraph that contains the insertion point. To display a list of all the AutoText entries, hold down the Shift key while you click on the Entries button on the AutoText toolbar or as you point to AutoText on the Insert menu.

In addition, only the AutoText entries stored in the NORMAL.DOT template (or any other template that is loaded for use with all your documents) appear in the list. If you stored AutoText entries in any other template, those entries are available only when a document based on that template is active.

To edit an AutoText entry, insert the entry in your document, and then make the desired changes to the entry. Select the entry (including the paragraph mark if you want to save the entry's formatting), and either click on the New button on the AutoText toolbar or choose Insert ➢ AutoText ➢ New (Alt+F3). Choose OK in the Create AutoText dialog box, and then choose Yes to redefine the entry you selected.

Background

To make your online documents and Web pages more interesting, you can add a background with a color, gradient, texture, or picture for Word documents that are displayed in Online Layout view. These backgrounds are specifically used for viewing on your screen, and do not print.

To display a background for an online document:

1. Click on the Online Layout View button beside the status bar or choose View ➢ Online Layout.

2. To display a background color, choose Format ➢ Background. Then do one of the following:

   - Click on the color in the palette that appears.

   - Choose More Colors to display the Colors dialog box, click on a color in the graphic that appears on the Standard tab, and then choose OK.

   - Choose More Colors, and then create a new color by clicking in an area on the Custom tab in the Colors dialog box. Choose OK in the Colors dialog box.

3. To display a background fill in an online document, choose Format ➢ Background ➢ Fill Effects to display the Fill Effects dialog box, and then choose one of the following options:

   - To display a gradient in the background, click on the Gradient tab, select One Color or Two Colors, and then choose the corresponding color in the Color 1 or Color 2 palette. If you choose One Color, drag the scroll button along the Dark/Light scroll bar to adjust the contrast in the gradient. Alternatively, choose Preset, and then select one of the built-in color combinations in the Preset Colors drop-down list. Select the direction of the shading in the gradient in the Shading Styles area, the pattern used in the gradient in the Variants area, and then choose OK.

   - To display a texture in the background, click on the Texture tab, click on one of the built-in background textures, and then choose OK. Alternatively, choose Other Texture to display the Select Texture dialog box, select the name of the file that contains the background texture you want, and then choose OK.

   - To display a pattern in the background, click on the Pattern tab, select the pattern in the Pattern area, choose a color in both the Foreground and Background palettes, and then choose OK.

- To display a picture in the background, click on the Picture tab, and then choose Select Picture to display the Select Picture dialog box. Select the name of the file that contains the picture, and then choose OK.

4. Choose OK in the Fill Effects dialog box.

Bookmark

Use bookmarks to name a selection or location in a Word document. You can then move quickly to the location, calculate numbers, mark pages for an index entry, or create cross-references.

Creating a Bookmark

When you create a bookmark, you assign a name to a selection or a location in your document. Bookmark names can be as long as 40 characters, must begin with a letter, and can contain numbers. Although you cannot include spaces in a bookmark name, you can use the underline character.

1. Select the text or item, or move the insertion point to the place in your document where you want to insert a bookmark.

2. Choose Insert ➢ Bookmark to display the Bookmark dialog box.

3. Type a name for the bookmark in the Bookmark Name text box.

4. Select Add to add the bookmark name to the list box.

You can delete a bookmark that you no longer need. Use any of the following methods to delete a bookmark in your document:

- If you assign a bookmark name that is already in the document to a new bookmark, the original bookmark with that name is deleted.

- Choose Insert ➢ Bookmark, highlight the name of the bookmark you want to delete, and then choose Delete to delete the bookmark but leave its marked text in the document.

- Select the bookmark bracket and its marked text, and then press Backspace or Delete to delete both the bookmark and its marked text.

When you display bookmarks in a document, they appear as square black brackets around selected text or as a large I-beam for a marked location. To display bookmarks in all your documents, choose Tools ➢ Options, and select the View tab. Select the Bookmarks checkbox in the Show area, and then choose OK.

To move to a specific bookmark in your document:

1. Choose Insert ➢ Bookmark.

2. In the Sort By area, select either Name (to display the bookmark names alphabetically in the Bookmark Name list box) or Location (to sort the bookmark names in the order of their locations in the document).

3. If necessary, select the Hidden Bookmarks checkbox to display the names of hidden bookmarks, such as cross-references, in the Bookmark Name list box.

4. Highlight the name of the bookmark in the Bookmark Name list box, and then choose Go To. If the bookmark is a location, the insertion point moves to the location. If the bookmark is selected text, the text is selected when you move to it. Choose Close to return to your document.

Editing a Marked Item

Keep the following points in mind when editing an existing bookmark:

- When you copy a bookmark or part of a bookmark to a location in the same document, only the text or item is copied, not the actual bookmark.

- When you copy a bookmark and paste it in another document, both documents will have the same bookmarks.

- When you cut a bookmark and paste it in a location in the same document or a different document, both the text or item and the bookmark move to the new location.

- If you cut or copy a bookmark to another document and that document already has a bookmark with that assigned name, the bookmark will not be pasted into the document. The original bookmark with the name will keep its name and location.

- If you delete part of a bookmark, the undeleted portion of the item stays marked.

- You can add text between any two characters in a bookmark, and it will become part of the bookmark.

- To add text at the beginning of a bookmark, add text just before marked text.

- If you want to add text at the end of bookmark text, type the text, then select all the text and the bookmark brackets. Choose Insert ➢ Bookmark, and then choose Add.

- When you add a new row at the end of a marked table, the inserted row is included in the marked table.

Borders and Shading

You can add borders and shading to selected paragraphs or to a page in a Word document, selected cells in an Excel worksheet, or to a selected text box or graphic in PowerPoint. Borders are lines that surround the cells, paragraphs, pages, or graphics boxes. Shading is the amount, color, and pattern of the fill inside the borders.

Applying Borders and Colors in Excel

Use either the Borders and Fill Color buttons on the Formatting toolbar or the options on the Border and Patterns tabs in the Format Cells dialog box to apply borders and colors to selected cells in an Excel worksheet. If you display the Patterns tab in the Format Cells dialog box, you can also select a pattern to apply to the selection.

To quickly apply borders and colors to a selection:

- Click on the Borders drop-down list button on the Formatting toolbar to display a palette of borders, and then click on the border you want in the palette. Alternatively, click on the Borders button when a graphic of the border you want to apply appears on it.

- Click on the Fill Color drop-down list button on the Formatting toolbar to display a color palette, and then click on the color in the palette.

Follow these steps to apply a border and color to a selection using the options in the Format Cells dialog box:

1. Choose Format ➢ Cells (Ctrl+1) to display the Format Cells dialog box.

2. Select the Border tab.

3. In the Presets area, choose None, Outline, or Inside to specify the location for the border.

4. Choose any of the following options for the border:

    - In the Border area, click on any of the buttons to toggle its border.

    - Choose the border's line style in the Style area.

    - If necessary, select a color for the border in the Color palette.

5. Select the Patterns tab, and then choose any of the following options:

    - Select a color for the background of the selection in the Color palette.

    - If necessary, select a pattern for the background of the selection in the Pattern palette.

6. Choose OK to apply the border and color.

Applying Borders and Shading in PowerPoint

Because PowerPoint is primarily a graphics program, there are several ways to change the border and fill of a selected graphics object, graphics box, or text box. To do so, click on the Slide View or Notes Page View button to change to either view.

To quickly apply borders, fill, and shading to a selected object, use the following buttons on the Drawing toolbar:

- Click on the Line Style or Dash Style button to display a list of line styles, and then select the line to use for the border.

- Click on the Line Color drop-down list button, and then choose a color for the border in the palette.

- Click on the Fill Color drop-down list button, and then choose a color for the object's fill in the palette.

- Click on the Shadow button, and then choose the object's shadow format in the palette.

- Click on the 3-D button and then choose a three dimensional format for the object's border.

To specify exact borders and colors for a selected object:

1. Choose Format ➤ Colors And Lines to display the Format AutoShape dialog box.

2. To apply a fill to the object, choose any of the following options in the Fill area:

   - Select its background color in the Color palette.

   - Choose More Colors in the Color drop-down list, click on the standard color you want, and then choose OK in the Colors dialog box.

   - To make a solid color fill less intense, select the Semitransparent check box.

   - Choose Fill Effects in the Color drop-down list, specify the gradient, texture, pattern, or picture on the corresponding tab in the Fill Effects dialog box, and then choose OK.

3. To apply a border to the object, choose any of the following options in the Line area:

   - To apply a color to the border, select a color in the Color palette, or choose More Colors, click on the standard color you want, and then choose OK in the Colors dialog box. Alternatively, choose Patterned Lines, select a color in the Foreground and Background palettes, choose the border's pattern in the Pattern list box, and then choose OK.

   - Choose the style of the border in the Style drop-down list.

   - To apply dashed lines, choose a pattern in the Dashed drop-down list.

   - Adjust the value in the Weight text box to specify the size of the lines in the object's border.

   - Select the style for a connector line between two objects in the Connector drop-down list.

4. Choose OK in the Format AutoShape dialog box to apply the specified border, colors, and fill.

Applying Borders and Shading in Word

You can add borders and shading to a paragraph or an item such as regular document text, text in a cell or frame, the actual cell or frame, or a table. You can also add a border to the pages in a document.

The borders and shading you apply to a paragraph can either surround only the text (if the paragraph is a short line of text) or extend between the paragraph indents. You can adjust the width of extended paragraph borders or paragraph shading by adjusting the indentation.

Use any of the following methods to specify which item is to receive a border or shading:

- To apply a border or shading to a paragraph, activate only the paragraph—even if it is in a cell or a frame—by selecting it or positioning the insertion point in it.

- To apply a border or shading to a table cell, including its contents, activate the cell.

- To apply a border to a table, select the table.

- To apply a border to a graphic or frame, or shading to a frame, select the graphic or frame.

Display the Tables and Borders toolbar to quickly apply predefined borders or shading to a paragraph, table cell, table, or frame. To display the Tables and Borders toolbar, click on the Tables and Borders button on the Standard toolbar or choose Format ➤ Borders And Shading ➤ Show Toolbar.

Use the following buttons and drop-down lists on the Tables And Borders toolbar to apply the corresponding border and color:

- Select a line style for the border in the Line Style drop-down list.

- Select the thickness of the border in the Line Weight drop-down list.

- Select a color for the border in the Border Color palette.

- To apply a border to the selection, click on the Border drop-down list button to display a palette of borders, and then click on the graphic of the border you wish to apply.

- To apply a fill color within the border, select the bordered item, click on the Shading

Color drop-down list, and then click on the background color in the palette that appears.

You can customize the borders you apply to an item, apply a shadow border, move the borders in relation to the selection, or apply borders to a page using the options in the Borders And Shading dialog box.

1. Activate the paragraph or item to which you want to apply a custom border or shading.

2. Choose Format ➤ Borders And Shading to display the Borders And Shading dialog box.

3. Select either the Borders or the Page Borders tab, then choose any of the following options to customize and apply a border:

   - To define the type of border to place around the item, choose None, Box, Shadow, 3-D, or Custom in the Setting area.

   - Select the style of line you want for the border in the Style list box.

   - Select a color for the border in the Color drop-down list.

   - Choose the border's width in the Width drop-down list.

   - In the Preview area, click on the position or the corresponding button where you want to add a top, bottom, left, right, inside, or outside border, or to remove the current border.

   - Select the item, such as Paragraph or Whole Document, to which to apply the border in the Apply To drop-down list.

   - If you are creating a paragraph border, choose Options, adjust the amount of space in points between the borders and the paragraph in the From Text area, and then choose OK.

   - If you are creating a page border, choose Options, then select either Edge of Page or Text in the Measure From drop-down list to define the relative position of the border. In the Margin area, adjust the amount of space in points between each border and each edge of the page or between the text and each border. If you chose Text in the Measure From drop-down list, select *Align paragraph borders and table edges with page border* to arrange paragraph borders and table edges along the border of a page, and select the Surround Header and Sur-

round Footer checkboxes to include headers and footers in the border. Select the Always Display in Front checkbox to position a page border on top of any text or objects that appear in the position for the border. Choose OK.

4. To apply and customize the shading for the object, select the Shading tab, and then choose any of the following options:

   - In the Fill area, choose one of the colors in the palette, or choose None to remove all shading from the item.

   - In the Patterns area, select a shading density or pattern to apply to the object in the Style drop-down list. If necessary, select a color for the shading or pattern in the Color drop-down list.

   - Select the item to which to apply the specified shading in the Apply To drop-down list.

5. In the Borders And Shading dialog box, choose OK.

Bullets and Numbering

Use bullets to indicate list items in PowerPoint or Word. In Word, you can also automatically number paragraphs or display them in an outline numbered list.

Adding Bullets to Presentation Text

The easiest way to add bullets to text in a presentation is to change the layout of the slide. Select one of the AutoLayouts that contains a bulleted list. You can also select the text box of an unbulleted item, and then click on the Bullets button on the Formatting toolbar.

You cannot select the bullets or numbers you insert into a presentation or document because they are automatic. However, you can remove automatic bullets or numbers by toggling the feature off in selected paragraphs.

Adding Bullets and Numbering in a Word Document

To quickly insert bullets or numbers before selected paragraphs or the paragraph that contains the insertion point, click on the Bullets or Numbering button on the Formatting toolbar.

To specify a format for the bullets or numbers:

1. Select the list text, or move the insertion point where you want to begin a bulleted or numbered list.

2. Choose Format ➤ Bullets And Numbering to display the Bullets and Numbering dialog box.

3. Choose the Bulleted, Numbered, or Outline Numbered tab, and then select one of the samples on the tab.

4. Choose OK in the Bullets And Numbering dialog box.

You can stop the numbering in a list, then restart it for a shorter list, or you can add, copy, and delete list items. Numbering for the list will automatically update when you make changes to your list.

• To remove bullets or numbers from a list or list item, select the list or item and click on the Bullets or Numbering button. Alternatively, select the list or item, then either right-click on the selection and choose Bullets And Numbering or choose Format ➤ Bullets And Numbering, and choose None. Numbering will automatically be updated for list items that still have numbering format.

• To restart numbering in a numbered or outline numbered list, select the list or item and then either right-click on the selection and choose Bullets And Numbering or choose Format ➤ Bullets And Numbering. Choose Restart Numbering in the List Numbering area on the Numbered or Outline Numbered tab, and then choose OK.

• To add a new item to the list, position the insertion point just before the location where you want to insert an item, press Enter, and then type the item.

Change Case

To change the case of selected text in PowerPoint and Word:

1. Select the text whose case you want to change, and then select Format ➤ Change Case to display the Change Case dialog box.

2. Select an option and choose OK.

To change the format of selected text in a Word document to small caps or all caps, choose Format ➤ Font, select the Small Caps or All Caps option in the Effects area on the Font tab, and then choose OK.

Columns

You can add newspaper columns to a Word document or part of a document. Newspaper columns are columns that let text flow from the bottom of one column to the top of the next column.

Columns can be of equal or unequal widths. When you insert columns in a document, you can format the whole document in multiple columns, or automatically add a section break to the portion of the document you want to be columnar.

To view columns in your document, you must be in Page Layout view or Print Preview.

Inserting Columns in Your Document

To quickly create equal columns in the current document section, click on the Columns button on the Standard toolbar, drag to highlight the number of columns you want, and then click on the Columns palette.

To create custom columns:

1. Position the insertion point where you want to create columns.

2. Choose Format ➤ Columns to display the Columns dialog box.

3. In the Presets area, select One, Two, or Three as the number of equal columns, or Left or Right as the position of the smaller column for columns of unequal widths.

4. If necessary, choose any of the following options to further define the appearance of the columns:

   • Adjust the value in the Number of Columns text box to specify the number of columns you want.

   • If you selected columns of unequal width in the Presets area, you can adjust the measurement that specifies the width of each column in the Width text box. To specify the amount of space that appears between columns, adjust the measurement in the Spacing text box.

- Select the Equal Column Width checkbox to quickly format the columns with equal width. Clear the checkbox for columns of unequal width.

- Select This Section, This Point Forward, or Whole Document as the portion of the document to be columnar in the Apply To drop-down list.

- Select the Line Between checkbox to create a line between the columns.

- When This Point Forward is selected in the Apply To drop-down list, select the Start New Column checkbox to add a column break in the position of the insertion point.

5. Choose OK in the Columns dialog box.

You can also edit some column features using the horizontal Ruler, shortcut keys, or menu commands.

- Drag the left or right column marker to change the width of the column.

- Drag the indent marker to align it with the column marker to remove indents from the paragraph that contains the insertion point. Or select an indented paragraph in a column, either right-click on the selection and choose Paragraph or choose Format ➢ Paragraph, and then change its indentation to 0.

- To start a new column, position the insertion point where you want to insert a column break, and then press Ctrl+Shift+Enter. Or position the insertion point, choose Insert ➢ Break, select Column Break, and then choose OK.

- To balance the lengths of columns on a page, position the insertion point at the end of the column you want to balance and choose Insert ➢ Break. Select Continuous, and then choose OK.

Comments

Use comments to describe complex formulas or provide explanations for items in an Excel worksheet. Excel allows you to enter text comments, which are indicated by a red triangle in the upper right corner of the cell to which they are attached. You can display the text of a com-

ment by positioning the mouse pointer over the cell, and print the comments when you print the worksheet. Each of Excel's comments contains the name of its author.

You can also insert a comment on a slide in a PowerPoint presentation. A comment appears as a yellow text box with the author's name at the top, and is positioned in the top left corner of the active slide. When you insert a comment on a slide, the Reviewing toolbar appears by default. Click on the Show/Hide Comments button to hide the comments in the presentation.

In Word, comment marks are formatted as hidden text, and each comment mark in the document appears with the initials of its author, which are entered by default in the Initials text box on the User Information tab of the Options dialog box during Setup. You must have a sound board, speakers, and a microphone installed on your system to insert voice notes.

Comments appear in your document with a light yellow highlight. Click on the Show/Hide ¶ button on the Standard toolbar to toggle the display of comment marks in your document. Select View ➢ Comments to toggle the display of both the comment marks in your document and the note window on your screen.

Inserting a Comment in Excel

Choose Tools ➢ Auditing ➢ Show Auditing Toolbar to display the Auditing toolbar.

1. Select the cell to which a comment is to be added.

2. Click on the New Comment button on the Auditing toolbar, or choose Insert ➢ Comment to display the Comment text box.

3. Type the text of the comment in the box.

4. Click on another cell to enter the note.

To manage the display of comment indicators in all workbooks, choose Tools ➢ Options, select the View tab, choose None, Comment Indicator Only, or Comment & Indicator in the Comments area, and then choose OK.

To edit a comment, select the cell to which it is attached, and then choose Insert ➢ Edit Comment to display the Comment text box with the insertion point in it. You can use the regular editing techniques to insert, replace, or delete text in the comment, and then click in another cell to enter the changes.

To delete a comment, select the cell to which the comment is attached, and then choose Edit ➢ Clear ➢ Comments.

Inserting a Comment in PowerPoint

If you wish, right-click on any displayed toolbar, and then choose Reviewing to display the Reviewing toolbar.

1. Activate the slide on which to insert a comment, and then click on the Insert Comment button on the Reviewing toolbar or choose Insert ➢ Comment to place the comment's text box on it.

2. Type the text of the comment in its text box.

3. Click anywhere outside the comment text box when you are finished.

Inserting a Comment In Word

Text in the comment pane can be edited when the pane is active. Text in the document window can be edited when the window is active. To switch between the comment pane and the document window, press F6 or click in the document window or comment pane. Comment marks are automatically renumbered whenever you insert, copy, or delete an comment.

To insert a text or voice comment:

1. Select the text or position the insertion point where you want to insert a comment.

2. Choose Insert ➢ Comment. A hidden comment mark containing the number of the comment and the initials of its author is inserted in the document, and the comment pane containing the insertion point opens at the bottom of your screen.

3. To insert a text comment, type the text of the comment, and add any formatting you wish to the text in the comment pane.

4. To insert a voice comment:

   • Click on the Insert Sound Object button in the comment pane to display the Sound Object dialog box.

   • Click on the Record button in the Sound Object dialog box and then speak into your microphone to record your comment. If necessary, check your sound board's documentation for instructions on recording a sound object.

   • Click on the Stop button in the Sound Object dialog box when you are finished recording your comment.

5. When you are finished inserting or editing the comments, close the comment pane by choosing Close (Alt+Shift+C).

To insert a comment that is both text and voice, insert the text portion of the comment first. Then move the insertion point just after the text and add the voice comment.

To delete a comment, select the comment mark in your document and press the Delete key.

To copy a comment, select the comment mark in the document pane, and then click on the Copy button on the Standard toolbar. Position the insertion point in the location in the document where you want to place a copy of the comment and click on the Paste button.

Listening to or Viewing Comments

To play back a voice comment, double-click on a comment mark in the document or select View ➢ Comments to display the comment pane, and then double-click on the sound symbol of the comment you want to hear.

Follow these steps to display the text of a comment:

1. Double-click on the comment mark you want to view, or choose View ➢ Comments to display the comment pane.

2. If necessary, highlight the name of the reviewer whose comments you want to see in the Comments From drop-down list.

3. If necessary, scroll through the list until the comment you want to see is displayed.

Cut, Copy, and Paste

Use the Cut or Copy commands or buttons on the Standard toolbar in any of the Microsoft Office applications to cut or copy text, tables, graphics, charts, or any item in your database, worksheet, mail message, presentation, or document to the Clipboard. You can then use the Paste command or button to paste the item into the same file or another file.

Cutting, Copying, and Pasting a Selection

When you cut or *move* a selection, you remove the selection from your document and place a copy of it on the Clipboard. When you copy a selection, it remains in the document and a copy is placed on the Clipboard. You can paste the current contents of the Clipboard into your document as many times as you wish.

The current contents of the Clipboard are replaced with the new selection each time you cut or copy a selection.

1. Select the item you want to move or copy.

2. Click on the Cut button on the Standard toolbar, or choose Edit ➢ Cut (Ctrl+X) to remove the selection from your document and place a copy of it in the Clipboard. Or click on the Copy button on the Standard toolbar or choose Edit ➢ Copy (Ctrl+C) to copy the selection to the Clipboard while the original stays in your document.

3. Position the insertion point in your document where you want to place a copy of the contents of the Clipboard.

4. Click on the Paste button on the Standard toolbar or choose Edit ➢ Paste (Ctrl+V) to place a copy of the contents of the Clipboard in the position of the insertion point.

Database

You can create a database in either Access or Excel, and then either insert the database into a Word document or create a report using the data in the database. You can also filter and insert records from a Word database, such as a merge data source file, into a Word document.

A database consists of tables of records that contain all the information about a specific person or item.

Records are composed of fields, which define each individual type of information in a record.

Creating an Access Database

To create a new database in Access:

1. Click on the New Database button on the Database toolbar, or choose File ➢ New Database (Ctrl+N) to display the New dialog box.

2. Highlight Blank Database in the list box on the General tab, and then choose OK.

3. Type a name for the database in the File Name text box, and then choose Create in the File New Database dialog box. Access automatically adds the .mdb file extension.

4. The Database window appears with the Tables tab active. Choose New to display the New Table dialog box.

5. Choose Table Wizard to have Access create a database from a template, and then choose OK to display the Table Wizard dialog box.

6. Choose any of the following options:

   • Select Business or Personal as the type of template you want to appear in the Sample Tables list box.

   • In the Sample Tables list box, select the name of a table that contains field definitions similar to the type you want.

   • Highlight the name of one field in the Sample Fields list box, and then click on the > button to add it to the Fields In My New Table list box. Or, to add all the fields in the selected table template, click on the >> button.

   • If necessary, highlight the name of a field in the Fields in My New Table list box, and then click on the < button to remove it from the list. Or, to remove all the field names from the list box, click on the << button.

7. Choose Next to display the next Table Wizard dialog box. Type a name for the table in the corresponding text box, and then select either Yes, Set a Primary Key for Me, or No, I'll Set the Primary Key.

8. Choose Next, and then choose Modify the Table Design, Enter Data Directly into the Table, or Enter Data into the Table Using a Form the Wizard Creates for Me.

9. Choose Finish to display the table in the design you created.

You can enter data for each record in the cells of the table, or into the field text boxes in a form.

If you select New Table in step 5 to create a new, blank table, you must name and define the fields yourself, and specify the type of data the fields will contain.

If you choose one of Access's built-in database templates with which to create the database, all the database items, including the tables, forms, reports and queries, are automatically created for you.

Creating an Excel Database

Use an Excel worksheet to organize associated data by rows into labeled columns in a *list*. Excel automatically identifies a list as a simple database with the rows of data as records and the columns of data as fields. The column labels in the first row, called the *header row*, are part of the list, even though they are not items in the list.

There are several points to keep in mind when you create a list:

- Place each list in a separate worksheet. However, you can store many lists on different sheets of a workbook.

- Position a list in a worksheet so there is at least one blank column and row between it and other data in the worksheet.

- Do not leave any blank rows between the header row and the items in the list. Instead, format the text in the header row so it appears different from the formatting of the items in the list, or add a solid border to the bottom edge of the cells that contain the labels to divide the column labels from the list items.

- Do not place essential data to the left or right of a list, because it may be hidden when you filter the list.

To create a list in Excel:

1. Select a new worksheet tab in a workbook.

2. Enter the column labels in the first row of the list, and then apply a format to the labels that is different from the format for the data.

3. Apply the same format to each cell in a column of the list. For example, in a Date field, format each cell in the column except the cell in the header row.

4. Optionally, select the range of cells that contains the list, including the column labels, and choose Insert ➣ Name ➣ Define to display the Define Name dialog box. Type a name for the list in the Names In Workbook text box, and then choose OK.

Entering Records in a Database

In both Access and Excel, you can enter data directly into each cell of a table or list:

- Select the cell in an Access table or an Excel worksheet into which you want to enter data, and then type the data. Press Tab to enter the data and move to the next table cell. To move to the previous cell, press Shift+Tab.

- Enter the data in the list without blank spaces at the beginning of any cell.

- Use uniform capitalization so you can sort the list later.

Inserting a Database into a Word Document

Once you have created a database and entered records into it, you can select which fields of data you want from the data source and filter the selection of records to be inserted into a table in a Word document. You can also format the table to meet your needs, and have Word update the table if the data source changes.

1. Position the insertion point where you want the database to appear in your document.

2. Right-click on a displayed toolbar, and then select Database to display the Database toolbar.

3. Click on the Insert Database button on the Database toolbar to display the Database dialog box.

4. Choose Get Data to display the Open Data Source dialog box.

5. If necessary, select the name of the folder that contains the database file in the Look In drop-down list.

6. If necessary, select the type of files to display in the Look In list box in the Files of Type drop-down list. Then, highlight the name of the database file to be used as the data source in the list box and choose Open.

7. If necessary, select Query Options to display the Query Options dialog box, and then select the necessary options to define and sort specific information that is to be inserted from the data source.

8. If necessary, select Table AutoFormat and select the name of the predefined table format you want to use in the Formats list box.

9. Choose Insert Data to display the Insert Data dialog box, and then choose any of the following options:

   • Choose All to insert all the records that meet the selection criteria. If no selection criteria is specified, all the data source records are inserted.

   • Type the number of the first record in the range of records you want to include in the table in the From text box, and the number of the last record in the range in the To text box.

   • Select the Insert Data As Field check box to insert the specified source data as a database field. When the table is inserted as a field in your document, you can update changes made to the data source in your Word document.

10. Choose OK to insert the database into your document.

If you insert the database as a field in your document, each time you update the database you will lose any table formatting you have applied to the table. To update a database with a selected table format, you must reinsert the database and the table format in your document. If you edit a table inserted as a Database field, your changes will be lost when you next update the field.

E-Mail

You can send an online workbook, presentation, or document file to other people for their comments,

revisions, or to fill in a form via electronic mail or *e-mail*. You can choose how the file is sent—to each person simultaneously, or you can *route* it (send it to selected people in a specific order). If the document is routed, the revisions and annotations inserted in the file by all the reviewers are collected in the file. You can also insert a text message with the document.

Sending a File Online

When you send a file online, it appears as a message in the recipient's Inbox folder, located in Microsoft Outlook.

To send the active file:

1. Choose File ➤ Send To ➤ Mail Recipient to display the Message dialog box with the file's icon inserted in the message area. If the Choose Profile dialog box appears, choose OK to select Microsoft Outlook in the Profile Name drop-down list.

2. Select To to display the Select Names dialog box.

3. If necessary, select a different address book in the Show Names from The drop-down list.

4. Highlight a name in the Type Name or Select from List list box, and then choose To to place the name in the Message Recipients list box.

5. Repeat step 4 for each person to whom the file is to be sent. The names in the Message Recipient list box are automatically separated by semicolons.

6. To send a copy of the message to a person, highlight the name of the person in the Type Name or Select from List list box, and then choose Cc to place it in the corresponding Message Recipients list box.

7. Choose OK to place the names in the Message dialog box's To and Cc text boxes.

8. If necessary, type the subject of the online message in the Subject text box.

9. If necessary, click in the message area, and then type the text of a message you want to include with the file.

10. Click on the Send button on the Outlook Send Mail toolbar, or choose File ➤ Send (Ctrl+Enter) to send the message and the document.

If you want others to suggest revisions or add comments to a file, send it online and add a routing slip. To do so:

1. Activate the file you want to send, and then choose File ➤ Send To ➤ Routing Recipient to display the Routing Slip dialog box.

2. Your name appears in the From area of the Routing Slip dialog box. Choose Address, and then select the name of the address book that contains the names of the people to whom you want to send the file in the Show Names from The drop-down list.

3. Select a name to whom to send the file in the Type Name or Select from List list box, and then choose To to place the name in the To list box.

4. Repeat step 3 for each person to whom the file is to be sent, and then choose OK to return to the Routing Slip dialog box.

5. If necessary, click on the ↑ or ↓ Move button to arrange the names in the To list box in the order you want the file to be routed to each recipient.

6. If necessary, type the subject of the file in the Subject text box.

7. Type any messages or instructions to the file's recipients in the Message Text text box.

8. In the Route to Recipients area, choose One after Another to send the file to the people in the order they are listed in the To list box, or choose All at Once to simultaneously send a copy of the file to all the people in the To list box.

9. Select the Return when Done checkbox to have the file returned to you when the last person closes it.

10. If One after Another is selected, select the Track Status checkbox to receive a message when the file is forwarded to the next person on the list.

11. Choose (None), Tracked Changes, Comments, or Forms to define how to protect a Word document from any changes to its text in the Protect For drop-down list.

12. Choose Route to send the file. A message appears in the status bar when the file is being routed.

To return to your document in order to edit it before you send it, choose Add Slip. When you have finished editing the document, select File ➤ Send To ➤ Next Routing Recipient, and then choose OK to send the document.

Envelope

Use Word's Envelope feature to quickly print an envelope for a document. Word will automatically insert the return and delivery addresses.

Addressing and Printing an Envelope

To print an envelope with a delivery address entered in the active document:

1. If the document contains more than one address, select the mailing address.

2. Choose Tools ➤ Envelopes and Labels to display the Envelopes and Labels dialog box, then select the Envelopes tab.

3. If necessary, type a different return address in the Return Address text box. Or select the Omit checkbox to omit printing the return address on an envelope.

4. Insert the envelope in the printer in the position shown in the Feed area.

5. If necessary, select Options to display the Envelope Options dialog box. Then, change any of the envelope options on the Envelope Options tab, and choose OK.

6. Select one of the following options:

    • To print the envelope, choose Print.

    • To add a section to the beginning of a document that contains the envelope formatting, select Add to Document.

    • To insert any changes made if you already have an envelope section in a document, select Change Document.

Field

A field is the most basic unit of information in a database. Databases are composed of *records*, which contain all the information about an item. Records are composed of *fields*, the individual pieces of information in each record. For example, in a database that contains customer names and addresses, each customer's information is contained in one record. The record itself may include fields for the first name, last name, street address, city, state, and zip code.

Defining a Field

Fields are defined in a database. In a table in Access or Excel, the field names appear as labels at the top of each column. In an Access form, the field names appear as labels beside the text or graphics box into which the data for the field is entered.

In Access, there are several types of fields that can be defined, depending on the type of data that will be entered in the field. These include the text, memo, number, date, time, currency, AutoNumber, Yes/No (or Boolean), OLE object, hyperlink and lookup fields.

In Excel, the type of data in a field is defined only by the number format you assign to the column of data.

Naming a Field

Use a descriptive name for each field in a database to help you remember what information you need to enter in the field:

- In Access, field names can consist of up to 64 characters, including spaces. However, if you want to use expressions, SQL statements, or macros in the database, do not include spaces in a field name. Underscores can be used instead of spaces in the field names.

- In Excel, field names can consist of up to 255 characters, including spaces.

File Management

Each Microsoft Office application has several commands useful for managing your files.

Closing an Open File

In all Office applications, you can close the active file without exiting the application. Because each open file uses memory in your computer, close any files when you are finished working on them.

1. Select File ➤ Close or click on the active file's Close box.

2. If you have made any changes to the file since you last saved it, a message appears asking if you want to save the changes. Choose Yes to save the file, No to close the file without saving the changes, or Cancel to return to the application and continue working on the file.

3. If you choose Yes for a file that you have not saved previously, the Save As dialog box appears. Type a name for the file in the File Name text box, and then choose Save.

Creating a New File

1. Click on the New Database button on the Standard toolbar in Access; choose File ➤ New Database in Access and File ➤ New in Excel, PowerPoint, and Word; or press Ctrl+N in Access and PowerPoint. The New dialog box appears in Access, Excel, and Word, and the New Presentation dialog box appears in PowerPoint.

2. Follow the appropriate steps below:

- In Access, select one of the database templates on the Databases tab, and then choose OK. Type the name for the new database file in the File Name text box, and then choose Create. Answer any questions in the Database Wizard that appears, and then choose Finish to have Access create the database. The Main Switchboard for the file appears.

- In Excel, highlight one of the workbook templates on the Spreadsheet Solutions tab, and then choose OK.

- In PowerPoint, highlight one of the templates on either the Presentation Designs or Presentations tab, and then choose OK. If you choose a template on the Presentation Designs tab, the New Slide dialog box appears. If you choose a template on the Presentations tab, the title slide for that presentation appears.

- In Word, choose the name of a template or Wizard from one of the template tabs, select Document in the New area, and then choose OK.

When you click on the New button on the Standard toolbar (or press Ctrl+N) in Excel and Word, a new blank workbook opens in Excel, and a new document based on the Normal template opens in Word.

Inserting a File

You can insert a file in the active Word document at the position of the insertion point:

1. Select Insert ➤ File to display the Insert File dialog box.

2. If necessary, select a different drive on which to find the file in the Look In drop-down list, and then select the folder that contains the file in the Look In list box.

3. If necessary, select the type of file to insert in the Files of Type drop-down list.

4. Highlight the name of the file to be inserted.

5. To insert a portion of the selected file, type the name of a bookmark or the range name in the Range text box.

6. To link the inserted file to the active file, select the Link to File checkbox.

7. Choose OK.

Opening a File

Each of the Microsoft Office applications uses a similar procedure to open a file that has been saved on your disk. To quickly open one of the last four opened files, choose File ➤ *File Name*. To open any file:

1. Click on the Open button on the Standard toolbar, or choose File ➤ Open (Ctrl+O) to display the Open dialog box. In Access, select File ➤ Open Database (Ctrl+O) to display the Open dialog box.

2. Highlight the name of the file in the Look In list box.

3. If necessary, select Access's Exclusive checkbox to open the selected database file so no one else can modify the objects in the database.

4. Choose Open.

Saving a File

To save the current file in Excel, PowerPoint, and Word for the first time:

1. Click on the Save button on the Standard toolbar, or choose File ➤ Save (Ctrl+S) to display the Save As dialog box.

2. If necessary, select a different drive on which to save the file in the Save In drop-down list, and a different folder in which to store the file in the Save In list box.

3. If necessary, select the type of file to save in the Save as Type drop-down list.

4. Type the name for the file in the File Name text box.

5. If necessary in PowerPoint, select the Embed True Type checkbox to embed the fonts in the presentation so they can be displayed on a system without those fonts installed.

6. If necessary in Excel or Word, select Options to display Excel's Save Options dialog box or the Save tab in Word's Options dialog box. Choose any appropriate options, and then choose OK.

7. Choose OK in the Save As dialog box.

Each time you click on the Save button or choose File ➤ Save (Ctrl+S) to save an existing file, the Save As dialog box will not appear. To save an existing file to a new file name, select File ➤ Save As to display the Save As dialog box, type a new name in the File Name text box, and choose OK.

In Access, you can save a new design of the active database object (table, form, report, query, or module) using File ➤ Save (Ctrl+S). Use File ➤ Save As/ Export to save the database object to an external file or to make a copy of it with a new name.

In Excel, use File ➤ Save Workspace to save a list of the sizes and positions of all open workbook files to the resume.xlw file. Open the resume.xlw file when you want to use the saved workspace.

Find and Replace

Use Find and Replace to search for and select text or other characters, formats, special characters, and other items in Access, Excel, PowerPoint, and Word and replace the found item with a specified item.

Finding Items

Follow these steps to search for a specific item (comparable options in each application's Find tab or dialog box are described below):

1. Choose Edit ➤ Find (Ctrl+F) to display one of the following dialog boxes:

   - In Access, the Find in Field *Field Name* dialog box appears.

   - In both Excel and PowerPoint, the Find dialog box appears.

   - In Word, the Find tab in the Find and Replace dialog box appears.

2. Type the text or characters to find in the Find What text box. Or select one of the last three items searched for in PowerPoint, or one of the last seven items in Word, in the drop-down list.

3. In Word, choose More to display additional options on the Find tab.

4. In Access and Word, choose Down, Up, or All in the Search drop-down list to specify the direction in which to search. In Excel, choose By Rows or By Columns in the Search drop-down list.

5. In Access, select Any Part of Field, Match Whole Field, or Start of Field in the Match drop-down list to narrow the search to a specific part of the field. In Excel, select Formulas, Values, or Comments in the Look In drop-down list to specify the items to be searched.

6. Choose any of the following options to narrow the search results, depending on the active application:

   - Select the Match Case checkbox to find an item with the exact uppercase and lowercase letters as those in the Find What text box.

   - Select the Find Whole Words Only checkbox to find only text that is a whole word.

   - Select the Use Wildcards checkbox to use advanced search operators and expressions in Word.

   - Select the Sounds Like checkbox to find homonyms of the text in the Find What text box.

   - Select the Find All Word Forms checkbox to broaden the search to additional related terms.

   - Select the Search Fields as Formatted checkbox in Access to find an item based on the format assigned to the field.

   - Select the Search Only Current Field checkbox in Access to search for the item in only the active field.

   - Select the Find Entire Cells Only checkbox in Excel to search for a cell that contains the same characters as those in the Find What text box.

   - In Word, choose Format, select Font, Paragraph, Tabs, Language, Frame, or Style to display each command's dialog box, and then choose the formatting for which to search in the corresponding dialog box. Or choose Highlight to search for characters that are highlighted. You can also search for formatting only, without searching for any text.

   - Choose No Formatting in Word to remove all specified formatting from the search.

   - Select Special in Word, and then choose a character in the pop-up list to enter in the Find What text box.

7. Choose Find Next to start the search. The first instance of the item you are searching for is selected.

8. If necessary, select Find Next to find the next instance of the item.

9. To edit the found item, select Close, or choose Replace to display the Replace tab or dialog box.

10. When the beginning or end of the file is reached during the search process, a dialog box appears asking if you want to continue the search. Select Yes to continue the search back to the location of the insertion point.

11. Choose OK to remove the message box that appears to tell you when the search is complete.

12. When you have finished searching for the document item, select Close or press Esc.

To repeat the last search after the Find dialog box is closed, press Shift+F4 to search without opening the dialog box.

In Word, you can edit your document while the Find and Replace dialog box is displayed. Click in the document window or press Alt+F6 to activate the document window. Click in the dialog box or press Alt+Shift+F6 to activate the dialog box when you have finished.

Replacing Items

To replace a found item with specific characters, display the Replace tab or dialog box:

1. Select Edit ➤ Replace (Ctrl+H), or choose Replace in the Find or Find and Replace dialog box to display the Replace dialog box or tab.

2. If necessary, type the text to be found in the Find What text box.

3. Type the text to replace a found document item within the Replace With text box.

4. Choose any of the options in the active application's dialog box to define and limit the search. The options are described above in "Finding Items."

5. Choose Find Next to start the search and highlight the first instance of the item.

6. Choose either of the following options:

   - To replace the highlighted item with the characters in the Replace With text box, choose Replace.

   - To find the next instance of the document item without replacing the currently highlighted item, choose Find Next.

7. Repeat step 6 as necessary.

8. When the beginning or end of the file is reached during the search process, a dialog box appears asking if you want to continue the search. Select Yes to continue the search back to the location of the insertion point.

9. Choose OK to remove the message box that appears when the search is complete.

10. Choose Close or press Esc to return to the file.

Select Replace All to automatically find all instances of the search item and replace it with the characters in the Replace With text box.

To delete the item for which you are searching, remove all the characters from the Replace With text box, then choose Replace.

Font

You can apply a different font and size, or other text attributes such as bold or italic formatting, to selected text in Access, Excel, PowerPoint, and Word. You can also change the default appearance of the characters you type.

Applying Fonts to Characters

Use the drop-down lists and buttons on the Formatting toolbar (displayed by default in Excel, PowerPoint, and Word) to change the font and size, and to apply Bold, Italic, Underline, and special effect formats to characters. You can also display the Font dialog box or tab in PowerPoint or Word, and the Font tab in the Format Cells dialog box in Excel, to format selected text.

To apply fonts and attributes to selected text using the options on the Formatting toolbar:

- Choose the name of the font in the Font drop-down list.

- Click on the Bold or Italic button to apply the attribute.

- Choose a size for the font in the Font Size drop-down list.

- In PowerPoint, click on the Increase Font Size button to change selected characters to the next largest size in the list.

- In PowerPoint, click on the Shadow button to apply a shadow to the text.

- Click on the Underline button to apply a single underline.

- Click on the Font Color button in Excel to apply the color on the button. Alternatively, choose a color in the Font Color palette.

To apply fonts and attributes to selected text using the options in the Font dialog box:

1. Choose Format ➤ Font or Format ➤ Cells (Ctrl+1), and then select the Font tab in Excel and Word. The Format Cells dialog box appears in Excel, and the Font dialog box appears in PowerPoint and Word.

2. Choose any of the following options:

- Choose the name of the font in the Font list box.

- Choose Regular (the default for each font), Bold, Italic, or Bold Italic in the Font Style list. Not all of the style options are available for every font.

- Choose a size for the font in the Size list box.

- Choose one of the underline attributes in the Underline drop-down list.

- Click on one of the colors in the Color palette. The text will display in color on a color monitor, and print in color on a color printer.

- In Access, choose the language script for the selected font in the Script drop-down list.

- In Excel, select the Normal Font checkbox to set all the attributes of the selected cell to the Normal style.

3. To apply special effects, select any of the following checkboxes:

- Strikethrough draws a line through text that does not have a revision line through it. Double Strikethrough draws two lines through text that does not have a revision line through it.

- Superscript raises the text above the baseline.

- Subscript lowers the text below the baseline.

- In PowerPoint, enter a percentage by which superscript or subscript text should be raised or lowered in the Offset text box.

- In PowerPoint, select the Underline checkbox to apply an underscore character to text.

- Shadow applies a shadow effect to text.

- Outline displays the text with only an inner and outer border.

- Emboss applies a raised effect to selec-ted text.

- Engrave displays the text as if it were imprinted into the page.

- Small Caps displays all the text in reduced size capital letters.

- All Caps displays the text in regular size capital letters.

- Hidden hides the text in the document, so it will not appear on-screen or in a printed document.

4. If necessary, select the Default for New Objects checkbox in PowerPoint to use the current settings for the text in all new objects.

5. Choose OK.

Changing the Default Font

In Access, the default font and style are set in each field's control property sheet.

In Excel, specify the default font by choosing Tools ➤ Options, and then choosing the General tab. Select the font name in the Standard Font drop-down list and the size in the Size drop-down list, and then choose OK.

In PowerPoint, select the Default for New Objects checkbox in the Font dialog box to use the selected font and attributes as the default font.

In Word, the default font and size are determined by the style that is applied to a paragraph. To change the defaults in the current document template to the options set on the Font, Character Spacing, and Animation tabs in the Font dialog box, select Default on the corresponding tab, and then choose Yes to confirm the changes.

Format Painter

Use Format Painter to copy the formats of selected text and characters to other text in Excel, PowerPoint, and Word, or to copy control formats to another control in Access.

Copying Formats to Characters

To copy the formats applied to existing characters or controls:

1. Select the characters or control whose formatting you want to copy.

2. Click on the Format Painter button on the Standard toolbar.

3. Select the text or control to which the format is to be copied. As the text is highlighted, the format is copied to it.

4. Repeat steps 2 and 3 for each set of characters to which you want to copy the format.

To copy the format of selected text to several locations, double-click on the Format Painter button, and then select each occurrence of the text to which the format is to be copied. Click on the Format Painter button again to toggle it off when you are finished.

If you copy a paragraph mark in Word, you can paste the paragraph style and any additional formats applied to the paragraph to other text. If a paragraph mark and some text in the paragraph are selected, the formats applied to the paragraph and the formats applied to the selected text are copied.

Formula

Use formulas in Access, Excel, and Word to automatically calculate values. In Access, formulas are called *expressions*, and are entered in text boxes called *calculated controls*. Formulas can be entered in calculated form fields in a Word form, in a Formula field code, in a bookmark, and in a table with Table ➤ Formula.

Entering Formulas in Excel

One of the basic uses of a worksheet is to perform calculations on values. Use a formula entered in a cell in Excel to automatically calculate operations and display the results in the cell.

A formula must begin with an = (equal sign). You can use numbers (constants), cell references, or range names as the values in formulas. Use the following arithmetic or comparison operators to indicate what operations are to be performed with the values: + (addition); - (subtraction or negation); / (division); * (multiplication); % (percent); ^ (exponentiation); = (equal to); > (greater than); < (less than); > = (greater than or equal to); < = (less than or equal to); < > (not equal to).

By default, formulas are not displayed in a worksheet, but the results of formulas are. To display a formula entered in a cell, select the cell; the formula will appear in the formula bar. To display

formulas in a worksheet (instead of their calculated results), choose Tools ➤ Options, choose the View tab, select the Formulas checkbox in the Window Options area, and then choose OK.

Use parentheses to indicate which set of values is calculated first in a more complex formula. Otherwise, Excel performs calculations in the following order: negation, percent, exponentiation, multiplication and division, addition and subtraction, text joining, and comparison.

To edit a formula, select the cell that contains the formula, and then click in the entry area of the formula bar to position the insertion point, or press F2 (Edit) to place the insertion point at the end of the data in the cell. Use any of the following methods to edit the formula:

- Move the insertion point by either click-ing in a different location or by pressing ← and →.

- When the insertion point is positioned where data is to be added, type the new data.

- To delete the character to the right of the insertion point, press Delete.

- To delete the character to the left of the insertion point, press Backspace.

- Drag to highlight any characters to be replaced, and then type the new characters.

- To enter the edited data, press Enter or click on the Enter Box on the formula bar.

FTP

File transfer protocol (FTP) is a convention that allows files to be moved from one location to another over the Internet or an intranet. If you have an account that allows you access to the Internet, or if your company has an intranet, you can add an FTP site to the list of Internet sites. The list allows you to quickly access a site, and you can display the list from within any of the Microsoft Office applications.

1. Click on the Open button on the Standard toolbar, or choose File ➤ Open to display the Open dialog box.

2. Select Add/Modify FTP Locations in the Look In drop-down list to display its dialog box. You can find the Add/Modify FTP Locations icon below the Internet Locations icon when any drive letter is selected in the Look In drop-down list.

3. Type the name of the FTP site in the Name of FTP Site text box.

4. Select either of the following options in the Log On As area:

- Choose Anonymous to log on to a site that allows anyone to visit.

- Choose User, and then type your password to log on to a site for which visitors must have been assigned user privileges.

5. Choose Add to add the FTP site to the list displayed in the FTP Sites list box.

6. Choose OK to close the Add/Modify FTP Locations dialog box.

You can also perform the following actions when the Add/Modify FTP Locations dialog box is displayed:

- To edit the address or logon information for an FTP site, highlight the site in the FTP Sites list box, and then choose Modify. Make the necessary changes in the dialog box, and then choose Add.

- To delete an FTP site from the list, highlight its address in the FTP Sites list box, and then choose Remove.

To open one of the FTP sites, double-click on its icon in the Open dialog box [when Internet Locations (FTP) appears in the Look In list box]. You can then double-click on the folder in which the file is stored to display its contents. Double-click on the name of the file you want to open.

Go To

Use Go To to move quickly to another location in the same file in Access, Excel, and Word. In Excel, you can also move to a location in another open workbook file. When Go To is used, the insertion point moves to the location specified.

Going to a Location in an Access Database

To move to a specific record in the active form, table, or query:

1. In Form view or Datasheet view, press F5, and then type the number of the record in the text box at the bottom of the form or datasheet.

2. Press Enter to move to the specified record.

Or you can use the following methods to move to specific records:

- Click on the First Record button at the bottom of the form or table, or choose Edit ➤ Go To ➤ First to move to the first record.

- Click on the Last Record button at the bottom of the form or table, or choose Edit ➤ Go To ➤ Last to move to the last record.

- Click on the Next Record button at the bottom of the form or table, or choose Edit ➤ Go To ➤ Next to move to the next record.

- Click on the Previous Record button at the bottom of the form or table, or choose Edit ➤ Go To ➤ Previous to move to the previous record.

- Click on the New Record button at the bottom of the form or table, or choose Edit ➤ Go To ➤ New Record to begin a new record in the database.

Going to a Location in an Excel Worksheet

To select the cell or range specified:

1. Choose Edit ➤ Go To (F5) to display the Go To dialog box.

2. Select the name of a range in the Go To list box, or type the reference of the cell to select in the Reference text box.

3. If necessary, select Special to display the Go To Special dialog box, select one of the following options, and then choose OK to select each occurrence of the specified item in the selected worksheet or range:

- To select each cell that contains a note, select Comments.

- To select each cell whose value does not begin with = (equal sign), choose Constants.

- Select Formulas, and then specify which cells to highlight by selecting any of these checkboxes: Numbers (selects cells that return a number); Text (highlights cells that return text); Logicals (highlights cells that return TRUE or FALSE values); and Errors (highlights cells that return error values).

- To select every empty cell, choose Blanks.

- To select the range around the active cell bounded by blank cells, choose Current Region.

- To select each cell in the array that contains the active cell, choose Current Array.

- To select all the graphic objects in the worksheet, choose Objects.

- To highlight the cells in each row that are different from the cell used for comparison in that row, choose Row Differences.

- To highlight the cells in each column that are different from the cell used for comparison in that column, choose Column Differences.

- To highlight cells that are referred to by the formula in the active cell, choose Precedents. Then choose Direct Only to highlight only the direct precedents, or All Levels to select all precedents of the formula.

- To highlight cells that contain formulas that refer to the active cell, choose Dependents. Then choose Direct Only to highlight only direct dependents, or All Levels to highlight all the dependents of the active cell.

- To move to the last nonblank cell in the worksheet, choose Last Cell.

- To select only cells that are not hidden, choose Visible Cells Only.

- To select cells that contain conditional number formats, choose Conditional Formats. Then choose All to select all the cells that contain conditional number formats, or Same to select all the cells that contain the same conditional number format as the selected cell.

- To select cells for which data validation is specified, select Data Validation. Then choose All to select all the cells for which data validation is specified, or Same to

select all the cells for which the same data validation as that in the selected cell is specified.

4. If necessary, choose OK in the Go To dia-log box.

Before choosing Go To Special, select one cell in a worksheet to select every occurrence of the specified item in the worksheet, or a range to select every occurrence of the specified item in the range.

Going to a Location in a Word Document

When you want to move quickly to another location in a document, you can go to a specific document item.

1. Use one of the following methods to display the Go To tab in the Find And Replace dialog box:

   - Double-click on one of the first two sections on the status bar.

   - Click on the Select Browse Object button below the vertical scroll bar and then click on the Go To graphic.

   - Choose Edit ➤ Go To (F5).

2. Highlight the document item to which you want to move the insertion point in the Go To What list box.

3. To go to the next specified document item, choose Next; to go to the previous item, choose Previous. Or type the number of the item in the Enter *Document Item* text box, then choose Go To to move the insertion point to that item.

4. When you are finished moving to document items, select Close.

Alternatively, press Shift+F5 to quickly move to the last three positions of the insertion point.

Header and Footer

Headers can be displayed and printed in the top margin of each page of a printed document in

Access, Excel, PowerPoint, and Word, and footers can be displayed and printed in the bottom margin of each page. The method used to add headers and footers to a file depends on the active Microsoft Office application.

Creating a Header or Footer in Access

You can create headers and footers in Access as controls on both forms and reports. To create headers and footers, the form or report must be in Design view. Page, form, and report headers and footers can be created only in pairs.

There are five sections in a form in Design view, four of which are headers and footers. Create the following kinds of headers and footers for a form:

- Use a form header to display instructions for using the form, or to display buttons that allow the user to open other forms or perform another task. A form header appears at the top of the form in Form view, and at the top of the first page when the form is printed.

- Create a page header to display the same information, such as the title of the database, at the top of each printed page.

- Create a page footer to display the same information, such as the page number or date, at the bottom of each printed page.

- Create a form footer to display instructions for using the form, or buttons that allow the user to perform specific tasks. The form footer appears at the bottom of the form in Form view, and at the bottom of the last page when the form is printed.

To display the form and page headers and footers:

1. Display the form in Design view.

2. Choose View ➢ Page Header/Footer to display the form's page header and footer. The form's header and footer are displayed by default.

A report can contain up to seven different types of sections, six of which are headers and footers. Create the following kinds of headers and footers for a report:

- Use a report header to display items, such as a company logo or the title of the report, only once at the top of a report. It appears before the first page's page header when the report is printed.

- Use a page header to display items at the top of every page in the report.

- Use a group header to specify items, such as a name for a group, at the beginning of a group of records in the report.

- Use a group footer to specify items, such as a total for the group, at the end of each group.

- Use a page footer for items, such as page numbers, that will appear at the bottom of each page in the report.

- Use a report footer for items that pertain to the entire report, such as the report's total. A report footer appears before a page footer at the end of the printed report.

To create a header and footer for a report:

1. Display the report in Design view.

2. Choose View ➢ Page Header/Footer to display the report's page header and footer. The report's header and footer are displayed by default.

3. To add a group header or group footer, select View ➢ Sorting and Grouping to display the Sorting and Grouping dialog box.

4. Select the field or expression on which to sort in the drop-down list for the first item.

5. In the Group Properties area of the Sorting and Grouping dialog box, select Yes in the Group Header and Group Footer property areas.

To remove an unwanted page, form, or report header or footer, do one of the following:

- Position the mouse pointer over the section heading in Design view until the mouse pointer turns into a resizing pointer, and then drag the section to change its height to none.

- Change its Visible property to No.

To remove a group header or footer, choose No as the Group Header or Group Footer property in the Sorting and Grouping dialog box, and then choose OK to confirm the removal.

Creating a Header or Footer in Excel

A header and footer appear by default on each page printed in an Excel file. However, you can customize the header and footer for any portion of a workbook that is printed.

To create a header or footer in Excel:

1. Click on the Print Preview button on the Standard toolbar, and then choose Setup, or choose File ➢ Page Setup to display the Page Setup dialog box.

2. Choose the Header/Footer tab.

3. Choose one of the predefined headers and footers in the Header and Footer drop-down lists. Alternatively, choose Custom Header or Custom Footer to display the corresponding dialog box.

4. Type the text for the header or footer in the Left Section, Center Section, and Right Section text boxes.

5. If necessary, do any of the following:

   - Click on the Font button to change the font and attributes of selected text.

   - Click on the Page Number button to insert the page number in the position of the insertion point.

   - Click on the Total Pages button to insert the total number of pages in the position of the insertion point.

   - Click on the Date button to insert the system date in the position of the insertion point.

   - Click on the Time button to insert the system time in the position of the insertion point.

   - Click on the Filename button to insert the name of the file that contains the worksheet being printed.

   - Click on the Sheet Name button to insert the name of the worksheet being printed.

6. Choose OK in the Header or Footer dialog box to return to the Page Setup dialog box.

7. Choose OK in the Page Setup dialog box to insert the specified header and footer in the document.

The header and footer appear on the screen only when the area being printed is displayed in Print Preview view.

Creating a Header or Footer in PowerPoint

Header and footer information can be added to a slide, notes page, handout, and outline. Slides have only footers; notes pages and handouts have both headers and footers. To apply a footer to only one slide, you must activate the slide before you insert a footer. The headers and footers you insert on notes pages and handouts appear on every page in the presentation.

You can change the appearance or position of header or footer information when the presentation is displayed in Master view. Any changes made to the handout master are also applied to the outline view of the presentation. However, you cannot insert additional characters in any of the header or footer placeholders because the placeholder becomes unusable. You must replace unusable placeholders by reapplying the master's styles.

To insert a footer on slides, notes pages, and handouts:

1. Choose View ➢ Header And Footer to display its dialog box.

2. Choose any of the following options on the Slide tab:

   - Select the Date And Time check box to insert the date or time in the left corner of the footer on the slides. Then select either Update Automatically and choose the date or time format in the drop-down list, or Fixed and type the date or time in the text box.

   - Select the Slide Number check box to insert the sequential number of the slide within the presentation in the right corner of the footer on the slides.

   - Select the Footer check box to insert text in the center of the footer on the slides, and then type the text in the text box.

   - Select the Don't Show On Title Slide check box to suppress the display of any footer items on the presentation's title slide.

3. Choose any of the following options on the Notes And Handouts tab:

- Select the Date And Time checkbox to insert the date or time in the right corner of the header on notes pages and handouts. Then select either Update Automatically and choose the date or time format in the drop-down list, or Fixed and type the date or time in the text box.

- Select the Header checkbox to insert text in the left corner of the header on the notes pages and handouts, and then type the text in the text box.

- Select the Page Number checkbox to insert the page number in the right corner of the footer on notes pages and handouts.

- Select the Footer checkbox to insert text in the left corner of the footer on the notes pages and handouts, and then type the text in the text box.

4. Choose Apply To All to insert the specified header and footer in all slides (except the title slide if the Don't Show On Title Slide check box is selected) and in all notes and handout pages. Alternatively, select Apply to apply the specified footer on the active slide.

To change the position of a header or footer:

1. Choose View ➤ Master ➤ Slide Master, Title Master, Handout Master, or Notes Master to display that item in Master view.

2. Drag the placeholder to a different location on the slide or page.

3. Optionally, select the placeholder and then use the options available on the Formatting toolbar or Format ➤ Font to change the attributes applied to the text.

Creating or Editing a Header or Footer in Word

Use Word's Header and Footer toolbar to easily create, move between, and display the header or footer in a document. You can use a negative indent to print a header or footer in the left margin.

1. Select View ➤ Header and Footer to display the Header and Footer toolbar. The header area of the current page is activated.

2. Type the text for the header of your document, using Word's regular formatting techniques to format your text.

3. Click on the Switch Between Header and Footer button on the Header and Footer toolbar to activate the footer.

4. Type the footer text and apply the appropriate formatting.

5. Choose one of the following options on the Header and Footer toolbar, to quickly insert the corresponding item in the position of the insertion point:

- Click on the Insert AutoText button, and then select one of the AutoText entries in the pop-up list that appears to insert that entry in the header or footer.

- Click on the Insert Page Number button to insert automatic page numbers in the header or footer.

- Click on the Insert Number of Pages button to insert the total number of pages in the document or section.

- Click on the Format Page Number button to display the Page Number Format dialog box, in which you can change the appearance of the current page numbers.

- Click on the Insert Date button to insert the current date.

- Click on the Insert Time button to insert the current time.

6. If necessary, click on the Page Setup button to display the Page Setup dialog box, in which you can change any of the page layout options for your document.

7. When you are finished creating or editing the header and footer, click on the Close button (Alt+Shift+C) on the Header and Footer toolbar to remove the toolbar and return to your document.

Click on the Show/Hide Document Text button on the Header and Footer toolbar to display or hide the regular text in your document while you are editing the header or footer.

If you want to edit the text or update a field code in a header or footer, you must activate the header or footer and display the Header and Footer toolbar, using either of the following methods:

- In Page Layout view, double-click on either the header or footer.

MASTER'S REFERENCE

H

- In Normal view, select View ➤ Header and Footer.

Creating Different Headers and Footers in Word

To make the first page header and footer different from those in the rest of the document:

1. Choose View ➤ Header and Footer to activate the header and display the Header and Footer toolbar.

2. Click on the Page Setup button on the Header and Footer toolbar to display the Page Setup dialog box, and choose the Layout tab.

3. Select the Different First Page checkbox in the Headers and Footers area, and then select OK in the Page Setup dialog box.

4. If necessary, create the header and footer that is to appear on the first page. To omit a header and footer on the first page, leave the areas blank.

5. Click on the Show Next button on the Header and Footer toolbar to move to the next header area, and then create the header for the rest of the document. Click on the Switch Between Header and Footer button to activate the footer area, and then create the footer for the rest of the document.

6. Click on the Close button (Alt+Shift+C) on the Header and Footer toolbar to return to your document.

To make odd and even page headers and footers different:

1. Follow steps 1–2 above.

2. Select the Different Odd and Even checkbox in the Headers and Footers area, and then select OK.

3. If necessary, click on the Show Previous or Show Next button on the Header and Footer toolbar to move to an even page number. Create the header and footer that is to appear on even pages. Click on the Switch Between Header and Footer button as necessary.

4. Click on the Show Previous or Show Next button on the Header and Footer toolbar to move to an odd page number, and then create the header and footer that is to appear on odd

pages. Click on the Switch Between Header and Footer button as necessary.

5. Click on the Close button (Alt+Shift+C) on the Header and Footer toolbar to return to your document.

If you create headers and footers in documents that contain more than one section, all the headers and footers will be the same for the entire document because the sections are connected. The phrases "Header - Section *N*" and "Footer - Section *N*" appear in the top left corner of the corresponding area, and the phrase "Same as Previous" appears in the top right corner of the header or footer area.

To create different headers and footers for a section, you must disconnect the previous section's header and footer. All subsequent sections will then have the same header and footer as the section after the broken connection, unless you break the connection for those sections as well.

To create sectional headers and footers:

1. Position the insertion point in the section for which you want different headers and footers, and then choose View ➤ Header And Footer.

2. Click on the Same as Previous button on the Header and Footer toolbar to break the connection to the previous section.

3. Select the header, press Backspace or Delete to delete the text, and then create the new header.

4. Click on the Switch Between Header and Footer button to activate the footer, select the footer, press Backspace or Delete to delete the text, and then create the new footer.

5. If necessary, move the insertion point into the next section and repeat steps 2–4.

6. Click on the Close button (Alt+Shift+C) on the Header and Footer toolbar to return to your document.

To reestablish the connection with the section before the section that contains the insertion point, click on the Same as Previous button on the Header and Footer toolbar.

Help

The Microsoft Office applications come with extensive online help. Depending on your immediate need for help, you can ask the Office Assistant a question, search for keywords, request help on a specific document item, or read step-by-step instructions on how to perform a task.

Asking a Question

If you need help performing a specific action, you can ask the Office Assistant for help using your own words. To do so:

1. Click anywhere in the Office Assistant, or choose Help ➤ Microsoft *Application* Help (F1) to display the Office Assistant's dialog box.

2. Type your question in the text box.

3. Choose Search to display a list of available topics that are pertinent to your question.

4. Click on the blue dot beside the topic you wish to read to display the Help window for that topic.

The Help window contains the following objects to assist your search for help:

- Some help topics include a button on which you can click to obtain information about a subtopic mentioned in that topic.

- You can click on any text that appears in green with a dashed underline to display a definition of that text.

- Click on the Help Topics button on the Help window's toolbar; the Index tab in the Help Topics dialog box will appear. Type the first few characters of the topic in the *Type the first few letters of the word you're looking for* text box, highlight the topic you want to see in the list box, and then choose Display.

- When the Help Topics dialog box is displayed, you can also search for a topic by a keyword. To do so, click on the Find tab, type the keyword in the *Type the word(s) you want to find* text box, highlight the topic you want to see in the list box, and then choose Display.

Getting Context-Sensitive Help

You can easily obtain some useful information for a command or an option in a displayed dialog box. To do so:

- Click on the menu that contains the command, and then, in the drop-down menu, drag until the command is highlighted. Then press Shift+F1 to display information about that command.

- Click on the Help button on the displayed dialog box's title bar. When the mouse pointer changes into a pointer with a question mark attached, click on the option for which you want information.

Getting Help from the Microsoft Network

If you have a modem and Internet account, you can get reference information about any of the Microsoft Office applications directly from Microsoft.

1. Choose Help ➤ Microsoft on the Web, and then select one of the topics in the drop-down list that appears to activate your Internet access software.

2. Choose the command that allows you to connect to the Microsoft Page you selected.

3. Click on the icon that is labeled with the type of support you want.

HTML Document

HyperText Markup Language, also called HTML, is the procedure used to create documents that are published on the World Wide Web. HTML documents include formatting tags and graphics that can be used to link to reference information. You can create HTML documents in Word, and view them with a Web browser. You can also convert HTML documents into regular Word documents.

Creating a Web Page

Create a Web page the same way you would any other Word document. You can apply a background format to a Web page, and insert hyperlinks to other documents.

1. Click on the New button on the Standard toolbar to open a new document.

2. Type any text and insert any hyperlinks and graphics for the Web page.

3. If necessary, choose Format ➤ Background, and click on a color for the background in

the palette that appears. Alternatively, choose Fill Effects and then select a gradient, texture, pattern, or picture for the background.

4. Choose File ➢ Save to display the Save As dialog box. Select HTML Document in the Save As Type drop-down list.

5. Type a name for the Web page in the File Name text box, and then choose Save.

Opening a Web Page in Word

Word contains a file converter that automatically opens a file saved in HTML format as a regular Word document. Once the file is open, you can save it as a regular Word document.

1. Click on the Open button on the Standard toolbar or choose File ➢ Open (Ctrl+O) to display the Open dialog box.

2. Select HTML Document in the Files of Type drop-down list.

3. Highlight the name of a file with the .html extension in the Look In list box.

4. Choose Open.

When you open a document that was saved in HTML format, only the text and placeholders for graphics appear in the document window. To view the Web page as it will appear when published on the Internet, you must have a Web browser, such as Microsoft Internet Explorer or Netscape Navigator.

To display an HTML file in your Web browser, choose File ➢ Open, and then double-click on the name of the file.

Hyperlink

A hyperlink allows you to jump to related information in the same or a different file. Hyperlinks can be used in Access, Excel, PowerPoint, and Word. They are particularly useful when presenting information in files on your company's intranet or the Internet.

In an Access database file, a hyperlink allows you to jump to an object in a database, to a file on your computer or on your network, or to an address on your intranet or the Internet.

In an Excel spreadsheet, you can insert a hyperlink consisting of text, a graphic, or a worksheet function. When you click on the hyperlink, you jump to the destination file or address.

In a PowerPoint presentation, a hyperlink can be used to jump to a different slide, a different presentation, a custom show, an Excel worksheet, a Word document, or an intranet or Internet address. You can use either the click method to jump to the location, or position the mouse over the hyperlink to perform the associated action. You can also associate two actions with a hyperlink, using both the mouse over and the click method to perform each action.

A hyperlink is a field code you insert in a Word document or a Web page that allows you to jump to related information in the same or a different file. The item you select to be the hyperlink appears as the result of the field code. Hyperlinks are often used to jump to multi-media files that contain sounds and videos, and to other text documents. The document a hyperlink jumps to can be on your hard drive, on a network drive, or an address on the Internet.

1. Choose one of the following options, depending on the application in which the hyperlink is to be inserted:

- In Access, display the form in Design view, and then click where you want to insert the hyperlink.

- In Excel, select the cells to use as the hyperlink.

- In PowerPoint, select the text that is to be the hyperlink.

- In Word, select the text or graphic that is to be the hyperlink.

2. Click on the Insert Hyperlink button on the Standard toolbar or choose Insert ➢ Hyperlink (Ctrl+K) to display the Insert Hyperlink dialog box.

3. Type the path of the file this hyperlink will jump to in the Link to File or URL text box. Alternatively, choose Browse and then select the name of the file to automatically enter its path in the text box.

4. To jump to a specific location within the file, type the name of the location (such as the bookmark or range name) in the Named Location in File text box. If the file to which the hyperlink will jump is a Word document, choose Browse to display a list of names, and then select the name of the bookmark to automatically enter it in the text box.

5. To specify that the location of the file containing the hyperlink may be moved, select the Use Relative Path for Hyperlink check box.

6. Choose OK.

The selected text is changed into the hyperlink display text, which appears as blue underlined text in your document. When you position the mouse pointer over the hyperlink display text, the mouse pointer appears as a pointing finger and the path to the file to which the hyperlink jumps is displayed in a yellow note. Click on the hyperlink text to jump to the specified file. If the file is a Word document, the Web toolbar is automatically displayed.

Labels

Create mailing and other types of labels in both Access and Word. In Access, use the Mailing Label Report Wizard to design the labels. In Word, use the options on the Labels tab in the Envelopes and Labels dialog box to create one label or an entire page of the same label. You can also use Mail Merge to create different labels using the records in a database.

Creating Labels in Access

To create mailing labels with Access's Mailing Label Wizard:

1. In the Database window, select the Reports tab.

2. Choose New to display the New Report dialog box.

3. In the drop-down list, highlight the name of the table or query that contains the records that will be used to create the text of the labels.

4. Choose Label Wizard in the list box, and then choose OK.

5. The Label Wizard dialog box appears. Select the desired label size in the What Label Size Would You Like list box. Then, if necessary, choose English or Metric in the Unit Of Measure area, and Sheet Feed or Continuous in the Label Type area.

6. Choose Next, and then select the font, size, color, and other attributes in the next dialog box.

7. Choose Next, then select the field whose data is to appear first on the label in the Available Fields list box, and click on the > button to insert it in the Prototype Label area. Insert a space or punctuation mark if necessary.

8. Repeat the field selection process in step 7 to insert each field in the necessary position in the Prototype Label area, and then choose Next.

9. Highlight the field on which to sort the labels in the Available Fields list box, and then click on the > button to insert it in the Sort By list box.

10. Repeat step 9 for each field on which to sort the labels, and then choose Next.

11. Type a name for the label report, and then choose whether to display the labels as they will appear when printed, or to change the label design.

12. Choose Finish to either display the labels or switch to Design view.

13. If the labels are displayed, click on the Save button on the Form Design toolbar or choose File ➤ Save (Ctrl+S) to save the report. If the labels are displayed in Design view, save the report after any changes are made.

Creating Labels in Word

Word allows you to print one label or a page of labels with the same text. You can select one of Word's built-in label definitions, which were created based on many different Avery label types and sizes, or you can customize a label definition to use with another brand of labels whose dimensions are not among those in the list.

Before you select a type of label, select and set up the printer on which the labels will be printed. The selected printer driver determines how the labels will be set up and printed.

To print the labels:

1. If necessary, select the address you want to print.

2. Choose Tools ➢ Envelopes and Labels to display the Envelopes and Labels dialog box, and then select the Labels tab.

3. Selected text appears in the Address text box. Choose any of the following options to change the address in the Address text box:

   • Type the text you want to appear on the label in the Address text box.

   • Select the Use Return Address checkbox to print the default return address.

   • Select the Delivery Point Bar Code checkbox to include the POSTNET bar code on a mailing label printed on a dot-matrix printer.

4. Click on the Label area of the dialog box or select Options to display the Label Options dialog box.

5. Select any of the following options to define the label and printer specifications, and then choose OK.

   • In the Printer Information area, select Dot Matrix or Laser to define the type of printer that is set up. If Laser is selected as the type of printer, highlight the location in which the labels will be fed to the printer in the Tray drop-down list.

   • Highlight the kind of label you are using in the Label Products drop-down list.

   • Select the manufacturer's product number for the label in the Product Number list box. A description of the label appears in the Label Information area.

   • Choose Details to display the *Type and Number* Information dialog box to customize the selected label. Make any necessary changes, and then choose OK.

   • Choose New Label to display the New Custom *Printer* dialog box, specify the measurements for the custom label, and then choose OK.

6. In the Print area of the Labels tab, select Full Page of the Same Label to print the text in the Address text box on each label on the page of labels. You can also select Single Label to print the text on only one label, and then adjust numbers in the Row and Column text boxes to define the position of the label on the page of labels.

7. Choose Print to print the page of labels or the single label. Or, choose New Document to place a full sheet of labels in a table in a new document, and then save the document.

You can also use Mail Merge to print labels if you have created a data file.

Letter Wizard

Use Word's new Letter Wizard to create personal and business letters in various formats. Letter Wizard helps you gather all of the essential items in a letter except its body, and automatically places them in the correct location for the letter format you select.

To create a letter:

1. Click on the New button on the Standard toolbar to open a new document.

2. Choose Tools ➢ Letter Wizard to display the Letter Wizard dialog box.

3. Choose any of the following options on the Letter Format tab:

   • To insert a date in the letter, select the Date Line checkbox and then select the date format in the corresponding drop-down list.

   • To insert a header and footer on each page of the letter except for the first page, select the *Include header and footer with page design* checkbox.

   • Choose a layout for your letter in the Choose a Page Design drop-down list.

   • Select Full Block, Modified Block, or Semi-Block as the style for the letter in the Choose A Letter Style drop-down list.

   • To format the letter so it will fit on your letterhead, select the Pre-printed Letterhead checkbox. Then select the location in which the letterhead is positioned in the *Where on the page is the letterhead?*

drop-down list, and adjust the value in the *How much space does the letterhead need?* text box to specify the distance from the letterhead to the edge of the page.

4. Click on the Recipient Info tab, and then specify any of the following:

   - Select the name and address of the recipient in the Address Book. Alter-natively, type the recipient's name in the Recipient's Name text box, and the recipient's address in the Delivery Address text box.

   - Type the salutation in the Example text box in the Salutation area. Alternatively, select one of the example styles beside the Example drop-down list, and then select an example in the drop-down list. The available examples depend on which style you select.

5. Click on the Other Elements tab, and then specify any of the following options to include in the letter:

   - Select the Reference Line checkbox, and then select one of built-in reference lines in the corresponding drop-down list. Alternatively, edit a selected reference line or type a different reference line.

   - Select the Mailing Instructions checkbox, and then select one of the built-in instructions in the corresponding drop-down list. Alternatively, edit a selected instruction or type a different one.

   - Select the Attention checkbox, and then select one of the built-in attention lines in the corresponding drop-down list. Alternatively, edit a selected attention line or type a different one.

   - Select the Subject checkbox, and then edit the subject line or type a different one.

   - Select the name of each person to whom to send a copy of the letter in the Address Book. Alternatively, type the name of each person who will receive a copy in the Cc text box.

6. Click on the Sender Info tab, and then choose any of the following options to complete the letter's format:

   - Select the name of the sender in the Address Book. Alternatively, type the name of the sender in the Sender's Name text box. The current user's address automatically appears in the Return Address text box. To enter a different return address, replace the contents of the Return Address text box. If your letterhead contains your address, select the Omit checkbox to prevent it from being printed in the letter.

   - To define how the letter's closing will appear, select one of the built-in closings in the Complimentary Closing drop-down list; select or type your title in the Job Title drop-down list; select the name of your company in the Company drop-down list; select your initials in the Writer/Typist Initials drop-down list. If necessary, select the Enclosures checkbox, and then adjust the value in the corresponding text box to indicate the number of enclosures in the letter.

7. Choose OK to insert the elements you specified in the new document.

The new letter appears in the document; you can immediately begin to type the body of the letter where "Type your text here" is selected.

Look Up Reference

You can have Excel, PowerPoint, and Word automatically look up information in Microsoft Bookshelf or Microsoft Bookshelf Basics using the new Look Up Reference feature. To do so:

1. Choose Tools ➤ Look Up Reference to display the Look Up Reference dialog box.

2. Select the reference to use to look up information in the Available Reference Titles list box.

3. Choose one of the following options in the Search area:

   - Choose Keyword, and then type the keywords on which to search for information in the Text text box.

   - Choose Full Text, and then type a specific string of text for which to search in the reference in the Text text box.

   - Choose None to perform the search from within the reference.

4. Choose OK to open the specified reference.

5. If necessary, insert the selected reference's CD in your CD-ROM drive, and then choose OK to remove the message box requesting that you do so.

Macro

Create or record macros to automate tasks that you perform regularly. In Access, macros can be assigned to forms, reports, sections, and controls. In Excel and Word, macros can be assigned to shortcut keys or toolbars for easy access. Each Microsoft Office application comes with useful macros that are assigned to toolbar or button bar buttons.

Use Access's Macro Builder to create a macro in a form or report in Design view, or create a macro in the Macro pane of the Database window. Use Excel's Visual Basic toolbar and Word's Macro Record and Macro toolbars to record a macro.

Access's macros are stored as database objects in the database file. In Excel, macros can be stored in the workbook in which you intend to use them, or in the Personal Macro Workbook, so they will always be available. Word's macros are stored by default in the Normal.dot template.

Creating and Running an Access Macro

In Access, you can create macros as database objects to make forms, reports, tables, and other database objects work together. For example, you can create a macro to print a monthly summary report or to open a report while you are working in Form view. Macros can also be used within other macros.

The macros you create as database objects are written in Visual Basic. You can also type Visual Basic instructions in macros.

Access database macros consist of *actions*, the events that the macro is to perform, and *action arguments*, the specific information that is necessary to carry out each action.

To create and run an Access macro:

1. Click on the Macros tab in the Database window to display the Macro pane, and then choose New to display both the Macro window and the Macro Design toolbar.

2. Select the first action for the macro in the Action drop-down list. Alternatively, display the Database window beside the Macro window, and drag a table, form, query, report, or macro from the Database window into a row in the Action list in the Macro window. An action is automatically added to open the table, form, query, or report, or to run the macro.

3. Click on the first argument for the action in the Action Arguments pane of the Macro window, and then, in its drop-down list, type or select the appropriate option for the argument. A brief explanation of the current argument appears in the area beside the arguments.

4. Repeat step 3 for each argument for the first action.

5. Optionally, type an explanation for the selected action on the corresponding line in the Comment area of the Macro Window. (Press F6 to move the insertion point between the Action/Comment pane and the Action Arguments pane in the Macro window.)

6. Repeat steps 2 through 5 to enter each step in the macro.

7. Click on the Save button on the Macro Design toolbar or choose File ➤ Save (Ctrl+S) to display the Save As dialog box. Type a name for the macro in the Macro Name text box, and then choose OK to save the macro as a database object.

8. To run the macro, click on the Run button on the Macro Design toolbar. To run a macro on the Macros tab in the active Database window, highlight the name of the macro and then choose Run.

To describe the purpose of a macro, leave the first row in the Action column blank, and type the description in the first row in the Comment column. Begin the macro in the second row in the Action/Comment pane of the Macro window.

The order in which the actions appear in the Macro Window is the order in which the actions are carried out when the macro is run. If the actions do not appear in the correct order, click on the row selector to select the entire row containing the action, point to the center of the row selector, and drag the row to a different position in the list.

To edit a macro, click on the Macros tab in the Database window, highlight the name of the macro in the Macro pane, and then choose Design. Follow the steps used when creating a macro, above, to add new actions on blank lines in the Macro window. If necessary, move the actions to the correct position in the Action list, and then save the changes you made to the macro.

To insert a blank row above the row that contains the insertion point in the Action/Comment pane of the Macro window, click on the Insert Rows button on the Macro Design toolbar or choose Insert ➤ Row. To delete the row that contains the insertion point, click on the Delete Rows button on the Macro Design toolbar or choose Edit ➤ Delete Row. Any characters in the row will also be deleted.

To delete an action, click on the row selector, and then choose Edit ➤ Delete Row.

Recording and Running an Excel Macro

In Excel, you can create macros to perform tasks that you often repeat. You can record often-used commands and keystrokes with Excel's Macro Recorder, or write macros in Visual Basic, Microsoft Office's macro language. When you are recording a macro in Excel, display the Visual Basic toolbar to make your work easier.

For a macro to run, it must be in a Visual Basic module—a special sheet in a workbook for storing macros—in an open workbook file. When you record a macro, Excel automatically inserts it in module in the workbook you specify.

A macro can be stored in the current workbook, so it is available whenever you are working in it; in a new workbook, which you must remember to open before you use the macro; or in Excel's Personal Macro Workbook, which is always open

(but hidden), and which Excel controls automatically. If you create or edit a macro in the Personal Macro Workbook, Excel automatically displays a message asking if you want to save any changes you made to the Personal Macro Workbook when you exit Excel.

To record and run an Excel macro:

1. Click on the Record Macro button on the Visual Basic toolbar, or choose Tools ➤ Macro ➤ Record New Macro to display the Record Macro dialog box.

2. Optionally, type a descriptive name for the macro in the Macro Name text box, and a brief description of the macro's function in the Description text box.

3. To assign a shortcut key to use to run the macro, type a letter in the Ctrl+ text box in the Shortcut Key area.

4. In the Store Macro In drop-down list, select Personal Macro Workbook, New Workbook, or This Workbook as the location in which to store the macro.

5. Choose OK in the Record Macro dialog box. The Stop Recording toolbar appears.

6. If necessary, click on the Relative Reference button on the Stop Recording toolbar to use relative instead of absolute references in the macro.

7. Perform the actions and select the commands necessary for the macro, and then click on the Stop Recording button on the Stop Recording toolbar or choose Tools ➤ Macro ➤ Stop Recording.

8. To run the macro, click on the Run Macro button on the Visual Basic toolbar, or select Tools ➤ Macro ➤ Macros (Alt+F8), to display the Macro dialog box. Then highlight the name of the macro in the Macro Name list box and choose Run. Alternatively, press Ctrl+*letter*, where *letter* is the shortcut key you assigned to the macro.

You can create a toolbar for your macros, and then assign each macro to the toolbar. Click on the corresponding button on your macro toolbar to run the macro.

You must display a macro's module on your screen to edit it. If the macro is stored in the Personal

Macro Workbook, you must unhide the workbook before you can edit the macro. To display the Personal Macro Workbook (after you have created a macro in it), choose Window ➤ Unhide, select Personal.xls in the Unhide Workbook list box, and then choose OK.

To edit a macro, choose Tools ➤ Macro ➤ Macros (Alt+F8) to display the Macro dialog box, highlight the name of the macro in the Macro Name list box, and then choose Edit to display the module that contains the macro.

To delete a macro, choose Tools ➤ Macro ➤ Macros (Alt+F8), highlight the name of the macro in the Macro Name list box, and then choose Delete.

Recording and Running a Word Macro

In Word, you can record the commands and keystrokes used to perform a task you often repeat. Use the mouse to select menu commands or to scroll while recording a macro, but not to select text or move the insertion point in the document window.

As you record a macro, Word uses the Visual Basic programming language to compile the macro. You can also type Visual Basic instructions to create more complex macros in Word, including instructions that cannot be recorded.

If you accidentally record something in a macro, immediately click on the Undo button on the Standard toolbar or select Edit ➤ Undo. The undone action will not play back when the macro is run.

To record and run a Word macro:

1. Choose Tools ➤ Macro ➤ Record New Macro or double-click on REC on the status bar to display the Record Macro dialog box.

2. Type a name for the macro in the Macro Name text box, and a description in the Description text box.

3. If necessary, select All Documents (Normal .dot) or the active template in the Store Macro In drop-down list as the location in which to store the macro.

4. Optionally, select Toolbars or Keyboard as the method to access the macro in the Assign Macro To area, and then perform the steps necessary to assign a toolbar button or keystroke combination to the macro.

5. Choose OK in the Record Macro dialog box to display the Stop Recording toolbar. While you are recording, the mouse pointer appears with a graphic of a cassette tape.

6. Select the commands and type the keystrokes necessary for the macro.

7. Click on the Stop Recording button on the Stop Recording toolbar, or double-click on REC on the status bar to stop recording the macro.

8. To run a macro, choose Tools ➤ Macro ➤ Macros (Alt+F8), highlight the name of the macro in the Macro Name list box and choose Run. Alternatively, click on its toolbar button, or press its shortcut keys to run the corresponding macro.

9. If necessary, choose Cancel in the Macro dialog box to return to your document.

To temporarily stop recording the commands and keystrokes in a macro, click on the Pause Recording button on the Stop Recording toolbar. Click on the Pause Recording button again when you are ready to resume recording your macro.

To edit a macro you have recorded, choose Tools ➤ Macro ➤ Macros (Alt+F8) to display the Macros dialog box. Then highlight the name of the macro in the Macro Name list box, and choose Edit.

To delete a macro, select Tools ➤ Macro ➤ Macros (Alt+F8) to display the Macros dialog box. Then highlight the name of the macro in the Macro Name list box, and choose Delete.

Margins

Margins define the distance from the edge of the paper to the beginning of the text or data on a printed page. The minimum margins that can be set depend on the size of the paper and the printer being used. Some items, such as headers, footers, and objects inserted in a frame, can be printed in the margins. Margins can be defined for Access forms and reports, Excel worksheets, and Word documents.

Setting the Margins for an Access Form or Report

To specify the margins for a printed form or report in Access:

1. Open the database file that contains the form or report.

2. Highlight the form or report whose margins are to be changed in the corresponding pane of the Database window. Then choose Open for a form or Preview for a report.

3. Choose File ➤ Page Setup to display the Page Setup dialog box.

4. Type the measurement for the Left, Right, Top, and Bottom margins in the corresponding text box in the Margins area.

5. Choose OK to set the margins for the active database object.

To set different default margins for all new database objects, choose Tools ➤ Options, select the General Tab, type the distance from the edge of the paper in the Left Margin, Right Margin, Top Margin, and Bottom Margin text boxes, and then choose OK.

Setting the Margins for an Excel Worksheet

To quickly set the page margins, adjust column widths, and adjust the distance between the header and footer and the top or bottom edge of the page in an Excel worksheet:

1. Click on the Print Preview button on the Standard toolbar, or choose File ➤ Print Preview to display the active worksheet in the Print Preview window.

2. Choose Margins to toggle on the display of margin and column width handles.

3. Position the mouse pointer over one of the handles until it appears as a cross with two arrows (the arrows point in the directions in which you can move the handle), and then drag the handle to adjust the margin, column width, or the position of the header or footer on the page.

To set exact margins for a printed page containing the current worksheet:

1. Choose File ➤ Page Setup to display the Page Setup dialog box, and choose the Margins tab.

2. Specify the Top, Bottom, Left, and Right margins in the corresponding text boxes.

3. Specify the distance from the edge of the page for the header and footer in the Header and Footer text boxes.

4. To center the data on the printed page, select the Horizontally and Vertically checkboxes in the Center on Page area.

5. Choose OK to define the margins for the current worksheet.

Setting the Margins in a Word Document

In a Word document based on the Normal.dot template, the top and bottom margins are set at 1 inch and the left and right margins at 1.25 inches by default. You can set margins for each section of a Word document.

To quickly set the margins in the current section of the active document, use the ruler in either Page Layout or Print Preview view.

To set exact margin measurements, adjust the position of the header or footer, or create a binding offset, follow these steps:

1. Position the insertion point in the section of the document whose margins you want to change.

2. Choose File ➤ Page Setup, and choose the Margins tab in the Page Setup dialog box.

3. Specify the Top, Bottom, Left, and Right margins in the corresponding text boxes.

4. If necessary, choose any of the following options, and then choose OK in the Page Setup dialog box:

   - In the Gutter text box, specify the amount of additional space to allow for the binding margin of a document. The gutter is added to the Left or Inside margin.

   - In the From Edge area, specify the distance from the edge of the page for the position of the document's header and footer in the Header and Footer text boxes.

- In the Apply To drop-down list, choose This Section, This Point Forward, Selected Sections, Selected Text, or Whole Document as the portion of the document whose margins are to be reset.

- Select the Mirror Margins checkbox to change the widths of the inside and outside margins for facing pages, if printing is to appear on both sides of the paper. In the Inside text box, specify the distance from the left edge of the paper to the left edge of the text on the odd-numbered pages, and from the right edge of the paper and the right edge of the text on the even-numbered pages. In the Outside text box, specify the distance from the right edge of the paper to the right edge of the text on the odd-numbered pages, and from the left edge of the paper and the left edge of the text on the even-numbered pages.

- Choose Default to change the default margins in the current template to the settings specified on the Margins tab, and then choose Yes to confirm the change.

Microsoft Office Shortcut Bar

Each time you start Windows, the Microsoft Office Shortcut Bar runs automatically, because Setup placed it in the Windows StartUp group. By default, the Shortcut Bar with small buttons is displayed near the top right corner of your screen. When any of the Office applications is active and maximized, the Microsoft Office Shortcut Bar appears on its title bar. You can drag the Shortcut Bar to another screen edge, minimize it, or hide it.

Customizing the Shortcut Bar

The Microsoft Office Shortcut Bar contains buttons that launch certain features, such as MS Outlook and the Microsoft Bookshelf Basics. You can add or remove buttons on the toolbar or change the display of the toolbar. You can also design additional customizable Shortcut toolbars and access them from the Office Shortcut Bar.

1. Click on the Microsoft Office icon on the Microsoft Office Shortcut Bar, and then choose Customize to display the Customize dialog box.

2. Select the appropriate tab to make changes to the Shortcut Bar's view, buttons, or settings, and to create other toolbars.

3. Make any changes necessary, and then choose OK in the Customize dialog box to implement the changes.

The following options can be changed in the Options area on the View tab:

- Select the Large Buttons checkbox to enlarge the icons on the Shortcut Bar and its other toolbars.

- Select the Show ToolTips checkbox (selected by default) to display the name of the application when you point to a button on the Shortcut Bar.

- Select the Show Title Screen at Startup checkbox to display the Microsoft Office dialog box when the Microsoft Office Shortcut Bar starts.

The following options can be changed on the Buttons tab:

- Choose Add File or Add Folder to display a search dialog box for adding items not included in the default Shortcut Bar lists.

- In the Show These Files As Buttons list box, select the checkbox beside any application that is to appear on the toolbar specified in the Toolbar drop-down list to place its icon on that toolbar.

- In the Show These Files as Buttons list box, highlight the name of an application whose toolbar button or position on the Shortcut Bar is to be changed, and then click on the ↑ or ↓ Move button to change its location.

- In the Show These Files as Buttons list box, highlight the name of an application whose toolbar button is to be removed, and then choose Delete.

The following options can be changed on the Toolbars tab:

- In the Show These Folders as Toolbars list box, select the checkbox of an application item or folder to create its toolbar, and then choose Add Toolbar to browse through your applications for additional items to add to it.

- Choose Add Toolbar to create a new toolbar to place on the Microsoft Office Shortcut Bar.

- Choose Remove to delete the highlighted folder in the Show These Folders as Toolbars list box.
- Choose Rename to rename the highlighted folder in the Show These Folders as Toolbars list box.

Object Linking and Embedding

Use Object Linking and Embedding (OLE) to exchange data between files. OLE is particularly useful in the Microsoft Office Professional applications, which are designed to be used together. You can link or embed graphics, equations, worksheets, and drawings in a file created in any Microsoft Office application, and then edit the selected object in the file.

A linked object contains information that remains connected to its original file. By default, each time it is changed in its original file, the linked data is automatically updated when you open the file containing the link.

An embedded object becomes part of the file in which it is placed. To edit an embedded object, double-click on it to open the application in which it was created, and make any necessary changes. The changes you made appear when you return to your file.

Creating and Embedding an Object

In Access, you must display the form or report in Design or Preview view before you can embed an object in it.

1. Position the insertion point where you want to embed a new object, select Insert ➤ Object to display the Object dialog box, and then choose Create New or the Create New tab.

2. Select the kind of object you want to embed in the document in the Object Type list box.

3. Choose from the following options to define how the object is displayed in your document:

   - To display the object in the drawing layer in your Word document, select the Float Over Text checkbox. Objects in the drawing area can be positioned in front of or behind document text. Clear the checkbox

to position the object at the position of the insertion point.

   - To display the object as an icon in your document, select the Display as Icon check box.

4. Choose OK to open the application used to create the object.

5. Create the object.

6. Click in the document outside the object to embed the object and return to your file.

7. Click on the Save button on the Standard toolbar to save the file with the embedded object.

The method used to embed the object and return to your file will vary slightly from one application to another. For example, if the object is a Word Picture, click on the Close Picture button on the Word Picture toolbar.

Editing an Embedded Object

1. Double-click on the object in your file, or select the object and then choose Edit ➤ *Type of* Object ➤ Open.

2. Make any necessary changes to the object.

3. To update the object and return to your document, click in the file outside the object.

Linking or Embedding an Existing File

1. Position the insertion point where you want to embed the object in your file.

2. Choose Insert ➤ Object and select the Create from File tab.

3. Type the path and name of the file to be embedded in the File Name text box, or select Browse to display the Browse dialog box, select the name of the file in the Look In list box, and then choose OK.

4. Choose from the following options to define how the object is displayed in your file:

   - To link the specified file to the active file, select the Link to File checkbox. Clear the checkbox to embed the file in the active document.

- To display the object in the drawing layer in your Word document, select the Float over Text checkbox. Objects in the drawing area can be positioned in front of or behind document text. Clear the checkbox to position the object at the position of the insertion point.

- To display the object as an icon in your file, select the Display as Icon checkbox.

5. Choose OK to embed or link the object in your document.

6. Save the active document with the embedded or linked object.

Linking or Embedding Part of a File

The source file must be saved before you can link or embed selected data in it to the active file.

1. Position the insertion point where you want to link or embed the object in your file.

2. Open the source application and file, then select the data to be linked or embedded.

3. Click on the Copy button or choose Edit ➢ Copy (Ctrl+C) in the source application, and then click on the Microsoft Office application button on the Windows 95 Taskbar to switch back to your file, or choose Window ➢ *Name Of File* to return to the object's destination file.

4. Select Edit ➢ Paste Special to display the Paste Special dialog box.

5. Choose either of the following options:

- To embed the object in the active file, choose Paste, and then highlight the first item in the As list box that includes "Object" in its name.

- To insert the selected data into the file as a link, choose Paste Link .

6. Choose one of the following options in the As list box to specify how to link the data in your file:

- To link the contents of the Clipboard to the file as a graphic, select *Application Name* Object.

- To link the contents of the Clipboard to the file as text data with its current formatting, select Formatted Text (RTF).

- To link the contents of the Clipboard to the file with no formatting, select Unformatted Text.

- To link the Clipboard contents to the file as a graphic, select Picture.

- To create a hyperlink to the source file, select *Application* Hyperlink.

7. Choose from the following options to define how a linked or embedded object is displayed in your file:

- To display the object in the drawing layer in your Word document, select the Float over Text checkbox. Objects in the drawing area can be positioned in front of or behind document text. Clear the checkbox to position the object at the position of the insertion point.

- To display the object as an icon in your document, select the Display as Icon checkbox.

8. Choose OK.

Modifying the File Format of an Embedded Object

If an embedded object is in a file format that you want to change or whose application you do not have, you can convert the file to a format that is available on your system.

An embedded object appears as a picture of the data you have embedded. However, all the data is still in the object. To reduce the size of a file with an embedded object, you can sometimes convert an object into a graphic. If you do, the original data is no longer embedded in the object, and the object can only be edited as a drawing.

1. Select the object that is in the file format you want to change.

2. Choose Edit ➢ *Type Of* Object ➢ Convert to display the Convert dialog box.

3. Select the format you want for the object in the Object Type list box. To convert the selected object into a graphic, highlight Picture in the Object Type list box.

4. Choose Convert To to permanently convert the file format, or Activate As to temporarily convert the file format.

5. If you chose Convert To in step 4, choose from the following options to define how the object is displayed in your document:

- To display the object in the drawing layer in your Word document, select the Float over Text checkbox. Objects in the drawing area can be positioned in front of or behind document text. Clear the checkbox to position the object at the position of the insertion point.

- To display the object as an icon in your document, select the Display as Icon checkbox.

6. Choose OK.

Modifying a Link

You can break an established link, reconnect a link to a file that has been moved or renamed, store the link as a picture in your file, specify how the link will be updated, update the link yourself, or lock a link in your file.

1. Activate the file that contains the link, and then choose Edit ➤ Links to display the Links dialog box.

2. Choose any of the following options to modify a link, and then choose OK:

- The name and source file, the range of the linked item, the name of the source application, and the update option of each link in the document are displayed in the Source File list box. Highlight the link you want to modify. Hold down the Ctrl key as you click on additional links to select more than one.

- In the Update area, choose Automatic to update the selected link whenever the source is changed, or Manual if you want to update the selected link in your document.

- Select the Locked checkbox to prevent the highlighted link from being updated. Clear the Locked checkbox when you want to update the link.

- Select the Save Picture in Document checkbox (selected by default.) to save the link as a picture of the linked data in your Word document rather than the actual information. Clear the checkbox if the link is a graphic and you want to reduce the size of your document. However, the link will take longer to display because Word must interpret the data in the source file and then create the picture.

- Choose Update Now to update all the highlighted links in the Source File list box.

- Choose Open Source to open the source document of the selected link to edit its data.

- Choose Change Source to display the Change Source dialog box for links you lost when a source was moved or renamed, and then select the name of the file you want to link in the Look In list box. The name or range of the item that is linked appears in the Item text box. If necessary, type a different name or range for the link, and then choose Open.

- Choose Break Link to break the link between the selected file and your Word document. The current data remains in your Word document, but it can no longer be updated.

You cannot reconnect a broken link as you can restore a link that was lost when the source file was moved or renamed. Instead, you must reestablish a link that is broken by mistake.

Outline

Switch to Outline view in Excel, PowerPoint, and Word to display important data or text in the current worksheet, presentation, or document, or to create a new outline. When you create an outline in Excel, the outline symbols appear. When you are in Outline view, the Outline toolbar appears to the left of the active window in PowerPoint, and just above the active window in Word, replacing the ruler.

Using Outline View in Excel

You can create an outline in Excel to display worksheet data in a summary report. In an Excel outline, as much data as necessary can be hidden or displayed.

In a worksheet outline, ranges of rows or columns are grouped, with each group containing the detail and summary data. An Excel outline can have up to eight levels of vertical and horizontal groups.

To create an outline:

- When worksheet data is arranged with detail data directly above or to the left of summary data and formulas, select the data to be grouped, and then choose Data ➤ Group And Outline ➤ Auto Outline to create an automatic outline.

- Choose Data ➤ Group And Outline ➤ Group to create an outline using detail data that is selected in either rows or columns.

- Select a cell in a list, and then choose Data ➤ Subtotals to automatically subtotal and outline the list items.

The selected data appears with outline symbols above and/or to the left of the data.

- Click on one of the *row* or *column level* symbols to display a specific level of data.

- Click on the *row* or *column level bar* to hide the corresponding detail rows or columns.

- Click on the *hide detail* symbol to hide the rows or columns indicated by its level bar.

- Click on the *show detail* symbol, to display hidden detail rows or columns.

To have Excel apply automatic styles to each level of data that is to be outlined before you create the outline, select the data to be outlined, choose Data ➤ Group and Outline ➤ Settings to display the Settings dialog box, select the Automatic Styles checkbox, and then choose OK. To apply automatic styles after you've created an outline, display the Settings dialog box, and then choose Apply Styles. To change the formatting for a level, change the style for that level.

To remove an outline or part of an outline, select the range that contains the outline, and then select Data ➤ Group And Outline ➤ Clear Outline.

To hide the outline symbols in a worksheet, select the range that contains the outline, choose Tools ➤ Options, choose the View tab, clear the Outline Symbols checkbox, and then choose OK.

Using Outline View in PowerPoint and Word

In PowerPoint and Word, the text in an outline appears in *levels*, or different amounts of indentation. A title or heading appears at the first level (no indentation) and subsequent data appears at the next level (one indent). Up to five levels of indentation in PowerPoint and up to nine levels of indentation in Word are possible.

Switch to PowerPoint's Outline view to create or display only the text of a presentation. The title and text on each slide in a presentation appear beside the number of the slide and the slide icon. If a slide contains a graphic, small pictures appear on the slide icon.

Switch to Word's Outline view to display only document text to which one of Word's heading or paragraph styles was applied. You can also create an outline for your documents, and then fill in the paragraph text later.

To change to Outline view in PowerPoint and Word, click on the Outline View button beside the horizontal scroll bar of the presentation or document window, or choose View ➤ Outline.

Use any of the following buttons on PowerPoint's and Word's Outlining toolbar to work with text in an outline:

- Click on the Promote button (Alt+Shift+←) to increase (move to the left) the level of the current heading, title, or text.

- Click on the Demote button (Alt+Shift+→) to decrease (move to the right) the level of the current heading, title, or text.

- In Word, click on the Demote to Body Text button (Ctrl+Shift+N) to change a heading into paragraph text.

- Click on the Move Up button (Alt+Shift+↑) to move the selected item up one line. The moved item remains in the same outline level.

- Click on the Move Down button (Alt+Shift+↓) to move the selected item down one line. The moved item remains in the same outline level.

- Click on the Expand button (Alt+Shift++) to expand the text on a single selected slide in

PowerPoint or the active level of heading text in Word. Double-click on the Expand button or the plus icon to expand all the heading text in a Word outline.

- Click on the Show All button (Alt+Shift+A) to expand the text on all slides in a PowerPoint presentation.

- Click on the Collapse button (Alt+Shift+2) to collapse the text on a single selected slide in PowerPoint or the active level of heading text in Word. Or, double-click on the Collapse button or the minus icon to collapse all the heading text in a Word outline.

- Click on the Collapse All button (Alt+Shift+1) to collapse the text on all slides in a Power-Point presentation.

- Click on the Expand All button to expand the collapsed text on all slides in a PowerPoint presentation.

- Click on the Summary Slide button to create a slide containing the titles of selected slides in a PowerPoint presentation.

- Click on the All button (Alt+Shift+A) to expand all the heading and paragraph text in Word. To expand the outline to only a specified level, click on the button that displays the corresponding level number.

- Click on the Show First Line Only button (Alt+Shift+L) to toggle the display between the first line of the current paragraph and the whole paragraph in Word.

- Click on the Show Formatting button (/ on the numeric keypad) to toggle the display of character formatting in the outline.

- Click on the Master Document View button to display the outline in that view and to display the Master Document toolbar in Word.

You can also drag the slide or plus or minus icon beside an item to the left to promote it and any paragraph text, or to the right to demote it. To promote or demote only paragraph text, drag the paragraph icon (the small black or gray square) to the left or to the right. As you drag, a vertical line appears on the screen. Release the mouse button when the line is in the location in which you want the outline item.

In addition, you can also drag the slide or plus icon up or down to move the heading and body text. Drag Word's minus icon or the paragraph icon up or down to move only the heading or the

paragraph text. As you drag, a horizontal line appears on your screen. Release the mouse button when the line is in the location in which you want the outline item.

When you print an outline in PowerPoint, it is printed just as it appears on your screen, including the slide numbers and icons, and the text formatting. Use View ➢ Master ➢ Handout Master to add a header and footer to each printed page.

In Word, only the headings and body text that appear on your screen are printed. Use View ➢ Header and Footer to add a header and footer to each printed page.

To automatically number the headings to which one of Word's built-in styles have been applied in an outline, choose ➢ Bullets and Numbering, and then select the numbering style to be used in the outline on the Outline Numbered tab.

Page Numbering

You can add automatic page numbers to the printed pages in an Access form or report, an Excel worksheet, the footer on a slide, notes page, or handout in a PowerPoint presentation, or a Word document.

Numbering Pages in Access

To number the pages in an Access form or report, insert a text box control in the position in which the page numbers are to appear, and then enter the page property in the text box:

1. Highlight the name of the form or report on the Form or Report pane in the Database window, and then choose Design.

2. Click on the Text Box button in the Toolbox, and then click in the location on the form or report in which you want to place the text box.

3. Click in the new text box, then click on the Properties button on the Form Design or Report Design toolbar to display the property sheet dialog box for the new text box, and select the Data tab.

4. Click in the Control Source text box, and then type **=Page** to number the pages of the form or report.

5. Click on the property sheet dialog box's close box to close it.

6. Click on the Save button on the Form Design toolbar, or choose File ➤ Save (Ctrl+S) to save the changed design of the form or report.

The text box for the page number appears on each page of a form (for each item in the table or query on which the form is based) or report.

Numbering Pages in Excel

By default, page numbers appear in the footer on each printed page in Excel.

To change the starting page number when printing the current worksheet, choose File ➤ Page Setup, select the Page tab in the Page Setup dialog box, type the number that is to appear on the first page in the First Page Number text box, and then choose OK.

Numbering Pages in Word

Page numbers in a Word document are usually placed in its header or footer. However, you can also place page numbers in a text box within the header or footer, and then drag the text box to any position in the document. The header or footer will expand as you drag, depending on the new location.

1. Position the insertion point in the section of the document where page numbering is to be added.

2. Choose Insert ➤ Page Numbers to display the Page Numbers dialog box.

3. Choose any of the following options to insert page numbers:

   • In the Position drop-down list, select Top Of Page (Header) or Bottom Of Page (Footer) as the location for the number on each page.

   • In the Alignment drop-down list, select Left, Center, Right, Inside, or Outside as the position between the left and right margins for the number on each page.

• Select the Show Number on First Page checkbox to display the page number on the first page of the document or section.

4. To change the format of page numbers, choose Format, choose any of the following options, and then choose OK in the Page Number Format dialog box.

   • If necessary, select the format for the numbers in the Number Format drop-down list.

   • To insert the chapter number just before the page number, select the Include Chapter Number checkbox. If necessary, highlight a style for the chapter number in the Chapter Starts with Style drop-down list, and choose the character to be used as the separator between the chapter and the page numbers in the Use Separator drop-down list.

   • Select Continue from Previous Section to maintain consecutive numbers in adjacent document sections, or enter the number on which the section's page numbering is to begin in the Start At text box.

5. Choose OK in the Page Numbers dialog box.

Page Setup

The page setup defines the way each page in an Access form or report, an Excel worksheet, PowerPoint slides, notes pages, and handouts, and a Word document appears when it is printed—including the margins, page layout, paper size, and the printer's paper source. The available paper size and source options depend on the printer that is set up to be used in all Windows applications.

Setting Up the Page

1. Activate the file whose page setup you want to change. In Word, you can also position the insertion point in the document section whose page setup you want to change.

2. Choose File ➤ Page Setup to display the Page Setup dialog box.

3. If necessary, specify the arrangement of each page as Portrait (the pages are taller than they are wide) or Landscape (the pages are wider than they are tall) on the Page or Paper Size tab. In PowerPoint, select the orientation in the Slides and/or Notes, Handouts & Outline area for the view to be printed.

4. Select a predefined paper size in the Paper Size or Slides Sized For drop-down list. In PowerPoint and Word, you can also enter a measurement to define the Width and Height of the slide or paper.

5. Select from the many options to further define the page setup. Options include Scaling, Print Quality, and Page Order, depending on the application in use.

6. Choose OK in the Page Setup dialog box.

Print

The printer that is currently set up for all Windows applications is the one that will be used to print the active Access database object or Binder, Excel, Outlook, PowerPoint, or Word file. When it is printed, the object or file will appear as it is displayed in the Print Preview window in each of the Microsoft Office applications.

Always save a file before you print it. That way, in case of any kind of system error, a copy of the file remains on your hard disk.

Printing a File

To print the current file or a selection in the file using the current settings in the Print dialog box, click on the Print button on the Standard toolbar.

To change the settings in the Print dialog box and then print the file:

1. If necessary, select the portion of the file to be printed.

2. Choose File ➤ Print (Ctrl+P) to display the Print dialog box, with the name of the printer that is currently setup displayed in the Printer area.

3. Specify the number of copies to be printed in the Number of Copies text box.

4. If multiple copies are specified in Access, PowerPoint, and Word, select the Collate checkbox to print one entire copy of the file, object, or selection, before automatically printing the next entire copy.

5. Choose from a variety of options, depending on the active Microsoft Office application.

6. Select OK in the Print dialog box to print the file, object, or selection.

In both PowerPoint and Word, you can specify some default printing options to use for all the printing you perform in those applications. To do so, choose Tools ➤ Options, and then select the appropriate options on the Print tab.

Print Preview

Use Print Preview to display an Access database object, an Excel worksheet, an Outlook object, or a Word file exactly as it will appear when printed. The portion of the file that appears in the Print Preview window depends on both the location of the insertion point in the active file and which part of the file is specified as the portion to be printed in the Print dialog box.

Changing to Print Preview

To switch to Print Preview in Access, Excel, Outlook, and Word, click on the Print Preview button on the Database or Standard toolbar, or choose File ➤ Print Preview.

The Print Preview window appears along with the Print Preview toolbar or button bar. Use the buttons on the toolbar or button bar to change the appearance of the page or otherwise manipulate the appearance of the file in the Print Preview window.

The following options are available in the various Print Preview windows:

- Click on the Print button to print the file or object with the default print settings. In Excel, choose Print to display the Print dialog box.

- Click on the Zoom button to reduce the size of the displayed page. Click on it again to return it to its enlarged size.

- To display one page of the document at a time, click on the One Page button.

- To display two pages of the document at a time, click on the Two Pages button.

- To display more than two pages at a time, click on the Multiple Pages button, and then highlight the number of pages.

- Click on the Zoom drop-down list, and then select a percentage to change the size of the page displayed relative to its real size.

- Click on the Close button to close the Print Preview window and return to the selected display of the file or object.

- Click on the Zoom or Magnifier button to display the page in its actual size.

- Click on the Setup button to display the Page Setup dialog box for the worksheet file.

- Click on the Next button to display the next page that will be printed.

- Click on the Previous button to display the page before the currently displayed page.

- Click on the Margins button to toggle on the display of the handles for margins, the position of the header and footer, and the width of each column.

- Click on the Page Break Preview button in Excel to rearrange the page breaks in the displayed worksheet.

- Click on the View Ruler button to display both the horizontal and vertical rulers in Word. To hide the rulers, click on the button again.

- If only a small amount of text appears on the last page of a Word document, click on the Shrink To Fit button to reduce the size of the font so the document can be printed on one less page.

- Click on the Full Screen button to hide everything on the screen except the document and the Print Preview toolbar. Click on the button again or press Esc to display all the screen elements.

Click on the Next Page or Previous Page buttons on the vertical scroll bar in Word or drag the scroll box to scroll through the document. Or press PgUp or PgDn to scroll through the document while it is displayed in Print Preview.

Repeat

Commands you select and formatting changes you make are stored in Excel, PowerPoint, and Word until you perform any action, except when you select a different cell or move the insertion point. You can repeat the last command or action that was performed in the active cell or at the

position of the insertion point. In Word, you can even repeat the last characters you typed after the insertion point is repositioned.

To repeat the last command or action:

1. Perform the action, select the command, or type new characters.

2. Select the cell or position the insertion point where you want to repeat the action.

3. In Excel, click on the Repeat button on the Standard toolbar. Or, in Excel, PowerPoint, and Word, choose Edit ➢ Repeat *Edit* (F4).

Share

You can specify that the active database or worksheet be shared. A shared file can be opened and edited simultaneously by multiple users on a network.

In Access, each new database file you create is shared with others who have permission to enter data in it by default. In Excel, you can specify who is allowed to share an open file.

Sharing a Workbook

When a workbook is shared, Excel automatically keeps a *change history*, a record of all the changes made to it, who made each change, and when each change was made. You can specify how long Excel maintains the change history. The change history can be viewed directly on the worksheet, or in a *history* worksheet, which lists the changes and allows you to filter them.

When a workbook is shared, there are several features you cannot use. For example, you cannot delete a worksheet in a shared workbook, merge cells, insert or delete blocks of cells, insert or edit graphics or hyperlinks, change or apply a password to any part of the workbook, or create or edit macros.

1. Activate the workbook you want to share, and then choose Tools ➢ Share Workbook to display the Share Workbook dialog box.

2. On the Editing tab, select the *Allow changes by more than one user at the same time* checkbox.

3. If necessary, highlight the name of an editor of the workbook in the Who Has This Workbook Open Now list box, and choose Remove User to disconnect the editor from the workbook.

4. On the Advanced tab, choose any of the following options:

   • In the Track Changes area, choose Keep Change History for Days, and then specify the number of days in the text box. Alternatively, choose Don't Keep Change History if you do not want a record of the changes made by all the workbook's editors.

   • In the Update Changes area, choose When File Is Saved to display the changes made by other editors when you save the file. Alternatively, choose Automatically Every Minutes, and then specify the interval in the text box to see the changes saved by other editors. Then choose either Save My Changes And See Others' Changes to save your changes and display others' changes at the specified interval, or Just See Other Users' Changes to display the changes made by others without saving your changes to the workbook.

   • In the Conflicting Changes Between Users area, choose Ask Me Which Changes Win to allow you to review conflicting changes and decide which change to save. Alternatively, choose The Changes Being Saved Win to save your changes without reviewing any conflicts.

   • In the Include in Personal View area, select the Print Settings checkbox to save the print settings you specified for the workbook. Select the Filter Settings checkbox to save the filtering settings you specified for the workbook.

5. Choose OK in the Share Workbook dialog box.

Sort

To change the order of selected data, you can perform a *sort* on it (rearrange it numerically, alphabetically, or chronologically). Data in Access, Excel, and Word can be sorted automatically with options you specify. Slides in a PowerPoint presentation can be sorted manually.

When you sort data, you arrange it in ascending order (lowest to highest or A-Z) or descending order (highest to lowest or Z-A).

Sorting Data in Access

In Access, sorting the records in a table, form, or query changes the order in which the records are displayed. Sorting the records in a report changes the arrangement of the data in the report. The records can be sorted by the data in one field in either ascending or descending order, or by the data in multiple fields in both ascending and descending order.

To display the records in an open table or form by sorting the records by the data in one field, position the insertion point in the field, and then click on the Sort Ascending or Sort Descending button on the Table Datasheet or Form View toolbar, or select Records ➤ Sort ➤ Sort Ascending or Sort Descending.

To sort the records displayed in a query by the data in one or more fields, display the query in Query Design view, and then specify the order in which to sort the data in the Sort row for the field or fields. The data is sorted in the left-most sort field first, and then sorted by the subsequent sort fields from left to right in the QBE grid.

To sort the records in a form or table by the data in multiple fields:

1. Open the form in Form view or the table in Datasheet view.

2. Choose Records ➤ Filter ➤ Advanced Filter/ Sort to display the Filter/Sort toolbar and the Filter window with a QBE grid for the selected form or table.

3. Drag the first field on which to sort the records into the Field row in the grid in the bottom pane of the Filter window.

4. In the Sort row for the field, select Ascending or Descending as the sort order in the drop-down list.

5. Repeat steps 3 and 4 for each field that contains the data on which to sort the records.

6. Click on the Apply Filter button on the Filter/ Sort toolbar, or choose Filter ➢ Apply Filter/ Sort to display the records in the form or table in the specified order.

Although the records are displayed in the form or table in the order specified, they are stored in the form or table in the order in which they were entered. To save the display of the records in a table in the specified order, create a query with the necessary sort order.

To undo the sort and redisplay the records in the form or table in the order in which they were entered, choose Records ➢ Remove Filter/Sort.

The data in a field that was used to sort records in a report can also be placed in a *group*, a collection of related data. Each group can contain summary information about its data in a header or footer. The summary information can be the result of a calculation, such as the total number of items in the group.

To sort the records that will appear in a report:

1. Open the report in Design view.

2. Choose View ➢ Sorting and Grouping to display the Sorting and Grouping window.

3. Select the name of the first field on which the data is to be sorted in the first cell in the Field/ Expression column.

4. Select Ascending or Descending in the first cell in the Sort Order column to specify the sort order for the first field.

5. Repeat steps 3 and 4 for each field on which the data in the report is to be sorted. Up to ten fields can be used to define the sort order.

6. To create a group, position the insertion point in the field to be grouped in the Field/ Expression column, and then set any of the following properties for the group in the Group Properties pane:

- In the Group Header drop-down list, select Yes to add text or graphics at the top of the selected field's group.

- In the Group Footer drop-down list, select Yes to add text or graphics at the bottom of the selected field's group.

- In the Group On drop-down list select the appropriate Text, Date/Time, or Numeric

option to specify how the data is to be grouped. The options that appear depend on the type of data in the field.

- In the Group Interval text box, type a number to specify the interval that is necessary for the property selected in the Group On drop-down list.

- In the Keep Together drop-down list, select No (the default) to print the group without forcing the header, details, and footer to appear on the same page; Whole Group to print the group's header, details, and footer on the same page; or With First Detail to print the group's header on a page if the first detail will also fit on the page.

7. If necessary, add controls to the group's header and footer.

8. Click on the Sorting and Grouping window's Close button to close it and return to the report in Design view.

9. Click on the Save button on the Report Design toolbar or choose File ➢ Save (Ctrl+S) to save the changes to the report.

Sorting Data in Excel and Word

You can sort selected data in an Excel list to organize it in alphabetical, numerical, or chronological order. All the data in each row is rearranged in the list according to the *sort order*—the order specified for data in selected columns of the list.

In Excel, data is sorted first by numbers and dates, then by text values, with numbers formatted as text sorted before the text. The logical values TRUE and FALSE are sorted next, then error values in the order in which they occur in the list, and finally empty cells.

In Word, you can sort up to three types of information in paragraphs, lists separated by commas or spaces, or table rows. Numbered lists are automatically renumbered after a sort. Items that start with punctuation marks or other symbols are sorted first, followed by items that start with numbers, then items that start with letters. Uppercase letters precede lowercase letters in the sorted list. Subsequent characters decide the sort order of items that begin with the same character, and subsequent fields decide the sort order if list items that contain the same data in a field.

To sort data:

1. Select a cell in an Excel list, and then choose Data ➤ Sort to display the Sort dialog box. Or select the items to be sorted in a Word document, and then choose Table ➤ Sort to display the Sort dialog box.

2. Choose any of the following options to perform the sort:

   - In the Sort By drop-down list in Excel, select the column label. In Word, choose the field name, column, or Paragraphs as the first type of data on which to sort the selection, and then choose Text, Number, or Date as the kind of data to sort in the Type drop-down list. Choose Ascending or Descending as the sort order.

   - In the corresponding Then By drop-down list, select the second, and if necessary, third column label or type of data on which to sort. In Word, choose the type of data to sort in the corresponding Type drop-down list. Select Ascending or Descending as the sort order for the second and third items being sorted.

   - In the My List Has area, select Header Row to disregard the first row of selected data while sorting an Excel list or a Word table, or all rows in a Word table that are defined as heading rows. Or select No Header Row to sort all rows of data in the selection.

3. If necessary, choose Options to display the Sort Options dialog box, select any of the following options, and then choose OK.

   - Select a *custom sort order*, a nonalphabetic or nonnumeric sort order, for the data in the column specified in the Sort By drop-down list in Excel's Sort dialog box in the First Key Sort Order drop-down list.

   - In an Excel list, select the Case Sensitive checkbox to sort words that begin with an uppercase letter before words that begin with the same lowercase letter. In Word, select the Case Sensitive checkbox when Text is the type of data specified in the Type drop-down list.

   - In Excel, select Sort Top to Bottom (the default for a list) to sort the list or the rows by the data in a single column, or Sort Left to Right (the default for a pivot table) to

sort the data or the columns by the data in a single row.

   - To sort text outside a table in Word, choose Tabs or Commas as the separator character, or choose Other and type the separator character in the text box.

   - In Word, select the Sort Column Only checkbox to sort a column of table data or text in a newspaper-style column.

   - In Word, select the language whose sorting rules you wish to use in the Sorting Language drop-down list.

4. Choose OK in the Sort dialog box.

To return the list to its original arrangement, click on the Undo button on the Standard toolbar before you perform any other command or action.

Spelling and Grammar

Use Microsoft Office's Spelling tool to catch typographical errors or misspelled words in your Access tables, forms, and queries, Excel worksheets, PowerPoint presentations, or Word documents. Each of the applications uses the same dictionaries and spelling tools.

You can create both custom dictionaries in which to add special terminology that is not in the main dictionary (to prevent it from being questioned), and exclude dictionaries to question the spelling of words in the main dictionary.

Checking the Spelling in the Active File

Both PowerPoint and Word automatically check the spelling of each word as you type. A wavy red line is placed under every word that is not in any of the open dictionaries.

To check the spelling of a word underlined with a wavy red line, right-click on the word to display its Spelling shortcut menu, and then select one of the words that appear in bold at the top of the menu. Or, choose any of the following options:

   - Select Ignore All to ignore each word spelled the same way in the document.

   - Select Add to add the word to the custom dictionary.

- Select AutoCorrect, and then select the word to insert each time you type the underlined word.
- Select Spelling to display the Spelling dialog box.

Double-click on the Spelling and Grammar Status button on the status bar to select the next word underlined with a wavy red line and to display its shortcut menu.

When you display the Spelling dialog box in Access, Excel, PowerPoint, and Word, each word in the file that is not in the main or custom dictionaries, or that is in the exclude dictionary, is highlighted in succession in your document.

1. Click on the Spelling button on the Standard toolbar or choose Tools ➤ Spelling (F7) to highlight the first misspelled word after the position of the insertion point, and to display the Spelling dialog box.

2. The word that is highlighted in a Word document appears with bold red characters in context in the Not in Dictionary text box. In the other applications, the highlighted word appears in the Not in Dictionary area or text box. Choose any of the following options:

   - Select the spelling that you want to use in the list of suggested spellings in the Suggestions list box, or directly edit any of the text in the Not in Dictionary text box.
   - Choose Change to change the text that appears in the Not in Dictionary text box in your document.
   - Choose Change All to change the spelling of each occurrence of the word highlighted in your document to the spelling that appears in the Not in Dictionary text box.
   - Choose Undo to return the text in the Not in Dictionary text box to its original spelling.
   - Choose Ignore to disregard the spelling of the word that is highlighted in your document.
   - Choose Ignore All to disregard the spelling of each occurrence of the word that is highlighted in your document.
   - Choose Add to place the highlighted word in the selected custom dictionary.

   - Choose AutoCorrect to automatically add the highlighted word to the list of Auto-Correct entries. Then, each time you type the word followed by a space, it will be replaced with the spelling selected in the Suggestions list box.
   - Choose Undo or Undo Last to restore the change you made to the last word that was highlighted in your document.

3. Choose Cancel or Close to close the Spelling dialog box and return to your document.

To check the spelling of a single word, select the word and then click on the Spelling button on the Standard toolbar to display the Spelling dialog box (or a message box if the word is in one of the open dictionaries).

Creating and Using a Custom Dictionary

If you often use technical terms or other words that are questioned by Spelling, create a custom dictionary that contains words that are not in the main dictionary. Words placed in a custom dictionary will be questioned in your files only when they are not spelled the way they are in the custom dictionary.

Microsoft Office comes with a custom dictionary, and you can create additional custom dictionaries to use. The custom dictionaries are Word documents, and can be edited using the same techniques you use in regular documents.

1. In a Word document with at least one misspelled word, click on the Spelling button on the Standard toolbar or choose Tools ➤ Spelling (F7), and then choose Options to display the Spelling & Grammar tab in the Options dialog box. Or choose Tools ➤ Options and select the Spelling & Grammar tab.

2. Choose Dictionaries to display the Custom Dictionaries dialog box.

3. Choose New to display the Create Custom Dictionary dialog box, with the contents of the Proof folder displayed in the Save In list box. Type a name in the File Name text box, and then choose Save to create a new custom dictionary file.

4. If necessary, choose any of the following options to manage your custom dictionaries:

- Highlight a dictionary in the Custom Dictionaries list box, choose Edit, and then choose OK to open the custom dictionary as a document. Edit the dictionary as necessary, and then click on the Save button on the Standard toolbar to save the dictionary. Click on the document's close box to close the custom dictionary file.

- Choose Add to display the Add Custom Dictionary dialog box, where you can add a custom dictionary file that is stored in a different path to the Proof folder.

- Choose Remove to delete the highlighted custom dictionary from the list in the Custom Dictionaries list box. The dictionary file is not deleted from your hard disk.

- If you have created a custom dictionary to check the Spelling of words in another language, select the language in the Language drop-down list.

5. In the Custom Dictionaries list box, select the checkbox of each custom dictionary you want Word to open and use during a Spelling check.

6. Choose OK in the Custom Dictionaries dialog box.

7. Choose OK in the Options dialog box. If necessary, choose Cancel in the Spelling dialog box to return to your document.

Word's automatic spell-checking feature is turned off each time you edit a custom dictionary. To turn it back on, select the Check Spelling as You Type checkbox on the Spelling & Grammar tab in the Options dialog box, and then choose OK.

Creating a Dictionary of Excluded Words

By default, any words that are in the main dictionary are not questioned during a Spelling check. To question correctly spelled words because you prefer a different spelling, create an exclude dictionary to be used with the main dictionary.

The exclude dictionary has the same filename as the main dictionary, but it has the .exc extension. For example, if you are using the US English dictionary, the main dictionary file name is Mssp2_en.lex. The exclude dictionary associated with it is named Mssp2_en.exc.

1. Click on the New button on the Standard toolbar or press Ctrl+N to open a new document based on the Normal.dot template.

2. Type a word you want to exclude and press Enter to start a new paragraph.

3. Repeat step 2 for each word you want to add to the exclude dictionary.

4. Select Table ➣ Sort to display the Sort dialog box, and then choose OK to arrange the words in alphabetical order.

5. Click on the Save button on the Standard toolbar or choose File ➣ Save (Ctrl+S) to display the Save As dialog box.

6. In the Save In drop-down list, choose the C:\Windows\Msapps\Proof folder or the C:\Program Files\Common Files\Microsoft Shared\Proof folder as the location in which to store the exclude dictionary file.

7. Choose Text Only (*.txt) in the Save As Type drop-down list.

8. Type a name for the exclude dictionary (usually Mssp2_en.exc) in the File Name text box.

9. Choose Save in the Save As dialog box, and then choose Yes in the resultant message box to save the file in Text Only format.

The next time you type a word that is in the exclude dictionary, Spelling places a wavy red line under it in a presentation or document. If you check the Spelling in a file, the words in the exclude dictionary will be highlighted in your document.

Setting the Spell- and Grammar-Checking Options

You can also set the spell-checking and grammar-checking options:

1. In Word's Spelling dialog box, choose Options to display the Spelling & Grammar tab in the Options dialog box. Or choose Tools ➣ Options and select the Spelling & Grammar tab.

2. Choose any of the following options to use when checking the spelling in a document:

- Select the Check Spelling as You Type checkbox to turn on automatic spell-checking.

- Select the Hide Spelling Errors in Current Document checkbox to suppress the display of the wavy red line that appears under misspelled words while you are creating or adding text to a document.

- Select the Always Suggest Corrections checkbox (selected by default) to have Word display suggestions for the correct spelling of the word highlighted in the document in the Spelling dialog box's Suggestions list box. In Access, select the Always Suggest checkbox in the Spell Options dialog box; in Excel, select the Always Suggest checkbox in the Spelling dialog box; in PowerPoint, select the Always checkbox on the Spelling tab in the Options dialog box.

- Select From Main Dictionary Only to display suggestions from the main dictionary rather than any open custom dictionaries.

- Select the Ignore Words in UPPERCASE checkbox to have Word disregard words typed in uppercase letters during the Spelling check. In Access, select the Words in UPPERCASE checkbox in the Ignore area in the Spell Options dialog box; in Excel, select the Ignore UPPERCASE checkbox in the Spelling dialog box; in PowerPoint, select the Words in UPPERCASE checkbox in the Ignore area on the Spelling tab.

- Select the Ignore Words with Numbers checkbox to have Word omit words that have numbers during the Spelling check. In Access, select the Words With Numbers checkbox in the Ignore area in the Spell Options dialog box; in PowerPoint, select the Words with Numbers checkbox in the Ignore area on the Spelling tab.

- Select the Ignore Internet and File Addresses checkbox to have Word omit those items during a spelling check.

- Click on the Custom Dictionary drop-down list to make sure that all the custom dictionaries you wish to use appear in the list.

- In Access, Excel, and PowerPoint, select the name of the custom dictionary to which to add words in the Add Words To drop-down list.

3. Choose any of the following options to use when checking the grammar in a Word document:

- Select the Check Grammar as You Type checkbox to turn on automatic grammar checking.

- Select the Hide Grammatical Errors in This Document checkbox to suppress the wavy green line that appears below potential grammatical errors.

- Select the Check Grammar with Spelling checkbox to have Word check both spelling and grammar.

- Select the Show Readability Statistics checkbox to have Word display the readability statistics after a grammar check.

- Select the style of writing that is used in this document so the correct grammatical rules will be applied during a Grammar Check in the Writing Style drop-down list.

- To change the style and grammar rules for the selected writing style, choose Settings, and then change any necessary option.

4. Choose Check Document to check both the spelling and grammar again and to remove all the words from the current session list for which you chose Ignore All in Word's Spelling dialog box.

5. Choose OK in the Options dialog box. If necessary, choose Cancel in the Spelling dialog box to return to your document or file.

Style

To present data in Excel worksheets and Word documents with consistent formatting, apply *styles*, defined groups of formatting commands, to the data or text. When a style is applied, each format in the style is simultaneously applied to the selection. Some built-in styles come with Excel and Word.

In Excel, all styles are cell styles. However, a defined style can be applied to an entire worksheet. Cell styles can include any of the formatting that can be applied to a cell using the options on the tabs in the Format Cells dialog box.

There are two types of styles in Word—paragraph styles and character styles. Paragraph styles control all the formatting in a paragraph, including the font and size, line spacing, alignment, tab stops, and the borders and shading. The format applied to a paragraph is stored in its paragraph mark. Character styles are created using the options in the Font dialog box.

Applying a Style in an Excel Worksheet

To apply an existing style in Excel:

1. Select the cells to which you want to apply a defined style.

2. Choose Format ➢ Style to display the Style dialog box.

3. Select the name of the style to apply in the Style Name drop-down list.

4. Choose OK.

To quickly apply currency, percent, or comma style to selected cells, click on the Currency Style, Percent Style, or Comma Style button on the Formatting toolbar.

Applying a Style in a Word Document

When you create a new document, select a template that contains the styles to use in the document, and then apply styles to all the document text. If a style is modified, the formatting of all the text to which the style is applied in the document will be changed.

To apply a paragraph style, position the insertion point in the paragraph or select more than one paragraph. To apply a character style, select the text to which the style is to be applied.

Use one of the following methods to choose a style:

- Select the name of the style in the Style drop-down list on the Formatting toolbar. Paragraph styles appear with a ¶ symbol in the Style drop-down list on the Formatting toolbar and in the Styles list box in the Styles dialog box. Character styles appear with an **a** in both lists.

- Choose Format ➢ Style to display the Style dialog box, select the name of the style in the Styles list box, and then choose Apply.

- Press the shortcut keys assigned to the style.

Copying Styles in Excel

You can copy styles from one open workbook file to another:

1. Activate the workbook to which the styles are to be copied.

2. Choose Format ➢ Style, and then choose Merge to display the Merge Styles dialog box.

3. Highlight the name of the workbook that contains the styles to be copied in the Merge Styles From list box.

4. Choose OK in the Merge dialog box.

5. Choose OK in the Style dialog box to return to the workbook.

If there are any styles in the active workbook with the same names as the styles being copied, Excel displays a message asking if you want to replace the current styles with the copied styles. Choose Yes to replace all the styles, or No to keep the current styles in the active file. Choose Cancel to cancel the copy procedure.

Copying Styles in Word

You can copy styles from a document or template to a different document or template to save time and to make sure the styles are exactly the same in both:

1. Choose Format ➢ Style, and choose Organizer to display the Organizer dialog box.

2. If necessary, select the Styles tab.

3. Highlight the name of the style in the In *File Name* list box. Press Ctrl as you select to highlight multiple names in the list box.

4. Choose Copy to copy the selected style to the To *Template* list box.

5. Choose any of the following options to manage the styles:

    - Select the name of the file or the template that contains the styles to be copied in the In *File Name*'s Styles Available In drop-down list. Then select the name of the template to which the styles are to be copied in the To *Template*'s Styles Available In drop-down list.

- Choose the corresponding Close File button to close the document or template file that contains the styles in the In *File Name* list box or to close the template that contains the styles in the To *Template* list box. Each button changes to Open File so you can open a different document or template file.

- Choose the corresponding Open File button to display the Open dialog box, and then open a new document or template file. The names of the styles in the file or template appear in the In *File Name* and To *Template* list boxes.

- Choose Delete to remove the highlighted style from the document or template. Select Yes to confirm the deletion.

- Highlight a style to be renamed or to which an alias is to be added, and then select Rename to display the Rename dialog box. Type a different name in the New Name text box, or type a comma and an alias, and then choose OK.

6. Choose Close in the Organizer dialog box.

You can rename a style to change the name of a style you created, or to give a built-in style, which cannot be renamed, an *alias*. Select Format ➤ Style, highlight the current name of the style in the Styles list box, and choose Modify. Type a new name for the style in the Name text box, or insert a comma after the name and then type the style's alias. Choose OK in the Modify Style dialog box.

Creating or Modifying a Style in Excel

In Excel, styles are stored in the workbook in which they were created. If you modify the formatting in a style, the formatting is automatically applied to all the cells in the workbook to which the style is applied.

1. Activate the workbook in which styles are to be created or modified, and then select the cells for which a style is to be defined.

2. Choose Format ➤ Style to display the Style dialog box.

3. To create a new style, type a new name in the Style Name text box, and then choose Add.

4. Choose Modify to display the Format Cells dialog box.

5. Select any of the formatting that is to be assigned to the style, and then choose OK in the Format Cells dialog box.

6. The formatting selected on each tab in the Format Cells dialog box appears in the Style Includes area of the Style dialog box. If necessary, clear the checkboxes of any of the tabs whose formats will not be in the style.

7. Choose OK to define the style and apply its formatting to the selected cells.

To delete a style other than one of Excel's built-in styles, select Format ➤ Style to display the Style dialog box, select the name of the style in the Style Name drop-down list, and then choose Delete.

Creating or Modifying a Style in Word

You can create your own styles to use in documents based on the template in which the style is stored.

To create a style using formatting applied to existing text:

1. Position the insertion point in the paragraph, or select the text whose formatting is to be saved as a style, and then format the text.

2. Click in the Style text box on the Formatting toolbar to highlight the name of the current style.

3. Type a name for a new style, and then press Enter.

To create an entirely new style or modify an existing style:

1. Choose Format ➤ Style to display the Style dialog box.

2. To modify an existing style, highlight the name of the style in the Styles list box.

3. Choose New or Modify to display the New Style or Modify Style dialog box.

4. If necessary, type a name for the style in the Name text box.

TABLE | **1115**

5. If you are creating a new style, select Paragraph or Character in the Style Type drop-down list.

6. Select a style that is similar to the style being created or modified in the Based On drop-down list.

7. Select the style to be automatically applied to a new paragraph begun after the style is applied in the Style For Following Paragraph drop-down list.

8. Optionally, select Shortcut Key and assign a key sequence to the new style.

9. Choose Format, and then select the formatting to be assigned to the style.

10. Select the Add to Template checkbox to make the style available for any document based on the same template.

11. Select the Automatically Update checkbox to have Word automatically change the definition of the style when you apply formatting to paragraphs in the style, and to update the paragraphs to which the style was applied.

12. Choose OK in the New Style or Modify Style dialog box, and then choose Apply in the Style dialog box.

To remove a style from the current document, choose Format ➤ Style to display the Style dialog box, select the name of the style in the Styles list box, and then choose Delete. If the selected style was a paragraph style, the formatting for any paragraph to which the style was applied is changed to Normal style. If the style was a font style, the style is removed from any characters to which it was applied.

Although you can redefine Word's Normal style, all new documents are based by default on the Normal.dot template, and many existing styles in other templates are based on the Normal style. Instead, modify the Normal style and save it to a different name. Then apply the new style as necessary.

Table

Use tables instead of tabs in Word documents that contain columns of data, for text that is positioned in side-by-side paragraphs, or to place graphics beside text. Tables are made up of rows and columns of data entered into cells. The cells' contents are individual paragraphs, and can be formatted with the same methods as those used to format any paragraph. (An Access table datasheet and Excel worksheet are also tables composed of rows and columns.)

To move the insertion point to the next cell in a table, press Tab. To insert a tab character in a cell, press Ctrl+Tab. Set tab stops in a table cell with the Ruler or with Format ➤ Tabs. The measurements entered in the Tabs dialog box are relative to the margin of the cell, not the margin of the page.

Calculating Numerical Data in a Table

You can create simple spreadsheets in a Word table, and then perform calculations on the table data by entering formulas. For example, click on the AutoSum button on the Tables and Borders toolbar to have Word calculate as a sum all the values above or to the left of the cell into which you enter the formula.

You can use the same types of cell references as those in Excel to specify the cells whose values you want to calculate. In a Word table, the columns are lettered and the rows are numbered.

Cell references in a Word table are always absolute, and must be enclosed within parentheses in the formula. Use cell references to specify values in cells other than those above or to the left of the cell that contains the formula.

1. Position the insertion point in the cell where the calculation's results will appear, and then choose Table ➤ Formula to display the Formula dialog box.

2. Type the formula in the Formula text box, preceded by an equal sign. Alternatively, either select one of Word's built-in functions in the Paste Function drop-down list and then add the necessary arguments in the function's parentheses, or select the name of a defined bookmark to use in the formula in the Paste Bookmark drop-down list.

3. In the Number Format drop-down list, select a format for the calculation's result.

4. Choose OK in the Formula dialog box.

Creating a Table

By default, a table in your document will include table borders, which are printed when you print the document. If you remove the default table borders, the table's gridlines—which are non-printing characters—are displayed. Select Table ➢ Gridlines to toggle the display of gridlines in a table on your screen.

Click on the Show/Hide ¶ button on the Standard toolbar to toggle the display of the end-of-cell mark (which indicates the end of each cell's contents) and the end-of-row mark (which indicates the end of each row).

To create a simple table:

1. Position the insertion point where you want to place the table, click on the Insert Table button on the Standard toolbar, highlight the number of rows and columns for the table, and then click on the palette to create the table. Or choose Table ➢ Insert Table to display the Insert Table dialog box.

2. Choose any of the following options to define the appearance of the table, and then choose OK.

- Adjust the value in the Number of Columns text box to define the number of columns you want in the table.

- Adjust the value in the Number of Rows text box to define the number of rows you want in the table.

- Adjust the measurement in the Column Width text box to define the width of each column in the table. If you select Auto, the table columns are evenly adjusted between the left and right margins.

- Choose AutoFormat to display the Table AutoFormat dialog box. Select the format for the new table, and then choose OK. The name of the format applied to the table appears in the Table Format area.

To create a complex table, choose Table ➢ Draw Table or click on the Tables and Borders button on the Standard toolbar to display the Table and Borders toolbar, and then draw a table, one cell at a time.

You can also convert the data in a table into regular text in the document. To change tabular data into regular document text:

1. Select the table rows that contain the text you want to change into paragraphs, and then choose Table ➢ Convert Table to Text to display the Convert Table to Text dialog box.

2. Select Paragraph Marks, Tabs, or Commas, or choose Other and type a character in the text box to separate the text that is in each cell.

3. Choose OK.

To create a table using existing document text, add paragraph marks, tabs, or commas in the text as separators, and then select the text that is to be changed into table text. Choose Table ➢ Convert Text to Table to display the Convert Text to Table dialog box, which is similar to the Insert Table dialog box. Select the separator you inserted in the text and then choose OK. The separated text will be placed in individual cells in the table.

Creating Table Headings

Table headings are the data that you want as the "title" of the table. The headings consist of data that is entered in the first row of the table (the *header row*) unless a manual page break is inserted in the table.

You can merge two or more cells to place a table heading in one cell that spans several columns in the first row of a table. When cells are merged, their contents are converted to paragraphs within a single cell. You can also split a selected cell (usually a merged cell) to divide its contents according to the number of paragraph marks in the cell. If there is only one paragraph mark, the text is placed in the left cell and empty cells are added to its right.

TABLE | **1117**

To merge or split cells:

1. Select at least two cells to merge or one cell to split.

2. Choose either of the following options:

   - Choose Table ➤ Merge Cells or click on the Merge Cells button on the Tables and Borders toolbar to merge the cells.

   - Choose Table ➤ Split Cells or click on the Split Cells button on the Tables and Borders toolbar to split cells.

The data in the heading row in a table is not automatically repeated across hard page breaks. However, you can have Word repeat the heading row in tables that contain soft page breaks, and automatically update heading text that is edited.

To create a table heading:

1. Select the row or rows, starting with the first table row, that contain the text to be used as headings.

2. Choose Table ➤ Headings.

To remove the heading text that was updated across soft page breaks, select the original row or rows you selected as the table headings, and then choose Table ➤ Headings to toggle off the headings.

Editing a Table

The table's appearance can be changed to fit your data.

To delete cells, rows, or columns:

1. Select the cells to be deleted, or a cell in each row or column to be deleted, and then choose Table ➤ Delete Cells to display the Delete Cells dialog box.

2. Choose one of the following options, and then choose OK.

   - Select Shift Cells Left to move the remaining cells in the row to the left after the deletion.

   - Select Shift Cells Up to move the remaining cells in the column up after the deletion.

   - Select Delete Entire Row to delete the row that contains the selected cell.

   - Select Delete Entire Column to delete the column that contains the selected cell.

Select an entire row or column, and then choose Table ➤ Delete Rows or Table ➤ Delete Columns to delete the selection.

To insert cells, rows, or columns in the table:

1. Select the number of cells, rows, or columns in the position in which new ones are to be inserted in the table.

2. Click on the Insert Cells, Insert Rows, or Insert Columns button on the Standard toolbar, or choose Table ➤ Insert Cells, Rows, or Columns. If you selected cells, the Insert Cells dialog box appears.

3. Choose one of the following options, and then choose OK.

   - Select Shift Cells Right to insert cells in the position of the selection and move the originally selected cells to the right.

   - Select Shift Cells Down to insert cells in the position of the selection and move the originally selected cells down.

   - Select Insert Entire Row to insert a row(s) and move the original selection down.

   - Select Insert Entire Column to insert a column(s) and move the original selection to the right.

If you selected rows, the rows are moved down to make room for the inserted rows. If you selected columns, the columns are moved to the right so the new columns can be inserted.

You can also use either of the following methods to add a row or column:

- With the insertion point in the last cell, press Tab to add another row at the end of a table.

- Select the end-of-row marks and then click on the Insert Columns button on the Standard toolbar to add a column on the right edge of the table.

To quickly change the width of a column, position the mouse pointer on the column's boundary (the border or gridline), and then drag it to the left to decrease the width or to the right to increase the width. As you drag, the mouse pointer appears as two vertical lines with horizontal arrows attached.

MASTER'S REFERENCE

T

To change the column width with the mouse:

- Drag the column boundary to change the width of the column to the right of the column in proportion, so the overall width of the table is not changed.

- Hold down the Shift key while you drag or drag the table column marker on the Ruler to change the widths of the column and the table.

- Hold down the Ctrl key while you drag the column boundary to change its size, and to simultaneously change all columns to the right to the same width without changing the width of the table.

- Choose Table ➢ Distribute Columns Evenly or click on the Distribute Columns Evenly button on the Tables and Borders toolbar to change the width of selected columns or cells so they are equal.

To change the width of a column or a cell to exact specifications:

1. Select the cells or columns whose widths are to be changed.

2. Choose Table ➢ Cell Height and Width, and then choose the Column tab.

3. Select any of the following options, and then choose OK.

   - Specify the width of the selected cell or column in the Width of Column Number text box.

   - Specify the amount of blank space between the column boundaries and the cell contents in the Space between Columns text box.

   - Choose Previous Column to select the previous column in the table.

   - Choose Next Column to select the next column in the table.

   - Choose AutoFit to automatically adjust the widths of selected columns to their minimum widths.

To quickly change the height of a row, display the table in Page Layout view, and then drag the row marker at the lower edge of the row on the vertical ruler. The size of the table changes proportionally.

To quickly change the height of several rows so they are of equal height, select a cell in each row, and then choose Table ➢ Distribute Rows Evenly or click on the Distribute Rows Evenly button on the Tables and Borders toolbar.

To specify the exact row height and set other row formatting options:

1. Select the row to be changed.

2. Choose Table ➢ Cell Height And Width, and then choose the Row tab.

3. Change any of the following options, and then choose OK.

   - In the Height Of Row *Number* drop-down list, select Auto to allow Word to adjust the height automatically; or select At Least, and then specify a minimum row height, or Exactly, and then specify an exact row height in the At text box.

   - Specify the distance from the left margin to the left edge of the row in the Indent from Left text box.

   - Select the Allow Row to Break across Pages checkbox (selected by default) to let a table split across a page break at the selected row.

   - In the Alignment area, choose Left to align the row along the left margin, Center to align the row between the left and right margins, or Right to align the row along the right margin.

   - Choose Previous Row to select the previous table row.

   - Choose Next Row to select the next table row.

Formatting a Table

Use Table AutoFormat to apply predefined styles to a new or existing table, and to size the table automatically:

1. Position the insertion point in the table, and then click on the Table AutoFormat button on the Tables and Borders toolbar or choose Table ➢ Table AutoFormat to display the Table AutoFormat dialog box.

2. Highlight the predefined border and shading format for the table in the Formats list box.

3. Choose any of the following options to define the format for the table, and then choose OK.

- In the Formats to Apply area, select the corresponding checkbox to apply the Borders, Shading, Font, or Color specified in the format. To automatically adjust the size of the table to fit its contents, select the AutoFit checkbox.

- In the Apply Special Formats To area, select the corresponding checkbox to apply special formats to Heading Rows, the First Column, Last Row, and Last Column, depending on the selected format.

To place text or a graphic between table rows, position the insertion point in a cell in the row at which the table is to be divided, and then choose Table ➤ Split Table. A paragraph mark is inserted above the row where the table is split. Delete the paragraph mark to reunite the table.

You can also align the contents of selected cells. To do so, click on the Align Top, Center Vertically, or Align Bottom button on the Tables and Borders toolbar.

To number selected cells, click on the Numbering button on the Formatting toolbar. The cells are consecutively numbered from left to right across the rows.

Selecting Cells, Rows, Columns, or Data

There are several ways to select items in a table:

- Drag over text in a cell to select the text.

- Click in the *cell selection bar* (the left margin of the cell) to select the cell.

- Click in the *row selection bar* (the left page margin beside the row) to select a row. Or choose Table ➤ Select Row to select the entire row that contains the cell in which the insertion point is positioned.

- Position the mouse pointer on the column's top gridline until it appears as a heavy, black downward-pointing arrow and then click to select the column. Or, choose Table ➤ Select Column to select the column that contains the cell in which the insertion point is positioned.

- Hold down the Shift key while you click on another cell, row, or column to extend the selection.

- Hold down the Shift key while pressing ↑, ↓, ← or → to extend a selection.

- Choose Table ➤ Select Table to select the entire table.

- Press Tab to select the contents of the next cell, or Shift+Tab to select the contents of the previous cell.

Tabs

By default, Word's tab stops are set at each 0.5 inch between the left and right margins. To insert a tab character and move to the next tab stop, press Tab.

To toggle the display of tab characters and other nonprinting characters on your screen, click on the Show/Hide ¶ button on the Standard toolbar.

Setting Tab Stops

1. Position the insertion point in the paragraph whose tab stops you want to change.

2. Select Format ➤ Tabs to display the Tabs dialog box.

3. Choose any of the following options, and then choose OK.

- Type a location for a new tab stop in the Tab Stop Position text box, or select an existing tab stop in the list box.

- Adjust the measurement in the Default Tab Stops text box to reset the distance between the default tab stops for each paragraph in the entire document.

- In the Alignment area, choose Left to align the text to the right of the tab stop, Center to align the text at the center, Right to align the text to the left of the tab stop, Decimal to align the decimals within text at the tab stop, or Bar to place a vertical bar at the tab stop.

- In the Leader area, select None, Dots, Dashes, or Underline as the repeating character you want to appear before the tab stop.

- Choose Set to set the tab stop that appears in the Tab Stop Position text box.

- Choose Clear to remove the tab stop that appears in the Tab Stop Position text box.
- Choose Clear All to remove all tab stops in the selected paragraph except the tab stops set in the Default Tab Stops text box.

To quickly set tab stops in the paragraph that contains the insertion point, click on the Tab Alignment button on the left side of the horizontal Ruler until the type of tab you want to set is displayed on the button, and then click in the position for the tab on the Ruler.

Template

You can use a template file to save the styles, formatting, and text that you use in Word documents that are similar to each other. You can also place AutoText entries and macros used for similar documents in the template. To create a document using the styles, formatting, text, AutoText entries, and macros that are saved in the template file, open a new document based on the template.

Access databases can also be created using one of the built-in templates. Excel comes with a template you can use to create invoices. PowerPoint presentations are also based on templates that define the background, colors, and text format used for a presentation. You can save the structure of a database, spreadsheet, or presentation that you often use as a template in the corresponding application.

Creating a Document Based on a Template

Word's template files are stored in various folders in the C:\Program Files\MSOffice\Templates folder. By default, all new documents are created with the Normal.dot template.

To create a document based on a different template:

1. Select File ➤ New to display the New dialog box.

2. Select the tab that describes what type of document you want to create.

3. Click on the icon of the template you want to use to display its contents in the Preview area.

4. If necessary, select Document (selected by default) in the Create New area.

5. Choose OK.

By default, the templates appear as captioned icons in the list box that appears on the tab that is displayed in the New dialog box. Click on the List button to display the templates' icons and captions in a list; click on the Details button to display the templates' icons with details such as the size and type of each template file, and the date each was last modified; or click on the Large Icons button to return the list box display to the default captioned icons.

Creating a New Template

1. Select File ➤ New to display the New dialog box.

2. If necessary, select the tab that describes what type of document template you want to create, and then select the icon of the template on which to base the new template.

3. Choose Template in the Create New area, and then choose OK.

4. Make the necessary changes to the template. For example, type any text, create any macros or AutoText entries, define the page setup, customize the toolbars or menus, and create any styles necessary for the documents that will be created based on the template.

5. Click on the Save button on the Standard toolbar, or choose File ➤ Save (Ctrl+S) to display the Save As dialog box. Word automatically selects the Templates folder in which to store the file, and adds the .dot extension to the name you enter in the File Name text box.

6. If necessary, double-click on the folder in which to store the new template file in the Look In list box. Alternatively, place the template file in the Templates folder so it will appear on the General tab in the New dialog box.

7. Type a name for the template in the File Name text box.

8. Choose Save in the Save As dialog box.

9. Click on the Document Close button or choose File ➤ Close to close the new template file.

To edit a template, open the .dot file that contains the template, and then make the necessary changes as you would in a regular document file:

1. Click on the Open button on the Standard toolbar, or choose File ➤ Open (Ctrl+O) to display the Open dialog box.

2. Select Document Templates (*.dot) in the Files of Type drop-down list.

3. If necessary, select the C:\Program Files\MSOffice\Templates folder in the Look In drop-down list, and then double-click on the folder in the Look In list box that contains the template you want to edit.

4. Highlight the template file to be edited in the Look In list box.

5. Choose Open in the Open dialog box.

6. Make the necessary changes to the template.

7. Click on the Save button on the Standard toolbar to save the template to the same file name.

8. Click on the Document Close button, double-click on the Document Control icon, or choose File ➤ Close to close the edited template file.

Text Box

Insert a text box in which to place text or a graphic in PowerPoint presentations and Word documents. Text boxes are placed in the drawing layer so they float above existing text. Text boxes do not automatically expand to accommodate their contents, but you can resize them as necessary.

You can convert a Word text box into a frame. Frames will expand to accommodate their contents, or you can resize frames. By default, document text will wrap around a frame.

To see how a text box or a frame appears along with its contents, click on the Page Layout View or Online Layout View button by Word's horizontal scroll bar to change to that view. Alternatively, click on Word's Print Preview button on the Standard toolbar to change to Print Preview.

Inserting a Text Box

1. Choose Insert ➤ Text Box. In Word, the mouse pointer changes into a crosshair.

2. In PowerPoint, click in the position on the slide in which you want to insert a text box. In Word, position the crosshair at the top left corner of the location where you want to insert the text box, and then drag down and to the right.

When you insert a text box, it is selected in your presentation or document—handles appear around its crosshatched borders. In Word, the insertion point is positioned in the text box so you can enter text in it, and the Text Box toolbar appears. Text boxes appear by default without a border in PowerPoint, and with a thin black line around the border in Word. You must resize text boxes in PowerPoint to fit your text.

Moving or Formatting a Text Box and Its Contents

To edit or move a text box or frame and its contents, you must first select the text box or frame. To do so, click on its border.

Type and format the text in a text box the same way you do in your document. In Word, you can also apply styles to the text in a text box, and either use the indent markers on the horizontal Ruler or choose Format ➤ Paragraph to indent a selected paragraph within a text box. Alternatively, right-click on a text box to display its shortcut menu, and then choose one of the available commands to format its contents.

The mouse pointer changes shape in relation to the text box or frame according to what function it can perform:

- If the pointer is placed along its border, it appears as a positioning pointer with a four-headed arrow, and you can drag the text box or frame to any position on the page.

- If the pointer is placed inside the text box or frame, it appears as an I-beam, and you can either click in the text box to edit the text or select its contents.

- When you place the pointer on one of its handles, a two-headed sizing pointer appears. Drag the handle away from the center of the text box or frame to make it larger, or toward its center to make it smaller.

To format a selected text box to the exact specifications you want in your document:

1. Select Format ➤ AutoShape in PowerPoint
   and Format ➤ Text Box in Word to display
   the Format AutoShape or Format Text Box
   dialog box.

2. Choose any of the following options:

   - Adjust the options on the Colors and
     Lines tab to format the lines around the
     border of a text box.

   - To resize a selected graphic, adjust the
     options on the Size tab.

   - To move a text box, adjust the options on
     the Position tab.

   - To specify the way text will wrap around the
     text box in your document, adjust the
     options on the Wrapping tab in the Format
     Text Box dialog box.

   - To specify the distance between the text
     box and the document text, adjust the val-
     ues in the Left, Right, Top, and Bottom
     text boxes on the Text Box tab.

   - To change the text box into a frame,
     choose Convert to Frame on the Text Box
     tab in the Format Text dialog box, and
     then choose OK in the message box that
     appears.

   - To change the appearance of a callout,
     choose Format Callout on the Text Box
     tab in the Format Text Box dialog box.

3. Choose OK in the Format AutoShape or Format Text Box dialog box.

You can also use the buttons on PowerPoint's
Drawing toolbar to create and format a text box
on a slide.

To format a selected Word frame:

1. Convert a text box into a frame.

2. Choose Format ➤ Frame to display the Frame
   dialog box.

3. Choose any of the following options:

   - In the Text Wrapping area, select either
     None to break the document text above
     the frame and allow the text to continue
     below the frame, or Around to allow text

to flow around the frame. There must be at
least 1 inch between the margin or column
boundary and the frame for the text to
wrap completely around the frame.

- In the Size area, select Auto in the Width
  drop-down list to allow a frame to span
  from the left margin to the right margin,
  or select Exactly and then adjust the measurement to an exact width for the frame
  in the At text box. In the Height drop-
  down list, select Auto to allow the frame
  to be as tall as the height of its tallest contents. Or select At Least to specify the minimum height for the frame, or Exactly to
  specify the exact height for the frame, and
  then adjust the measurement in the At
  text box.

- In the Horizontal area, type a measurement
  in the Position text box or select Left,
  Right, Center, Inside, or Outside as the
  position for the frame in the Position drop-
  down list. Then select the frame's position
  on the page in relation to the specified
  position in the Relative To drop-down list.
  The position can be relative to a margin,
  the edge of the page, or a column. Adjust
  the amount of space that will separate the
  frame from surrounding text in the Distance from Text text box.

- In the Vertical area, type a measurement
  in the Position text box or select Top, Bottom, or Center in the Position drop-down
  list to specify the frame's position on the
  page in relation to the location specified
  in the Relative To drop-down list. The
  position can be relative to a margin, the
  edge of the page, or a column. Adjust the
  amount of space that will separate the
  frame from surrounding text in the Distance from Text text box. Select the Move
  with Text checkbox to move the frame
  vertically on the page as you add or delete
  paragraphs in the document. Select the
  Lock Anchor checkbox to anchor the
  frame to a specific paragraph.

- Choose Remove Frame to remove the
  selected frame. The contents of the frame
  are moved to the paragraph above the one
  where the frame was located.

To remove the frame and delete its contents,
select the frame and press Backspace or Delete.

Text Direction

By default, the text is oriented horizontally from left to right in your files. You can change the orientation of the text in worksheet cells and in table cells, callouts, text boxes, and AutoShapes.

Changing the Text Direction in Excel

1. Select the cells in which the text direction is to be changed.

2. Choose Format ➤ Cells (Ctrl+1) to display the Format Cells dialog box, and then choose the Alignment tab.

3. In the Orientation area, adjust the value in the Degrees text box until the text is rotated in the direction and amount you want. Alternatively, select the Vertical text option to rotate the text 90° from the top to the bottom of the cell.

4. Choose OK.

Changing the Text Direction in PowerPoint

1. Select the text box that contains the text to be rotated.

2. Choose Format ➤ AutoShape, and then choose the Text Box tab.

3. Select the Rotate Text within Autoshape By 90° to have the text flow from the top right corner to the bottom right corner of the text box.

4. Choose OK.

Changing the Text Direction in Word

To quickly change the direction of the text in a selected Word table cell, callout, text box, or AutoShape, click on the Change Text Direction button on the Tables and Borders toolbar until the A on the button is pointing in the direction you want for your text.

Alternatively, you can use the following method to change the direction of the text:

1. Choose Format ➤ Text Direction to display the Text Direction - *Item* dialog box.

2. Click on one of the following options in the Orientation area:

- Choose the horizontal Text graphic to position the text so that it flows from left to right in the object.

- Choose the vertical - top to bottom Text graphic to position the text so that it flows from the lower edge of the item to its upper edge.

- Choose the vertical - bottom to top Text graphic to position the text so that it flows from the upper edge of the item to its lower edge.

3. Choose OK.

Toolbars

In Access, Excel, PowerPoint, and Word, toolbar buttons provide easy access to often-used commands, macros, AutoText entries, fonts, and styles.

You can change the position of a displayed toolbar: Drag it onto the work area of your screen to make it a floating toolbar, which can be resized. Or drag a displayed toolbar to place it vertically along the left or right edge of the window.

Creating or Editing Toolbars

You can edit any of the built-in toolbars or create entirely new toolbars to use:

1. Right-click on one of the displayed toolbars, and then select Customize in the shortcut menu, or choose View ➤ Tool-bars ➤ Customize to display the Customize dialog box.

2. Choose any of the following options:

- In the Toolbars list box on the Toolbars tab, select the checkbox of any toolbar you want to display.

- To create a new toolbar, choose New on the Toolbars tab, type a name for the toolbar in the Toolbar Name text box, and then choose OK to return to the Customize dialog box.

- Highlight a built-in toolbar that has been changed in the Toolbars list box, choose Reset, and then choose OK to return it to its original defaults.

- Highlight a custom toolbar in the Toolbars list box, choose Delete, and then choose Yes to confirm that the toolbar is to be deleted.

- Select the Large Icons checkbox on the Options tab to increase the size of the displayed toolbar buttons.

- Select the Show ScreenTips on Toolbars checkbox (selected by default) to display the name and a short description of a button's function when the mouse points to it.

- Select the Show Shortcut Keys in Screen-Tips checkbox to display keyboard shortcuts in ScreenTips.

3. Choose Close.

Customizing a Toolbar

1. Display the toolbar you want to customize.

2. Right-click on one of the displayed toolbars, and then select Customize in the shortcut menu, or choose View ➤ Tool-bars ➤ Customize to display the Customize dialog box.

3. Choose the Commands tab.

4. In Word, select the template in which you want to save the changes in the Save In drop-down list.

5. Perform any of the following actions:

- To add a button, select an item in the Categories list box. If the item has built-in buttons, they are displayed in the Commands area. Highlight a button and then choose Description to see a description of its function. Drag the button from the Buttons area to its new location on a displayed toolbar.

- To delete a button from a displayed toolbar, drag the button off the toolbar.

- To move a toolbar button on a displayed toolbar, drag the button to a different location or toolbar.

- To copy a button, press Ctrl while dragging the button to a different location or toolbar.

- To customize the selected button, choose Modify Selection, select Edit Button Image to display the Button Editor dialog box, and then make any changes necessary. Alternatively, choose Change Button Image in the Modify Selection pop-up menu to display a palette of images, and then click on the image for the button. To place text on the button, choose Text Only (Always) in the Modify Selection pop-up menu.

6. Choose Close to return to your document.

Track Changes

You can track the changes made by others to a worksheet or document.

When you track the changes made to an Excel worksheet, the workbook is automatically shared with others, and the change history is saved with the workbook. Any changed cells appear with a blue border and a blue triangle in the upper left corner. When you position the mouse pointer over a changed cell, a note indicating the change made to it appears.

The changes made to a Word document appear both on screen and in the printed document in the form of underline and strikethrough characters. If more than one person revises a document for which you are tracking changes, their track change marks appear in different colors. The name of the reviser and the date and time of the change is displayed when track changes are reviewed.

Comparing Versions of a Worksheet or Document

If you have two Excel workbooks or Word documents with different filenames or that are in different directories, you can compare the original file to the edited version and add tracked change marks to the edited document.

1. With the edited file active, choose Tools ➤ Merge Workbooks in Excel, or Tools ➤ Track Changes ➤ Compare Documents in Word. Choose OK in Excel to save the active workbook.

2. Select the name of the original version of the file in the Look In list box, and then choose OK or Open. The changes made in the edited version appear as tracked change marks in the edited file.

You can accept or reject the tracked changes that appear in the edited document the same way you do in a revised worksheet or document.

Highlighting Changes In an Excel Workbook

1. Choose Tools ➤ Track Changes ➤ Highlight Changes to display the Highlight Changes dialog box.

2. Select the Track Changes while Editing checkbox.

3. Choose any of the following options:

   - Select the When checkbox (selected by default) and then choose Since I Last Saved, All, or Not Yet Reviewed to specify which changes are to be highlighted. Alternatively, choose Since Date, and then specify the date in the text box.

   - Select the Who checkbox, and then select Everyone, Everyone but Me, or your name as the person(s) whose changes are to be highlighted.

   - Select the Where check box, and then specify the name of the range or sheet where the changes are to be highlighted.

   - Select the Highlight Changes On Screen checkbox (selected by default) to indicate which cells were changed directly on your screen.

   - Select the List Changes on a New Sheet checkbox to create a Change History sheet in the workbook. This option is only available after the workbook has been saved as a shared workbook.

4. Choose OK in the Highlight Changes dialog box.

Highlighting Changes in a Word Document

When track change marking is turned on in a document, you can display or hide change marks and modify the format of the marks. Word keeps track of changes even if they are not displayed in the document.

To quickly turn on track change marking in the active document, double-click on TRK on the status bar.

To specify the track change marking options:

1. Select Tools ➤ Track Changes ➤ Highlight Changes to display its dialog box.

2. Select the Track Changes while Editing checkbox to turn on track change marking in the document.

3. If you want to suppress the display of track change marks on your screen, clear the Highlight Changes On Screen checkbox.

4. To suppress the printing of the track change marks, clear the Highlight Changes in Printed Document checkbox.

5. To change the format of the track change marks in the document, choose Options to display the Track Changes tab, choose any of the following options, and then choose OK.

   - In the corresponding Mark drop-down list, select the character or attribute with which to mark inserted and deleted text, changed formatting, and to indicate which lines of text were revised.

   - In the corresponding Color drop-down list, select the color to apply to inserted and deleted text, changed formatting, and for revision lines.

6. Choose OK in the Highlight Changes dialog box.

To turn off track change marking in the document, clear the Track Changes while Editing checkbox and then choose OK in the Highlight Changes dialog box.

You can also choose Tools ➤ Options, and then select the Track Changes tab to change the format of the track change marks.

Merging Tracked Changes in a Document

When others have added comments or tracked changes to your document, you can insert their marked comments and changes in the original document. By default, Word assigns one of eight colors to the comments and tracked changes. If more than eight reviewers revise the document, the same colors are used again.

To merge the tracked changes made by others to your document:

1. Activate the revised document.

2. Choose Tools ➤ Merge Documents to display the Select File to Merge Into Current Document dialog box.

3. Select the name of the original document in the Look In list box, and then choose Open to merge the tracked changes into the original document.

If you sent a document to all reviewers simultaneously by electronic mail, double-click on the document's icon when the mail is returned. Choose OK to confirm that you want to merge the tracked changes, then choose OK again to merge the tracked changes into the original document. Repeat this process for each reviewer's document.

Reviewing Tracked Change Marks

You can review each tracked change and either accept or reject its inclusion in the worksheet or document.

1. With the revised worksheet or document active on your screen, choose Tools ➤ Track Changes ➤ Accept or Reject Changes.

2. Specify which changes to review in the Select Change to Accept or Reject dialog box in Excel, and then choose OK to review the changes. In Word, specify which changes to review in the Accept or Reject Changes dialog box.

3. Choose any of the following options:

- In Word, choose → Find to highlight the next marked change, or ← Find to highlight the previous marked change.

- To include the proposed change in your document, select Accept. To remove the marked change, choose Reject.

- To change the acceptance or rejection of the last marked change in Word, choose Undo.

4. When you are finished reviewing the marked changes, select Cancel or Close to return to the worksheet or document.

To accept or reject all the tracked changes without reviewing them first, select Accept All or Reject All in the Accept or Reject Changes dialog box, and then choose Yes to confirm the acceptance or rejection of the tracked changes.

Undo/Redo

You can use Undo to reverse the last several actions you performed, and Redo to reverse the last action or the last several actions you canceled.

- To reverse your last action, click on the Undo button on the Standard toolbar or choose Edit ➤ Undo (Ctrl+Z).

- To reverse your last several actions in Excel, PowerPoint, and Word, choose the Undo drop-down list on the Standard toolbar, and then highlight the action you want to undo.

- To immediately reverse the last undone action in Excel, PowerPoint, and Word, click on the Redo button on the Standard toolbar or choose Edit ➤ Redo (Ctrl+Y).

- To reverse the last several cancellations in Excel, PowerPoint, and Word, choose the Redo drop-down list on the Standard toolbar and then select the action you want to reverse.

Versions

You can save multiple versions of a document in a single file instead of saving each version in a separate file. When you use Word's new Versioning feature, Word saves snapshots of the changes made instead of saving the entire version of the document.

Managing Document Versions

The versions of the active document can be opened for review, editing, and printing, or you can delete a version you no longer need.

1. Choose File ➤ Versions to display the Versions in *Filename* dialog box.

2. Highlight the version of the document to be managed in the Existing Versions list box.

3. Select any of the following options for the selected version:

- Choose Open to open the highlighted version of the document. Both the originally opened version and the highlighted version appear in tiled windows on your screen, and the highlighted version is active.

- Choose Delete, and then choose Yes to delete the highlighted version.

- Choose View Comments to display the View Comments dialog box with the full text of the comments that were entered by the highlighted version's author, and then choose Close to return to the Versions in *Filename* dialog box.

4. If necessary, choose Close to return to your document.

Saving a Version of a Document

1. Choose File ➤ Versions to display the Versions in *Filename* dialog box.

2. Choose Save Now, type your comments in the Comments on Version text box, and then choose OK in the Save Version dialog box.

3. Click on the Save button on the Standard toolbar to save your document.

Each new version you save appears at the top of the Existing Versions list box in the Versions in *Filename* dialog box. Multiple versions of a document increase the size of its file.

To have Word automatically save a new version of the document each time it is closed, select the Automatically Save a Version on Close checkbox, and then choose Close to return to your document. Click on the Save button on the Standard toolbar to save the document.

You can also save the a version of the active document by choosing File ➤ Save As, and then choosing Save Version to display the Save Version dialog box. Type your comments in the Comments on Version text box, and then choose OK.

Saving a Version as a Separate File

You can save an open version of a document in a separate file. Do so when you want to compare two versions of a document, or when sending a version for review by other editors so they cannot open other versions of the document.

Each time you open a highlighted version of the document, its name appears along with the date and time the version was created, and "version" on its title bar. When you save the version, you can either specify a different filename or accept the filename assigned to the version.

1. Choose File ➤ Versions to display the Versions In *Filename* dialog box.

2. Highlight the version of the document to be saved as a separate file in the Existing Versions list box, and then choose Open.

3. Click on the Save button on the Standard toolbar.

4. If necessary, type a different name for the file in the File Name text box.

5. Choose Save to save the version to the specified filename.

View

In Access, Excel, PowerPoint, and Word, change the way your data appears on screen and the way you work with the data by changing the view. Each view is designed for a specific task.

Changing the View in Access

Each time you open a database file in Access, the Main Switchboard window appears, allowing you to enter or preview data or exit the database. You can also view the actual database objects from within the Database window. To activate the Database window, click on the Database Window button on the Form View toolbar.

With the Database window active, use any of the following methods to change to the corresponding view:

- Click on the Tables tab or choose View ➤ Database Objects ➤ Tables to select a table that contains the records on which to work, create a new table, or edit an existing table.

- Click on the Queries tab or choose View ➤ Database Objects ➤ Queries to select a defined query, create a new query, or edit the definition of an existing query.

- Click on the Forms tab or choose View ➤ Database Objects ➤ Forms to select an existing form to open or design, or to create a new form for the database.

- Click on the Reports tab or choose View ➤ Database Objects ➤ Reports to select an existing report to preview or design, or to create a new report for the database.

- Click on the Macros tab or choose View ➤ Database Objects ➤ Macros to select an existing macro to run or design, or to create a new macro for the database.

- Click on the Modules tab or choose View ➤ Database Objects ➤ Modules to select an existing module to run or design, or to create a new module for the database.

To display the active database object in Design view so you can edit its format or structure, click on the Design View button on the toolbar that appears for the object.

Changing the View in Excel and Word

- In Word, click on the Normal View button by the horizontal scroll bar or choose View ➤ Normal to work more quickly as you create, edit, and format your documents. In Normal view, the formatting applied to text appears on screen, but the page layout does not. To work even faster while in Normal view, limit the number of font sizes and the alignments and spacing available. To do so, select the Draft Font checkbox on the View tab in the Options dialog box.

- In Word, click on the Online Layout View button by the horizontal scroll bar or choose View ➤ Online Layout to make it easier to read a document on your screen. Online Layout view is useful when reading or editing the text of a document.

- In Word, click on the Page Layout View button by the horizontal scroll bar or choose View ➤ Page Layout to display and edit a document just as it will appear when printed. Use Page Layout view to make any necessary formatting changes to the document's appearance.

- In Word, click on the Outline View button on the horizontal scroll bar or choose View ➤ Outline to control how much of the document is displayed. In Outline view, you can easily change the arrangement of text in the document or the structure of the document.

- In Word, click on the Master Document View button on the Outlining toolbar or choose View ➤ Master Document to control the arrangement of subdocuments in a long document.

- Click on the Print Preview button on the Standard toolbar or choose File ➤ Print Preview to display the worksheet or document at a smaller magnification to see its overall appearance before it is printed. In Excel, you can change the width of columns, the page margins, and the position of the header and footer while you are in Print Preview.

- Choose View ➤ Full Screen to display more of the worksheet or document on the screen. All toolbars, menus, scroll bars, rulers, and the status bar and Windows 95 Taskbar are removed. Click on the Full Screen button that appears in its own toolbar while you are in Full Screen view or press Esc to redisplay the screen items.

Changing the View in PowerPoint

- Click on the Slide View button by the horizontal scroll bar or choose View ➤ Slide to display only the active slide in a presentation. You can edit the appearance of the slide, and add graphics and text to it. To display a different slide while in Slide view, drag the scroll box on the vertical scroll bar until the number of the slide appears, and then release the mouse button.

- Click on the Outline View button by the horizontal scroll bar or choose View ➤ Outline to display only the text on each slide in the presentation in an outline. Use Outline view to create and edit the text that will appear on each slide in the presentation.

- To display miniaturized versions of each slide in the presentation, click on the Slide Sorter View button by the horizontal scroll bar or choose View ➤ Slide Sorter to change to Slide Sorter view. You can easily change the order in which the slides appear in the presentation, and set the timings and transitions for each slide to control its appearance on the screen during a slide show.

- To display the active slide in the presentation with room to add notes for the slide below it, click on the Notes Page View button by the horizontal scroll bar or choose View ➤ Notes Page to change to Notes Page view. Use Notes Page view to create speaker notes for the presentation.

- Click on the Slide Show button to run an electronic slide show using the slides in the active presentation. Or choose View ➤ Slide Show to display the Slide Show dialog box to set up the options before running the slide show.

- Click on the Black and White View button on the Standard toolbar or choose View ➤ Black and White to see how a slide will look when printed on a black-and-white printer.

Zoom

You can adjust the magnification of the data displayed on-screen in Excel, PowerPoint, and Word.

Enlarge the magnification to make the data easier to read, or reduce it to display the overall effect of an entire slide or page.

Adjusting the Magnification

The percentage of magnification is the amount the data is reduced or enlarged on your screen in relation to its real size. The magnification appears only on your screen, not on a page printed while the magnification is in effect.

To enlarge or reduce the magnification of the data displayed on your screen, select a different magnification in the Zoom drop-down list on the standard toolbar, or type a different percentage of magnification in the Zoom text box. Alternatively, follow these steps:

1. Choose View ➤ Zoom to display the Zoom dialog box.

2. Select one of the predefined options in the Magnification or Zoom To area, or specify the percentage of the size of the data displayed in the Custom or Percent text box.

3. Choose OK in the Zoom dialog box.

INDEX

Note to the Reader: Throughout this index **boldfaced** page numbers indicate primary discussions of a topic. *Italicized* page numbers indicate illustrations.

W

What's New in Office 97

New Excel, PowerPoint, and Access Features

Excel

Multiple-Level Undo - Multiple-level Undo is no longer a feature reserved for Word. Excel Workbooks now have the ability to undo multiple actions.

Collapse/Expand Dialog Boxes - Selecting ranges while using Wizards is easier with the ability to collapse a dialog box.

Natural Language Formulas - Create formulas that reference your headings without having to create named ranges.

Range Finder - When viewing cells with formulas, the cells referenced in the formulas become highlighted in colors that match the color of the reference in the formula.

Visual Printing - Get it right the first time. New Page Break view and draggable page breaks make it easier to adjust the page output correctly the first time you print.

Conditional Formatting - New formatting option allows a cell to be formatted based on its value.

Rotating Text - Sometimes you need a font to read at an angle; with new rotating font formats, you can do just that.

Single-Click Selection - Working with charts is a bit more intuitive now that you no longer need to double-click on a chart in order to select or format one of its components.

Chart Types - More chart types are now available in Excel to provide you with more options to get your point across.

Data Validation - Cells can now be set to accept only data that meets certain validation conditions.

Visual Basic Development Environment for Macros - This is a separate yet integrated interface for creating and editing Excel macros.

PowerPoint

Presentation Advice with Office Assistant - Get all of your tips and suggestions for creating better-looking presentations directly from the Office Assistant.

Custom Shows - Create multiple presentations within a single PowerPoint file to accommodate different audiences.